Architecture and Empire in Jamaica

Architecture and Empire in Jamaica

Louis P. Nelson

Yale University Press   New Haven and London

Published with assistance from the Annie Burr Lewis Fund.

yalebooks.com/art

Designed by Leslie Fitch and Tina Henderson
Printed in China through Oceanic Graphic International, Inc.

Library of Congress Control Number: 2015930491
ISBN 978-0-300-21100-9

A catalogue record for this book is available from the British Library.

This paper meets the requirements of ANSI/NISO z39.48–1992 (Permanence
of Paper).

10 9 8 7 6 5 4 3 2 1

Jacket illustrations: (front) Pierre Eugène du Simitière, "Triumphal Arch at
the Decoy" (detail of fig. 5.6); (back) Mount Plenty Great House (detail of
fig. 0.3).

Frontispiece: Colbeck Castle (fig. 2.19).

Dedicated to the people of Jamaica

Contents

Acknowledgments

It is with a great debt of gratitude that I cross the finish line on this book. Begun more than five years ago, this book has benefited from conversations with an extraordinary array of colleagues, friends, students, librarians, archivists, and others. I have done my best to cover them all below, but certainly there are some I've overlooked.

This book was born from a longstanding commitment to the field analysis of everyday architecture, which in this instance took the form of a summer field school held on the north coast of Jamaica every summer for almost a decade. Over the course of those summers, more than one hundred students traveled with me to live in Jamaica for a month spending days recording historic architecture and nights swatting mosquitos. I would like to thank them each by name: Jasper Adams, Jesse Adams-Doolittle, Sara Anderson, Stephanie Arbieto, Hunter Armstrong, Sela Bailey, Hannah Beckman, Katherine Boles, Eryn Brennan, Sarah Brummett, Kristin Buchanan, Stephanie Burcham, Margaret Burke, Sam Carr, David Casteel, Alisha Clark, Jonathan Coble, Robert Cox, Katherine Cullinan, Colin Curley, Anna Danz, Erika deBroekert, Eduardo Diaz-Etchevehere, James Dunnigan, Sarah Eissler, Elizabeth Engel, Adam Erby, Robert Erickson, Tahinee Felix-Marin, Stephanie Fernandez, Jason Fox, Marina Freckmann, Laura Frye, Molly Garfinkel, Mike Goddard, Grace Goldstein, Jennie Graves, Margaret Hansen, Jennifer Harris, Ethan Heil, Kristen Hennings, Rachel Himes, Rachel Jessup, April Johnson, Matthew Jungclaus, Katie Klepper, Kosova Kreka, John Kupstas, Erin Kuykendall, Anna Kvan, Alexandra Lauzon, Lawrence Lazarides, Tran Le, Yun-Fong Lin, Jennifer Lindblom, Jordan Matthews, Todd Mattocks, Lindsay McCook, Molly McDonald, Meagan McFadden, Maureen McGee, Elizabeth McGinley, Meghan McLoone, Francis McMillen, Elizabeth Milnarik, Amy Moses, Noel Mukubwa, Effie Nicholaou, John O'Hara, Jennifer Pack, Camila Quinteros-Casaverde, Philip Redpath, Kelsey Reynolds, Elizabeth Rice, Julie Robert, Rachel Robinson, Jerold Rosema, Alison Ross, Blythe Rowe, Kedryn Samson, Maria Sanchez-Carlo, Tommy Schaperkotter, Lauren Shepulski, Richard Sidebottom, Charles Smith, Deborah Smith, Kathleen Smith, Kristen Sparenborg, Mark Stephongzi, Todd Stovall, Jackie Taylor, Jessica Terdeman, Anh Thai, Katherine Thaxter, Sarah Thomas, Kimberly Toney, Alyssa Turner, Jessica Underhill, Jessica Vanecek, William Watkins, Leah Werner, Christoph Wilhelm, Michael Wsol, Steven Yena, and Chris Young. Among these students, a handful played critical roles as research assistants and colleagues. Hayden Bassett, first an undergrad on the field school and now a Ph.D. student at William and Mary, has read numerous chapters of this book and offered very useful feedback and criticism. Brian Cofrancesco played a critical role in helping to organize the research that undergirds this book. Emilie Johnson, Edward Barnes, Whitney Martinko, Ivor Connelly, and Josi Ward were an extraordinary research team, and they are all important scholars with very promising futures. And, of course, I am especially grateful for the summers spent in the field with Ed Chappell, whose commitment to the careful recording of historic architecture is surpassed by none.

The chapter structure of this book began to emerge in a seminar on the architecture of the Caribbean that I offered at the University of Virginia in the fall of 2010.

Those students played such an important role in helping me to think through the organization of this material that I'd like to thank them as well: Kate Crawford, Jamie Frieling, Gray Graham, Ben Hays, Stephanie Langton, Ed Barnes, Laurin Goad, Justin Grieving, Katy Lassdow, Kristin Rourke, and Doug Sefton.

The final push to produce the book would not have been possible without the extraordinary contributions of Jason Truesdale and Zhifei Cheng, both of whom produced drawings and illustrations, and, especially, of Mike Mitchell, who gave a year of his life to this book managing illustration permissions, editing endnotes, building a bibliography, and responding to my never-ending curveball requests.

The book has also benefited from the extraordinary support of a number of Jamaicans who remained committed to supporting my research. Valerie Facey has been a longstanding cheerleader, champion, and colleague in the effort to understand Jamaica's architectural heritage. The same is true of Ivor Connelly and Kevaughn Harding. Without enthusiasm and encouragement from these three Jamaicans, this book would not have happened.

Of course, the research was supported by institutions and their staff and faculty in the United States, in the Caribbean, and in Britain. The invitation to spend the eight months of the 2011–12 academic year at the Rothermere American Institute at Oxford University as a research fellow gave me the time to produce the first drafts of many chapters. I am also indebted to the librarians, curators, and archivists of the following institutions: Archives of Jamaica; Bodelian Library; Bristol Museum and Art Gallery; British Library; Cambridgeshire Archives; Glasgow City Archives; Huntington Library; Institute of Jamaica, Island Record Office; Jamaica National Heritage Trust; Lewis Walpole Library; Library of Congress; National Gallery of Jamaica; National Library of Jamaica; National Maritime Museum; National Museums Liverpool; Pierpont Morgan Library; Public Record Office, Kew; UVA Special Collections; Victoria and Albert Museum; West Indies Collections of UWI Library; and the Yale Center for British Art. I am especially indebted to the private owners of the Storer Sketchbook and the D'Simitiere sketches for allowing me to carefully study and to publish these incredibly important visual sources.

And various chapters benefited from feedback after presentations to the following: American Society for Eighteenth Century Studies; Department of Art History at the College of William and Mary; Department of Art History at the University of Delaware; Department of History of the University of Ghana, Legon; Early American Seminar at the University of Virginia; Georgian Society of Jamaica, London; John Carter Brown Library; Oxford University Architectural History Seminar; Rutgers British Studies Center; Savannah Symposium; and the Society of Early Americanists.

The shape of this book and the quality of its insights and arguments were all vastly improved by the contributions of colleagues in the field. I am indebted to each of the following for reading various chapters of this book and providing helpful feedback: Alex Bremner, Cary Carson, John Crowley, Douglas Fordham, Maurie McInnis, James Robertson, and Dell Upton. Worthy of very special mention is Robert Barker, whose indefatigable commitment to exacting research and his encyclopedic knowledge of eighteenth-century Jamaica was enormously helpful in the research and writing of this book.

And, lastly, I am indebted to the extraordinary team at Yale University Press for their patience and shepherding through the production of this book. Final thanks go to Katherine Boller, Heidi Downey, and Tamara Schechter, and my fantastic editor, Deborah Bruce-Hostler.

FIG. 0.1 Laura Facey, *Their Spirits Gone Before Them,* 2006.

Introduction

Thousands of black bodies give the hull a haunting presence. Lined with row upon row of figurines, a simple wooden canoe rides the current of sugarcane that carries it. Laura Facey's *Their Spirits Gone Before Them* (2006) is a tour de force, simultaneously political and historical commentary and agent of healing (fig. 0.1). The viewer's immediate reference is the familiar late eighteenth-century broadside illustrating the interior of a slave ship, the *Brookes*, during the middle passage (fig. 0.2). The numbing repetition and anonymity of the bodies and the unrelenting presence of the cane immediately connect the work to Jamaica's tragic history of slavery. Yet the boat is not a slave ship but a canoe, like the thousands used every day by the island's fishermen. And the figures are not of the enslaved but the emancipated, miniatures of the artist's monumental *Redemption Song* figures that dominate the entrance to Kingston's Emancipation Park. It is a work about the past, about slavery, but it is also—as the artist insists—a work about the future, "transcendence, reverence, and strength." Like many Jamaicans, Facey understands herself in part through her past, through Jamaica's past. But unlike many Jamaicans, Laura gives that past a form, a shape, an architecture.

First exhibited in Kingston, *Their Spirits* has now crossed the Atlantic to dominate the main exhibition gallery of the International Slavery Museum in Liverpool. Were it also to show in Accra or Lagos, the piece would travel the historical circuit that connected these places so closely through the eighteenth century, when Jamaican sugar plantations, West Africa's dungeons, and Britain's country houses were inextricably linked. In her willingness to exhibit in England, Facey courageously reminds British viewers of their implication in the project of slavery and, by extension, the project of empire. This book shares much in aspiration with Facey's work. It looks squarely in the face of the same history. It also seeks to demonstrate through shape, form, and meaning that the artifacts of the Jamaican landscape are powerful tools for the interpretation of its history. Like Facey's discovery of telling power in the everyday object of a canoe, this book enlists generally unremarkable historic buildings in the writing of a monumental history. And like the canoe, this volume on Jamaican architecture is not—and could not have been—bounded by that island's shores.

I learned about Facey's powerful work standing in her gallery, the large hall of the Jamaican sculptor's

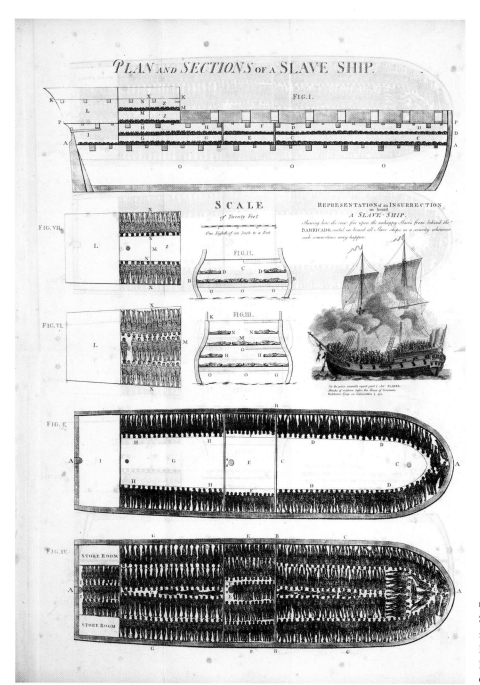

FIG. 0.2 "Plan and Sections of a Slave Ship," London, 1789. Lithograph, 10.98 × 16.4 in. (27.9 × 41 cm). Reproduced by permission of The Huntington Library, San Marino, California.

late eighteenth-century house in remote St. Ann Parish (fig. 0.3). Built between the 1760s and 1780s, Mount Plenty is a "Jamaica house," a local building form that markedly departed from anything familiar to British memory. It was very much a product of Jamaica's particular history and distinctive culture, a Creole form. It was shaped by the challenges, even violence, of life in early colonial Jamaica. The low, sweeping roof offers the least resistance to hurricane-force winds, while the broad eaves originally sheltered cooling piazzas on all four sides of

the house. While their main living floors are wide open and breezy with louvered jalousies, many houses of this sort sit atop fortified masonry foundations, strongholds of refuge in times of attack. Yet within this local envelope, Mount Plenty's interior is richly ornamented with refined eighteenth-century consoles and architraves. It would also have been fitted out with fine furniture from England, textiles from the eastern Mediterranean, and ceramics from China. Sparer today, the original interior would have exhibited the occupant's participation in Britain's empire of goods. The builders of Mount Plenty housed some of their enslaved Africans in a barracks, emulating the housing associated with the broader agricultural improvement phenomenon reshaping Britain's landscape in the same century. For these reasons, Mount Plenty is the perfect place to begin because these three themes—violence, empire, and identity—gave shape and meaning to both this building and this book.

Architecture and Empire in Jamaica is the first scholarly analysis of Jamaican architecture of the long eighteenth century. Generally spanning from the Port Royal earthquake of 1692 to emancipation in 1838, the book introduces the prevailing architectural types found in early colonial Jamaica and then argues that through these buildings Jamaica played a leading role in the formation of both the early modern Atlantic and the emergent British Empire. Rooted in a close reading of hundreds of carefully measured field drawings—generated during more than a decade of field schools producing on-site documentation—and a careful analysis of private accounts and public records, the book is both architectural history and a social history of spaces.[1] Characters in the story include a range of people: elite planters, middling overseers, free blacks, and recently enslaved Africans. So, too, with spaces; from shop windows filled with newly imported finery from England and India to the whipping posts in the market square, the material realities of these spaces determined the contours of everyday life in Jamaica.[2] That everyday life labored always under the island's predominant institution: slavery.[3] So much so that one early nineteenth-century writer noted that "all people are regarded according to their appearance," by which the author meant skin color.[4] While Virginia never boasted a black majority, Jamaica claimed the largest enslaved African population in the empire; Jamaica's blacks outnumbered whites by at least eighteen to one, in some parishes by thirty to one.[5]

As the chapters to follow will show, Jamaican slavery had a profound impact on the island's built environment. This has led to a continued—and understandable—focus on plantations as the predominant spaces of colonial Jamaica.[6] Slavery made many free white Jamaicans very rich; by the middle of the eighteenth century, Jamaicans would be the wealthiest Britons outside of Britain. As historian Trevor Burnard has shown, the average white man in Jamaica was more than thirty-six times wealthier than the average white man in the thirteen mainland colonies.[7]

Only four men in all of New England and the middle colonies had wealth that exceeded the wealth of the *average* white Jamaican. And the richest planters were far richer than all others; the top 10 percent of the island's whites owned two-thirds of the island's wealth. This extraordinary wealth and its concentration at the top meant that Jamaica's economic structure generated a small, elite class of extremely wealthy men with money enough to travel to Oxford for education, undertake grand tours of the continent, and marry into aristocratic English families.[8] *Architecture and Empire in Jamaica* is the story of wealth, slavery, and everyday life as told through the lens of Jamaica's buildings and landscapes.

Even so, this book reaches beyond Jamaica. As championed by Pulitzer Prize–winning historian Bernard Bailyn, Atlantic history—the study of the early modern Atlantic world—has emerged as an important critical historical frame.[9] Studies have ranged from religious subjects such as the "first great awakening" to the economic machine of the transatlantic slave trade. But those few architectural histories that attend to the Atlantic typically do so by presuming a unidirectional flow of people and ideas from east to west.[10] By connecting the Caribbean first to West Africa and then to Britain, this book takes capital flow as its broadest frame and makes explicit the material, economic, and political connections around the Atlantic. British slavers purchased Africans from barrel-vaulted dungeons under castles erected along the coast of West Africa and then sold them to Jamaican merchants who kept them in barrel-vaulted cells under their own houses. Some English and Scottish emigrants to Jamaica, or the sons and grandsons of those emigrants, benefited extraordinarily from Jamaica's economic structure and built great houses for themselves first in Jamaica and eventually in Britain, many designed by Britain's leading architects. But capital flow is not the only map for transatlantic circulation. British slavers resident on the coast of West Africa experimented with housing in much the same way as did their counterparts in Jamaica.

Paul Gilroy has recently introduced to the conversation the critical reimagining of the Atlantic world as the Black Atlantic.[11] *Architecture and Empire in Jamaica* engages the architectural history of the Black Atlantic in two ways. The opening chapter articulates the architectural parameters of the four stages experienced by Africans caught in the web of slavery: capture, containment, transportation, and sale. But the book also engages the black experience of the sugar plantation, the late eighteenth- and early nineteenth-century architectural practices of free blacks in Jamaican urban centers, and the emergence of a pan-Caribbean free black architectural practice that connected communities across the Caribbean and even to the coastal rim of mainland North America. Europeans were not the only travelers around the Atlantic. First as enslaved Africans and then as freedmen, blacks also traveled; this project takes a serious look at the complex webs of relationships between their experiences and identities and architecture. Unlike earlier architectural histories of the early modern Americas, *Architecture and Empire in Jamaica* assumes a continuous circulation of people, ideas, and capital around and across the Atlantic.

If Jamaica was a central cog in the machinery of the Atlantic world, it was also a major—if perpetually under-recognized—component of the British Empire. The long-standing model has subdivided the British Empire into first and second empires bisected at the Seven Years War, the first as Atlantic, colonial, and mercantile and the second as Asian, driven by conquest and direct rule.[12] As a result, histories of the British Empire often overlook Jamaica, which fits comfortably into neither.[13] But more recent work contests that view, seeing colonialism and conquest as unfolding and contingent practices ranging from the late sixteenth through the late nineteenth centuries.[14] In this view, Jamaica is not an odd outlier, but in fact a central hinge of empire. As the following chapters will demonstrate, eighteenth-century architecture in Jamaica resurrected fortified domestic house forms from seventeenth-century Ireland and directly connected Jamaica to the Gold Coast of West Africa. Furthermore, recent scholarship has moved to examine the "connected worlds of empires," recognizing that empires are often adjacent, even overlapping, and that for this reason they learn from one another.[15] Reinforcing this model, the chapters that follow demonstrate that the architecture of early colonial Jamaica reveals the interconnectedness of the British and Spanish empires in the Caribbean. Just as Jamaican merchants regularly sold slaves in Havana, the colonnaded streets of Kingston reminded visitors of "old Spanish towns," while galleried plantation houses built by English planters derived from those left behind by their Spanish predecessors.[16]

Douglas Fordham has recently argued that the British Empire has also become an important subject in the study of early modern British art. As his state of the field essay makes very clear, historians and art historians alike have embraced Benedict Anderson's 1983 description of nations as "imagined communities."[17] For example, Maya Jasanoff's award-winning *Edge of Empire: Lives, Culture and Conquest in the East, 1750–1850* brings to the fore the important role played by individuals and objects in the incorporation of first India and then Egypt into the British Empire. Yet the few significant works to focus exclusively on the visual culture of Jamaica include Steeve Buckridge's *Language of Dress: Resistance and Accommodation in Jamaica, 1760–1890* and the monumental *Art and Emancipation in Jamaica*, edited by Tim Barringer, Gillian Forrester, and Barbaro Martinez-Ruiz.[18] Derived from a huge exhibition, the latter is the most intensive study of the visual culture of early colonial Jamaica and is particularly important because it engages a variety of worlds of experience, including objects and essays that range in topic from Afro-Jamaican music and festivities to picturesque landscape painting. This emphasis on the making of empire through visual culture has also carried through to architectural histories.[19] As is evident by its title, empire stands at the heart of *Architecture and Empire in Jamaica*; this will lead many readers to expect public buildings, courthouses, and fortifications to leap from its pages. Yet these are all missing from the pages that follow; this is a book focused almost exclusively on domestic architecture. In so doing it implicitly argues that the work of empire is not just the work of the state. The work of private individuals is just as much the work of empire as the publicly funded projects of the state. These chapters demonstrate how this can be true. Until now, the role of architecture in the story of Britain's empire in the Caribbean was unrecognized.[20] *Architecture and Empire in Jamaica* closes this critical gap.

This volume also makes methodological claims by standing squarely in a decades-long tradition of field-based research on everyday architecture.[21] As already suggested, this volume would not have been possible without the decade of work examining everyday architecture in Jamaica with a team of fifteen to twenty students for a month every summer. After documenting scores of buildings through careful measured drawings one comes to recognize that architecture is evidence of everyday life. This is especially so in preprofessional early modern contexts like early America, where individuals and communities struggled to adapt to a wide range of new circumstances and experienced high levels of cross-cultural interaction. Since the 1980s, scholars of early America

FIG. 0.3 Mount Plenty Great House, St. Ann Parish, Jamaica, late eighteenth century.

have published award-winning work demonstrating how architecture and material culture create a new body of evidence in the writing of early American social, cultural, political, and religious histories. Yet, surprisingly, this rich source of new evidence has yet to find its way into the writing of histories of the region of early America most profitably characterized as the dynamic periphery: the British Caribbean. Furthermore, this book embraces a history of architecture concerned more with use of space than with design and production.[22]

This focus on space depends on four methodological convictions. First, that the meanings of spaces are not always determined by their production. Sometimes the experience of a space, if such an experience can be suggested, is far more important than its production. Second, that the writing of history benefits from the rigorous examination of the spaces where events took place; too frequently historians generate disembodied narratives that divorce events from place. Third, that the most important meaning of architecture is often found in the

various human networks—social, economic, and political—that tied those spaces one to the next. And fourth, that spaces engage multiple domains of human experience simultaneously. By this I mean that individuals are defined by a range of personal characteristics: race, enslaved or free status, local versus visitor, class—elite or common sort—and that these characteristics reshape the meaning of a space for each person. As a result, there is no single "meaning" of a space. First through careful documentation and analysis of real spaces, then through the commitment to interpret these spaces through multiple, historically grounded lenses of perception, this book is a social history of architecture.

ARRIVALS

The book's first chapter opens in front of Dixcove Castle, in what is now Ghana, with an introduction to the places of capture, containment, transportation, and sale of the hundreds of thousands of Africans who found their way to Jamaica against their will. In an examination of the ways in which slavery began to transform architecture across Africa, chapter 1 argues that Jamaica's seemingly insatiable demand for enslaved laborers reshaped places and spaces in Africa. Africans created the spaces of the coffle as they ensnared victims for sale to European traders. Dungeons erected along the coast by Europeans transformed over time as enslaved people became increasingly valuable commodities. Carpenters refitted the holds of ships and erected deck-top barricados to manage and contain the enslaved through the middle passage. The chapter closes in the surviving Kingston courtyard and seasoning pen of slave trader Thomas Hibbert. The property of Jamaica's leading mid-eighteenth-century slave merchant, the courtyard penned thousands if not tens of thousands of Africans over the course of the eighteenth century. Hibbert's house in Kingston cannot be understood on its own; it is only rightly understood as the final in a string of historically interdependent spaces that began hundreds of miles inland from Africa's west coast.

VIOLENCE

After the opening chapter, the next seven chapters are organized into three thematic sections. The first frames early colonial Jamaica as a landscape of violence. In an economic system dependent on slavery imposed within a tropical context inextricably shaped by sweltering heat, devastating hurricanes, and the ever-present threat of earthquakes, violence—both human and natural—was a defining feature of everyday life. Stewart Castle is one of an extensive collection of fortified houses erected by Scottish "sojourners" in the island's northern (frontier) parishes in the second half of the eighteenth century. These houses followed an even earlier English tradition of building houses with prominent corner towers as a means to assert dominance and authority over a contested landscape. The castellated houses betray both the historical reality of conquest—the English seized Jamaica from the Spanish in 1655—and the haunting persistence of fear. British Jamaicans lived under the constant threat of attack, including raiding Maroons, attack by the Spanish or French, and most especially, slave insurrection. Chapter 2 examines the architectural evidence of these anxieties and goes on to argue that this was not the first contested landscape so conquered by the British. Comparing examples from Jamaica and Ireland, the chapter reveals the striking historical parallels between early seventeenth-century Ireland and eighteenth-century Jamaica. Both places

were considered barbarous, contested marchlands, to use American historian Bernard Bailyn's term, and their shared architectural responses reveal quite clearly their shared history.[23]

But human assault was not the only form of violence that defined life in early colonial Jamaica. Chapter 3 opens with the townhouse erected in Falmouth, Jamaica, by Anglo-Jamaican planter John Tharp in the 1790s. With a sturdy masonry foundation and timber-framed and nogged (brick infill) upper story, the house is decidedly out of character with the fashionable neoclassical designs executed by James Wyatt, whom Tharp had hired for earlier work on his English country house in Cambridgeshire. This chapter demonstrates how Tharp's house responds very directly to more than a century of experimentation by builders adapting to the violence of the tropical climate, including oppressive heat, devastating hurricanes, and violent earthquakes. Over time, British Caribbean architecture adopted hurricane-responsive profiles and roof-shapes and earthquake-responsive foundations and wall engineering. All the while, the same builders learned to negotiate the piercing violence of the Caribbean sun and its oppressive heat. As a building form found first in early eighteenth-century Kingston, the "piazza" soon appeared on planters' houses across the island, emulating in part the earlier tradition in the Spanish Caribbean. The piazza was not just about comfort, as early moderns believed that the heat of the sun could kill. Together these two chapters foreground the violence that framed early colonial life on the island; tall towers, low roofs, and sheltering piazzas stand witness to the persistent anxiety that framed everyday life.

EMPIRE

The second section expands on the book's central theme of empire. While much has been said about the British Empire in India, this section examines an earlier episode of empire through colonialism, agriculture and industry, wealth and refinement, and mercantile exchange. A Jamaican commentator understood the dependence of the empire on Jamaica: "The sovereign of Great Britain holds an interest in Negroes . . . for his revenue is very greatly benefited and supported by the produce of their personal labor." He continued that the labor of enslaved Africans undergirded "the nation at large"; the work generated by Jamaican plantations set manufacturers to work producing the machinery of the sugar works, mariners necessitated by the vast shipping required to move goods, slaves, and sugar around the Atlantic, and artisans providing clothes and other stuffs for the enslaved workforce.[24] Between his numerous travels to England in the 1780s and 1790s, John Tharp completely rebuilt Good Hope, his plantation seat in Trelawny Parish, including new water and cattle mills, an expanded sugar works, new warehouses, and a new overseer's house, all of which survive. Taking a lead from Tharp's rebuilding of Good Hope, chapter 4 positions the Jamaican plantation in two historical narratives that are traditionally confined to the British mainland: "agricultural improvement" and the Industrial Revolution. Tharp's rebuilding efforts were not unique; in fact he only exemplified the pervasive and almost continuous process of experimentation and improvement that shaped Jamaica's plantations through the eighteenth century. And as many historians have now come to recognize, the sugar plantation was more industrial than it was agricultural. To that end, this chapter examines the physical fabric of the Jamaican sugar plantation as a contingent example of both agricultural improvement and the Industrial Revolution, and in this way, it resists the convenient separation of Jamaica from Britain. Chapter 4 closes with discussions of punishment and surveillance, essential tools in the management of an enslaved labor force generating Britain's greatest source of colonial wealth. The chapter situates the Jamaican plantation as an engine of empire that ran on improvement, industry, and oppression.

In the midst of that machinery and oppression, mid-eighteenth-century white Jamaicans labored hard to demonstrate their personal refinement as leaders, not victims, of the empire. Chapter 5 opens at Colbeck Castle's monumental ruins to provide an introduction to Jamaica's wealthiest planters—all actively participant in Jamaica's powerful colonial assembly—in the middle decades of the eighteenth century. Some of the wealthiest rebuilt Italian Renaissance palaces in the Jamaican plains. Other Jamaican sons positioned themselves at the avant-garde of British aesthetics. In addition to building country houses and funding publications in the arts, Jamaicans planted expansive—and civilizing—picturesque gardens, complete with masonry triumphal arch follies. Through political action in their assembly and through the arts of architecture and gardens, Jamaica's planters understood their island not as an agricultural outpost subsidiary to the motherland but as a tropical frontier awaiting the inscription of empire.

Chapter 6, the final one under the theme of empire, turns to consumption and the world of stores to examine Jamaica's participation in what T. H. Breen has called the empire of goods. The Jamaican merchant house and store was the nexus of diverse interdependent social, racial, and economic landscapes, each working to align or differentiate individuals—merchants, white and mixed-race women, sailors, and slaves—in particular, if perpetually repeated, encounters. Often proximate to the town wharves, these houses were usually adjacent to the socially marginal spaces of sailors, free black hawkers, and enslaved day laborers. The ground-floor shop was a place of established commercial exchange that opened onto commercial streets that offered a respectable shopping-scape for the purchase of refined consumables. And the house was a place dedicated to the performance of those goods, while the back lot provided a place of labor for the team of enslaved domestics that served the family. The wharves, the streets, and the shops of Jamaican port towns were lively, complex places of commerce whose material forms played a critical role in shaping the social and racial dimensions of commercial exchange. The store and the street of stores directly connected Jamaican towns to the world of goods that materialized the empire.

IDENTITY

The final two chapters on Jamaica turn attention to the formation of colonial identities evident in the architecture of the early nineteenth century, as those who remained in Jamaica engaged the project of "becoming" Jamaican, to enlist Robert Blair St. George's use of the term.[25] Chapter 7 opens by claiming that Jamaicans had by the end of the eighteenth century established a shared architectural formula for a distinctive type, the "Creole" or "Jamaican house." Limited to a few large rooms, always a single floor of living space, and usually fronted or encircled by a piazza on three or four sides, the Jamaica house became a distinctive marker of that landscape by the end of the century. The chapter examines the ever-present hall that persisted in Jamaican houses well after it fell from favor in houses elsewhere across Britain and British America. It also became a place known for the practice of "creolizing," or reclining on a porch with elevated feet. Depending extensively on letterbooks and probate evidence, the chapter examines the piazza as a social space and the emergence of distinctive furniture forms such as the Campeche chair, as architecture was becoming Jamaican.

Part of this process of becoming was manifest in the cultural circumstances of interracial coupling, ambivalence, and violence. These conditions—especially the constancy of white on black rape—produced an extraordinarily complex racial hierarchy and almost shocking degrees of white-to-white hospitality, conditions Trevor Burnard calls egalitarian tyranny.[26] The chapter closes by situating the prevalence of the Jamaican house as a response to the island's white-to-white hospitality. In an environment where whites were so threatened and outnumbered by the enslaved majority, architecture could not afford to segregate whites by class.

The second chapter on identity examines a distinctive collection of small, well-built, two-room frame houses that all appear to date from the early decades of the nineteenth century. Always on back streets and in marginal neighborhoods, these buildings survive in great numbers. Archival research suggests that they were built by the island's very large free black population, often women, raising very interesting questions about free black agency, the role of free black women in urban environments, and the complexities of free black identity formation in a slave society. Chapter 8 then identifies the large numbers of very similar houses found across the greater Caribbean in these same decades, exploring the emergence of a region increasingly defined by buildings associated with a growing free black population. Over time, black and white cultural practices were less different and the lines between wealthy free blacks and middling overseers were slowly blurred, if never erased.[27] This chapter concludes by considering the wide range of houses and buildings erected by the ever-growing free black population into the early nineteenth century. Jamaican or "Creole" houses and the board houses erected initially by the island's free black population, then, were not buildings shaped entirely by the tropical climate but things socially produced, shaped by the complexities of interpersonal relationship and identity formation in a socially and racially unstable landscape.

DEPARTURES

The closing chapter carries the reader back to the British Isles by opening at the quay of the West India Docks on the Isle of Dogs, just down the Thames from London. Begun in 1800, the construction of the docks was driven by Jamaican merchants and planters Robert Milligen and George Hibbert, nephew and heir to Thomas

Hibbert of chapter 1. The scheme was also underwritten by John Tharp, known to readers from chapters 3 and 4. The extraordinary scale of the project, by far the largest dock system of its day, made clear the material reach of Jamaican cachet in the capital. And sugar money poured into Bristol, Liverpool, and Glasgow as well. But Jamaican wealth did not stop at the docks. As the chapter demonstrates, Jamaican money funded prominent townhouses and country estates, many by Robert Adam and other major architects. Chapter 9 examines the work of Jamaican-associated patrons then living in Britain. If the story of Jamaica and its architecture in this telling begins with the capture and containment of African slaves, it concludes with the rebuilding of late eighteenth- and early nineteenth-century Britain.

◆ ◆ ◆

While the chapters of this book generally unfold along a broad chronological sweep, early British Jamaica was dramatically transformed in the decades between 1760 and the late 1790s; that period—the same that witnessed the construction of Mount Plenty—deserves specific attention. The first trigger for change began on Easter morning, 1760. Inspired by a plan to supplant British colonial rule with a reconstituted African state, Tacky's Rebellion included at least fifteen hundred Africans and was the largest insurrection in the Caribbean until the Haitian Revolution, with residual outbreaks lasting until October of 1761.[28] In obvious ways, this event played a critical role in focusing the island's white population on the issue of safety. It is not a surprise that the greatest concentration of defensive houses appear in the 1760s. The year 1780 witnessed the landfall of Jamaica's deadliest hurricane, followed immediately by the worst decade for hurricane damage in the eighteenth century. The 1790s would be the decade in which Jamaica's architecture clarified its hurricane resilience in form, materials, and structure. Anxiety and alarm shaped late eighteenth-century Jamaica more acutely than it had in the half-century before.

Other assaults came in the form of economic and moral pressure. The first of these was the economic isolation resulting from the American Revolution, an event described by historians as *the* transformative event for the eighteenth-century Jamaican economy.[29] And in the 1790s, abolitionists in Britain began to organize and call for the termination of the slave trade, threatening to undermine the economic structure of the plantation machine that produced such enormous wealth. The next year, slaves on the French island of Saint-Domingue initiated a fourteen-year war that resulted in huge losses of life and the eventual establishment of a black government on that island. Not surprisingly, these are also the same decades for which historians report increasing rates of absenteeism, the departure from Jamaica for Britain of those rich white planters who could afford to do so.[30] While the scope of absenteeism is disputed, there is general agreement that Jamaica saw the greatest rates of absenteeism in the Caribbean through the later eighteenth and early nineteenth centuries. And over these same decades, Jamaican towns saw the rapid increase of their population of free blacks—individuals, often of mixed race—who had in various ways wrested themselves from slavery. The increasing numbers of free blacks and the rising power of attorneys and overseers assuming the responsibilities of absentee landowners meant that Jamaica's elite by the end of the eighteenth century included fewer clearly aspiring British gentry than at midcentury. In light of these circumstances, the preeminent Jamaican historian Barry Higman has argued that Jamaica's "First Empire optimism" persisted only into the 1780s.[31] Taken together, these factors resulted in a Jamaica of 1800 that was really very different from the Jamaica of the 1750s. At midcentury, Jamaica's wealthiest planters and merchants were all still resident on the island and they were still working to build Jamaica into the tropical front of the British Empire. Yet a half-century later, the island was governed by a white West Indian Creole elite, less committed to refinement than to personal leisure and hospitality to other whites. By the end of the eighteenth century, Jamaica had faded in the British imagination, abandoned by the wealthiest, mocked by the motherland, and overtaken in evocative power by India, but that is a topic for a different book. This history begins in Ghana.

1   Coffle, Castle, Deck, Dock

The gleaming white fort rises dramatically from the promontory overlooking the coastal town of Dixcove, Ghana, much as it has for more than three centuries (fig. 1.1). Visitors arrive in town and park at the base of the hill, climbing to the fort on foot. The path wends up the side of the hill and diverts to the west toward the small parade ground that stands between the front of the fort and the sea. Two massive, diamond-shaped bastions stand to either side of a heavily rusticated door, which opens through the solid, unbroken masonry of the curtain wall into the front courtyard of the fort. In the back corner of an interior courtyard is an arched opening into the northeast bastion, accessed by three steps. The small chamber behind is closed not by a door but a heavy iron gate (figs. 1.2, 1.3). No more than two hundred feet square, this was the slave room dedicated to the containment of Africans intended for the Atlantic slave trade. Merely 2 percent of the total square footage of the whole compound, this small cell was a critical component of the sequences of such spaces in forts operated along the west coast of Africa by England and other European powers. It played a vital role in the highly lucrative system of transatlantic slavery that defined the coastline of West Africa

and that sustained the sugar production of the British— and French, Dutch, Danish, and Spanish—West Indies for well over a century.[1]

The so-called slave holes of the English fortifications lining the west coast of Africa were and are horrifying.[2] "There was nothing to be heard but the rattling of chains, smacking of whips, and the groans and cries of our fellow men," reported Ottobah Cugoano, an emancipated slave who would later publish an account of his life. But these prisons were not the only spaces experienced by enslaved Africans in the long journey from Africa to Jamaica. While historians have dealt with many dimensions of the slave trade—and this chapter depends extensively on the published scholarship of a number of excellent historians—architectural historians have left the spaces of enslavement largely untouched.[3] This chapter situates the castles of West Africa as the second in a series of four critical spaces experienced by enslaved Africans from the moment of capture to their final sale to a British Caribbean planter: coffle, castle, deck, dock.[4] In this view, the spaces of the slave trade are very much the product of those social and economic relationships governing capture (and resistance to capture), containment,

FIG. 1.1 Dixcove Fort, Dixcove, Ghana, begun 1683.

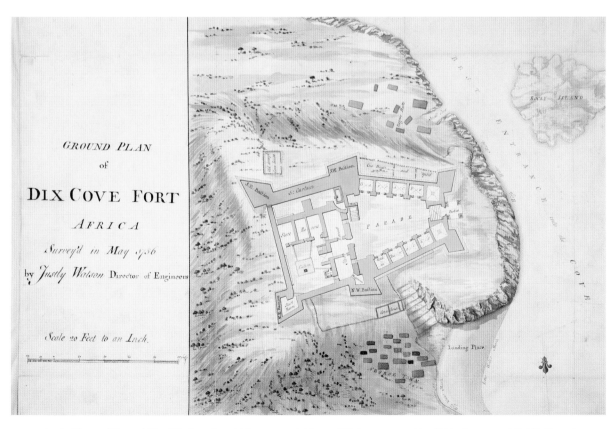

FIG. 1.2 Justly Watson, "Ground Plan Dix Cove Fort Africa surveyed, May 1756." Ink on paper, 11½ × 18½ in. (29 × 47 cm). Public Record Office, London.

transfer, and the sale of people. Understood as agents in the economic and social relationships of exchange, these spaces—in canoes, ships, and buildings—are components of a machine of production dedicated to the generation of "the slave," the fuel that drove the sugar plantation, the economic engine of early colonial Jamaica. In tracking sequences of spaces, I do not pretend to suggest that this chapter reports a "typical" experience; variations over space and time and among personal dispositions mean such an attempt is folly.[5] But the telling that follows describes in its component parts the reality for many who traveled against their will from Africa to the Caribbean on British slavers. Based on fieldwork in Ghana and on a careful examination of documentary and visual records in England, Ghana, and the United States, this chapter reconstructs the spatial experience of the enslaved, examining when possible not just the physical spaces but also the spatial experience of the senses, so powerfully captured by Cugoano.

West Africa's coastal forts and their associated spaces are rightly understood as spaces engaged in the economic processes of slave making—transforming a person into a commodity.[6] It is no accident that the definitive study of the Royal African Company—that organization that oversaw England's Africa trade until 1750—was written not by a social or political historian but by a historian of business in a series on emergent international capitalism.[7] The decisions made by Europeans along the west coast of Africa and by their African partners were motivated by economic self-interest, and over time it became increasingly clear that the highest profits lay in the production of slaves. This economic machine matured through the eighteenth century, generating finely tuned processes of exchange and function-specific architecture to support that machine. Understood as an economic process, slave making had a number of important factors that drove the decisions of enslavers. One was valuation; central to this process was the recognition that individuals became more valuable as they traveled further in the process from capture to final sale in the Americas. Allied with this is that some goods have higher value potential over other goods; in early modern African slave making this translated to gender, age, and health. A younger healthy male had far greater value potential than an older sickly female. Another reality is that damaged goods are less valuable, creating an incentive to protect your investments from damage. While deeply inhumane, these are the factors that drove many decisions in the early modern West African trade; to ignore this reality is to write poor history.

COFFLE

The first act of enslavement was, of course, capture. Enslaved Africans were sometimes the loot of war. In 1682, John Barbot, a French Huguenot who traveled West Africa in the late seventeenth century and later published his account, reported that one English trader had recently purchased three hundred Africans "almost for nothing, besides the trouble of receiving them at the beach in his boats." This was a huge number, the result of a recent war: "The Commenda men brought them from the field of battle, having obtained a victory over a neighboring nation, and taken a great number of prisoners."[8] Nonetheless, as recent historical scholarship has made clear, most Africans sold into slavery were not legitimate prisoners of war but victims of internal legal processes, debt, famine, or, most commonly, kidnapping.[9] One English observer by the name of Bowman wrote, "We often saw several thousand men in full war paint march inland where they stormed the villages, set the houses ablaze and caught the inhabitants." Francis Owen, another English trader, described how an African trader "went out with his troops,

FIG. 1.3 "Slave hole" gate at Dixcove Fort.

FIG. 1.4 "Representation of a Lott of Fullanis . . ." Samuel Gable logbook, 1793. National Maritime Museum, Greenwich, England.

set three sides of a village ablaze, placed his soldiers at the fourth side to grab those inhabitants who ran out of the flames."[10] One young Jamaican slave reported to his owner that his village was attacked by a marauding party who "came in the night, and set fire to the houses, and killed most of the inhabitants with guns and cutlasses—particularly the old."[11] Especially as the eighteenth century unfolded, kidnapping became the primary mode of slave production across West Africa as African traders worked to meet the escalating demand for enslaved Africans from their European trading partners.

Surviving African accounts of capture, of course, are rare. That written by Ottobah Cugoano, published in 1787 as part of the emerging critique of the slave trade, offers a rare glimpse into the experience of an African boy. Playing with friends, Cugoano was assaulted by "ruffians" who claimed the boys had "committed a fault against their lord" and must travel with them to answer for this fault. Threatened with weapons, the boys submitted and walked

for two days to what was likely a market town, where they were divided among the houses of locals, colluders in the plot. After spending six days in that town, he was eventually conveyed under the direction of another trader to a town populated with white men near the coast. The next morning, the trader took him into the castle under the presumption of obtaining some trade goods, but it was in the castle that young Ottobah came to fully understand his kidnapping.[12] Asa-Asa, another African boy, relayed how his hometown was attacked and burned by invaders. They pillaged for two days and then carried off all the survivors in a coffle of about twenty.[13] It is not surprising that these accounts come from children. The increasing numbers of older children sold into slavery over the course of the eighteenth century have led some historians to see kidnapping supplanting war as the primary means of introducing persons into the slave trade market, especially as the value of adolescent males—unwounded by war—surpassed the value of all other categories of potential slaves.[14] Adam, an enslaved African in Jamaica, reported that after a succession of trades, his final purchaser collected twenty boys before sending the coffle to the seacoast for sale to the captain of a ship.[15] Millions of Africans were delivered to the coast, some as a consequence of war or crimes in their villages, but as the century unfolded most were delivered to coastal factories by armed raiding parties through a method called "grand pillage"—being stolen from their homes as they slept, worked, or played.[16]

Once captured, the enslaved African was bound to a coffle in the forced march from the point of capture to trading posts along the coast. A remarkable early representation of such a gang appears in a watercolor sketch drawn by Captain Samuel Gable into the logbook of the *Sandown*, an English ship that slaved in Sierra Leone in 1793. Entitled in part "Representation of a Lott of Fullanis bringing their slaves for sale to the Europeans," the image shows a collection of drivers armed with bows and arrows marching seven captives in a gang along the horizon of the picture plane (fig. 1.4). The implements of restraint in the gang are the diagonal yokes that reach from the waist of one captive to the neck of another. Other slaves are carrying large baskets on their heads, likely filled with food and essential supplies, or sometimes other trade items such as ivory tusks, which had to be carried with the coffle during the days, weeks, and sometimes months of a march.[17] But historical analysis suggests that the coffle was much larger than the few people represented in this image, ranging from dozens to up to eight hundred enslaved in a single caravan of coffles.[18]

The yokes were the target of much criticism among abolitionists by the late eighteenth century. Thomas Clarkson's *Letters on the Slave Trade*, published in 1791, included plates illustrating variations on the yoke (fig. 1.5).[19] In the simplest version, Clarkson reported, Africans are bound around the neck by two pieces of wood fastened to each other at the ends. Such individual devices prevent escape by creating an impediment to the escapee who cannot quickly run through the dense forest. A second version shows a single yoke with crutches at each end, one for each of two people. The third has a crutch at one end and a twisted rope at the other, by which it is hung around the neck. "It is reported to be so heavy," Clarkson writes, "that it is extremely difficult for the person who wears it to walk, much less to escape or run away." The only way to manage the weight of the log was to rest the crutched end of the yoke on the shoulders

of the person before. In Clarkson's account the straight end of the yoke is tied around the person's neck; in the captain's sketch, it appears to be secured around the waist.[20] Some accounts suggest that rather than yokes, some Africans were bound neck to neck in chains with their hands bound behind the waist or to their sides.[21] In this fashion, most coffles walked from their point of capture to the coast. Evidence of the torture of this march was clear to Carl Wadstrom when he noted the "mangled bodies of several [Africans who had just arrived], whose wounds were still bleeding . . . a most shocking spectacle."[22] The march to the sea was gruesome. Historians' estimates of mortality vary widely, but it is absolutely clear that not all who began the journey would live to see the ocean.[23]

While evidence is scant and uncertain, historians generally agree that most Africans came from within a few hundred miles from the coast but that some traveled great distances, from as far as Timbuktu, approximately one thousand miles from the closest forts or factories on the Gold Coast.[24] Hans Christian Monrad indicated that "most of the slaves that are sold in Guinea [the Gold Coast] come from Ashantee, Fantee, Acutim, Crepee, and Dunko . . . all these places lie more or less south of the Sahara."[25] The majority of Africans sold into slavery were victims of complex African trading networks that brought captives from across the interior to the coast.[26] Ghanaian historian Akosua Perbi has determined that early modern Ghana had at least nine major trade routes by which captives were channeled to the coast.[27] Most of the interior routes passed through Kumasi; one of the major spurs from Kumasi led directly to Cape Coast. Those traveling substantial distances likely passed through one of the interior's many market towns. Perbi has identified as many as sixty-six market towns in Ghana, most of which probably engaged in the trade of slaves.[28] The accounts of capture reported by enslaved Africans to planter Bryan Edwards reinforce this understanding. Cudjoe journeyed for two months before arriving at the coast; Adam traveled as a captive for a month, while Oliver, who was traded to other Africans six times, reported that he came from a village "far from the sea."[29] Captives became commodities in the network that spread broadly across west and central Africa. Asa-Asa, for example, reported that he had been sold six times over the course of about six months, "sometimes for money, sometimes for cloth, and sometimes for guns," before he arrived at the coast.[30]

The largest and most important market town in what would become modern Ghana was Salaga, located approximately three hundred miles inland from Cape Coast. This critical town enjoyed a very important position. Situated between the two branches of the Volta River, Salaga was easily accessible from the coast. The town was also the terminus for two branches of the trans-Saharan trade routes and was the market town with the greatest access to North Africa.[31] Salaga was also politically important as the major market town under the rule of the Asante, after their capture of the town in 1744. The Asante were one of the major slavers providing Africans for the transatlantic market, and the Salaga market became a major point of exchange.[32] Recent archaeological investigations have uncovered evidence of the courtyard of the large slave warehouse as well as water dams and cisterns used to bathe slaves before sale.[33] As described by Perbi, the

Salaga market was divided into two sections, foodstuffs and slaves. The majority of the foodstuffs were sold in the morning, while the sales of people usually took place in the afternoons, a lag that gave traders time to organize their "stock" by gender and age and to assess their value. Some period accounts suggest that the daily opening of the slave market was announced by a town crier, who had to be paid by traders to announce sales.[34] This was an experience often repeated; many if not most people would be housed in slave camps and sold multiple times at markets in Africa before their final arrival at the sea coast.[35]

Research on the internal trade of the Bights of Biafra and Benin, the regions that would become southeastern Nigeria, suggests that traders there also depended on a vast network that penetrated deep into the African interior.[36] The diary of Antera Duke, one of the leading African traders in Old Calabar in the Bight of Biafra, indicates that he exploited a trading network that ranged over thirty thousand square miles and that most of his slaves came from market towns near the fringes of that region, many from the Camaroon grasslands, most having already traveled great distances.[37] David Northrup's work on this region suggests that many Africans, if not a majority, were brought from at least as far as Bauchi, a major market town more than five hundred miles from the coast, although the last one hundred fifty miles were surely traveled by canoe on the Niger or Cross Rivers.[38] Many of these enslaved Africans also passed through the market town of Idah, near the critical junction of the Niger and Benue Rivers. The market in Idah occurred every ten days, was attended by as many as six thousand people, and witnessed the sale of approximately three hundred enslaved Africans at each market.[39]

If travel by land in a coffle was the experience of most enslaved Africans, some were also transported from market to market via canoe. This was certainly the case for those in Gambia and the Bight of Biafra, both regions dominated by major river systems. Fashioned from the trunk of a single enormous tree, these canoes could be as large as eighty feet long and could hold scores of paddlers, raiders, and captives.[40] When preparing for a raiding expedition, these canoes were fitted out with a range of weaponry including "two guns, which were three pounders, fixed upon a block of wood; one in the canoe's stern and one in the bow."[41] Fleets of up to twelve canoes would depart on expeditions that could last three weeks, returning with as many as thirty enslaved Africans per canoe.

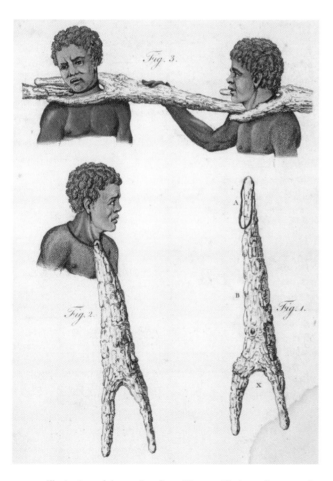

FIG. 1.5 Illustration of slave yokes, from Thomas Clarkson, *Letters on the slave-trade, and the state of the natives in those parts of Africa, which are contiguous to Fort St. Louis and Goree: written at Paris in December 1789, and January 1790.* London: Printed and sold by J. Phillips, 1791. Harvard Libraries.

These canoes were a critical component of slaving in Old Calabar; Equiano noticed that some people seemed to live out of their canoes, which were fitted out with "household utensils and provisions of all kinds . . . [some] staid and cooked in theirs, and laid in them all night."[42] In such canoes, the first captives traveled for weeks, as described by one sailor with "their Arms generally pinioned behind their backs with Grass Ropes. They are made to lie down in the Bottom frequently of a wet canoe."[43] In Gambia and the Bights of Benin and Biafra, most of the enslaved arrived at their final African destination via canoe; along the Gold Coast that arrival was on foot as part of a coffle.

Before arriving at a coastal fort, most coffles would pass through the castle town: "Their streets and roads . . . are only poorly kept clean so there is a right good smell," wrote Johannes Rask in the early eighteenth century. But he then asserted that their courtyards are "usually very neat and clean" and that trees planted along the streets "provide a comfortable shade and a lovely appearance so that every negeri looks like a small green grove."[44] Occupants of the town included the majority of the castle slaves, or those slaves owned by the castle—not intended for resale—purchased to undertake work in the fort.[45] One report from 1749 lists 379 slaves for Cape Coast Castle, all listed by name and occupation, which ranged from washerwoman to brick mason.[46] African and European traders had houses and offices in town; they frequently paid a regular fee to house in the prisons of the castle those slaves they intended to sell to ship captains. Centuries-old multistory masonry buildings are likely the remnants of such traders' houses (fig. 1.6). Predating the erection of the castle, the town itself became a socially and economically complex entity thoroughly integrated into the workings of the castle.[47]

At some point, however, the coffle came in sight of the castle. As described by one European observer, the castles appeared to be "chalk mountains, especially when the sun shines directly on them."[48] The first sight of the castle was a terrifying prospect, for at that moment enslaved Africans came to understand their fate; as one firsthand European observer wrote, "To be exported is, for them, synonymous with being murdered."[49] He continued, "sometimes a gag is placed in the slave's mouth, which is forced wide open, in order to keep him from shouting. . . . This intractability among the slaves as they approach the coast also has its origin partly from their conviction that they are going to be shipped out to places where they will be eaten."[50] Others, like young Cugoano, were tricked into

FIG. 1.6 European slaver's house, Elmina, Ghana.

approaching the castle. "Those who are brought without knowing the fate that awaits them there . . . are violently fallen upon in the forts and dragged into the slave holes. . . . They, especially the women, throw themselves to the ground, shriek, stretch their hands over their heads and turn their eyes to heaven."[51]

CASTLE

At only two hundred square feet, the slave hole in the northeast bastion of Dixcove Fort is hardly the vast dungeon often assumed to be part of the forts along the Gold Coast. And while this space is the result of mid-eighteenth-century rebuilding, the amount of space dedicated to the containment of enslaved Africans at Dixcove and most other forts was never very large. In part, this is because at the point of their construction in the later seventeenth century, the trade in slaves was only one growing dimension of the broader Africa trade undertaken from these forts. Dixcove was also just one component of a system of forts along the coast built by the Royal African Company in the late seventeenth and early eighteenth centuries. These forts represented footholds by the English on various parcels of land granted by treaties between the English and various local kings. They were not independent operations. Most, like Dixcove, were satellites, extensions of the largest and central fortification at Cape Coast.[52]

Given its remarkably advantageous site the castle at Cape Coast was from the 1670s onward the center of English trading interests along the West African coast. Through the seventeenth century, the fort housed a garrison never smaller than fifty men and often over one hundred. The fort also boasted an officer corps of ten to fifteen and as many as thirty castle slaves.[53] The Royal African

Company lost its monopoly on the Africa trade at the end of the seventeenth century, but it continued to oversee the maintenance and construction of forts along the West African coast until the middle of the eighteenth century.[54]

Physically dominating the landscape, forts created the sense of a secure site for the high-stakes buying and trading of slaves. A substantial percentage of indoor space in most remote forts was given over to warehouses for storage of the various European and East Indian goods used in the Africa trade.[55] One account by Dane Hans Christian Monrad, penned between 1805 and 1809, reported that the castle warehouses stored those things considered most valuable by African traders, especially "guns . . . gunpowder, shot, flint stones, iron, lead, swords, knives of various kinds, all manner of cotton, calico, salem puris [a cotton cloth from India], silk cloth, woolen caps, quantities of beads, mirrors, and . . . tobacco, rum, brandy and cowries."[56] While the particulars vary from account to account, it is quite clear that the most valuable trade item across Africa was guns.[57] It was critical that fort warehouses remain filled with ready trade items to continue to entice African traders to choose that fort over others.[58] But some forts also offered a containment space for small lots of captives during negotiations between castle governors and African traders. The fort at Elmina was described as having a "slave yard" in the early eighteenth century, suggesting an enclosed yard rather than a dedicated dungeon.[59]

Careful examination of early plans and of the surviving fabric of Dixcove and of many other forts makes it clear that these forts never dedicated a large space for the housing of enslaved Africans. They were always understood to be suppliers to the primary trading post at Cape Coast Castle. In fact, Dixcove's placement ensured its importance not so much as a slave fort—although it was one—but as a guard over a supply of essential natural resources. A heavily forested site provided lumber, a natural bed of limestone-sourced masonry building materials, and a natural spring made it an excellent location for ship refreshment and repair.[60] As a result, its role in the slave trade was largely as a point of temporary holding and transfer.[61] Of course, captives passed through Dixcove or other fortifications and factories along the coast, but they were only in transit. Records of the Royal African Company from 1678 suggest that between April and December of that year, Cape Coast housed 1,854 Africans for sale, quite obviously not all at the same time: 366 arrived from Anamabu, 330 from Egya, 166 from the fort at Accra, and the same number from

Winnebah; the rest are unaccounted for but probably came from small factories along the coast or from traders delivering directly to Cape Coast.[62]

Cape Coast was the central site dedicated to the storage and sale of Africans through the period of the lawful English trade in slaves. Unlike the smaller fortifications, Cape Coast had an underground dungeon with substantial capacity.[63] These dungeons were created by the English expansion of the fort in the 1680s; they were little more than the quarry from which the stone for the curtain walls and new bastions had been extracted. The massive hole, it seems, was vaulted and paved over to create a central parade ground.[64] One account from 1682 describes the dungeon as a "mansion . . . cut out of the rocky ground, arched and divided into several rooms; so that it will conveniently contain a thousand Blacks, let down at an opening for the purpose." The advantage of keeping the enslaved underground was "good security to the garrison against any insurrection."[65] A 1756 plan of the castle shows a number of ventilators in the floor of the courtyard, extending all the way across the parade grounds, presumably inserted to deliver more light and fresh air into the spaces below (fig. 1.7). These ventilators suggest that these dungeons were vast indeed, spanning the width of the parade ground. Inspection of the surviving fabric of the fort suggests that some portion of the series of chambers under the courtyard and the seaward curtain wall were these first dungeons. These chambers had no natural light except that leaking in through the single openings in the roof vaults through which slaves would be raised and lowered (fig. 1.8). While period descriptions suggest that the dungeons were intended to hold up to a thousand captives, records suggest that they actually held far fewer. One account from the turn of the eighteenth century, for example, records only four hundred Africans held in the dungeons of Cape Coast.[66] With or without the ventilators, the conditions must have been unthinkable. Even up in the best apartments, one factor wrote in 1708, "there is never a dry room to lye in."[67]

The early history of the British forts along the west coast of Africa falls into two major eras: their formation under the Royal African Company and their restructuring and expansion under the Company of Merchants Trading to Africa, which took over control of the fortifications in May of 1751. This change was driven largely by the press to undermine the official royal monopoly on the British slave trade held by the Royal African Company at its founding.

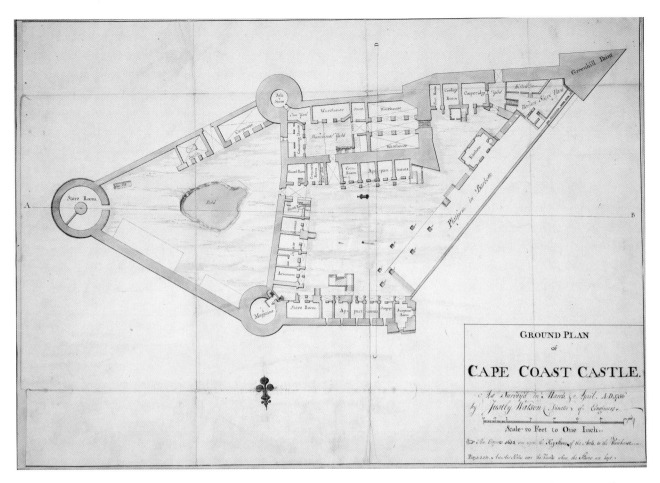

FIG. 1.7 Justly Watson, "Ground Plan of Cape Coast Castle, 1756." The ventilators are the squares opening through the courtyard pavement. Ink on paper, 18.5 × 27 in. (47 × 69 cm). Public Record Office, London.

In the later seventeenth century and in full drive by the early eighteenth century, merchants—many from Bristol and London but eventually Liverpool as well—launched voyages independent of the Royal African Company; this change saw the company's slow demise.[68] Founded in 1750, the Company of Merchants Trading to Africa took over the West Africa trade and offered a major restructuring of the slave trade. The newly founded company was open to anyone who wanted to enter the slave trade. Parliament agreed to pay a yearly grant to the company for the maintenance of the British forts along the coast of West Africa. A London-based African Committee of three men, one representative each from London, Liverpool, and Bristol, received the monies and then gathered the necessary materials, men, and other resources and sent them to Cape Coast to be distributed to the various forts as necessary.

Through the 1750s and 1760s, the Company of Merchants spent a great deal of time and resources assessing and improving the physical condition of the

fortifications and building new forts. In 1756, the company informed the governor of Cape Coast Castle that "the ruinous condition of the Forts in general, is a matter of great concern to us."[69] That same year, the company sent engineer John Appleby to Africa to oversee the reconstruction of the forts with the instruction that he was to be in charge of all designs "except you shall find it necessary from the opinion of the governor and council at Cape Coast Castle to make any Alterations in the Lodgements for Slaves or any of the inner Apartment."[70] The company wished the fortifications to be made substantial "making good use of lime, and not clay as formerly," objecting to the mud-walled construction of so much of the fort construction under the Royal African Company.[71] In 1758, the company required reports from the chiefs of each fort assessing the material conditions of the company's forts along the coast. Letters sent in 1760 suggest that those chiefs had not repaired or upgraded the conditions of the forts to the expectations of the company.[72]

Under the Royal African Company, the fortifications had been understood as trading posts where Europeans could engage in business transactions with African traders. One of the increasingly lucrative markets, of course, was the trade in slaves. In the seventeenth and early eighteenth centuries, many forts housed captives not in dungeons but in stockades called slave yards or barracoons outside the fort walls.[73] Under the Company of Merchants, the fortifications become installations dedicated almost exclusively to the trade in slaves, and the architecture responded to the changing priorities. For the first time, fort plans show slave containment cells. Plans also demarcate slave yards—now used for daily exercise—and identify ventilators for prisons below. Records from the second half of the century demonstrate that the sick from among the enslaved were sent out of the castle into town to recover, so as not to contaminate the rest of the African captives. One 1753 letter from the castle governor to a ship's captain reports that the eighteen Africans being held in the castle were all in good health but that three others had been sent to town, and two of them had already died. A 1770s listing of castle rules reports that no sick slave was to remain in the castle.[74] Such attention to conditions was quite obviously driven not by general concerns for welfare but by the economic incentive to preserve the value of an investment. Remote forts were refitted with secure slave cells for more effective containment. New forts were built at points central to the slave trade, and a new set of dungeons were built at Cape Coast, which remained the British flagship fort. Under the Company of Merchants, the forts became slaving machines.

The reconstruction undertaken by the Company of Merchants in the extensive expansion of the castle at Cape Coast produced new dungeons and warehouses flanking a new, carefully managed route channeling the enslaved from the dungeons to the ships. Designs for the new dungeons in a defensive spur were prepared in 1768 and construction was completed soon thereafter. Five vaulted chambers were built into this large new double bastion that overlooked the sea (fig. 1.9). A parade-ground door opened into a tunnel that led down into the chambers, connecting with the second chamber in the sequence of five (fig. 1.10). Each of the five chambers was sheltered by a massive masonry barrel vault, illuminated by an end wall window, and fitted out with a sewage gutter that ran down the spine of the complex (figs. 1.11, 1.12, compare with 1.7). An archaeological excavation of the entire dungeon undertaken in 1972 unearthed food debris, body ornaments, and other evidence that demonstrated that all five chambers were used for human containment.[75] The first chamber was structurally isolated from the rest by a small opening that originally had a lockable door. Unlike all the others, that chamber has a brick-laid floor and a much more sophisticated drainage system for more effective cleaning out of waste. Castle governors kept a regular practice of purchasing Africans in advance for ship captains and

FIG. 1.8 Courtyard and parade ground, Cape Coast Castle, Cape Coast, Ghana. The square opening to the left of the stairs is an entrance into the early dungeons. The ventilators can be seen to the far right on the edge of the courtyard.

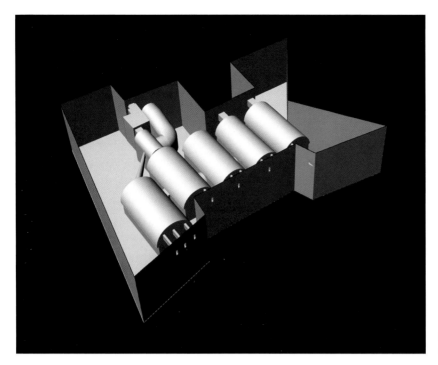

FIG. 1.9 Still from digital model of the ca. 1770 dungeons, Cape Coast Castle.

owners, and sometimes even planters in the Caribbean. It is possible that these preselected individuals were housed in this chamber of better quality, both to differentiate them from the rest of the captives and to help ensure the health of those individuals who had already become an investment.[76] Similarly, the last of the chambers also had evidence of a lockable iron gate with evidence for shelving, while the three middle chambers were all open one to the next. The specific features of the final chamber suggest that like the first chamber it was dedicated to particular functions and not likely used for general containment of slaves. Through the sequence of all five, the packed earth floor slopes from either side toward the single conduit for waste that runs down the middle of the rooms. And although they are now blocked up, the last three chambers had large window openings near the crest of the roof vault—presumably with iron bars—allowing far more light into these dungeons than in the earlier set underneath the courtyard. The first chamber also has a curious shaft leading from the entrance passage into the chamber, probably intended to filter in some natural light. In all five, small ventilators on the walls opposite the windows were intended to allow some airflow through the chambers.

Much larger than the previous dungeons, far better lit and with far greater capacity for airflow, more easily accessed and more easily cleaned than the former dungeon site, the new dungeons were—according to

contemporary descriptions—capable of holding upward of two thousand people, doubling the capacity of the earlier dungeons. But as was the case with the earlier descriptions, the claimed capacity of the dungeon was far higher than the reality of persons held in these spaces in any moment in time. The massive *Voyages: The Transatlantic Slave Trade Database* by David Eltis and Martin Halbert, funded by the National Endowment for the Humanities, has made available an extraordinary body of numeric information about the slave trade.[77] A recent query of the database has allowed a collection of data about every slaver voyage that departed from Cape Coast Castle from 1685 to 1807. Data

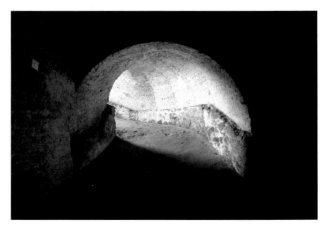

FIG. 1.10 Entrance tunnel descending into the ca. 1770 dungeons, Cape Coast Castle.

FIG. 1.11 Interior of the fourth chamber, Cape Coast Castle dungeons. The end wall window to the courtyard has been closed in.

from the *Voyages* records make clear that the reconstruction of the dungeons by the Company of Merchants was in response to the greater demand on the fort. Under the Royal African Company, from 1685 to 1749, Cape Coast Castle provided an average of 517 enslaved Africans per year, with the heaviest supply in a sharp spike in the 1720s with an average of 1,265 slaves per year. Those shipments increased rapidly under the Company of Merchants, who supplied from Cape Coast an average of 842 slaves per

year in the 1750s and then a sharp increase to an average of 1,514 slaves per year in the 1760s. Clearly in the face of that increase, the Company of Merchants felt the need to outfit the fort by building dungeons in the late 1760s in response to the heavier demand and to better ensure the health (and value) of their investments. And they were right. The number of enslaved Africans departing from Cape Coast each year jumped to an average of 1,847 in the 1780s and peaked in the 1790s at an average of 1,998 per year.

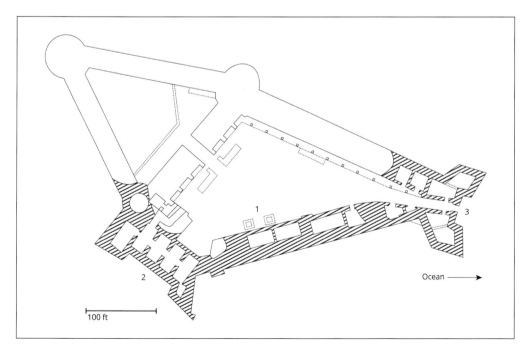

100 ft

Ocean ⟶

FIG. 1.12 Plan of Cape Coast Castle. (1) Air vents into the seventeenth-century dungeon; (2) 1768 dungeons; (3) 1777 horn work and warehouses.

Even so, these better-lit and roomier dungeons were still dungeons. Accounts suggest that upon arrival at the fort, Africans were "struck into chains," meaning bound by chains into gangs of ten to twenty. Individuals so struck remained in their gang until sold to a ship.[78] Cugoano's account of his own capture in 1770 is the sole account of the experience of containment in Cape Coast's dungeons. He was kept in the prison "for three days, where I heard the groans and cries of many, and saw some of my fellow captives." The separation from and then reunion with his friends betrays the reality of multiple African traders and multiple routes to this single dungeon space. Describing a still dark and likely very damp, cavernous space, his account reports more on what he heard than what he saw: "When a vessel arrived to conduct us away to the ship, it was a most horrible scene; there was nothing to be heard but the rattling of chains, smacking of whips, and the groans and cries of our fellow men. Some would not stir from the ground, when they were lashed and beat in the most horrible manner."[79] The sharp sounds of whips and the low groans or loud cries certainly echoed through the cavernous chambers of Cape Coast's dungeons.

But contrary to Cugoano's account, which reports that his coterie of slaves remained in the dungeons for the three days of his containment, other records suggest that by the second half of the eighteenth century enslaved Africans were spending the majority of their days not in the dungeons but in the courtyard or parade ground of Cape Coast and other castles.[80] Like the drive to build healthier dungeons, this decision was likely motivated by the drive to preserve the health of the captives as a means of sustaining their resale value. A 1756 plan of Cape Coast demarcates the newly established yard for enslaved women, just above the large bastion called Greenhill's Point. Records report that the large parade ground dominating the rest of the castle's open interior was used as a yard for male slaves, although they remained bound in lots of ten or twenty. These yards created an outdoor space for slaves to take in some fresh air and exercise. Accounts also suggest that the captives were driven down to the ocean once or twice daily for washing.[81]

Long days in the courtyard were occasionally interrupted by the sights and sounds of everyday life. Castle records report on an assortment of tropical animals kept in the castle as pets, from chimpanzees to parrots, and once even a leopard called Sai.[82] This menagerie added variety to the generally monotonous soundscape. Vultures, circling to collect scraps from butchering, frequented the castle, as

did voracious biting red ants.[83] The hours were marked by the regular ringing of the castle bell.[84] In the evenings, after the return of the enslaved to the dungeons, the rattle of chains was a constant sound that echoed enough to be heard constantly throughout the apartments above.[85] The monotony of the bells was occasionally broken by the fife and drum corps who played for newly arrived visitors, special events in the governor's hall, and the frequent funerals of officers.[86] The monotony would also have been broken by the screams of newly arrived coffles or the regular flogging of castle slaves or of merchants' slaves from town, often sent to the castle for whippings.[87]

The announcement of the arrival of a ship's captain by the fife and drum corps meant the likelihood of a sale. In the courtyard, the castle slaves would wash and oil the bodies of Africans to be sold, "either chained or loose, so that they form a circle." The buyers then undertook a thorough examination of the bodies of those offered for sale. "The slave must open his mouth wide, show his teeth; they smell in his mouth, and look very carefully into his eyes; he must perform all manner of movements with his arms and legs; the secret parts are examined, during which I have seen many, especially young Negresses crying." After the inspection, the buyer "marks those slaves he has chosen with a piece of white chalk right across the head."[88] But not all submitted to inspections. One 1767 account from the Dutch fort of Elmina reported that when the slaves were ordered from the dungeons into the yards they "cut their own throats: one Negroe even cut the throat of his wife and then his own; the yard of the noble company's chief castle was thus turned into a bloodbath."[89] Barring such violent resistance, the victims might be branded right after sale, "as the seller often sees a chance to exchange the sold slave for one of inferior quality."[90] Those selected and branded were then sent out of the castle to canoes waiting on the shore.

The process of moving those recently sold out to the canoes was entirely restructured by a second major construction at Cape Coast Castle in the later eighteenth century: a new set of warehouses completed in 1777 (see fig. 1.12).[91] Letters from the governor to the Company of Merchants in London make it clear that the company prepared designs for the new construction but that the governor rejected them, preferring to build to his own design. "I am now erecting a fortification in the form of a horn work," he wrote to the company. He hoped that they "will not blame me for deviating from Mr. Hipperley's design, and be enabled at the same time to see the impropriety of Mr. Oxbridge's plan." He was quite pleased with the new construction given that the "old warehouses are likely to fall soon, there are in [the new spur warehouses] space to contain all that used to be put in the old warehouse," including "all the liquors, provisions, and store that will ever be in the castle at one time."[92] These new warehouses were built in the form of a "horn work" or protrusion from a fort flanked at the opening by flared bastions. This new horn work was also a new channel by which the recently sold could be securely marched out of the fort and toward the canoes waiting outside the castle walls. The new construction included an increasingly constrained passage that gently slopes down from the height of the parade ground to an exterior platform only a few steps above the beach. In addition to the gradual constriction of the passageway, which limited the damage possible from the press of panicked captives, there was also a sentry box immediately above it (figs. 1.13, 1.14).

From this position, a guard would have easy surveillance over the stream of enslaved and could shoot if required. The investment of so much attention to a passage out to the sea clearly suggests that those few minutes of transfer from courtyard to ship were fraught with anxiety for both captor and captive.

DECK

The view of the ocean and the slave ship surely incited a range of emotions. Equiano wrote of his experience in the 1760s: "The first object which saluted my eyes was the sea, and a slave ship, which was then riding at anchor. . . . These filled me with astonishment, which was soon converted to terror, when I was carried on board."[93] As the majority of people sold into slavery came from Africa's interior, few had ever seen the ocean, a European, a sailing ship, or the ever-present sharks that favored factory sites and followed slave ships.

FIG. 1.13 View down the 1777 horn work to the ocean gate with surveillance window of sentry box above, Cape Coast Castle.

FIG. 1.14 View from the sentry box over the passage to the ocean gate, Cape Coast Castle.

The first leg of the middle passage was the transit from shore to ship.[94] In many cases this passage was undertaken via canoe provided by African merchants and manned by free African "canoemen," or else it was via the yawl or longboat carried on the ship.[95] For the enslaved headed to those ships anchored in the calmer waters of a river delta, this voyage was brief and generally uneventful, as represented in a vignette of a 1760s print of the Bristol slaver the *Southwell* anchored off the coast of West Africa (fig. 1.15). In the scene three male slaves in a coffle are loaded into a canoe. To the landside, the British captain and the African slaver—both wearing the British tricorn as a sign of their mutual empowerment—shake hands to complete the trade, shaded by another African carrying an umbrella. Near the ship, enslaved Africans scramble out of a canoe and labor to board the *Southwell* having apparently crossed without calamity. For most, however, the passage was harrowing and occasionally fatal. Without the protection of a harbor or river, ships along the Gold Coast and the Windward Coast typically anchored well past the surf in a band of coastal waters commonly called "the roads," at times as much as a mile offshore.[96] Canoes used to pass through the surf were usually fashioned from one single, large tree and could shuttle as many as twenty captives, who usually remained chained in pairs for the voyage to the ship.[97] For the majority, of course, the ocean was unfamiliar and terrifying, and reports of resistance, small-scale insurrection, and suicide of those boarded on canoes are numerous. Fear of the ocean was justified, especially in the stormy season from April to July.[98] Overloading of canoes or the violence of the surf sometimes resulted in an overturned canoe. Chained in pairs and often unable to swim, captives would perish by drowning or were attacked by sharks.[99] As one observer wrote, "Predatory sharks are to be found here by the thousands; it is not seldom that the negroes are devoured by them when their canoes capsize or they fall overboard. I myself have been witness to such a dreadful sight."[100] Sometimes captives threw themselves overboard willingly. One English captain reported, "The Negroes are so willful and loth to leave their own country, that they have often leap'd out of canoes . . . into the sea, and kept underwater till they are drowned."[101]

Once on board the deck of the ship, the Africans were stripped naked, if they had not been already, and were inspected by the captain and the ship's surgeon if the ship retained one.[102] This inspection took place under a thatched shelter that was built to shade most of the deck

during the wait along the African coast; such a thatched shelter is on the deck in the vignette to the right in the print of the *Southwell* (see fig. 1.15).[103] The inspection was humiliating and terrifying. Equiano's description of the experience is a rare report:

> I was immediately handled and tossed up, to see if I were sound, by some of the crew, and I was now persuaded that I had got into a world of bad spirits and they were going to kill me. Their complexions, too, differing so much from ours, their long hair, and the language they spoke united to confirm in me this belief. Indeed, such were the horrors of views and fears at that moment that if ten thousand worlds had been my own, I would freely have parted with them all to have exchanged my condition with that of the meanest slave in my own country.[104]

Those remaining on board were then usually shaved and sent into the prisons below deck; those rejected by the captain or the surgeon boarded the canoe once again for the return journey to the shore.[105] While the intention was clearly to strip Africans of everything but their own bodies, work by Jerome Handler has demonstrated that enslaved Africans were frequently able to transport small personal effects.[106]

Since Africans were usually loaded on ships soon after their purchase by the captain, those purchased early in a ship's season along the coast had a long and miserable waiting period before the ship departed. Ships often remained offshore for at least three months, sometimes as long as a year, waiting to collect a full cargo of captives.[107] Because captains widely believed that the newly enslaved were more likely to engage in insurrection or suicide while the coastline was still in sight, captives might be kept below deck from the time of purchase to the time of departure from the coast.[108] Historians suggest that just as many if not more Africans died while waiting to depart as during the middle passage itself, as a result of this long wait often entirely below deck.[109] After some months, the ship would be filled to capacity, and the captain would set sail. Under horrific conditions, millions of enslaved Africans eventually left the coast of Africa on European and American slavers and began the months-long voyage of the middle passage to the Americas.[110]

The slaves were delivered to a wide range of ships that were usually converted for this use.[111] Everything from small sloops and schooners to very large ships were used in the slave trade. Among the smallest on record was a

FIG. 1.15 Nicholas Pocock, "The Southwell Frigate, Trading on the Coast of Africa," 1760s. Monochrome drawing on paper, mounted. Bristol Museum and Art Gallery.

ten-ton vessel reported in 1761 intending to carry only thirty captives from Africa to St. Kitts.[112] The largest was the *Parr*, a 566-ton ship purpose-built in 1797 in Liverpool for brothers Thomas and John Parr of that city. Designed to carry seven hundred enslaved and a crew of one hundred, the *Parr* was a floating fortress and dungeon.[113] The average tonnage of slavers before 1725 was 179 tons, but this average slowly increased over time.[114] Through the seventeenth and into the eighteenth century, the majority of British vessels used in the slave trade were built in London. In the early eighteenth century the center of construction shifted to Bristol, only to be overtaken by Liverpool by the 1750s.[115] By the later eighteenth century, a few American ports, especially Charleston, began to overtake Liverpool, largely because of their easier

access to abundant and inexpensive wood.[116] While the historical record about slave voyages becomes increasingly complex and more complete, the material record remains very thin. Not a single slaver ship survives and only two slaver wrecks have been identified and excavated. The *Henrietta Marie*, an English slave ship, sank off the coast of Florida in 1700 and the *Fredensborg* ran aground in southern Norway in 1768. Neither was carrying enslaved Africans when they ended their voyaging, yet the excavators of the *Fredensborg* have uncovered the cannon that would have been fired as enslaved Africans were loaded, and barrels of animal bones that reveal that the crew were fed salted meats, including beef, veal, and mutton, although incisions in the bones indicate that the best cuts were removed before shipping. The excavation also shed light on the material culture of the Atlantic trade, including fine ceramics, likely for use by the officers, bindings for a prayer book and psalter, elephant and hippopotamus tusks, and three hundred mahogany planks, likely Jamaican mahogany, which plays an important role in this book's concluding chapter.[117]

It was in Liverpool in the middle decades of the century that purpose-built ships like the *Parr* were first constructed (fig. 1.16).[118] These ships tended to be slightly larger in scale than ships intended for other purposes, to accommodate the increased width and height required for below-deck stowage of slaves. Slavers were built with copper lining to protect the hull from wood-boring worms common in the tropical waters off the coast of Africa. Slaver-builders generally replaced deck hatches with grates that would allow some minor airflow down into the prisons below.[119] Lastly, slavers were usually designed to include a range of air ports along the sides of the ship that when opened allowed some airflow into the below-deck prisons. But, of course, these air ports could only be opened in calmer seas.[120] Such air portals are visible in the 1780s portrait of a Liverpool slave ship by William Jackson, now in the Merseyside Maritime Museum in Liverpool (fig. 1.17). The construction of purpose-built slavers accounted for the major economic boom in Liverpool in the last two decades of the slave trade. Between 1787 and 1807 Liverpool shipbuilders produced 469 vessels, twenty-one ships per year.[121]

Slavers usually dedicated the greater part of the space on the main deck for the stowage of their human cargo. While the size of shipments generally increased over time, the average number of enslaved Africans on a British slaver was about 230. Probably as a result of demand, shipments to Jamaica were usually a bit larger, averaging about 270.[122] Often shipped in ratios of two to one, men were separated from women and were housed in the largest space, usually between the main mast and the bow of the ship. When ordering a purpose-built ship from a shipbuilder in Newport, Rhode Island, Joseph Manesty requested "5 feet twixt Decks" for holding captives, a typical space allotted for this purpose.[123] This space was subdivided by a platform that extended from the walls of the ship about six feet into the room, leaving less than two and a half feet of vertical space for those men lying on or under the platform. The men were almost always bound wrist and ankle—and sometimes by the neck—in pairs. Archaeological evidence from the excavation of the slaver *Henrietta Marie*, which sank in 1700, produced ninety sets of shackles of various sizes (fig. 1.18). Some were clearly for restraining the ankles of large men while others were sized for women and still others for the wrists of children.[124] In 1804, the *Connecticut Sentinel* carried an advertisement for the sale of "300 pair well made Shackles" and "150 iron collars" for the "confinement of slaves," presumably those recently used on an American slaver.[125] In his account of the middle passage, Equiano reported the

FIG. 1.16 Eighteenth-century dry docks, Liverpool, England.

FIG. 1.17 William Jackson, *A Liverpool Slave Ship*, 1780s. Oil on canvas, 40 × 50 in. (102 × 127 cm). Merseyside Maritime Museum, Liverpool, England.

"galling of the chains" that rubbed raw the flesh of arms, legs, and necks. As described by Alexander Falconbridge: "In each of the apartments are placed three or four large buckets, of a conical form, being near two feet in diameter at the bottom, and only one foot at the top, and in depth about twenty-eight inches; to which, when necessary, the negroes have recourse."[126] These "necessary tubs" tapered to reduce splashing and spillage during rough seas.[127] Shackled in pairs, captives had to request the indulgence of their shackled partner to vomit from seasickness or otherwise relieve themselves.

This "apartment" was separated from that of the women first by a very strong bulkhead and then often a passage that allowed the crew access to the lower hold of the vessel. Between this passage and the stern was a smaller prison, also defined by a strong open grating and outfitted with an intermediary platform, for the women and sometimes children as well. The women's prison on the 1793–1794 voyage of the *Sandown* was in the place of some "state rooms" that were disassembled by carpenters on the southward voyage to accommodate the women's space.[128] Women were less frequently kept in chains. Larger vessels had a range of small chambers for the captain, the first mate, and often the surgeon, underneath

the quarterdeck.[129] One passenger aboard a slaver in 1801 reported that he and the captain slept in a small chamber at the very stern of the ship, a space they shared with twenty-five enslaved girls who slept on the floor below their hammocks. The surgeon and the first mate shared their cabin with twenty-nine boys who also slept on the floor.[130]

The drive to maximize profits meant that ships' captains often filled these prisons with an extraordinary number of Africans.[131] By comparing the actual square footage of the prisons of ships with their slave manifests, abolitionist Thomas Clarkson determined that Africans were limited to three or four square feet of space, many limited vertically to only two feet, eight inches.[132] Analysis of the shipping records of the Royal African Company suggests that the conditions assessed in the late eighteenth century were much improved over those of the late seventeenth century, when the cost per slave was still quite low and there was little financial incentive to maximize survival rates.[133] In any season, the conditions were surely brutal. Equiano reported that individuals were "so crowded that each had scarcely enough room to turn himself."[134] Sailors reported packing in Africans each evening, even to the point of "adjusting their arms and legs."[135] Men and women were often stowed in a spooned position,

FIG. 1.18 Leg irons, eighteenth century. Acquired with the assistance of the Heritage Lottery Fund. National Maritime Museum, Greenwich, London, Michael Graham-Stewart Slavery Collection.

alternating head to toe, to maximize space. Such unbeliev-able conditions resulted in the passage of the Dolben Act in 1788, which capped the number of enslaved Africans on British slavers to five for every three tons of ship.

The most famous image of the packing of Africans on a ship, of course, was the abolitionist image drawn of the *Brookes* (see fig. 0.2).[136] The *Brookes* was purpose-built for the slave trade in Liverpool in 1781 for slave merchant James Brookes, Jr. Originally drawn by Captain Parrey, R. N., for the purpose of investigating the size of slaver ships, the plan of the *Brookes* was redrawn in 1789 showing both the main deck and the intermediate platform, which had been left off from Parrey's representation. The text made very clear that the image was a polemic, not actual documentation of reality, but inferred that reality would be even worse. The text noted that the image did not include the "poopoo tubs" usually situated in the middle of the rooms, the posts supporting the intermediate plat-forms, or the passage between the prisons giving sailors access to the other cargo and ballast in the lower hull. But its most powerful blow came when it indicated that the image included only the legal allowance of 482 slaves while the captain's manifest reported that the *Brookes* car-ried 609 slaves on its most recent voyage (1786–1787) and a stunning 740 the previous year, a 50 percent increase over its legal capacity of 482. Together the image and text argued that the density of people as represented in the plan of the *Brookes*—shown able to lie on their backs, not spooned on their sides—paled in comparison to the real experience of the majority who crossed the Atlantic. The power of the image was in its unreality.

In an attempt to preserve health and to reduce the stench generated by the atrocious conditions, the "neces-sary tubs" were emptied each day while the slaves were up on deck and the prisons were scrubbed down by sailors or slaves about twice a week with sand or vinegar.[137] By the later eighteenth century, as purpose-built ships became more common, ships were outfitted with air ports along the side of the hull and with windsails over the gratings. Commonly noted by the 1780s, windsails were tubes of canvas kept open at the top to catch air and then secured around the mouth of a deck grating "to convey a stream of fresh air downward into the lower apartments of the ship."[138] Even with such interventions, Equiano reported that the stench from the heat and poor ventilation, the sweat, vomit, blood, and necessary tubs "almost suffocated us." Sailors described it as "putrid."[139] As a result, many of the enslaved fell ill. Sick Africans were often separated from those in the prison to avoid contagion. Sick men often slept in the longboat on the upper deck and sick women were stowed in the half-deck, the rest of the spaces on deck being taken by sailors in hammocks.[140] Under questioning in the House of Commons, one captain reported having a specially fitted out hospital berth. The log of the *Sandown* also reveals that sick Africans and sail-ors alike were housed in a "Doctor's list."[141] But such berths were rare.[142] While estimates vary, most scholars suggest that African mortality on the middle passage was approxi-mately 12 percent; those shipped in the seventeenth century died at rates of up to 24 percent. Of the many mil-lions who left Africa's shores, more than one in ten would die in transit.[143] Deceased slaves and crew were generally "consumed by sharks, devouring with great dispatch the dead bodies . . . as they are thrown overboard," as reported by one sailor.[144] The wretched stench, mingled with the suffocating heat and the moans and shrieks of the dying made this floating prison a living hell.

During calm weather, the enslaved were brought from the holds of the ship to the upper deck for spans of eight to twelve hours.[145] Men were usually then kept in chains of ten as a greater deterrent against suicide.[146] As below, the hours above deck were spent segregated by gender, with the men toward the bow and the women to the stern. The mechanism for segregation was the barricado, a massive wooden wall, often ten feet high, that bisected the ship front to back, sometimes along the edge of the quarterdeck, and extended two feet over the sides.[147] The barricado was usually constructed by carpenters during

the voyage from England down the coast of Africa.[148] Its primary function was not to separate men from women but to serve as a protection for the crew during an insurrection. The barricado usually had a small door that allowed only one person to pass at a time. During daytime hours guards stood watch over the slaves from atop the wall while others manned a set of cannon positioned behind the wall at small openings. John Newton, the slave trader turned hymn writer, noted on one voyage that the barricado was outfitted with cartridges for four swiveling blunderbusses, which he believed "would make a formidable appearance on the main deck, and will, I hope be sufficient to intimidate the slaves from any thoughts of insurrection."[149] Another witness noted the "cannons which are positioned along the decks so that, in case of riot, they can sweep the entire deck; and since they are

BARRICADO, erected on board all Slave Ships, as a security whenever such commotions may happen.

See the privy council's report part I. Art: SLAVES.
Minutes of evidence before the House of Commons.
Wadstrom's Essay on Colonization §. 471.

FIG. 1.19 Carl Wadstrom, "Representation of an insurrection aboard a Slave Ship," from *An Essay on Colonization, particularly applied to the Western Coast of Africa, with some Free Thoughts on Cultivation and Commerce.* London: Printed for the author by Darton and Harvey, 1794. Reproduced by permission of The Huntington Library, San Marino, California.

loaded with grapeshot, they can shoot everything down in a moment. In such cases, the sailors rush, partly into the rigging and to the topsail where there are, on certain ships, a sack of caltrops that they strew out over the deck."[150] One 1790s image of a slaver during an insurrection shows the barricado separating the armed crew who stand on the quarterdeck firing into the group of unarmed Africans on the main deck (fig. 1.19). The ever-present barricado was a material reminder of an African's condition as a slave.

Another distinctive feature of slaver ships, or Guineamen, was the expanse of netting that surrounded the edge of the ship, positioned to prevent captives from jumping overboard.[151] One captain, William Miller, noted in his journal of 1764 that "the People Emp[loy]'d about netting and other necessarys" prior to taking on slaves.[152] In his instructions to his Rhode Island shipbuilder, Joseph Manesty directed that the ship's ribs were to be "left high enough to Support Rails all round the Vessel," probably to hold netting during the middle passage.[153] Equiano described that his ship had nettings but that they failed to prevent three people from jumping overboard during his voyage.[154]

The consistent erection of the barricade and the netting were the material reminders to both crew and the enslaved of the persistent impulse among the enslaved to resist their condition. Some resisted the routines of everyday life. Daytime hours were usually filled with a variety of regular activities, including the two daily meals and the forced dancing, an activity intended to provide exercise. Staple food often varied by region: rice from Senegambia, corn from the Gold Coast, and yams from the Bights of Benin and Biafra.[155] Food was usually served on the main deck from a single bowl to groups of ten slaves.[156] Those who refused to eat as an act of resistance were force-fed. Those who refused to dance were subject to the cat-o'-nine-tails. The ship's deck was also the stage for the public torture of those slaves discovered plotting an insurrection. As bloody events, numerous examples too graphic to relay here have survived in the historic record.[157] Huge numbers of enslaved Africans did actively resist their enslavement through suicide and insurrection.[158] Others persevered during the two to three months of the middle passage.[159] They waited most days above deck, separated by gender, carefully guarded from behind a prison wall, and forced to eat and to dance; they endured most nights below deck pressed naked against two others on the bare boards of a wooden platform, constantly suffused with the heat of hundreds of bodies in confinement and the smell of, if not contact with, vomit and human waste.

BLOCK

The great majority of British and American slave ships made their way to the Caribbean. Through the closing years of the seventeenth century, those ships generally made for Barbados, the largest consumer of slaves at the time. Barbados was then eclipsed by Jamaica, which would boast the largest demand for African labor of any British colony. Through the course of the eighteenth century, Jamaica received one third of all Africans imported on British slaving ships; such was the consumption in the 1790s that Jamaica commanded a full one half of the British trade, approximately twelve thousand Africans per year for that decade.[160] If Port Royal was the principal port of call in Jamaica in the seventeenth century, Kingston took that role through the eighteenth century, docking almost 90 percent of all slavers.[161] Historians Trevor Burnard and Kenneth Morgan have estimated the worth of Kingston's trade in enslaved Africans at £200,000 per year, an astonishing sum roughly equivalent to $40,000,000 in modern currency.[162]

Once they arrived in port, slavers began to sell slaves as soon as a sale from the deck could be arranged, following the earlier shipboard practice of selling indentures for servants.[163] Eighteenth-century Jamaican newspapers report numerous shipboard sales of slaves. In May 1779, for example, "Four Hundred and thirteen choice Young Slaves" were advertised for sale on board the *Molly*.[164] The following year, "475 choice young Coromantee, Fantee, and Shantee NEGROES" from Anamaboe (Fort William), were advertised for sale "On board the ship *Rumbold*."[165] "Notice is hereby given," read another advertisement from August 1788, "that such SLAVES as remained unsold aboard the Brig FANNY, John Muir, Master will be exposed to sale every day on board the said vessel, until the whole are disposed of."[166] Ship sale remained the primary method of sale through the eighteenth century in both Kingston and in smaller port towns.[167] In 1784, John Tharp, a major planter and minor slave trader, sold Africans directly from the deck of his ship, the *Tharp*, as it sat in the harbor of Falmouth, Jamaica.[168] An analysis of Tharp's estates from his 1805 inventory indicates that he owned Africans from a wide range of ethnic groups, including Mandingo, Coromantee, Chamba, Moco, Nago, Angola, Wakee, Chago, Banda, Pawpaw, Canya, and Congo. Likely a substantial number of these people arrived on Tharp's own ship.[169]

The preparation of the enslaved for the days of the sale included shaving their bodies and rubbing them down with oil in an effort to hide blemishes.[170] Such efforts frustrated purchasers like Thomas Thistlewood, who complained, "They shave the men so close and gloss them over so much that a person cannot be certain he does not buy old Negroes."[171] The presentation of Africans naked was practiced throughout the period to allow purchasers to investigate their health, as made clear by one late seventeenth-century observer: "When they are brought to us, the Planters buy them out of the Ship, where they find them stark naked, and therefore cannot be deceived in any outward infirmity."[172] Once again naked and intimately inspected, the experience incited "sorrow, melancholy, and despair," in the words of one victim.[173] Shaved, oiled, and standing naked before the gaze of consumers, Africans' already unnerving experience of the sale was occasionally rattled by the outbreak of disagreements over price, which sometimes turned violent among purchasers or between purchasers and sellers.[174] Equiano reported that the noise and clamor of the sale and the visible eagerness of the buyers "served not a little to increase the apprehensions of the terrified Africans."[175]

At these sales, family members, if they had been transported together, or shipmates who had survived together the hellish experience of the middle passage, were permanently separated. "Here daughters are clinging to their mothers, and mothers to their daughters, bedewing each others naked breasts with tears . . . and some will be still weeping for their native shore, and their dear relations and friends, and other endearing connections which they have left behind."[176]

Historical evidence about the structure of the sale itself is limited. In some instances, it appears the captain or factor organized a scramble, where some portion of the upper deck was sheltered with canvas sails. The Africans stood in rows. At a certain signal, the prospective buyers rushed the slaves and marked those preferred for purchase before their competitors could do the same.[177] It was this kind of sale that was described so powerfully by Equiano, who wrote of the gut-wrenching cries of those being separated from family and friends.[178] More recent historical scholarship suggests that most sales from the decks of ships were not by scramble but individually orchestrated, or, less frequently, through auctions,

both engineered to produce the greatest gains for sellers.[179] Slaves not yet sold from the deck of the *Molly*, for example, were "put up in lots agreeable to the purchasers" and offered for sale by public outcry "At Daniel Major's Wharf."[180] In most cases, the seller made available the healthiest and most valuable Africans first and these often sold in fairly large lots to wealthier planters or merchants. Then over the course of the sale, less valuable Africans— older or sickly individuals—would be readied and these more commonly sold individually or in smaller lots much later in the sale.[181] The reality of individually agreed-upon sales is reinforced by the fact that sales usually lasted more than a month, often up to fifty days or more.[182] The captain of the ship *Sandown*, which sat in Kingston harbor in 1794, complained that his slaves "go off very slowly (Market glutted)"; upon arrival he noted with anxiety that there were already three thousand Africans on the market. His records indicate that it took a full month to clear his ship of the enslaved.[183] In such situations, some—usually those who had been able to remain the healthiest through the voyage—departed the ship fairly rapidly. Others, however—those who had suffered sickness but not death— often remained onboard for weeks longer waiting for sale.

Research by Trevor Burnard and Kenneth Morgan has demonstrated a significant shift in the slave sale process over the course of the eighteenth century. Most Africans sold in the seventeenth century were sold in small lots or singly and their purchasers appear to have been those who would be their immediate owners.[184] By the early eighteenth century, however, the majority of Africans were purchased in much larger lots, usually between ten and forty but often as large as one hundred or more, although a significant proportion continued to be sold singly or in small lots. Certainly the Royal African Company functioned this way; in early eighteenth-century Jamaica the company transformed an old fortification into a slave pen where newly imported Africans were fed and prepared for sale.[185] By the early eighteenth century, the Royal African Company was selling slaves from a building in town referred to as the "African house" rather than from the decks of ships.[186] Kingston's merchants quickly followed suit, purchasing larger lots of Africans off ships and reselling them to planters, who increasingly recognized the risk in purchasing new slaves directly from the deck of a ship.[187] Not only were newly arrived Africans highly prone to sickness and death, they also were more valuable once they acclimated to their new circumstances, an intentional process called seasoning.[188] Writing from Jamaica in 1790, planter William Beckford admonished those new to the purchase of enslaved labor that it was impossible "to preserve and domesticate, in three years, more than one out of four who shall turn out a really industrious and efficient slave."[189] The Assembly of Jamaica directed in the early 1790s that the sale of all newly arrived Africans "shall be conducted on shore," permanently moving the sales from ships to merchant houses in town.[190] Over the course of the eighteenth century an internal, or retail, slave market emerged in Kingston, introducing an intermediary step between ship and plantation.[191]

The emergence of a retail market meant that an increasing number of Africans spent a season in the yards of merchants before they were sold to the planters who would ultimately take them to plantations. Such was the experience reported by Equiano upon his arrival in Bridgetown, Barbados. Soon after arrival, he was prepared for an onboard inspection by potential purchasers. Soon thereafter he was taken ashore to the "merchant's yard" where "we were all pent up together like so many sheep in a fold, without regard to sex or age." Burnard and Morgan argue that a 1745 poll tax in the city of Kingston recorded twenty-five slaveholders in that city who owned thirty or more slaves, numbers that suggest that these Africans were "almost certainly intended for resale."[192] In such merchant yards, new arrivals were intermingled with Creole, or Caribbean-born, slaves, speeding the seasoning process.[193]

Evidence of this shift to sale from merchant houses appears in the Kingston newspapers. In 1779, one merchant house offered "Ten Prime New Negroes" for sale "at the Subscriber's Vendue Store."[194] Another offered "Twenty Young Gold Coast NEGROES" for sale "at the Subscriber's Stand, the corner of King Streets and Harbour Street."[195] The same process was true of merchant houses elsewhere: earlier, a 1739 advertisement in the *South Carolina Gazette* announced that there was to be a sale of Africans "at Mr. Wragg's House . . . in Charlestown."[196] Wragg had been involved in the business of purchasing large lots of Africans for resale since at least the mid-1720s.[197] In the same year, the *South Carolina Gazette* announced to readers that "a fine cargo" of Africans "will be kept at the house built by the late Charles Hill, Esq.,."[198] In 1761, readers learned that a lot of two hundred "fine Rice Coast Negroes" would be sold from "Mr. Ranstowle's house or store" in Charleston.[199]

One such merchant house still survives in Kingston (fig. 1.20). Thomas Hibbert, from a wealthy cotton manufacturing family, arrived from Lancashire in 1734 and became involved in the slave trade almost immediately. Within two decades, he was mid-eighteenth-century Kingston's largest slave trader—even though, as James Robertson has shown, Hibbert was directly involved in an open debate over the morality of the African slave trade in which it was decided by a majority that the trade "was neither consistent with sound policy, the laws of nature, nor morality."[200] In the single season of September 1751 to May 1752, his merchant house, Hibbert and Spriggs, purchased 3,358 slaves from slave ships for resale, probably netting £4,130 in that single season.[201] Inspired by his extraordinary success, Hibbert soon began the construction of a massive new townhouse and yard, which stood completed by 1755. Some decades later, after Hibbert had forged a partnership with his nephew George Hibbert, the *Royal Gazette* announced that "thirty-eight SEASONED NEGROES" were offered for sale; inquirers were directed to "THOS HIBBERT and Nephew," then operating out of the mansion house on Duke Street.[202]

A careful investigation of the cellar of that house makes clear that it was fitted out for the purpose of housing slaves sometime soon after the assembly moved the sale of slaves from ships to shore. By this point, circa 1800, the changes to the basement were undertaken by Hibbert's nephew George, who first partnered with and then inherited his uncle's slave trading business and his Kingston townhouse-headquarters. The transformation included the installation of a barrel-vaulted cell, security for which required masons to close up a number of windows (figs. 1.21, 1.22). The newly vaulted chamber was secured by a single strong door and illuminated through a single barred window opening. The installation also required the creation of a contained circulation route from the vault through the ground floor of the building to the rear yard. In this process, a number of openings built as windows were transformed into doors allowing human passage while new walls were installed to block passage elsewhere. The circulation route would have delivered slaves directly into the rear courtyard of the house where potential purchasers seated or standing on the rear piazza would have a convenient view over the lot. The approach to the same space by purchasers, of course, was very different (fig. 1.23). Given the extraordinary purchasing patterns first of Hibbert and Spriggs, then of Thomas

FIG. 1.20 Hibbert House, Kingston, Jamaica, begun 1755.

FIG. 1.21 (below) Plan of the cellar of Hibbert House before installation of slave cell, ca. 1755.

FIG. 1.22 (right) Plan of the cellar of Hibbert House after installation of slave cell, ca. 1790. The dashed line shows the new route from the cell to the rear yard.

FIG. 1.23 (below right) Plan of the ground floor of Hibbert House. The dashed line shows the likely route of planter-customers passing through the house to the rear piazza overlooking the rear yard.

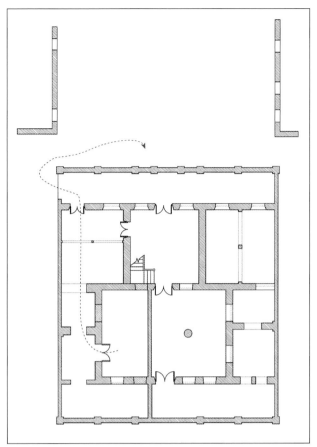

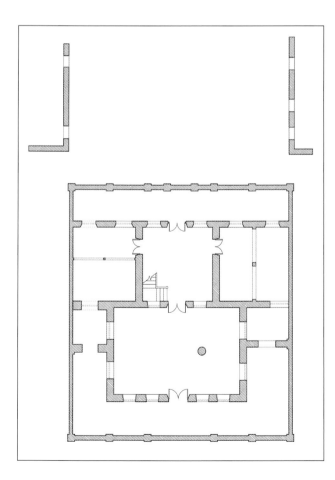

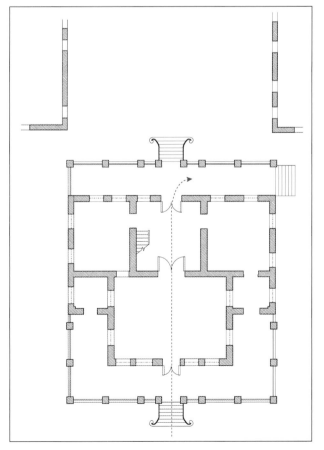

Hibbert and Nephew, and finally of George Hibbert, the ground floor cell and the rear yard were certainly among the first Caribbean spaces known by many hundreds if not thousands of newly arrived Africans.[203]

The rear yard and broad rear gallery of Thomas Hibbert's fine house in Kingston were likely the place of sale for thousands of the Africans sold by him and his nephew over the course of the eighteenth century (fig. 1.24). After settling on a price, Jamaican planters likely proceeded down the rear piazza where they could collect the slaves they had just purchased and leave the property through the side gate (fig. 1.25). Once purchased and delivered to the plantation, slaves were partially dressed, an osnaburg linen frock and trousers for the men and blouse and skirt of the same for women.[204] Covering their nakedness, clothes marked the end of the one hell, that of life as a slave under transport, and the beginning of another, the life of a plantation laborer. Yet if they had survived the march of the coffle, the containment of the castle, and the horrors of the middle passage, huge numbers of enslaved Africans—approximately 15 percent, higher than that of the middle passage—would not survive their first eighteenth months on the plantations. Sale to a planter in the Caribbean was no insurance of survival.

The installation of a containment cell in the cellars of the Hibbert townhouse and headquarters directly connected that building to the horrible series of spaces that spanned the Atlantic Ocean. Kingston's Hibbert House, now the headquarters of the Jamaica National Heritage Trust, is a very important national landmark, not just because of its rare survival as an eighteenth-century townhouse but because of its connections to the slave trade, to the middle passage, to Dixcove and Cape Coast Castle, and to market towns and slave routes across early modern West Africa. The Hibbert cellar was the first Jamaican architecture known by many thousands of Africans, the final stop in their passage from freedom to slavery.

FIG. 1.24 View of rear courtyard of Hibbert House. Slaves offered for sale would emerge from under the piazza to the far right while potential buyers would be likely seated on the piazza overlooking the courtyard.

FIG. 1.25 View down the rear piazza of Hibbert House to the side yard gate and the street beyond.

2   Castles of Fear

Until fairly recently, the ruins of Stewart Castle were almost completely lost in the bush of Jamaica's north coast. Less than a mile from the major east–west highway, the site of the early great house was known by locals but visited by almost no one else (fig. 2.1). The approach to the site takes visitors to a sharp turn off the narrow, pocked, and dusty backcountry road just as the monumental ruins come into view. At first blush, the site is a bewildering mass of roofless stone walls. But after some time a few distinguishing features come into view. Standing prominently in the complex are tall square towers, two embedded in the house complex and one freestanding. A very large yard enclosed by an eight-foot-high wall dominates the far side of the house ruins, with the footprints of other buildings within. Tall thin slots called loopholes—originally intended for firearms—cut through the masonry on all sides. What is now a sprawling ruin was once an imposing, if curious, plantation great house.[1]

Stewart Castle appears to have been constructed in two phases (figs. 2.2, 2.3). Dominating the first phase was a large rubble limestone two-story house measuring twenty-eight feet by twenty-four feet. Significantly, the house had only one room per floor. This first phase included two square towers, each approximately fifteen feet square, standing twelve feet distant from the main house, one to the northwest and the other to the southeast. That these towers were designed to provide military defense for the house is made explicit in the gun loops that open through almost every elevation, allowing both direct and enfilade fire. Archaeological evidence suggests that this phase of the house probably dates to the 1760s, soon after the plantation was patented by Scottish émigré James Stewart I in 1754.[2] The house was significantly expanded in the late eighteenth century by his son, James Stewart II, who encased the early house with rooms on three sides, built a third freestanding tower fitted out with a cannon port, dug in a massive water cistern, and raised a huge courtyard wall eight feet in height complete with thirty-six gun loops positioned every ten feet along the length of the new wall.[3] Broken glass set in mortar still runs along the crest of the wall. Born in 1763, James Stewart II served Trelawny Parish as the custos for many years. He was also a leader of the local militia and was a lieutenant colonel in the Maroon War of 1795. In these years, he undertook the massive expansion of his father's house into the footprint that remains on site today. As built by James Stewart I

FIG. 2.1 Stewart Castle ruins, Trelawny Parish, Jamaica, begun 1760s.

and expanded by his son, Stewart Castle was a house site explicitly intent on military defense.

Stewart Castle has few peers in the American colonial context; it is a far cry from contemporary Georgian planters' houses in the Carolinas or Virginia. The few known fortified houses in the mainland colonies were erected in the frontier context of the seventeenth century. An excellent example was the manor house erected by Nathaniel Pope called Clifts plantation on the Northern Neck of Virginia. The single-story earthfast wooden dwelling was encircled by a timber palisade complete with two diagonally positioned corner bastions. John Hallowes built a similar earthfast timber house in Westmoreland County, Virginia, in the 1660s. During the unrest of Bacon's Rebellion (1675–1676), he added two palisaded bastions accessible from within the house (fig. 2.4). The handful of other known earthfast palisaded houses were built along Virginia's rivers through the seventeenth century.[4] Sometime in the 1640s, Samuel Desborough built

a two-story frame house in Guilford, Connecticut. The house was contained within a strong fence and gatehouse that one architectural historian has convincingly interpreted as defensive.[5] Palisades and bastions all gesture to the instability of the seventeenth-century colonial American landscape, a landscape that historian Bernard Bailyn has called a contested and barbarous marchland.[6] A rare eighteenth-century example is Wormsloe, built by Noble Jones outside Savannah, Georgia, in the late 1730s when the location was a frontier (fig. 2.5). The house was encased in tall tabby perimeter walls fitted out with raking loopholes.[7] But these few exceptions prove the rule; houses across the mainland colonies were generally not fortified, and they were almost never fortified in the eighteenth century.

Lacking cousins in mainland America, the closest correspondents for Stewart Castle are a collection of houses built in medieval and very early modern Scotland. Glenbuchat Castle, built in the late sixteenth century by

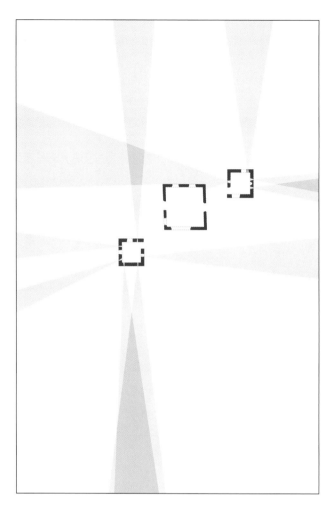

FIG. 2.2 Plan of Phase 1 of Stewart Castle (1760s) showing fire range through loopholes.

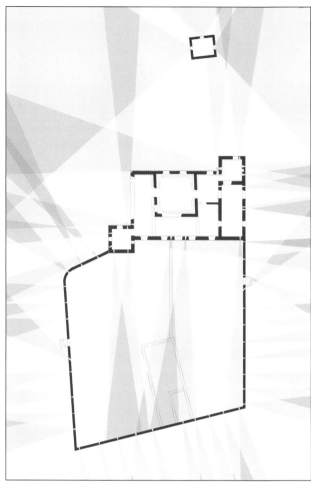

FIG. 2.3 Plan of Phase 2 of Stewart Castle (1790s) showing fire range through loopholes.

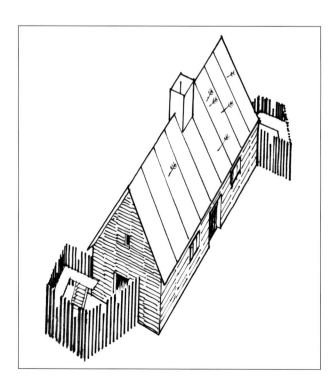

John Gordon, is a central single-chamber, multistory tower flanked at two corners by square towers, in plan very similar to the late eighteenth-century Stewart Castle in Jamaica (fig. 2.6). Appearing as early as the twelfth century, Scottish tower houses were commonly constructed and occupied by middling gentry into the middle of the seventeenth century.[8] While some are many stories tall and boast complex plans, the majority of Scottish tower houses are actually fairly small in scale, often only a few stories with one room per floor.[9] The greatest concentration of these smaller tower houses date from the late sixteenth and early seventeenth centuries and are found in the Scottish Border counties.[10] Relative to their earlier counterparts, most of these tower houses have larger

FIG. 2.4 Axonometric of John Hallowes House, ca. 1660s, Westmoreland County, Virginia. Colonial Williamsburg Foundation.

FIG. 2.5 Model of 1730s house and site at Wormsloe, outside Savannah, Georgia.

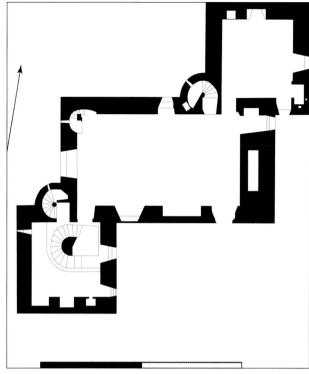

FIG. 2.6 Plan of Glenbuchat Castle, Aberdeenshire, Scotland, late sixteenth century.

windows and thinner walls since threats came not from invading siege armies but lightly armed raiding parties. Most tower houses originally boasted a walled courtyard, called a barmkin, although few examples have survived. Z-plan houses like Glenbuchat were more recent variants on smaller tower houses and included two towers positioned on opposite corners of the house, typically fitted out with gun loops protecting the elevations of the house.[11] The Z-plan house became common in Scotland in the middle of the sixteenth century, and appeared most commonly in rural, contested territories.[12] This chapter enlists these buildings as a way of telling the historical continuities between landscapes of fear—to use Yi-Fu Tuan's phrase—in Scotland, Ireland, England, and Jamaica.[13]

◆ ◆ ◆

Defensive domestic architecture was pervasive across eighteenth-century Jamaica. Numerous houses, especially in the northern and western parishes, have clear evidence for loopholes through their foundations (fig. 2.7). Like so many defensible houses, Winefields, a late eighteenth-century house in St. Ann Parish, sits atop a prominent

FIG. 2.7 Artist unknown, untitled view of a Jamaican great house, from the Storer Sketchbook, 1820s. Note the loopholes that alternate with the piers of the foundation. Private collection.

FIG. 2.8 Winefields, St. Ann Parish, Jamaica, late eighteenth century.

hillock in the landscape cleared of vegetation on all sides (fig. 2.8). The siting not only provides spectacular views and access to breezes but also gives occupants a distinct situational advantage in combat. The broad open footprint of the upper floor is supported by a thick-walled masonry foundation of two chambers. The door opening through the original foundation wall is still flanked to

either side by equidistant splayed holes approximately a foot tall and foot wide at their inside edge (fig. 2.9). These loopholes are central components of a defensible stronghold in the cellar of the house. The foundation walls of a number of other houses across Jamaica have similar openings; those in the cellar walls of Bromley are another example (fig. 2.10). While some of these might also have

FIG. 2.9 Foundation walls of Winefields with loopholes flanking the main door. When built, this was an exterior wall.

FIG. 2.10 Foundation wall with embedded loopholes, Bromley, St. Ann Parish, Jamaica, late eighteenth century.

doubled as ventilation holes—such holes are common in masonry foundations for this purpose—in these cases they are clearly participant in the construction of a defensible house site (fig. 2.11).

The perceived need for defense frequently surfaces in the documentary record. Writing in the late 1760s, Edward Long reported that planters along the north coast who had been regularly plundered by Spanish privateers learned to make their houses defensible by installing loopholes. In such a way, Long reminds his readers, these planters "in guarding against the insults of foreign enemies . . . are fortified also against internal ones," a

not so veiled reference to Jamaica's enslaved majority.[14] In another account, Long reported that "an enterprising man" had patented three hundred acres and enjoyed some prosperity from within his "defensible house."[15] And in Westmoreland, a house called Bluehole, "which commands an extensive prospect over the sea . . . is a modern building, constructed of stone, fortified with two flankers, and loop holes for musquetry, and defended, besides, toward the sea with a barbette battery of six guns, nine-pounders."[16] Long was not the only author to note the Jamaican proclivity for defense. Thomas Thistlewood, an eighteenth-century planter, commented frequently on defensive measures in his thirty-year diary, describing one raised house with a long piazza as being fortified, presumably through the masonry walls of the foundation. Another house in Thistlewood's telling was fitted out with "port holes" for defense.[17] And John Stewart, writing in the early nineteenth century, described the houses of Jamaica's planters as generally outfitted "with loop holes for muskets, as a defense in case of a sudden insurrection of the slaves, a danger of which the white inhabitants were formerly in perpetual apprehension."[18]

Another less obvious example of this phenomenon is the house at Hamden plantation in Trelawny Parish. The house was built between 1777 and 1783 by Archibald Stirling of Scotland, who oversaw his family's properties in Jamaica. It was intended to serve as the seat of the family's major holdings in sugar agriculture along the

FIG. 2.11 Detail of ruinous loophole in foundations of the great house at Orange Valley, Trelawny Parish, Jamaica, late eighteenth century.

island's north coast.[19] Happily, an elevation of the unusual two-and-a-half-story masonry house survives in archives in Glasgow. The elevation includes put-luck holes for the installation of framing for the porch that now graces the front of the building (figs. 2.12, 2.13). Although neither the eighteenth-century drawing nor a careful inspection of the building as it stands today reveals clear measures of defense, a written account by a visitor to the house makes evident that the house was once outfitted in this way. Writing in 1804, Scotsman Phillip Barrington Ainslie commented on a visit to Hamden. In his account he noted that "the windows were all glazed, and on each side of them were loopholes for defense, which were also on each side of the entrance doors." The house stood raised on a full cellar, "and as a further means of defense, there were loopholes, or apertures, cut in the floors of the hall and bedrooms, to allow a fire of musketry being kept up against any assailants gaining possession of the cellars and rooms of the ground floor of the house."[20] So while many Jamaican planters structured their foundations as a defensible stronghold, the Stirlings took the opposite approach, working to make the main floor defensible against assailants from within the cellar.

The persistent focus on martial defense of plantation housing surfaced in the 1760s for a Jamaican context. One of the houses in a 1770s book of designs produced for a Jamaican client included a defensible house intended for a rural situation (fig. 2.14). It included four corner flankers surrounding a simple building core of three rooms. One of the flankers contains stairs down to the ground floor, the walls of which were fitted out with regularly disposed circular loopholes on all elevations, mirroring in function, if not in form, the foundations of Winefields and other Jamaican houses. And, for further defense, the house was surrounded by an open moat "dry or filled with water." The advantage of this house, the architect reported, is that access is gained solely via a drawbridge, which makes the house very easily defensible. Rather than installing moats, Jamaican planters usually positioned their houses on steep sites, as with Winefields. Although D'Albaret was a French architect who had never been to Jamaica, his designs conform to the common pattern of installing a defensible stronghold within the cellar. In sum, the physical and documentary record is clear: houses in early colonial Jamaica were designed with the explicit intention of personal defense. Jamaica was an embattled landscape.

The British occupation of Jamaica was from its inception marked by a sense of martial contest. Unlike any other British colonial holding in the region it was forcibly taken from another major European power—the Spanish. While the English were able to take the capital of Spanish Town easily, without a single casualty, control of the rest of the island took another five years of bitter guerilla warfare with small bands of Spanish resistance fighters, familiar with the landscape, surprising English troops. When the Spanish eventually departed, they left behind

FIG. 2.12 Hamden plantation, Trelawny Parish, Jamaica, late eighteenth century.

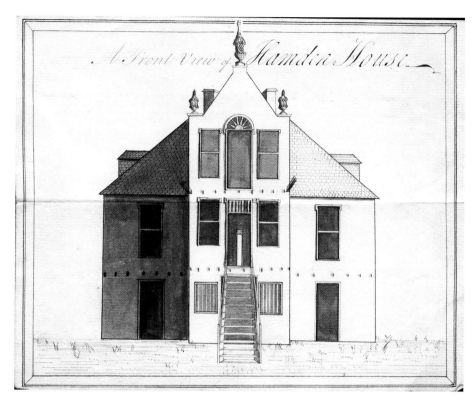

abundant evidence of their occupation: government buildings, churches, and houses, most of which the British colonials occupied and slowly adapted to their own uses.[21] Such material memories of the Spanish remained evident in the landscape long enough into the eighteenth century for the island's early historian, Edward Long, to author a long and detailed description of their construction.[22] As historian James Robertson has demonstrated, English colonials practiced English government in Spanish public buildings for almost a century of occupation. These material remains appear to have haunted British colonials who wrote frequently of Spanish ghosts who rode "to and fro on a full carre[e]r" down streets and around city squares.[23] By day and by night, English colonials were reminded that their island was taken by conquest.[24]

But the threats were not past. Jamaica's sugar plantations enslaved the largest population of Africans, and the island had a greater disproportion of blacks to whites than any other British colony by the early years of the eighteenth century.[25] Enslaved Africans were the majority population in Barbados by 1660 and in South Carolina by 1720.[26] While Virginians owned a large number of African slaves, their numbers were never greater than the colony's white occupants.[27] The disparity was by far the greatest in Jamaica, where by the 1710s, blacks

outnumbered whites by eight to one.[28] The number of Africans on the island more than doubled between 1700 and 1750 and increased again by a factor of five by the end of the century, when the imbalance had reached thirteen to one across the island, with some rural parishes reaching thirty to one.[29] The Caribbean slave-based agricultural economy had distinct implications for the physical nature of the plantation landscape as perceived by apprehensive British planters. The heat and humidity, the dense and lush vegetation, and the exotic flowers, animals, and birds more closely approximated Africa than foggy England. One Englishman noted that the seemingly innumerable slaves in Jamaica were summoned to their labors not by European bells but "by the sound of a Conche-shell." He also noted that thatched huts on this tropical island made "every Plantation look like a little African city."[30] Writing in the 1740s, James Knight described the life of a planter in Jamaica as defined by "great anxiety and trouble." The large populations of slaves, he continued, generate "great uneasiness and vexation."[31] In a predicament of their own making, Jamaica's planters were fearful of their African slaves, sustaining a latent anxiety fueled by racial tension.

The distinct racial imbalance of Jamaica had sharp implications for race relations; by the late seventeenth century, slave riots became increasingly common.

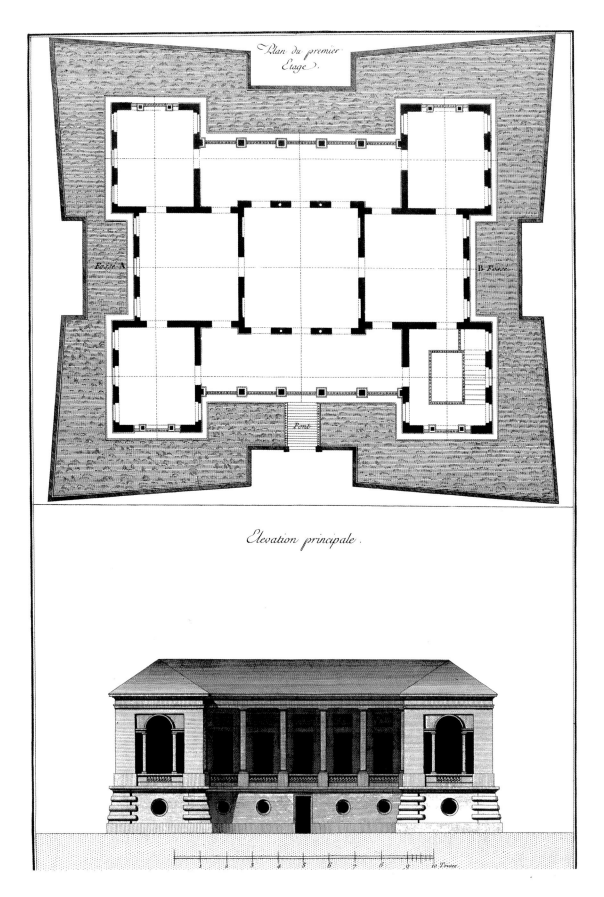

FIG. 2.14 M. D'Albaret, *Différents projets relatifs au climat et à la manière la plus convenable de bâtir dans les pays chauds, et plus particulièrement dans les Indes occidentales* (Paris, 1776), Plate XI. University of Maryland Library.

Jamaica's greatest insurrection was Tacky's Rebellion of 1760.[32] Requiring secret communications between large numbers of Akan slaves in five or more parishes across the island, the insurrection's sophisticated organization was astonishing. As described by Edward Long, the rebellion was the complete reimagining of the island's geopolitical organization. It was to include "the entire expiration of the white inhabitants; the enslaving of all such Negroes as might refuse to join them; and the partitioning of the island into small principalities in the African mode; to be distributed among their leaders and head men."[33] The insurrection unfolded over the weeks of May 1760 and as it moved, the fire of rebellion concentrated on the greatest symbols of white authority: great houses and overseers' houses. Thistlewood reported on May 29 that rebellious slaves had torn down the great house at Jacobsfield. That evening he looked on from the safety of Savannah-la-Mar, watching another great house burning in the distance.[34] In a much smaller rebellion just a few years later, rebels burned houses on plantations in the eastern parishes of the island.[35] An insurrection plot discovered in 1769 included the plan to burn the city of Kingston.[36] Of nineteenth-century insurrections, the Baptist rebellion of 1831 was also notorious for the burning of great houses. As Michael Craton's research has shown, Jamaica was the most common site of slave insurrections in the entirety of the British Caribbean, including twenty-two rebellions between 1655 and 1832, six of which involved thousands of slaves.[37] Jamaican planters knew the threat of insurrection was real, and that threat played out in the real spaces of plantation landscapes.

The decades of greatest rebellion peaked around the 1760s.[38] By the second half of the eighteenth century an increasingly wealthy and powerful class of British planters was fully aware of the African threat to their hegemony, especially from the *Cormantin* Negroes" who, according to Edward Long, were notorious for their "martial ferocity."[39] Writing in response to a recent insurrection plot, one early nineteenth-century visitor wrote from Kingston exclaiming: "This town at present has a very warlike appearance, the Militia being all called out. They parade the streets every hour."[40] Throughout the eighteenth century, slaves who threatened the established order were delivered severe corporal and often capital punishment. Tacky's Rebellion in 1760 was followed by a horrific sequence of public executions.[41] Physical reminders of that punishment marked the landscape; severed heads left on poles, often for years, were only the most gruesome examples. Jamaica was rife with potential and actual violence.

British colonials in Jamaica also faced the persistent reality of guerilla attacks from the island's Maroons, escaped slaves who had reestablished themselves in two free communities, the Windward Maroons in the rugged mountains of upper Portland Parish and the Leeward Maroons to the west.[42] These Maroon populations became a formidable presence as their numbers grew after a series of late seventeenth-century slave insurrections.[43] Regular raids on colonial plantations by Maroons proved a continuous nuisance among the British through the early eighteenth century. In his advice to settlers of the intended new port city of Antonio on the island's north coast, engineer and city planner Christian Lilly instructed the settlement to position its guard not toward the water to defend the port from sea invasion but toward land to "defend against rebellious Negroes."[44] British troops were regularly engaged in campaigns to locate and capture these Maroon communities. They failed. In 1739, the British colonial governor signed a treaty with the two communities of Maroons, recognizing their independence as a nation in exchange for their promise to return any future escaped slaves, bringing the half-century of incursions to a temporary peace. Even so, one 1740s writer when speaking of the Maroons was certain "their number does not diminish, many others [slaves] going over to them every year."[45] Even as late as the early nineteenth century the Maroons were cast as primitive savages by fearful white Jamaicans; one visitor was anxious about the Maroons whom he understood to live "in caves and dens in the forests and mountains."[46]

And lastly, Jamaica was a prized British possession in a region also occupied by the French, the Spanish, and rogue pirates. Settlements along the east coast of the island had been attacked by the French in 1694, an episode that lived long in Jamaican memory. Those same settlements remained ruinous until the middle of the eighteenth century.[47] James Knight noted in 1742 that many Jamaicans along the north coast were continuously "under some apprehensions of being invaded by the French. . . . People are backward in settling there afterwards as it lay very much exposed to the Enemy, and is within twenty-four hours' sail of the French settlements on Hispanola [*sic*]."[48] Thomas Thistlewood's midcentury diary offers numerous accounts of raids or the fear of raids on Jamaican plantations by French and Spanish marauders.[49]

Edward Long noted in the 1770s that many of the planters in St. Ann Parish had been attacked by Spanish privateers during the midcentury wars, "in order to plunder the inhabitants of their Negroes."[50] In the late eighteenth century, renewed hostilities between the English and the French and Spanish reawakened the fear of invasion.[51] And as Richard Pares argued in 1963, war is a social institution, one with implications well beyond battles and campaigns.[52] War, or at least the fear of attack or invasion from slaves, Maroons, or foreign enemies, was a persistent threat throughout the eighteenth century. Historian Trevor Burnard argues flatly, "Jamaica was a society at war."[53] That martial character shaped the built environment in Jamaica, not just in the seventeenth century but throughout the period of slavery.

Jamaica was not Britain's first embattled colonial landscape. The Norman invasion of Ireland in the twelfth century marked the beginning of more than seven centuries of Anglo-Norman and eventually British assertion of political and cultural authority in Ireland. The early centuries were marked by sporadic seizure of lands in southern Ireland by Anglo-Normans and the establishment of an elite who controlled a substantial percentage of Irish landholdings. As a result of centuries of such occupation, by the sixteenth century an established network of "old English" families coalesced in Munster and controlled large portions of southern Ireland into the seventeenth century. These families remained distinct from their Irish subjects, even if they shared their Catholic faith. The Irish in the north, by contrast, were far more successful in resisting these incursions and set up consistently stronger military resistance.

In 1534, the native Irish and their "old English" counterparts actively resisted Protestant English authority in Ireland, leading one historian to note that "Ireland in 1534 was a land of constant war."[54] Local skirmishes abounded and climaxed in a two-week campaign by English troops to seize the stronghold of Kildare at Maynooth to suppress the uprising and break Irish home rule. But the fall of Kildare did not stop the fighting; other rebellions persisted through the 1530s.[55] Soon thereafter newly empowered English Protestants challenged the authority of Ireland's old English families, and in 1536, Henry VIII began a new series of English military campaigns into Ireland. Under Henry VIII's Kingdom of Ireland, the traditional political authority of the old English Catholics was questioned, and under Elizabeth I, directly challenged.

During and after the Desmond Rebellions (1569–1583), the old English families in Ireland refused to pay taxes to support the English army sent to suppress Irish uprisings. Once again, these rebellions pitted Irish "rebels" against the English army; Humphrey Gilbert suppressed the rebellion with brutal force and gruesome displays of subjection, exhibiting "the heads of dead fathers, brothers, children, kinsfolk and friends."[56] Further north through the 1570s, Nicholas Malby as military governor of Connacht undertook to suppress what he saw as the lawlessness of his region. Like Gilbert before him, Malby executed young and old and burned whole villages suspected of harboring rebels.[57]

The "plantation" of Munster, begun in the 1580s, was the first systematic attempt at English colonization in Ireland.[58] In Munster, extensive Irish landholdings in the south—in the modern counties of Limerick, Cork, Kerry, and Tipperary—were confiscated and resettled with English colonists called undertakers, largely from the southwest of England.[59] Clearly threatened by the English presence, Hugh O'Neill, the Earl of Tyrone, began assembling an army in the late 1580s. By 1593 Tyrone was in communication with Philip II of Spain to secure an alliance against England. Through the 1590s, the Gaelic Irish nobles continued their alliances with each other against English control; supported by a number of Gaelic lords, the earl launched open war on the English state in Ireland in 1598, catching the English unprepared and resulting in a major victory for the Irish.[60] In 1601 the Spanish landed at Kinsale with the intention of reinforcing the Irish, but the resistance eventually collapsed under the military response by the English under Lord Mountjoy, who conquered the Irish forces at the Battle of Kinsale and settled on terms with the Spanish.[61] One historian has noted that by 1600 Ireland "contained plentiful evidence of devastation and decay," all the result of the "incessant military campaigns and guerilla warfare conducted between the English and Irish."[62]

Prior to the 1590s the Irish in the northern region of Ulster had more successfully resisted military and cultural incursion and had remained fiercely Gaelic. Aggressive military campaigns into Ulster during the Nine Years War (1594–1603)—including wholesale burning of crops and the starvation of thousands—not only asserted English claims of authority over the region but also launched an aggressive campaign of colonialism in the north. In 1607 a confederation of Irish chiefs departed Ulster for Spain in an effort to gain an ally against the English. In their absence, the English governor seized their lands. Resistance by northern Ireland's chiefs eventually led to the seizure of all land held by native Irish landowners and the foundation of the Ulster plantation by King James I (James VI of Scotland) in 1609. As a result of the aggressive, carefully orchestrated colonization campaign in the first two decades of the seventeenth century, northern Ireland was marked by the construction of plantation castles and houses by predominantly Scottish settlers.[63] Those who received two thousand acres were required to build a castle and a bawn, a fortified, unroofed enclosure usually used for protecting cattle. Those receiving fifteen hundred acres had to build a house and bawn. Those with only one hundred acres were to build at least a bawn. In 1609 James I banned all Catholics in Ireland from holding office. By the 1630s most of the old English families were forced to confirm their land titles, often in the absence of deeds; their claims to the land were directly contested and many families lost their landholdings.[64] These campaigns laid the groundwork for late sixteenth- and early seventeenth-century plantation Ireland, where newly transplanted English and Scottish Protestants established and governed privately held plantations. British colonialism in Ireland had begun in full force.

In the midst of violent resistance, the English actively constructed the Irish as primitive barbarians. Francis Bacon would assert that Ireland was "the last of the daughters of Europe," waiting "to be reclaimed from desolation and a desert (in many parts) to population and plantation; and from savage and barbarous customs to humanity and civility."[65] The image of incivility that came to characterize the Irish was framed largely in terms of warfare. Spenser's *Faerie Queen* painted a terrifying picture of the primitive Irish:

> . . .with outrageous cry
> A thousand villeins round about them swarmed
> Out of the rocks and cave adjoining nye:
> Vile caitive wretches, ragged, rude, deformed,
> All threatening death, all in straunge manner armed;
> Some with unwieldy clubs, some with long speares,
> Some rusty knives, some staves in fier warmed.[66]

By the end of the sixteenth century, the English would see Ireland as a wasteland occupied by primitive peoples fated for subjugation. By the end of the seventeenth century, the English had invaded Jamaica and continued that campaign of claiming and dominating a landscape, only this time the dangerous "savages" were the enslaved Africans and self-emancipated African Maroons brought to Jamaica against their will. In this way, Ireland and Jamaica were part of a continuous colonizing process, one that shaped these landscapes—both "barbarous marchlands," places witness to brutal conditions—in very particular ways. Historian Bernard Bailyn has rightly suggested the mutuality of experience between the Irish and Native Americans at the hands of the English.[67] The dependence of fortified house sites in seventeenth-century British America on earlier English building strategies in Ireland has been explored most recently by Robert Blair St. George.[68] His careful analysis of bawns in northern Ireland and in New England demonstrates both actual historical and conceptual connections between these aggressively colonized zones. Archaeologist James Delle has undertaken a similar comparison of settlement sites in Ireland and the Blue Mountain coffee plantations of Jamaica.[69] That Bailyn's marchlands encompass the Caribbean is seen in the frequency of slave revolts across the seventeenth-century Caribbean as well as in an Irish laborers' rebellion in the Leeward Islands in 1692.[70] Although Bailyn is not concerned with architecture, surviving buildings and landscapes—often overlooked historical evidence— strongly substantiate his characterization of these places as violent. The evidence from Jamaica expands our understanding of this correspondence.[71] Examples from Jamaica demonstrate that the English and the Scots employed different material strategies; that the power of defensive architecture is simultaneously real—actually martial—and symbolic, burdened with social message; and finally that the condition of being a marchlands persisted in Jamaica through the eighteenth century, much later than is apparent on the American mainland. To understand how, we return to our evidence: the buildings themselves.

◆ ◆ ◆

If loopholes were a common defensive mechanism, one of the more prominent forms of defense at Stewart Castle and in houses across Jamaica was the construction of towers. The earlier form of defensive house in Jamaica is a central square house core framed by four symmetrically disposed corner towers. Stokes Hall, erected in the late seventeenth century at the eastern tip of the island, stands atop a dramatic bluff overlooking the vast fields of St. Thomas Parish (fig. 2.15). The building's most notable features are the four equally disposed corner towers, each fitted out

FIG. 2.15 Stokes Hall, St. Thomas in the East Parish, Jamaica, late seventeenth century.

with loopholes facing out over the edges of its hilltop site and along the flanks of the building, providing cover for the windows and doors. The house was probably built by Luke Stokes, an early property owner in Jamaica and late seventeenth-century governor of Nevis in the Leeward Islands. A mid-eighteenth-century account reports that the site of this and other Stokes properties in this parish were all burned in a French attack in 1693 and remained in ruins to the time of that writing.[72] Edward Long noted in 1774 that the ruined plantation house at Stokes Hall "still commemorated" Governor Stokes and his mid-seventeenth-century colony, which had removed from Nevis to Jamaica in 1656.[73] Little survives of the main block of the house at Stokes Hall except the foundations of a few walls that divided the interior into multiple chambers. The shells of the building's four corner towers, on the other hand, remain largely intact. Single-chambered, the towers each have only one window opening to the outside, flanked by tall thin loopholes intended for defense of the house.

The house with four corner features was a common building form erected by English elites in the eighteenth century, especially in the parishes very near Kingston and Spanish Town. The clearly defensive function of this plan type remained prominently fixed in the public imagination through the eighteenth century. The 1763 Craskell and Simpson map of Jamaica is an extraordinarily detailed representation of the island and represents Jamaica's many military barracks scattered across the island.[74] And

even though Edward Long's descriptions make clear that they were quite varied in form and armament, the symbol used by the cartographers to represent these military installations was a small square with four corner flankers, in form much like Stokes Hall. That same form was also proposed by Long in both word and image as the public building type to be erected in the many towns he imagined would be built across the island as populations increased. In the very center of his plan for such a town, Long included a "hall for public business, built with loop holes, and flankers for defense" (fig. 2.16). He further noted that all the houses were to be built "at least two feet above the surface, and guarded with loop holes."[75]

Over the course of the eighteenth century Jamaican planters erected a number of houses with corner flankers or pavilions. An important example is Halse Hall in Clarendon Parish, erected in the eighteenth century with a rectilinear core and four solid corner pavilions (fig. 2.17). Philip Pinnock's house at Richmond, his St. Ann estate, was "surrounded with a spacious piazza, supported by columns of the Ionic order; at the four angles are pavilions."[76] Two others include Philip Pinnock's spectacular great house near Half-Way Tree, just north of the city, and Robert Turner's house in Kingston (fig. 2.18). But the most obvious example, of course, is Colbeck Castle (fig. 2.19; see fig. 5.20). Two features suggestive of a martial origin are the circular windows of the south tower's lowest story. While the loopholes in Stoke's Hall are tall thin openings,

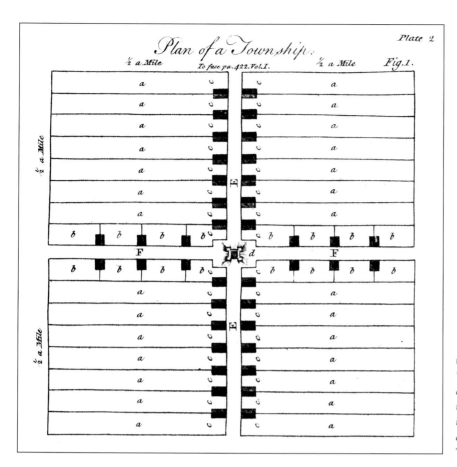

FIG. 2.16 Edward Long, "Plan of a Township," *The History of Jamaica, or, General survey of the antient and modern state of that island: with reflections on its situation, settlements, inhabitants, climate, products, commerce, laws, and government* (London: Printed for T. Lowndes, 1774).

Colbeck's circular windows seem to recall versions such as those that line the ground floor of the defensive house published in D'Albaret. Yet, a number of features seem to mediate against such an interpretation. The circular windows are far too large to actually function to protect the person firing from within the house. The windows also appear only on the three publicly visible elevations—the northern elevation has large rectilinear windows on the ground floor—suggesting that the circular examples are

HALSE HALL

FIG. 2.17 Halse Hall, now drastically altered. Reprinted from Frank Cundall, *Historic Jamaica: With fifty-two illustrations* (London: Published for the Institute of Jamaica by the West India Committee, 1915).

positioned for visual effect, not functionality. Such a desire to appear defensive, rather than being actually defensive, suggests that Colbeck's towers carried some symbolic function. Earlier work on Colbeck has suggested that its "castellated" form might be part of the English practice of erecting Spenserian mock castles.[77] In English examples these castles are ornamental and not functional, participants in the romance of chivalry, courtly combat, jousting, and neomedieval literature like the *Faerie Queen*.[78] An example is Lulworth Castle, Dorset, erected by Lord Howard Bindon in 1607 (fig. 2.20).[79] Lulworth was a "little pile which he [Bindon] hopes to prove pretty." The writer continues describing the house as in the form of "a castle of the imagination," hardly a house built for defense.[80] But such a context of romantic indulgence in chivary-dense literature seems, and in fact is, a world away from Colbeck Castle. Mock jousting and readings of Spenser are hard to imagine in eighteenth-century Jamaica.

There is an alternative context for the construction of post-medieval castles that could more comfortably extend to include these corner-towered buildings of early colonial Jamaica. If new-built "castles" provided a stage for the

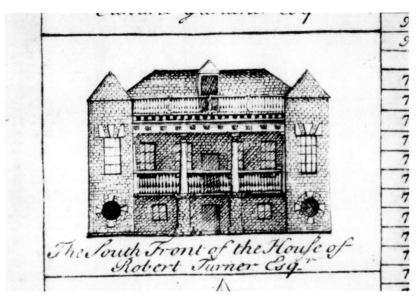

FIG. 2.18 "The South Front of the House of Robert Turner, Esqr." Detail from Michael Hay, plan of Kingston, ca. 1745. Ink on paper, 13 × 16 in. (33 × 41 cm). Library of Congress.

reenactment of chivalric rituals as the prevailing interpretation supposes, they also recalled the elevated social status of the English nobility. Beginning with the dissolution of the monasteries under Henry VIII, England witnessed a massive reorganization of the landscape between the sixteenth and eighteenth centuries.[81] Dana Arnold has very effectively argued that eighteenth-century English elite depended on ownership of land and the construction of a great house to establish or preserve membership in England's privileged social circles.[82] The construction of a "country house" on these new estates secured the identity and the authority of the family and its patriarch in and over the landscape.[83]

By the eighteenth century, English monumental houses with four corner towers had been associated with land-based authority for centuries. An excellent late medieval example is the 1434–1446 *donjon*, or central tower, of Tattershall Castle, in east Lincolnshire (fig. 2.21). Built by Ralph Cromwell, the Lord Treasurer to Henry VI, Tattershall Castle was outfitted with large, hardly defensible traceried windows not as a fortification to withstand siege but as a symbol of lordly status.[84] In continuity with

FIG. 2.19 Colbeck Castle, St. Catherine Parish, Jamaica, third quarter eighteenth century.

FIG. 2.20 Lulworth Castle, Dorset, England, ca. 1607.

FIG. 2.21 Tattershall Castle, Lincolnshire, England, 1434–46.

the late medieval tradition, many later country houses were also built with corner towers. Perhaps the most abundant evidence for this practice is seen in the many houses of the late sixteenth and early seventeenth centuries designed by Robert Smythson. As Mark Girouard has suggested, these massive new houses were generally built not by England's well-established families or those long associated with the aristocracy but by the wealthy "new" gentry, most newly rich through the acquisition of former monastery lands, profit from law, or success in commerce.[85] These families had a need to demonstrate their wealth, to make clear their claim to substantial landholdings—and by extension, to make claims to an elite social status and to secure rank or political stature. Probably the clearest example is Wollaton Hall, erected in 1580–1588 for Francis Willoughby, whose family wealth depended on extensive coal deposits on their vast landholdings (fig. 2.22).[86] An inscription on the exterior of the house reads, "Behold this house of Sir Francis Willoughby, built with rare art and bequeathed to the Willoughbys. Begun 1580 and finished 1588."[87]

The house now standing as Bourton House in Gloucestershire is an eighteenth-century rebuilding on the footprint of an early seventeenth-century house. The early building, with a rectilinear core framed by four strong corner towers, was built by Sir Nicholas Overby, a lawyer of increasing prominence in the early seventeenth century.

FIG. 2.22 Wollaton Hall, Nottinghamshire, England, 1580–88.

The construction of his house precedes his elevation to the knighthood in 1621 by only a few years. Another example is Chastleton in Oxfordshire. In 1604 prominent London lawyer Walter Jones purchased the Chastleton estate from Robert Catesby, the mastermind of the Gunpowder Plot. Demolishing Catesby's house, Jones erected a house not unlike that of Bess of Hardwick—a Smythson

commission—if much smaller. Significantly, the house stands bookended by tall crenellated towers that prominently project from the main block of the house. While not placed at each corner, the prominence and ornamentation of these towers situates them comfortably in the larger tradition. In both examples, lawyers purchased large estates and immediately built new houses defined by towers. Plas

FIG. 2.23 Plas Teg, Flintshire, Wales, begun 1610.

FIG. 2.24 John Vanbrugh, Blenheim Palace, Oxfordshire, England, 1705–24.

Teg is a great house built in northern Wales in 1610 by Englishman Sir John Trevor (fig. 2.23). Trevor enjoyed a number of official posts in London in the 1590s that generated for him both wealth and prestige; in 1597 he became a Minister of Parliament and a year later he was Surveyor of the Navy.[88] The construction of his house was a natural outgrowth of his rise to political prominence. The house has four tall corner towers dramatically amplified by the small spires at the corner of each tower. Yet the building is clearly not military in nature. The only gun loops in the walls of Plas Teg are in the form of the builder's initials along the garden side of the house. Various versions of houses with corner towers also appear in architectural drawings from across the seventeenth century, including a number in the drawings of architect John Thorpe, suggesting that the symbolic significance of corner towers was widely recognized through the century.[89]

Archaeologist Matthew Johnson offers a useful frame for understanding the English castles of the fifteenth and sixteenth centuries. He argues that the houses of the elite became more potently discursive in the late sixteenth century. In exactly the same season when the cultural systems that sustained the medieval castle were dissolving, the symbolic image of the castle was established. In this way, new "castellated" houses like Wollaton or Plas Teg, which gestured to the martial but were not actually defensible, were built to correspond to older castles like Tattershall with the intent of being viewed as a collective, "a conscious attempt

to invoke values seen as being under threat."[90] His most powerful evidence to this end is the partial destruction or "slighting" of castles that had been royalist strongholds of the aristocracy—defensible and indefensible—as enforced by Parliament after the English Civil War of 1642 to 1649.[91]

But the tradition persisted and the bold use of corner towers reemerged after the Civil War in both Scotland and England. In the 1680s and 1690s, Scottish architect William Bruce designed a wave of great houses defined by corner towers, including Balcaskie, Thirlestane Castle, Drumlanrig Castle, and others. Panmure House was built in the early 1670s with very prominent corner towers and was published in *Vitruvius Britannicus,* as was Drumlanrig Castle. In light of this tradition, Charles McKean has convincingly argued that the persistence of castellated features on Scottish houses of the sixteenth and seventeenth centuries was in pursuit of the "nobility" conveyed by the castle, even (or maybe especially) when the forms were clearly useless for military defense.[92] In the hands of eighteenth-century English architect John Vanbrugh, corner towers became explicitly connected with ennoblement. An excellent example is Blenheim Palace with its four enormous corner towers, the great palace given to John Churchill soon after he was established as Duke of Marlborough in thanks for his military successes in the War of the Spanish Succession (fig. 2.24). Built for a man of less wealth than his peerage, the palace stands on the royal demesne of Woodstock, a huge tract of land that had been

FIG. 2.25 Hagley Hall, Worcestershire, England, ca. 1751.

under royal governorship since Henry I. That corner towers and crenellations on Vanbrugh's designs were associated in the architect's mind with ennoblement is made clear in a letter that he wrote to the Earl of Manchester about the redesign of Kimbolton Castle: "As to the outside I thought 'twas absolutely best to give it something of the castle air tho' at the same time to make it regular. . . . I am sure this will make a very *noble* and masculine show and is of as warrantable a kind of building as any" (emphasis added).[93] The infatuation with castles extended, of course, to the architect's own house, a gothic fantasy on the south side of the Thames in Greenwich.

Corner towers appear on the most important Palladian houses of the eighteenth century as well. Four square corner towers define both Wanstead and Houghton, identified by eminent English architectural historian John Summerson as the two most important models for eighteenth-century English country houses.[94] Built in the early 1750s, the great house at Hagley Hall is also defined by four tall corner towers, in this case for a man who was both the descendant of and brother of Jamaican governors (fig. 2.25). As Summerson observed, the form of this house "is a deep rooted formula which has travelled through English taste," one that "sank very deep into the popular consciousness."[95] As English architectural historian Michael Thompson has argued, this tradition was not just fashion; a "castle air" was an ennobling practice that depended on a long tradition connecting the castle with the land to "enhance the authority of a landowner," well into the eighteenth century.[96]

Furthermore, a distinctive and consistent characteristic of these early modern country houses in Britain was the use of *square* corner towers. Square towers self-consciously signaled a departure from the practical defensiveness of Britain's royal military castles, which more often employed the more strategic round towers. In early modern England and Scotland, square towers gestured to those same features on early private houses erected by local nobility to secure and defend their claim to their landholdings.[97] As Thompson has suggested, "A fortified residence [i.e., a medieval tower house] was a privilege accorded to great landowners." Only large landowning elites were allowed to build such residences and they typically served "as the administrative centre for a large area."[98] Once the actual need for military defense of the land had passed, sixteenth-, seventeenth-, and eighteenth-century architects and builders enlisted castellated features and especially square corner towers to evoke not just chivalric romanticisms but to assert their patrons' claims to social and political status.

If the towered country houses had symbolic associations with ennoblement in the heart of Britain, their association with control of and authority over landholdings seems to have been particularly acute at the edges of empire. Michael Thompson has observed that the square tower as a visual form—usually a well-defended tower house—was, not surprisingly, most common in the British landscape in those regions where land had been most hotly contested, along the Welsh and Scottish borders (fig. 2.26).[99] Thompson argues that the house with square corner towers was all the more responsible for asserting authority over contested or threatening landscapes. One of those landscapes, of course, was Ireland. The country house with four corner towers appears intermittently across Britain through the early modern period; there is a pronounced spike in the construction of this form in southern Ireland between the 1580s and 1620, decades immediately following the foundation of the Munster plantation and the widespread seizure of land by English Protestants.

While earlier generations of Anglo-Normans had erected a few buildings of this type in southern Ireland—the fifteenth-century Barrycourt is an example—the greatest concentration of such buildings appeared around the early seventeenth century. There are at least ten surviving examples erected in the decades between 1590 and 1650.[100] Significantly, all but one of these houses were built by Englishmen, some by newly arrived colonial clergy and military officers, others by old English families who

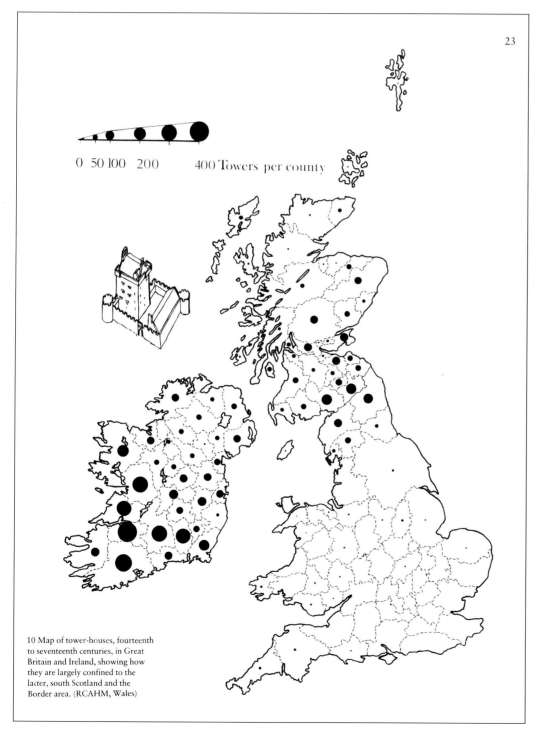

23

0 50 100   200   400 Towers per county

10 Map of tower-houses, fourteenth to seventeenth centuries, in Great Britain and Ireland, showing how they are largely confined to the latter, south Scotland and the Border area. (RCAHM, Wales)

FIG. 2.26 Map of Britain identifying densities of tower houses. Reprinted from M. W. Thompson, *Decline of the Castle* (Cambridge: University Press, 1987), 22.

had occupied Ireland for centuries. The profusion of the form in southwest England and the heavy population of Munster by settlers from that region of England in the plantation period have led English architectural historians to link the proliferation of the form in Ireland to the English occupation in the early seventeenth century.[101]

The earliest examples in this wave of construction were all built by newly transplanted English settlers. Rathfarnham was erected sometime just before the turn of the century by Adam Loftus the Elder (fig. 2.27).[102] Born and raised in Yorkshire, Loftus was the Protestant archbishop of Dublin and Lord Chancellor of Ireland, the highest judicial office in Ireland under Elizabeth I, from 1581 to his death in 1605. He built Rathfarnham Castle on lands confiscated from the Eustace family in 1583 as a result of their participation in the Second Desmond Rebellion. Although much altered in the late eighteenth century, the essential form of the towered house survives from the original construction of the building in the late sixteenth century. The house's corner towers are not square but slightly canted to take the more defensible form of a bastion. Although removed in the eighteenth century, the house originally exhibited crenellations along

its parapet. These martial features were put to the test in 1600 when the house underwent assault from Irish attackers during the Nine Years War, another effort by Irish Catholics to unseat English Protestant rule. Rathfarnham probably served as a model for the construction of Raphoe in County Donegal, built by John Leslie in 1636 following his appointment as bishop of Raphoe in 1633.

Another corner-towered house was built by Charles Blount, Lord Mountjoy, in County Tyrone in northern Ireland in 1602. Blount served as English Lord Deputy, the direct representative of the English regent and senior executive in Ireland, for the early years of the Ulster plantation. Famous for his shrewd and often ruthless military tactics, Blount brought the Nine Years War to an end at the Battle of Kinsale, the decisive victory over Irish clan leaders and the (temporary) end of Irish military resistance. Mountjoy, built in the opening years of the Ulster plantation and framed by four imposing towers each fitted out with gun loops, is indicative of the most monumental fortified architecture erected by the English (fig. 2.28). Edward Blaney's castle at Monaghan, built in the same years and not far removed from Mountjoy, suggests that Blount's highly defensive house was a model for the fortified houses of other English soldiers who remained in Ireland after the conquest. Its function as a defensible house against an understandably hostile Irish population is quite clear. The two very high-profile plantation era buildings of Rathfarnham in Dublin and Mountjoy in Ulster, each built in the early years of the plantation era by leading new English political authorities, served as exemplars for the defensible English house that persisted in Ireland for decades.

These monumental houses erected by English authorities are joined by another important example built between 1610 and 1618 by Richard Burke, Earl of Clanricarde, a leading member of Ireland's old English.[103] With close ties to the English court and of Anglo-Norman ancestry, Burke had been educated at Christ Church, Oxford. As an adult he traveled between London, Ireland, and his English property in Kent.[104] At the founding of the Ulster plantation in northern Ireland, Burke fought alongside English general Lord Mountjoy, defeating the Irish rebellion at the battle of Kinsale. His prominence at the English court was recognized in his position as the only Catholic allowed to hold office in seventeenth-century Ireland.[105] In 1603 he married Frances Walsingham, widow of the Earl of Essex, availing himself of a great English fortune. In the years following, Burke built two houses,

one in England and the other in Ireland. The first, his house at Somerhill in Kent, is fairly typical of houses of its class, U-shaped with large window bays (fig. 2.29).

Portumna, the house he built in Ireland in 1609 in County Galway, was something else entirely (fig. 2.30). In the context of the rising challenge to Catholic old English families in Ireland, Burke built a large, three-and-a-half-story house with projecting corner towers in an explicitly English mode. The house was partially defensible: gun loops in the cellar defend the front of the house and loops in the sides of the projecting towers defend the front door. But with only slightly projecting towers, very large windows, and with the crenellations interrupted by curvilinear gables, Portumna's castellation is not military but symbolic. In the heat of the contest over their cultural and political authority and their claims to the land, Richard Burke and many old English families built houses that simultaneously asserted their English identity and defended their claim to land ownership.

The claims to authority asserted by this house form are probably best evident in the construction of Kanturk in northern County Cork, begun in the same years as Portumna (fig. 2.31). Constructed with substantial corner towers with fairly large windows, quoining, and an elaborated classical doorframe, the house is highly refined. The

FIG. 2.28
Mountjoy, County Tyrone, Ireland, begun 1602.

FIG. 2.29 Somerhill, Kent, England, ca. 1605.

lack of gun loops or even windows in the towers flanking the sides of the house undermines any interpretation of the house as primarily defensible. Its symbolic meaning is made clear in the fact that Kanturk is the only house of this type built in the early seventeenth century by a man of ancient Irish heritage. MacDonagh McCarthy enlisted the architectural language of colonial power, but to great frustration. Objections to the construction of such a house were so great among his English counterparts that he was never allowed to complete it.[106] The symbolic significance of this form was well understood by new and old English and Irish alike.

But the form was not only symbolic. A number of other houses that rise in southern Ireland were built by

FIG. 2.30 Portumna, County Gallway, Ireland, 1609.

old English families with explicitly defensive corner towers. Two examples suffice. From the early 1630s, only a few years apart and a few miles apart, the Long family's Mountlong Castle (begun 1631) and the Archdekin family's Monkstown Castle (begun 1636) both have substantial corner towers boldly projecting from the rectilinear core of the house and rising to full masonry gable ends (see fig. 2.32).[107] In addition to their pronounced towers, both buildings feature very small windows and appear in general more defensible than the earlier example at Portumna. Both houses were built immediately after "The Graces," a set of agreements negotiated in 1628 between Charles I and a delegation representing old English families in Ireland.[108] Seeking to demonstrate their faithfulness to the English crown, old English families hoped to find favor with Charles I, whose wife Henrietta Maria was Catholic. A number of these graces dealt specifically with land tenure and were favorable to the old English retention of land grants. In return, old English families committed funds to support the English government in Ireland. But the implementation of these graces by the Irish government over the next ten years was uneven, resulting in the eventual failure of the old English families to ultimately achieve their goal of security for their land titles. Built in the years when this failure was unfolding, both Mountlong and Monkstown are material responses to anxious circumstances. Through their symbolically English plan the houses assert political association with Rathfarnham and Portumna. But their numerous gun loops and clearly defensive manner convey their pessimism over legal resolution to the question of land tenure. Ultimately that pessimism would be justified. Both houses are associated with individuals who were directly involved in armed resistance to English Protestant rule. John Long of Mountlong was established as High Sheriff of Cork in 1641 after the Confederate rebellions of that year briefly returned Ireland to Catholic rule. He was hung in 1653 after the fall of Ireland to Cromwell's army. John Archdekin of Monkstown was an officer in the army of King Philip IV of Spain and fought alongside the Spanish against the English. Almost twin constructions, these two houses enlisted the towered form first as evidence of their claim to ancient "English" authority, and also as strongholds to militarily defend old English claims to landholdings. When an eighteenth-century member of the Archdekin family, then spelled Archdeacon, removed to Jamaica to establish a plantation adjacent to Stokes Hall (fig. 2.15), he would have recognized the older building as being not entirely unlike Monkstown, his ancestral home.[109]

◆ ◆ ◆

FIG. 2.31 Kanturk, County Cork, Ireland, ca. 1609.

FIG. 2.32 Monkstown, County Cork, Ireland, ca. 1636.

The corner-towered house in Jamaica and southern Ireland represented one form; houses with diagonally opposed towers, like Stewart Castle in Jamaica, present a second, slightly later type. As built by Scottish planter James Stewart I, Stewart Castle was a compact house block with a single room per floor and two freestanding towers (see figs. 2.1, 2.2). While the house block had fairly large window openings, the towers were both fitted out with gun loops facing all four directions, with careful sightlines along the main elevations of the house. When expanded by James Stewart II, the main house block was enclosed on three sides, filling in the open space left by his father between the house and the towers (see fig. 2.3).[110] The surviving walls of the expanded house with their multiple gun loops, as well as the original sightlines from the corner towers, make clear that the concern for defense remained. The two older towers were now incorporated into the footprint of the main house. The son's new, third tower stood some distance from the house, but this time to the west; in addition to its gun loops and port for small cannon in its upper story, the ground floor of the tower functioned also as a privy. To the east, the younger Stewart's massive enclosed courtyard—with its eight-foot wall topped with mortared broken glass and lined with gun loops at ten-foot intervals—reiterates that defense was a primary concern for both father and son.

In both its early (ca. 1760s) and later (ca. 1790s) phases Stewart Castle is an exemplar of early colonial Jamaican houses built with defensive towers providing gun loops with sightlines along all flanks of the main house. While it is among the most extraordinary examples, it is not atypical. An early house at Kew Park, St. James Parish, has a small, rectilinear core flanked by two tall square towers on opposite corners, in an arrangement much like that of the 1760s Stewart Castle (fig. 2.33). Intact gun loops make clear that these towers were defensive in nature. The same is true of the diminutive and early house ruin called Edinburgh Castle, St. Ann Parish, built soon after the arrival of its builder, Lewis Hutchison, in the 1760s (figs. 2.34, 2.35).[111] Although they are rounded (rather than squared as in most examples), the attached corner towers of Edinburgh Castle closely resemble the placement of the towers at Kew Park. Archaeological excavations of Auchindown Castle in Westmoreland Parish reported on the site "two imposing castellated towers" connected by a tall wall that likely defined an enclosed courtyard.[112] In another example, a freestanding tower similar to that erected in the second phase of construction at Stewart Castle appears in an early nineteenth-century print of Montpelier plantation in St. James Parish. Many late eighteenth- and early nineteenth-century houses erected in Jamaica's western and northern parishes were designed with defensive towers sometimes attached to the house on opposite corners or sometimes freestanding at some distance. Some also had enclosed yards or

FIG. 2.33 Kew Park, Westmoreland Parish, Jamaica, late eighteenth century. Note the loopholes flanking window openings.

bawns defended by tall masonry walls fitted out with gun loops.

The 1748 inventory recorded for a plantation great house called Stewart's Fort in St. George Parish indicates that the house boasted a great hall, a great room, a blue room, and piazzas as well as three bastions: a stone bastion, Dr. Stewart's bastion, and the overseer's bastion. The first had a bedstead, chest of drawers, and various table linens, and also two cutlasses and two blunderbusses. The overseer's bastion was also fitted out with a bedstead and table, as well as two guns, two more blunderbusses and a "Speaking Trumpet." Dr. Stewart's bastion was, not surprisingly, the finest, including a bedstead and fittings, a table with other furniture, fine specimens of silver, and, again, two blunderbusses and two pistols.[113] These chambers were the most well-fitted with arms; positioned at or near the corners of the main rooms of the house, unquestionably intended for defense, these substantial masonry bastions functioned as rooms in a house all the while invoking the capacity for military defense.

While this building type is widespread in the early modern era, there is a striking correlation between these west and north coast defensive great houses—which all appear to date from the mid and late eighteenth and early nineteenth centuries—and planters recently emigrated from Scotland.[114] Scottish family and place-names abound, such as Stewart, Ainslie, Sterling, Auchindown,

Edinburgh, and Hutchison. Historian Alan Karras has examined in detail the community he refers to as the Scottish sojourners to Jamaica.[115] He describes these men as second and third sons of middling and educated Scottish families who traveled to Jamaica with the specific intention of making a livable fortune and returning to Scotland. This was, however, a hope that few actually realized.[116] Karras notes that the immigration of Scottish sojourners to Jamaica began in earnest in the 1740s—certainly in part exacerbated by the failed Jacobite rebellion—and escalated through the eighteenth century. As a result of the lateness of their arrival relative to their English counterparts, most of these Scottish planters purchased land in the frontier regions of the west and north coasts, principally Westmoreland, Hanover, St. James, Trelawny, and St. Ann parishes. By the end of the eighteenth century, all of these parishes had a 25 percent or more Scottish landowning population.[117] This density, Karras argues, led to mutually reinforcing webs of relationships among Scottish professionals and planters. This support also worked to reinforce kinship networks and to distinguish Scots in Jamaica from their English counterparts, at least through the second half of the eighteenth century.[118]

The houses erected in Jamaica by these Scottish sojourners are surprising. By the second half of the eighteenth century, the majority of middling educated Scottish families were building for themselves in Scotland

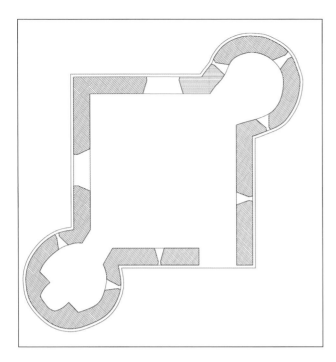

FIG. 2.34 Plan of Edinburgh Castle, St. Ann Parish, Jamaica, late eighteenth century.

single- or double-pile "Georgian" houses with symmetrical front elevations and plans with central passages flanked by large, well-lit chambers.[119] In short, the houses of most middling Scots were not fundamentally different from those of their English counterparts. The houses erected by a number of Scottish sojourners to Jamaica, however, drew upon older, more defensive architectural

traditions long inscribed in the Scottish landscape, especially the tower house and the Z-plan house.

Jamaica's Scottish sojourners chose not to build for themselves genteel Georgian country houses with central passages and large glazed sash windows such as those most of these émigrés would have known in Scotland. In building tower houses and Z-plan houses, both of which were largely abandoned as forms for new buildings in Scotland by the middle and late eighteenth century, they drew upon memories of the defensive architecture of their homelands. The main house erected at Stewart Castle by John Stewart I was a tower house—a substantial house with a single room per floor—and Stewart's Fort, Edinburgh Castle, and Kew Park were all derivatives of the Scottish Z-plan house. In all cases, the choice to reject fashionable options in favor of defense was a clear reflection of Scottish anxieties about personal safety in Jamaica's hostile environment. And the concentrated appearance of these houses in the 1760s is not at all a surprise; this was the same decade of the greatest number of Jamaica's slave rebellions. Hoping to reside but a while, these planters erected houses like those that had defended Scottish landholdings for centuries.

As with the larger towered houses of Munster, the smaller more defensive houses of northern Jamaica have clear correspondence with Scottish-built settler houses of northern Ireland. Examples survive among the collection of planter houses erected at the dawn of the seventeenth

FIG. 2.35 Edinburgh Castle, St. Ann Parish, Jamaica.

century in County Fermanagh, a territory at the southwest edge of Ulster.[120] Begun by Scot Malcolm Hamilton in 1616, Monea is among the most impressive (fig. 2.36). The substantial two-and-a-half-story masonry house is defined by the two round towers that flank the end-wall entrance into the house. The gun loops in the house walls and those of the end towers were reinforced by a twelve-foot wall defining a hundred-foot-square courtyard, or bawn, itself defended by rounded corner towers. These Irish forms derive from earlier Scottish tower houses, such as the well-preserved late sixteenth-century Claypotts Castle (fig. 2.37).[121] In 1619 Scot John Hume began his plantation house at Tully as a rectilinear two-story stone house with a large bawn, defined and defended by square corner towers. Termon, built in 1615, is a single-tower house in Donegal with a corner stairtower that doubles as a defensive work. The tower stands at one edge of a large bawn defined by two more corner fortifications.[122] These examples demonstrate the type: compact rectilinear masonry house, sometimes with

appended towers, surrounded by a bawn defended by a tall masonry wall, usually boasting additional corner towers, all features with the ever-present gun loops.[123] While some time has been spent on the particularly Scottish features of these fortified houses, the more helpful acknowledgment for our purposes is that Scots were directly involved in the settlement of the Ulster plantation and that they brought with them a long-lived tradition of fortified houses.[124]

◆ ◆ ◆

There are some extraordinary parallels between the plantation houses of early seventeenth-century Ireland and mid-eighteenth-century Jamaica. Both are marked by two types of towered houses. Just as Munster in southern Ireland boasts a large number of English-built manor houses defined largely by four prominent corner towers, so too is that form predominant in the older, mostly English parishes of Clarendon and St. Dorothy in Jamaica. Built by both old and new English in Ireland, the house with four corner towers was sometimes a practical measure, but always a symbolic gesture of English claims to authority over the land. As a result of this history, the symbolic power of Jamaica's towered houses becomes all the more clear. Drawing from a centuries-long practice in the British landscape, newly wealthy planters in Jamaica asserted their status and authority over the landscape. The parallels between Jamaica and Ireland are evident not only in the architecture of English elites but also in that of their Scottish counterparts. Just as Ulster in northern Ireland exhibited a number of Scottish-derived tower houses, usually with appended or freestanding defensive flankers, often connected via a bawn wall, so, too, is this form evident in Jamaica, again built largely by Scots.

Immigrating Scots were not unfamiliar with the militarization of houses in a colonial context. The immigration of Scots to Jamaica in the eighteenth century was in many ways a repeat of an earlier emigration of Scots into northern Ireland in the very early seventeenth century. But by the time they began to immigrate to Jamaica during the second half of the seventeenth century, Scots had not been actively building defensive houses in Scotland for more than a century. Even so, Stewart Castle, a house and bawn built in the latter half of the eighteenth century on the north coast of Jamaica, seems quite obviously to draw from this model, its plan almost entirely absent from the English gentry houses of the period but common in the Scottish fortified tower housebuilding tradition.

FIG. 2.36 Monea, County Fermanagh, Ireland. ca. 1616.

FIG. 2.37 Claypotts Castle, near Dundee, Scotland, 1569–88. The Z-plan house has a rectangular core and two circular towers. Note also the cellar loopholes.

The architectural parallels between the two colonies suggest that alone among Britain's colonial territories, Ireland and Jamaica share a distinctive model for colonialism in Britain's early empire. Occupation of both islands by the British was a process hotly contested by "others." As a result, if Ireland was the contested frontier of the English empire in the early seventeenth century, Jamaica took on that role by the late seventeenth century. In both cases, British occupation of the land depended on seizure of land, a process accompanied by forcible resistance from *indigenes*. In Ireland, that resistance took the form of armed rebellion through the late sixteenth and early seventeenth centuries. In Jamaica, resistance to British occupation was first presented by the Spanish colonizers from whom Jamaica was seized, then by the island's population of Maroons, descendants of Africans enslaved by the Spanish who fled during the seizure of Jamaica by the English. The Maroons offered periodic and violent resistance to English control of the island and remained a consistent threat until the 1739 peace treaty recognizing Maroon nationhood and independence. As was the case for architecture in Ireland, the towers on houses in Jamaica were sometimes actually defensive, as at Stokes Hall, but always intended as a symbolic claim to political authority and control of the land.

Jamaica bore the scars of Spanish conquest and the persistent threat of Maroon attack, foreign invasion, and slave insurrection, realities that had a profound impact on the *mentalité* of its colonial residents. The British colonial presence in Jamaica was marked by a profound uncertainty, an unrelenting anxiety that found expression in their architecture. Jamaica's early towers betray a concern for fortification in a landscape seized from, claimed by, and still occupied by "others." But if the constant pulse of anxiety is one form of fear, the other is alarm.[125] The correspondence between the efflorescence of fortified Scottish houses along the north coast in the 1760s was a direct response to the alarm engendered by the numerous insurrections of that decade, most especially Tacky's Rebellion that began on Easter morning of 1760 and continued through to at least October of the following year. Inspired by a plan to supplant British colonial rule with a reconstituted African state, Tacky's Rebellion included at least fifteen hundred Africans and was the largest insurrection in the Caribbean until the Haitian Revolution.[126] The intensely fortified houses of the 1760s were the result of the clear alarm incited by this monumental event, especially in the more remote regions of the north and west. Such an event, of course, fueled the anxiety that continued to shape architectures of defense into the nineteenth century. The houses built by Scottish and English planters demonstrate the coherence of a marchlands mentality and, furthermore, that planters first in Ireland and then in Jamaica were themselves agents of empire.

3   Heat and Hurricanes

Until the recent construction of the vast cruise ship terminal that landlocked the building, John Tharp's townhouse in Falmouth overlooked the harbor of this late eighteenth-century port town on Jamaica's north coast. The low one-story house sitting high on a raised masonry foundation faced a long wharf and yard on which thousands of pounds of goods moved to and from ships each year (fig. 3.1). Born in 1744 as the eldest son of a wealthy Jamaican planter, Tharp inherited plantations in Hanover Parish and enough wealth to travel to England for his education, at Eaton and Trinity College, Cambridge.[1] After returning to Jamaica in 1766, he began building a massive plantation empire. He was also involved in the slave trade; in 1784 he posted an ad in the local newspaper announcing the sale of 440 "Fantee, Ashantee, and Akim" slaves from the ship bearing his name then anchored in Falmouth harbor. In December of that year he advertised another 425 slaves for sale.[2] The house at Tharp's wharf would have been the first building that enslaved Africans would encounter in the new world; the remains of a stronghold in the cellar might have confined Africans waiting for sale. Tharp's house thus participated directly in the violence of slavery, but this chapter focuses on a different violence.

Built by one of Jamaica's wealthiest planters in the closing years of the eighteenth century, Tharp's townhouse adopted a number of distinctive characteristics—especially a low building envelope, intermixture of materials, and multiple low roof systems—that it shared with many other structures across the Caribbean. The Tharp house stands on a masonry foundation tall enough to allow a storehouse underneath. The front elevation of that foundation is laid in tight courses of very precise ashlar blocks.[3] Resting on that foundation is a single living floor of rooms whose exterior skin was always plastered and scored to look like stone. Underneath that visible surface, the building walls were timber-framed posts, sills, and plates infilled with courses of brick, a technique called nogging (fig. 3.2). Sheltering those rooms of the main floor are a series of four low roofs, three of which are visible from the main northern elevation. Tharp's master carpenter sheltered each room or suite of rooms with single, hipped roofs; the final result is a building that departed dramatically from the tall elegant townhouses built for elites in Bristol, Philadelphia, or other major port cities across the British world. Tharp's house was entirely a product of the Caribbean. But it would be

FIG. 3.1 John Tharp House, Falmouth, Jamaica, ca. 1790.

FIG. 3.2 Elevation drawing of Tharp House showing the nogged wall construction. The circles show the locations of original iron straps.

FIG. 3.3 Francis Sandys, Chippenham Park entrance lodges and gates, Chippenham Park, Cambridgeshire, England, 1790s.

wrong to presume that this house is simply provincial; it was built for a patron who would work in the mid-1790s with British architects James Wyatt and Francis Sandys on the reconstruction of Chippenham Park, his Cambridgeshire country house (fig. 3.3).[4] The architecture of Tharp's Jamaican townhouse was quite intentional, not unaware of fashionable neoclassical design but attentive to different circumstance: the terrifying violence of the Caribbean climate. This chapter examines the architectural response of British builders in the Caribbean to climate, especially the oppressive heat and the destructive force of the hurricane.[5]

◆ ◆ ◆

The Caribbean's seventeenth-century colonials quickly recognized one shared reality: it was really hot. While some simply reported on the region's "sultry heat," others complained that "the climate is so hot . . . and the heat of the sun so great, that it will melt a ship's pitch and shrink her planks."[6] That heat changed the daily rhythms of life. One Englishman writing from late seventeenth-century Jamaica noted that merchants commonly "shut up their shops" at noon only to reopen again at three in the afternoon when "the brezes begin to fan the earth strongly." It was common, he said, "to sleep in the heat of the day," emulating the cultural practices of the region's Spanish colonials.[7] But the Caribbean heat was not just uncomfortable, it could also be deadly, leading to dehydration and heatstroke. And as historian Karen Kupperman has

demonstrated, seventeenth-century British settlers to the West Indies presumed an intimate connection between climate and the body's humors; a dramatic change in climate could, they thought, have detrimental effects on health.[8] Many believed that the sun had the power to render them gravely ill by melting their body's fat within them. Sweating could debilitate one's stomach and other organs.[9] The tropical sun could do violence to the body, even kill.

But the challenges of weather in the tropics were not limited to the heat. The destructive potential of hurricanes was already apparent to settlers in the Leeward Islands by the late 1630s, when one account reported that upon the approach of a hurricane, colonists fled their houses for the protection of "holes, Caves, pits, Dens, and hollow places of the earth . . . which places are good harbours and defences against the Hurry-Cano."[10] Initially, settlers to Jamaica from the eastern Caribbean thought the more westerly island less susceptible to hurricanes. John Taylor, among Jamaica's most important chroniclers, wrote in the late 1680s that Jamaica was "much more serean and happy than the Windward Islands (Barbadoes, Neives, Antego, Saint Christopher) which at a certaine time of the yeare are much damnified by tempestious hirocladons or huricans."[11] Taylor would be right, for a time. Through the seventeenth century, Jamaica experienced only two major storms, far fewer than in the Leeward Islands or Barbados. But the tranquility was short-lived. In the opening decades of the eighteenth century, the island was buffeted by a series of powerful storms. The 1712 hurricane presented colonials with "the most Melancholy and dismal Prospect, many houses in the Towns, as well as in the Plantations being blown down, other uncovered, and none without some damage."[12] Describing the capital of Kingston after the 1722 storm, the *Weekly Jamaica Courant* reported, "Near one-half the Houses are thrown Down or Shatter'd to such a degree they are Irreparable, and few or none have escaped without some Damage, in so much that the town appears in a Ruinous Condition." The devastation was particularly acute near the wharves, which were "all destroyed and most of the Sugars and other Commodities that were there are all washed away."[13] Writing in the late 1730s, James Knight noted for his readers the particular devastation of the storms of 1712, 1722, and 1726; another account noted that in a 1733 hurricane many "were killed by the falling down of their Houses."[14] As it turned out, Jamaica was just as susceptible to the wrath of hurricanes.[15]

In self-defense, colonials found it necessary to adapt their buildings to the Caribbean's heat and hurricanes. While the relationship between architecture and climate is a topic that has been addressed by historians of architecture, these discussions usually focus on the origins of the porch and diffusion narratives across the Caribbean and coastal America.[16] This chapter takes a more focused look into the piazza in Jamaica, arguing that it coalesces from a variety of sources; and the chapter examines how colonials built buildings that had the capacity to withstand hurricanes and earthquakes. The previous chapter reviewed the architectural response to the violence of slavery; this chapter examines the ways British colonials enlisted their buildings to combat the violence of weather and natural disasters in the Caribbean. The first half of the chapter examines the ways that seventeenth-century colonials responded to heat and hurricanes across the Caribbean, from Barbados to the Leeward Islands to Jamaica. The second half of the chapter focuses more specifically on the development of architectural strategies to heat and hurricanes in eighteenth-century Jamaica.

SEVENTEENTH-CENTURY SHADES

One of the first material accommodations to the heat of the Caribbean by the earliest British colonials was one learned from the region's native inhabitants: sleeping in a hammock (fig. 3.4). Described as cotton beds made in the "Indian style," hammocks were common across the

early British Caribbean; they appear frequently in probate inventories from seventeenth-century Port Royal as well as in accounts from early eighteenth-century St. Christopher (commonly called St. Kitts).[17] While one writer from early Barbados suggested that hammocks were used only by servants, other commentators suggested otherwise.[18] John Taylor, writing from late seventeenth-century Jamaica, noted that planters and servants alike "rest for the most part in swinging hammocks made of cotton, or netts of silkgrass."[19] Antoine Biet, a French traveler to Barbados, observed, "When an English lady sees someone pass by she freely asks if he needs anything. She invites him into the house, has him sit in a hammock . . . and she immediately brings some brandy or any other drink that is desired."[20] Evidence for colonials' use of hammocks persists well into eighteenth-century Jamaica. The probate inventories of Robert Thurger (1712) and Robert Nedham (1739), for example, include hammocks in addition to fine feather beds in their best bedchambers.[21] In the 1750s, Thomas Thistlewood kept a hammock hanging in his hall for guests and visitors.[22] But simply sleeping in hammocks, although a widespread seventeenth-century practice, was not enough to mediate the heat. Englishmen in the Caribbean had to transform their houses.

In his dissertation on life in mid-seventeenth-century Barbados, Richard Ligon lambasted English settlers on that island for not building houses that responded specifically to the region's heat. Prior to his arrival, he had presumed that housebuilders would have built houses with "thick walls, high roofs, and deep cellars," but to his surprise they erected "timber houses, with low roofs, so low, as for the most part of them, I could hardly stand upright with my hat on, and no cellars at all." But his greatest critique was leveled at the fact that most builders built houses with very solid walls "stopping, or barring out the wind." Opening the houses to the breezes, he argued "should give them the greatest comfort, when they were neer stifled with heat." Ligon observed that the winds in Barbados always came from the east. For this reason, settlers on that island should always build houses with openings to that direction "thereby to let in the cool breezes, to refresh them when the heat of the day came." But to his astonishment, he found that most settlers closed up their houses to the east and opened them to the west, facing the afternoon sun. As a result, "those little low roofed rooms were like Stoves, or heated Ovens." Upon inquiring about this practice he learned that the

wind brought with it driving rains from the east and those rains kept the interiors of their houses perpetually wet. Desiring to keep the east side of their houses closed up to keep out the rains, they opened the west sides to allow as much airflow as possible.[23]

In order to mediate this problem, Ligon offered a number of recommendations in his treatise. The first was to open the house to the east and install shutters on that side to close out the rains. He also recommended planting fast-growing palmetto trees to "interpose so between the Sun and house, as to keep it continually in the shade." When planting such trees, he recommended, place them a little distance from the house and encourage them to grow tall, "for shades that are made by the highest trees,

FIG. 3.5 Robert Smythson, Hardwick Hall, Derbyshire, England, 1590–97. An original gallery spans between the towers on the garden front of the building.

are undoubtedly the coolest, and freshest, by reason it keeps the heat farthest off."[24] But most particularly, he recommended attending to the form and orientation of the house. If one is building a smaller single house where all the rooms are arranged in a linear fashion, then it must be positioned on an east–west line, with the longer elevations to the north and south. Such an orientation would expose the least elevations to the sun in the morning and evening and give optimum shade to the house through the course of the day. Such buildings should have "walks" on either side; from the sixteenth century, the term referred to spaces dedicated to walking, in a garden or in an ambulatory or cloister, adjacent to buildings and sheltered by a shed roof, often open to one side.[25] While not common, such features were not unknown in England; the very late sixteenth-century walk at Hardwick Hall in Derbyshire is an excellent example (fig. 3.5).

But if one had the capacity, Ligon continued, it was advisable to build a double house, an arrangement where the rooms are organized in two adjacent and attached flanks, each flank sheltered by its own roof. In this design, the building creates its own shade as the "West side is not visited by the Sun in the morning nor the East in the afternoon." Yet, he acknowledges, the double roofs and the gutter between them tend to heat constantly over the

course of the day and "will so warm the East side of the House, as all the shade it has in the afternoon will not cool it, nor make it habitable."[26] Experimentation with double houses and thermal management was under discussion in London in these same years, but the far greater heat in the Caribbean amplified the needs for an architectural response.[27]

Over the course of the seventeenth century, most builders learned that temperature in a house was reduced by increasing airflow and creating shade, and they experimented with both. One way to increase airflow was to make the walls as permeable as possible. In the earliest decades of the century, this was accomplished in a variety of ways. In 1652, the "best houses" in Barbados were two-room and wood-framed with a thatch roof, while "the upper part of the house is open at the side so that air can flow through."[28] Two years later, a visitor to St. Kitts reported that the boards on the walls of houses on that island were "not closer together than one can pass a hand out and in between each board in order that the air may be able to blow in to cool the people staying within."[29] A midcentury description of the churches on the French islands of the Caribbean noted that on these buildings "all the siding . . . has openings to allow the air to pass." By the end of the seventeenth century, some builders on St. Kitts sheathed their houses with woven mats or cane, creating walls that could be opened or closed depending on conditions. Edward Warner Sevion, for example, lived in a twenty-four-by-twelve-foot thatch-roofed house that was "matted round." John Abbot had a house of the same size with one stone wall, "ye other End & Sides matted."[30] In doing so, these European builders emulated the region's native Taino (see fig. 3.4). Cheap and air-permeable, walls of matting or caning seemed a logical choice.

One of the critical decisions seventeenth-century housebuilders had to make was how to handle windows. As suggested by Ligon's criticisms of planter houses in Barbados, increasing airflow through windows was complicated by rain, "[for they have] no glass to keep it out."[31] His solution—installing shutters that could close the window opening—avoided using glass, which seemed impractical to many, "because of the hot climate of the country, for one is obliged to keep the doors and windows open to allow for breezes, with the intention of cooling the house; one only closes them at night."[32] Many buildings across the Caribbean, even large public structures, had unglazed window openings. The church in Basse-Terre on French St. Kitts was a wood-framed building on a stone foundation, but "instead of Glass-windows there are only turned pillars; after the fashion of a balcony."[33] Francis Rogers noted in the very early eighteenth century that in the Jamaican town of Port Royal, "most of the houses, especially the public ones, have no glass, but large deep window frames all open or a little lettic'd, for coolness."[34] Similarly, a mid-eighteenth-century observer commented that no buildings in Spanish Town had glazed windows save the governor's house.[35] Even to this day, early houses on the Windward Island of Dominica—initially colonized by the French but claimed by the English in 1763—offer very little evidence of sash windows. Like their counterparts across the British Caribbean, the vast majority of early houses on that island still have only interior louvered shutters with solid shutters outside.

In addition to increasing airflow, early builders also worked to create shade by erecting structures of the same name. From the early seventeenth century, English usage of the word often referred to mats or blinds over windows or pent roofs over doors.[36] But among settlers to the Caribbean, the term was expanded to refer to a more substantial shelter that accomplished the same feat. Easily erected, shades were lightly framed structures intended to provide places of intensive labor some shelter from the

sun, and were in use by Taino, Africans, and Europeans through the late seventeenth century (fig. 3.6).[37] As is demonstrated by the 1706 St. Kitts claims for damages after a French raid on the island, such structures were appended to houses and other buildings as a transitional space from inside to out.[38] Philip Vorchild's thirty-by-eighteen-foot house was expanded by two shades, one in front that measured fourteen by eight feet and a rear shade that ran the whole length of the house and was boarded "under foot." To add the shade alongside an English house required little more than removing the vertical wall boarding of another common English housing feature, the shed. In addition to shades, sheds also appear in the accounts. Jedidiah Hutchinson had a thirty-six-by-eighteen-foot dwelling house of two rooms that was expanded by a shed "boarded and shingled" (meaning enclosed with board walls and shingle roof) along the shorter end wall. The same was true of Elizabeth Winder's house, which boasted two large sheds, and Godwin Bantanon's house, which had three sheds, also "boarded and shingled." Enclosed for security, these sheds were typical of those found all over England in the seventeenth century. The 1706 accounts from St. Kitts make clear that by the end of the seventeenth century, builders in the British Caribbean distinguished between an enclosed shed and an open shade, both of which appeared as appendages to houses.

While many shades must have required little more than earthfast posts, thatch roofs, and dirt-floored spaces, some appear to have been more finely finished, suggesting that rather than places of labor, they might have been conceived of as extensions of the polite spaces of the house. John Davis's fifty-two-by-sixteen-foot house had a hall paved in tile and two board-floored chambers. Significantly, his house also boasted a shade that was paved with tile, connecting the space of the shade with that of the hall. The 1679 accounts for the construction of a new glebe house for the parish of St. John in Barbados offer evidence of a shade that was even more substantial. The forty-by-twenty-one-foot, two-story stone house was to have a "porch building" on the front and a "stair building" behind (in this way, the building was much like Bacon's Castle in early Virginia). To either side of the rear stair building stood a fourteen-by-twelve-foot shade built out of stone.[39] The substantial nature of the shades on the glebe house is reinforced by the fact that the upper floor boasted shade chambers, rooms immediately above the ground-floor shades. Yet for all their substance, they

1. *Negre qui ejambe le tabac.*
2. *Negre qui torque le tabac.*
3. *Negre qui le met en rolle.*
4. *Tabac a la pente.*

Tom. 4. pag. 496.

FIG. 3.6 Jean-Baptiste Labat, *Nouveau voyage aux isles de l'Amérique* (Paris: P. F. Giffart, 1722). John Carter Brown Library at Brown University.

might still have been associated with work; one of the shades on the Barbados glebe house had a chimney and oven. Another contemporary and surviving house on the same island has physical evidence for the same arrangement. The two-story masonry building that now serves as the principal's house for Codrington College has a sophisticated classical elevation and a spectacular porch entry to the front.[40] But for our purposes, the building has a rear stair tower just like the glebe house, and to either side of that tower are substantial masonry platforms that might easily have accommodated flanking shades, much like the tile-floored shade on John Davis's house on St. Kitts.[41]

As the seventeenth century unfolded, concentrations of houses became towns and eventually cities. The increasing wealth and density of cities generated new problems for housebuilders in the Caribbean. While smaller towns like those on St. Kitts remained largely built of timber and single-story in nature, Bridgetown, Barbados, and Port Royal, Jamaica, took on decidedly urban forms with multistory masonry houses often built cheek by jowl with neighbors. Whereas glazing was rare on rural houses through the century, cities populated by more well-traveled merchants introduced greater pressure to conform to cosmopolitan fashions. As wealth increased, glazed widows became increasingly desirable. As late as the 1660s, Jean-Baptiste du Tertre informed his readers that in the Leeward Islands "I have only seen glass in the window openings of the governors' houses."[42] But by the final decade of the seventeenth century, glass windows were becoming quite common in the English Caribbean. Hans Sloane, describing Port Royal in the 1680s, reported that "the houses built by the English are, for the most part, brick, and after the English manner," a design he describes as "neither cool, nor able to endure the shocks of an earthquake."[43] In the 1680s, when Port Royal was near its economic zenith, many of its multistory masonry houses had glazed windows.[44] Early eighteenth-century Port Royal had many smaller houses with no glass windows but there were "some handsome large houses of the merchants, with sash windows."[45] By contrast, accounts from early St. Kitts make it clear that only the very wealthiest on that island had sash windows in their houses.[46] Even though glazing had the obvious detriment of blocking airflow, wealthier urban merchants in the English Caribbean began to install sash windows by the early eighteenth century, if not a few decades before. Even as late as the 1740s, an observer noted that St. John's Antigua only had "some glass windows."[47] But, of course, the installation of glazing and sash windows was a conscious preference for fashion over comfort on the part of housebuilders; such windows admitted light and the heat of the sun and even with the lower sash raised, they impeded airflow. Perhaps to compensate, property owners in cities, like their counterparts on plantations, embraced the practicality of shade structures. In her work on the early Leeward Islands, Daphne Hobson has suggested that shades were found in those islands primarily on urban sites.[48] The documentary evidence from late seventeenth-century Port Royal in Jamaica reveals numerous references in deeds and lease agreements to shades in urban backlots.[49] Creating a shaded space immediately behind the house and in the rear work yard of urban lots, shades seem to be places of labor intended to create sheltered workspace in the yard, rather than places of repose or extensions of the better rooms of the house, a function they would gain in the eighteenth century.[50]

SEVENTEENTH-CENTURY HURRICANES

If the oppressive heat seemed ever present, colonial lives were occasionally punctuated by the arrival of storms such as they had never known in the British Isles. The response by the majority of colonials was almost immediately to

build houses with low profiles. In the middle of the 1660s, Charles de Rochefort suggested that European settlers in the Caribbean generally "built after the same manner as those in their own Countries." The only marked difference was "they are but one or two Stories high at the most, that they may the more easily resist the winds, which sometimes blow in those parts with extraordinary violence."[51] Colonel Stapleton, governor of the Leeward Islands, wrote in 1676 that in Charlestown, the capital of Nevis, "there were good dwellings and storehouses built with country timber, not exceeding 60 feet long and 20 broad, story and a half, the Hurri-Canes having taught the people to build low."[52] Numerous failures had taught them that tall buildings fared far worse in hurricanes than did low, sprawling ones. This seemed especially true in the cluster of small islands in the northeastern Caribbean, including St. Kitts, Nevis, Montserrat, and Antigua. First colonized in the 1620s, these islands experienced a number of violent storms through the seventeenth century, and settlers appear to have accommodated to hurricanes fairly quickly. In a hurricane in 1681 on St. Kitts, Christopher Jeaffreson noted that "a great part of the roof of my dwelling house began to fly away."[53] As suggested by the surviving roof framing system on an early house on adjacent Nevis, housebuilders might have begun to include wind braces by the later seventeenth century to better secure against such loss (fig. 3.7).[54] By the middle of the seventeenth century, with decades of experience under their belt, English settlers in the eastern Caribbean had learned the most important lesson about architecture in hurricane-prone circumstances: build low.

As they began to respond to the realities of hurricanes, some colonials noted the resilience of houses erected by the region's indigenous populations. "It hath been found by experience that these Huts [of the native Taino], being round and having no place open but the door," Rochefort wrote, "are commonly spared when the highest houses are removed from one place to another."[55] The most detailed European visual sources of early Taino architecture are a handful of images from the collection of late sixteenth-century watercolors from the Francis Drake manuscript, now in the Pierpont Morgan Library.[56] A second excellent collection of early images appears in Fernández de Oviedo y Valdés, *La Historia general y natural de las Indias.*[57] These collections represent a wide range of buildings built by indigenous West Indians, most likely late sixteenth-century Taino. A number of the images depict fairly small

FIG. 3.7 Roof framing at the Hermitage, Nevis, Leeward Islands. ca. 1700.

circular buildings with steep conical roofs made from light rafters covered with matted plantain or other large leaves (see fig. 3.4).[58] The roofs are supported by earthfast posts with forked tops which carry the structure's horizontal members. These images represent two variations in wall surfaces. One is sticks or reeds woven through the vertical earthfast posts, and the other a woven matting that encircles the building. Rochefort's descriptions of indigenous construction technologies agree with the Drake and Oviedo images quite closely. The houses of the Caribbean's indigenous population are, he tells us, supported by "pieces of wood planted in the ground, over which they put a roof of Plantane-leaves or Sugar-canes,

or some herbs which they can so dispose and intermix one among another, that under that covering which reaches to the ground, they are secured against rain and all injuries of the weather." He goes on to report that these roofs last three to four years "unless there happens to be a Hurricane." The roofs were constructed of a sacrificial material that was easily replaced after such a storm. Once the sheathing blew off, the load from the wind nearly disappears, leaving the structural frame largely undamaged, even if the contents of the house are lost.[59] A recent Caribbean-wide analysis of all Taino archaeological sites has convincingly suggested that the vast majority of indigenous architecture was rounded or oblong.[60]

While not drawing from centuries of experience with hurricanes, West Africans building in the seventeenth-century Caribbean also erected earthfast buildings. Evidence for the architectural patterns of seventeenth-century Africans is very limited, but they did not differ significantly from those of their eighteenth- and early nineteenth-century counterparts (figs. 3.8, 3.9).[61] One early nineteenth-century sketch of an African house site in Jamaica shows two houses, one complete and the other an earthfast vertical post frame under construction (fig. 3.10). Douglas Armstrong's excavations at Drax Hall and Seville plantations have uncovered the building sites of a number of eighteenth-century houses occupied by enslaved Africans, which he describes as earthfast in construction

FIG. 3.8 Reconstructed mud-walled slave quarter, Seville plantation, St. Ann Parish, Jamaica.

FIG. 3.9 Isaac Mendes Belisario, *Highgate, Jamaica*, ca. 1836–42. Oil on canvas, 17¼ × 23¼ in. (43.8 × 59.1 cm). National Gallery of Jamaica.

with wattle-and-daub walls and likely thatched roofs. They measured approximately twenty feet long by fourteen feet wide and were composed of two rooms.[62] The foundations of one late eighteenth-century quarter at Drax Hall suggested a building that was a bit different. Probably also of wattle-and-mud construction, the Drax Hall house had three chambers, including a larger central hall and two flanking chambers. The main entrance into the building was centrally located on the long elevation and opened directly into the hall.[63] The archaeological and historical record suggests that three-room plans were less common. Like most eighteenth-century observers, Bryan Edwards suggested that the typical house was only of "two apartments," and he indicated that the whole house usually measured fifteen to twenty feet in length.[64] Matthew Lewis agreed, noting that the houses were generally of two rooms, "one for cooking and the other for sleeping."[65]

Houses with mud walls and palm thatch roofing were things of curiosity for many eighteenth-century British observers. While their surviving accounts are certainly

colored by the pro-slavery or abolitionist perspective of their authors, taken as a whole they do offer some useful contours of typical building practices. Most accounts report that the houses are "composed of hard posts driven into the ground."[66] Since builders saw no need to shape the posts, most were left unsquared, or hewn flat on only one face. The ends of the posts were usually burned before being driven into the earth to slow the pace of rot. In a practice unchanged since the seventeenth century, most housebuilders used the "largest posts with forks" to support the middle and end of the house. If nails were not available, "a notch is cut in the top of each post to receive the wall plates." Eighteenth-century houses boasted rafters "flatten'd at the upper-ends" spanning from the plate to the ridge and secured in place with wooden pins. The whole of the house frame was lashed secure with vines "which the wood[s] afford of various sizes in great abundance."[67] Once the frame was erected, the posts were then "interlaced with wattles and plaister," to infill between the posts and form a wall.[68] This was accomplished by

FIG. 3.10 Artist unknown, sketch of African house under construction in Jamaica, from the Storer Sketchbook, 1820s. Private collection.

weaving small sticks between every two posts in alternate directions and "nailed on each side of every post." Once the posts were entirely filled, the "interstices among the wattles are filled with clay and earth, into which some fibers of dried plantain leaves are rubbed to render the same more cohesive." Both the interior and exterior of each wall was "plaistered smoothly with the same composition."[69] Plastering both interior and exterior was almost universal on wattle houses through the nineteenth century.[70] Some early nineteenth-century accounts and sketches suggest that wattle houses also had what were described as foundations. But rather than building foundations in the traditional sense, as where a house frame rests on a masonry foundation, these were stones placed around the base of the exterior walls to offer support to the earthfast posts and to hinder erosion by rain.[71]

The roofs were almost always of thatch of the palm tree or coconut tree descending from either side of a horizontal ridge pole with some bending from one side down to the opposite side of the roof, "in such a manner as affords no admittance for the rain to penetrate."[72] When possible, "the leaves are twisted or plaited to the strong stem on which they grow."[73] This layering and bending over the ridge is continued "until the roof is deemed sufficiently thick to carry off the water, which in the rainy season falls with great violence."[74] Thatch was celebrated by English observers as "an admirable covering, forming a lasting and impenetrable shelter against the sun and the rain."[75] In most cases the eaves project well past the walls "to shelter the walls from rain."[76] While some quarters appear to have had hipped roofs in the early nineteenth century, most had simpler gable roofs.[77] In most cases, tall thatch roofs are carried by walls defined by earthfast vertical posts.

The houses built by West Africans seemed to perform well in hurricanes. In the midst of a hurricane on St. Kitts,

Jeaffreson and his slaves escaped the plantation dwelling house, whose roof had blown away, to a "little hut . . . which sheltered us from the violence of the storm." The hut "rocked like a cradle" but it survived the storm.[78] A later observer farther south on Guadeloupe reported that in a hurricane "the most solid buildings tumble down; whilst the villages of the little huts of the negroes stand unhurt."[79] Writing in the late 1730s, Charles Leslie, for example, noted that during hurricanes, white Jamaicans would often "retire into the Huts of the negroes, which are built exceedingly low and elude the Shocks of the Tempest."[80] While it might be the case that architectural engineering of the buildings was a factor, site also played a role; plantation houses were often raised on deforested hillocks while quarters were more often positioned in low, sheltered sites. With permeable walls and roofs that allowed air pressure to equalize in and around a building, these less substantial houses often stood when the less permeable walls of more substantially built houses collapsed under the extreme differences in air pressure that accompany hurricane-force winds. Framed by typical early modern racial prejudices, the region's colonists were surprised to learn that their more substantial houses would collapse while those of the Taino and the Africans stood strong.

But the English colonials' interest in African architecture in Jamaica was vastly overshadowed by the impression made by the buildings left by the Spanish. Even during the English conquest of the island, one observer wrote that Spanish houses "are but one storie height Becas the Harrie Cane, for doth many times com and give them a visit."[81] These observations persisted through the eighteenth century. The *Weekly Jamaica Courant* exclaimed after the 1722 hurricane, "It is remarkable that those Houses built by the Spaniards received very little damage, tho' 'tis now 67 years since the conquest of the Island; Consequently those buildings are of much Older date. From whence we may conclude that they had met with accidents of like Nature, that put them on that manner of Building."[82] Similarly James Knight noted that while the Spanish houses survived two "dreadful hurricanes" those built by the English "were either blown down or very much shattered." Knight also wrote that the Spanish houses were no more than twelve feet high and rested on "principal posts fixed in the ground 6 or 7 feet deep, the roofs hipped covered with canes and tiles laid in mortar."[83] If settlers in the seventeenth-century Leeward Islands

took heed of the building practices of the region's native inhabitants, many of their eighteenth-century counterparts in Jamaica took none at all.

English colonials in the Leeward Islands knew the architecture of the native Taino and of enslaved Africans well; those in Jamaica knew African and Spanish architecture well. The extent to which seventeenth-century English settlers in the Caribbean knowingly adopted these building practices is unclear. The 1706 St. Kitts accounts, which record in careful detail the housing stock of that island at the very beginning of the eighteenth century, suggest that most colonials lived in houses not unlike their native and African counterparts. While some wealthier planters were building substantial framed houses, the middling majority were still living in buildings that seem to quite closely approximate Rochefort's description of the early settlers' houses: "sustained by only four or six forks planted in the ground, and instead of walls are encompassed and palizado'd only with reeds, and cover'd with Palm or Plantane leaves." What is significant about this is that houses of mountain timber, thatched and caned, were still a common option as late as 1706, reinforcing Rochefort's claim that the "weak structures" of the first settlers are "still to be seen." Through the seventeenth century, the majority of the white population of St. Kitts lived in shelters that differed very little from the houses of the first settlers, houses that Rochefort described as "much after the same manner as the natural Inhabitants of the Country." The St. Kitts claims demonstrate that these materials remained common options for British housebuilders in the Leeward Islands throughout the seventeenth century.[84] And, by extension, they differed little from houses erected by the indigenous Taino, enslaved Africans, or vanquished Spanish.

Thus most houses built by seventeenth-century English colonials were of earthfast timber with thatch roofing; they were also fairly small in size. A handful of the 1706 claimants from St. Kitts lived in one-room houses, but as historian Daphne Hobson has determined, of the St. Kitts claims for which some information about room structure can be determined, three quarters of the dwellings had either two or three rooms.[85] In this way, the houses of most English settlers to the seventeenth-century Caribbean corresponded closely with those of natives and Africans not only in materials but also in scale. The clear preference among English settlers for hurricane houses of earthfast posts and cane walls suggests that they believed such technology to be better suited to weathering a storm.[86] The long persistence of earthfast construction in the region into the eighteenth century also suggests a long-standing preference for the technique when other, more fashionable options were becoming available.

But not all English colonials chose to build in wood, let alone earthfast wood. In the closing decades of the seventeenth century, many settlers opted to transition from timber houses—whether framed or earthfast—to masonry. Although expensive and affordable by only the wealthiest, masonry was celebrated for its capacity to resist hurricane-force winds. One of the first substantial masonry houses in the Leewards was the French governor's mansion on St. Kitts. Charles de Rochefort, in describing the building, noted that

> the Indians, who never had seen a Structure of any such material, look'd on it at first with a great astonishment, and having attempted to shake it, by the strength of their shoulders, but not stirring it, they were forc'd [to] acknowledge, that if all Houses were so built, the Tempest which they call the Hurricane would not prejudice them.[87]

George Welch reported in 1671 that houses on Nevis were "commonly of late . . . built of Stone, and but one Story high."[88] Just one year later, however, most builders in the Leeward Islands would reconsider the safety of masonry houses. The year 1672 saw the first of a series of late seventeenth- and early eighteenth-century earthquakes across the Caribbean.[89] Soon after that first major earthquake, the governor of the Leeward Islands informed London readers that colonists had previously preferred "stone buildings, but the earthquakes having thrown them all down, they build with timber only except the boiling houses for sugar, which in part must be built of stone."[90] The high mass and low tension strength of masonry led to widespread severe damage to the region's masonry buildings in earthquakes.[91] In 1690 another quake struck the nearby island of Nevis with similar results. As one Nevis resident wrote,

> All the Houses in Charles Town that were made of Brick or Stone, dropt a sudden from the Top to the Bottom in perfect Ruins. Those that were made of Wood were no less violently shaken, but stood, however; which shew'd that the Rivetings of wooden Structures are far stronger, and are not so easily disjoynted as the Co-augmentations of Cement and Mortar.[92]

This quake reached across the narrow channels that separate these islands. Christopher Codrington II, writing from nearby Antigua about the same event, complained that on that island "Scarce any stonework in these islands has escaped damage and I myself am a loser to the value of £2000."[93] If stonework was a lifesaver in a hurricane, it could be devastating in an earthquake. Colonists in the Leeward Islands faced some difficult choices.

In 1688, some years after the 1672 earthquake on Montserrat far to the east, colonial observers in Jamaica noted their first tremors on the island. Jamaica was "subject to earthquack," although they had "not bin so frequent as formerly, neither hath it don any considerable dammage." "On Sunday the 19th of February 1688," John Taylor wrote, "there happened at Porta Royall a strong earthquack which continued for about the space of three minutes. The inhabitants were much afright'ned thereby, for it threw down three housses, and shatter'd the tiles off most houses, and did much damage to glass windows, and to glasses, and earthenware in shops."[94]

But the 1688 tremors would only be a foretaste of the terrible earthquake of 1692, which leveled the city of Port Royal—Jamaica's principal seventeenth-century city—sinking a large part of the town leagues underwater and killing approximately four thousand people, nearly half of the population.[95] Just before noon that day,

> the sand in the street rose like the waves of the sea, lifting up all persons that stood upon it, and immediately dropping down into pits; and at the same instant a flood of water rushed in, throwing down all who were in its way; some were seen catching hold of beams and rafters of houses, others were found in the sand that appeared when the water drained away.[96]

By the early 1690s, Port Royal had become the fastest growing city in the British Caribbean. Numerous sources attest to the wealth and prosperity of the town built on the end of a long spit of land that created an enormous safe harbor. Rapid growth, the general presumption of climatic and seismic safety, and great wealth meant that after only a few decades, "most of the buildings [were built] after the English manner and 3 stories high."[97] British Jamaicans built a growing city with tall masonry buildings interspersed with lower frame sheds, shops, and tenements.[98] On that fateful day in 1692, however, these structures, tall and short, came crashing down in the course of minutes. The 1692 earthquake was followed by regular tremors between 1700 and 1707 and occasional earth-quakes in later decades. Early eighteenth-century Jamaica had a century of experience on which to build; from the regular assault of hurricanes, the unleashed devastation of the late-century earthquakes, and the resilience of native, African, and Spanish structures, colonial builders learned to keep the height of their buildings to a minimum. Writing of Jamaica in the late 1730s, Charles Leslie noted that even "the Gentleman's Houses are generally built low, of one story, consisting of five or six handsome apart-ments. . . . In the Towns there are several Houses which are two-stories; but that way of Building is disapproved of, because they seldom are known to stand the shock of an Earthquake, or the Fury of a Storm."[99] Jamaicans had learned their lesson.

EIGHTEENTH-CENTURY PIAZZAS

When the earthquake of 1692 sank much of Port Royal into the ocean, refugees from the earthquake fled to the mainland and began occupying the broad, flat plain on the mainland side of the harbor. Soon thereafter the site was designated as the new city of Kingston, intended to replace the much reduced city of Port Royal as the island's major mercantile center; lots in the new city were avail-able for purchase by 1693.[100] In the opening years of the eighteenth century the city's new grid plan markedly differentiated the city from its predecessor.[101] The best representation of the city appears in a map produced in about 1745 (fig. 3.11). Unlike the winding streets of Port Royal or the capital city of Spanish Town, the streets of Kingston were broad and straight: King Street, the major north–south street, and Queen Street, the major

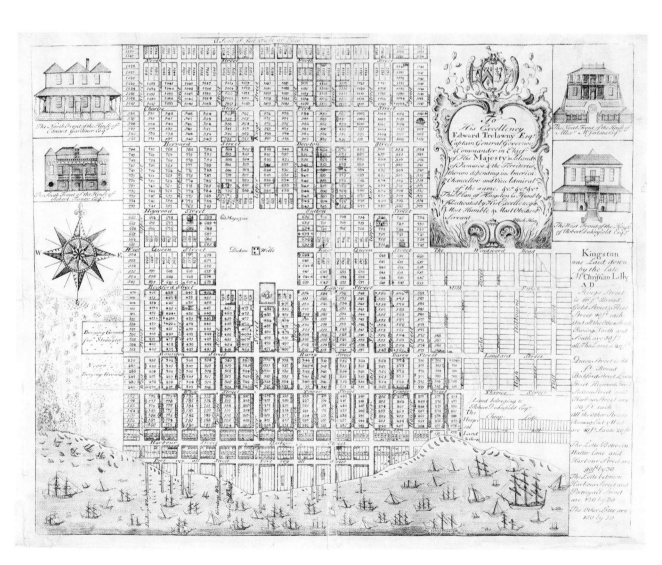

FIG. 3.11 Michael Hay, plan of Kingston, ca. 1745. Ink on paper, 13 × 16 in. (33 × 41 cm). Library of Congress.

FIG. 3.12 Dominic Serres the Elder, *The Piazza at Havana*, 1762. Oil on canvas, 41 × 56 × 3½ in. (104.5 × 142.5 × 8.7 cm). National Maritime Museum, Greenwich, London.

east–west street, were each sixty-six feet broad while other streets were fifty, thirty, or twenty, depending on their prominence. These urban passages were a conscious departure from the streets of Port Royal, a city crammed onto the tight end of a narrow peninsula. Relocating the city allowed Jamaican merchants to reimagine their urban fabric. One of the critical features that appears in the city from its reimagination as Jamaica's great postearthquake city was urban piazzas, covered walks fronting houses. Robert Lodge's probate inventory, for example, already reported in 1714 that his new Kingston house was fronted by a "peaza" and his was not unique.[102] By the 1740s, visitors to the city noted that Kingston's streets "are wide and regular. . . . The Buildings are but two Stories, cover'd with Shingles, sashed and glazed, with Piazza's before every House."[103] Another observer noted in 1742 that the "Piazzas before every house" allowed someone to "walk from one end to the other without going in the sun but in crossing streets."[104] The installation of piazzas on building facades and the use of the new term "piazza" instead of the

seventeenth-century term "shade" marked these features as something new, something heretofore unknown in the British Caribbean.

With its large central square and straight streets, Kingston fairly closely emulated the ordinances of the Laws of the Indies, a set of urban planning guidelines for new cities in the Spanish Americas. The laws were first published by Philip II in 1573 and were republished in their most widely dispersed form by Charles II as *Recopilación de las Leyes de los Reynos de las Indias* (Compilation of the Laws of the Kingdoms of the Indies) in 1680, just over a decade before the planning of Kingston.[105] The central planning feature of the laws was a large central plaza, not unlike Kingston's large central square. In fact, Kingston's central square seems to reflect Spanish urbanism in the Caribbean, as it had few equivalents in earlier English urban planning. One of the distinguishing features of Spanish Caribbean urban squares and their corresponding thoroughfares was the practice of sheltering sidewalks from the sun. The Spanish laws dictated that "the whole plaza and the four main streets diverging from it shall have arcades, for these are a great convenience for those who resort thither to trade."[106] Such features had been clearly in place in Cuzco, Lima, and Mexico City since the late sixteenth century or by the seventeenth century, when painted views of these cities show arcades lining one or more sides of the plazas.[107] Arcades also became defining features of Havana, Cuba, just to the north of Jamaica, by the early eighteenth century.[108] The 1762 painting of Havana's main piazza by Dominic Serres the Elder clearly illustrates the arcades, piazzas, and galleries that distinguished Spanish cities in the region (fig. 3.12).[109] The new piazzas of Kingston are material evidence of the interconnectedness of the British and Spanish Caribbean; one visitor to Kingston, in fact, noted that with its covered walkways it "reminds me very much of many of the towns I saw in Spain."[110]

Travel to Spanish and Portuguese colonial ports around the region had been common for Port Royal's residents, especially among the large concentration of Jewish merchants living there who had mercantile and family connections to Sephardic merchants in other cities.[111] The Jamaican connection to Spanish Cuba was already in place through Jewish merchants in seventeenth-century Port Royal who traded in Cuba; those connections expanded manifold in the opening decades of the eighteenth century. In 1713 Kingston merchants received the *Asiento,* giving the English South Sea Company the exclusive right to provide slaves to the Spanish Americas, while private merchants dramatically increased their provision of slaves, if illegally. Historians estimate that a full two-thirds of slaves provided to Cuba arrived illegally through Kingston merchants.[112] Put simply, British merchants in the newly rising city of Kingston would have been quite familiar with Havana and its urban architecture; there is no reason to think that this familiarity did not play a role in shaping the newly emerging British port city of Kingston.

Even so, the Spanish Caribbean was not necessarily the singular inspiration for Kingston's piazzas. Covered walkways in English urban settings appeared as early as the late medieval period; examples from the fifteenth century and later include the Rows in Chester, the Butterwalk in Totnes, an unnamed stretch in Ludlow, and the Pentice in Winchester (fig. 3.13). And presumably there were many others that are now lost. In the case of the Pentice in Winchester, material and documentary evidence suggests that some of the overhanging upper stories with sheltered walkways below date to the fourteenth century.[113] An early 1417 Winchester reference to posts supporting an overhang seems to refer to an earlier version of the sheltered walkway now on that site.[114] Significantly, all of the buildings in the Pentice and in these other English examples originally served ground-floor commercial functions. Since the colonnaded and sheltered commercial street—as

FIG. 3.13 The Pentice, Winchester, Hampshire, England.

FIG. 3.14 Pierre Eugène du Simitière, "Vista de la Procession que fue hecha en la Havana . . ." Engraving. Consider the balconies captured to the far right. Private collection.

the forerunner to the Caribbean piazza in the eighteenth century—was not unknown in early modern English towns, the accommodation of such forms in Kingston would not necessarily have been perceived as Spanish.

Kingston's distinctive urban piazzas might have found their origin closer to home. Many wealthier merchants in seventeenth-century Port Royal installed balconies overlooking the street from their second-floor chambers. As reported by one observer immediately after the 1692 earthquake in Port Royal, "only Eight or Ten remained from the Balcony upwards above Water."[115] The writer's use of the feature as a baseline measurement suggests that the majority of houses in Port Royal boasted such balconies. Port Royal's balconies come into clearer focus through the late seventeenth-century building accounts for Robert Sneed's intended townhouses in the city. He was to build "three or four substantial houses, fronting to the harbor, each to have a cookroom and a house of office, with a balcony to each house fronting the sea to the northward, of eight

feet long and three and a half feet in the cheare." Eight feet by three and a half feet was no small balcony. The Sneed houses were also to be provided with "a sufficient penthouse even with the balcony," suggesting that the large balconies were intended to be shaded, creating a breezy and shaded retreat opening into the best upper room of the house.[116] The appearance of balconies on late seventeenth-century houses in Port Royal is striking because they appeared on houses in London only a few decades earlier—the balcony, a new platform for self-display, was not a common feature on London townhouses until the early eighteenth century.[117] As with piazzas, Jamaican merchants in Port Royal likely adopted balconies from the architecture of their Spanish counterparts, who had been installing balconies on their multistory urban houses in the region since the sixteenth century (fig. 3.14).[118] While these balconies were surely intended to provide merchants in the port towns a place from which to survey the comings and goings of ships, they also offered escape from the hot still air of closed townhouse chambers. Balconies became so indicative that sale advertisements distinguished some urban houses as a "balcony house."[119]

The penchant for covered balconies in seventeenth-century Port Royal might have established a precedent for a distinctive form of piazza in early eighteenth-century Kingston. One eighteenth-century observer noted that the fronts of most buildings in Kingston "are shaded with a piazza below, and a covered gallery above."[120] This particular double-story design reveals an integration of forms: piazzas from Havana or ports town in England, and the covered balconies of earlier Port Royal. The building blocks for these eighteenth-century piazzas were already in place before Kingston was laid out. Having learned the cooling benefits of large balconies cantilevered off the fronts of houses in seventeenth-century Port Royal, housebuilders in early eighteenth-century Kingston took advantage of the intentionally straight and wide streets of that new city to expand the size of those balconies by supporting them on posts, creating a covered space immediately off the second-floor chambers of their houses as well as a shaded walkway underneath. Robert Dunkinfield's house, as represented on the 1745 Hay map of Kingston, is wrapped in a piazza that includes a knee wall limiting passage from the street, claiming the space as private, not part of the public right of way (fig. 3.15). Edward Gardiner's piazza was open (fig. 3.16).

The feature that clearly distinguished the sheltered walks lining the streets of newly rising Kingston from medieval covered walks in England, urban arcades in seventeenth-century Spanish cities, or the covered balconies of seventeenth-century Port Royal was the use of the term "piazza." The term obviously derives from the Italian word for the large open squares found in Italian cities. But while "piazza" in English was sometimes parallel to its Italian usage, its far more common meaning at the time referred to the arcaded galleries that lined the edges of urban squares. The first and most famous application of this form in London was Inigo Jones's Covent Garden, designed in the early 1630s. Covent Garden was a large open square lined with townhouses fronted with arcades; soon after their construction, these arcaded walks were almost immediately referred to by contemporaries as "piazzas" (fig. 3.17). In 1642, for example, one London advertiser invited subscribers to "meet in the Piazzas of Covent Garden."[121] English travelers took this understanding of the term with them when they went abroad; one Gilbert Burnet, in describing some townhouses in Switzerland in 1686, noted "that one walks all the Town over covered under Piazza's."[122]

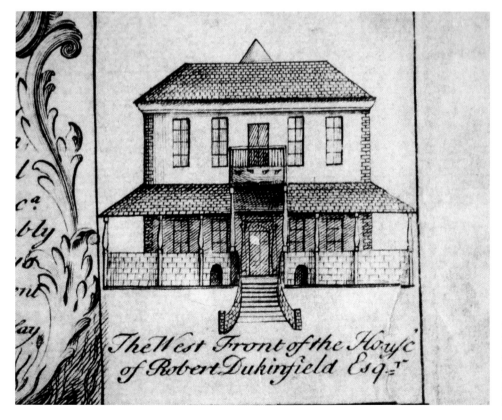

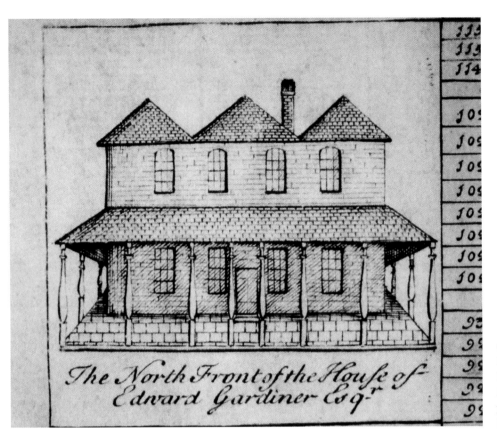

FIG. 3.16 "The North Front of the House of Edward Gardiner, Esqr." Detail from Michael Hay. Map of Kingston, ca. 1745. Ink on paper, 13 × 16 in. (33 × 41 cm). Library of Congress.

Piazzas below and galleries above were also a distinguishing feature of the houses lining the primary commercial streets of Falmouth, laid out on the north coast in the closing decades of the eighteenth century. The town's earliest datable architecture includes the Moulton Barrett House, erected in 1795 (fig. 3.18). Like so much of the architecture of that period, the building has a masonry lower floor with a frame upper story projecting out over the street and supported by a range of columns. But an early nineteenth-century painting of another of these houses in Jamaica suggests that there was certainly some variation within the type (fig. 3.19). Down the street to the left in the image stands a two-story masonry house with a frame gallery and piazza, painted white and green, appended to the front. In this instance and in the right foreground, the gallery is enclosed all around with louvers. Other examples down the street show open double piazzas, while right next door a one-story frame shop has a piazza over the sidewalk as well. The centerpiece of the painting is the large shop and house of the harbormaster. With a masonry arcade running along one side and a wooden piazza along the other, the building is a striking example of the type. Over Market Street, the building projects a typical gallery enclosed by jalousies, but along the Duke

Street side the jalousies give way to an open piazza, here shaded by cloth sheets stretched between posts. This image suggests the continuing practice of sheltering sidewalks with piazzas executed in a variety of strategies. After their first appearance along the streets of Kingston, piazzas spread to other towns on the island quite quickly; they took on a number of different forms, from covered pedestrian space to an entirely privatized extension of interior living space.

Soon after piazzas appeared along Kingston's streets, colonials in Jamaica also transfered the form to houses in the rural context. Through the opening decades of the eighteenth century, Jamaican probate inventories reveal plantation houses not with "shades" as per their seventeenth-century counterparts in the Leeward Islands but with "shade rooms." The probate records make quite clear that these were enclosed and securable rooms—not open or partially outdoor spaces—but with easy capacity for ventilation. Thomas Belchin's "Shead room" included the best bed in the house, more valuable even than the bed in the "Great Room," while George Walden's 1727 inventory included a number of valuable items, including the best bed in the house, in his "shade room next the sea."[123] And while shade rooms are almost ubiquitous on rural

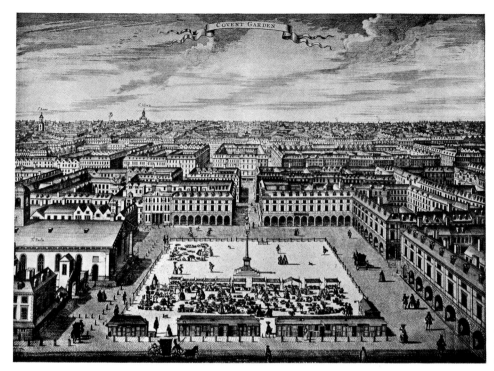

FIG. 3.17 Sutton Nichols, "Covent Garden," ca. 1720. Library of Congress.

FIG. 3.18 Moulton Barrett House, Falmouth, Jamaica, ca. 1795. The half walls enclosing the piazza are a later alteration.

FIG. 3.19 Artist unknown, *View of Falmouth*, ca. 1800. Oil on Canvas, 1.28 × 1.87 in. (3.25 × 4.75 cm). Aaron and Majorie Matalon Collection. National Gallery of Jamaica.

houses from the first half of the eighteenth century, spaces identified in inventories as "piazza" are very rare through the same decades, further reinforcing the development of the form and its name in Kingston before its translation to plantation houses.

The earliest examples of piazzas on rural houses in Jamaica are not on English buildings but on the houses left behind by Jamaica's Spanish settlers. In his *History of Jamaica*, Edward Long asserts that in early Spanish Town "the Spanish houses had no piazzas originally," claiming the urban piazza as an entirely English form.[124] But in this claim he oversimplifies. Sixteenth-century Spanish townhouses in the region commonly included a recessed loggia on the front of the house, creating a sheltered space just off the street.[125] If not on the front as a piazza, there is abundant evidence that sixteenth- and seventeenth-century Spanish builders appended galleries to the sides or patios (inner courtyards) of their houses.[126] These early galleries tended to be very narrow in width and clearly intended to facilitate the circulation

of people and air; they were not outdoor living spaces. In his seventeenth-century description of Jamaica, Hans Sloane described a typical rural Spanish house as "one story high having a porch, a parlor, and at each end a bed room with small rooms behind for closets." While in this instance the porch might refer to an enclosed entry chamber, called a *zaguan*, such transitional spaces were more typical on larger urban houses and not on smaller rural farmhouses. Sloane's use of the term "porch" here seems actually to refer to the more modern sense, a generic covered approach to the entrance of a building. Sloane's Spanish house with a porch might correlate more closely with sixteenth-century houses excavated by archaeologist Kathleen Deagan at Puerto Real, which she describes as having only a few chambers arranged linearly with a porch or gallery sheltering the main entrance.[127] Sloane also noted in one instance that an English planter was living outside of Kingston in an abandoned Spanish house. Rather than just reporting a porch, Sloane described the house as "all galleried around."[128] The Spanish house was probably not unlike those captured in Frans Post's mid-seventeenth-century paintings of Portuguese Brazil (fig. 3.20).[129]

Seventeenth-century English planters appear never to have built rural houses with full piazzas or galleries, but the form was increasingly embraced by English planters by the 1730s and was common by midcentury. Charles Leslie, who described piazzas on urban residences in Jamaica, noted in 1740 that planters' houses "have generally a Piazza, to which you ascend by several Steps, and serves for a Screen against the Heat, and likewise is a way of enjoying the Benefit of any Coolness in the Air."[130] Leslie is unclear as to whether that piazza only fronts the house or wraps the house on multiple sides. Slightly later, the form was common elsewhere in the British Caribbean; writing from Antigua, Janet Shaw noted that "every house has a handsome piazza."[131] Interestingly, this general chronology appears also to characterize the adoption of the form—called galleries, rather than piazzas—among the French in the region. Scholars have demonstrated that Fort Louis on the mainland Gulf Coast was populated with houses distinguished with galleries along a single elevation as early as 1702.[132] Galleries are common in New Orleans by the 1720s and fully peripteral galleries appear on rural houses by the middle of the century.[133] British planters appear to have been slower to adopt the form than their French and certainly their Spanish counterparts.

The documentary and visual evidence makes clear that the piazza fronting a house or fully encasing a house on all sides was a feature commonly found first on urban houses at the beginning of the eighteenth-century and on rural plantation houses by midcentury. A review of Jamaican probate inventories reinforces this chronology; piazzas are common on Kingston houses from the 1710s but they appear commonly on rural houses only by the 1750s. Whereas some scholars have suggested that the piazza simply appears fully formed in the middle of the eighteenth century, it seems far more plausible that piazzas evolved from seventeenth century shades, common features on urban buildings but not unknown on rural examples.[134] Rear shades and large front balconies were common in seventeenth-century Port Royal; Kingston's broad open streets allowed the translation of those forms into the more fashionable urban piazzas, sheltered spaces adapted from London and recreated in Jamaica's newly established port city. The major formal difference was that while seventeenth-century shades were generally dirt-floored, early eighteenth-century piazzas were floored, elevated off the ground. The appearance of shades on seventeenth-century rural houses and a full gallery on at least one Spanish house in Jamaica encouraged the speedy

FIG. 3.20 Frans Post, *Brazilian Landscape with a Worker's House*, ca. 1665. Oil on wood, 18½ × 24¾ in. (46.99 × 62.86 cm). Los Angeles County Museum of Art.

expansion of the English piazza from urban to rural houses. The increasing popularity of these forms over the opening decades of the century meant they were commonplace by the 1740s. And as seventeenth-century builders adapted shades that evolved into eighteenth-century piazzas, so too was there a transformation between the centuries in strategies for architectural response to hurricanes and earthquakes.

EIGHTEENTH-CENTURY ANTISEISMIC ARCHITECTURE

English housebuilders in the seventeenth-century Caribbean took a fairly simple approach to designing hurricane-resistant architecture, building houses with low profiles. Their eighteenth-century counterparts brought to the challenge a greater interest and concern for the strength of various materials and the structural capacity of building systems. The eighteenth century is generally recognized for the launch of modern scientific inquiry, especially as it relates to structures and architectural engineering.[135] While there is not nearly enough evidence to provide a clear picture, there is enough to suggest that eighteenth-century Jamaican builders were participant in a transatlantic inquiry into structural design that would actively resist the devastations of hurricanes and earthquakes. Bernard Forest de Belidor's 1729 *Science des ingénieurs* was the first comprehensive, widely published resource to examine architecture as engineering, in the scientific analysis of the structural capacity of materials and the best means to calculate the strength of various building systems, especially of wood framing systems.[136] Its republication through the eighteenth century is evidence of its importance, and while there is not yet evidence that Jamaican housebuilders owned or were reading copies of Belidor, they clearly were studying the forces unleashed on structures during earthquakes and hurricanes and experimenting with building materials. In his *History of Jamaica*, Jamaican Edward Long offered his late eighteenth-century readers a number of recommendations on building for disaster. The shocks of earthquakes, he noted, were horizontal, not vertical as was often supposed. Buildings "erected on a rocky foundation, are subject to be less injured by [earthquakes] than those built on other soils; and more particularly those which stand on a loose sandy texture, contiguous to the sea." Possibly in pursuit of building stronger foundations, the Jamaican Assembly republished in Jamaica in 1775 a French treatise on cement, entitled *A Practical Essay, on*

Cement and Artificial Stone.[137] The assembly was surely interested in this volume as it promised "durable construction." No other colonial eighteenth-century assembly would undertake a similar task. Furthermore, numerous Britons in Jamaica undertook to study the "curious" building systems that had been left behind by the Spanish. As early as the late seventeenth century, Sir Hans Sloane connected the earthfast framing systems of the Spanish to earthquake-resiliency:

> The Spaniards who inhabited this island and those neighboring built their houses very low and they consisted only of ground rooms, their walls being made of posts which were as much buried under ground as they stood above, on purpose to avoid the danger which attended other manner of building from earthquakes.[138]

But the most careful observations of Spanish houses came from Edward Long. Writing in 1774, he noted that at least fifty Spanish houses remained in Jamaica and that "their duration for so long a time in defiance of earthquakes and hurricanes, some of which, since the English settled here, have been so violent as to demolish several more modern buildings, is demonstrative proof of Spanish sagacity." He continued by exploring in detail their design and materials, illustrating the discussion with an image (fig. 3.21). Spanish houses in Jamaica boasted frames constructed of dense tropical hardwoods "well-seasoned and hardened in smoak." The wooden posts, usually six or eight inches thick, were sunk into the ground at least three feet. These posts were then infilled with brick and the walls plastered. The buildings had rafters that were only eighteen inches apart covered in canes and lashed with the bark of mangrove trees. This substrate was covered in mortar and sheathed in pantiles, which made the roofs much stronger than the shingles of their English counterparts. As a result, the houses were extremely durable and because of their heavy pantile roofs they were far cooler in the day and warmer at night than the English houses, although heavy roofs were a detriment in seismic conditions. The English, Long concluded, "consult neither their personal security, their convenience, their health, nor the saving of a most unnecessary expense" by "neglecting these useful models."[139] He certainly understood that the survival of Spanish buildings meant that they should be a model for new architecture on the island.

The response to hurricanes by Jamaica's builders in the eighteenth century reached well beyond the simple

View of a Spanish Building.

Published as the Act directs 1.st June 1774.

R. B. Godfrey sculp.

FIG. 3.21 Edward Long, "View of a Spanish Building," *The History of Jamaica, or, General survey of the antient and modern state of that island: with reflections on its situation, settlements, inhabitants, climate, products, commerce, laws, and government* (London: Printed for T. Lowndes, 1774), vol. 1. Harvard Libraries.

◆ ◆ ◆

admonition to build low that had characterized building through the seventeenth century. As suggested by the Tharp townhouse in Falmouth, architecture of eighteenth-century Jamaica generally betrays a handful of carefully considered design options: broad masonry foundations, mixed building materials, and low roof heights. As suggested by the Jamaican Assembly's initiative to republish a French treatise on cement and the careful analysis of the structural systems of surviving Spanish architecture, these choices were part of a carefully studied strategy to navigate the devastating effects of hurricanes and earthquakes. The brick-filled timber-framing of Tharp's house on the coastline of Falmouth harbor is among the earliest known examples of this building strategy in the English architecture of the island. Commonly called "Spanish wall" by modern Jamaicans, it appeared in British building practices in the late eighteenth century and persisted as a common building strategy into the twentieth century. Aware of the persistent threat of hurricanes and earthquakes, Anglo-Jamaican builders actively implemented this form of disaster-responsive architectural design.

The most famous natural disaster of the eighteenth-century Atlantic was certainly the 1755 Lisbon earthquake. Beginning at 9:40 on the morning of November 1, the city was struck first with three tremors, then flooded by a massive tidal wave, struck by a fourth tremor, and then subjected to a fire that burned for six days. Tens of thousands died. In the months that followed, newspapers around the Atlantic carried reports and engraved images of the devastation. Soon thereafter Sebastião José de Carvalho, the Marquis of Pombal, declared martial law and launched a massive rebuilding of the city on a grand and expansive new plan.[140] He pursued an alliance with Great Britain and requested supplies and troops to defend the weakened city against France and Spain, long enemies of Portugal. By 1762, George III was actively supplying troops and English merchants regularly shipped building materials from Bristol, Liverpool, and London for the reconstruction of the Portuguese capital.[141] Pombal imposed a new modern city plan over the ruins of the ancient city and assigned the most recent manual in the

FIG. 3.22 *Gaiola* system exposed in a café in Lisbon.

science of engineering—Belidor's *Science des ingénieurs*—as required reading in the Lisbon military academy. One of the distinctive features of Pombaline architecture was its intentional earthquake-responsive structural design.

The rebuilding of Lisbon was not the first major effort at building seismic-responsive architecture. Historians have identified intentionally earthquake-responsive architecture in East Asia as early as the twelfth century.[142] The earliest documented historical earthquake-resistant building material in the colonial Americas was *quincha*, cane-reinforced adobe, in seventeenth-century Lima. This system of reinforced adobe was required of all new construction after the 1746 earthquake in Lima.[143] Yet the most important scientific advances in seismic-responsive architecture would take place in the aftermath of the Lisbon earthquake. Architects and engineers there undertook to build in a manner that would best survive the assault of the next earthquake—the result was the famous *gaiola*, or caged building of late eighteenth-century Lisbon. In this system, a structural wood-frame cage embedded along the inner face of the masonry shell of the building held the masonry in place during an earthquake, while the masonry walls protected the wood from the inevitable fires (fig. 3.22).[144] Soon after the 1783 earthquake in Calabria, Italy, architect Vincenzo Ferraresi worked to intermix building materials to greatest antiseismic effect.[145] In this system, lateral wooden braces framed by vertical posts and horizontal sills and plates were embedded in the masonry to give the exterior walls greater lateral resistance, in a manner close to mixed-material construction in the contemporary Caribbean. And like the earlier Spanish houses in Jamaica, the Italian *casa baraccata* was earthfast. The system was required by law for all new construction in the Calabrian capital. Investigation of surviving examples demonstrates that the majority of buildings included an integrated frame and masonry system, but one that was far less elaborated than evidenced in Ferraresi's design.[146]

A similar system of integrated wood frame and masonry was recommended by the French architect D'Albaret in his 1776 book on construction in the West Indies. Plate III of his book illustrates the technique (fig. 3.23). Published after the Lisbon earthquake but before the published designs of the *casa baraccata*, D'Albaret recommends erecting "sturdy posts rising from the base in the corners" and that these should rest on "sturdy pieces of wood" that rest on the masonry foundations. He recommends that the walls be thirteen inches thick with four-inch walls of bricks on each face and an open space between these brick walls "to lighten the load."[147] The masonry foundation and frame upper story gave the building some of the resistance desirable in hurricane conditions without the fear of brick walls collapsing onto those taking refuge inside. The wood frame superstructure provided the building some flexibility in the face of hurricane winds and, even more importantly, during earthquakes. There is no clear evidence whether D'Albaret was informed by antiseismic architectural technologies, but the appearance of such a detailed structural system does beg the question. Certainly D'Albaret would have known and read Belidor's *Science des ingénieurs.* It was in the 1770s that Edward Long observed the earthquake-resilience of the mixed-material Spanish buildings remaining in the island. And it is not insignificant that similar mixed-material and possibly antiseismic wall systems appear in Jamaican architecture by the end of the century. After the various earthquakes that rocked certain regions of the Caribbean in the late seventeenth and early eighteenth centuries, Jamaicans likely knew that integrated frame and masonry wall systems were central to antiseismic structural experimentation in Europe.

But in the Caribbean, antiseismic walls had to be integrated with hurricane-resistant foundations and roofs. Writing in the middle decades of the eighteenth century about houses in the Leeward Islands, a Moravian missionary noted that broad masonry basements "not only provide for the enjoyment of shade in the open air [by providing space for a piazza] but also . . . give the buildings a bigger foundation and thereby make them more resistant to the winds of storms."[148] Edward Long noted "the expediency of building low houses," but continued by making sure his readers knew that these should be "raised on a foundation not exceeding three or four feet."[149] Earlier, writing from Jamaica in 1731, the military engineer Christian Lilly described a house he was designing for a

client in Spanish Town. Lilly mentioned specifically that the builders should follow his instructions that the foundations be "very strongly and firmly laid, as also the several walls carried up to some distance above ground."[150] Thomas Thistlewood recorded in his journal that three of his enslaved masons spent their day underpinning "an end and a side of my house."[151] One notable advantage of this choice was that substantial masonry foundations could serve as a hurricane shelter. As early as the 1730s, the great house at Worthy Park included in the basement a "Hurrycane House."[152] Writing later in the century, William Beckford in his *Descriptive Account of Jamaica* mentioned his experience of a hurricane. Late in the storm, he noted, "we were driven, in the evening of the hurricane, from the apartments above stairs to take shelter in those below."[153] Masonry basements, some even with loopholes, provided safe refuge in times of attack, as suggested by the previous chapter, and safe haven from storms.

If they provided occasional shelter, the primary responsibility of masonry foundations was to reinforce the building against collapse. In 1725, the vestry of St. Peter's Anglican Church in Port Royal, Jamaica, began the *fourth* church erected by that parish in the course of only fifty years. The three earlier structures on the site had all suffered under a battery of natural disasters, including the devastating 1692 earthquake, a fire in 1702, and hurricanes in 1712 and 1722. In an effort to erect a church that would better withstand natural disasters, the parish erected a

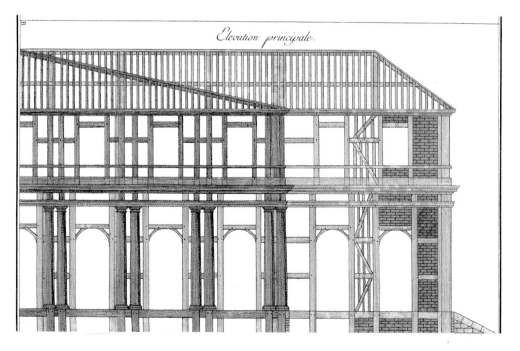

Elevation principale.

FIG. 3.23 Detail of framed and nogged construction from M. D'Albaret, *Différents projets relatifs au climat et à la manière la plus convenable de bâtir dans les pays chauds, et plus particulièrement dans les Indes occidentales* (Paris, 1776), Plate III. University of Maryland Library.

FIG. 3.24 Hyde Hall, Trelawny Parish, Jamaica, ca. 1820. The ground floor is ashlar masonry while the primary living floor above is nogged.

compact church on the plan of an extended Greek cross measuring eighty feet east to west and seventy-two feet north to south. The walls of the 1725 cruciform building are over four and a half feet thick at ground level—far more than necessary to support the twelve-foot walls and the roof of a fairly small cruciform church that spans only twenty-six feet. The thickness of the walls approximates that used by builders of powder magazines rather than churches.

While many buildings took the height of foundations up a full story, it became common practice in Jamaica to rest a timber-frame house on a strong and substantial masonry foundation. Hyde Hall (ca. 1820) is typical of plantation construction (fig. 3.24). Like the Tharp House, Hyde Hall's upper story was plastered and intended to emulate stone, but its nogged upper story rested on a very substantial masonry ground floor (fig. 3.25). The widespread embrace of masonry foundations and timber-framing above took place in the 1780s. By 1808, John Stewart would write that "the houses in this island are of various forms and construction." He follows this statement with a summary of the two basic variations: "Some have

stone foundations, others are built entirely of wood."[154] A full masonry house was not listed among his options.

Housebuilders knew that houses erected in flood-prone sites needed even stronger foundations. John Taylor noted that rising waters "much damnified the eddiffices and buildings towards the seaside by washing and spoyling their foundations."[155] Rising waters from the 1722 hurricane undermined house foundations, giving "continual and just Apprehensions of the Houses falling, as in effect half of them did, and buried their inhabitants."[156] The *Jamaica Weekly Courant* reported that in another hurricane, the houses near the sea were all "washed away," destroyed not by wind but water.[157] In 1763, Lieutenant Colonel James Robertson commented on the practice in British Florida of raising houses on pillars to escape the frequent flooding brought on by violent gales.[158] Long argued that rivers were also dangerous during an earthquake and "buildings situated on their banks are more severely affected than others which are remote from them."[159] For Knight, Long, and other observers, one of the major lessons to be learned from the tidal surges of hurricanes and from the dramatic failure of houses in Port Royal during the 1692 earthquake was the necessity of very strong foundations, especially when one was building a house along the waterfront or in other sandy or low-lying conditions.

Over the same decades in the 1700s, Jamaicans reconsidered their roof framing systems. The roof of the 1760s Hibbert House in Kingston is nothing short of incredible. A vast M roof shelters the main block of the house, which extends from the rear porch to more than half of the footprint to the rear of the house (fig. 3.26). This substantial principal rafter framing system has four major trusses and collar beams that help to carry the raised central plate that runs down the spine of the system. The massive scale, the finished stairs that reach the attic, and evidence for shelves and partitions all suggest that this rear portion of the roof system was intended as usable space from its inception. The front of the house is then sheltered by a single roof of substantial king post trusses running parallel to the M roof behind. This system accommodates the coved ceiling in the main entertaining room of the front of the upper floor. Two lightly framed common rafter

FIG. 3.25 Interior of Hyde Hall with exposed nogging, ca. 1820.

gable roofs run perpendicular to the main stretch of roof at each end, terminating in the smaller end gables of the front elevation. These various roofs run in different directions, creating a well between the systems that was a certain problem in seasons of heavy rain. Internal lead gutters running from that well through the roof to the outside offered a simple and probably unsatisfactory solution to rainwater management (fig. 3.27). The final solution is a hodgepodge of different systems seemingly cobbled together to cover the building's huge footprint.

The roofing system sheltering Hyde Hall is something quite different. A simple, common rafter hipped roof stands over each of the building's major sections (fig. 3.28). Three of these roofs are visible from the front elevation: the ends of the two roofs spanning the flanking rooms stand at each end framing the side elevation of the hipped roof over the front flank of core rooms. The subdivision of a large roof area was understood to be a valuable feature by the closing decades of the eighteenth century. In 1788, the *Savanna-la-Mar Gazette* carried an advertisement for a house for sale, "40 by 45 feet square . . . having three distinct roofs built of the best materials."[160] The solution presented at Hyde Hall was simpler, cleaner, and lighter than that realized on the Hibbert House: adjacent low, hipped common rafter systems with rain gutters between. Evidence from a variety of sources suggests that over the first half of the eighteenth century, elite houses grew dramatically in scale. By mid-century, roofing systems were heavy and complicated, struggling to shelter ever larger houses. As suggested by the differences between these two roofing systems, however, Jamaican carpenters made significant adjustments over the second half of the eighteenth century, resulting in much simpler, less complicated, and lower profile roofs.

One reason for this shift might very well have been economic. Tropical hardwoods that were often used in wall framing were rot- and insect-resistant but were also heavy and hard to work. Raised well above the wet conditions of moist foundations, roofing systems were the most likely to be constructed of lighter imported lumber. The 1706 St. Kitts claims make clear that there was a vigorous practice of importing building timber by the end of the seventeenth century.[161] Valentine Percivale and Philip Vorchild both submitted claims for Leeward Island houses "framed of New England Timber." John Park lost a house of "Carolina Cedar, framed at Carolina" suggesting in this case the importation of not just raw building materials but a whole house frame. This was a practice of course

FIG. 3.26 M roof of
Hibbert House, Kingston,
Jamaica.

not just in the Leeward Islands but across the Caribbean.
In March 1665 the Jamaican Assembly proposed an act
prohibiting the importation of "New-England boards,"
presumably to give a competitive advantage to those
working to develop local sources of lumber in the newly
settled colony.[162] Imported woods used for house framing
appeared most frequently in roofing; the use of smaller

lengths of regularly sized lumber would have dropped
that cost significantly. The result would be a rise in simpler, smaller, common rafter roofs.

The primary reason, however, for the emergence of
timber-framing on masonry houses—and houses with
smaller roofing systems—was increased attention to
hurricane-responsive design. Small, low, hipped roofs are

FIG. 3.27 Lead gutters in
roof system of Hibbert
House, Kingston, Jamaica.

FIG. 3.28 Common rafter system in Hyde Hall, Trelawny Parish, Jamaica, ca. 1820.

more aerodynamic, demonstrating greater resilience in hurricane-force winds. (Hipped roofs also offer greater bracing during the racking of an earthquake.) In a gable roof, when the wind is parallel to the ridge, the roof framing can topple like dominoes. In a hipped roof, the sloping ends serve to brace the interior structure.[163] Builders also worked hard to create greater rigidity at the corners of the

roofing system by installing iron straps as corner braces (fig. 3.29). Jamaican patrons might also have recognized that replacement of a section of smaller, segmented roofs was easier and cheaper than wholesale replacement of a large and expensive roof. Jamaicans preferred to build piazzas with independent, lightly framed roofing systems, creating roof profiles that often revealed a double pitch, as is nicely illustrated in George Robertson's painting of a small frame house (fig. 3.30). Such independent systems meant that the piazza roof was sacrificial and in a hurricane might be ripped from the building without compromising the roof over the main structure. This strategy worked for Thomas Thistlewood, who was relieved that a 1786 hurricane "tore off the piazza roof and some shingles from the body of the house," but left the main roof intact.[164] Such separation of roofing systems became the norm on the island by the end of the eighteenth century.

When Jamaican builders began their examination of hurricane- and earthquake-resistant architecture in the 1770s, they were soon given many reasons to continue that pursuit. The late decades of the eighteenth century were a crucible for housebuilders in Jamaica. The 1780 hurricane

FIG. 3.29 Iron strap securing the corner of the house frame at 32 Duke Street, Falmouth, Jamaica.

FIG. 3.30 George Robertson, *Two Gentlemen Surveying Their Estate in Jamaica,* early 1770s. Image courtesy Sotheby's.

was widely recognized as the island's most devastating storm of that century.[165] As his house was slowly blown apart by the storm, Thomas Thistlewood and many of his enslaved Africans stood against the single standing wall of his house pelted by the rain "which came like small shot." After the storm he surveyed the plantation:

> The external face of the earth, so much altered, scarce know where I am. Not a blade of grass, nor leaf left, or tree, shrub or bush. The face of the earth looks as it does at home in winter, after a week's Black Frost. The morass & beds of logwood, &c. appear as if fire had passed through them & those trees that are left standing, have all their limbs broke off.[166]

But it was followed soon thereafter by many more. In the 1780s alone, the island was struck by nine hurricanes. Four more followed in the 1790s. Such an intense and concentrated buffeting from hurricanes happened nowhere else in the early British Caribbean.[167] The next greatest concentration of hurricanes had been the group of seven

to strike the Leeward Islands in the 1660s, when houses were still mostly one or two rooms with few demands beyond the simplest roofing systems. Soon after the devastating Jamaican hurricane of 1780, Thomas Thistlewood reported that "Mr. James Robertson declares he is afraid to fall asleep, as such dreadful hurricanes and confusion present themselves to him, as far exceed the real one. Just so with myself and several others, the nerves so affected."[168] Hurricanes had a psychological effect on those who survived them but memories could be short. When hurricanes struck with greater frequency, anxieties persisted, sustaining a building culture that made climate responsiveness a higher priority. Late eighteenth-century Jamaican housebuilders adopted alternative strategies in order to build houses that might weather more successfully the assaults of nature. Each strategy emerged in different moments across the century; all were in place by the last decades of the century, all in time for John Tharp's building program for a new house on his property along the wharf in Falmouth.

4   Plantations and Power

A twenty-minute drive south from Falmouth leads along a backcountry road to Good Hope, John Tharp's plantation seat.[1] Passing the steep drive up to the great house, the road leads between a remarkable stone warehouse and a grandly ornamented if diminutive lodge down toward the rushing waters of the Martha Brae River. Just before the river on a flat parcel to the right stands a substantial cut-stone building that now serves as an orange-packing plant. A tall central doorway surmounted by a graceful segmental arch flanked on either side by similarly scaled windows clearly defines this as a building of significance. This was Good Hope's boiling house, where scores of enslaved Africans labored day and night in near furnace-like conditions to purify cane juice, separating molasses and other residue from the thick cane syrup that would cure into crystalized sugar (fig. 4.1). Contemporaries considered full-time labor in the boiling house the unhealthiest of all roles among the enslaved on a sugar plantation.[2] It was the heart of the plantation sugar works, an aggregate of at least one mill, the boiling house, and a curing house. Working sequentially, these buildings housed the interdependent stages essential to the refining process. These were spaces of forced labor where scores of toiling Africans fed cane through the mill, stirred copper cauldrons of boiling syrup, and hauled hogsheads. Accounts from Good Hope give us some of these individuals' names; somewhere near the curing house, the cooper Oxford, for example, a seventy-nine-year-old African-born Cormantee, continued to make barrels for the export of sugar even in his advanced age.[3] When slaves began cutting cane from a field, the sugar works were set into action running continuously until that harvest was complete.

Good Hope's boiling house was among Jamaica's grandest because it belonged to one of Jamaica's wealthiest planters. In 1766, when John Tharp returned to Jamaica after completing his British education, he purchased Good Hope plantation, just inland from Falmouth, as one of the first steps in what would become a massive plantation empire in Trelawny Parish.[4] Over the coming decades, Tharp purchased eight other plantations in the parish—Covey, Lansuinet, Merrywood, Pantrepant, Potosi, Top Hill, Wales, and Windsor—in addition to properties in St. Ann and Westmoreland parishes. By 1791, Tharp owned almost all the property bordering on the Martha Brae River and was by that point among the largest slave owners on the island with close to three thousand slaves on

FIG. 4.1 Good Hope boiling house, Trelawny Parish, Jamaica. Mid-eighteenth century, expanded ca. 1802.

FIG. 4.2 Original front of Good Hope great house, Trelawny Parish, Jamaica.

his many properties; he was one of only four Jamaicans who owned ten or more sugar plantations.[5] With his wealth and position secured, Tharp began in the 1790s to completely refashion his plantation seat of Good Hope. One of his major projects was the massive expansion of the mid-eighteenth-century house on the property into the substantial—even sprawling—great house that stands on the site today. The original house was a long, narrow masonry building that now stands as the left flank of the enlarged house (figs. 4.2–4.4). In the same campaign, he built a counting house behind his great house, a privy that doubled as a garden folly, and a coach house halfway down the hill (fig. 4.5). All of these buildings were fashioned from white Jamaican limestone laid in tight ashlar coursing with rusticated quoins along the building edges. The final product was a great house site that is nothing short of spectacular.

As implied by the development of his sugar works and boiling house, Tharp's massive rebuilding campaign was not limited to the great house site. In 1794, he hired a military surveyor to complete an exacting and detailed plat of Good Hope; the commission of the plat was likely tied to his plans to return to England that year (fig. 4.6). The plat shows the expanded great house, the counting house, the privy, and the coach house all on an outcropping fairly far removed from the sugar works. The plat also records that Tharp had erected a massive new store or warehouse uphill from the sugar works; the building carries a date stone of 1790. Soon after 1794 he directed the construction of a small lodge opposite the warehouse, likely as a post for bookkeepers to oversee the contents of each wagon as it made its way from the warehouse down to Tharp's wharf in Falmouth. Also shown on the plat is a new overseer's house standing not far removed from the slave village. While he was rebuilding his great house site, Tharp invested an enormous amount of money in the sugar works—the boiling house and the curing house—which appear on the 1794 plat clustered adjacent to the river.

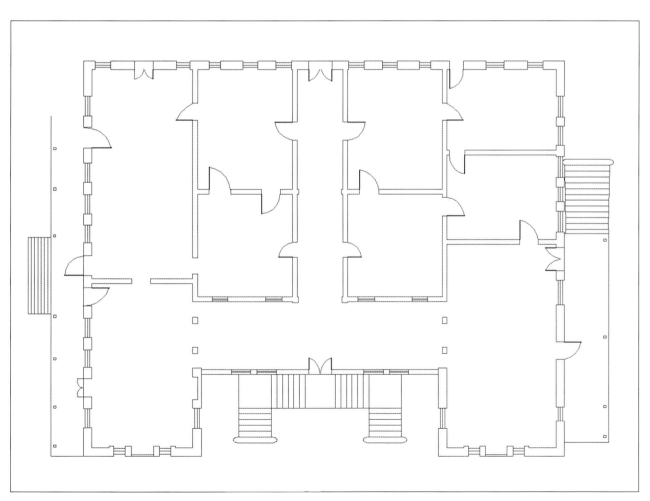

FIG. 4.3 Plan of Good Hope great house. The mid-eighteenth-century building is the long left flank; the rest was added by Tharp sometime in the 1790s.

FIG. 4.4 Good Hope great house, Trelawny Parish, Jamaica, begun mid-eighteenth century, expanded ca. 1790s. The original house is the left flank.

Across the river stands the water mill, from which sugar juice flowed across the Martha Brae to the boiling house in a channel carried by iron brackets on the large masonry posts of the bridge crossing the river (fig. 4.7).[6]

And, finally, a number of long narrow buildings were likely trash houses, used to dry the crushed cane stalks for reuse as fuel. The plat also reveals fields of sugarcane subdivided into parcels separated by paths radiating through the fields from the works, giving enslaved laborers the quickest routes of access from the fields to the mill. As was typical, these fields were divided into plots of ten to twenty acres each with fifteen-foot paths between, wide

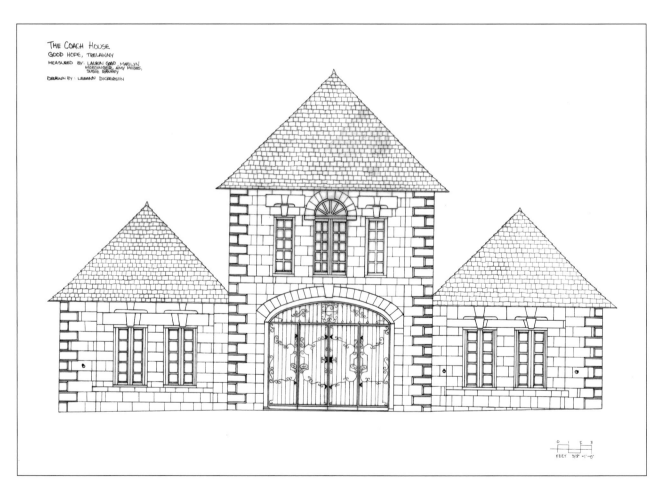

FIG. 4.5 Coach house, Good Hope plantation, Trelawny Parish, Jamaica, ca. 1790s.

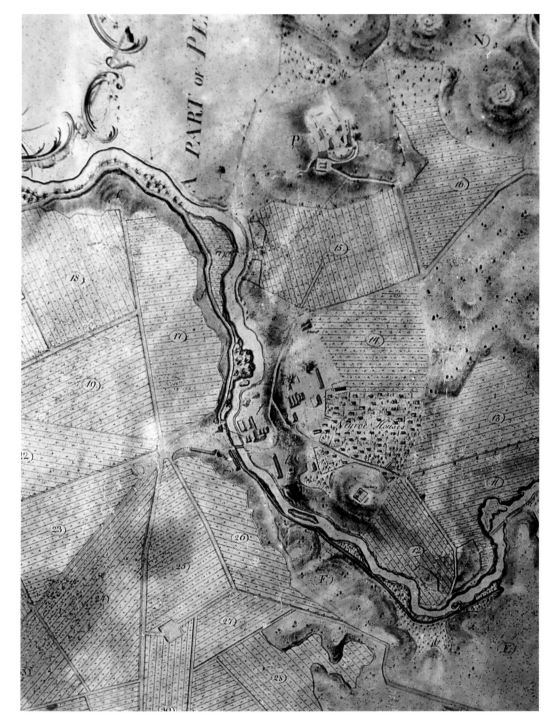

FIG. 4.6 John Henry Schroeder, "A Plan of Good Hope Estate" (detail), 1794. The great house complex is on the outcropping to the top of the image, labeled *P*. The boiling house and curing house are the cluster of buildings immediately adjacent to the river. The mill is on the opposite bank. The overseer's house is the large building at the bend in the road, between the sugar works and the "Negroe Houses." Private collection.

enough to allow slave-driven carts to gain access to any field being harvested.[7] Over the course of a single decade, John Tharp completely rebuilt Good Hope, a project he documented in the plat that he carried with him back to England. And, while elegant, his campaign was not a response to changing architectural fashion. He was improving. The 1794 plat and the many buildings from Tharp's reconstruction of the plantation in the late eighteenth century survive as an extraordinary record of the modern Jamaican sugar plantation, which depended on the labor of almost four hundred enslaved people by the early nineteenth century.[8]

FIG. 4.7 Bridge crossing the Martha Brae River, Good Hope plantation, Trelawny Parish, Jamaica, ca. 1800. The bridge columns each carry an iron bracket that supported a sugar channel that led from the mill on one side of the river (right) to the boiling house on the other (left).

IMPROVEMENT

The huge cast-iron wheel of Good Hope's water mill still turns, although all of the milling machinery it once powered has long disappeared (fig. 4.8). Originally, an axle from the center of the wheel powered the huge cylindrical drums in the mill that were used to crush the sugarcane, extracting the cane juice from the "trash," the tough fibrous crushed cane stalks. This was exhausting and fast-paced work; numerous accounts report that sugar mills were typically outfitted with an ax to sever the limb of the tired laborer whose hand or arm was accidentally drawn in-between the drums.[9] The milling could not be stopped just to save the arm of an African. A small window for the channel that carried the freshly crushed cane juice over the river to the boiling house on the opposite bank is still visible in the wall of the otherwise solid masonry mill house. Visible on the 1794 plat and still extant in the landscape upstream from the mill is a small, masonry-lined

FIG. 4.8 Good Hope water mill, Trelawny Parish, Jamaica.

channel that led to a weir and sluice gate that fed as constant a flow of water as possible. The sluice gate allowed an operator to redirect water in the aftermath of a heavy rain, so as not to overpower the waterwheel and damage the millworks. Careful examination of the Good Hope plat reveals the upstream watercourse used to channel a consistent stream of water to the mill and a viaduct that follows downstream, even passing through a hillock (see fig. 4.6). Standing just above and behind the water mill is the huge octagonal masonry platform of a cattle mill, a necessary backup to the water mill in the case of drought. Tharp's water mill is material evidence of the constant press among Jamaican planters to play their part in the broad phenomenon of "agricultural improvement."

In 1776, one Jamaican planter proclaimed that "prodigious practical improvements [in sugar agriculture] have been made."[10] In much the same vein and just two years earlier, Edward Long argued that among planters "a spirit of experiment has of late appeared, which by quitting the old beaten track, promises to strike out continual improvements."[11] He would continue by arguing that while the construction of "expensive and magnificent works" was evidence of the present transformation, the improvement of the Jamaican plantation would necessarily go far

beyond just enlarged mills and boiling houses. He emphasized the centrality of the works as he argued for the centrality of the plantation in the economy of the empire. If, as the next chapter will argue, Edward Long's view of the Jamaican landscape was framed by the picturesque, he was also a planter and his perspective on the landscape was simultaneously framed by agricultural improvement. One of the many topics addressed by Long in his *History* was an estimate of the investment necessary for and value of a typical plantation. In that discussion he articulated the numbers of acres planted in various crops, the number of enslaved necessary to work those fields, and the capital investments necessary to produce a crop of a certain size and value.[12] In the same years, Charles Taylor, one of Long's contemporaries, began to exact an economic calculus on the plantation by determining ratios of laborers to land and laborers to product.[13] When given the responsibility of extensively rebuilding the sugar works at Golden Grove plantation, Charles Taylor began by rebuilding the mills.[14] For Taylor, improvement was economic. Early examples of this concern for the improvement of sugar works include the plans for a mill, boiling house, and curing house published by Pierre Labat in his 1724 *Nouveaux voyages aux isles de l'Amérique* (figs. 4.9–4.11).

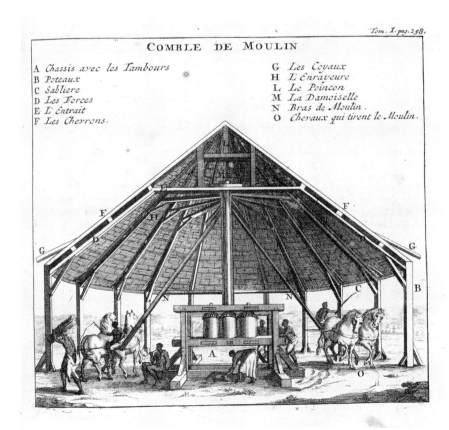

FIG. 4.9 Animal mill. Pierre Labat, *Nouveaux voyages aux isles de l'Amérique*, 1724. University of Virginia Special Collections.

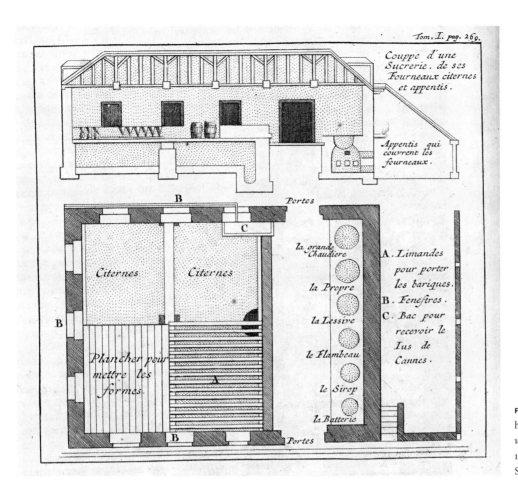

Tom. I. pag. 269.

Couppe d'une
Sucrerie. de ses
Fourneaux citernes
et appentis.

Appentis qui
couvrent les
fourneaux.

Portes

B   C

Citernes   Citernes

la grande
Chaudiere   A. Limandes
pour porter
la Propre   les bariques.
B. Fenestres.
la Lessive   C. Bac pour
recevoir le
le Flambeau   Ius de
Cannes.
Plancher pour
mettre les   le Sirop
formes.
la Batterie

B

B   Portes

FIG. 4.10 Plan of a boiling house. Pierre Labat, *Nouveaux voyages aux isles de l'Amérique*, 1724. University of Virginia Special Collections.

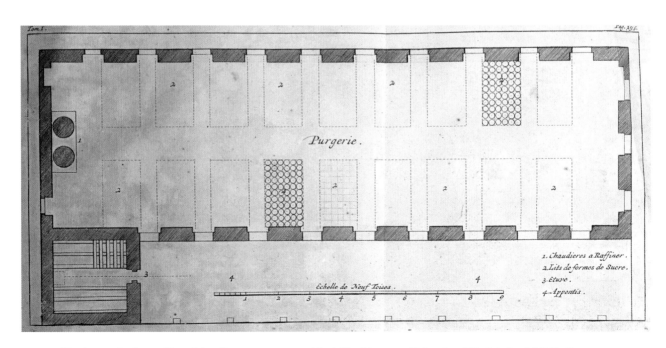

Tom. I.   Pag. 295.

Purgerie.

Echelle de Neuf Toises.
1   2   3   4   5   6   7   8   9

1. Chaudieres a Raffiner.
2. Lits de formes de Sucre.
3. Etuve.
4. Appentis.

FIG. 4.11 Plan for a curing house. Pierre Labat, *Nouveaux voyages aux isles de l'Amérique*, 1724. University of Virginia Special Collections.

Other planters engaged improvement through better management and oversight of plantations.[15] One essential tool for better management was the plantation plat; Barry Higman has identified a radical spike in their numbers from the second half of the eighteenth century.[16] In the final years of the century, Jamaican planters introduced a new species of sugarcane of Tahitian origin that matured more quickly and produced more sugar per acre of cane.[17] Many of these improvements were the result of a drastic spike in published literature on sugar planting, mirroring the efflorescence in the same decades of literature on agricultural practice in Britain.[18] With new buildings, a new sugarcane species, new views of the plantation via cartography, and new systems of calculating profit, late eighteenth-century planters enlisted their buildings and landscapes to demonstrate their participation in the agricultural improvement movement.[19]

This press toward improvement was driven by greed. Although some early planters discussed the possibility of establishing centralized works that might serve multiple plantations—freeing each planter from the capital investment of having to build his own works—that model, which had seen success in Brazil, never took hold in the British Caribbean.[20] From the beginning of British sugar production in Barbados, each planter generally chose to erect his own works. Such a substantial investment, of course, required a very large plantation to support, and as a result, by the middle of the eighteenth century, there was almost no such thing as a small sugar planter in the British Caribbean. The rapid expansion of Jamaican sugar plantations meant that through the first half of the eighteenth century, most planters could take advantage of recently cleared virgin soil, minimizing the need for crop rotation or manuring. By the later eighteenth century, planters needed to know the best methods of improving their reused fields.[21] While British Jamaica always had large plantations—of an average 260 acres in the late seventeenth century—the number of very large plantations expanded rapidly over the first half of the eighteenth century, reaching well over a thousand acres by midcentury.[22]

The choice to erect individual sugar works on each plantation was also driven by the need to deliver newly cut cane to the mill with speed. Sugarcane spoiled quickly; for best quality, cane stalks had to be crushed soon after they were cut, and cane juice had to be boiled within hours of the canes being crushed or it would begin to ferment.[23] But careful timing was required also over the course of the year. Unlike European agriculture, in which the growing season was generally limited to a part of the calendar year, Caribbean sugar took fourteen to eighteen months to ripen and could be planted year round, although it grew best during the two rainy seasons in May and November.[24] The opportunity to decouple the growing cycle from the seasonal calendar allowed planters to plant fields and deliver cane to the sugar works in rotation so that, as described by one commentator, the crop "may come in one field after another," as "it is necessary to have a constant succession of ripe canes."[25] Such rotations allowed planters to make greater use of their sugar works, "otherwise the work will stand still."[26] Into the 1780s, Jamaican field slaves were not cutting canes in January and August; by the 1790s, they were cutting throughout the year.[27] As a result, once a field was brought to harvest, the mills and boiling house would run continuously for days and nights on end until all harvested fields had been processed. Divorced from the rhythm of natural seasons, or even the cycles of labor and rest incorporated within the church calendar, the experience of labor on the sugar plantation was monotonous and relentless, a continuous staged cycle of cutting, crushing, boiling, curing, cutting, crushing, boiling, curing. The sugar plantation realized the very modern drudgery of industrial efficiency. The plantation was a machine.[28]

Rising concerns for efficiency drove both the design of plantations and the imposition of new regimes of labor management. The need to deliver cut cane to the mill as quickly as possible necessitated a centralized model of plantation organization. In 1769, just as he was planning his return to England, Edward Long hired cartographer James Blair to produce a plat of his own plantation, Lucky Valley. In many ways, this plat is typical of late eighteenth-century examples, representing fields, roads, settlements, and wooded sections of the property. But in one way it is strikingly different. It includes a series of concentric circles in quarter-mile intervals radiating from the sugar works near the center of the plantation.[29] Blair's plat reveals the increasing recognition by planters that plantations with centralized works allowed the fastest transport of cut cane to the mill.[30] The same impulse is revealed in the radial paths represented on the plat of Good Hope (see fig. 4.6). In his careful analysis of eighteenth- and early nineteenth-century plats of Jamaican plantations, historian Barry Higman has argued that most plantations were governed by a general organizational principle of concentric zones radiating from the settlement core, which included the great house, the slave village, and the sugar works.[31] While this spatial-conceptual model was never explicitly articulated by Jamaican planters, the plat of Long's Lucky Valley demonstrates that Long and his peers were certainly thinking about the spatial implications of organization, efficiency, and production on a sugar plantation. The concern for expedient delivery of cane to the mill paralleled new regimes of plantation management that included careful recording of work schedules and time discipline. Justin Roberts has found that clock-based modes of plantation management emerged on the Caribbean sugar plantation well before it appeared in other agricultural or industrial contexts.[32]

One of the most important decisions to be made by a sugar planter was to determine the design and power source of his sugar mill. The rapid adoption of the vertical cylinder animal-powered mill in the very earliest Jamaican sugar mills is evidence of its far greater efficiency over mills that employed two horizontal cylinders or even millstones commonly found in sugar mills in early seventeenth-century Barbados.[33] In his 1687 treatise on Jamaica, John Taylor described Jamaican mills as "composed of three large iron rowlers, which turn one against another, the two outermost of which move round against the middlemost, which is fix't" (see fig. 4.9).[34] Before the early eighteenth century the rotation of the cylindrical rollers was generally powered by a team of mules, made available by the large stocks of horses and asses abandoned by the Spanish.[35] The mid-seventeenth-century embrace of the vertical triple-barrel cane mill meant that British sugar planters employed a more sophisticated milling technology than was commonly found in England even a century later.[36] As they established sugar plantations in the closing decades of the seventeenth century, British planters in Jamaica knew that they were enlisting the most recent technology in milling, a system that remained in place well into the next century.

Eighteenth-century planters recognized that the quantity of sugar produced per acre depended in large part on the efficiency of the milling process. One of the first changes took place in the form and materials of the rollers that crushed the cane. By the middle of the eighteenth century, the power source for the mill turned all three rollers, the two outer rollers geared from the middle one.[37] Plans for mills with three moving rollers were published by Bryan Edwards in *A History, Civil and Commercial, of*

the British Colonies in the West Indies, as "An Improved Sugar Mill," but such mills were already in production many years before; the powered rotation of all three rollers allowed slaves to work systematically, passing each cane stalk through the mill twice to extract the maximum juice from each stalk.[38] The other change in Jamaican animal mills was the shift from mules to stronger and more compliant cattle.[39] The major transformation came, however, with the 1794 introduction of the horizontal three-roller mill, one that was both more durable and easier for animals to drive. It also distributed the crushing space across the face of the entire roller, rather than concentrating it in the center. Planters paid close attention to any potential efficiencies gained by well-maintained or improved mills; 93 percent of all Jamaican patents related to sugar production registered between the 1760s and the 1780s were for mills.[40] And by the early 1800s, the rollers were manufactured entirely of iron, rather than iron-clad wood.[41]

Other changes in milling came from alternative power sources. While there is evidence for experimentation with steam power for driving sugar mills in Jamaica as early as 1768, steam did not come to predominate in the region until well into the nineteenth century. The predominant migration over the eighteenth century was from cattle power to water power.[42] This was especially true in Jamaica, which boasted far more rivers cascading through the landscape than either Barbados or any of the Leeward Islands. Eighteenth-century planters in Jamaica quickly came to recognize that water mills were far more efficient.[43] In his discussion of Golden Grove plantation in the 1760s, historian Barry Higman makes quite clear the centrality of water to the sugar plantation even by that date. In a section entitled "Water Wars," Higman argues that water resources were a point of "competition and conflict, even cooperation" among planters in late eighteenth-century Jamaica.[44] By 1763, 382 Jamaican sugar plantations still depended on cattle mills but 150 had built water-powered mills; the trend would continue in force through the century.[45] The rapid expansion of the use of water mills in Jamaica in the final quarter of the eighteenth century was a direct response to changes in design; between 1770 and 1800, the all-iron water-wheel quickly replaced wood and iron wheels across England and Jamaica.[46] In his 1793 treatise on the British Caribbean, Bryan Edwards asserted that the building of first importance to a sugar plantation was the water mill.

He continued by instructing his readers that if there were no source for a water mill, planters should erect either a windmill and a cattle mill or two cattle mills in its stead, presuming the greater efficiency of water mills.[47] By the early nineteenth century, in fact, access to water to run a water mill was presumed essential for any land that would support a successful plantation.[48] In his *Jamaica Planter's Guide* of 1823, Thomas Roughley presumed that plantations required both a centralized sugar works and a water-powered mill and that if the terrain did not allow this convergence, "a course should be leveled for one," suggesting that planters build an extensive aqueduct, bringing water from a natural source to the centralized mill.[49]

The construction of a watercourse and water mill was not an easy undertaking; the construction of one weir in the 1760s required forty enslaved laborers working for three weeks.[50] Given Jamaica's torrential rainfall, canals needed to be lined in stone if they were to have any permanence. In 1770, Daniel Moore petitioned and won from the Jamaican Assembly the right to bring water to the mill on his plantation via an extensive aqueduct and a half-mile brick-lined tunnel through an adjacent mountain range.[51] The construction of a water mill often required that water be conveyed via an aqueduct, like the impressive one at Mona plantation (now the University of the West Indies—Mona campus) (fig. 4.12).

Maps, views, and surviving ruins make clear that many late eighteenth-century planters undertook such capital-intensive construction in order to build a water-powered sugar mill. An 1804 map of the island by James Robertson identifies numerous aqueducts leading from rivers to water mills, but likely the most striking is the aqueduct in James Hakewill's view of Trinity Estate, which Hakewill describes as completed in 1797 and "at once an object of utility and ornament" (fig. 4.13). The particular topographic constraints on water meant that even with aqueducts, water mills never overtook cattle mills in total numbers, and most planters who invested in water mills also maintained a cattle mill for times of drought.[52]

Probably the most profound change in milling technology came in the shift from the undershot to the overshot waterwheel. Undershot waterwheels were driven entirely by channeling water from the source through the mill to turn the wheel by the energy of the moving water; the overshot waterwheel gained its efficiency by introducing the water at the top of the wheel, adding gravity to the power of the water flow, rather than simply submerging the wheel into moving water (fig. 4.14). The improvement of overshot wheels for millworks, turned by both the kinetic power of moving water and the potential energy of the weight of the water itself, was demonstrated in 1759 in published scientific experimentation.[53] Construction of an expensive

FIG. 4.12 Aqueduct at Mona plantation, St. Andrew Parish, Jamaica.

FIG. 4.13 James Hakewill, "Trinity Estate," from *A Picturesque Tour of the Island of Jamaica* (London: Hurst and Robinson, 1825). The prominent aqueduct powers the plantation's water mill; the cone of the now obsolete windmill stands to the far right of the complex. Harvard Libraries.

aqueduct that led from a more elevated water source was needed to deliver water to the top of a waterwheel; the known potential efficiency of the overshot wheel after 1760 convinced many Jamaican planters to invest in the construction of aqueducts and to consider the elevation of their water sources. One observer writing in 1790 noted that "upon hilly estates there are in general I think, more water-mills than there are upon the plains," reflecting the propensity to build overshot water mills in variable terrain and cattle mills in flatlands.[54] From its introduction in the mid-eighteenth century and with various refinements over the following decades, the water mill was a major site of improvement on the Jamaican sugar plantation.

But improvement also implicated broader changes. The late eighteenth-century Jamaican sugar plantation boasted three new building types: trash houses, slave hospitals, and slave barracks. From the late seventeenth century, commentators noted that sugar planters in Barbados and the Leeward Islands used trash—the leaves and the unusable uppermost portion of each cane stalk—as fuel for the boiling house furnaces. The migration toward the use of trash as a fuel source was driven largely by the rapid deforestation that followed the expansion of sugar cultivation on these smaller islands; Jamaica, heavily forested and much larger, did not face the same pace of deforestation. Many Jamaican planters continued to open

FIG. 4.14 Overshot water wheel, Tryall plantation, St. James Parish, Jamaica.

up new plots for sugar on their existing plantations into the 1740s.[55] But over the course of the eighteenth century, most planters in Jamaica faced the reality of decreasing supplies of easily available wood, and they embraced the efficiency of reserving the otherwise useless by-product of cane cultivation for fuel. The result was an increasing need for a place to store and dry the trash before its use in the furnaces; plantations began to include trash houses as part of the sugar works complex.

The typical trash house was a long, low building of masonry piers supporting a shingled roof, with wooden frames between each pier. Bryan Edwards argued in 1807 that every plantation should be outfitted with two trash houses, each 120 feet long by 30 feet wide, with stone foundations, open sides, and a shingled roof supported by stone pillars—not unlike the trash house at Virgin Valley.[56] In his slightly later manual for Jamaican planters, Thomas Roughley insisted that trash houses be up to one hundred feet long and forty-five feet wide, well roofed with cupolas along the whole length of the building "to allow the exhalations from the green trash to pass off freely." Roughley also indicated that the house should have doors only at the two ends, allowing slaves to pack the trash as compactly and as high as possible on either side of a central aisle. He continued that the possibility of fire was always great with trash houses, so an ideal location was for them to be separated from the works by a stream of water, creating a firebreak and providing a ready supply of water for extinguishing the flames.[57] In their streamlined form and reuse of by-product, trash houses realized modern efficiency in the machine.

The second building type to appear more regularly on Jamaican plantations was the slave hospital. Documentary records suggest that these infirmaries, earlier called in the West Indies hot-houses, were not uncommon by the middle of the eighteenth century.[58] Writing in 1788, John Lindsay declared it "a strange idea that some [planters] have imbib'd, that . . . a [hospital] should be contrived so disagreeable and inconvenient . . . that a good Negroe when really sick, will patiently work till he falls in the field, rather than go through the ordeal" of a miserable hospital.[59] The early Jamaican hospital was not entirely restorative. As implied in Lindsay's comment, many planters intentionally erected bleak hospitals in an effort to make them as unappealing as possible. Hospital inventories reveal that sick slaves commonly slept on the floor, without bedding. These buildings were outfitted with iron bars on the windows and strong, lockable doors

to accommodate their simultaneous function as a site of confinement; planters believed that severely limiting movement would discourage feigned sickness among slaves. Some hospitals were even outfitted with stocks.[60]

While hospitals had been a fixture of the Jamaican plantation since midcentury, a handful of planters erected very large and substantial examples in the closing decade of the eighteenth century. The examples at Good Hope and Orange Valley are just two of the most spectacular, and they correspond closely to the parameters set out for hospitals by contemporaries. The substantial slave hospital at Good Hope plantation has the remarkable survival of an architect's plan, showing the clear differentiation between men's and women's halves of the building (fig. 4.15). An analysis of John Tharp's 1805 inventory suggests that in that year almost sixty of his enslaved Africans were employed in this hospital in some fashion, including "doctors, attendants, assistants, hospital men, hospital women, those attending yaws children, those attending yaws negroes, field nurses, nurses for children with swelled knees, nurses for children, those nursing children, midwives, and those attending children."[61] This list includes one of Tharp's most valuable slaves, Will, a Jamaican-born doctor, valued at £250.[62] The huge and elegant slave hospital shell surviving at Orange Valley was also originally divided into two equal halves (fig. 4.16). Bryan Edwards argued that each plantation needed a hospital for sick negroes, including "a room for lying-in women, a room for confining disorderly negroes, a shop for the doctor, and one or more store rooms for securing provisions."[63] The ruins of the Good Hope hospital reveal quite clearly a rear strongroom for securing rebellious slaves; it has ventilation gaps that allow airflow but that bend in the middle of the thick masonry wall, denying passage of any light or large objects. Writing slightly later, Thomas Roughley described hospitals as necessarily strong and commodious with "wholesome water running through pipes." He insisted that the hospital have twin spaces, separating men from women as is the case at Good Hope and Orange Valley. Roughley also argued that hospitals should be outfitted with piazzas "so slaves can walk around." Windows must be "iron barred on the outside," but for health and comfort the hospital should have a fireplace in each room and whitewashed interiors. Roughley argues against the inclusion of stocks in the hospital as this "allows the transfer of disease." He recommends that planters build isolated purpose-built stocks with strong hinges,

FIG. 4.15 Archibald Campbell, "Plan of the Hospital for the Sick Slaves upon Good Hope Estate," 1798. Ink on paper, 22½ × 18½ in. (57 × 47 cm). Cambridgeshire Archives.

iron bars, and many locks to "make confinement more irksome and dreaded."[64] Other accounts suggest that hospitals were often fitted out with stocks and chambers for solitary confinement.[65] Seen through the lens of improvement, slave hospitals were simultaneously spaces of confinement and a repair shop for broken laborers, an effort to better sustain the continuous production of the sugar works. John Tharp's large and elegant hospital was a choice driven more by concerns for financial health and the consistency of his labor force than ease of life among his slaves.

Improvement even extended to the residences of enslaved Africans. Through most of the eighteenth century the majority of the enslaved resided in villages that became the center of their world (fig. 4.17). Generally clusters of houses, each positioned on its own parcel and supported by an aggregate of smaller sheds and pens, the village was the site of a wide range of everyday activities. Many late seventeenth- and early eighteenth-century descriptions reported that enslaved Africans slept in groups outside their quarters: "They lay themselves naked on the ground all round their fire, the whole family together in a confused manner to sleep."[66] Later writers noted the presence of an indoor bedstead and by late in the eighteenth century it was presumed by most writers that Africans slept

FIG. 4.16 Slave hospital ruins, Orange Valley, Trelawny Parish, Jamaica, ca. 1790s.

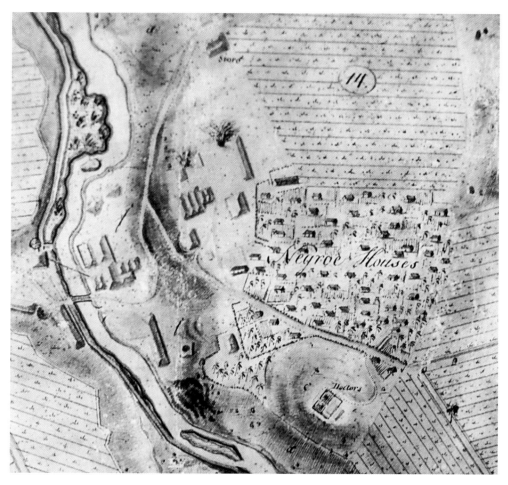

FIG. 4.17 John Henry Schroeder, "A Plan of Good Hope Estate," detail of the slave village site, 1794. Private collection.

indoors. Their bed frames, noted one commentator, were a platform of boards, "frequently made of cleft cabbage-tree stems," and the bed, a mat covered with a blanket.[67] In order to reduce the need for joinery, the posts of the bed, like those of the house, were "fixed in the earth." The mats were generally made of the "long ribs of the plantain leaf . . . stripped of the dry foliage."[68]

Another daily activity, of course, was cooking. While some commentators suggest that Africans used one of their two chambers for cooking, most evidence suggests that enslaved men and women prepared their meals outside their house, usually in an earthenware pot supported by three rounded stones.[69] Many writers observed the cookery used by slaves, some noting their African manufacturing traditions.[70] "Some negroes are expert in manufacturing pots and other common vessels," wrote one observer. He continued by noting that the pots, which Africans called *yabbas,* bore a "coarse glazing" and were "convex at the bottom without a ring as ours." Houses often had jugs as a reservoir of fresh water. To protect against contamination, "their water jar is raised from the ground, on a stem of a small tree with three prongs, fixed in one corner of their house."[71] Africans also used "calabashes of different sizes [which serve] very tolerably for plates, dishes, and bowls," but also for ladles and "vessels for holding grain, spirits, &c."[72] The principal cooking pot was usually supported by a "trivet . . . of three large stones."[73] By the middle of the eighteenth century, some planters provided iron pots for their slaves, although they were usually shared between two or more slaves.[74] Africans also built a roasting spit of "two forked sticks, placed in the earth at a due distance from each other."[75] Their houses eventually included European imported ceramics, metal utensils, and, on occasion, even tea pots.

While planters often provided "new negroes" with some provisions, including rice, plantains, and maize, seasoned slaves or Creole slaves cooked most of their own food from their own provisions.[76] The predominance of the pot—either earthware or iron—was in large part due to the predominance of stewing as a primary cooking method among Africans.[77] Broths depended on vegetables grown in yards and provision grounds, including callaloo, okra, plaintains, yams, cocos, and peppers, all seasoned with small amounts of salt fish or pork. Combined and stewed, seasoned heavily with hot peppers, this meal came to be called pepper-pot by the later eighteenth century.[78] Africans also cultivated fruit trees including coconut, orange, plantain, papaw, lime,

star-apple, mango, breadfruit, and bananas.[79] Often a mortar and pestle were used to beat boiled tubers into a small cake that served as a starchy side. Small graters found in archaeological excavations of the village site at Montpelier suggest that spices and coconut might have been used to flavor dishes as well.[80]

The village was also, of course, the site of events of great importance, specifically births and deaths within the community. A number of sources make clear that a newborn child was not considered viable until it had survived the first nine days, time spent entirely inside the mother's house.[81] As Kamau Brathwaite has argued, the birth of a child was often attended with the burial of the placenta near the house of birth; often a small tree was planted at the site establishing a connection between the child, the tree, and the house. The house site was also highly important at the time of death. Deceased enslaved Africans were occasionally buried in the immediate vicinity of their house and garden, sometimes even under their bed.[82] In this practice, the documentary record is substantiated by house-yard burials from the archaeological record.[83] Douglas Armstrong excavated four burials associated with early to mid-eighteenth-century house-yard sites from Seville plantation, providing information about burial practices and the use of coffins and grave goods.[84] The village was typically the site of elaborate mourning practices. On the death of one of his slaves, Thomas Thistlewood reported that the slave's wife "killed a heifer, several hogs, &c. to entertain her company with." The company spent an entire day and night "singing &c. at the Negro houses," possibly encouraged by the eight gallons of rum provided by their master.[85] Another account reports that "the body put in the ground; all the while they are covering it with Earth, the Attendants scream out in a terrible manner, which is not the effect of Grief, but of Joy; they beat on their Wooden Drums and their Women with their Rattles make a hideous noise."[86] But the celebration of the death of a master was equally riotous. Thistlewood noted that upon the occasion of the death of his nephew, the slaves of the village blew on a shell over the river and "afterwards in the Night 2 guns fired with a loud huzza after each." The overt celebration of the death of an oppressor was noted by Thistlewood as only "Strange Impudence."[87]

The village site was also the locus for the practice of Obeah, a complex belief system that involved spirits in the events of everyday life.[88] In one early nineteenth-century report, a visitor reported on a conversation with an elderly slave who suggested that charms and talismans were common: "The old patriarch said, that 'formerly people minded the *puntees,* hung up in trees and grounds as charms to keep off thieves."[89] Individuals described as Obeah-men or Obeah-women would have a regional reputation and could wield significant authority over other slaves in that district.[90] Obeah was also enlisted in assaults on whites. In one report, a slave had thrown a headless fowl down a well in an effort to exact revenge on his master for sending his sister to work as a field slave.[91] Such an act was understood to be common Obeah practice; the plantation well became a point of weakness in the machinery of the plantation, a point assaulted by particularly aggravated slaves. The practice of Obeah required numerous talismans, including "blood, feathers, Parrots Beaks, Dogs Teeth, Alligators Teeth, broken Bottles, Grave Dirt, Rum, Egg-shells," among other objects given supernatural power.[92] Such a range of objects meant that particularly active Obeah practitioners transformed their quarters into a veritable market of such items, as was described by one Jamaican planter in a 1775 account from his own plantation:

> Upon hearing [of the report of an Obeah woman] he repaired directly with Six White Servants to the old Woman's House, and forcing open the Door, observed with whole Inside of the Roof (which was thatch), and every Crevice of the Walls, stuck with the Implements of her Trade, consisting of Rags, Feathers, Bones of

Cats, and a thousand other Articles. Examining further, a large earthen Pot or Jar, close covered, was found concealed under her Bed—It contained a prodigious Quantity of round Balls of Earth or Clay of various Dimensions, large and small, whitened on the Outside, and variously compounded, some with Hair or Rags or Feathers of all sorts, and strongly bound with Twine; other blended with the upper section of the skulls of Cats or stuck round with Cats Teeth and Claws, or with Human or Dogs Teetth, and some Glass Beads of Different colours.[93]

Upon the discovery, the planter burned the house to the ground and sold the woman to slave traders from Cuba.

But by the later eighteenth century, some planters began to disrupt the village community by building barracks-style housing that removed enslaved Africans to linear, organized, and equally disposed housing units. John Baillie, for example, built a range of quarters at Roehampton in what he described as barracks, "to distinguish them from houses with each of them ground around them; a barrack is a range of houses, or a row of houses, not detached."[94] Standing not far from the main house at Phoenix plantation is a longitudinal building that was once a row of four quarter chambers, each with a door opening onto the shallow stoop that faces toward the main house and a window opening through the rear wall of each room (fig. 4.18). Another example survives at Mount Plenty

FIG. 4.18 Barracks quarters, Phoenix plantation, Trelawny Parish, Jamaica.

FIG. 4.19 Barracks quarters at Mount Plenty plantation, St. Ann Parish, Jamaica.

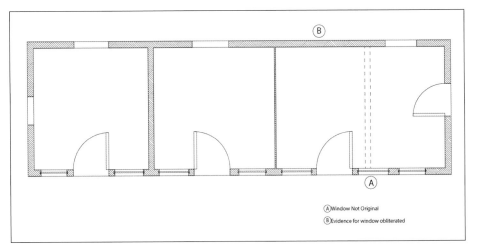

Ⓐ Window Not Original
Ⓑ Evidence for window obliterated

FIG. 4.20 Plan of barracks at Mount Plenty plantation.

FIG. 4.21 Slave barracks at Arcadia plantation, Trelawny Parish, early nineteenth century.

FIG. 4.22 Front passage of Arcadia barracks with doors flanked by jalousies opening into each chamber.

plantation, this one fronted by a piazza (figs. 4.19, 4.20). A much grander version of the same type survives at Arcadia plantation (fig. 4.21). In this longitudinal, raised building, a single staircase rises to a centrally located door which in turn opens into a passage. Opening onto that passage are four doors flanked by jalousies, each opening into a private, noncommunicating chamber (fig. 4.22). At each end of the passage is a larger chamber with windows opening on three sides, fine door and window trim, and coved ceilings.

The earliest reference to quartering in attached units appears in a 1774 description of a wattle and thatch row, but barracks-style housing does not appear commonly in Jamaica and across the Caribbean until the 1790s.[95] In his examination of slave quartering in the Danish West Indies, William Chapman finds abundant evidence for the construction of such barracks beginning in the 1790s and lasting well into the early nineteenth century.[96] So much so, in fact, that he asserts that almost all of St. Croix's quartering was rebuilt between the 1790s and the early 1830s. The architectural similarities between barracks in Jamaica and St. Croix and their simultaneous appearance

in the 1790s collectively reinforce Chapman's claim that these new building forms derive from broader "improvements" to workers' housing across the British Empire. Surviving 1790s examples from England include the rows of duplexes at Chippenham Village built by John Tharp for the laborers on his English country estate in Cambridgeshire (fig. 4.23). These were all likely inspired by conversations around agricultural improvement in England that first took visual expression in John Wood's 1781 publication, *A Series of Plans for Cottages or Habitations of the Labourer.* In that volume, which was republished in 1792 and again in 1806, Wood not only offers designs for laborers' houses but he also advocates for improved conditions (fig. 4.24).[97] Interestingly, Tharp undertook purpose-built housing for his English but not his Jamaican laborers, who continued to live in individual houses as suggested by the plat.

Another change to slave housing was the erection of more permanent quarters, either nogged or even in stone. Recent archaeological excavations by Hayden Bassett at the village site at Good Hope have unearthed substantial

quantities of brick with plaster on the broken faces, evidence of its use as nogging infill. The same village site has revealed abundant nails that were likely used to secure clapboard siding, suggesting the extensive use of these materials by the early nineteenth century.[98] Stone quarters also begin to appear in Jamaica and on other Caribbean islands in the early years of the nineteenth century.[99] As was the case at Montpelier, the construction of stone quarters soon after the abolition of the Atlantic slave trade in 1807 likely revealed the intentional involvement of the planter in the design and construction process. In the absence of the renewable source of labor, planters recognized the need to preserve the health and longevity of their workforce. Improved housing was one means. Stone slave quarters also reveal far greater regularity and linear alignment compared to housing built of other building materials.[100] Those at Roehampton were all a standard sixteen by twenty-four feet; the documentary record for Montpelier indicates that all stone quarters were uniformly shingled rather than covered in thatch.[101] The construction of stone barracks likely reveals the preferences of the planter, not those of the enslaved, but even if these forms are inspired by the broader practices of agricultural improvement, in Jamaica they played a particular role in diminishing slave agency and in asserting control over enslaved laborers.[102]

Late eighteenth-century trash houses, slave hospitals, and slave barracks joined the overshot water-wheel as features that visibly distinguished the later eighteenth-century sugar plantation from earlier examples. "Improvement," as it has been generally understood in the history of early modern Britain, was a phenomenon focused on the transformation of British landscapes to render them well suited to increasingly intensive farming. In this view, improvement is understood to mean a transformation of forms and processes intended to improve productivity. Understood in this way, Jamaican planters actively participated in the improvement of the later eighteenth-century sugar plantation; Jamaica's plantations were not at the periphery of empire but in fact stood at the inventive front edge of British improvement, industry, and control. But as Richard Hoyle's recent volume of essays reminds us, improvement was also about land ownership, access, enclosure, and managerial practices, all driven toward the end of increased profits for the few.[103] In the early modern period, the "good" of improvement was largely undisputed. And this was especially true in places like Jamaica where local rights and customs offered no resistance to the cult of improvement. But we need also to remember that improvement, as Richard Drayton has argued, was imperial: "[It] promised that people and things might be administered, in the cosmopolitan interest, by those who understood nature's laws. European power, joined to the scientific mastery of nature, would necessarily confer the greatest good on the greatest number."[104] Sometimes those who pressed for improvement justified coercion and even violence.[105]

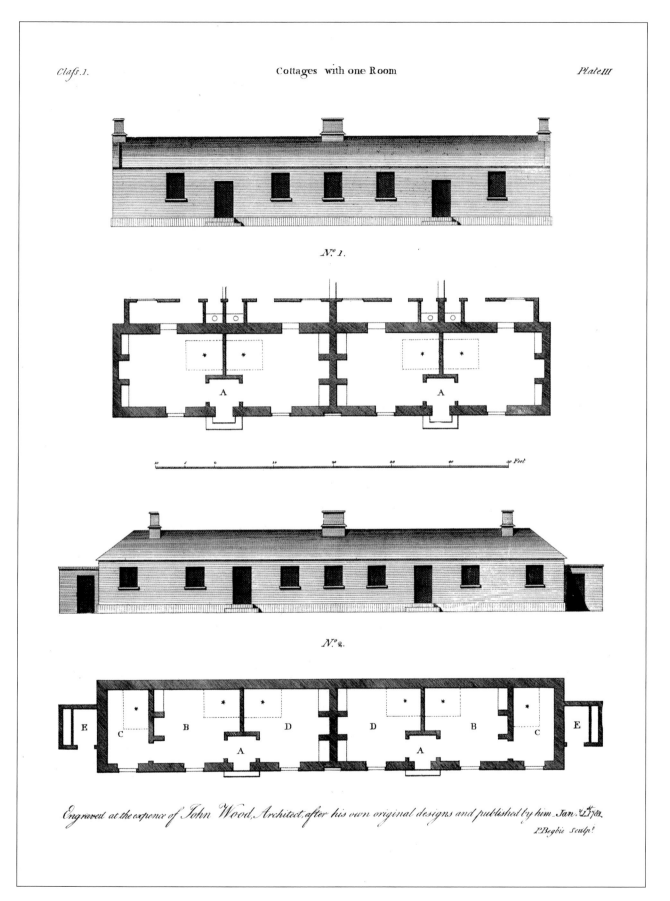

N.º 1.

N.º 2.

Engraved at the expence of John Wood, Architect, after his own original designs and published by him Jan.ʳʸ 1ˢᵗ 1781.

P. Begbie Sculp.ᵗ

FIG. 4.24 "Cottages with One Room," from John Wood, *A Series of Plans for Cottages or Habitations of the Labourer either in Husbandry or the Mechanic Arts* (London: J. J. Taylor, 1781), Plate III. Harvard Libraries.

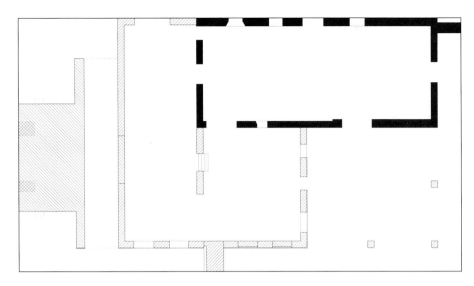

FIG. 4.25 Plan of Good Hope boiling house, Trelawny Parish, Jamaica. Mid-eighteenth-century boiling house in solid black, 1802 expansion is hatched.

INDUSTRY

John Tharp's boiling house, as it stands today, is a late eighteenth-century three-fold expansion of an earlier boiling house that stood on the property through the century.[106] Careful examination of the building's plan reveals that the grander elevation of the building encased an earlier mid-eighteenth-century boiling house that likely stood on the site when John Tharp purchased the property in 1766 (fig. 4.25). Measuring thirty-seven feet long by sixteen feet wide, the mid-eighteenth-century boiling house was already a fairly large, industrial-scale building. But Tharp's expansion substantially enlarged the building to sixty-four feet long by thirty-four feet wide. When in the flush of refining, this boiling house disgorged smoke and heat, running continuously through night and day as teams of exhausted slaves ladled scalding hot syrup from one cauldron to another. The boiling house was the epicenter of the plantation and the center of concerns for "clock time consciousness," to use Justin Roberts's useful phrase.[107] The boiling house was so central, in fact, that some sugar works included an office for the overseer with a window directly overlooking the boiling house (fig. 4.26). In an annual letter of report, one overseer assured the plantation owner that "the Boiling House has been my constant residence all day as soon as light would permit work to be done."[108] And, as at Good Hope, Jamaica's boiling houses were usually paired with equally large curing houses, where enslaved Africans poured the thick syrup into heavy clay molds to cure into crystal cones. The curing house at Orange Grove plantation in Trelawny Parish bore so much weight that external buttresses were added soon after its construction. In scale and complexity of form and process, these buildings were not agricultural but industrial.

The defining feature of the boiling house was the sequence of four or five cauldrons—called coppers for their preferred material—used to reduce and refine the sugar juice and to eliminate impurities (fig. 4.27). In the case of the early boiling house at Good Hope, these

FIG. 4.26 Venetian window in office of the works at Orange Valley, overlooking the boiling house, ca. 1800.

cauldrons would likely have lined the southern long wall of the building. As the juice boiled in each copper, impurities rose to the surface and the sugar boiler—the highly skilled slave entrusted to the task—would determine when a worker with the ladle might begin to skim the impurities off the surface of the juice.[109] The role of boiler at Good Hope in the 1820s was probably fulfilled by a man named Price.[110] Once purified in that copper, the workers ladled juice into the next, slightly smaller copper and repeated the process. All the while other enslaved Africans maintained the fires below, feeding fuel through tunnels underneath and behind the coppers. In order to best purify the juice, the sugar boiler and fire-man needed to attend carefully to the heat of the fire, so as to neither crystalize the juice too soon or to over-boil the cauldron. In the seventeenth century each of the coppers was heated over its own furnace, fueled from an opening on the outside of the building.[111] But by the early eighteenth century, Jamaican planters began to build a single furnace and flue that heated all the coppers simultaneously, an innovation labeled a "Jamaica train," although it seems to have appeared first in Barbados.[112]

While the form of the furnaces in the earlier Good Hope boiling house is no longer legible, that in the later eighteenth-century expansion was certainly a Jamaica train. The long narrow chamber that runs along the west end of the building has just beyond it a masonry tunnel along the outside. This tunnel sheltered the access of those stoking the furnaces to the series of flue-holes that opened below each copper. Those five coppers were fed by a single fire that spanned under the entire range, vented at the far northern end. As each copper required at least seven feet for useful operation, boiling houses were often thirty-five feet long or more. The new boiling house in Good Hope measures thirty-four feet from end to end; Bryan Edwards, writing in the late eighteenth century, offered the dimensions of a standard Jamaican boiling house as forty-five feet by twenty-two.[113] When the coppers lined an end wall, the middle of the building was opened as a thoroughfare and the opposite end was dominated by a large sunken cistern for the scum from the coppers. While not definitive, it is possible that the expansion of the boiling house at Good Hope was in some way related to the desire to install a much larger and more sophisticated Jamaica train, the remnants of which still survive under the floor of the orange-packing plant. This massive masonry building would have been a regular place of labor for dozens if not scores of men and women at a time; French, Hannibal, Clarissa, Charlotte, Friday, Jack, and Yorkshire are just some of the people for whom this was a regular site of everyday life and labor.[114]

The major by-product of this process was molasses, which was commonly incorporated into the slave diet as a cheap source of energy. But molasses could also be distilled into rum, generally for local consumption. While there is clear evidence for major distilleries by the nineteenth century, most plantations had small-scale distilleries. By the eighteenth century, Jamaica was the leading producer of rum in the British Caribbean; archaeologist-historian Frederick Smith chronicles the history of its production and consumption among all Jamaicans, free whites and free and enslaved Africans alike.[115] Just as the dried trash was reintroduced into the system as fuel, so too molasses was not a discarded by-product; it was creatively reincorporated into the system.

Having passed through the series of coppers, the refined cane juice was then poured into earthenware sugar cones, sixteen inches wide at the mouth and twenty-six to twenty-eight inches long, open on the top for pouring and with a small hole at the point plugged by a stick or rag. These cones were then placed in rows in a well-secured curing house. The large curing house at Good Hope stands immediately behind the expanded boiling house. After the sugar began to cool and crystalize, a process which usually took about two days, slaves extracted the stick, allowing the residual molasses to drain from each cone.[116] Once the molasses had fully drained, the cones were dried through the work of a "gentle fiere made in the midle of the house for about a daie and a night, by which the sugare is cuered, dried and becomes perfect sugare of a bright collour and good grain."[117] Curing the sugar could take up to a month. Once it was cured, enslaved Africans loaded the sugar into hogsheads to be stored in a warehouse for export. The warehouse at Good Hope was at the top of the hill, halfway between the sugar works and the road up to the great house site.

Like the boiling house, the curing house was a substantial building. As with the boiling house, a large and well-lit building was advantageous, but the curing house required windows that allowed close management of airflow. Through the curing process, the windows were to remain airtight so that the sugar would not dry too quickly.[118] In his *History of the Island of Barbados,* Richard Ligon published an extraordinary model for a curing house, a model surely known by many early planters in Jamaica.[119] With a main block measuring forty feet wide by one hundred feet long, Ligon's curing house is a very large building. The main floor was to be lined with rows of frames, each frame holding a single sugar cone for curing. In order to allow circulation around the cones, the rows were to be arranged to either side of a "great passage"

with narrow aisles to either side. If the building was to have an upper story on the same plan, the floor was to be tightly sealed to prevent the breakage of an upper story cone from spoiling the sugar curing in those below.[120] The curing house was also to have a ground floor comprising a network of gutters intended to catch molasses draining from the cones above and to convey it to cisterns situated in each of the four corners of the building. Accounts from eighteenth-century Jamaica suggest that many planters made do with much smaller curing houses, usually immediately adjoined to the boiling house.[121]

Obviously, a sugar works was a substantial capital investment. In the late 1760s, Simon Taylor, the overseer of Golden Grove plantation, wrote to the plantation owner that he could expect a sharp rise in profits since the recent completion of a new sugar works, an important point since the owner had been "at a very great expense in your works," even though "nothing has been done to them more than was necessary."[122] As in all cases, the machinery of their works—the millworks, the coppers, and so on—had to be ordered and shipped from Britain at no minor expenditure.[123] In the 1770s, Edward Long estimated that a beginning planter would need to invest £600 sterling in the construction of a *temporary* sugar works just to begin processing. The assumption was that this works would, of course, need to be replaced after three or four years, even while making in those first years nothing but rum. The investment in enslaved labor, Long estimated, would be more than twice that cost.[124] In his 1790 *Descriptive Account of the Island of Jamaica,* William Beckford argues that "it is not in the power of every planter (indeed it is in the ability but of very few), to erect a new set of works, although upon the foundations of the old, and upon the most contracted plan, without feeling the pressure of it for many years at least, if not for ever."[125] And near the turn of the century, Bryan Edwards estimated that only £30,000 sterling would launch a sugar plantation "with a fair prospect of advantage."[126]

The investment of a sugar works was not just in buildings but also machinery. Richard Ligon warned his mid-seventeenth-century readers that planters needed to take great care of the sugar mill, which he called the "Primum Mobile of the whole work."[127] This included a great deal more than just providing the ax to cut off a hand or arm ensnared in the drums. Planters would want to regularly inspect "the Rollers, the Goudges, Sockets, Sweeps, Cogs, or Braytrees," because if any of these failed "the whole work stands still." The same would be true of the equipment in the boiling house, where the brick platforms that carried the coppers might crack or break "by the violence of the heat from the Furnaces." Again, such a mishap meant "a stop in the work, till that be mended." Another threat was the burning of the coppers or the breaking of the iron bars that support the floor of the furnace, always possible when red hot. In each case, the single failure, he warns, brings the entire process to a halt, "for all these depend on one another, as wheels in a Clock."[128] And bringing the process to a halt meant a significant financial loss as all cut cane would be spoiled before the machinery could be repaired. Replacing a burned or cracked copper, for example, would take at least fifteen days, assuming a replacement was on hand.[129] In preparation for a harvest to begin in five days' time, enslaved "Masons, Millwrights, and Coppersmiths" were all "busy repairing the works" on Colbeck, according to one early nineteenth-century visitor.[130] In his comparison of the sugar works to a clock, Ligon recognized not only the delicacy and interdependence of the machinery of a sugar plantation but also the time discipline required for fiscal success.[131] But it was also important to make sure that you enlisted the work of slaves who knew how to operate the machinery, because mishaps were often fatal. As described by one planter: "If a stiller slip into a rum-cistern, it is sudden death; for it stifles in a moment. If a mill-feeder be catched by the finger, his whole body is drawn in, and he is squeezed to pieces. If a boiler gets any part into the scalding sugar, it sticks like glue, or birdlime, and 'tis hard to save either limb or life."[132] As a result, preserving the lives of those more skilled slaves working in the sugar works was important for smooth and profitable operation. As historian Justin Roberts has argued, planters "flinched more at the loss of labor than at the loss of life."[133]

Sugar processing in the British Caribbean required capital investment in substantial landholdings, large buildings and complicated machinery, and heavy as well as skilled labor organized in gangs on schedules to ensure that the appropriate labor was available at each stage of the process. As early as 1750, Samuel Martin told his readers that the success of the plantation depended, "as in a well-constructed machine," in the "right disposition of the main springs, or primary parts." The plantation machine was "compounded of various wheels, turning in different ways, and yet all contributing to the great end proposed."[134] The size of the coppers and their sequential

nature meant that seventeenth- and mid-eighteenth-century boiling houses were buildings of production that were significantly larger than any industrial sites in Britain until the late eighteenth century; historians of Britain's industrial landscape report that most industrial buildings from the earlier eighteenth century "differed little [in scale] from domestic buildings."[135] The scale and complexity of an eighteenth-century Jamaican sugar works looked more like a factory than contemporary industrial sites in Britain.

While the traditional line of argument identifies the third quarter of the eighteenth century as the launch of England's Industrial Revolution, more recent scholarship, largely framed in historical-economic terms, has come to question the notion of a temporal threshold, arguing instead for a gradual emergence of industrialization in England over the course of the eighteenth century.[136] Additionally, industrialization has historically been located in the motherland. But a number of recent historians of the Caribbean have rightly noted that the sugar plantation, while agricultural in genesis, was decidedly industrial in process. In Sweetness and Power, Sidney Mintz argued that the discipline central to the successful operation of a sugar plantation and the combination of agriculture and processing on a single site is one of the central features of industrialization.[137] Mintz further argued that the complexity of the process required the organization of the labor force into "interchangeable units," another dimension of industrialization. Barry Higman demonstrates that sugar planters discussed their slaves as if they were components of a large machine, observing that slaves wore out over time and that overwork often killed slaves, an event that disadvantaged the efficient operation of the plantation.[138] That the boiling house was a major center of British industrialism was a point powerfully reinforced in an early nineteenth-century image of one such building on Antigua, burning, as they often did, through the night (fig. 4.28). The industrial nature of sugar production was not lost on the artist James Robertson, who within a few years painted two major sites of British industry: the sugar works of Jamaica and the ironworks of Shropshire.[139] Mintz, Higman, and now many others have convincingly argued that sugar processing in the early British Caribbean prefigures the industrialization of late eighteenth-century Britain; if Jamaica was shaped by and shaped agricultural improvement, the same can be said for industrialization.[140] As this discussion makes clear, these

FIG. 4.28 William Clark, "Exterior of a boiling house," from *Ten Views in the Island of Antigua: in which are represented the process of sugar making, and the employment of the Negroes, in the field, boiling-house and distillery* (London: T. Clay, 1823). Yale Center for British Art, Paul Mellon Collection.

two phenomena cannot be properly understood in their British context in Britain alone; the Jamaican plantation was a crucible for both improvement and industrialization in Britain.

CONTROL

In his extensive reconstruction of Good Hope, John Tharp built an overseer's house not near his own house on the great house site but on a steep outcrop overlooking the sugar works and near the slave hospital and the village site. The building is large, with a full cellar underneath the main, single story of living quarters. The interior is organized around a central passage which provides direct access to four chambers of equal size, suggesting that the house might have housed multiple individuals, all of generally equal status, rather than just a single overseer (fig. 4.29). The rear of the building is dominated by a large common hall with windows that provided immediate oversight of the sugar works, although that view is today obscured by the regrowth of the dense Jamaican forest. The front of the building is dominated by a curious enclosed but well-ventilated porch or lobby, a feature that appears on numerous other overseers' houses of the later eighteenth century. Importantly, this is the chamber closest to the slave hospital and the village site, suggesting that it served in some fashion as a space of interaction between the white overseers and their enslaved African charges, a liminal zone partly interior and partly exterior,

within the overseer's domain but well removed from private chambers.

One of the most critical features of an overseer's house was its position in the landscape. Recent research on overseers' houses on both sugar and coffee plantations in early colonial Jamaica has determined that physical position on an elevated site was critical to the house as a type.[141] The goal appears to have been the capacity for surveillance over the works. By the end of the eighteenth and the early nineteenth century, these material practices were written into proscriptive literature. William Beckford directed that the overseer's house was to be situated "on an eminence overlooking the works"; Thomas Roughley offered an extensive description of the Jamaican overseer's house, which should, he argued, be compact, convenient, and not over-roomy. It was important that it be "raised sufficiently high from the foundation, with good masonry work, to admit of suitable stores underneath, to keep all the plantation store and supplies in"; most importantly, "it should be placed so, that all the works can be seen from it."[142] Elevation of the building site was essential to allow the overseer to survey the plantation, most especially the operations of the sugar works. The 1790s overseer's house at Good Hope conforms exactly to these expectations. As revealed in an 1830s painting of the property by Joseph Kidd, the house enjoyed easy oversight of the sugar works along the river below (fig. 4.30).

Bearing in mind the relationship between architecture and landscape in Jamaica and control of the ever-growing

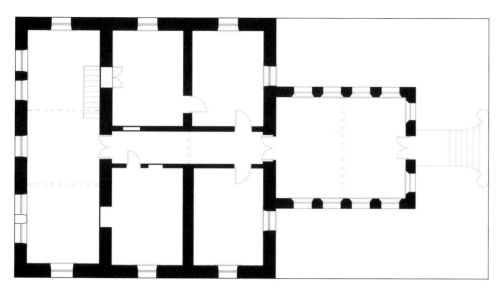

FIG. 4.29 Plan of the overseer's house at Good Hope, Trelawny Parish, Jamaica.

FIG. 4.30 Joseph Bartholomew Kidd, *Good Hope*, 1835–36. The new overseer's house is the large building at the front of the hill overlooking the sugar works. The large building opposite it is the new slave hospital. The view also shows the sugar duct running from the mill over the river to the boiling house. The great house site is in the far distance. Private collection.

African labor force, it is significant that the overseer's house at Good Hope had almost no capacity for surveillance over the slave village; in this and other examples the topography does not allow it. In her thesis examining the viewsheds from the overseer's house at Stewart Castle, Lyndsey Bates came to the same conclusion: that house oversaw the works, not the village.[143] Ignoring the village might seem an odd choice, especially given the regularity of insurrections in the Caribbean more generally and in eighteenth-century Jamaica specifically.

Driven by concerns for the productivity of their land, most early planters housed enslaved Africans on land that was not well suited to planting. Africans commonly found themselves living on low, swampy, mosquito-infested land or on slopes steeper than was desirable for cultivating sugar, in either case usually with poor soil for growing provisions.[144] This practice of doling out undesirable land persisted through the eighteenth century. Yet in describing the village on his own plantation in the early nineteenth century, Matthew Lewis reported that "each house is surrounded by a separate garden, and the whole village is intersected by lanes, bordered with all kinds of sweet smelling and flowering plants."[145]

As described in detail in chapter 3, the buildings were generally two chambers defined by walls of earthfast posts, wattle and mud walls, and a thatched roof. In the interior, the height of the roof was "barely sufficient to admit the owner to walk in upright." The floor was generally of packed earth, "which is commonly dry enough," but which when not dry "might possibly transmit noxious exhalations in the night."[146] Visitors also noted that of furniture, "they have no great matters to boast," but this was to be expected since in their view the Africans' "habits of life" required little; most had only a "small table," with "two or three low stools."[147] But the presumed paucity of possessions of many accounts is strongly contradicted by other historical and archaeological evidence. As Barry Higman and others have shown, slave quarters were often filled with a wide range of goods, both locally made and imported.[148] Common in houses were the African-derived and Jamaican manufactured yabbas, bowls made from local clay, pit fired, and coarsely glazed.[149] But excavations have also uncovered large quantities of imported ceramics and glass—including some tea or coffee pots—as well as some metal utensils. Houses were also filled with furniture, musical instruments, marbles, and stashes of money.[150] There is also abundant evidence for increasingly sophisticated clothing;

excavations unearth plain and fancy buttons as well as thimbles and sewing scissors.[151] Historical archaeologists and historians have pointed to the fancy dress donned by some slaves in the later eighteenth and early nineteenth centuries as evidence of their increasing capacity to negotiate their enslavement in creative ways.[152] While earlier scholars presumed that imported goods were likely given by planters, there is increasing evidence that even in the eighteenth century these items were purchased by slaves using money they earned through profit from provision grounds and other income-generating mechanisms.[153] Slaves found it necessary to protect their property from theft; Thistlewood's journals abound with accusations among slaves of thieving from one another.[154] It also appears that slave quarters sometimes had locks, but the common intrusion into houses by masters surely rendered these locks useful only against other slaves.[155]

Many observers also noted that Africans maintained a fire in or outside their houses almost continuously. Most obviously, this was for cooking. But the fire was also maintained "within doors during the night, without which a Negro cannot sleep with comfort." The fire "is made in the middle of one of the two rooms"; devoid of a chimney, "the smoke makes its way through the door or the thatch."[156] The fires obviously provided a little light, which was supplemented with tin oil lamps fueled with the oils of various nuts.[157] There is little evidence that early quarters had any windows.[158] Another writer noted that during the rainy season these indoor fires and smoke "prove an excellent safeguard to those within, against the injuries of a vitiated atmosphere."[159] This was especially important since so many slaves in Jamaica occupied "marshy soils"; hence the smoke of the fire was also "intended to disperse the muskeetos."[160] In an effort to keep the "numerous and rapacious" rats from devouring their meat and fish, they suspended it in a "half cylinder of bark with the round site uppermost, the rope to which their food is appended passing thro this up to the ridge pole"; this was usually positioned "immediately over the fire." Africans built rat traps "that prove very effectual in destroying that noxious animal."[161] Some Africans also built ovens for baking "by scooping hollows in perpendicular sides of a bank; and covered with a shade of sticks & leaves to keep off rain." Frequent firing of the earthen hole in the bank served to harden the interior into a functional oven.[162]

These houses usually stood on their own individual plot of ground, and collectively these plots composed the village.[163] As described by James Knight, "The nigro houses to the number of 80 or 100 . . . makes every plantation appear like so many villages."[164] The evidence also suggests that Africans were usually free to locate their house according to their personal preference; villages were "seldom placed with much regard to order," revealing an organic planning pattern that incorporated the personal agency of the occupants rather than that of the planter.[165] This was especially true in the case of extended families, where those with strong kinship relations occupied a cluster of houses usually surrounding an enclosed yard.[166] Each plot was fenced off from its neighbors by enclosures of pales "to confine their stock at night."[167] In some cases these fences were very tall and visually impermeable, protecting the activities of the yard from the vision of even mounted passersby.[168] As Sidney Mintz has argued, these house yards defined discrete units where many enslaved Africans spent a substantial portion of their nonwork daily living.[169] Some parcels included hog sties "built with logs piled up piramidally in squares, crossing at the ends and covered with boughs at the top," and other "huts, kitchens, or pens."[170] Freestanding kitchens as well as pigsties were also noted at Montpelier by the early nineteenth century.[171] In order to drain waste water, the sties were "generally situate on the side of a hill."[172] This characterization was reinforced archaeologically by Douglas Armstrong's work at Drax Hall plantation, where he found that houses usually took advantage of topography.[173]

A collection of the sty, other pens, and a kitchen often created "a little court surrounding [the] cottage."[174] Critical to the house site was the yard garden, providing some provisions for those in the house but also a means for generating revenue. As Hakewill argued, "With their surplus produce, and their pigs and poultry, they supply even to the distance of Anotto Bay, and from this traffic derive a very considerable profit."[175] Africans commonly grew fruit and vegetables such as yams, cassava, maize, plantains, bananas, breadfruit, mangoes, and oranges, and kept pens for poultry as well as hogs.[176] These slave villages, "being always intermingled with fruit-trees . . . the Negroes' own planting and property," were often described as picturesque by late eighteenth-century British observers.[177]

Having planted gardens and improved houses, enslaved Africans became quite attached to their individual parcel of land. In his description of one plantation in Jamaica, James Hakewill remarked that parcels of land assigned to slaves are passed "from father to son . . . who

regard their houses and provision grounds . . . as an inheritance." There was "visible grief in all our Negroes," wrote Thistlewood upon the notification of the removal of the village from one site to another.[178] In listening to a land dispute in an early nineteenth-century village, one author noted, "the negro maintained that his own grandfather had planted the tree, and had a house and garden beside it, and he claimed the land as his inheritance."[179] Jamaican slaves commonly believed that the land they occupied belonged to them.[180] As many historians of slavery have noted, the provision of land to each African increased their autonomy while shifting the responsibility for provisioning shelter and basic foodstuffs from the planter to the laborer. Using money generated through jobbing, or their provision grounds, or their own bodies, slaves were able to generate some cash and capital that allowed them to transform their own housing, gradually replacing mud-walled houses with board houses or even nog-walled houses with shingled roofs and wood floors. The architecture and landscape of the quarters of enslaved Africans in Jamaica seem to suggest that they enjoyed a fair degree of autonomy in the spaces of their own domiciles. But that independence stood in stark contrast to their experience in the places of labor, either in the fields or in the sugar works.

The early Jamaican sugar plantation was an extraordinarily profitable machine. But it was also a machine whose efficiency depended wholly on a compliant work force. Jamaican planters knew that much was at stake, for as Edward Long and all planters recognized, the labor of slaves "is the foundation of [our] riches."[181] But if that workforce was so central to the health of the planters and even the nation at large, it was also a potential tinderbox. One rebellion in Jamaica reinforced the baldly honest sentiment of one planter: "However they may disguise it, [slaves] hate their masters and wish them destroyed."[182] As a strategy, British planters enlisted the plantation as a landscape of control, exercising authority over the enslaved majority through fear, which the early Jamaican historian Bryan Edwards described as "the leading principle on which all governments in slave societies are supported."[183]

From their first encounter with Africans through to emancipation, Jamaican planters used corporal torture as a means of punishing those who resisted their slavery. From their inception, plantations were sites of corporal discipline. John Taylor's description of Jamaica in 1687 noted that if any slaves "committed robbery, prove sullen, or refuse to work," they were bound hand and foot to the whipping post "which they have in all plantations." The whipping was followed by a salt rub, which proves so painful it "forces 'em to their work againe." If their infraction was more serious, planters and overseers substituted molasses for the salt and left the slave to "stand for some time for the wasps, merrywigs and other insects to torment."[184] The practice of securing an African to a post via rope or bilboes—iron wrist and ankle restraints—for whipping was common throughout the period of slavery, as was the practice of covering the bloody body of the victim with lime juice, pepper oil, molasses, salt, or anything else that might amplify the pain. Thomas Thistlewood also used human feces, which he rubbed on the faces of disciplined slaves. On occasion he required one slave to urinate into the face and mouth of another.[185] His most extreme version of these practices, however, was called Derby's Dose, when the flogging and salt pickle rub was followed by the order for one slave to defecate in the open mouth of the victim, who was then "immediately put in a gag whilst his mouth was full" and the gag left in place for hours.[186] As Trevor Burnard has demonstrated, white planters and overseers in eighteenth-century Jamaica knew no real limitations to the punishments they might exact.[187] Slaves under discipline were often imprisoned for a time afterward, usually overnight in the plantation cookhouse; there is scant evidence for purpose-built punitive spaces or "stock rooms" in the early nineteenth century.[188] While cookhouses do appear on plantation plats, their function as spaces of solitary confinement emerges only through a careful reading of the documentary record. Whipping posts, sites of terrible corporal discipline and essential features for the management of a sugar plantation, never appear on plantation plats.

From whipping posts to town center gallows, Jamaica was a landscape of death. Many towns had places of public execution, and on occasion such executions extended also to the landscapes of plantations. In May of 1764, Thistlewood noted in passing that "a Negro wench hanged at Savannah la Mar today." A few years later he noted that "Stompe . . . was burnt alive this evening, and his wife (Dr. Frazier's Polly, a mulatto) was hanged." Just months later, he recorded, "as I was coming home [from Savannah la Mar] they were hanging two Rebel Negroes." On another occasion, a "stout Negro man . . . is gibbetted alive in the [Savannah la Mar] Square," hanged in an iron cage from a post and left to die of thirst and exposure.[189] An astonishing sketch of a double gibbet, one side empty, the other not, was completed in the 1760s by a European traveler to Jamaica (fig. 4.31). Among the most horrible executions recorded by Thistlewood was of the surviving mutinous Africans from Tacky's Rebellion in 1760. One slave, condemned to be burned alive, was "made to sit on the ground, and his body being chained to an iron stake, the fire was applied to his feet." Thistlewood was amazed as the man's courage: "he uttered not a groan, and saw his legs reduced to ashes with the utmost firmness and composure." Other slaves were simply hanged.[190] These public executions had an afterlife that marked the plantation landscape. In 1774, Thomas Thistlewood noted that "the head of Gold, the Rebel, carried to Leeward this evening, to be put up as a terror," a reminder to slaves of the consequences of rebellion.[191] In the early nineteenth century another sugar planter openly acknowledged "the necessity of terror to coerce . . . obedience."[192] Such terrors were not uncommon and were to be found along roadways and on plantations.[193] On one occasion, Lady Nugent reported that if she had not already promised her attendance at church, "I would not have gone, for we were obliged to pass close by the pole, on which was stuck the head of a black man who was executed a few days ago."[194] In another incident, the head of one of Thistlewood's slaves—a thief and a persistent runaway—was put on a pole and "stuck . . . in the home pasture."[195]

White male power was exacted in particular ways on enslaved women. The names of many of the female slaves at Good Hope suggest that their physical appearance was noticed by the white men who named them: Beauty, Grace, Venus, and Plaything.[196] As Trevor Burnard has demonstrated, planters and overseers raped female enslaved Africans as a mechanism of social control.[197] Thomas Thistlewood's diary records sexual activity with 138 women in his thirty-seven-year tenure in Jamaica. And while it is clear that Thistlewood had preferred sex partners, he was never monogamous. On numerous occasions, Thistlewood raped women as punishment for transgressions. While the extent to which his sexual predation was typical is uncertain, it is clear that he and many other men regularly preyed on enslaved women. His most frequent victims were his own slaves; not a single woman he owned escaped his advances save the very young and the very old. But the fact that he raped sixty-three slaves who were owned by others is evidence enough that planters

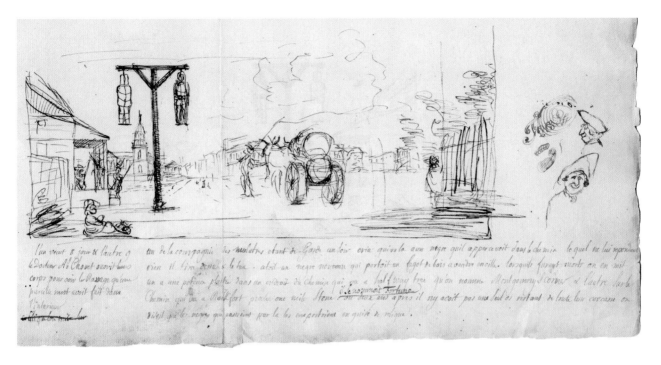

FIG. 4.31 Pierre Eugène du Simitière, untitled Jamaican scene, ca. 1760s. Ink on paper, 8 × 13 in. (20 × 30 cm). The gibbet is at the left in the image. The Library Company of Philadelphia.

and overseers felt free to prey on women for pleasure or discipline beyond those they owned.[198] The constant reality of rape meant that for enslaved women, the plantation became a landscape of fear in a way unknown by their male counterparts. Women fell victim to Thistlewood in the curing house, in the wash house, in cane fields, on the loading dock, on a hill overlooking the sea, on the garden bench, and in their own provision grounds.[199] In a 1751 account, Thistlewood reports having sex with Flora "among the canes." He likely happened upon her, as he indicates "she [had] been for water cress." He raped Ellin "in the garden" where just the day before she had been "weeding in the garden." Thistlewood even raped women in the houses of other slaves.[200] Like his assaults on Flora and Ellin, the vast majority of these attacks were unanticipated by the women who bore the brunt of his predations. In response, enslaved women surely navigated the plantation in a way that attended to this fear. Many who had been raped on the garden bench—one of Thistlewood's favorite spots—would surely have avoided the garden when they thought he might be present. Furthermore, those who undertook to leave their own plantation without permission risked rape if they were caught traveling illegally and alone.[201]

But over the course of the eighteenth century, the explicit violence to black bodies came under question. In 1781, for example, the Jamaican Assembly outlawed mutilation and dismemberment as forms of discipline.[202] While the degree of amelioration remains in question, the late eighteenth century brought increasing moral anxiety about corporal and capital punishment.[203] In the context of gradual and uneven moral uncertainty about torture, planters added a second mechanism to suppress slave resistance and to support the smooth operations of the plantation: surveillance. The capacity to see was from the beginning focused on spaces of labor, not the spaces of residence. In the 1752 *Art of Making Sugar,* for example, the author makes it clear that sugar should be planted in straight rows so as to better "inspect the negroes employed in weeding the canes, etc."[204] And slowly the person undertaking surveillance began to change. Most seventeenth- and early eighteenth-century planters in Jamaica oversaw their own plantations. Yet by the middle decades of the eighteenth century—not entirely disconnected from the rising numbers of Scottish immigrants—more planters began hiring overseers rather than doing that work themselves. Probate inventories of planters' houses from the first half of the century make occasional references to a

FIG. 4.32 George Robertson, "A View in the island of Jamaica, of Roaring River Estate, belonging to William Beckford Esqr: near Savannah la Marr." Engraving, 19.48 × 26.57 in. (49.5 × 67.5 cm). London, 1778. John Carter Brown Library at Brown University.

room given over specifically for use by an overseer.[205] But as their wealth increased, later eighteenth-century planters came to see themselves as country gentlemen, preferring to hire overseers to actually manage the day-to-day operations of the plantation. Inventories of plantations from the second half of the century replace the overseer's room with an overseer's house.[206] The introduction of the person of the overseer over the course of the eighteenth century foregrounded oversight—or surveillance—as central to plantation management.[207] And by extension the later eighteenth-century overseer's house not only symbolized white authority—as did the planter's great house— it also offered easy surveillance over the plantation.

Overseers' houses were commonly outfitted with piazzas, and while these features surely helped to mediate the heat, they also served to facilitate surveillance. Thomas Thistlewood's journal recorded in 1754 that his newly built overseer's house boasted both front and back

piazzas. Upon traveling to another plantation some years later, he notes that the overseer was keen to show him the view from his piazza.[208] But the view in question was surely not just the picturesque landscape; overseers and owners had a particular interest in the ability to survey the activity of the plantation, especially the ongoing labor in the sugar works. William Beckford's description of an overseer's house presumed the presence of "a front and a back piazza," spaces for comfortable viewing of the works (fig. 4.32).[209] The literal oversight and management of the plantation from the piazza was increasingly assisted through the use of timepieces, spyglasses, and telescopes. In 1754, Thistlewood had two of his slaves flogged for "meddling with my watch and telescope," both of which were kept on the piazza.[210] Overseers managed shifts by clock time as early as the early eighteenth century, well before similar regimes appeared in factories in England or on plantations in Virginia or South Carolina.[211] One late eighteenth-century visitor to a Jamaican sugar plantation recognized that the overseer took meticulous accounts of hours and recorded daily logbooks but that "he has no Clock, nothing but an Hour Glass to put the people to work by."[212] The precision of managerial timekeeping was remarkable in the absence of a watch or clock. In the 1788 probate inventory of John Lord's plantation, the only object listed at the overseer's house was "a spyglass," provided for the overseer to more fully execute his responsibilities.[213] Telescopes, or spyglasses, appear commonly alongside hourglasses in probate inventories of the period; by the second half of the eighteenth century they are ever-present on piazzas and balconies.[214] In his tour through Jamaica in 1823, Cynric Williams found himself sitting on a piazza disturbed by a commotion from the vicinity of the sugar works: "I looked through the spy glass (a very usual piece of furniture in every piazza) towards the quarter whence the noise of the whip appeared to come, and observed a black man laid on the ground, and two drivers flogging him."[215] The telescope allowed the overseer exceptional views into the workings of the plantation; the presence of a watch or hourglass allowed the imposition of time discipline over a process that depended heavily on careful timing.[216] A third object found on overseer's piazzas was the plantation plat. An inventory of one overseer's house, for example, included "an old plan of the estate" recorded "on the front piazza"; as Barry Higman has argued, the plantation plat became a significant management tool allowing overseers to "see" the plantation in entirely new ways.[217] Over the course of the eighteenth century, the piazza had become a convenient stage for surveillance.

One dimension of surveillance that played a critical role in control was the practice of ticketing and branding. Mid-eighteenth-century slaves, for example, were required to have a ticket of passage from their owner for travel beyond the bounds of their plantation. Trespass had its dangers: Thomas Thistlewood "set traps of nails in boards in the paths through the thatch against the Lime-Kiln provision ground"; in order to protect his own slaves, he "acquainted all my Negroes of them."[218] Many planters enlisted the watchful eyes of their peers in the collective surveillance of the enslaved through branding.[219] Thistlewood was so frustrated with one slave who made a persistent practice of running away that he branded her on the forehead, forever marking his ownership of her.[220] Early newspaper advertisements make clear that branding

was fairly common: "Anthony, a Mandingo, RS on right shoulder," or "York, a Coromantee, to Mrs. Slack, at Falmouth, the brand marks on his shoulders are illegible," or "Jack, a Congo, marked BL left shoulder."[221]

As surveillance became an increasing concern in Jamaica, some planters worked to extend this control to the architecture and organization of the slave village, but with very limited success. As suggested by the plat of Good Hope, the village there was an aggregate of small plots of land, each containing a single house separated from the next by a fence. There is no evidence of linear or orthogonal organization. Using plats as a data set, Higman has determined that only 22 percent of villages were organized in straight streets, with a concentration between 1790 and 1810.[222] In 1790 William Beckford noted the increasing tendency to build quarters in streets: "It is the custom now to have [quarters] built in straight lines, constructed with some degree of uniformity and strength, but totally divested of trees and shrubs."[223] The absence of trees and shrubs, so important to the slave yard gardens, allowed unobstructed sightlines. In his assessment of the slave village at Seville, Douglas Armstrong argues that the positioning of the street was oriented to "maximize planter surveillance and control."[224] While most Africans were free to locate their houses where they willed within their village, on some plantations they went into barracks or linearly aligned streets or rows of houses, especially in the decades following 1790.[225] Thus some Jamaican planters and overseers adopted planning strategies that were far more common on the American mainland than in the British Caribbean.[226] Yet, throughout the period of slavery in Jamaica, the organization of villages into streets remained the exception, not the norm.

Documentary evidence, though scant, suggests that slaves resisted their relocation from villages into linearly aligned streets or barracks. When John Baillie erected at Roehampton stone barracks that he believed "far superior . . . to the ordinary Negro house," his slaves "refused to occupy them, stating, that they were so much exposed to their neighbors, they did not like to let them know what they were doing on all occasions."[227] While planters might have directed the construction of streets or rows on sites devoid of large vegetation, allowing greater surveillance over those spaces, enslaved Africans fought back by building kitchens, sheds, and other buildings adjacent to their houses, disrupting the rigid linearity and restoring their privacy. Baillie would later write that although he built a slave village of houses uniform in size and shape, their occupants "got a fashion among them, and would not make fires in several of their houses; they spoiled my range by putting kitchens or outbuildings in front of some of them for themselves."[228] But careful assessment of topography suggests that planters were far more concerned with views over the sugar works than with the capacity to even see—not to mention see *into*—the slave village. As a result, surveillance as a strategy remained largely focused on the operations of the works and most Africans in Jamaica found themselves able to shape their own domestic spaces as they wished.

In sum, early planters very explicitly used sites of terror—whipping posts, cookhouses, garden benches—as mechanisms for controlling the enslaved majority. But planters and overseers increasingly subjected the plantation landscape to surveillance; the Jamaican overseer's house was explicitly a place of surveillance over a complex sequence of events that would result in astounding wealth for only a few. The overseer's house was the center of a complex machine that depended on the principles of institutional, industrial management so eloquently articulated by Michel Foucault in *Discipline and Punish*. The Jamaican overseer's house realizes the principles of surveillance that Foucault suggests are central to the formation of docile bodies necessary for modern industrial economies, a form of surveillance ultimately realized in Jeremy Bentham's 1790s panopticon, a circular prison.[229] Emergent mechanisms of time discipline and the making of docile bodies were central to the working of the panopticon and to the Jamaican plantation. But in many ways, the drive toward surveillance was undermined by the planters' primary concern not for the workforce but for the product, as they carefully surveyed the sugar works and generally ignored the village. Neither planter nor slave was ignorant of the fact that the plantation depended entirely on the coerced labor of the enslaved. Slaves exercised their own agency to resist their condition; blocking viewsheds with pigsties was only one of many strategies used to defend their privacy and thwart the eye of the overseer. They resisted by stealing their own labor as runaways, depending on the help of Obeah, sometimes even assaulting whites individually or in small groups. But resistance surfaced most clearly through outright rebellions, which consistently targeted the architectures of oppression; during insurrections whites watched as great houses burned.[230]

5   The Arts of Empire

To find Colbeck Castle, a visitor has to have a keen sense of direction and just a bit of faith. The final road to the site is little more than a long dirt path, fairly well removed from the paved roads and highways of the south coast. Approaching the ruin, the visitor gets the clear sense that this is no ordinary British colonial house. Four corner towers, each rising a full three stories, frame the large stone house while elegant double arcades range from tower to tower on all four elevations (fig. 5.1). Striking circular windows on the ground floor of the south towers—absent from the north towers—signal the south as the front elevation. Positioned on a slight rise above the vast expanses of St. Jago, Jamaica, an open plain of more than fifty thousand acres of rich alluvial flatlands in St. Catherine Parish, the ruin stands in the midst of a huge square terrace (fig. 5.2). For the American visitor used to visiting refined "Georgian" townhouses in Philadelphia or the grand plantation houses of early Virginia, or the English visitor accustomed to elegant country houses, this building is something entirely different. Colbeck is certainly distinctive, yet it is not an aberration. This remarkable building opens a window into a largely unexplored realm: the forms and meanings of elite architecture of

eighteenth-century Jamaica and their place in the shifting contours of the British Empire.

Mid-eighteenth-century Jamaica's elites were no bystanders in the colonial project, but powerful political players in Jamaica and in London. Among the most prominent Jamaican politicos was William Beckford, enormously wealthy from his family's Jamaican plantations, twice lord mayor of London, and very close friend and ally to William Pitt, later England's prime minister.[1] Beckford was a leader among a growing circle of powerful, Oxford-educated Jamaican elites, most of whom returned to Jamaica after their education. By the middle of the eighteenth century, the increasingly powerful Jamaican Assembly contested the local authority of the royal governor, the Governor's Council, and, by implication, the Crown.[2] The politically complicated contest of the 1760s Privilege Controversy pitted the assembly, asserting the authority of their own constitution, against the royal governor, William Lyttleton, who argued that local authority was subject to royal grace and that royal decrees overrode local statutes. Even though the governor dissolved three successive assemblies, the Jamaicans won the contest, leading to Lyttleton's removal and the appointment of a

FIG. 5.1 Colbeck Castle, St. Catherine Parish, Jamaica, third quarter eighteenth century.

Jamaican scion—and former member of the assembly—as lieutenant governor. As historian Jack Greene has argued, this political contest was evidence of the fervent view of Anglo-Jamaicans of their identity as Britons living "under a British constitution, with the same guarantees of government by consent and rule of law enjoyed by those in the home islands. . . . The astonishing intensity and determination with which Jamaicans articulated and defended this view," Greene continues, "was a measure of the extraordinary importance that they attached to that crucial feature of their identity."[3] They depended on friends and associates in powerful circles in London; their political work resulted in the affirmation of the authority of the Jamaican Assembly and the withdrawal of the royal governor from the island in 1766. "By the 1760s," Trevor Burnard tells us, Jamaicans "were at the pinnacle of their power within British politics."[4]

Recognizing their position as the most powerful players in Great Britain's colonies, Jamaican elites worked to reframe Britain's political geography.[5] The prevailing seventeenth-century view of empire, when the British colonies were in their infancy, generally understood "the plantations" as adjuncts to the British Empire, which resided first in England and by the early eighteenth century in the British Isles. But as historian David Armitage has recently argued, those boundaries expanded in the second quarter of the eighteenth century toward a pan-Atlantic understanding of the British Empire. In this collective view of the empire the colonies of mainland America, those in the Caribbean, and in some cases the forts and factories along the west coast of Africa were incorporated in an organic whole with England, Wales, Scotland, and Ireland. Central to this reframed empire, Armitage argues, was a collective British identity that coalesced a full generation after the Anglo-Scottish Union of 1707. Even more significantly, this reimagining of the empire was a political ideology forged in the colonies.[6]

Contingent with their identities as political leaders at the avant-garde of empire, elite Jamaicans actively worked to shed the identity of "colonial," preferring instead the identity of Briton in Jamaica, a subtle but to them important distinction.[7] Part of this identity was self-fashioning as refined British citizens. In addition to being rich and politically astute, Jamaican elites were also the most well-traveled Britons in the Americas. The *Dictionary of British and Irish Travelers in Italy, 1701–1800* records two Jamaicans on grand tour as early as the 1720s.[8] It records sons of thirteen other Jamaican families on grand tour in later decades, five in the 1740s, 1750s, or 1760s, four in the 1770s, and four more in the 1780s and early 1790s.[9] And there were surely many more who evaded notice. Over the course of the century, a majority of Jamaican sons who had been educated in England then traveled to the continent on grand tours, and thereafter moved frequently between Jamaica and Britain. Jamaicans were certainly citizens of the world, to adopt David Hancock's phrase.[10] But their work to shape the British Empire and their place therein was an ideology, and ideologies are both constructed and enacted.[11] Elite Jamaicans worked

to demonstrate themselves as worthy Britons by exploiting their transatlantic identities in undertaking monumental scholarly expeditions, building "gentleman's seats" worthy of their station, and translating the wild, dense growth of Jamaica's mountains and bush into an Anglo-tropical "picturesque" landscape. These were material acts of refinement employed to resist the violence and provincialism that so clearly marked Jamaica throughout the eighteenth century. Historians have been primarily concerned with the political and economic dimensions of elite Jamaican ideologies. This chapter argues that this same circle of men enlisted their wealth and refined aesthetic sense to demonstrate their role as British sophisticates, participants in a refined British citizenry. Jamaican elites would have been pleased to read of themselves in 1756, described as

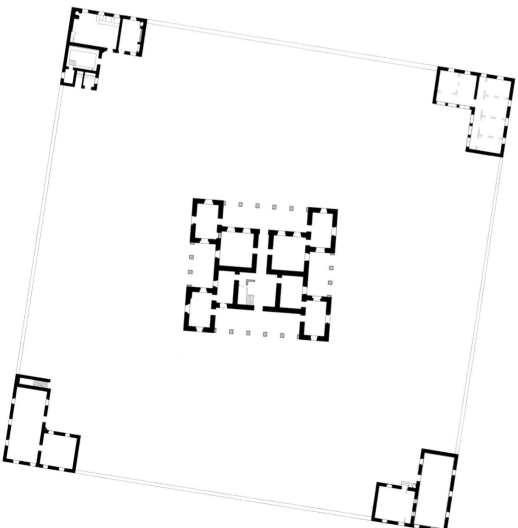

FIG. 5.2 Plan of Colbeck Castle terrace.

men of good taste, as much learning, and as well acquainted with the world, as may be met with in any part of Europe; nor is it uncommon to find those who (though never out of the Island) shine in many parts of life, with as much delicacy and judgement, as if they had been bred in the most polished courts.[12]

ARCHAEOLOGY

Unlike William Beckford, whose interests were generally toward political ends, Jamaican-born James Dawkins was a scholar whose archaeological expeditions positioned him at the center of British tastemakers. Dawkins was the eldest son of Henry Dawkins and Elizabeth Pennant Dawkins, daughter of Edward Pennant, chief justice of Jamaica. James was heir to an estate of twenty-five thousand acres, most of which was made up of plantations in Clarendon Parish on Jamaica's south coast.[13] After graduation from Oxford, Dawkins spent years traveling extensively on the continent, where he mingled with numerous Jacobites in exile and secured his identity among them.[14] From Rome in 1749, he organized a trip with an Oxford friend, John Bouverie, as one of the first serious archaeological explorations of the eastern Mediterranean.[15] As the principal heir of the family's Jamaican plantations, which yielded a gross income of £60,000 per annum, he was easily able to finance such an expedition.[16] Leaving Naples in the early summer of 1750, the expedition leader and patron was joined by Robert Wood, experienced traveler

and scholar of classicism, and Giovanni Borra, an architectural draftsman. In the preface to his later publications of the excursions, Wood reports to his readers that he agreed to accompany Dawkins because of his patron's "love of antiquities." They traveled on the *Matilda*, a ship fitted out in London with a full library including "all the Greek historians" and "other books of antiquities," mathematical instruments, and presents for the Turkish grandees who Dawkins expected would serve as local hosts.[17] The party toured the Aegean, the coast of Asia Minor, Egypt, and the Levant, places where "architecture had its origin," recording inscriptions and taking marbles with them "whenever it was possible." Architecture, however, "took up our chief attention."[18] By March 1751, they had traveled to Syria and visited the ancient ruins of Palmyra and Baalbek. After documenting those sites through carefully executed measurements, they left for Greece.

In June, the team arrived in Athens, where they joined James Stuart and Nicholas Revett, who by then had been at the project of documenting ancient Greek ruins for three months.[19] After a few days in Athens, Dawkins and Wood traveled with Stuart throughout the region, eventually returning to Athens for a thorough investigation of the ruins there; Stuart captured those investigations in his drawing, "James Stuart, James Dawkins, and Robert Wood at the Funerary Monument of Philopappos," eventually published in *Antiquities of Athens* (fig. 5.3). Leaving Stuart and Revett, the team returned to Naples in the summer

FIG. 5.3 Nicholas Revett, "James Stuart, James Dawkins, and Robert Wood at the Funerary Monument of Philopappos," from *Antiquities of Athens* (London: Printed by John Haberkorn, 1762). University of Virginia Special Collections.

of 1751. The voyage's journal suggests that Dawkins was not just a traveling patron but the expedition's leader, an engaged scholar, and passionate recorder of ancient sites.[20] Wood, in fact, reports that Dawkins was "so indefatigable in his attention to see everything done accurately, that there is scarce a measure in this work that he did not take himself."[21] As a result of their commitment to accurate documentation, Dawkins and Wood, together with the more well-recognized Stuart and Revett, laid a foundation for modern fieldwork in classical archaeology.[22]

Upon their return, Dawkins offered critical financial support to Robert Wood to support his publication of their findings, which ultimately appeared in both English and French as *The Ruins of Palmyra* in 1753 and *The Ruins of Baalbec* in 1757. Plates from these volumes made the critical step of representing the sites in their existing condition, simultaneously picturesque and unrestored. Offering the first systematic recordings of ancient classical ruins beyond the Italian peninsula by British or European scholars, both volumes included detailed architectural drawings of sites and remains that had been previously unknown in Britain or the Continent. Greatly expanding the West's understanding of ancient architecture, these books became the "quintessence of architectural taste."[23] The books established a model against which all later archaeological work would be compared; Robert Adam acknowledged as much in the introduction to his own treatise on Diocletian's Palace at Split (Spalato).[24] Their significance to eighteenth-century European neoclassicism cannot be overestimated.

While in the midst of these two projects, Dawkins also offered generous financial support to James Stuart and Nicholas Revett to complete and publish their work in Athens.[25] The two men returned to England in 1755 and lived for some time in Dawkin's London townhouse.[26] The lengthy list of subscribers at the beginning of the first volume of *Antiquities of Athens* names a few more generous individuals, those who purchased more than one set. Some subscribed for two "setts"; as evidence of his extraordinary support for the project, James Dawkins alone was listed as receiving "20 setts." And Dawkins was certainly connected with a Jamaican circle in London; the only two subscribers associated with Britain's colonies were two governors of Jamaica, William Lyttleton and Colonel Haldane. Both friend and patron to James Stuart, Dawkins appears to have purchased a large number of the gouaches painted by the artist in preparation

for the publication of *Antiquities*.[27] Like Wood's volumes, *Antiquities of Athens* had an enormous impact on English taste in the second half of the eighteenth century. These efforts earned Dawkins great renown and election as a Fellow of the Royal Society and nomination as a member of the exclusive Society of the Dilettanti.[28]

Upon his return to England in 1754, Dawkins—indicative of Anglo-Jamaicans abroad—established himself among the landed English gentry by purchasing a large estate in Southampton, and was that same year elected a Member of Parliament.[29] While in England, he developed a friendship with fellow-Jamaican and heir William Beckford.[30] By this time James Dawkins's younger brother Henry was also in England, having completed his own grand tour in 1750. Henry would eventually marry Lady Juliana Colyear, the daughter of the Earl of Portmore. Like his brother, Henry established himself among the English landed gentry by purchasing an English estate and like his brother was elected a Member of Parliament. Like the Beckfords, the Dawkins brothers understood themselves to be English landed gentry with significant interests in both England and Jamaica. They moved easily between both countries.

James Dawkins—the eldest of four brothers—had become the patriarch of the family when his father Henry died in 1744 (his younger brother William, who had remained on the island as the family representative, died in 1752 at the age of twenty-six).[31] In 1755, Dawkins planned a return trip to Jamaica and in preparation, he drafted a will. The most notable line of the will allows for £10,000 sterling, a lavish sum to be sure, to construct a new house on his Southampton estate, to be designed by his "good friends" James Stuart and Nicholas Revett.[32] Such a commission, had it been realized, would have resulted in the first country house fully designed in the new Greek taste. He also left £100 per annum to support Robert Wood. Finally, £500 was to be dedicated to the founding and support of an academy of painters, sculptors, and architects. Given the transatlantic identities of elite Jamaicans, Dawkins was among friends immediately upon his return to Jamaica. He likely visited his good friends Charles Price and Henry Moore soon after his arrival.[33] Price would soon be Speaker of the Jamaican Assembly, and Henry Moore would become governor.[34] And soon after his arrival Dawkins also demonstrated his commitment to his peerage and homeland by founding an academy for the instruction of "wealthy white sons."[35] But Dawkins

FIG. 5.4 Gavin Hamilton, *James Dawkins and Robert Woods Discovering the Ruins at Palmyra*, 1758. Oil on canvas, 122 × 153 in. (309.90 × 388.60 cm). National Gallery of Scotland.

survived in Jamaica only two years. He was buried at his family estate, Old plantation, in Clarendon Parish.[36] The world of ancient antiquarians mourned; no less than Johann Winkelmann proclaimed that his death was "a loss for the arts and sciences."[37] Soon after, Gavin Hamilton was commissioned to represent Wood and Dawkins's landmark expedition in paint (fig. 5.4). Evidence of Dawkins's impact on his home island appears most clearly on the 1765 Craskell and Simpson map of Jamaica, which identifies numerous plantations with names such as Aleppo, Palmyra, Parnassus, and others recalling locales documented by Jamaica's own traveler-scholar.[38] Dawkins, empowered by Jamaican sugar wealth to undertake extraordinary expeditions, played a definitive role in founding classical archaeology, and he had financially supported the publications that would transform British architecture. He was no provincial.

LANDSCAPE

Charles Price was a third-generation Jamaican who at the time of his death was the largest landowner in Jamaica.[39] His grandfather, Francis Price, had arrived on the island with Robert Venables as part of the English capture of Jamaica from the Spanish. As with most Jamaican sons, Price was educated at Oxford (Trinity College), after which he took a seven-year grand tour. On the continent from 1724 to 1730, Price was the first Jamaican recorded on grand tour. He returned to Jamaica and quickly entered politics. He was much admired as an orator and became a celebrated Speaker of the Jamaican Assembly, serving in 1745 and again from 1756 to 1763.[40] In the midst of that service, Price led the colonial assembly through a political maelstrom that pitted the island's planters and the assembly against Kingston's merchants and their champion, then Governor Knowles. Resolved in favor of the assembly, Price oversaw Knowles's departure from the governorship and his replacement by Henry Moore, also a planter (for his service to the island, Moore was elevated to baron after his service as governor in 1762).[41] Price's stature on the island was greatly enhanced in 1768 when he too was given the title of baron by King George III, signifying his elevation to a position many elites in Jamaica deeply desired: English nobility.[42]

Drawing on and exhibiting his wealth and his taste, Charles Price spent decades installing a truly impressive garden landscape that expressed the picturesque aesthetic at the Price family seat, called "The Decoy." The years during which Price had been in England and on the continent on grand tour witnessed a revolution in landscape design, the celebration of the picturesque mode. Price's friend, Edward Long, reported that The Decoy was "one of the greatest curiosities" of Jamaica. After briefly mentioning the house of wood, he continues by celebrating the "very

FIG. 5.5 Capability Brown, garden rotunda at Croome Court, Worcestershire, England, 1754–57.

elegant garden disposed in walks" shaded by coconut, cabbage, and sandbox trees. He continued by noting that the garden "is decorated, besides, with some pretty buildings." Foremost among these was "an octagonal saloon richly ornamented on the inside with lusters, and mirrors."[43] The "saloon" was probably not unlike the rotunda designed by Capability Brown and erected in the 1750s at Croome Court in Worcestershire (fig. 5.5). Long notes that the various trees in the prospect had been planted "dispersed in different parts to enliven the scene." Architectural follies were not uncommon in the gardens of Jamaica's planter elites; the garden of the house on New Seville was "prettily laid out; and decorated with a stone-temple, elegantly designed in the modern taste."[44] But not all gardens were in the picturesque manner; the Pinnocks' plantation, Richmond, boasted a large formal pleasure garden laid out in neat walks centered on a fountain and enlivened by a labyrinth.[45] Some others were experimental: "Gentlemen of the island [have introduced] exotic plants and trees from the East-Indian and American continents, . . . such kinds as have been most celebrated for their medicinal . . . qualities."[46]

While nothing of the garden landscape at The Decoy survives today, a view of a triumphal arch was captured in the sketchbook of a traveling artist. In the early 1760s, Swiss-born artist Pierre Eugène du Simitière spent two years in Jamaica and made a number of sketches of the landscape around him. His images include spectacular landscape views and urban scenes in Kingston.[47] The artist shows us a planter—likely Price—seated in a Windsor chair, contemplating the beauty of the landscape from under the shelter of an extraordinary garden folly in the form of a triumphal arch (fig. 5.6). The massive tripartite structure with flat-roofed sides flanking a raised arched centerpiece appears almost too spectacular to have been built in Jamaica in the eighteenth century. Yet, the verso of the painting has a lightly inscribed line: "Decoy, St. Mary, juin 1761." Surely a reference to the same structure, Edward Long also notes at The Decoy "a grand triumphal arch" at the end of a long walk, "from which the prospect extends over the fine cultivated vale of Bagnals, quite to the Northside sea." One material survival from the gardens at The Decoy—now relocated to a park in Port Maria—is a massive, fifteen-foot-tall marble column carried by a marble pedestal ornamented on each face with an allegorical representation of one of the four continents, surely a reference to Price's perception of himself as a man

FIG. 5.6 Pierre Eugène du Simitière, "Triumphal Arch at the Decoy," June, 1761. Private collection.

of at least the Atlantic, if not the world.[48] Charles Price chose to spend his leisure time and great wealth on a picturesque landscape, complete with follies, columnar monuments, garden saloons or pavilions, and a triumphal arch.

The picturesque was an eighteenth-century visual and linguistic aesthetic that understood real landscapes, especially those revealing presumed natural irregularity—and paintings of such landscapes—as compositionally beautiful. But the picturesque had political implications as well; historians of the English picturesque garden have rightly linked the rise of that garden tradition to the process of land enclosure.[49] Enclosure and privatization of common fields and the aggregation of smaller farms allowed larger landowners to remove productivity to the fringes of properties, opening up acreage immediately around country houses for aesthetic landscapes. Furthermore, the laboring classes were incorporated into the aesthetic; essential to the picturesque was the "delightful" irregularity of the

view together with the animation of the scene by peasants, invariably cast as happy and productive. The rise of the picturesque tradition in Jamaica built on these cultural and political tactics but included as well the cultural responsibility of the picturesque to civilize the wilderness. The establishment of gardens began with the imposition of order through cartography, as discussed in the previous chapter. But once the land was known, it could be subdivided into productive and aesthetic plots; the great expanse of Jamaica's largest plantations and the diversity of its landscape offered an abundant resource for Jamaican elites to enact what in their view were the civilizing and refining powers of the picturesque.

Jamaica's landscapes were also the stage for the maturing science of botany. London surgeon Dr. Anthony Robertson, supported by the London-based Society of Arts, spent more than a decade studying the island's natural history in the late 1750s and early 1760s. James Wiles, one of the gardeners from Captain William Bligh's second voyage, stayed on in Jamaica as a curator of a botanical garden where specimens from the voyage were cultivated. England-trained physician William Weston spent years in Jamaica documenting the island's plant species and sending specimens back to the motherland; he maintained a lengthy correspondence with British naturalists and published a paper on his research in the Transactions of the American Philosophical Society. Readers will remember from the previous chapter that Thomas Thistlewood cultivated an expansive garden, which for many enslaved women was a regular site of rape. In that same garden, Thistlewood experimented with new plants, working literally to implant Jamaica with British cultivars. And he was not alone; agricultural and botanical experimentation was widespread across the eighteenth-century Jamaican landscape. As Jill Casid reminds readers in *Sowing Empire*, the cultivation of a colonial garden was a stage for scientific experimentation but even more a platform for colonial authority over exotic landscapes.[50]

The newness of the Jamaican landscape also allowed the wealthiest to purchase landmark sites for personal enjoyment. Much like Thomas Jefferson's much later purchase of Natural Bridge, Price purchased a site of natural grandeur in the hopes of preserving it for elite pleasure. The object of his affection was the cascade of the White River, which was described by Edward Long as "grand and sublime. The fall is said to exceed in grandeur that of Tivoli, or any other in Europe, though much inferior to that of Niagara." Long continues by reporting that Price found it so beautiful that he "would not suffer the least alterations to be made to it." In order to more perfectly enjoy the site, however, Price "formed a club of gentlemen, and built a range of apartments on a pretty lawn just fronting the cascade," where they met for a few weeks each year to engage in pigeon hunting.[51] Price's probate inventory suggests that the house at The Decoy included a hall and bedchambers, all well furnished but not luxurious. The only distinguishing feature was the collection of forty-eight prints and landscapes that hung on the walls of his hall.[52] Price was clearly enamored with the aesthetic power of landscape. While remarkable in number, the fact of landscape prints was not; John Gale, a wealthy planter who died in 1750, had hanging on the walls of his hall "15 views of Stow Gardens."[53] It was surely in the spirit of this tradition of landscape painting that Price hired du Simitière to undertake "An exact representation

of the Cascade at the White River" which he had the artist inscribe as a gift for King George from "His Humble Servant, Charles Price." Charles Price spent much of his leisure time investing in the remaking and representation of Jamaica's landscape, simultaneously taming it and incorporating it into the empire.

It is clear that Price used his garden in a manner similar to that intended for contemporary gardens in England. Long tells us that Price was "extremely attached to this place and spent much of his time here, making it the abode of cheerfulness and hospitality." Long described it as "the temple of social enjoyments," writing that it was "constantly open to the reception of worthy men . . . and few gentlemen of rank . . . quitted this island without having passed some of their time at Decoy."[54] Price's death in 1772 was mourned by many but by few as much as his son, also Charles Price, who erected a grand monument carrying an inscription to his father's memory. The younger Price also penned a poem entitled "The Decoy" dedicated to his father; its first two stanzas evoked the idea of a haven:

> To dust and suffocating heats,
> Well pleas'd, we bade adue;
> To taste your garden's rural sweets,
> And pay respects to you.
>
> Peace to this calm, sequester'd seat,
> Where art and nature vie,
> To decorate your lov'd retreat,
> And charm the mental eye.[55]

Drafted by a son who was raised in this emotive, picturesque landscape, Price the younger surely understood the dialogue between art and nature that his father presumed would create a place of leisured repose. Planter, politician, and landscape enthusiast, Price played a significant role in translating an English garden aesthetic to the tropical context of the Caribbean and in enlisting that landscape as a space—for a very privileged minority—of repose, quietude, and healing, much in the English fashion. In the simultaneous realities of two landscapes in Jamaica—the relentless press of sugar production with its terrible toll on human life and limb and the escapist sentimentality central to these picturesque gardens—the astonishing contrast only amplifies the searing truth of early capitalist systems. As one space of production afforded the second space of repose, so, too, did the space of repose provide psychological escape from the first; the adjacency of these landscapes exposes the symbiosis of capitalist exploitation.

Through the course of the eighteenth century, British planters in Jamaica worked tirelessly to transform the wilderness of tropical Jamaica into a refined Anglo-Jamaican paradise—most, like Price, through the installation of picturesque gardens.[56] Others, like Thistlewood, commanded authority over the landscape through botanical experimentation. But a few tamed the jungle through words. Edward Long was born in Cornwall, England, in 1734, the second son of an Englishman who owned Jamaican plantations and properties in Cornwall and London.[57] The Longs had been substantial planters in Jamaica since the late seventeenth century. In 1757, at the age of twenty-three, Long traveled to Jamaica for the first time and soon thereafter married Mary Ballard Beckford, a wealthy heiress of the Beckford family.[58] After his arrival, his elder brother conveyed to him some plantation property, most importantly Lucky Valley Estate, which lay immediately adjacent to Friendship, a Dawkins plantation in Clarendon Parish.[59] (Long's plat of Lucky Valley figures in the argument of the previous chapter.) Long's sister Catherine Maria was wife to Henry Moore, governor of Jamaica upon Long's arrival.[60] By marriage and physical proximity Edward Long was intimately connected to Jamaica's most important planter families.

But Long was not just a planter. He remained on the island for twelve years, serving in the Jamaican Assembly from 1761, briefly as Speaker of the Assembly in 1764. He was also a critical figure in the Privilege Controversy. In 1764, Long conspired with Thomas Fearon and a few others to draft an address to the Crown to assert the privileges of the Jamaican Assembly and to request that the king check the governor's "arbitrary exercise of power as chancellor."[61] Both as a member and Speaker and then as one of the clearest agitators in the Privilege Controversy, Long was intimately involved in the defense of the power and authority of the Jamaican Assembly. But in 1769, due to deteriorating health, he left the island never to return. In his final years in Jamaica, Long must have been busy taking extensive notes; in 1774 he published his monumental *History of Jamaica, or General Survey of the Antient and Modern State of that Island*, a richly detailed three-volume treatise on the island's political, cultural, economic, and natural history.

While Long's *History* has been a source for scholars on a range of topics from colonial politics to natural history

to slavery—he has been described as "the father of English racism"—he is also rightly noted as a keen observer and describer of the Jamaican landscape.[62] In remarkable passages, Long describes Jamaica's most spectacular natural sites. The island's extensive limestone deposits created, over millennia, deep caverns explored by some but first described by Long.[63] Not surprisingly, his narratives of these spaces engage the sublime. He describes the mouth of one cave as "extremely Gothic in appearance," with two arched entrances that looked like "ancient doorways . . . sunk by time or accident to within two feet of their lintels." And there he begins his imagining of the cave as an ancient cathedral with a "niche about four feet in height . . . which might as well be supposed intended for the reception of a madonna," below which was a "proper reservoir for holy water." Upon entering he was struck by the appearance of the "stalactic and sparry matter" that glistened and "reflected the most rich and splendid appearance imaginable." The chamber's roof was supported by columns and the whole appeared to be "in the true Gothic taste." The cathedral was even inhabited by a feature in the form of "a venerable old hermit, sitting in profound meditation, wrapped in a flowing robe, his arms folded, and a beard descending to his waist." After providing the hermit with facial features in chalk, Long's party descended into the labyrinth before them, expecting "no less, at every turn, than to pop upon Cerberus, or some other horrid inhabitant of Pluto's dominion." They continued nearly a quarter mile, inspecting the various "cloysters and apartments" as they progressed. "The famous Cretan labyrinth did not," Long assures his readers, "contain half the turns and windings which branch through every part of this infernal wilderness."[64] After exploration, Long emerged successfully, evidently surpassing the heroism of Theseus, ready to transcribe his view of Jamaica's subterranean landscape.

If the island offered the sublime, it also proffered places of healing. The "salutary virtues" of the hot spring waters at Bath, Jamaica, had been known to settlers since the late seventeenth century, having famously healed Governor William Beeston. The road to the spring was (and remains) not easily accessible; travel by carriage was up a mountain pass "from one side of which, the eye is terrified by the view of a river foaming several hundred feet below," with a "lofty precipice of solid rock" on the other. The spring issues forth in the midst of an extraordinary pool deep enough for swimming and surrounded by dense vegetation. Long reports that the best manner

FIG. 5.7 Pierre Eugène du Simitière, "A View of the Houses at Bath," early 1760s. Private collection.

to take the waters is to stand about three feet from the fissure from which they erupt "and receive it immediately from the hand of the drawer" in quantities of about a half-pint. The water is "naturally light" and "sparkles when received in the glass." Upon consumption, it "diffuses a thrilling glow over the whole body." The benefits of the waters were many: correcting capillary obstructions and disorders of the breasts; restoring appetites and the natural actions of the bowels; invigorating circulation; strengthening the nerves; and always allowing "an easy sleep at night."[65] Ignoring the difficulty of access, elite Jamaicans made the journey to the salubrious spot throughout the eighteenth century, so much so that by the 1760s a number of houses had been erected near the spring to accommodate visitors (fig. 5.7). Demonstrating the tight interrelationships of this small group of elites, Edward Long's friend Charles Price had served as a commissioner for the 1747 construction of a bathhouse at the site.[66]

Grottos and healing hot springs were among the more extraordinary sites in Jamaica but Long reserved his highest praise for the island's picturesque landscapes. In one passage, he describes a villa overlooking "a diminutive vale,"

> through which the high road passes, and extends its narrow prospect to another delightful, rising spot, of a circular form, and fringed with stately trees. A number of kids, lambs, and sheep, are pastured in the glade, or roam on the sides of the adjacent hills, which are fenced in with a wall of craggy mountains, richly cloathed with wood. In rural charms few places exceed this little spot.[67]

In another passage Long describes a scene one side of which "is girt about with romantic hills and woods; the other . . . is washed by the sea; the middle sweep is graced with scattered clumps of trees and underwood"; he explicitly identifies the view as "very picturesque and beautiful," connecting his passages to contemporary landscape theory.[68] While this is not atypical of the types of descriptive material offered in travel accounts from this period, it is notable that Long's *History* includes such passages so soon after the 1768 publication of William Gilpin's *Essay on Prints,* which broadly articulated the principles of the picturesque.[69]

In one passage, worthy of quoting in full, Long essentially defines and demonstrates the picturesque in Jamaica:

> Not far is Orange Cove . . . beautiful beyond description. So various, so picturesque, and so admirably fine, is the combination of all the detail which unites in forming this landscape; and the whole so nicely interwoven and disposed; that it seems almost impossible for either painter or historian to give anything like a faithful sketch of it. Here has nature exerted all her plastic powers, in laying out and arranging the groundwork; and art has likewise put forth her whole skill, in vying with or assisting her in the machinery, composed of a thousand decorations. Wherever the passing eye delights to wander, it meets with a succession of objects, throughout an extent of many miles, equally new, striking, and lively. In one division is seen a wide plain, richly carpeted with canes of the emerald tint, differently shaded, and striped with fringes of logwood, or penguin-fense, or, instead of this border, with rills of crystal water. In another rises a high-swelling lawn, smooth and fertile, whose gently sloping bosom is embellished with herds and flocks, and whose summit is crowned with Negroe-villages, or clumps of graceful trees. Here, on a neighboring hill, is a windmill in motion; boiling houses, and other plantation buildings, at the foot: there in the various duties which cultivation excites are labourers, cattle, and carriages; all briskly employed. In addition to these animated scenes is a boundless prospect of the sea which skirts the distant horizon toward the North; and, on the other hand, a wood-capped battlement of hills, that shuts in the Southern view.[70]

At Orange Cove, Long would have us see, a viewer could take in the very best of a picturesque view graced with windmills and other necessities of rural, agricultural life and animated by brisk and productive "laborers." Jamaica was a long way from England, but given a shared vocabulary, Long implied, the Caribbean island was simply an exotic extension of the other. Art historians have recently come to understand the picturesque as a metropolitan mechanism for taming exotic or unruly landscapes, first the Lake District, then Scotland and Wales. Long's dissertations on the Jamaican landscape make clear that it, too, was a landscape tamed by British "civility," a place worthy of empire.[71]

Among the most affecting passages from Long's discussions of landscapes are his descriptions of The Decoy, which included the notations "very elegant garden disposed in walks"; "flower and kitchen-garden filled with the most beautiful varieties"; and "clumps of graceful cabbage trees dispersed in different parts, to enliven the scene." All this in what had just years before been "a gloomy wilderness."[72] Through his mastery of the arts of landscape design, Price had civilized Jamaica. Edward Long's *History*, and by extension his passages on the picturesque, were well read across Jamaica; even Thomas Thistlewood noted that he had purchased and read the *History*.[73] Long was followed by the illegitimate William Beckford (cousin of Lord Mayor Beckford), who included in his 1790 treatise *A Descriptive Account of the Island of Jamaica* numerous descriptions of picturesque scenes on the island.[74] In some part catalyzed by these descriptions, later eighteenth- and early nineteenth-century Jamaicans were flush with language of the beautiful, the picturesque, and the sublime. Houses advertised for sale in the newspapers were celebrated as having "commanding extensive and beautiful prospects."[75] The houses of African laborers were consistently described in a manner similar to the words of Lady Nugent, wife of the governor, in the opening years of the nineteenth century: "little huts up the sides of the hills, each having a piazza in front, and a little garden, looking really picturesque."[76] One Scottish traveler to Jamaica described a house and site in the Blue Mountains as "without any exceptions the most romantic place I have seen." He continued by exclaiming: "The sublime grandeur of the lofty Blue Mountains whose aspiring summits seem to invade the regions of the ether towers in majestic grandeur over the mountain the cottage is built on; luxuriant scenery everywhere courts the eye of the traveler."[77] English colonials had enlisted follies, prospects, and descriptions to transform the wildness of the Jamaican landscape into the stuff of the picturesque, the beautiful, and the sublime; the picturesque aesthetic had conquered, tamed, and incorporated the tropics into the British Empire.

ARCHITECTURE

Edward Long also turned his pen to the subject of architecture, noting that only in the decade or so before the publication of his volume (1774) had Jamaican planters attended to sophisticated architecture:

> It is but of late, that the planters have paid much attention to elegance in their habitations: their general rule was, to build what they called a make-shift; so that it was not unusual to see a plantation adorned with a very expensive set of works, of brick or stone, well executed; and the owner residing in a miserable, thatched hovel, hastily put together with wattles and plaister, damp, unwholesome, and infested with every species of vermin. But the houses in general, as well in the country-parts as in the towns, have been greatly improved within these last twenty years. The furniture of some of them is extremely costly; and others constructed in so magnificent a style, and of such durable materials, as to shew that they were not intended for a mere temporary residence.[78]

Certainly before the 1760s, any planter returning to Jamaica from an English education must have been dismayed at the poor quality of the architecture on their island, Kingston excepted. While the rest of the island was littered with small planters' houses, Lord Adam Gordon described Kingston as a "very considerable Town . . . large and very well Inhabited with many Sumptuous houses, with Gardens and Offices in Proportion."[79] Over the course of the first half of the century, the island's major port had grown to become one of Britain's most important colonial trading centers. The town enjoyed spectacular economic prosperity in the 1730s and 1740s, and by the 1750s Kingston was a large, booming port city with seemingly unbounded economic energy.[80] Certainly the grandest houses on the island in the early decades of the century were those of Kingston's merchants.[81]

Two remarkable examples of such houses were used as illustrations on a mid-1740s map of the city. The most striking is "the House of Robert Turner, Esq.," a one-story house on a raised basement that is defined at each end by two-story towers rising higher than the house and sheltered by independent roofs (see fig. 2.18). Smaller but not unlike Colbeck Castle, the Turner house has distinctive circular windows that open through the ground-floor level of each tower and a grand, classically ornamented gallery connecting the two towers across the face of the house. With a tall balustrade, the roof was accessible. Robert Turner's 1743 will reveals him to have been an important factor for the South Sea Company.[82] A codicil to his will dated July 1743 mentions specifically the construction of "a new dwelling house" which he directs to be completed if he should die before finishing it. As a sign of his prominence in the city, Turner was buried in the chancel of the Kingston Parish church.

A second, spectacular house was that of Kingston merchant Alexander MacFarlane. This two-story house was related in form to Turner's but instead of independently roofed towers, MacFarlane's house had two projecting end pavilions and a recessed center all under a single roof (fig. 5.8). The continuation of a railing across the entirety of the upper floor suggests the possibility of a gallery across that entire front. The dark shading of the middle three bays, however, clearly refers to a deeply recessed center and a gallery with decking supported by swelling vase-like posts. A roof balustrade betrays MacFarlane's rooftop access, which would have been essential to accommodate the use of his extensive collection of astronomical equipment. This view also reveals a front garden and corner buildings and a fence along the street, signaling that the house sat back from the street by some distance. MacFarlane was described as an "ingenious and learned mathematician"; he fitted up his house as an observatory, and his election as a Fellow of the Royal Society in 1747 attests to his prowess as an astronomer.[83] He was also an occasional representative to the colonial assembly.[84] MacFarlane's will demonstrates that he had numerous Scottish contacts, many of whom were beneficiaries; the University of Glasgow received all of his telescopes and other astronomical and mathematical instruments.[85]

The only surviving example of a mansion house built by a Kingston merchant is Thomas Hibbert's residence on Duke Street, the building that concluded our opening chapter (see fig. 1.20). Completed by 1755, the first phase of construction included a house core with a most unusual plan including a large front chamber flanked by very small offices and a range of rear chambers, the center of which is a grand stairhall (see fig. 1.23). The plan of the upper floor mirrors that of the lower with the exception that

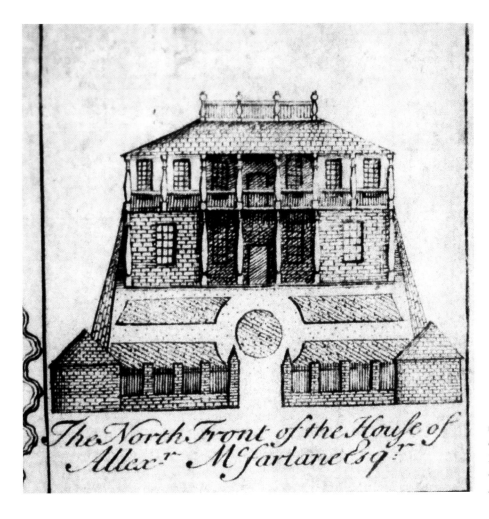

FIG. 5.8 "The North Front of the House of Allexr Mcfarlane, Esqr." Detail from Michael Hay, plan of Kingston, ca. 1745. Ink on paper, 13 × 16 in. (33 × 41 cm). Library of Congress.

FIG. 5.9 Interior of Thomas Hibbert House, ground-floor archway and stair beyond.

the front chamber upstairs boasts a soaring tray-vaulted ceiling. Careful investigation of the foundations suggests that the front and rear piazzas were certainly added in a second building campaign, but that might have happened very soon upon the completion of the building core. Outfitted in mahogany throughout, from stair details to flooring, the interior of the house is rich and sumptuous (fig. 5.9).

But the most extraordinary house in Kingston—or more properly in the Kingston suburbs—was the great house erected just outside the city by Phillip Pinnock, another important Kingston merchant.[86] Pinnock's prominence is attested to by his membership as one of the founding members of the Jamaican Association, a collection of eleven of Jamaica's most powerful planters and merchants. This association was gathered together in

1751 as a self-appointed cabinet to advise then Governor Trelawny on issues of internal governance or judicial proceedings. While the association was generally representative of the legally instituted Jamaican Assembly, it had absolutely no legal status, suggesting the remarkable political confidence of Pinnock and other Jamaican elites.[87] Pinnock would later serve as Speaker of the Jamaican Assembly in 1768 and again in 1775.

Pinnock's suburban villa appears in a small detail of a Du Simitière sketch of the plains of Half-Way Tree, likely taken from the tower of St. Andrew's Church in that parish.[88] Almost dropped off the page, had the artist cropped the image differently, the Italian villa stands remade for the Jamaican landscape (fig. 5.10). In his cipher book, Du Simitière reports producing this series of views from and around Pinnock's house outside Kingston.[89] In his *History of Jamaica,* Edward Long reports that the "chief ornament" of Half-Way Tree "is a very magnificent house, erected here a few years since by Mr. Pinnock." In Long's assessment, it vies "in the elegance of design, and excellence of workmanship, with many of the best country seats in England." Long asserted that the stone from the Hope River was "far more beautiful" than Portland stone.[90] Those invited inside would be delighted by the "mahogany work and ornaments," which exhibited "singular beauty." But if its appearance was striking to the average passerby, only a gentleman might recognize the building's inspiration.

Pinnock's house reimagined a mid-1560s villa design by late Renaissance architect Andrea Palladio. The front

elevation and ground-floor plan of the Italian architect's designs for a grand house for Venetian Gianfrancesco Valmarana had been published as Plate XLII in his *Four Books of Architecture* (fig. 5.11). In his description of the house, Palladio notes that the house has four towers "in the angles of the house."[91] Palladio describes the loggias, which span double height between the corner towers across the front and rear, as being of the Ionic order. As revealed in the elevation, the ground floors of the front towers have tall, arched openings and the roof is ornamented with classical figures. All of these same features appear also in the Du Simitière sketch: corner towers with a double height portico between, arched openings on the ground floor of the towers, and prominent roof ornaments. Emulating Palladio's villas, of course, was a popular pursuit among England's landed gentry; Chiswick House and Mereworth are but two examples. In directly emulating a Palladian model, Pinnock aligned himself not only with his elite Jamaican peers but, more importantly, with his English peers, among whom he presumed membership. Sadly, Pinnock appears to have overreached. A notice in the *Royal Gazette* for March 20, 1786, announced that "that spacious and elegant mansion near Half-Way Tree, built by the Hon Phillip Pinnock, Esq., deceased, and which is supposed to have stood him upward of £25,000 has lately been purchased at a very low rate and is now taking down for the purpose of sending the materials off the island."[92]

Into the 1750s, Jamaica's merchants appear to have outpaced their planter friends in elegance of architecture.

FIG. 5.10 Detail of Pierre Eugène du Simitière, "View in the Island of Jamaica," early 1760s. Private collection.

Writing in the 1770s, Jamaican historian Edward Long asserted that generations of planters in Jamaica had lived in makeshift houses, expending most of their resources on their sugar works. A rare exception was Drax Hall, that family seat erected in the remote parish of St. Ann by the Barbados-derived Drax family. In 1742, James Knight described Drax Hall as "the best and compleatest House in the Island."[93] Even so, the house was a fairly simple two-story pile five bays wide and three bays deep. If Kingston's merchants were building elegant and fashionable houses in Kingston in the 1740s, very few planters followed suit. But as Edward Long argued, the 1750s and 1760s had seen planters' houses "greatly improved," many of them constructed in magnificent style. One of these was surely that of Andrew Archedekne, whose stone house was built according to plans he obtained during his Italian grand tour.[94] In 1776, Englishman William Hickey visited Jamaica, where he was entertained at the house of Dr. Bonynge at Bushy Park in St. Dorothy Parish, which he described as having "the grandeur about it of a palace," with "a noble portico at the head of a large flight of stone steps that led to the principal entrance." He also stayed at the St. Ann plantation house of Robert Richards:

> This mansion . . . being of the best masonry, [is] built in the modern style of architecture, and had the advantage of two stories. The furniture was neat and handsome. Mr. Richards told me it had been planned and erected under the particular direction of his first lady, who, from her partiality to the spot, resided there the

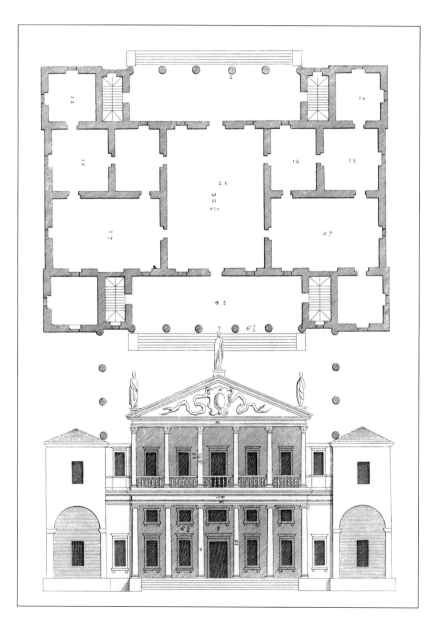

FIG. 5.11 "Villa Valmarana," from Andrea Palladio, *Four Books of Architecture* (London: Printed for R. Ware, at the Bible and Sun, on Ludgate-Hill, 1738). University of Virginia Special Collections.

greater part of the year. . . . Adjoining the house was a spacious and admirable garden, both kitchen and pleasure, so well laid out that it would not have disgraced a gentleman's seat in England.[95]

As can be seen in these examples, the middle decades of the century mark a veritable revolution in plantation great house architecture on the island.

Thomas Fearon served as the chief justice of the island from 1756 to 1764—longer than any other eighteenth-century chief justice—and as Speaker of the Jamaican Assembly in 1764.[96] Fearon was so well respected by his peers that one described him as possessing talents "so extraordinary, that it is almost impossible for the most impartial pen to do justice to them." Although he never traveled overseas, he claimed a "more comprehensive and accurate knowledge of places, persons, and things, in Great-Britain, Europe, and . . . throughout the known world, than most other gentlemen, who have had the opportunities of being personally acquainted with them." Through his personal study, he was esteemed "among the first ornaments of this country."[97]

Fearon had long occupied a typical plantation house in Clarendon unworthy of notice. Yet in his description of Thomas Fearon's seat, contemporary Edward Long mentioned that from this house one could see innumerable "beauties of nature." One prospect offered a "long wavy [vista] adorned with the lively verdure of canes, interspersed with wind-mills and other buildings." Another view presented "pasture-land, dotted with cattle and sheep, and watered with rivulets." Yet a third brought to the eye the slave village, where "peace and plenty hold their rein."[98] Yet very near to this older house, Fearon had more recently (presumably in the 1760s) erected a new mansion "of more modern and elegant construction." The villa boasted a huge hall fifty feet in length, twenty in width, and twelve feet tall, entered through a Tuscan portico of twelve or fifteen feet square. Opposite the portico, another door opened onto a rear gallery that offered a view "along an avenue between two gently rising woods, that have a solemn and silent grandeur."[99] At the height of his career, the island's chief justice and most respected scholar had built for himself a modern house in the most elegant fashion situated in the midst of one of the island's most picturesque settings.

But a revolution in Jamaican architecture was most clearly imagined by planter John Blagrove. In 1756, at the age of three, Blagrove (1752–1824) inherited a vast

Jamaican sugar fortune, including the five plantations of Orange Valley, Unity, Pembroke, Magotty, and Cardiff Hall.[100] By the early 1770s, he had traveled to England to study at Eton and Trinity College, Oxford. Like so many before him he undertook a lengthy grand tour of the continent, including Venice, Siena, Rome, and Paris.[101] Upon his return to Jamaica in 1777, he married Anne Shakespear; the couple took up residence at his family's seat at Cardiff Hall and within a decade he was a member of the Jamaican Assembly. In 1805, Blagrove removed to England and purchased and rebuilt Ankerwycke House in Wraysbury, Buckinghamshire.[102] He later purchased Great Abshott House in Titchfield, Hampshire, as a second residence. He apparently remained in England until his death.

John Blagrove had a keen interest in the subject of architecture. In 1776, while on grand tour in Paris, he commissioned French architect M. D'Albaret to produce an architectural pattern book of newly designed houses well suited to hot climates, more particularly in the West Indies. The book was available in London bookshops by December 1776.[103] The introductory passages of the pattern book make it clear that the designs contained therein depend extensively on advice from D'Albaret's patron, the "English gentleman," Mr. Blagrove. D'Albaret was "encouraged by an enlightened enthusiast, who himself shed considerable light for me on the subject of air temperature and the materials that one can safely use in that climate." This was especially important since, in D'Albaret's words, the country intended to receive these houses was "unknown to me."[104]

The designs are astonishing; the volume includes plans, elevations, and sections for a total of nine villas as well as a discussion of materials and techniques for building in the tropics. While the elevations of the designs are quintessentially late eighteenth-century French, and unlike anything actually realized in Jamaica, the plans of the buildings very directly reveal Blagrove's hand. A plan not unlike two major houses erected in Jamaica in the 1760s, Hibbert House in Kingston and Rose Hall on the north coast in St. James Parish, is seen in D'Albaret's plate XIII (fig. 5.12; compare fig. 1.20). Both of the Jamaican houses were originally graced with double piazzas along the front that return partway down the sides. And while there are certainly some differences, the French architect's design is fairly close in its form with these two newly erected buildings on the island. This comparison is reinforced by the architect's statement that the idea for this design was

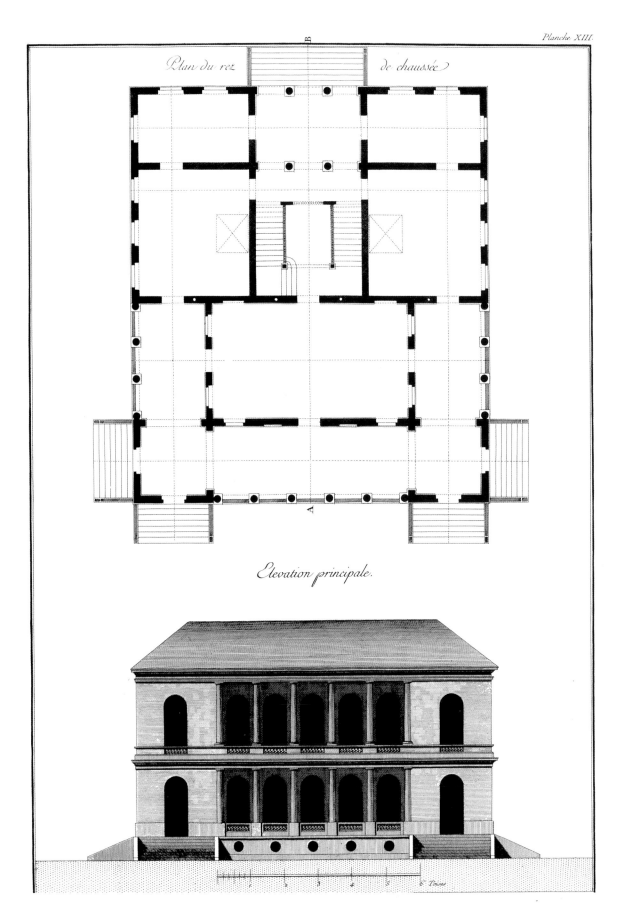

Plan du rez   de chaussée

Elevation principale.

FIG. 5.12 M. D'Albaret, *Différents projets relatifs au climat et à la manière la plus convenable de bâtir dans les pays chauds, et plus particulièrement dans les Indes occidentales* (Paris, 1776), Plate XIII. University of Maryland Library.

"provided by the Amateur," meaning Mr. Blagrove. It seems likely that Blagrove was thinking about known Jamaican houses when offering to D'Albaret the idea for the design.

But even when D'Albaret does not make such explicit reference, it does seem likely that Blagrove provided architectural references. For one design intended for a remote site far removed from neighbors, the architect designed a house with four corner pavilions graced with Venetian windows (see fig. 2.14). In a curious correspondence, the design emulates fairly closely that of Phillip Pinnock's two-story mansion on Richmond, his St. Ann estate, described by Edward Long: "At the four angles are pavilions, with Venetian windows corresponding to each other."[105] Plate XV presents a house with four strong corner towers, each independently roofed and connected to one another via loggias (fig. 5.13). This design is one of the book's most striking, and it is the second occasion where the architect gives credit for the design to his patron. In fact, Blagrove's interest in this design was so particular that the architect noted that he "was even able to have it constructed for him as a model about two years ago."[106] While the finished elevation is far more French than English, it is clear that the plan was closely modeled on Jamaican buildings like the house of Robert Turner in Kingston, or more obviously, Colbeck Castle. Suggested by Blagrove to D'Albaret, the presence of corner towers on this design amplifies the prominence of such features on houses in Jamaica. But the dependence of this particular design on recent Jamaican architecture goes even further. As represented in both plan and in section, the building's grand central hall was a large space dominated by a range of columns stepping out from the walls on all four sides. This space was described by Lady Nugent as an "Egyptian hall," a room type first described by the Roman architect Vitruvius but popularized by Andrea Palladio in text and image in his *Four Books of Architecture*. Palladio picked out the Egyptian hall as a space offering "admirable magnificence" for balls and assemblies. An Egyptian hall, according to Palladio, was a double-story height ringed by a march of columns below and a balcony or gallery above.[107] The design by D'Albaret is only one story in height.

There was only one other such space designed for a colonial building, a space recently designed for the King's House in Spanish Town. Edward Long described the "great saloon, or hall of audience," of King's House as well proportioned, measuring seventy-three feet long, thirty

feet wide and thirty-two feet high. As viewed from the north, or entrance, end of the room, a full range of seven giant Doric columns marched down the west side and a full Doric cornice ringed the entire room. The columns carried a balcony that overlooked the floor of the great hall. The east side of the room was ornamented with Doric pilasters; between each were bronze "busts of several antient and modern philosophers and poets, large as life," resting on gilt brackets. At the north end of the room, a balcony for an orchestra projected over the main door. At the south end of the room, massive portraits of "their present majesties" hung over folding doors that opened into spacious apartments generally used by the Governor's Council. Above the apartments was a large banqueting room "hung with paper and neatly furnished," which communicated with the saloon through an open window. In Long's estimation, the room was evidence that King's House was "the noblest and best edifice of its kind, either in North America or any of the British colonies in the West Indies."[108] Records of the assembly indicate that the room was outfitted in 1762 with thirteen mahogany settees, twenty-four mahogany Windsor chairs, twenty-four large gilt girandoles, fourteen bronze busts, and ten tables.[109] The grand saloon was clear evidence of Jamaica's midcentury self-fashioning as refined, even noble.

The large room installed in the King's House was very much an Egyptian hall, possibly the inspiration for the main hall of the building in plates XV and XVI of D'Albaret's volume. In depending on such academic sources, the real Egyptian hall of the King's House and the imagined example in D'Albaret stand in company with the only other surviving examples from the eighteenth century, Lord Burlington's Egyptian hall in new assembly rooms in York, England, first published in the 1767 edition of *Vitruvius Britannicus,* and the grand entrance hall at Holkham Hall, both from the 1730s.

The significance of Jamaican buildings as the model for the building in D'Albaret's plate XV cannot be overstated. The dominant feature of the designs for plans included in the book are strong corner towers or pavilions connected one to the other with loggias. While Robert Turner's house in Kingston and Colbeck Castle in St. Dorothy Parish both reveal strong towers at each corner, lower pavilions at building corners were an alternative. Halse Hall, the seat of the Halse family in Clarendon Parish, exhibited such corner pavilions as did Richmond, Phillip

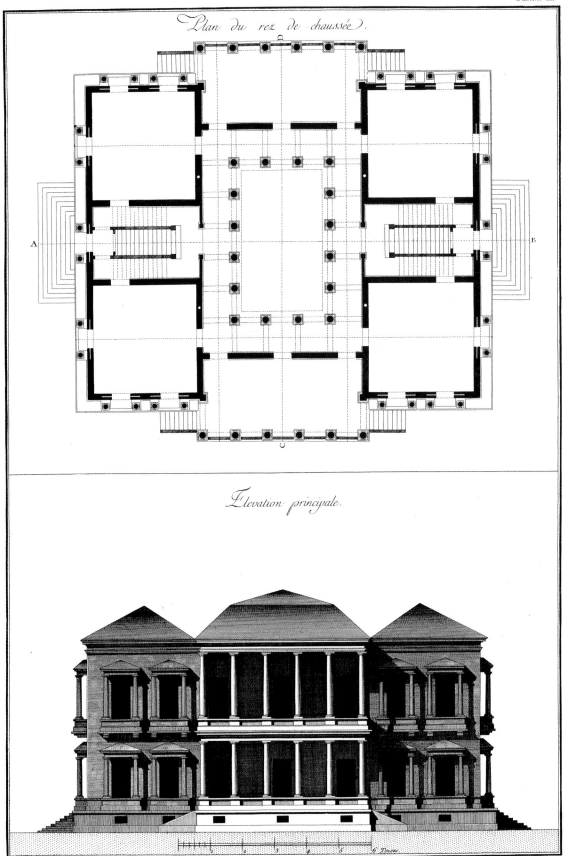

Plan du rez de chaussée.

Elevation principale.

FIG. 5.13 M. D'Albaret, *Différents projets relatifs au climat et à la manière la plus convenable de bâtir dans les pays chauds, et plus particulièrement dans les Indes occidentales* (Paris, 1776), Plate XV. University of Maryland Library.

Pinnock's great house in St. Ann. The significance of these features for Blagrove is reflected in the presence of strong corner elements in some version or another on no fewer than six of the nine designs. While in elevation these representations appear to be more like pavilions and less like towers as on Colbeck, there is no question that the arrangement of strong corner features (addressed in greater detail in chapter 2)—connected by open galleries—was intended by Blagrove to be a defining feature of a new architecture in Jamaica.

Blagrove returned to Jamaica in 1777 after his grand tour. He built a new house at his family's long-standing seat, Cardiff Hall; according to its datestone, the building was designed for Blagrove by Scottish architect John Forsythe in 1789. Less ambitious than the sprawling designs produced by D'Albaret, the house at Cardiff Hall is nonetheless grand (fig. 5.14). But in encasing the house with a single-story piazza on three sides, the plan also reveals the building's particular attention to the climate. The attention to classical refinement persists into the interior where the entrance hall is dominated by a march of columns and a staircase of particular grandeur (fig. 5.15).[110] But Blagrove did not limit his classical attentions to his house alone. The property also has a slave hospital that exhibits the same architectural language of classical refinement, especially in its use of Corinthian columns. And yet, as outlined in chapter 4, such hospitals were also used as spaces of confinement; the refinement was superficial, intended only as landscape ornament for visual consumption by the planter and his class. And on another Blagrove property, then known at Magotty, now Kenilworth, there stands the shell of classically detailed sugar works of the late eighteenth century, surely also erected under the patronage of Blagrove. These new plantation great houses signaled a revolution in architecture—real and imagined—on the island. Such a revolution positioned Jamaica as the sophisticated frontier of the expanding British Empire.

COLBECK CASTLE

It is in this context of exceptional attention to landscape and architecture that John MacLeod, a second-tier Scottish planter, built Colbeck Castle in a bid to rise into the ranks of Dawkins, Price, Long, Pinnock, and Blagrove. Colbeck Castle has long been believed a seventeenth-century building. Tradition associates the building with its namesake, John Colbeck (d. 1683), who was among the first English planters on the island. That Colbeck Castle's entire building program dates from the middle decades of the eighteenth century is reinforced by close physical examination as well as cartographic and documentary evidence. The site appears unoccupied on maps of the island drawn by Sheffield in the 1730s and 1740s and printed in 1755 or on the Craskell and Simpson map drawn in the late 1750s and published in 1765. Furthermore, the 1755 map includes a symbol for "Gentlemen's Seats" in addition to houses. Surely this ruin would be considered such a seat, but there is no such symbol anywhere close to the site of the current building on the map. On November 22, 1749, John MacLeod purchased the plantation ("Colobeck") from Bernard Henry. While the same purchase includes other plantations with improvements, none are noted at Colbeck.[111]

John MacLeod built the house he named Colbeck Castle as his principal residence in the early 1760s, in about the same years that he applied for heraldic arms as the chief of his branch of the MacLeod clan.[112] He was clearly aspiring, and by 1771, soon after the building's completion, he served on the vestry of St. Dorothy Parish with none other than Charles Price.[113]

Colbeck Castle's sequences of double arcades are surprising; such features are almost unknown on contemporary British country house architecture (see figs. 5.1, 5.16). Even so, Colbeck Castle's arcades are clear evidence of a sophisticated English architectural culture. Colbeck's form was adapted directly from plans, elevations, and sections published in Italian architect Sebastiano Serlio's early sixteenth-century treatise, *I sette libri dell'architettura* or *The Seven Books of Architecture*, first published in English in 1611. In that volume, the late Renaissance architect published two versions of a famous fifteenth-century country villa outside of Naples, the Poggio Reale. The first version represented the building as Serlio found it, and the second was an adaptation of his own design from the original. The original building was a perfect square with an open internal courtyard and four corner towers connected by loggias on all four elevations (fig. 5.17). The Serlio adaptation is,

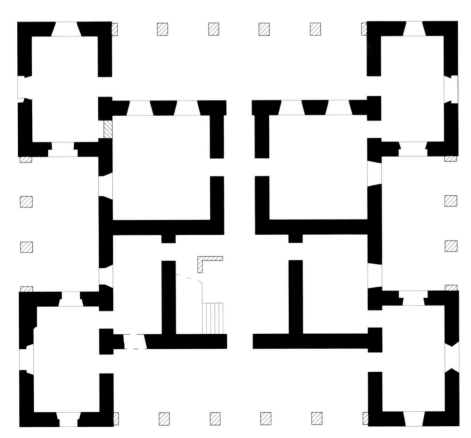

FIG. 5.16 Plan of Colbeck Castle, second (main) floor.

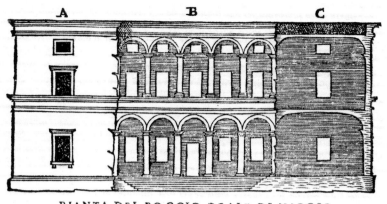

PIANTA DEL POGGIO REALE DI NAPOLI.

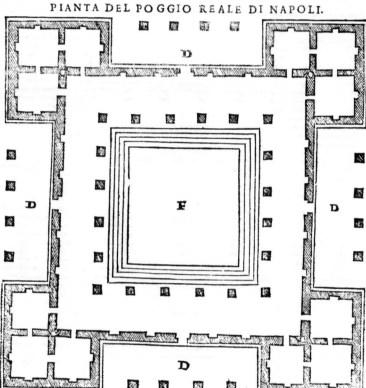

FIG. 5.17 Sebastiano Serlio, "Plan of the Poggio Reale in Naples." Original fifteenth-century plan. From *I sette libri dell'architettura* (London: Printed for R. Peake, 1611). University of Virginia Special Collections.

like Colbeck, a rectangle with two longer prominent elevations and two shorter side elevations. The corner towers appear on both versions (fig. 5.18). As in Serlio's adaptation of the original, Colbeck boasts five bays between the towers on each of the longer elevations and three on the shorter sides. For the design of the loggias, Colbeck adapts the double arcades seen in the interior courtyard elevation of the original to the exterior of the Jamaican building.

Along with the drawings for the Poggio Reale, Serlio offered a written defense for the excellence of this design based not only on its convenience as a modern villa but also on its capacity to manage the heat and light of the sun, surely a selling point in both Italy and Jamaica. "This building was intended for use during the very hot periods," he writes, " . . . the hall and the four chambers would always be cool, the sun being unable to enter." Serlio celebrated the power of architecture to ennoble; buildings like the Poggio Reale, he believed, were evidence of noble manners and grace.[114] Surely Colbeck's builder sought the same for himself. Colbeck's architecture draws directly from Serlio, a recognized authority for English builders of the seventeenth and eighteenth centuries. In doing so, John MacLeod participated in an important marker of eighteenth-century elite English identity, the adaptation from the ancients or from Renaissance authorities in the making of modern country houses.

One of the critical features of the building's design is the grandeur of the polite entrance sequence. Access

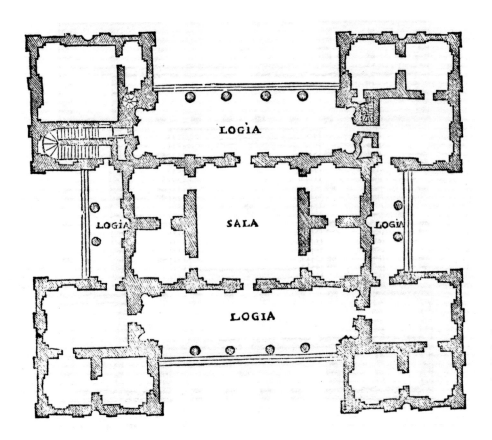

FIG. 5.18 Sebastiano Serlio, "Plan of the Poggio Reale in Naples." Serlio's adaptation. From *I sette libri dell'architettura* (London: Printed for R. Peake, 1611). University of Virginia Special Collections.

onto the house terrace from the south brought a formal visitor between the two southern corner buildings into what was surely a grand arrival roundabout (certainly when MacLeod's six-horse chariot was in use; yet, as Long suggests, a six-horse chariot was typical of "substantial inhabitants"—even shopkeepers, he reports, have "two-wheel chaises").[115] Passing through the building's main southern arcade gave direct access into a spacious, fully paneled stairhall with stairs rising to a landing dominated by a huge set of double doors. The double height stairhall as the first in a sequence of polite spaces conveyed a recognition of the staircase as an object of visual delight and a stage for the performance of dignity and grace.[116] The double doors opened into a large, fully paneled hall, which gave access to an adjacent paneled parlor and the second-floor bedchambers of the towers, spaces that were all plastered and fitted with wood chair rails and baseboards.

John MacLeod's 1775 probate inventory offers a detailed accounting of the building's contents in its early years of occupation.[117] In the spaces on the main floor, MacLeod housed most of his household furniture: numerous mahogany dining, breakfast, and dressing tables; six large bedsteads with beds and matching window and bed curtains; ten paintings and more than seventy-five framed prints; a billiard table; and a chamber organ. Together

with silver and other fine goods, these spaces conveyed his capacity for leisure, cultured refinement, and grand self-presentation.

The great hall opened onto the exterior arcades which, via other corner tower chambers, allowed circumambulation of the main floor; the adjacent parlor led to a small tower chamber with stair access to the roof. Rooftop decks then gave access from the third-floor chamber of the northwest tower to the uppermost chambers in each of the other towers. One of the more extraordinary features of Colbeck Castle would have been the views from the third-floor tower chambers. Scars in the masonry make it clear that access to the third floor was made available only through the northwest tower, that tower chamber immediately off the best chamber or parlor of the second floor. Ascending the stairs to the top of that tower provided privileged visitors the capacity to take in Jamaica's picturesque beauty. And from that tower, family and guests could circumnavigate the entire building via rooftop walkways that connected all four tower-top chambers. The plaster finishes and chair rails in these chambers betray their integration into the house's landscape of sociability. In addition to being a grand house in the manner of a great British country house, Colbeck also made available the distinctive British penchant for taking in the prospect from a house or the construction of estate landscapes in the picturesque mode.

The main house at Colbeck stands in the midst of a large, flat terrace defined by four L-shaped outbuildings. The two buildings in the forecourt appear to be fairly generalized, the southeast possibly functioning as a gatekeeper's or manager's lodge. The southwest (and northeast) flanker sits over a huge, well-secured, vaulted space. Together these buildings framed the more formal front face of the building while the two northern outbuildings define the rear work yard. The kitchen to the northwest is a functionally complicated building with three distinct spaces (fig. 5.19). The main block of the building was a kitchen and washroom. Each end of the large rectangular kitchen was dominated by a large open cooking fireplace. Physical evidence suggests that at least one of these was originally flanked by a bake oven. Both ends of the kitchen were also originally outfitted with stew stoves of three pots each with plastered hoods above to carry the heat and smells over to the main chimney flues.[118] Sauce pans, chocolate pots, and other specialty items listed in the kitchen in MacLeod's inventory betray the sophisticated culinary expectations of the family. There is also evidence for fitted dressers with wooden backsplashes along one wall and three stone-lined units for below-ground water storage. With two cooking fireplaces, multiple bake ovens, two stew stoves, and built-in dressers for food preparation and cold storage, this was a very sophisticated eighteenth-century kitchen.[119]

The wing extending to the south was a series of plastered polite spaces, conceptually an extension of the house. It was dominated by a sunken bath (fed by rainwater from the roof of the main house, passed via underground channels) together with a plastered changing room, and a pair of privies flushed by another channel from the main house and also by the overflow from the bath.[120] The edges of the main room have eighteen-inch ledges that just allow a person to walk around the perimeter of the pool to the changing room and the set of steps that descended into the pool from the southwest corner. Cold bathing had been resurrected as healthful in the very late seventeenth century

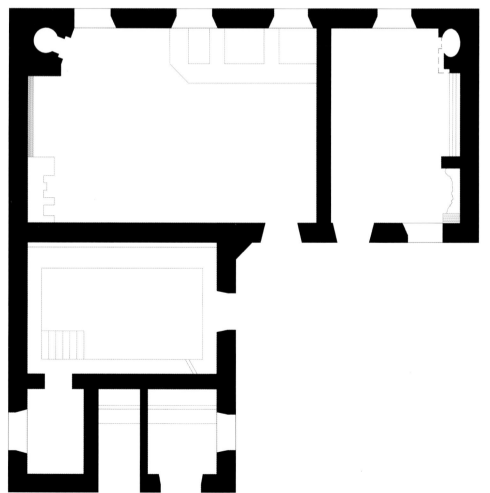

FIG. 5.19 Plan of northwest service building, Colbeck Castle. The kitchens are to the north (top) in this plan. The bathing room with its robing room is just to the south of the kitchens.

among London physicians. One of the early proponents of cold water bathing was John Floyer, who published on the subject in two treatises in 1697 and 1706. Cold water bathing, he argued, was a means of regaining "an ancient natural vigour, strength, and hardiness." Bathing houses were recorded in Jamaica in Port Royal as early as the late seventeenth century.[121] By the middle of the century, cold water bathing had become widely practiced for its healthfulness, especially for children and infants (although the presence of a cold-bathing pool in mid-eighteenth-century Jamaica is very surprising in that there are so few other colonial examples). Inspired by the wet mudpacks applied to feverish patients by Maroon healers, Dr. William Weston, the earlier-mentioned physician in Trelawny, began to prescribe cold baths for fevers in the early 1770s. Edward Long reported that elite Jamaican families bathed their children daily and then exposed them freely to the air; Long noted that "no part of the world can shew more beautiful children."[122] Cold baths were by then being offered as a remedy for a wide variety of ailments, even cancer. As the benefits of cold water were first embraced among Cambridge's natural philosophers, it is not a surprise that the earliest cold water pools were installed in fellows' gardens at Cambridge. While members of the middle class attended public baths and the lower classes visited local rivers or waterfalls, the elite had the capacity to build this convenience into their estates. By the 1730s, many English elites were installing cold baths on their country estates, usually in small bathing pavilions. While such cold baths on private property are unknown on the colonial American mainland, the presence of such a bath at Colbeck establishes even deeper connections between elites in Jamaica and their counterparts in Britain.[123]

Although fronted by an elegant range of arches, the northeast flanker was originally divided by masonry walls into a series of six equally sized chambers, each lit by a single window in the rear wall (fig. 5.20). These chambers each opened onto a front loggia mirroring in miniature the grand arcades of the main house. These barracks-style accommodations for enslaved house staff were common in mid-eighteenth-century Jamaica. MacLeod's Colbeck plantation included 355 men, women, and children listed as slaves. Those living up on the house terrace would surely have included "Dirty pit Peggy," the cook, "Mulatto Nancy, Black Nancy, Patty, and Katey" the washerwomen, and a few of the four drivers—Mars, Wambridge, Jack, or Virgil. It is also likely that some of the housemaids—Priscy,

Quadroon Nelly, or Little Betty—were also in this quarter. With the kitchen to one side of the rear yard, with its attendant butchering and cleaning of animals, and the quarters to the other side, the rear of the house functioned very much as a work yard, regularly occupied and crisscrossed by slaves performing the daily tasks of maintaining the household.

The extraordinary listings of goods housed "in the stores" (likely the vaulted chambers under the southwest and northeast corner outbuildings) reveal MacLeod's capacity to purchase and store high volumes of English goods. In addition to 140 gallons of rum, likely Jamaican-distilled, he stored 772 bottles of wine, mostly claret, and port, sherry, and Burton Ale. This together with salted hams, local beef, barrels of split peas, raisons, currents, and oatmeal. He also stored building supplies, including a hundred gallons of linseed oil and seventy gallons of tar in the same space as large lots of osnaburg, likely for slave clothes. In a separate chamber he stored a range of fine textiles, including chintz, damask, printed linen, and yellow and blue livery cloth, as well as red check to cover furniture. John MacLeod's house signaled an incredible degree of elite cultural currency, in a monument of sophisticated British architecture erected at the very fringe of empire. In constructing it, he followed the lead of his social superiors who worked so hard to deny their own peripheral status through elite social and aesthetic performance.

Yet if the construction of this house was a bid to step into the ranks of the island's elite, it failed. Already by the 1750s, the Longs, Prices, Blagroves, and others had been wealthy planters on the island for two or more generations. MacLeod's bid to erect a large and sophisticated house as a means of rising into these ranks was unsuccessful. John MacLeod was never elected to the assembly nor does he appear to have ever been elected to any major public office, save the vestry of his local parish. And, most tellingly, neither John MacLeod nor his great castle is mentioned in Edward Long's comprehensive three-volume history of the island. While Long discusses The Decoy and other plantations in some detail, the newly finished Colbeck was excised from the story. Soon after the construction of his house, MacLeod sent his sons to Britain for their education, and he expected them to stay. His will directed that upon his death, his great house on Colbeck plantation was to be sold. The island's elite were those from English families with a long history on the island, not newly arrived Scots, no matter how wealthy or sophisticated.

FIG. 5.20 View of the northeast outbuilding, Colbeck Castle.

• • •

"The island of Jamaica has never wanted of distinguished taste for the fine, as well as the useful and economical arts"; Edward Long argued that such sophistication was a result of the fact that "the island is so opulent."[124] In some ways, Jamaica could surpass England. "In manner of living, the English here differ not much from their brethren at home," Long argued, "except in a greater profusion of dishes, a larger retinue of domestics, and in wearing more expensive cloaths."[125] But this was not opulence for opulence's sake. Charles Price and his peers in Jamaica enlisted the arts to demonstrate that Jamaica was not at the periphery of empire but, in fact, in the avant-garde. In its wealthy, well-traveled, well-educated, and politically ambitious elite, Jamaica was by the middle decades of the century governed not by royally appointed representatives but by a small coterie of enormously rich planters. The eleven-man Jamaican Association included William Dawkins, Richard Beckford, Thomas Fearon, Phillip Pinnock, and Charles Price, among others. In these years, the Speakers of the Jamaican Assembly included Richard Beckford (1751), Edward Manning (1755), Thomas Hibbert (1756), Charles Price (1756), Charles Price, Jr. (1763, 1765, 1771), Thomas Fearon (1764), Edward Long (1768), and Phillip Pinnock (1769, 1775). Interrelated and enjoying privilege at the very top of a highly profitable economic system, this collection of a dozen or so men functioned as Jamaica's political oligarchy; their efforts can and should be seen as a collective effort to situate Jamaica as a leader in the newly reimagined British Empire. Immediately under this small oligarchy stood many planters, like John MacLeod of Colbeck, who aspired to membership in this circle. Most failed.

By the 1760s, Jamaica's planters understood quite well that they were vital to the empire's economic health. Edmund Burke's cousin William, made wealthy from investments in the East India Company in the 1760s, argued that the North American colonies and Britain's interests in Africa "must rise and fall exactly as the West-Indies flourish or decay."[126] The 1763 Treaty of Paris introduced into the British holdings a number of formerly French Caribbean islands, opening the door to increased investment in sugar planting and the sugar trade; within a decade, Grenada was Britain's second most valuable colony after Jamaica.[127] Jamaica's oligarchy could see that they stood at the leading edge—rather than the periphery—of empire. Certainly John Blagrove imagined such a readership for D'Albaret's 1776 volume of great houses for the British West Indies. Significantly, the book was not intended just for Jamaica but to provide models for new British great houses across the expanding Anglo-tropical empire. Blagrove's undertaking reveals an extraordinary confidence in Jamaica's future. Jamaica's planters enlisted the arts of architecture and landscape to "refine" the violence of the landscape in Jamaica and to reinforce their role in the empire's political geography. Even so, those aspirations would not survive the century.

6   Merchant Stores and the Empire of Goods

Now little more than a large, one-story masonry shell standing at the foot of Market Street in Falmouth, the Barrett House was one of the earliest and largest houses in town (fig. 6.1). Built in 1799, the once grand Barrett House was reduced by Hurricane Danny in 1997 into a pile of timbers in and around the ground-floor masonry. Before its collapse, the building boasted a second-story residence that projected out over the sidewalk, supported by a row of eight elegant columns. As the principal commercial street in town, Market was once lined with buildings of similar form, as revealed in Adolphe Duperly's early nineteenth-century lithograph of the street (fig. 6.2).[1] The house was likely built by Charles Moulton, son-in-law to Edward Barrett, who had owned and developed more than half the town in the preceding decades. Barrett had also conveyed a significant inheritance to his grandson (Charles Moulton's son) in his 1799 will, under the condition that his grandson change his last name to Barrett. Surviving on the site today is the seven-bay masonry shell of the ground-floor shop, with three tall doors originally opening into a single large store, and footings at the street-line marking the locations of the columns that carried the wood-frame upper-story residence (fig. 6.3).

Inside the masonry ground floor a transverse partition divided the large open store at the front from a shallow range of chambers behind. A single door centrally located in the cross partition led into a rear stair chamber that also gave access to the rear yard. A more prominent double door opened through that same partition from the large front store into a smaller rear chamber that likely served as a counting room. Predemolition drawings of the building reveal the clear contrast between the fine neoclassical finishes of the upper-story residence and the starkly plain finishes of the ground-floor shop. Preliminary archaeological investigation of the deep back lot suggests that this large yard also had a (now completely lost) complex of outbuildings that supported the residential functions of the upper story.[2] And finally, an 1844 plat illustrates the large wharf complex immediately across Market Street from the house, a complex leased and managed by Charles Moulton as early as 1786 (fig. 6.4).[3]

Market Street originated at the wharves and passed through town and south toward the many sugar plantations of the north coast. Looking southward down the street in the late morning, Duperly's view captures a wealthy white couple arriving in town by carriage, while

FIG. 6.1 Barrett House shell, Falmouth, Jamaica, 1799.

a number of black Jamaicans proceed through town on foot and small groups of men and women socialize at the street side and on corners. Cheek by jowl on both sides of this major thoroughfare stands a line of buildings whose collective form distinguished Market from other streets in town: ground-floor shops sit back from the street while upper-story residences carried by a march of columns reach out over the sidewalk, creating a public space that

was both sheltered from the elements and elevated above the thoroughfare of the street.

Serving as the commercial spine of Falmouth, Market Street boasted a number of large and well-stocked stores.[4] The commercial spaces of these buildings were distinctive enough to warrant comment by a Scotsman visiting Falmouth in 1802:

FIG. 6.2 Adolphe Duperly, "Market Street, Falmouth," 1844. Lithograph, 11 × 16 in. (28 × 40.7 cm). National Library of Jamaica.

FIG. 6.3 Barrett House, first floor and lot plan. A. originally a door; B. originally a door; C. stair rising into hall.

There appeared to be several large shops, or in Jamaican parlance, "stores" all open in front, and apparently filled with an *omnium gatherum,* consisting of silk mercery, woolen and linen drapery, hardware, saddler, groceries, etc. I observed in some of the larger of the stores several gentlemen, who I opined were leading men in the country, carrying on a lively conversation, which, doubtless, was increased by potations of sansgaree, which was freely circulating among them. Their costume was of an airy and light description, consisting of white trousers and waitscoats, with coatees of nankin and other light fabrics. They all wore hats with large broad brims, and in one or two cases, the crown was raised above the brim by a light wire or whalebone, thus admitting the air freely to the top of their caputs.[5]

As understood by this visitor, these "stores" were richly stocked with a wide range of goods; they were impressive commercial spaces. But they were also spaces occupied by "leading men" who used the stores as places of social gathering for drink, conversations, and a chance to escape the intense heat of the Caribbean sun. And these were not just masculine spaces. Writing in about the same years, James Stewart noted that elite Jamaican women "occasionally relieve the tedium of existence with a *shopping;* that is a rummaging over every shop, without any intention, perhaps, of buying anything: an amusement which the females here are as partial to as those of the first fashion in the British metropolis."[6] Commercial spaces used as social spaces were dominated by elite men and women who enlisted the environment of rich and abundant imports as a stage for self-definition as agents in the British empire of consumption.[7]

Most of Falmouth's stores were built in the short season between the foundation of the town in 1769 and the emancipation of slaves in 1838.[8] In these six short decades Falmouth expanded from a waterside hamlet to one of Jamaica's premier port towns.[9] The remarkable growth of Falmouth was noted as early as 1793 by commentator Bryan Edwards: "The rapid increase of this town and neighbourhood in the last sixteen years is astonishing. In 1771, the three villages of Martha-Brae, Falmouth, and the Rock, contained together but eighteen houses." But only two decades later, Falmouth alone boasted 150 houses. Edwards continued by noting that the town's growth was tied directly to the commerce of Falmouth's harbor: "Vessels which entered annually at the port of Falmouth [in 1771] did not exceed ten. At present it can boast upward of thirty capital ships, which load for Great Britain, exclusive of sloops and smaller craft."[10] Writing in 1793, however, even Edwards would not see the town's most explosive growth, which happened in the first decades of the early nineteenth century, especially after 1809, when Falmouth received free port status.[11] By 1810 Falmouth was Jamaica's busiest port after the capital of Kingston.

Jamaica's coastal towns played a crucial role as points of export for sugar and other plantation products and as markets for goods consumed in both towns and on the plantations. The greatest concentration of colonial merchants was in the capital city of Kingston, where extremely wealthy merchants competed with one another for transatlantic partnerships and with local planters for control of the colonial assembly.[12] Mercantilism and commercial activity were so important in Kingston, in fact, that almost one half of the labor in the city was in some way related to maritime activity. By comparison, maritime-related work comprised only one fourth of the total labor in early nineteenth-century Boston and New York.[13] But Jamaica's smaller port towns, like Falmouth, had more fluid boundaries. Unlike Kingston, where the lines between merchant and planter were often clearly

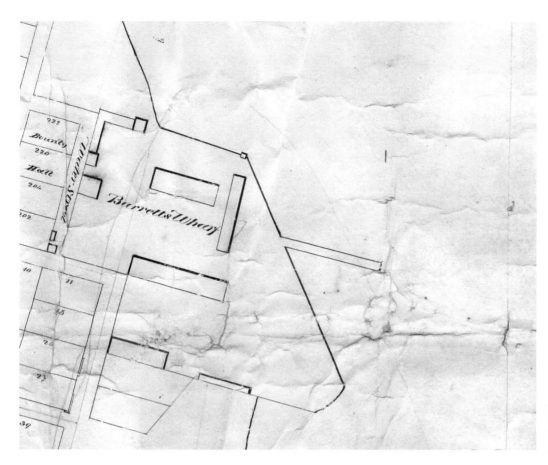

drawn and politically loaded, those roles in smaller towns were less distinct. As historian Barry Higman has demonstrated, Jamaica's port towns were closely connected to the immediate plantation context and the hinterland of pens where the enslaved butchered meats and grew local produce.[14] In these situations, elite families were often by necessity both planters and merchants.[15] And so, when our traveling Scot commented on the social life in Falmouth's stores he rightly noted that they were occupied by "the leading men in the country," of both town and plantation.

The Barrett family house, store, and wharf at the foot of Market Street was the nexus of numerous interdependent social and economic landscapes.[16] Through differences in building materials and the clear segregation of floors via the rear staircase, the merchants, clerks, and customers of the ground-floor commercial space were removed from the family residing in the residential spaces of the building's second floor. Cut another way, the refined spaces of family dining and elite entertaining upstairs depended on the service provided by enslaved laborers working in the back lot. And finally, the customers entering the store from the sheltered sidewalk on Market Street could hear from the wharf across the street the bawdy conversations of sailors unwinding from

lengthy voyages and the groans of slaves unloading heavy crates of stock. But if these three are social landscapes that segregated and differentiated, others conspired to unite. The Barrett store's street colonnade was made all the more effective when considered alongside similar colonnades that ran down the rest of Market Street. Together they created a collective space that was greater than the sum of its parts. The Barrett store was also in conversation with merchant houses elsewhere in the Caribbean, as merchants from different corners of the Caribbean responded to the demands of polite and leisure shopping.

In recent decades, historians have foregrounded patterns of consumption as a powerful cultural and political force in the shaping of the eighteenth-century Atlantic world. Foremost among these is T. H. Breen, who has gone so far as to assert that Britain fostered the birth of an "empire of goods," a vast system of commercial exchange that forced Britons around the Atlantic "to situate themselves within a larger conceptual framework, where mutual imagining, the product of rumor and exaggeration, fantasy and fact, spawned new perceptions of empire." For colonials, Breen argues, participation in the empire of goods gave shape to what it meant to be British.[17] It was an empire "not of formal institutions," he argues, "but of common men and women making decisions about the quality of their lives, [and] of thousands of people on the move."[18] This chapter situates the making of that empire of goods in real spaces called stores as well as on wharves and in streets—and through social practices called hawking and shopping. Published literature on merchant houses of this period has focused on the domestic and service functions of such buildings around the British Atlantic; this chapter will instead focus on the architecture of the store, the house, the street, and the wharf, to demonstrate that Jamaicans—elites, enslaved laborers, free blacks, and sailors—eagerly participated in the complex economies of transatlantic trade.[19] Spaces of trade, like the merchant houses of Falmouth, provided the stage for complex interactions of exchange and consumption and in building these architectures, Jamaicans undergirded Britain's empire of goods at the front edge of empire.[20]

THE FALMOUTH HOUSE-STORE

Howard Davis, in his recent monograph on this building type, rightly argues that the integration of commercial and residential functions into a two-story or more urban building has been and remains a global phenomenon with a wide range of local interpretations.[21] The many examples surviving in Falmouth—and for that matter across the early modern Caribbean—are an extraordinary collection distinct from other global varieties yet with some discrete variations within the greater Caribbean. Those in Falmouth were always two stories in height and often of masonry ground floors and timber upper stories in response to the threat of hurricanes and earthquakes. They usually incorporated a large, open ground-floor store with a few smaller chambers behind, sometimes an accounting room and often a stairhall. While many in the British context included a separate passage from the front of the building to a rear stairhall rising to the upper residential spaces, the older and more common pattern was for access to the rear stairhall either directly through the shop or via a rear entry.[22] This appears to be the pattern enlisted by merchants in the Caribbean. Few examples offer segregated access from the street to a rear stairhall. And Davis also reminds his readers that by the early nineteenth century these shops were usually dedicated only to finer goods; without that luxury, the stores in Falmouth and across the Caribbean continued in the older tradition of selling fancy goods right alongside foodstuffs and goods of more pedestrian quality.[23]

The Barrett house-store was among the earliest of this house form in Falmouth. Central to the building's form was that it served as the urban residence for the Barrett family. The building originally offered access to the residential upper floor of the house in two ways, through an enclosed staircase that rose off the sidewalk and via an internal staircase behind the open store of the lower floor. While very few of these sidewalk staircases survive

FIG. 6.5 Exterior of 7 Upper Harbour Street, Falmouth, Jamaica. The ground-floor store still has only wooden shutters, while the upper residential floor has fine tripartite sash windows.

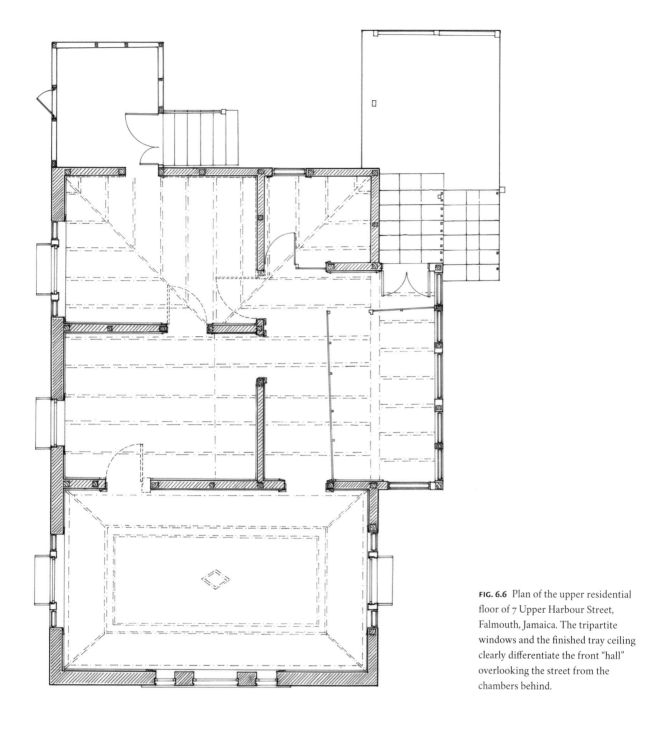

FIG. 6.6 Plan of the upper residential floor of 7 Upper Harbour Street, Falmouth, Jamaica. The tripartite windows and the finished tray ceiling clearly differentiate the front "hall" overlooking the street from the chambers behind.

anywhere in Jamaica, they were once a fairly common form in coastal towns. In the case of the Barrett House, this staircase rose to a large front room that spanned the entire width of the building. From its size—it was sixty feet wide—and its level of ornament, this was clearly the best room in the house. Usually called "the hall" well into the nineteenth century, the largest front room overlooking the street was the primary public entertaining space of these houses. Most often ornamented with a tray ceiling, the hall was airy and open, and usually lightly furnished.

It was generally the principal dining room as well as the retiring room through the course of the heat of the day. The front hall of the smaller house-store at 7 Upper Harbour overcomes its size in its richer degree of ornamentation, with neoclassical trim around the fenestration, a cornice under the tray ceiling, and an elegant tripartite window overlooking the street (figs. 6.5, 6.6). In his assessment of urban houses in the Danish West Indies, William Chapman rightly frames these spaces as the domain of women; these were the spaces where women were most able to practice their sociability.[24] The urban hall was the site of afternoon teas and evening dinner parties.

Most urban halls featured an ornamental arched opening into a central passage that reached back through the house toward the rear, flanked on both sides by bedchambers (figs. 6.7–6.9). The prominent opening served as a threshold between the public space of the hall and the more intimate spaces to the rear of the house. In this feature, the Barrett House was actually an outlier; its major ornamental arch opened into a central square

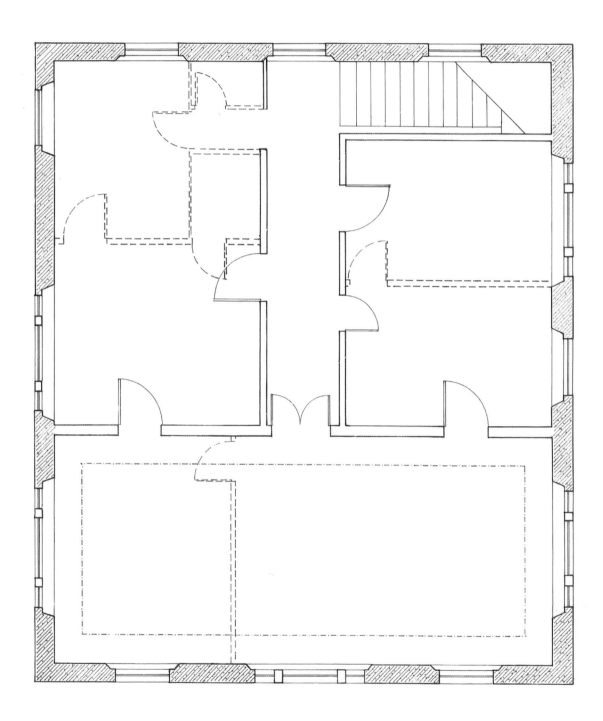

FIG. 6.7 Plan of Thomas Vermont House, 17 Market Street, Falmouth, Jamaica, residential upper floor. The large chamber overlooking the street was the hall. The partition in that room is a later installation.

FIG. 6.8 Hall of Thomas Vermont House, 17 Market Street, Falmouth, Jamaica.

FIG. 6.9 Typical arch defining the entrance into the hall from the passage, 7 King Street, Falmouth, Jamaica.

chamber that similarly gave access to a number of secondary bedchambers. The repetition of this form in both one- and two-story houses in Falmouth and across Jamaica in the late eighteenth and early nineteenth centuries resulted in a distinctive plan type that established consistent sociability. Their consistency helped Jamaicans understand how to navigate these spaces. Some houses included a front staircase, but almost all incorporated a stair rising to this domestic floor from the rear of the building.

The rearmost chamber of the ground floor in the Barrett House was a stairhall that opened into the store to the front, to the work yard behind the house, and rose to the domestic spaces of the upper story. In another example from Falmouth, the rear stair rose to a lighted landing that gave clear visual surveillance of the work yard from within the comfort of the house (fig. 6.10). This stair was a critical nexus of spatial flow for both the white family and the enslaved laborers who lived and worked on the property, for as one early nineteenth-century observer wrote, "An inhabitant of a West India town is, perhaps, a possessor of six, eight, ten or even a dozen slaves."[25] Comparable evidence from other port towns suggests that this assessment might be a bit high; average households often included three or four domestic slaves—mostly women—and often a few children. Larger urban slaveholders might also own skilled craftsmen who hired out and often lived off-site

FIG. 6.10 Rear elevation of the Moulton-Barrett House, Falmouth, Jamaica. The observation landing is centrally positioned in the elevation at the top of the rear stairs. The elevated chamber to the far left is a much later addition.

from their owners.[26] Barry Higman has estimated that as much as 50 percent of an urban slave population was made up of domestics.[27] And numerous accounts make clear that through the eighteenth century the majority of urban townhouses had at least a separate kitchen.[28] The low one-story building still standing behind the Thomas Davidson house is likely the shell of a kitchen building (fig. 6.11). Even a small, four-room house on Pitt Street has a surviving kitchen and slave quarter building (fig. 6.12). As Edward Long suggested in the late eighteenth century:

> Almost every dwelling-house throughout the island is detached from the kitchen and other offices; which, though different from practice in England, is a very judicious arrangement for this climate, where the fumes and smoak of the kitchen, and the stench of other necessary offices, would be intolerable in too near a neighborhood.[29]

Together with the kitchen, the rear lot also would include quarters for the slaves. As announced in the *Royal Gazette,* one house on Lower Street in Kingston was offered for sale together with its "large yard, wash house and negroe houses."[30] Documentary evidence suggests that some quarters were not unlike those found on plantations, either earthfast with wattle and mud or lightly framed, both with a thatch roof; none of these survive. By the early nineteenth century, the majority of urban domestics were housed in barracks-type buildings along the periphery of the lot.[31] The early Jamaican townhouse certainly accommodated enslaved domestics in quarters in the rear yard but the documentary record also makes clear that domestics regularly slept on the floors of bedchambers or just outside the bedchamber door of their primary charge.[32] The inventory of Jonathan Gale's house in Spanish Town, for example, includes in a closet a "parcel of Negro matt."[33] In relaying the account of a female "peeping tom," one nineteenth-century male visitor to Jamaica reported that "on seeing me move, [she] tumbled in her hurry over Ebeneezer, who was snoring at my door, which opened into the hall."[34]

The rear yards of these urban merchant houses were not unlike the very well-documented work yards of houses in eighteenth- and early nineteenth-century Charleston, South Carolina.[35] While all surviving examples in Charleston are brick, archaeological evidence suggests that through the eighteenth century, quarters in Charleston's back lots might also have been earthfast with thatch roofing, much like the houses found on plantations.[36] But it is also true that by the early nineteenth century, slaves in the Caribbean and in South Carolina lived

FIG. 6.12 18 Pitt Street, with kitchen and quarter dependency to its side (ca. 1820), Falmouth, Jamaica.

independently from their owners, often living in huts aggregated on urban lots. When there were more than four on a single lot, the lot was required by law to have a wall and a single gate, intentionally obstructing access.[37] In the eighteenth century, slave yards were interspersed among more refined house sites: Ann Storrow noted of Kingston in 1792, "the Town of Kingston has some beautiful houses in it . . . but you often see between two handsome houses an obscure negro yard which spoils the effect entirely."[38] Nineteenth-century towns and cities in Jamaica witnessed increased segregation of "negro yards" to urban peripheries.[39]

The Barrett House was among the earliest documented of the merchant house-store building type in Falmouth, and it represents the predominant form of that building type in town, but there are some variations worthy of note. Located in a prominent position at 17 Market Street, the building that now serves as the Falmouth post office is one of the finest examples of a merchant house-store in town (fig. 6.13). Thomas Robert Vermont, a senior resident magistrate of the parish, built the house sometime after he purchased this lot in September 1832. Vermont died in 1865 and left the house to Mrs. Mary Atkinson and her daughter Wilhemina [sic], who had tended to the house when Vermont was away in England.[40] Two stories of brick with bold architectural detailing, this building differs in both materials and detail from earlier masonry and frame merchant houses like the Barrett House down the street. The building is remarkable for its decorative details, such as the well-articulated classical door, the rough faceted masonry panels below smaller windows, and the quoins emulating heavy stone blocks that define the building's corners. Much like the earlier Barrett building, the Vermont house-store has a single large store space on the ground floor with exposed framing and very little architectural ornament. Unlike other examples of this form, however, this ground floor includes an unlit corner chamber that has only a single access; its lack of illumination and its very limited circulation suggest that it functioned as a counting room and safe. The security of the building was further reinforced by the iron bars used to close the ground-floor window shutters from the interior and a wrought-iron staple and bracket that barred the door. But even if the building dissents in its bolder aesthetic and its ground-floor safe room, its upper floor conforms almost exactly to the plan seen in example after example across town and across Jamaica (see figs. 6.7, 6.8). The tray ceiling of the large room overlooking the street through the triple sash window clearly announces it as the hall.

Built before Thomas Vermont's store, the double version of the building type now standing at the intersection of Market and Duke Streets was probably erected in the mid-1820s (fig. 6.14). Now entirely gutted on the interior, the significance of this example lies in its doubled form;

FIG. 6.13 Thomas Vermont House and Store, 17 Market Street, now the post office, Falmouth, Jamaica, mid-1830s.

FIG. 6.14 23 Market Street, Falmouth, Jamaica.

rather than being built for a builder-occupant, this building was clearly built with some dimension of speculation
toward a rental market. And as Howard Davis has suggested, fewer and fewer British merchants were actually
living above their stores by the early nineteenth century.[41]
The increasing segregation of the nineteenth-century city
meant that wealthy merchants preferred to move their
residence to more exclusive districts of the city occupied by their peers. While no documentary evidence has
surfaced to clarify the story of this particular example in
Falmouth, its doubled form suggests that at least half of
the building was intended for rental. But even within their
variation, there emerges among these port city buildings
a notable consistency of form and spaces; the remainder
of this chapter is dedicated to examining each of those
spaces in turn: the wharves, the stores, and the streets that
connected them.

WHARVES

Located directly opposite Barrett's house and store was
Barrett's wharf, which predated the construction of the
house by at least thirteen years and possibly predated
the foundation of the town in 1769. The detail of the 1844
town plan of the wharf shows the strong diagonal stroke
of the seawall interrupted only by the projecting dock
(see fig. 6.4). Dominating the middle of the wharf are four
massive rectangular buildings that likely served as warehouses to store the thousands of barrels of sugar that were
produced on Barrett plantations.[42] Another important

example is the remarkable 1805 plat of Alexander Lindo's
wharf in Kingston (fig. 6.15). Lindo's house stands to the
far north, to the right in the plat. Behind the house, spanning to the south toward the harbor, stood a large yard
flanked to the west by a single-story range of brick stores
and to the east by a longer, double-story range of brick. In
the midst of the yard ran yet another range of stores, these,
however, of frame. The ranges of stores all led to a rear-lot
gate that opened directly onto the pier of Lindo's wharf,
which had on it nothing more than a crane to assist in
loading departing ships with hogsheads of sugar.

But those warehouses were also used to store imports.
Factors often rented space on private wharves to store
the many items recently unloaded from ships and not yet
transferred elsewhere for sale. While detailed records
of imported items are rare, one very lengthy 1794 inventory of English goods shipped to Falmouth on board
the Jamaican vessel the *Martha Brae* by merchant John
Stogdon has recently come to light.[43] The list includes an
astonishing array of English-made items. In addition to
textiles, buckles, thimbles, buttons, and huge sums' worth
of ready-made clothes, the manifest included a wide range
of hats for men, women, and children, including four blue
beaver hats with elegant feathers, and a large assortment
of shoes and slippers. Fine housewares included decanters,
cruets, water and wine glasses, "blue and white cups," and
six large tureens, while household necessities ranged from
lamp oil to mosquito netting. The list included a large volume of spirits, including ale, port wine, cider, raspberry

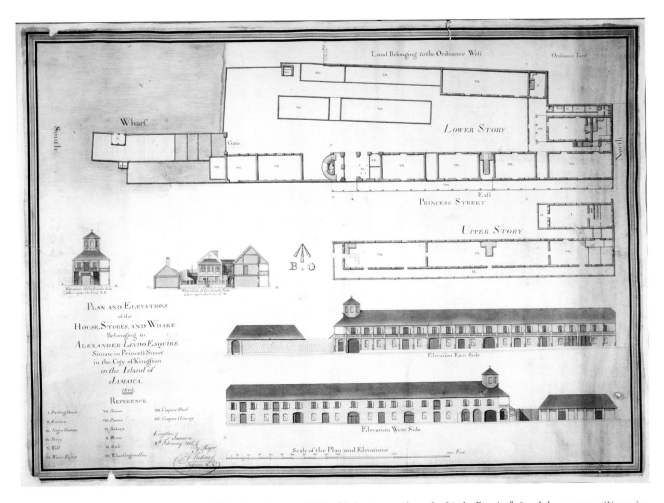

FIG. 6.15 Major Pechon, "Plan and Elevation of the House, Stores and Wharf Belonging to Alexander Lindo, Esquire," 1805. Ink on paper, 26½ × 37 in. (67.6 × 94 cm). Public Record Office, London.

brandy, and sherry wine. Sage, cinnamon, cloves, black pepper, mustard, ketchup, and soy were on offer as were staples like oatmeal. Small portable building materials were abundant, including a wide range of nails, handsaws, hinges, door locks, rope, and kegs of ground lead and Spanish Brown pigment. And lastly, evidence of Jamaicans' love of horses and horse racing, the inventory included a huge range of saddler supplies, including a large variety of bridles, saddles, and jockey fittings.[44] If Barrett's warehouses were filled with Jamaican sugar for export, they were also at times filled with the many imported goods made possible by the wealth generated from that very same sugar.

In addition to the very large warehouses, Barrett's wharf also included a range of smaller buildings around the edges and just outside: the shallow range at the south edge, the range set at 90 degrees to the northwest, and the two very small buildings perched immediately outside the wharf on Water Street. The two small buildings on Water

Street are certainly small shops or booths, much like the "vile hovels and disgraceful sheds, inhabited by free people of color, who keep petty huckster's shops, and by low white people, who vend liquors" described by one traveler. Such hovels and sheds "give rise to many disorderly scenes."[45] These small shops were similar to the booths that stood just outside and along the wall of Fort Balcarres, the town's military fortification, and—when in season—around the racetrack. One newspaper account noted with dissatisfaction that the regular horse races in Falmouth attracted "all classes from town and country" and that "the usual concomitants (vice and Sabbath desecration), have distinguished the conduct of the lower orders at the race course, where booths have been erected for many weeks past."[46] Such an account notes not only the temporary and impermanent nature of these booths but also the standard association among elites of those smallest of shops and booths with the lower classes and, by extension, presumed immorality and vice.

Such booths were themselves a more permanent solution to the broader Caribbean practice of selling at open-air markets, a practice undertaken on occasion by recently arrived sailors but dominated by the region's enslaved majority. Records for French Saint-Domingue (Santo Domingo, or Haiti) suggest that sailors often sold small, easily portable goods like soap, ribbons, and hardware from cloths spread directly on the ground, usually in and around the wharves.[47] But this practice was most closely associated with the enslaved selling goods and produce of their own manufacture. As reported by Thomas Atwood, writing about the practice on the island of Dominica,

> Sunday is the chief market day there, as it is in all the West Indies; on this day the market is like a large fair, the negroes from the plantations, within eight miles of Roseau come thither in great numbers, each one bringing something or other to dispose of for himself, often to the amount of three or four dollars; and many

of them, who bring kids, pigs, or fowls, seldom return home without fifty or sixty shillings, the produce of their articles.[48]

One early nineteenth-century print offers a view into such a Sunday market in Antigua (fig. 6.16). If the artist exaggerates the sense of chaos and stereotypes the black figures, he also represents well the broad practices of selling produce, poultry, livestock, and handcrafts while seated in the open space of the market. Falmouth's market was captured in a lithograph by Duperly in 1844 when he documented Water Square, the town's major public gathering space, on market day (fig. 6.17). In addition to the women seated in the foreground selling produce and wares in piles on the ground, other venders sell goods from covered pushcarts.[49] These pushcarts, a sales practice that has survived to the present, are the portable version of the booths and small shops that appeared around the city's racetrack, fort, and wharves, except these mobile versions

A NEGRO MARKET in the WEST INDIES.

FIG. 6.16 W. E. Beastall, "Negroes Sunday Market at Antigua," 1806. Lithograph, 13 × 17 in. (33 × 43 cm). The Lewis Walpole Library, Yale University.

FIG. 6.17 Adolphe Duperly, "Water Square," 1844. Engraving. National Library of Jamaica.

were likely managed by the town's free black or poor white populations who had less easy access to fixed space.

In some places the commercial nature of the waterfront was manifest in the construction of market buildings proximate to the wharves. The eighteenth-century market building near the docks in Roseau, Dominica, was described as wooden, "built on pillars of stone, between which are apartments for the butchers and fishermen . . . and the middle passage is for the loaded fish canoes, that they may be drawn up out of the heat of the sun while the fish is selling."[50] The building likely resembled that appearing in the background of Augustino Brunias's early nineteenth-century painting of that town (see fig. 6.26). Unlike dedicated markets of major cities, these markets were often built immediately adjacent to the city's wharves, simply as a means of giving material form and shelter to a practice that was already taking place in these locales.

If the small buildings lining the streets were booths or small shops, the shallow ranges of buildings on the wharf itself were probably shops as well, if more substantial. Shops on wharves were often let to ship captains whose cargo was not consigned to a particular merchant's store.[51] This use of the space of the wharves for the sale of goods was a strategy that competed directly with more established Falmouth merchants who in 1798 presented a formal complaint to the House of Assembly. The merchants argued that "transient traders . . . have been enabled to dispose of their goods and merchandise on lower terms than the resident traders." They were enabled to do so, these merchants argued, because they are not "subject to public and parochial taxes, store rent, and other expenses and charges."[52] From individual sailors hawking fine goods, slaves selling local products from pushcarts, and captains selling goods from small shops, the wharves were spaces of lively commerce and exchange.

This condition, of course, was not unique to Jamaica. In 1743, the front pages of the *South Carolina Gazette* published the report of a special commission dedicated to assessing the condition of Charleston's wharves; it gives some very useful insight into the architectural conditions of early modern wharves.[53] All of the wharves had buildings, most of which were being used as shops and a few even as dwelling houses. For example, Elizabeth Jeny's wharf boasted no fewer than three houses and a cooper's shop. William Elliott's wharf contained one house, three large stores, a smith's shop and store with a chimney, and a silversmith's shop with a chimney. Such an arrangement created a commercial alley offering a wide range of utilitarian and fine goods in that narrow space between the wharf and the city.

Mid-eighteenth-century advertisements in the *South Carolina Gazette* give further evidence of the shops and stores on Charleston's wharves.[54] By far the most prominent category of items for sale on the wharves was foodstuffs, followed by spirits and beer. The predominance of foodstuffs and spirits suggests that Charleston's shopkeepers sought to capitalize on the high demand for supplies for the many ships that passed through the harbor. Most craftsmen who worked from shops on the wharves offered services associated with shipping and the maintenance of ships: sailmakers, coopers, blacksmiths, and ship carpenters and painters were the majority. There were a few exceptions. William Wright was a gold- and silversmith

working on Trott's wharf in the early 1740s. Benjamin King worked on Simmons's wharf in the 1760s as a survey instrument maker and mender, and Thomas Floyd was a clockmaker on Burns's wharf in the same years. While offering high-end and fancy items, each of these artisans might also have benefited from working on the wharves.

Most of these shops offered their wares directly through the falling shutter of a shopfront window much like the booths erected at Falmouth's racetrack. One newspaper reference, reporting on a statute that limited encroachments on the streets, offers a brief glimpse into the character of shops in Charleston: shopkeepers may "suffer their stall boards (when their Shop Windows are set open) to turn over and extend Eleven Inches, and no more from the Foundation of their Houses."[55] Most shops on the city wharves were fronted by similar stall windows, a form identified by Dell Upton as the earliest form of Euro-American shopfront.[56] A simple concept and of ancient origins, late medieval examples of such stall windows can still be seen in the small shopfronts in the Shambles in York, England (fig. 6.18), where the street takes its name

FIG. 6.18 Medieval window stalls along the Shambles, York, England.

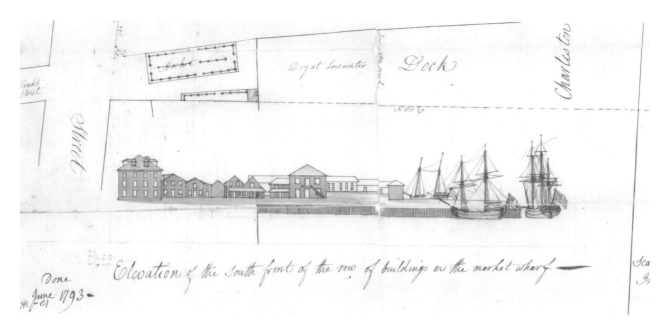

FIG. 6.19 "Elevation of the South front of the row of buildings on the market wharf," June 1793. Ink on paper. Register of Mesne Conveyance, Charleston, South Carolina.

from the distinctive boards, originally called shambles, the same term used to describe the butchers' district in seventeenth-century Bridgetown.[57]

A 1793 plat of a wharf in Charleston, South Carolina, offers an extraordinary view into the complexity of buildings that occupied early modern wharves (fig. 6.19). Adjacent to East Bay Street to the far left stands a three-story brick house with garrets and cellars and roofed in slate. In the middle of the wharf stands a two-story store of brick roofed in wood shingle, with an exterior staircase that rose to the second floor, suggesting open and unimpeded storage below and offices and counting rooms above. Standing between these two more substantial structures was a range of "stores, shops and shades of wood." The larger buildings on this plat and others were called stores but the smaller, narrow buildings were termed shops, some fronted by a "shade," presumably erected to shelter those standing at the open shop window considering a purchase. Wharves were far more than simply docking points for ships; they were also lively commercial districts that capitalized on the flow of goods and people on the waterfront.

The character of these spaces, of course, lent themselves well to the various activities of those considered the least reputable in the city, from sailors, to slaves, to prostitutes.[58] As asserted by one reformer, "In every seaport there is a large class of people of the most degraded character, whose support depend almost entirely upon

the vicious habits of Seamen."[59] A reading of the *South Carolina Gazette* from 1788 offers a glimpse of the crime that often accompanied wharves.[60] Theft in and around the wharves was rampant. All things associated with sailing—rope, sails, timber, paint, tackle, and even an entire mast—were reported stolen on regular occasion. The largest items commonly stolen were the many small boats and canoes used to navigate around the wharves and from the wharves to bigger ships anchored in the harbor. Fights among sailors that led to bloodshed were common. In October 1788, a fight between French and English sailors resulted in the death of one of the sailors by ax. In December, the battered body of a sailor was found floating among the wharves. Sailors also assaulted citizens near the wharves at night. For women, these assaults could become rape.

The wharves were home not only to sailors but also to large populations of enslaved laborers; historian Barry Higman has mapped the distribution of slaves in the port city of Kingston, Jamaica, and the overwhelming density of slaves was along the waterfront.[61] As a means of resisting their enslavement, slaves along wharves often engaged in crimes from petty theft to plotting grand insurrection. The circulation of ideas was dangerous; this was particularly true when those ideas reached large gatherings of the enslaved in urban markets, where people, information, and ideas circulated as easily as chickens and peas.[62]

As for petty theft, a Falmouth newspaper reported in

1826 that James Richards was being held on trial in the courthouse for his crime of "stealing crockery from a crate on Doman's Wharf." Found guilty, he was sentenced "to hard labour in the Workhouse for 3 months. To receive 50 lashes in the Water-square before going in, and another 50 at the expiry of his imprisonment." The close proximity of these commercial districts and crime is made evident in the highly public nature of Richard's punishment. All of his lashes were to take place "in the Water-square," exactly the same space where Falmouth's black population held their market.[63] The same was also true in Roseau, Dominica, where the market building included "public stocks for confinement of disorderly white people and negroes."[64] Slaves would also plot at much grander scales; the conversations that would become the foundations for the failed Denmark Vesey Rebellion in Charleston were all begun on the wharves, where large numbers of slaves enjoyed a certain modicum of freedom to congregate and share information.[65] For a port town's polite community, early modern wharves were at best unsavory and at worst very dangerous.

STORES

Differentiating themselves from the people of the wharves and their booths, Falmouth's elite erected stores along Market Street for the sale of both fancy goods and utilitarian staples in a far more respectable venue.[66] Measuring almost sixty feet wide and twenty-five feet deep, the ground-floor store of the Barrett house was among the largest commercial spaces in town. The only apparent ornamentation of the interior of this space was a range of four turned classical columns that helped to carry the ceiling framing across the depth of the chamber. The two elevations facing Market and Lower Harbour Streets were perforated with large windows, while the other two walls were almost entirely solid to accommodate shelving for the display of fine goods. In the absence of any other physical or documentary evidence, it seems reasonable to assume that the store included a number of stock display strategies, ranging from shelves to open crates in the middle of the floor. Significantly, Jamaicans' preference for the term "store" over the term "shop" clearly differentiated these wholly retail spaces from the smaller-scale retailing of shops on wharves and from the labor undertaken in an artisan's house-shop.

The "omnium gatherum" noted by the Scot is quite clear in various contemporary records.[67] In 1815, Arnold's

Repository in Falmouth advertised for sale in the *Cornwall Chronicle* a remarkably wide range of goods just imported from London. Customers could purchase diverse books, looking glasses, musical instruments, hair combs and powder boxes, fabrics, lace and other materials for sewing, and ready-made clothes including either black or brown beaver hats for ladies, and shoes for men, women, and children. Wealthier customers could also peruse the extensive range of jewelry: brooches, fashionable gold earrings and wedding rings, lockets, necklaces with earrings and bracelets to match, silver hunting watches, and elegant beads, including coral, amber, and gold. One could also purchase table, tea, or dessert spoons, snuffers, and spectacles in silver or tortoiseshell. But in addition to carrying all these very fancy and high-end goods, Arnold's Repository also sold "an extensive assortment of dry goods, hardware, etc, etc" and groceries including "Yorkshire hams, Gloucester and Cheshire cheese, brown stout, and old hock in excellent order."[68] From the best silks to ham and cheese, Arnold's Repository seemed to sell it all.[69] In a store in Falmouth, elite Jamaicans could purchase goods and foodstuffs that helped define their identity as Britons, participants in the empire of goods.

The predominance of textiles and ready-made clothes as the largest and most expensive stock in the Arnold's Repository advertisement is consistent with other contemporary records as well. The 1805 inventory of Jonas Hart's store in Montego Bay, Jamaica, comprised £734 worth of stock, more than half of which—£395—was textiles, sewing supplies, and ready-made clothing. Other expensive items included mahogany furniture ranging from a dining table and some desks to a mahogany bedstead with furniture, a silver teapot with full accoutrements, and a barrel organ. Among the more utilitarian were copper kettles, a cask of nails, and a lot of fishing hooks and line.[70] One uniquely local item was "one coconut, silver mounted," which is probably a reference to a distinctively Jamaican form, a coconut shell goblet with a silver stem and foot, one of which survives in a private collection. "Omnium gatherum" indeed.

The majority of fine goods were imported from Britain and her colonies. As a result of the Navigation Act, more than three quarters of the imported goods sold in Jamaican stores were of British origin, and another 16 percent were from Canada and the United States.[71] In terms of their goods for sale, these stores differed little from the stores in any town in England. While it seems quite clear that the large open-fronted stores of early Falmouth offered a wide range of stock, the means of organization and display within the store is entirely unknown. The complete absence of any interior store fittings in a townscape with a remarkably high level of architectural survival, in fact, suggests that Falmouth's stores were not entirely unlike the early open shops of mid-eighteenth-century merchants in larger cities like Charleston, South Carolina.

The 1764 probate inventory of Charleston merchant William Wilson sheds some light onto the spatial organization of a later eighteenth-century merchant's house and shop.[72] The inventory opens with a listing of items that appear to be stored on twenty-one shelves along the walls. These include textiles, tinwares, ceramics, collections of small items like thimbles, buckles, and buttons, and specialized items like spectacles, compasses, and weights and scales. The next section is a series of specialized items displayed in the "shew glass," likely standing in the shop window. These range from silver buttons and silver-edged cloth, sugar, and almonds to a box of Dutch toys. The remaining items in the inventory are all contained in six fairly large boxes and one trunk, likely filling the shop room floor or positioned along the walls under the shelves. Some of these were differentiated by contents, including only textiles, while others were very diverse, including everything from tobacco to decanters to looking glasses. As was the case for most late eighteenth-century merchants, luxury goods were sold from the same spaces as everyday wares. After writing the inventory of the shop, the appraisers moved to the (presumably other) "room below stairs." Equipped with a tea table, a mahogany dining table, and a desk and corner cupboard, this back room was fitted out for the necessary blending of business and entertaining that was so much a part of eighteenth-century commerce. The walls were hung with five large maps and a looking glass, further communicating the worldliness and refinement expected of an eighteenth-century merchant. Above stairs was a single room with three bedsteads for the merchant and his family and floor bedding for their slaves, among sundry other items. The integration of the shop into the space of the residence had been common for centuries in English practice and remained so through the eighteenth century.[73]

While counters and shelves had been commonplace in Charleston shops since the early eighteenth century, the increasing significance of the "show glass" in Charleston shops by the late eighteenth century is made very clear in

the daybook of Charleston painter and glazier Alexander Crawford.[74] His 1785 to 1795 daybook has regular notations of repairs to show glasses or the replacement of a regular window with a "bow window" to physically project store goods into the space of the passerby. Some show glasses were also finely finished to especially draw the eye; in 1793 Crawford painted a show glass with faux mahogany finish on the outside and a black interior. A similar process of increasingly sophisticated shop interiors and more prominent front windows, or show glasses, is evident in eighteenth-century towns across England as well. As scholars of the English shop have demonstrated, these increasingly refined spaces of the later eighteenth century accommodated new "polite" modes of shopping that included women as prominent consumers and that encouraged "window shopping" and browsing through goods.[75]

Constructed in the 1770s as a shop and residence but with a partially intact shop space dating from about 1800, the Geiger House in Charleston is a rare survival of an early commercial interior (fig. 6.20). The deep shop space is trimmed with a fashionable neoclassical cornice that stepped out from the wall to accommodate now-missing shelves or fixed cupboards. The cornice curved toward the back of the shop room as it moved toward the spectacularly framed glass-filled door with fanlight that gave access into the slightly elevated and heated back-shop or counting room behind.[76] In addition to participating in the growing significance of leisure shopping as a polite activity, this more elaborated interior highlights the emergence of the specialty shop in the later eighteenth century as a retail space selling a particular subset of finery, differentiated from the shop or store of merchants carrying a wide range of goods.[77] The large front chamber has a far higher level of refinement than do the larger open store spaces of Falmouth, which seem to be more a warehouse space by comparison. And, by extension, the absence of such spaces from Falmouth reinforces the documentary evidence that specialty retail shops like the Geiger shop in Charleston were not a common fixture in Falmouth.

Thus far, surviving architecture and documentary records from Falmouth offer no indication of such refined retail interiors.[78] Rather than feature bow windows and show glasses, merchants in Falmouth chose to keep their shops "all open in front." The street fronts of Falmouth's surviving stores all seem to have had multiple large double doors and shuttered windows between;

show glasses are nowhere to be seen. This opening of the front facade of stores in Falmouth parallels display practices among wholesale merchants in major port cities like New York and Philadelphia, and also among retail merchants in smaller ports across the Caribbean and in British-dominated port towns in Southeast Asia.[79] The lack of retail store display windows and finished interiors in Falmouth and other small towns across the British colonial world might be a result of those towns' small size. As Claire Walsh has argued, shops in London were burdened with the responsibility to influence the customer's judgment of the shop and of the reputation of the shopkeeper. Architecture did not carry such burdens in smaller markets where the reputations of both merchants and most consumers were well-known in the community.[80] Falmouth's small size, the practices among Jamaican merchants for the importation of a wide range of English-made goods, and the general Jamaican preference for the importation of refined goods (over the local generation of such goods as in South Carolina) all seem to have conspired against the emergence of refined, specialty stores like the Geiger store in Charleston.[81]

The lack of transparent store fronts might also be a result of the general anxiety about security that marked everyday life in colonial centers like Jamaica. There is, of course, a direct correspondence between the transparent display of goods and shoplifting; visibility and ease of access constituted a retail risk.[82] It is clear that solid masonry walls and heavy shutters locked from the inside are all that faced Market Street in nighttime hours. But such apparent impermeability was not enough to provide constant protection. At least one ingenious thief broke into a Falmouth store "by removing the bricks from under the sill of the window by means of a knife," working from the inside of a barrel. The burglar had positioned a barrel on its side under the windowsill with himself inside and "quietly carried on his work within it, so that had a person passed at the moment, they could have seen nothing but the barrel."[83] The growing volume and value of goods available in shops became an increasing temptation to those who did not have the means to participate in legitimate leisurely consumption, and Falmouth's large, masonry stores were an attempt to deter such theft.

STREETS

Among the most distinctive features of Falmouth's stores are the projecting piazzas or colonnades along the streets that sheltered the store fronts from the Caribbean sun, and when positioned cheek by jowl, created a shaded shopping street. The association of the piazza with mercantile exchange had a long history in Jamaican architecture. The seventeenth-century church in Port Royal was described in 1687, as having "at the north side of this church . . . a paved walk" over which is "built a good stonen gallerey, supported with large cedar pillars of ye Dorick order."[84] This was a space favored by Port Royal's merchants. The association of covered walks as sites of commercial exchange reemerged in Kingston. In his 1742 manuscript, James Knight described Kingston's public townhouse, a building dedicated to both law courts and public assemblies, as outfitted with "piazas" on all sides "where the trading people meet every day and is in the nature of an Exchange."[85] These two buildings, each the major public building of their respective city, appear to have made accommodations for shaded spaces for mercantile activities. In constructing piazzas on the front of their shops and houses in early eighteenth-century Kingston, it is possible that merchants were simply perpetuating and expanding forms already in place in seventeenth-century Port Royal.

As early as 1774, Edward Long noted that the fronts of most buildings in Kingston "are shaded with a piazza below, and a covered gallery above."[86] While many are heavily altered, examples of colonnaded house-stores survive along the major commercial street in St. John's, the capital and port city of (English) Antigua (fig. 6.21).

And a handful of similar buildings appeared along Waterfront Street in (Dutch) Paramaribo, Suriname, on the north coast of South America, after a major fire in 1821. This practice of sheltering the public way in front of the ground-floor shop, of course, is hardly unique to the Caribbean. In more monumental form, porticos or arcaded commercial streets and squares—called *portales* in Spanish—are found throughout southern Europe and across the Mediterranean, where they are also a response to climate. Similar arcaded streets could also be found in the newly developed sections of expanding seventeenth-century London, such as at Covent Gardens. Nineteenth-century examples appear also throughout colonial port towns in Southeast Asia, where buildings accommodate a "five-foot way" on the ground floor that creates a public walkway right along the street, sheltered from the elements by the second floor (fig. 6.22).[87] Via Spain, this form is manifest in Mexico and in the Spanish Caribbean, where merchants preferred to build masonry arcades; the Plaza Vieja in Havana, Cuba, for example, is ringed with commercial-residential buildings supported by recessed ground-floor arcades.[88] As suggested in chapter 3, the appearance of the Jamaican piazza has much to do with the adoption of that form and practice from the Spanish in Cuba. Yet, as Spiro Kostof has suggested, the arcaded commercial street reaches as far back as the ancient Roman Empire as an important component of urban commercial districts.[89] The notion of sheltering the public

FIG. 6.21 High Street, St. John's, Antigua.

FIG. 6.22 House-shops in Penang, Malaysia, nineteenth century.

space along primary commercial streets is a longstanding practice found across the globe, resulting in a fairly wide range of formal strategies.

The colonnaded commercial front of Falmouth's stores was not the only resolution to the problem of shading potential customers from the tropical sun.[90] In early Charleston, South Carolina, a statute forbade the erection of any encroachments on the street, allowing only for balconies that projected from a building no more than five feet.[91] An account of an accident involving the collapse of a balcony in the November 15, 1760, edition of the *South Carolina Gazette* commented with frustration on the practice of building balconies instead of street-front piazzas in Charleston: "Tis such a wonder that such accidents do not happen more frequently, as scarce any of the balconies in this town are supported with pillars, but rest solely on pieces of timber let into the ends or sides of houses, which rot at the ends into the houses."[92] The installation of a balcony that allowed outside access to residents of a second floor also created a shading device for the shop elevation and the public right of way below, much like canvas awnings would on fully commercial nineteenth-century buildings in Philadelphia, New York, and elsewhere.[93] Merchants in Marigot, the capital of French St. Martin, erected two-story masonry buildings fronted by covered balconies that were cantilevered from the building on beams and supported by spectacular iron brackets (fig. 6.23). Those in Bridgetown, Barbados, appear

to have preferred the balconies as well, although they are shallower and carried by scrolled wooden brackets, probably not unlike those erected in early Charleston.[94] Roseau, the capital of Dominica, first a French island but claimed by the British in 1763, has examples of both balconied and colonnaded shop fronts (figs. 6.24, 6.25). Whereas most port towns appear to prefer one strategy or the other, the presence of both in Roseau suggests the integration of both French and British practices. The effect of shading the sidewalk and the front of the store, of course, was the same in all these places, even if the architectural solution differed. In all cases, the buildings that stood along emerging commercial streets of Caribbean towns in the late eighteenth and early nineteenth centuries make clear that merchants in many diverse locations across the Caribbean were responding to the shared impulse to create comfortable and convenient shopping environments. They demonstrate that merchants in any locale tended to collectively agree on a shared strategy, reflecting the broader impulse among early modern merchants to create an ordered and unified commercial sphere.[95]

As merchants serving polite society erected buildings that shared a physical form, they did so in rows, creating streets dedicated to elite consumption.[96] One early nineteenth-century visitor to Kingston noted that "Port Royal street or Harbour Street . . . are the general resort of men of business, being composed of stores and counting houses."[97] As Martha Zierden's research has demonstrated,

FIG. 6.23 House-shop on rue de la République, Marigot, St. Martin, early nineteenth century.

Broad Street in Charleston emerged over the course of the eighteenth century as the preferred address for merchants in that city and became Charleston's polite shopping strip.[98] John Stobart has completed a similar analysis of Chester, England, and has noted the clustering of shops serving the elite on the town's two major streets, centered on the town's theater and public assembly rooms.[99] Merchants lobbied to have old and shabby medieval buildings torn down and replaced by new and regular (i.e., Georgian) facades. And in this way, the merchants building along Market Street in Falmouth—appropriately the dominant commercial street in town—engaged an unspoken social contract with one another; together they built houses that collectively transformed the character of the public sphere. The best evidence for this collective contract is the absence of fronting piazzas on the few

FIG. 6.24 House-shop on Church Street, Roseau, Dominica, early nineteenth century.

FIG. 6.25 House-shop on Church Street, Roseau, Dominica, early nineteenth century.

isolated examples of this building type on other streets in town. The fine little example on Upper Harbour Street, built in the 1820s, when piazzas were commonplace, stands entirely independent of other commercial house-stores and does so without a piazza (see fig. 6.5).

In addition to lobbying for better pavement and improved street lighting, merchants in Chester petitioned effectively in the last decades of the eighteenth century to have fairs and markets removed from the town's main streets, to create a more orderly and respectable commercial district.[100] In the late eighteenth century, for example, the city of Basse-Terre in Guadeloupe built a public promenade as part of a larger urban redesign.[101] As shops migrated toward greater material refinement and display, the streets they faced followed suit. In Falmouth and across the Caribbean, this move toward order and refinement was manifest in the formation of colonnaded commercial streets. If fashionable uniformity was the order of the day, the uniformity of the Caribbean commercial street was not a series of similarly proportioned shop windows under and between aligned belt courses and cornices but the regular march of columns down each side of the street. The result was a street-side colonnade, an architectural strategy that not only claimed the public way as semiprivate display space for merchandise but also sheltered potential customers from the intensity of the Caribbean sun.[102]

The importance of physical protection from the sun was particularly keen for elite women in the Caribbean, who were in these same years becoming a significant

factor in the culture of consumption.[103] This point is made quite plain in Augustino Brunias's 1770s painting of a market scene in Roseau, Dominica (fig. 6.26). In this image various market ladies sit on low stools selling everything from textiles to produce in a space framed on two sides by market buildings and on the third by a fabric shelter over a temporary booth. Dominating the middle of the scene is an exchange between two women, a seated vendor and a standing customer. The refinement and gentility of the customer are reinforced by the open space before her and by the gentleman seen just beyond her, giving her primacy in the picture. But probably most important for our purposes is the fact that she is shielded from the sun by a parasol held by a (likely enslaved) maidservant behind her. The difference in flesh tones is striking; she is singularly porcelain while most of the women in the scene are mulatto, and some exhibit even darker skin tones. The significance of preserving her "whiteness" is amplified not only by the act of a darker woman shielding a lighter woman from the sun but also by the stark whiteness of her dress; she is the only figure in the image dressed completely in white. In this market scene, this woman is singled out by her skin and risks darkening that skin through participation in leisure consumption.[104] The colonnaded streets of Falmouth and other Caribbean towns resolved this dilemma. Projecting balconies and, even more effectively, fully projecting upper floors functioned as sunshades, preventing the direct rays of the sun from penetrating the store interior and keeping the interior

FIG. 6.26 Augustino Brunias, *A Linen Market in Dominica*, 1770. 19⅝ × 27 in. (49.8 × 68.6 cm). Yale Center for British Art, Paul Mellon Collection.

cooler. The colonnades allowed potential customers, especially women, to stroll leisurely along the street, shaded from the rays of the sun.[105]

As demonstrated by a number of historians, the eighteenth century saw the slow decline of traditional markets and the increase of shops and stores as a response to growing consumerism and the emergence of shopping as a leisure activity.[106] Shops could be located in a variety of places in a cityscape, from wharves to main streets. If wharves were important commercial zones, they were also morally disreputable. In response, merchants in Falmouth and other towns in the greater British Empire worked to create an alternative, more respectable, commercial zone in socially "safer" spaces of the city. In Falmouth these shaded sidewalks worked to resist the common perception that the streets were beyond the bounds of polite society.[107] Market Street worked to be everything that the wharves and the market in Water Square were not: clean, attractive, and fashionable. Mirroring similar shifts in English towns, the sheltered

colonnades of Market Street's stores created a fashionable promenade where "parading and shopping could combine as status-acquiring activities in an environment free from heat and rain."[108] In the Caribbean, they also created spaces where men could convene in the deep shade of a cool store, reinforcing their distinction as elites differentiated from others in the public sphere. As a result, Falmouth's colonnaded commercial street was not just about physical comfort but about social comfort as well. Offering access to that deep shade, Falmouth's stores became sites where these elite men could segregate themselves from public space and engage in "lively conversation." Such conversations were claims on space; others who surely came into stores—women, nonlocals, nonelites, and nonwhites—were exposed as interlopers by their unwillingness or inability to participate. Similarly, the shaded and elevated space behind the colonnades created zones where women could participate in the burgeoning practice of leisure shopping safe from the intense racial and social intermixing of the wharves and protected from the darkening rays of the sun. The Barrett family house and store in Falmouth was an exemplar of architectural and social design in the Caribbean. It stood at the intersection of many landscapes and its physical form and location in the townscape helped those who used the store, the wharf, and the street to understand their place in Falmouth's complex social, racial, and economic hierarchy.

◆ ◆ ◆

Jamaica's enslaved and free blacks actively and creatively resisted these hierarchies. One of the most notable events in the Jamaican calendar is the Jonkonnu festival, which spans the days between Christmas and New Year's.[109] The festival was characterized by spectacular costume, "African masks," street parades and performances, and celebrations late into the night. With roots in West African religious rituals, by the early nineteenth century the festival had clear undertones of reversal and resistance to white authority.[110] One description of the event in early nineteenth-century Falmouth made clear the mimicry and reversal: "His Lordship, as well as several other distinguished characters, were personated by negroes in full costume."[111] These performances were of great interest to white Jamaicans; some even collected African masks, purchasing them for display in their houses.[112] One of the practices most shocking to white chroniclers was the practice of racial and spatial inversion. As Susan Davis has demonstrated in her excellent work on nineteenth-century Philadelphia, parades and street festivities are often closely aligned with critiques of established power structures through claims on the public space of the street by the disenfranchised and sometimes through outright mockery.[113] There is abundant evidence for these practices in the Jamaican Jonkonnu festival.[114]

In 1837, the English artist Isaac Belisario published a series of sketches that illustrate a number of the characters central to Jonkonnu festivals that he witnessed.[115] In one of these images, Belisario represents a figure named "Actor-Boy" in spectacular costume, with a whiteface mask and a wig, followed by a band (fig. 6.27). Belisario makes the point to situate this event in the street before the tall columns of a typical Jamaican merchant's house. Through costume, music, and spectacle, these black Jamaicans make an effective claim on the public sphere, which for the other fifty-one weeks of the year forced them to the social and economic margin. Under the protective mask of the festival, black Jamaicans felt empowered to speak

out against their oppression, but always in a guarded dance. As one chronicler described:

> The merriment became rather boisterous as the punch operated, and the slaves sang satirical philippics against their master, communicating a little free advice now and then; but they never lost sight of decorum, and at last retired, apparently quite satisfied with their saturnalia.[116]

But this spatial inversion, where blacks for a brief season seized control of the spaces of white authority, was not limited to the streets. During the festival, blacks, free and enslaved, were welcomed into great houses where they celebrated as equals with the white family.

> On these occasions, the slaves appear to be an altered race of beings. They show themselves off to the greatest advantage, by fine clothes and a profusion of trinkets; they affect a more polished behavior and mode of speech; they address the whites with greater familiarity; they come into their master's houses and drink with them; the distance between them appears to be annihilated for the moment.[117]

As was probably the case for many English observers, such inversion was at least uncomfortable, if not threatening: "They took possession of the house en masse, with the exception of our bedrooms. Such a motley assembly! . . . [which] continued till late the following day."[118] Another wrote: "They completely besieged my room, which opens on the garden, so that I was forced to remain a prisoner, and listen to their rude songs, which I should fancy must be very much like the wild yelling and screaming that we read of in African travels."[119]

The central character for the entire festival was the one wearing an elaborate house headdress, an object called the jonkonnu (fig. 6.28).[120] As shown in Belisario's image, the Jonkonnu character supports a highly fanciful, multistoried house with plumes rising from the top. One late eighteenth-century writer describes another example:

> They wear a representation of an edifice, sometimes very prettily devised and executed in the stile of a baby house, shewing different fronts with open doors, glazed windows, stair cases, piazzas & balconies, in which diminutive figures are placed. They now and then salute with the discharge of little guns placed in some of the buildings. Small looking glasses are also used to embellish the person.[121]

FIG. 6.27 Isaac Mendes Belisario, "Actor Boy" from *Sketches of Character: In Illustration of the Habits, Occupation, and Costume of the Negro Population, in the Island of Jamaica* (Kingston, Jamaica: Published by the artist, 1837). Yale Center for British Art.

Drawn after nature, and on stone, by I. M. Belisario   Printed by A. Duperly.

FIG. 6.28 Isaac Mendes Belisario, "Jaw-Bone, or House John-Canoe" from *Sketches of Character: In Illustration of the Habits, Occupation, and Costume of the Negro Population, in the Island of Jamaica* (Kingston, Jamaica: Published by the artist, 1837). Yale Center for British Art.

While the range of representation could be quite wide, these remarkable objects were marked by some commonalities. In particular, they were always manufactured specifically and annually for each festival. Scholars of the festival have tied the manufacture of the house to a religious ritual of West African origin that was devised to appease the spirits of the ancestors. The design and construction of the house is managed under spiritual consultation with the ancestors, accompanied by drink and food offerings. In some of the earliest ethnographic evidence on the festival, the jonkonnu is presented to the community on Christmas Day in the local cemetery, where the house represents the gathered community, living and deceased.[122] While this might well be the case, I'd like to make two simple observations that suggest an additional interpretation: (1) the figure wears a building that more closely approximates the architecture of the master rather than the architecture of the slave; and (2) the entire weight of the house rests on his head. He literally supports the house. In this way, the house might also be seen to represent the houses of elite whites. Or by extension, the house might be a surrogate for the houses, or even the bodies, of white elites.[123]

This alternative or additional reading of the jonkonnu house is made all the more significant when we consider the final act of the festival—at least in its late twentieth-century manifestations—once the jonkonnu is returned to the cemetery in early January. In more recent iterations, festival-goers reach a climax in their dance and suddenly the house is violently destroyed. Through a traditional West African lens, the house represents the gathering of the ancestors and its destruction, the appeasement of ancestral spirits for another year.[124] But if in Jamaica the jonkonnu house is or was a surrogate for white authority over black lives, the violence has a clear and subversive meaning.[125] The palpable anger and frustration that results from a long legacy of racial oppression finds temporary release. Physical violence to a symbolic surrogate, even to a festival headpiece, became an ultimate act of resistance.

◆ ◆ ◆

The distinctive merchant house-stores of Falmouth and other towns across Jamaica, and in various forms across the Caribbean, gave Britons the opportunity to participate in the British Empire through consumption. Rejecting the large glass fronts of stores elsewhere across the empire but incorporating their pronounced colonnades,

merchants built a public sphere of consumption that was distinctively Jamaican. These spaces worked to segregate as they differentiated shopping for internationally imported goods from the carts of local sellers and Sunday markets that offered products of local production. The power of elite spaces was recognized easily by the marginalized; the annual Jonconnu festivals that overtook public spaces claimed them for a time, all the while engaging in mockery of elite behavior and elite materialism. These spaces facilitated and shaped the arrival and departure of oceans of goods and people, a flow of exchange, segregation, and consumption that defined Jamaica's place in the empire of goods.

7   The Jamaican Creole House

Nestled in the dramatic hill country of St. Ann Parish, Mount Plenty is a remarkable survival (fig. 7.1). Built sometime in the third quarter of the eighteenth century, the house is now a spectacular residence and gallery space for a prominent Jamaican artist, and the main house of a large ranch managed by her husband. The eighteenth-century front of the house faced north, sheltered in shadow from the unforgiving southern sun, a common orientation in the Caribbean. The primary northern elevation is little more than a wall of louvered openings—called jalousies in Jamaica—interspersed with occasional sash windows, interrupted only by the central double doors. These open into a long narrow room that spans the front of the house (fig. 7.2). Open to the breeze, this gallery space is pleasant through most of the day. Two larger spaces, probably once used as a hall and bedchamber, stand behind this front gallery; two small corner chambers occupy the southeastern and southwestern corners. The house seems perfectly suited to its circumstances. But close inspection suggests that the house originally had a very different exterior envelope (figs. 7.3, 7.4). The range of jalousies and sash windows were all installed near the turn of the nineteenth century, closing in what

was originally an open piazza that ranged on at least three sides of the two-room house core; the east and west sides of Mount Plenty included "chambers" enclosed on three sides but defined on the fourth by only the columns and rails of the open piazza. In these spaces, intermediary walls complete with baseboards, cornices, and solid wooden doors divided the long front piazza from the two chambers on the side piazzas. Thus the two small corner chambers at the southeast and southwest corners had semiprivate piazzas of their own, just as the two primary chambers claimed the long front piazza. As reconstructed to its original appearance, the house at Mount Plenty resembles a house type found across Jamaica that became common by the third quarter of the eighteenth century: the Jamaican Creole house.[1]

◆ ◆ ◆

As early as 1765, an overseer charged with building a great house reported to his client in England that "both your mother and aunt have a great objection against the house having no piazzas." They considered the house plans he sent from England as unsuited to their circumstances; they preferred instead "a Jamaica house."[2] Writing soon

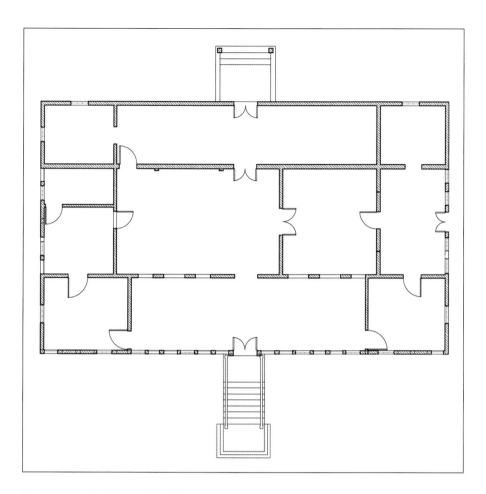

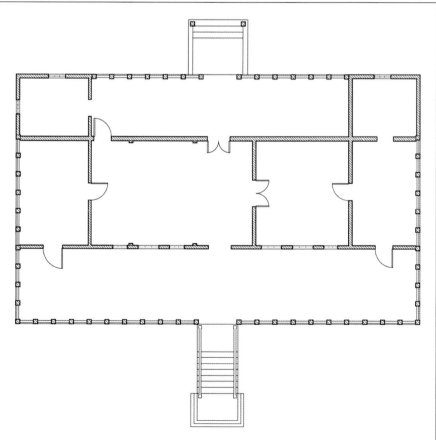

FIG. 7.1 (opposite, top) North elevation of Mount Plenty, St. Ann Parish, Jamaica, ca. 1770.

FIG. 7.2 (opposite, bottom) North gallery of Mount Plenty.

FIG. 7.3 (above left) Plan of Mount Plenty, St. Ann Parish, Jamaica, as it stood by the mid-nineteenth century.

FIG. 7.4 (left) Reconstructed plan of Mount Plenty, St. Ann Parish, Jamaica, late eighteenth century.

FIG. 7.5 Pierre Eugène du Simitière, "View in the Island of Jamaica," ca. 1760s. Private collection.

thereafter, Edward Long noted that planters on the island built in a standardized fashion: a house with a large hall flanked on either side by bedchambers, often with a shed with smaller rooms to the rear and a piazza to the front.[3] In September 1801, only months after her arrival, Lady Maria Nugent noted of one planter's house that it was "the usual one, of one story with a piazza." In a journal entry a few months later, she went so far as to name the type. Nugent breakfasted at Bushy Park, the house of one Mr. Mitchell. After describing a breakfast "in the Creole style—cassada cakes, coffee, tea, fruits of all sorts, pigeon pies, hams, tongues, rounds of beef, &c," she commented on his house, which was also "truly Creole" with rich mahogany woodwork and "galleries, piazzas, porticoes, etc."[4] But the most detailed description comes in the opening years of the nineteenth century from Matthew Lewis, more famous for his pen name Monk Lewis. He described planters' houses as "generally built and arranged to one and the same model." His own house was a wood frame building "partly raised upon pillars"; the elevated house "consists of a single floor." The dominant feature of the house, and of all houses of the type, was "a long gallery, called a piazza." Running across the front of the house, the piazza was "terminated at each end by a square room."[5] Similar buildings surface also in the pictorial record, such as that appearing in the foreground of a Du Simitière watercolor and in the background of a Philip Wickstead portrait, both from the 1760s (figs. 7.5, 7.6). In the Du Simitière watercolor, the two-story house appears to have ground-floor service spaces and upper-level living spaces. The whole of the building is wrapped on all four sides by a two-story gallery open below and ringed by a rail and balustrade above.

The distinctive house form emerged in Jamaica over the course of the late eighteenth century, first called "Creole" by British visitors—probably with an air of derision. "Creole" is a complicated term.[6] While one of the earliest uses of the term distinguished an American-born slave from an African-born slave, by the middle of the eighteenth century the term was also used by British

FIG. 7.6 Philip Wickstead, detail from *Portrait of an Unknown Jamaican Couple*, ca. 1760s.

visitors to the Caribbean to distinguish white West Indians from themselves.[7] Englishwoman Ann Storrow noted of her very first accommodations in Kingston, Jamaica, that they were directed by a "real creole to the back bone."[8] For Storrow a Creole was a person distinct in type from herself, and that distinction implicated more than just place of birth. Edward Long dedicated ten pages of his three-volume history to his discussion of the "native white men, or Creoles, of Jamaica," and another four pages to Creole women.[9] Significantly, he differentiates "Creoles, or natives," from "Europeans and other Whites." While he certainly categorizes both as "white" they were in Long's mind clearly distinct, even to the point of physical, genetic distinction, almost a different race. The men, for example, were tall and well-shaped but sometimes "inclined to corpulence." Among other distinguishing characteristics, they have high cheek bones and eye sockets "deeper than is commonly observed among the natives of England," a physical adaptation, he argues, to the intense glare of the tropical sun. Although they are "descended from British ancestors," they had become their own kind, physically differentiated from Britain-born Britons.[10]

Long attributed the distinction to climate: the heat had reshaped Creole bodies. The general beauty of the Creole children was a result of a childhood free of restraint. Girls were "not suffered to wear stays," and boys "are indulged in such a cool and unconfined attire, as admits the free extension of their limbs and muscles." But this lack of restraint generated remarkably unrefined habits. "We may see," he argues, "a very fine young woman awkwardly dangling her arms with the air of a Negroe-servant, lolling almost the whole day upon beds or settees . . . her dress loose, and without stays."[11] He also noted that "the natives of Jamaica are dancers from their infancy." And although there were medical proscriptions against such action, Long argued that Jamaicans, especially Jamaican women, were very fond of dancing.[12] John Stewart also argued that the Jamaican heat "naturally begets a languor, listlessness, and disposition to self-indulgence."[13] As Justin Greving has suggested, most later eighteenth- and early nineteenth-century authors followed Long's lead by suggesting that Creoles were distinct from their British cousins certainly by behavior but also in physical description.[14] In the popular imagination, Creoles were physically, socially, and culturally distinguishable from Britons born in the British Isles.

What remains ever present but entirely unspoken is the fact that the term also implicated racial boundaries.

When Maria Nugent described one house as "perfectly in the Creole style," the Creole nature of the house was shaped by black bodies: "A number of negroes, men, women and children running and lying about, in all parts of it. Never in my life did I smell so many."[15] Here to describe a house as Creole is not just architectural but racial. Nugent noted the extraordinary custom among enslaved Africans to sleep throughout the house, abiding very few spatial boundaries, a condition unsettling to someone reared in the spatial regulation of late eighteenth-century British households. But, also worthy of note, the penetration of slaves into the house is associated with the open, unregulated nature of the piazza, as galleries were a common place for slaves to sleep. And, as Christer Petley has recently demonstrated, the choice by a Jamaican planter to keep a white wife came with the material consequences of keeping up "appearances" in the form of an expensively equipped household. Social mores allowed those who chose the alternative of living with a black or a mixed-race "housekeeper" to live far more relaxed and moderate lifestyles in less properly appointed houses.[16]

Jamaica's racial intermixing was very well known. None other than Edward Long went so far as to chart the various stages of race by naming the "types" of children from various white and mixed-race matches.[17] Concern for racial intermixing generated increased anxiety in the later eighteenth century as the population of free people of color grew exponentially.[18] J. B. Moreton argued that "when deprived of the advancement of an European education, [Creoles] are assuming and presuming, negroefied, aukward, ignorant gewgaws."[19] For this opinion he depends on a long-held belief that white Creole children, when suckled by an African nurse, eventually speak "in drawling broken English, like the Negroes."[20] While not explicitly acknowledging the reality of interracial coupling, these authors located the "negroified" condition of Creoles in their physical, social, and certainly sexual proximity to Africans. Creole was simultaneously an architectural practice and one shaped by racial mixing, a mixing that caused British observers deep anxiety.

And it is no surprise that the characterization of white Creoles came into focus in the later decades of the eighteenth century, for these were also the years in which increasing numbers of wealthy Jamaican-born planters permanently removed to Britain. Historians have long debated the extent and importance of Jamaican absenteeism, generally seeing it as both extensive and destructive to the colonial project of building a stable, "anglicized" Jamaican society. But as Trevor Burnard has recently shown, this view often depends too heavily on eighteenth-century commentators rather than empirical data from the period.[21] His assessment makes clear that those who did leave were usually the very wealthiest and the largest landowners; by the end of the eighteenth century, absentee planters owned almost one quarter of the total acreage held in plantations. This shaped Britain, by establishing a swelling population of white West Indians moving in British elite circles, especially in London, a topic addressed in chapter 9. But rising absenteeism also shaped Jamaica. As noted in chapter 5, the construction of self-consciously fashionable houses and landscapes that responded to current British practice petered out in the closing decades of the eighteenth century. The departure of the very wealthiest from Jamaica left behind a more self-consciously Creole class of planters, managers, and attorneys as the island's powerbrokers. As a result, by the turn of the century the "Creole" had been clearly defined in the British imagination as West Indian–born, culturally distinct, racially blurred, given to physical indulgence, and lacking in refinement. Through the eighteenth century, ascription as "Creole" by a British speaker implied cultural derision; by the early nineteenth century, the term was commonly embraced by Jamaicans as a marker of self-identity. This identity was manifest in various cultural forms, language, dress, comportment, and for our purposes, houses.

The surviving architecture and the numerous written descriptions and visual images make clear that over the course of the later eighteenth century, Jamaicans generated for themselves a distinctive form of house, one comprising three typical features: (1) one-story living, (2) a large central hall flanked by smaller chambers, and (3) piazzas. As has already been argued in previous chapters, some of these features are, of course, a direct accommodation to climate. But the house form was not entirely driven by climate; these distinctive spaces became stages for a particular form of cultural performance, an informality that flew in the face of the spectacle of refinement and comportment that defined elite British social and cultural mores. The Creole house was itself a spectacle, a stage for the performance of an alternative sociability, one governed by physical comfort for whites and racial ambivalence—white hospitality, miscegenation, and the corporal punishment of black bodies.

SINGLE-STORY LIVING

The first and most distinctive feature of these commonly described houses was the limitation of polite living spaces to a single story. Quite obviously shaped by the lessons learned from dozens of hurricanes through the late seventeenth and eighteenth centuries, Jamaican planters knew that houses with lower profiles were generally more resilient to the ravaging winds of hurricanes and the devastation of earthquakes. The significance of this form to Creole identity is best revealed in the story of the house at Seville.

FIG. 7.7 Seville plantation, St. Ann Parish, Jamaica.

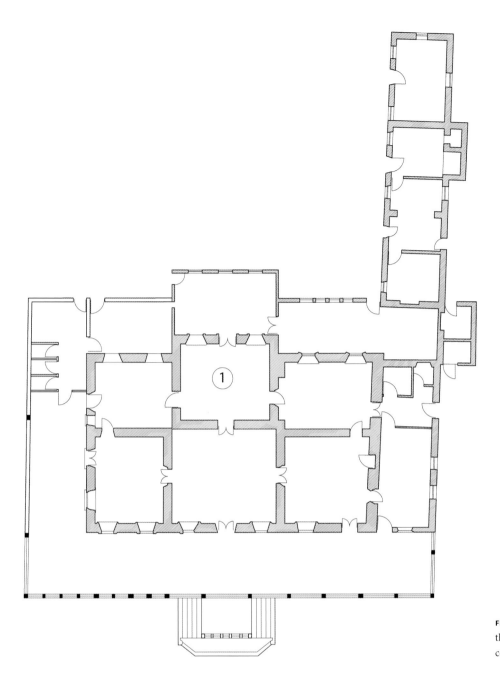

FIG. 7.8 Plan of Seville. The "1" marks the original stairhall before the conversion to a single-story house.

Easily accessible from the northern coastal road, Seville plantation in St. Ann Parish is one of the most important historic sites managed by the Jamaica National Heritage Trust (fig. 7.7). Just north of the coast road lies the archaeological site of the seventeenth-century Spanish settlement of Nuova Sevilla. Visitors can wander around the foundations of the governor's house and examine the remains of an ancient Spanish sugar works. A short drive up the entrance road leads past the huge iron waterwheel that powered the late eighteenth-century British sugar mill. From the mill, the road leads up to the great house site. Although there is to one side a reconstructed African slave quarter and to the rear the range of outbuildings that framed the work yard, it is the broad low great house fronted by a sweeping piazza that commands attention. But the house as it stands today is quite different from the house as it was built in the middle of the eighteenth century. Possibly begun as early as the 1720s but certainly completed by the mid-1740s, the British great house at Seville was originally a two-story masonry pile with six rooms per floor fronted by a broad thirty-foot-wide by fourteen-foot-deep piazza.[22] Eighteenth-century visitors ascended a set of stairs to the piazza, then passed directly into the hall, the largest room in the house. Two equally sized but smaller chambers stood to either side of this hall, and the tripartite arrangement was mirrored in the three rooms at the rear, the center of which was probably the stairhall to the upper story (fig. 7.8).

The Jamaican Creole House   **193**

The extraordinary and bold rusticated surround of the central door of the main northern elevation positions this building squarely in the robust Anglo-Georgian building tradition (fig. 7.9). Furthermore, the deep, six-room plan compares favorably with well-built two-story masonry gentry houses in England and the American colonies of the mid-eighteenth century. Beginning in the late seventeenth century, houses of the English gentry and aristocracy were commonly framed around a central two-room core of front hall and rear saloon, typically with a symmetrical flank of chambers to either side of this ceremonial core. Ragley Hall in Warwickshire, built in the 1670s by architect Robert Hooke, is an excellent, if grandiose, example. Scholars of architecture in early Virginia have noted numerous examples of this tradition surfacing in that colony. Carter's Grove, built in the mid-1750s for one of Virginia's most prominent tobacco planter families, exhibits a similar six-room floor plan (fig. 7.10). In this plan, the rear central chamber is dominated by the staircase—as was the case at Seville—but was separated from the front hall by only a broad arch. The midcentury house at Seville was squarely a product of this Georgian house-building tradition.

But sometime in the 1780s—probably the storm of October 1780—a massive hurricane extensively damaged the house at Seville. In the following months and years it was reconstructed into its current form; the entire upper floor was removed, the staircase extracted, and the small front piazza expanded to a much broader piazza encasing three sides of the house. It was this reconstructed house that was visited by then-governor Nugent and his wife in March 1802, when she described it as "Creole."[23] Resident in Jamaica for two years by the time of her visit to Seville, Lady Nugent had come to recognize that many Jamaicans lived in houses that were distinctive; they incorporated characteristics unfamiliar to someone raised in Britain. While she would not have known the house in its pre-hurricane state, in its single-story iteration with large central hall and broad piazza, it was to her emblematic of a Creole house.

One-story living did not always mean one-story houses. By the later eighteenth century, many of Jamaica's plantation houses were fully two floors, the ground floor relegated to service spaces, with access to the main-floor polite spaces usually rising via an exterior staircase. As Matthew Lewis described of his own house, "There is nothing underneath except a few store-rooms and a kind of waiting hall."[24] Hyde Hall, built of nogged walling over an ashlar masonry foundation, is an excellent example (see fig. 3.24). From the exterior, Hyde Hall seems self-evidently a two-story house; the architecture of the building worked very hard to convey that the house had only a single story for polite purposes. Visitors arriving in pleasant weather could ascend the long run of exterior

FIG. 7.9 Rusticated door surround at Seville, ca. 1740s.

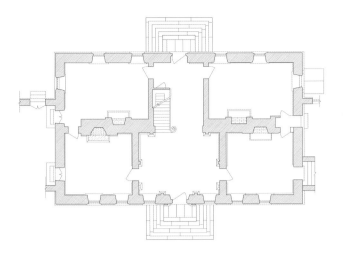

FIG. 7.10 Plan of Carter's Grove, outside Williamsburg, Virginia, 1750s.

stair to the main living floor. Those arriving in inclement weather would arrive under the shelter of the arcade, where a circular stone stair also gave direct access to the main floor (fig. 7.11). Once inside the main floor, visitors were presented with an unusually deep and long hall that passed right through to the building's rear piazza. In a planning tradition not entirely unlike that at Seville, this main public core was flanked to either side by pairs of more private chambers. All of these spaces contained by nogged walling stand above a full masonry ground floor of large bare chambers dedicated to the everyday work of

maintaining the house. While not universal, this strategy of elevating the polite spaces of the house over service spaces contained within a raised masonry foundation was not at all uncommon.[25]

THE HALL

Through the eighteenth century and well into the next, most visitors to Jamaica noted that the majority of houses were dominated by a large, well-ventilated hall.[26] As reported by one visitor: "A flight of stone steps . . . [leads] up to the front door, and he is immediately ushered into a spacious hall. . . . The large hall is characteristic of all Jamaican houses."[27] The centrality of the hall to the Jamaican house throughout the period in question is strongly supported by evidence from probate records: room-by-room inventories from the 1710s to the 1810s consistently begin with an inventory of the hall. This space was the primary hub of circulation. One weary traveler, upon entering an apparently unoccupied house, stepped from the piazza into the hall, then "from the hall into a suite of rooms to my left, which I traversed until the course of them brought me back to the hall." He then crossed the hall to make a "tour of the other side of the house."[28] The core function of the hall is clearly evident also in the surviving examples. In most cases, the room is open to both front and rear of the house. At Hyde Hall, the front stair opens into the large single hall, which runs

FIG. 7.11 Arcade stair, Hyde Hall plantation, Trelawny Parish, Jamaica, 1820.

FIG. 7.12 Arcadia, Trelawny Parish, Jamaica. ca. 1820.

through to the piazza along the rear elevation of the building. The main floor at Arcadia is approached through two exterior stairs that open directly into the hall (figs. 7.12, 7.13). Large central halls survive also in the visual record, as in the central hall at Belle Isle plantation, depicted in an early nineteenth-century watercolor (fig. 7.14).[29] In this view, the large hall with a tall coved ceiling and highly polished floors has chairs and mirrors along the walls and opens into a front gallery enclosed with sash windows and jalousies and likely filled with sofas and more comfortable furniture.

The persistence of the hall as the central living space of the Jamaican house through the eighteenth century is remarkable in light of changing planning practices elsewhere in the British world. Direct access from the exterior into the hall was certainly the most common arrangement for elite English houses through the seventeenth and early eighteenth centuries, both in the motherland and across the Anglo-American Atlantic.[30] But elites and aspiring elites began to embrace more complex house planning strategies in the opening decades of the eighteenth century, primarily through the introduction and embrace of the entrance hall among the aristocracy in England and the central passage plan among the gentry.[31] In the latter arrangement, the main door of the house opened not into the hall but a central passage, often filled with a stair rising to the upper story. This central passage then gave access

FIG. 7.13 Hall at Arcadia, Trelawny Parish, Jamaica, ca. 1820.

FIG. 7.14 Artist unknown, *Belle Isle House, Jamaica*, ca. 1820. Private collection.

to the sociable spaces of the house, sometimes still called a hall but more commonly called a parlor. By the middle of the eighteenth century, the central passage plan was the recognized preference among merchants in port towns and in rural contexts, from small country houses in southern England to plantation houses along the James River in Virginia. The central passage plan, for example, appears in colonial Virginia in the 1710s, and was a common building strategy among elites there by midcentury. As numerous architectural historians have demonstrated, the introduction of the central passage was an attempt to create greater social distance between elites and others. Architectural historian Mark Wenger reports a mid-eighteenth-century account from Virginia where a planter engages with one of his slaves not in the hall but in the passage.

> About ten an old Negro Man came with a complaint to Mr. Carter of the Overseer. . . . The humble posture in which the old Fellow placed himself before he

began moved me. We were sitting in the passage, he sat himself down on the Floor clasp'd his Hands together, with his face directly to Mr. Carter, & then began his Narration.[32]

As the hall became an increasingly refined space dedicated to the rituals of elite sociability, the introduction of the central passage became a social buffer, a space for engagement across social, economic, and racial boundaries. Significantly, middling and elite Jamaicans seem not to have embraced the central passage, preferring instead to retain immediate access from the exterior into the hall throughout the eighteenth and well into the nineteenth century. To this point we will return.

While Jamaican halls were usually centrally located in the plan of the house and were typically the largest room in that plan, they varied considerably in architectural finish. Some galleries and halls, like those in Mount Plenty, boasted plastered walls and rich architectural ornament (see fig. 7.2). But the console brackets supporting the modillion cornices and elegant door pediments in Mount Plenty are unmatched by plainer finishes elsewhere in the house. This odd juxtaposition of richly sophisticated and generally plain suggests that these ornaments were not fashioned by a carpenter on site but purchased from a shop in Kingston selling sets of imported ornament. Evidence for such importation appears in the Kingston newspapers:

> IMPORTED For sale at Sterling, Gost, and Charges, 24 Sash Frames and Sashes eight feet by four glazed with the best Crown glass with patent Brass Fastenings, Mahogany Window shutters, &c. also 2 pair Mahogany Folding Doors 10 feet by 2½ each with fine plate Brass locks with Drop Handles, &c. The whole being completed in the most elegant Modern Taste, by an approved workman at *Bath*.[33]

If merchants were importing sash frames and doors, they were certainly importing sets of architectural ornament as well. The ornamentation of the stairhall of Cardiff Hall in St. Ann Parish, the 1789 house built by William Blagrove, is spectacular and astonishing. Running along the Doric screen separating the front hall from the rear stairhall is a Doric cornice complete with bucrania (ox sculls) (fig. 7.15; see fig. 5.15). Sometimes, halls were richly painted in the most fashionable colors:

> J & H Stevensons [offer] a complete assortment of COLOURS for finishing and decorating Rooms, Halls, Staircases Lobbys, &c. . . . This kind of painting is particularly adapted to this climate, where vermin harbor in wainscot and behind papering.[34]

But most halls were generally very plain. One advertisement in the *Jamaica Mercury and Kingston Weekly Advertiser* for a house for sale noted that the finishes were to a Jamaican standard: "The doors and window shutters are all paneled, the shingles planed, and the laths and rafters planed, beaded and painted, and the whole completed in a neat and workmanlike manner."[35] Leaving the framing members, either studs or rafters, exposed to the interior was a common practice even in fashionable Jamaican houses by the late eighteenth century. In the same advertisement just cited, the shop was picked out as a special room because it was "neatly ceil'd."[36] While in meaner houses, this absence of a ceiling is less striking, it is entirely remarkable in grand houses like Arcadia. In the best chambers of this and other houses, elegant neoclassical ornamentation frames window and door openings and light beads trim summer beams, yet the absence of any ceiling gives view directly through to the underside of shingles (fig. 7.16). This absence was surely a response to the region's heat: open piazzas or jalousies introduced cooler air that forced warmer air up into the roof framing. The same

FIG. 7.15 Detail of Doric entablature in Cardiff Hall, St. Ann Parish, Jamaica, 1789.

FIG. 7.16 Interior, Good Hope plantation, Trelawny Parish, Jamaica.

practice extended also to walls. One house for sale noted that the walls were "framed and boarded on both sides," distinguishing these from the normal practice of boarding only one side of a partition wall.[37] Surviving examples demonstrate repeatedly that walls were often boarded on only the side facing the better chamber.

When the occasion lent itself, the floors of the hall were waxed and polished to a very high sheen. One visitor noted that upon the occasion of a party presenting her daughters to eligible bachelors, one Jamaican woman paid close attention to her floors: "The house was washed inside and outside; the floors and piazzas of fine cedar were rubbed with wax, and shone like polished mahogany."[38] As in the case of Wales in Trelawny Parish, the floors were often polychrome (fig. 7.17):

> The floor is made of the most beautiful of the native woods, in the selection of which much taste is displayed, as also in the arrangement, so that the various colours of the wood may harmonize or contrast well with each other. . . . Scarcely anything surprises a European more than to tread on floors as beautifully polished as the finest of our tables in our drawing rooms."[39]

John Stewart noted that the "smoothness of polish" on the floors "rival even the finest mahogany tables."[40] Always the largest room in the house, some Jamaican halls were finished handsomely with plastered and painted walls and rich architectural ornament, but the majority were fairly plain spaces, with exposed framing and polished floors.

The hall was usually the locus of entertaining, at least before the nineteenth century when probate records begin to show increasing interest in purposely named "dining rooms." When one traveler "took shelter at a plantation belonging to a Mr. Fraser from Inverness," he was pleased that the planter "entertained us in true West India style."[41] This "West India style" generally meant extravagant food and brilliant display of plate on tables housed in oddly simple or plain chambers. John Stewart informed his readers that "Creoles are not extravagantly expensive in their furniture; this is generally plain but genteel. Their sideboards and beaufets, however, display a costly brilliancy, in unison with the plentiful and splendid cheer which is spread on their dinner tables."[42] Similarly,

> there are some peculiarities in the habits of life of the White Inhabitants which cannot fail to catch the eye of an European newly arrived; one of which is the contrast between the general plenty and magnificence of their tables (at least in Jamaica) and the meanness of their houses and apartments; it being no uncommon thing to find, at the country habitations of the planters, a splendid sideboard loaded with plate, and the choicest wines, a table covered with the finest damask, and a dinner of perhaps sixteen or twenty covers; and all this, in a hovel not superior to an English barn.[43]

FIG. 7.17 Detail of floors in Wales, Trelawny Parish, Jamaica.

The meanness of the hall in this description very likely reflects the general absence of interior ornamentation and the usual absence of ceilings. But as suggested by this description, the simplicity of the space was counterbalanced by the overabundance in plate and food.

And "West India style" also meant presenting food unfamiliar to most European or British visitors. The food on the table was often described by visitors as "Creole." Bryan Edwards noted that he much preferred the "native growths" of Jamaica—including the chocho, okra, lima bean, and kale—to the "esculent vegetables" of Europe. He also favored plantains, yams, bananas, callaloo—"a type of spinnage"—cassava, and sweet potatoes. A mixture of these, he reported to his readers, with salted fish and hotly seasoned with cayenne pepper is a favorite of Jamaicans, both black and white.[44] Thomas Thistlewood served visitors roast beef and cheese as well as "crabs, shrimps, roast teal" at one feast. At a Christmas he served "stewed mudfish, and picked crabs, stewed hogshead, fried liver etc, quarter of roast pork with papah sauce and fresh potatoes. Bread roast yam, & plantains boiled." He finished the meal with "marshmelon, watermelon, oranges, French Brandy . . . punch and porter."[45] On other occasions he served "roast goose with paw-paw sauce."[46] As Bryan Edwards had described years earlier, John Stewart, writing in 1808, indicated that less formal meals included pepper pot:

> certain favorite viands, such as the black or land crab, shrimps, toasted green Indian corn, pepper-pot (a distinguished dish, made so hot with green pepper, that one can hardly endure it in the mouth), *tum-tum,* that is plantains beat into a kind of dough, and boiled in the pepper pot, and several other articles. This must be eaten with the assistance of the fingers alone; for knives and forks are on this occasion proscribed![47]

Jamaican tables were adorned with plentiful tropical fruits, turtle soups, rum drinks, and other consumables alien to Britains back home; they were also shaped by the close intermixture with African foodways, as the pepper pot and *tum-tum* suggest.

The spectacular finish of Jamaican floors would be all the more visible when the dining table was removed and the floor was made open for dancing, a common and popular Jamaican pastime. In fact, Moreton described both mixed-race and white Creoles as "amazing fond of dancing."[48] The music, however, was not familiar to most visitors: "Even if the music of the violins were better than

it is, it would be spoiled by the uncouth and deafening noise of the drums, which the negro musicians think is indispensable, and which the dancers strangely continue to tolerate."[49] The same would be true of the dancing. A satirical view of a ball in the King's House makes this point quite clear. "A Grand Jamaica Ball! or the Creolean Hop à la Mustic" makes explicit reference to the Creole nature of the dancing (fig. 7.18). In the image, Jamaica's ladies engage in all sorts of scandalous comportment: reclining most ungracefully, drinking to excess, dancing in a manner shocking to gentility. The top right vignette reports the eventual outcome of these dances: sex. Given their lack of composure, these ladies are, so says the satirist, utterly "charmless." And this event took place in the grand Egyptian Hall of the governor's house. If the erection of sophisticated architecture was intended to instill refinement, this room appears to have failed. The Creoles depicted here were represented as overindulgent and indecorous, even a bit sleazy. Dancing as preview to sex was made explicit in Thomas Thistlewood's diary when he noted that it was common to sprinkle pepper on the floor of a dance hall because "as soon as they begin to warm it rises and has such an effect upon the women's thighs, &c that it almost sets them mad and easy to be debauched."[50] The hall, standing literally in the center of the building as the central space of everyday life in the Jamaican house, was the locus of most meals and dancing, common events of everyday sociability among Jamaica's white population.

Even so, Jamaican houses provided a few smaller public spaces. The most common room appending the hall in rural Jamaican houses before the 1720s was often a room simply called "the chamber." James Tebber's house, inventoried in 1719, included a hall, a chamber, two shed rooms, and a cook room, this last probably in a separate building.[51] This two-room hall and chamber arrangement echoes the most common house core found across the British world through the seventeenth century and well into the eighteenth. But by the second decade of the eighteenth century, Jamaicans began to live in houses with an alternative plan.[52] As early as 1718, a house in the parish of St. Dorothy was described as fifty-six feet long and forty feet wide with a twenty-four by twenty foot hall, and one chamber "on each side" measuring sixteen by twenty each. The rear shed had two lodging rooms which likely flanked an open porch between.[53] James Herbert's 1726 inventory described his house as having a hall and a chamber to the left and right, together with a shade and an entry. In 1741, Joseph Heiser's house included

FIG. 7.18 "A Grand Jamaica Ball! or the Creolean Hop à la Muftee." Etching with hand coloring, 11⅜ × 19 in. (29.8 × 48.4 cm). Image courtesy the Walpole Library, Yale University

a hall together with a west room and an east room. The earliest surviving example of this plan is certainly Halse Hall, built sometime in the very early eighteenth century.

The plan was fairly common on Jamaican plantations by the time Thomas Thistlewood described the house he occupied as an overseer upon his first arrival on the island in 1750. The building was of wattle walls and thatch roof. Disposed into three rooms, the middle hall was the largest at eleven by fifteen feet, flanked on each side by a smaller chamber measuring eight and one half by fifteen feet. The hall had four doors, one each to the outside through the front and rear walls and one into each of the flanking chambers.[54] In the 1770s, Edward Long described typical houses as disposed into three divisions: "The centre room is a hall, communicating at each end with a bedchamber; the back part, usually a shed, is divided in the same manner, and communicates with the front, or principal hall, by an arch, which in some houses is wainscoted with mahogany."[55]

Long asserts quite directly that the tripartite plan of a large central hall and flanking chambers was Spanish in origin. After describing the plan, he reports "the English in general have copied the ichnography of the Spanish houses with great uniformity"; this is a view that remains broadly accepted in the scholarly literature.[56] Besides the English on the island of Jamaica, their French counterparts derived their "Creole" plan from Spanish predecessors.[57] The French in the Caribbean as well as in mainland Louisiana appear to embrace a distinctive planning tradition sometime in the early eighteenth century.[58] By the 1760s, one visitor to the French Caribbean asserted, "All of the houses are more or less made on the same pattern; only a few have an upper story; they consist only of a first floor." In this way they compare in form and plan quite closely with English houses in early colonial Jamaica. But the striking parallel appears also in the floor plan: "There are three rooms in a line; the middle one is sixteen to eighteen feet long; the two on the sides are sixteen feet long, the whole making a frontage forty-eight to fifty feet long and sixteen feet wide if we don't count the galleries going round the house that are at least six to seven feet wide."[59] What seems clear is that if the symmetrical tripartite plan was Spanish in origin, it was used broadly as a Creole plan by the middle of the eighteenth century, even in regions of the Caribbean with no early Spanish influence. The plan appears commonly, for example, in the eighteenth-century houses of St. Eustatius, an Anglo-Dutch island in the Leeward Islands with little exposure to the Spanish Caribbean. By the middle of the eighteenth century, the tripartite Spanish plan had become broadly used by Europeans of widely divergent origins across the Caribbean.

If the eighteenth-century Jamaican Creoles adopted their house plan from their Spanish predecessors, they also transformed it. The broad press for larger houses and increased numbers of rooms meant that late eighteenth-century builders often doubled the footprint of their houses from three to six chambers, creating a front and a back hall, with pairs of chambers to each side, much like the plan of Seville. Robert Dellap's 1768 inventory describes two chambers—one papered in yellow and the other in blue—to either side of the front hall. The back hall was similarly flanked by the "little east chamber" and the "little west chamber." The executors of James Rutherford's estate described his house as having a hall and a back hall with four other chambers, one each at the northeast, northwest, southeast, and southwest. Evidence from probate inventories suggests that houses with both front and back halls appear in the 1750s and remain common through the end of the century. Significantly, the rear hall became the dining room in inventories from the early nineteenth century, once that designation became more popular in Jamaican parlance. Resisting the temptation to add a second story and face the threat of natural disaster, most Jamaicans opted to expand horizontally, often doubling the footprint of the house with a flank of rooms to the rear that mirrored the arrangement of the more prominent larger rooms to the front.

THE CREOLE PIAZZA

Along with single-story living and the centrality of the hall, the third distinctive feature of houses in Jamaica was certainly the piazza. As demonstrated in chapter 3, piazzas appeared for the first time in large numbers lining the streets of Kingston, where they sheltered passersby and shaded the front rooms of urban shops and houses. During his visit to Jamaica in 1687, Hans Sloane noted that one English planter had taken up residence in a Spanish-built hacienda that was "all galleried around."[60] Thus before the piazza became a definitive feature of the Anglo-Jamaican Creole house, the earliest examples of such houses were likely abandoned Spanish haciendas. By the middle of the eighteenth century, piazzas were a common feature on English-built plantation houses—as they had appeared on urban houses decades before—and, as chapter 4 suggested, they served as a stage for plantation surveillance. Thomas Thistlewood offers regular references to piazzas on plantation houses of the 1750s. Immediately after his arrival on the island in 1750 and not yet familiar with the term "piazza," Thistlewood described one great house as having "wood columns on each side."[61] But soon thereafter he made common references to events taking place on the piazza of his own houses or those of others.[62]

Rural piazzas came in many forms. Many houses boast a piazza along only a single elevation. As in the case of the house at Phoenix plantation, the piazza often ranges along the front of the house (fig. 7.19). But in some cases, as at Hyde Hall, the piazza was moved to the rear of the house, serving as a final space in an entertaining sequence, rather than an initial place of welcome.[63] But the most distinctive form was when the piazza wrapped the house on three or even all four sides as in the case of the house in the Wickstead painting (see fig. 7.6). In another example, a piazza encircled William Beckford's Virgin Valley. While certainly prevalent across the island through the eighteenth century, few houses retain their early piazzas, many having been damaged by hurricanes and others later enclosed. But piazzas were not just observation points or mechanisms to mediate the heat, they were also tools of healthfulness and sociability.

Eighteenth-century piazzas derived in part from seventeenth-century "walks." In his diatribe against the architecture of early planters in Barbados, seventeenth-century commentator Richard Ligon recommended building alongside a Caribbean house "a walk," in the manner of an ambulatory or a cloister: a sheltered space alongside a building open to the outside, connecting the transitional indoor-outdoor space with the act of walking from its inception in the colonial architecture of the Caribbean. Walking, it should be noted, was also common practice in long galleries of British country houses and

FIG. 7.19 Phoenix plantation, Trelawny Parish, Jamaica.

in greenhouse conservatories in seventeenth-century England.[64] Certainly the earliest piazzas along Kingston's streets were intended as walks, allowing a person to traverse the city sheltered from the sun except at crossing intersections. But this role was complicated by the fact that each piazza was individually built by its respective property owner. As a result, the piazzas were inconsistently sized and positioned: "The piazzas are [irregular], so that a stranger or drunken man, of a dark night, unless he walk in the middle of the street, is liable to get his bones broke."[65] So even if for the convenience of the public, these urban piazzas were not appreciated by all who used them. But walking on eighteenth-century piazzas was not limited to the urban context. In his *History*, Edward Long spoke at length about the importance of walking for the preservation of health. "The morning air," he writes, "is here delightfully cool; and the most agreeable time for exercise is before, or just about, sun-rise." Early risers were advised to "exercise at this hour," so that they might "feel their bodies refreshed and vigorous . . . [and] suffer no inconvenience from the heat during the remainder of the

day." It was particularly important to Long that if his readers were to walk after sunrise, they "keep withindoors, or in the shade," to avoid "solar rays."[66] The obvious locale for such exercise was the piazza.

Lady Nugent frequently recorded in her journal that she or members of her family had undertaken their morning walk "in the piazza."[67] That the piazza was understood to be private space was made clear in one entry that noted "General N and I walked, in our dressing gowns . . . in the piazza." Her serious commitment to this health regimen was made clear in the same entry when she noted that they had walked "for an hour . . . before the sun rose."[68] Similarly, William Bartram, writing in 1765, described George Whitefield's 1739–1740 Orphan House in Bethesda, Georgia, just outside Savannah. The house was graced with "piazzas, ten feet wide, [which] project on every side, and form a pleasant walk, both winter and summer, round the house."[69] While the piazzas would certainly be "convenient in the Heat of summer," further evidence that these broad spaces were actually used as walks emerges from the pages of Whitefield's journal.[70] In describing the daily life of the orphanage the famous orator noted, "Generally once a day, if I do not, they [the masters of the house] walk with their respective charges, telling them of the glory of God in creation," resurrecting a sense of the ancient monastic use of the form.[71] The orphanage was described, often in derision, as "a seminary."[72] Maria Nugent mentioned in her journal that she often "read prayers to the family in the back piazza."[73]

❖ ❖ ❖

As walking platforms, piazzas were a response to health concerns. Fear of moist miasmic air required one to be able to open up a house during the day to healthful breezes but also to close out what was considered to be dangerous night air. Shed roofs around the house helped to cast rainwater away from the house, keeping the interior freer from moist air. Similarly, raising the building on elevated piers or foundations lifted the living floors of the house above the moist soils, to avoid miasmas. One "framed Dwelling-House" offered for sale in 1779 was "in a most healthy situation, raised seven feet from the ground on posts of hard timber."[74] This was so common by the late eighteenth century that a single-story house raised on piers was described in a sale advertisement as a "new built up-stair house."[75] Raised on piers, such a house created shelter for livestock; Cynric Williams commented that "all is on the ground floor, which is generally built, as in this case, on stone buttresses; so that if the piazza happens to have chinks, you can see the pigs that you hear grunt in their perambulations beneath."[76]

Many concerns about health were well articulated by Edward Long, who recommended building in timber as wooden houses were less prone to trap the climate's damp air. "Stone buildings," he argued, "without some precautions, are not wholesome habitations in the West Indies."[77] As a case in point, he offered the military barracks at Clarendon and Bath, Jamaica. These stone barracks "were found insalutary to the men lodged there." Porous stone, Long told his readers, imbibed and "transuded" moisture freely, while hard stone forced moisture to condense on its surfaces in damp weather. Both porous and impervious stone exposed inhabitants to the miasmic conditions found also in fogs and dews. If one chose to build in stone, it was important that the house "be surrounded with a shed, or piazza, to keep off the beating of heavy showers," to reduce the dampness. Furthermore, "the walls within should be lined with a facing of brickwork, plaistered,

or of boards, set off about 1 or 2 inches, leaving a space behind for the free circulation of air" and further protection from the damp.[78] Stone buildings, far more prone to retaining the damp of the climate than their frame counterparts, were perceived as less healthful.

That the piazza created a space that was simultaneously cool and healthful was not accidental, for in the minds of early eighteenth-century residents of the Caribbean, temperature, air, and health were closely interrelated. In 1740 Charles Leslie informed his readers that Jamaicans commonly referred to the sea breeze as *Doctor, and truly it deserves the Title,*" for refreshing breezes were life-giving. Without it, he asks, "how dismal would the Consequence be?" Leslie referred not to the discomfort of the heat but its association with dangerous air: "The hot and moist Temperament of the Air would soon bring on Plagues, and other Epidemical Distempers," common sources of death in early colonial Jamaica. Removing to the Caribbean freed Britons from a range of traditional killers, including smallpox and influenza. But the torrid zone came with its own set of new, deadly diseases: malaria, yellow fever, dysentery, dropsy, leprosy, yaws, hookworm, and elephantiasis, to name the worst.[79] Historian Trevor Burnard has suggested that the island suffered from an 11 percent mortality rate through the eighteenth century.[80] The best evidence for high mortality is the fact that whites in Jamaica never achieved a sustainable population; birthrates in the seventeenth and eighteenth centuries always lagged behind death rates.[81] Leslie continued, "These evils are Provided against by the Wise contriver of Things who has made these Gales to blow, and temper the Air, that we need not be afraid of such Evils."[82] For Leslie and his contemporaries, heat and death were directly associated: "the warm Climate makes the Place sickly." Thankfully, breezes restored life; piazzas became life-giving, essential for those who could afford to have them.[83]

Before the introduction of germ theory in the nineteenth century, the prevailing framework for understanding health was humoral theory, the belief that health was best preserved by keeping in balance the body's four humors—melancholy (black bile), phlegm, blood, and choler (yellow bile). One of the presumed threats leading to imbalance of these humors in the tropics was miasma, or bad air, which rose from moist and swampy soil, especially at night. In his three-volume *History of Jamaica,* published in 1774, Edward Long drew upon generations of experience and the prevailing theories of miasmic air to warn readers about unhealthy situations in a tropical climate. The first was a dramatic shift in temperature from "stifling heat" to a "chilling cold" in the evening. This shift was often accompanied by a heavy dew, evidence of "a swampy unwholesome soil." Another cause of miasma was thick fogs, which arose from "mud slime, and other impurities." He also warned against "swarms of large muskeetos, flies, and other insects, which attend putrid air and low unventilated places, where they delight to breed." One should also avoid settling in places "where butchers meat is soon corrupted," or "where a dead corpse becomes intolerably offensive." A final dangerous place was the channel of a dry river which often "emits a disagreeable smell, by night as well as by day, from putrid slime, dead fish and insects, and other corrupted substances." The most dangerous times were summer nights, when "the body is most liable to fevers, because of the alterations of the air." One should also avoid the early evening dew "which is most unwholesome and dangerous" because it "rises imperceptibly from the earth after sunset."[84] "The best preventative against the mischievous impressions of a putrid fog, a swampy or marshy exhalation," Long wrote, "is a close, sheltered, and covered place, such as . . . a house which has no doors nor windows facing the swamp."[85] Cool, crisp morning air, it was generally believed, was the least dangerous. While in actuality the greatest threat to health was from mosquito-borne infection, Long and his eighteenth-century counterparts assigned the danger not to mosquitoes but to damp miasmic air. English engineer Christian Lilly, who worked on military installations in Jamaica, advised an ailing friend on the island that he "must be careful not to take cold by being too free at the window," especially at night.[86] As late as the 1820s, new arrivals to Jamaica were still "cautioned . . . against the night air."[87] Houses that allowed access to healthy morning air, while simultaneously allowing protection from more dangerous evening air and dew, were the most desirable. As a result, Jamaicans erected piazzas that fronted houses that could still be sealed in the evenings by windows and doors. And they erected houses on raised foundations or piers to set them above the dangers of groundwater. James Phillippo described the typical Jamaican plantation house as usually of wood, raised on a "foundation of stone" or "on pedestals of stone or wood from two to six feet from the ground," a move he applauded as more healthful.[88]

The particular anxieties about the healthfulness or putridness of air in the Caribbean led to distinctive architectural strategies. One of the most important was increasing airflow through the house, allowing fresh air to displace damp putrid air. The importance of air circulation was known already in the seventeenth century. A Jamaican physician writing in that century believed that daytime sea breezes were good and healthful but that nighttime land breezes brought "stagnated Air, harbouring in mountainous Caverns and woody confinements," which caused "hot paroxysms."[89] These assumptions about healthfulness persisted through the eighteenth century. John Crowley has demonstrated that the importance of air circulation to health was first codified in the publications of army physician John Pringle.[90] His 1750 *Observations on the Nature and Cure of Hospital and Jayle-Fevers,* an attempt at a medical analysis of the problem of bad air, argued that ventilation was an important precondition to health, Pringle's recommendations, however, had been intuited by residents of the Caribbean for some time; the importance of ventilation and air circulation was well understood before 1750.

Besides serving as a stage for walking and healthfulness, the piazza was a locus of hospitality to other whites. From their first appearance in Kingston, Jamaican piazzas were outfitted with water for visitors. As early as 1712, Robert Thurger's piazza had "a large water jar framed."[91] William Sampson added to the water jar "a small hand basin," presumably to allow visitors to refresh their hands and face.[92] At the same time, many of these early eighteenth-century piazzas were still littered with artisan's tools, suggesting that early piazzas may have been places of welcoming but they were often places of work.[93] If Kingston houses boasted street-sheltering piazzas from the beginning of the eighteenth century, soon thereafter they were also outfitted with rear piazzas, and these presumably more private spaces became places of outdoor living and sociability. Hannah Sanders's Kingston house had a rear piazza with objects of work, brass weights, assortments of old pewter, tables and chairs, a buffet, and a cupboard, while the rear piazza on George Roberts's Kingston house included tables and Windsor chairs.[94] By midcentury the sociability of the rear piazza marked both urban and plantation houses. The rear piazza on Mathias Philpsale's plantation house was filled with two low compass-back Windsor chairs, one large mahogany claw table, a marble slab upon a mahogany frame, two-seater settees, one low mahogany stuffed leather seat, and two "India pictures."[95] Sarah Seymour served from her "tea china" on the rear piazza of her plantation house.[96] In plantation contexts, the sociability of the rear piazza quickly combined with the welcoming of the front piazza. Cynric Williams reported in the early nineteenth century that upon his arrival at one plantation, "I was ushered into the piazza, and presented to a middle-aged lady, his wife, who was still handsome and very agreeable."[97] Piazzas were commonly outfitted with backgammon and chess boards.[98] If in the early eighteenth century the piazza was understood to be primarily about protection from the sun and a transitional space of welcome into the house, by the end of the century it had become one of the critical spaces of sociability in the British Jamaican house, increasingly integrated into everyday life.

Thomas Thistlewood describes eating on the rear piazza of his house on numerous occasions. Writing in the 1770s, Edward Long described at length the delights of a piazza. "In the piazzas," he writes, "many families may be said to live the greater part of their time." The reason, of course, was that "the shade and refreshing breeze" rendered them far cooler than the rooms of the house.[99] Lady Nugent writes in her 1801–1805 journal about intimate conversations and small informal gatherings on the piazza. She describes a morning when she and her husband, governor of the island, privately discussed "many interesting arrangements," a conversation that took place "in the piazza, before breakfast." On another occasion, she was entreated by "a host of gentlemen, who were taking their sangaree in the piazza." Many of them were drunk by afternoon; she described the scene as "a picture for Hogarth."[100] She makes regular mention of dining; while most of the references are to informal meals taken on the piazza, a few describe much grander events. In April of 1802, for example she entertained twenty men at "a loaded table extending all the length of the piazza."[101] Similarly, early nineteenth-century inventories list piazzas with a range of objects including mahogany breakfast tables, sideboard trays, and a full sideboard and various implements for dining and tea.[102]

The piazza was also a place to relax racial boundaries. Lady Nugent agreed to let the "black servants" have "a dance in the back piazza." Later that same evening, she entertained a number of guests in the dining room while "the whole family [meaning the 'family' of house slaves] were assembled in the piazza."[103] Slightly earlier, Ann Storrow noted that the piazza was a place ideal for receiving informal visitors.[104] The piazza was an effective place

for seeing and being seen. Upon their arrival in Falmouth, Lady Nugent traveled to the house of General Bell, which overlooked the Sunday market, populated largely with black Jamaicans. Soon after their arrival, she noted that "we shewed ourselves in the piazza," in the manner of a head of state from the balcony of a government house. Nugent remarked that the market ladies selling "yams, coconuts, plantains, &c. and salt fish . . . laughed, danced, bowed, curtsied, and grinned and used every possible grimace to express their happiness in seeing us."[105] The piazza was also a perfect stage for seeing and surveillance. Nugent describes an early morning sitting in the piazza to watch the sun "rise most beautifully from behind the mountains."[106] From another piazza, she occupied herself by contemplating Mount Salus "over the plains of Liguanea."[107] Certainly Edward Long recognized that the piazza offered a nearly unobstructed view of the tropical landscape. As he wrote of a house in St. Catherine, "From the piazza of this house the eye takes in a view of the greater part of St. Catherine, St. Dorothy, and Clarendon, and the sea from St. Thomas in the East to Portland Point in the West."[108] But as earlier chapters made evident, Jamaica's picturesque beauty was tempered by persistent, if quiet, threats. Aware of a possible French naval invasion, Nugent reported that she had "walked in the piazza the whole day . . . looking continually toward the sea for the enemy."[109]

One particular activity came to characterize the Jamaican house and especially the piazza: the act of "creolizing." In the 1770s, Edward Long offered the first written description of the activity, although he does not use the term: "Nor can there be a more agreeable indulgence . . . than to sit in an elbow chair, with his feet resting against one of the piazza-columns; in this manner he converses, smoaks his pipe, or quaffs his tea, in all the luxury of indolence."[110] Rather than maintaining the upright posture prized among most British elites, elite white Jamaicans understood their relaxed comportment—even slouching—to signal their comfort with indulgence, even their right to engage "the luxury of indolence." The earliest visual representation of creolizing is a 1770s watercolor by George Robertson of what is likely an overseer's house on one of the Beckford estates (see fig. 3.30). While one man leans against the piazza post, the other "creolizes" in a low wooden chair, his feet elevated on the piazza post in the manner suggested by Long's description. And an anonymous author, writing in 1790, described the same for his British audience: "The manner in which [the

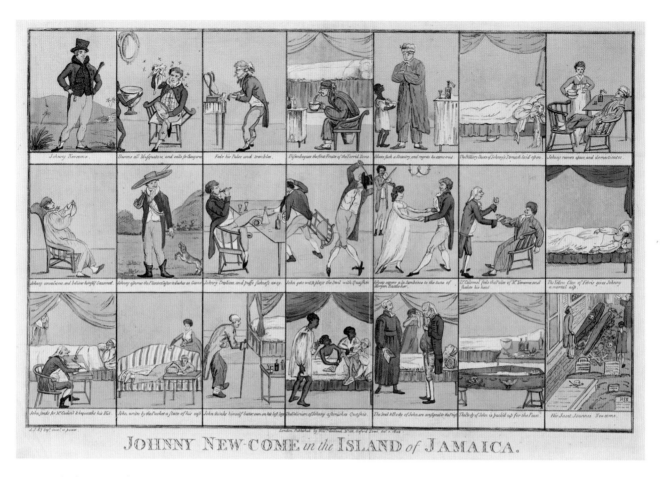

FIG. 7.20 Abraham James, "Johnny New-come in the Island of Jamaica," published by William Holland, London, 1800. In the first panel of the second register, Johnny convalesces in a tall, sloped chair, likely a Spanish chair. In the third panel of the second register, Johnny "creolizes." Etching with aquatint, hand-colored; plate mark: 13.79 × 20.43 in. (35 × 51.9 cm) on paper: 14.6 × 20.9 in. (37 × 53 cm). The Lewis Walpole Library, Yale University.

gentlemen] seat themselves, would strike you on the first view as ludicrous—they draw their chairs to the railing of the piazza, and fixing themselves nearly upon the end of their backbones, they elevate their feet into the air upon the highest rail above their heads."[111] The term "creolizing" had come into popular enough usage to appear on a satirical print of the character Johnny Newcome, published in 1800 (fig. 7.20). But if all the earliest references reserve this posture for men, the act of creolizing was no longer solely a masculine activity by the turn of the century. Lady Nugent herself mentions on one occasion that she spent the morning as she does most mornings: "writing, reading, and creolizing."[112] The term was defined slightly later by John MacLeod: "Creolizing is an easy and elegant mode of lounging in a warm climate; so called, because much in fashion among the ladies of the West Indies; that is reclining back in one arm chair, with their feet upon another, and sometimes upon the table."[113] An early nineteenth-century writer noted how his host addressed him after

"cocking up his legs in the Creole fashion on the table."[114] To creolize was to undertake a very relaxed body posture, reclined in a chair and with elevated feet, and from its popularization in the final quarter of the eighteenth century, creolizing was a posture of repose associated with the piazza.

The persistence of creolizing generated a new material culture: Jamaican probate inventories unrelentingly report the ubiquity of Windsor chairs soon after their introduction in the 1730s. Richard Moore's 1739 probate accounts, for example, list his set of "Winzor chairs."[115] Through the 1740s, Windsor chairs are commonly listed in the hall, but as plantation houses more commonly include piazzas in the 1750s and after, the set of Windsor chairs is generally listed on the piazza. And after the 1750s, they are often described as painted green.[116] Through the second half of the eighteenth century, Windsor chairs are generally described also in two types, either high- or low-backed. On occasion, they are described in greater detail, as in Mathias Philpsale's inventory, which reported his collection of "low compass back Windsor chairs" on the back piazza.[117] Such low compass-backed Windsor chairs are the most common forms used by cartoonists to illustrate the act of creolizing in turn-of-the-century satirical prints. Late eighteenth-century newspaper accounts suggest that many of these chairs were likely English made for the Jamaican market. One ad, for example, advertises an auction of furniture "all made in London by the most eminent Workmen and particularly adapted for this island, both by their elegance and goodness of materials."[118] And another announces the arrival of "green Windsor chairs," just imported from London.[119] But the distinctive patterning of the backsplat on many of the high-backed chairs and the fact that many are unpainted and made of mahogany suggest that many of the Windsors were Jamaican made (fig. 7.21).

If low compass-backed chairs were the most common chair form and the preferred type of chair for creolizing, alternative types also lent themselves more fully to

the increasingly popular body posture. John Stewart's 1750 probate inventory listed "2 Spanish chairs" on his piazza.[120] It is very likely that a mid-eighteenth-century "Spanish chair" was an X-frame chair with a curule base and leather seat, a form common in seventeenth- and eighteenth-century Mexico. Significantly, the vast majority of Spanish chairs before the eighteenth century have the leather seat spanning from side to side, limiting the capacity of the sitter to recline. But the rotation of the leather so that it drops from the back and continues to the front of the seat in the form of a sling is a distinctively Mexican form, an adaptation of the Spanish form to colonial circumstances. The earliest surviving example, called the March chair, dates from the 1730s. The 1750s "Spanish chairs" listed on John Stewart's piazza might be either the form from the Spanish Main, with the leather spanning from left to right, or they might just as easily be a Mexican form with the leather running from the crest down through the seat.

This distinctively Mexican chair form has come to be called a Campeche chair, and likely arrived in Jamaica through Cuba. While a survey of probate records does not suggest that these chairs were common in the eighteenth century, they abounded in the region soon after the turn

FIG. 7.21 High-backed Jamaican Windsor chair, early nineteenth century. Private collection.

FIG. 7.22 Jamaican Campeche chair. Private collection.

of the century. Surviving Jamaican examples all share a few common features, including a full leather sling that is suspended from a large and often richly shaped and ornamented crest rail and hangs from the side frames. By their very form these chairs' design presumes that the sitter's feet are resting on an elevated support. And they are almost always fitted with arms, convenient elbow supports for those choosing to read. Abraham James included in his ca. 1800 satirical prints figures seated in high-backed chairs that were clearly designed to accommodate "creolizing," suggesting that the form was just becoming more familiar in those years. Large numbers of Campeche chairs of Jamaican manufacture appear to date from the early nineteenth century (fig. 7.22).[121] Quite obviously, the use of Spanish chairs on midcentury piazzas and the eventual appearance of locally manufactured Campeche chairs in Jamaica easily accommodated the penchant for elevating one's feet in a posture of repose. These chairs facilitated the act of creolizing and thus the chair and the piazzas on which they appear are Creole forms. Since the act of creolizing predates the proliferation of the Campeche chair, it seems Jamaicans adopted the Campeche as a form well suited to their penchant for indolence.

The piazza, initially a practical response to heat and health concerns, quickly became the exemplary feature of Jamaican houses, a liminal space not outside but not inside, and came to characterize the life of whites in Jamaica. Unlike the English house, strictly ordered and carefully organized to support the orchestrated rituals of everyday life, the Creole house in Jamaica was apparently unconstrained. More than just the house of a person who had been born in Jamaica, it was, in fact, material evidence of very different social engagements and self-comportment. To be Creole was to be far less concerned with the rules of social engagement that characterized so much of life in elite cosmopolitan circles, and to be comfortable with a blurring of racial distinctions. The openness and spatial uncertainty of the Creole piazza manifested in material form the social and racial ambivalence that was indicative of Jamaican Creole society.

◆ ◆ ◆

Jamaican piazzas were sometimes open on all sides but in some instances, as at Mount Plenty, the corners were enclosed as chambers, spaces that came to be called pavilions in some elite examples. Edward Long described Richmond as a mansion "surrounded with a spacious piazza, supported by columns of the Ionic order; at the four angles are pavilions, with Venetian windows corresponding to each other."[122] John Stewart noted that the piazza on his house was "terminated at each end by a square room," much like the end rooms of Mount Plenty. These corner rooms were always finished with sash windows "on account of the rains."[123] Matthew Lewis reported that since tropical storms brought torrents that shifted with the wind "so suddenly from the one side to the other," the occupants of the house were obliged to shut all the blinds on the whole exterior. "Consequently," Lewis writes, "the whole house is in total darkness during their continuance, except the single sash-windowed room."[124] By the turn of the nineteenth century, many Jamaican houses were outfitted with small chambers at the corners, typically fitted out with sash windows. An early example of such a chamber appears in the low piazza-fronted building in the background of Du Simitière's watercolor sketch of Bath, Jamaica (see fig. 5.7).

These peripheral bedchambers were also the site of another distinctive Jamaican social practice: frequent sex, consensual or not. J. B. Moreton was quite direct in his commentary on this subject. Even the most "honorable gentlemen" had daughters, "lamb-like lasses," usually available for "sport" at the end of an evening: "When the ball of rigadoon is over, escort her to your house or lodging and taste all the wanton and warm endearments she can yield before morning."[125] And he further implied that some free women of color made themselves so available that they were insulted if his (presumably male) readers mustered any restraint.[126] The frequency of both consensual sex and rape in eighteenth-century Jamaica is made perfectly clear in the diary of Thomas Thistlewood, who recorded his sexual activity in great detail. Often he paid women; his most frequent partners were those women he kept as wives, three in sequence over the course of his life; only these women shared his bed. But he assaulted female slaves in the spaces of his own house and grounds.[127] Such profligate sexual activity was not confined to middling planters but was common among "gentlemen" as well.[128] And, as Trevor Burnard has demonstrated, drunkenness often led to gang rape.[129] The clear evidence of interracial sex and rape in colonial Jamaica, of course, is the rapid expansion of the island's mixed-race population, especially in the families of overseers and attorneys.[130]

◆ ◆ ◆

The piazza was a not stable form. Over time the Jamaican Creole house began to incorporate the piazza as a space internal to the house. Through most of the eighteenth century, piazzas were understood to be open sheltered spaces appended to the outside of the house. Like the original piazza at Mount Plenty, they commonly had a shed roof supported by a range of columns that usually had rails between to prevent injury from a fall. But over the course of the century, the piazza increasingly became a living space where families would spend many hours a day; in the later eighteenth century, these open spaces became visually enclosed from the outside, if still open to the breeze. While common by the end of the century in both written descriptions and images, jalousies or louvers are unknown through the first half of the eighteenth century. Even though screens and blinds were common in the Spanish Caribbean through the seventeenth century, the first known reference to them in English Jamaica seems to be the installation of jalousies on the King's House and the Assembly Building in Spanish Town in 1771.[131] The appearance of jalousies or venetian blinds in the closing decades of the century betrays the increasing desire to privatize the space of the piazza and screen the increasingly frequent social events taking place there from the gaze of those on the street. One house was advertised for sale in 1779, for example, with a porch "with Venetian blinds, which are also to all the windows."[132] Possibly a response to the enclosure of the piazza and the elimination of the open rails as footrests, mid-nineteenth-century Campeche chairs began to extend the arms to serve as footrests as well.

Evidence from urban piazzas suggests that sheets were commonly hung between piazza posts to protect sitters from the direct rays of the sun. But sheets were slowly replaced by more permanent jalousies, installed between columns to simultaneously admit air and deflect sun. Writing in the first years of the nineteenth century, John Stewart noted that the piazza was "either open or with jalousies."[133] In some images the open jalousies of the long front gallery are clearly visible beyond the large hall that dominates the center foreground. In fact, the slight closure of the gallery has allowed that space to become almost continuous with the central hall, separated by nothing more than an open arcade. In the view of the house at Frome, from the Storer Sketchbook—an extraordinary collection of early nineteenth-century pen and ink drawings and watercolor sketches from the western end

of the island—the roof structure clearly reflects the distinction between the house core and the range of spaces under the shed roof on all sides (fig. 7.23). The shed spaces are not open piazzas as at Bryan Castle or Virgin Valley, but rather enclosed galleries much as at Mount Plenty in its later condition. By the end of the eighteenth century, the open piazza appended to the exterior of the house became the fully integrated living space; still well ventilated via jalousies and still long and narrow, positioned along one or both of the two primary elevations of the house, the jalousied gallery-style piazza became the late eighteenth-century alternative to the porchlike outdoor space of the open-air piazza.[134]

In the same decades the spaces of the hall and the piazza became spatially and socially conflated. In his *West India Customs and Manners* of 1793, J. B. Moreton advises newly arrived employees of a plantation that they should avoid "loitering about the hall or piazza, for it may be displeasing to your employer; therefore retire to your room and read some good book."[135] He complains of Jamaican women who are often found "romping, or stretching and lolling, from sofa to sofa, in a dirty confused hall or piazza, with a parcel of black wenches, learning and singing obscene and filthy songs, and dancing to the tunes."[136] The early nineteenth-century account offered by Cynric Williams presumes that his readers understood that these spaces were contiguous, when he reports that he was awakened by "footsteps on the piazza to which my chamber windows opened"; he descibes the perpetrator, upon seeing him stir, running immediately from the piazza around the corner into the hall, where she tumbles over Ebeneezer snoring at Williams's door, "which opened into the hall."[137] The continuity of these two adjacent spaces is found in many other accounts as well.[138] Where the hall typically opens directly onto the piazza, physically linking these two critical public spaces of the house core, in many examples from the late eighteenth century a large arched opening connects the two spaces; by the early nineteenth century, even the arch had disappeared.

As the piazza became more enclosed, partition walls slowly dissolved and interior spaces of the house began to bleed one into the other. By the third quarter of the eighteenth century, Jamaica had seized upon the distinctive window of the jalousie. "The houses of towns in this climate cannot be too airy," claimed Edward Long. "On this account the jealousy-shutters [*sic*], as they are called, which freely admit the air, are very excellent

FIG. 7.23 Artist unknown, Frome Plantation, from the Storer Sketchbook, 1820s. Private collection.

contrivances; and no bed-chamber should be unfurnished with them."[139] Long noted that in the best houses of his day, "sashes are more generally in use; to which are added jealousy-shutters, or Venetian blinds, which admit the air freely, and exclude the sunshine."[140] One of the distinctive features of Jamaica's jalousies is that they could create a large, generally unobstructed space when the breeze was desirable, but could be easily closed to create a tight, overlapping board surface completely filling in the opening, closing out the dangerous night air and the torrential rains. The extraordinary view of the interior of Frome from the early nineteenth century offers a clear image of those spaces from within. The large open central hall is defined on two sides by board walls that separate private chambers to each side. A broad set of tripartite arches separates the hall from the gallery or piazza that ranges across the front of the house. The double doors of the front are flanked on each side by jalousies painted in the traditional green; in this case the jalousies open through walls unbroken by the columns of a piazza. What had been an exterior

space defined by columns had become by the early nineteenth century a chamber open entirely to the interior and separated from the outside by banks of jalousies.

In some cases, as in both of John Tharp's late eighteenth-century houses, interior walls also began to dissolve into jalousies, allowing airflow not just at the house perimeter, but between rooms as well (fig. 7.24). The airiness of the Jamaican house was intended to create for its inhabitants the greatest physical comfort and the best defense of their health, but the result was a social and racial openness that came under intense scrutiny and critique. One young male Jamaican traveler reported that upon his arrival in town, the innkeeper "scolded some younger damsels for peeping at me through the jalousies which communicated with the bed-chambers on each side of her hall."[141] For many English visitors, this openness was deeply unsettling. Upon arriving at his family's plantations in Jamaica, Matthew Lewis reported on the shocking nature of everyday life on the island, a sharp pen so delightful that his passage is worth reading in full.

The greatest drawback upon one's comfort in a Jamaica existence seems to me to be the being obliged to live perpetually in public. Certainly, if a man was desirous of leading a life of vice here, he must have set himself totally above shame, for he may depend upon everything done by him being seen and known. The houses are absolutely transparent; the walls are nothing but windows—and all the doors stand wide open. No servants are in waiting to announce arrivals; visitors, negroes, cats, dogs, poultry, all walk in and out, and up and down your living rooms, without the slightest ceremony. Even the temple of Cloacina (which, by the bye, is here very elegantly spoken of generally as "The Temple,") is as much latticed and as pervious to the eye as any other part of my premises; and many a time has my delicacy been put to the blush by the ill-timed civility of some old woman or other, who, wandering that way, and happening to cast her eye to the left, has stopped her course to curtsey very gravely, and pay me the passing compliment of an "Ah, massa! Bless you, massa! How day?"[142]

FIG. 7.24 Interior view of Good Hope great house, Trelawny Parish, Jamaica, ca. 1790, with jalousies between rooms.

FIG. 7.25 Wales plantation house, Trelawny Parish, Jamaica, early nineteenth century.

FIG. 7.26 Roehampton great house, St. James Parish, Jamaica, ca. 1810.

The jarring contrast between differing perceptions of privacy reminds us, as Gerald Pocius has shown, that privacy is an unstable category that is socially constructed and determined.[143]

The Jamaican house type emerged over the course of the eighteenth century, but it was a type was that not at all stable. Although most houses in late eighteenth-century Jamaica conform to the design options of polite spaces all on a single story, some raised over service spaces on the ground floor, a small handful of houses from this period abided by the forms and organization more commonly found across the British Atlantic world. Wales, Rose Hall, Roehampton, and New Hope are all examples of the two-story masonry house with a ground-floor entrance, an interior staircase, and polite chambers on both upper and lower floors (figs. 7.25, 7.26).[144] Significantly, these two-story masonry houses also rejected the use of piazzas or galleries, the intermixture of wood and stone building materials, and the large central hall. As a group, these buildings seem to consciously dissent from the local adaptations that came to define great house architecture on the island by the close of the eighteenth century. And although they are in the minority, there are enough to suggest that a small contingent of Jamaican planters wished to mark themselves as distinct from the local Jamaican tradition. But their dissent only functions to reinforce the norm; these buildings would not appear as distinctive if there were not such a clearly predominant tradition to define themselves against.

HOSPITALITY

There remains one significant question yet unanswered: How do we reconcile the fact that the extraordinarily open, fluid, and hospitable Jamaican Creole houses were built in exactly the same landscape and in the same decades—generally the later decades of the eighteenth century—as the monumentally anxious and closed castles of fear described in chapter 2? As a case in point, Mount Plenty, with its open piazzas and large hall, and Edinburgh Castle, with its small, tightly stacked chambers, attached corner towers, and loopholes, were built within ten miles of one another, and only decades apart. How can this be, when these houses are so drastically different? The narratives offered thus far would lead us to understand Edinburgh Castle as the product of a deeply fearful and anxious Scottish sojourner hoping desperately to survive Jamaica long enough to make a small fortune and return home, and Mount Plenty as the product of a Jamaican-born Creole building a house that successfully negotiates the Caribbean climate and communicates the builder's Creole identity. If the former is about anxiety and fear, the latter is about comfort and identity. To some extent this reading would be accurate. But that is not the whole story. Edinburgh Castle and Mount Plenty are two alternative responses to the landscape of fear that was eighteenth-century Jamaica. One option—that taken by many Scottish sojourners but by others as well—was intensive martial response, one of explicit fortification and self-defense. In this strategy, architecture's primary responsibility is to repel assailants. While variable by degree, this response is fairly self-explanatory. The architectural strategy evinced by Mount Plenty is a bit more difficult to read.

Mount Plenty, as a Jamaican Creole house, was a house designed to accommodate openness and hospitality. Jamaican Creole houses were defined by large open halls, almost universally rejecting the fashionable central passage plan increasingly common across Britain and her mainland American colonies in the same decades. If, as architectural historians have long argued, the central passage was a mechanism of social, economic, and racial distancing, then we might expect to see the central passage flourishing across Jamaica. As Jamaica's castles of fear demonstrate, many worked hard to establish such distance. It is insufficient to suggest that Jamaicans were simply ignorant of the central passage—they traveled frequently and were intimately connected to port cities around the Atlantic rim. It is also insufficient to suggest that Jamaicans could not afford the luxury of a central passage—earlier chapters have demonstrated their extraordinary wealth relative to their peers elsewhere across the British colonies. The embrace of a large open hall and the rejection of the central passage plan was a conscious choice.

A second conscious choice was the installation of small bedchambers on the piazza. As in the case of Mount Plenty, these small chambers are often fitted out with a single door giving access only from a side piazza; these chambers had no direct access into the main chambers of the house. The southwest lodging room at Mount Plenty had access only from the west piazza, which was in turn accessible from the main northern piazza or the chamber in the center of the house. The southwest room could have its own private piazza in those seasons when the room was occupied. This limited access accords with their typical function as registered in probate inventories: "lodging rooms." Such rooms were incorporated into the body of the house, but circumscribed access allowed them some degree of privacy and separation from the central spaces—chambers and piazzas—of the main house. William Sampson's 1741 inventory is among the earliest to report that his piazza was equipped with a "piazza room." Mathias Philpsale's 1750 inventory indicates that the chamber adjoining the piazza was outfitted with a low-quality bedstead while William Duncan's house had a "front lodging room" in the corner of the piazza in 1751. And such piazza rooms and shed rooms off the piazza with bedsteads and simple furniture are common throughout the rest of the eighteenth century. William James's 1808 inventory notes the "bedroom off the piazza."[145] From at least the 1740s through to the early nineteenth century, Jamaica's plantation houses were commonly outfitted with one or more private lodging rooms, typically immediately off the piazza, usually with private access. Again, Trevor Burnard's work provides a clue to the purpose of such spaces. In addition to being shockingly egalitarian, later eighteenth-century Jamaicans were also famously hospitable. As Burnard asserts, "Every commentator on white society in Jamaica noted that white Jamaicans were famed for their hospitality to both friends and strangers."[146] "Even [white] vagrants," noted William Beckford, "are seldom refused protection and food"; in 1750, Thomas Thistlewood extended his hospitality to a white traveler who "begged a Nights lodging and refreshments for his horse."[147] This extraordinary hospitality was atypical in early modern elite and aspiring elite British culture; Burnard argues convincingly that such hospitality reinforced the essential bonds between all Jamaica's white minority. Burnard also points out that virtually all of Jamaica's whites were slave owners, uniting all whites in the concern for supporting racial subordination. He further notes that the increasing numbers of skilled slaves undermined the Jamaican Assembly's attempts to attract poorer whites to Jamaica; most elite whites recognized the significance of keeping whites on the island in the face of growing numbers of slaves and free blacks.[148] As a result, the egalitarianism of the hall led quickly to the hospitality of the lodging room.

Both of these decisions—open halls free of social buffers and welcoming lodging rooms—signal the standing hospitality of the Jamaican Creole house. Early nineteenth-century Jamaican historian Bryan Edwards remarked on this hospitality: "A marked and predominant character to all the white residents" was "a display of conscious equality throughout all ranks and conditions." In the West Indies, Edwards continues, "the poorest white person . . . approaches his employer with an extended hand." Such familiarity across ranks would not have been tolerated in Britain. In determining the origins of such radical egalitarianism, historian Trevor Burnard argues we need not look any further than Edwards, who informs his readers that these conditions arose "from the pre-eminence and distinction which are necessarily attached to the complexion of a white Man, in a country where the complexion, generally speaking, distinguishes freedom from slavery."[149] Bernard rightly argues that this hospitality was not entirely benevolent but an attempt at white solidarity in a threatening black landscape. It is worth remembering here that Jamaican plantations bound the largest population of enslaved Africans in the British colonies; the island represented the greatest disproportion of blacks to whites through the eighteenth century.[150] Furthermore, as a result of its much higher mortality, the slave population in Jamaica was also substantially African born, while the proportions of African-born slaves in the Chesapeake dwindled dramatically over the course of the eighteenth century. Not only was there a greater proportion of slaves in Jamaica, but they exhibited greater cultural distance than did their counterparts in the Chesapeake. Not surprisingly, such marked differences resulted in much higher racial tensions and a greater propensity for slave revolt in Jamaica. In the English Caribbean at least seven revolts of fifty or more slaves arose between 1640 and 1713. During the eighteenth century, the majority of slave uprisings took place in Jamaica.[151] By contrast, Virginia experienced no major slave uprising until the nineteenth century. If there was any landscape in which whites might dispense with the boundaries of social exclusion it was Jamaica. The openness and hospitality of the Jamaican house was a necessity of white-Creole solidarity.

It is worth noting here that white Creoles might very well have considered their house slaves—most of them mixed race—to be participants in that solidarity, viewing them as welcome occupants of the spaces of the house, for as argued at the opening of this chapter, racial blurring was endemic in Creole practice and identity by the end of the eighteenth century. Recent archaeological analysis at John Tharp's Good Hope plantation, for example, has revealed a second, much smaller slave village site just behind the house on the crest of the hill.[152] If the location of the primary village near the works makes evident that it housed all those who labored at the works, the location of the second, smaller village suggests that it was reserved for the house slaves, physically segregated from those engaged in much more labor-intensive work below. This physical segregation points to the social segregation between two classes of enslaved people—laborers and domestics. Furthermore, we know that domestics were often the progeny of current or former masters of the plantation, so domestics were often, in a very real sense, the children of the white family. Indicative of this is the report in which Edward Long describes a scene: "We find [a fine young Creole woman] employed in gobbling pepper-pot, seated on the floor, with her sable handmaids around her," and her manner of speech, which is "whining, languid, and childish."[153] White planters and their

families—white and mixed race, free and enslaved—populated the various spaces of the Creole house. It is very possible that Jamaican planter solidarity included mixed-race house slaves in the desperate attempt to amass a defense against marauding Maroons or the insurrection of the far greater numbers of enslaved Africans who labored in the sugar fields.[154]

That these two strategies—the martial defense of Edinburgh Castle and the hospitality and solidarity of Mount Plenty—are shared architectural responses to the same social and racial landscape is best revealed in the architecture of houses that integrate both. The later eighteenth-century Winefields plantation, built within miles of Edinburgh Castle and Mount Plenty, appears at first glance to be a typical Creole house (see fig. 2.8). While the encircling piazzas were enclosed later, as has happened to so many of these houses, the break in the roofline and the evidence from the interior make clear that it was once very much like Mount Plenty. It exhibits a long exterior masonry staircase that once rose to the open piazza, which then opens into a suite of two interior rooms, likely a hall and a parlor. But opening through the floor of the back corner of the piazza is a small staircase that winds down into the raised masonry basement of the ground floor. The open airy piazzas of the upper floor transition down into thick masonry walls with heavily built doors flanked by carefully positioned loopholes. If the upper floor of the house corresponds easily to the Creole house type of Mount Plenty, the masonry walls of the foundations correspond equally to Edinburgh Castle. In Winefields, fortification and hospitality converge.

◆ ◆ ◆

The emergence of a locally forged "Jamaican house" happened in the extraordinarily challenging decades of the late eighteenth century, a season when white Jamaicans were under assault on many fronts. The first assault came in the form of the economic isolation and trade interruptions resulting from the American Revolution, an event described by historians as a profound and transformative event for the Jamaican economy.[155] By 1775, tensions on the American mainland were on the verge of the war of independence, a circumstance that Jamaican planters and Atlantic merchants knew would directly interrupt Atlantic trade; the war inhibited Jamaican access to commodities from the mainland, dramatically raising prices for basic necessities in Jamaica.[156] The postwar Navigation

Acts severely restricted Jamaica's legal trade with the new United States, establishing trade restrictions through the 1780s. The next assault came from Mother Nature; the devastating hurricane of 1780 was followed immediately by the worst decade of the eighteenth century for hurricane damage. The 1790s introduced the rising abolitionist call for the termination of the slave trade. These are also the same decades for which historians report increasing rates of absenteeism, the departure from Jamaica of those rich white planters who could afford to leave.[157] While the scope of absenteeism is disputed, there is general agreement that Jamaica saw the greatest rates of absenteeism across the Caribbean through the later eighteenth and early nineteenth centuries, with the obvious exception of St. Domingue in the decades following the Haitian Revolution. These factors and others led to what one historian has entitled the "fall of the planter class" in the late eighteenth-century British Caribbean.[158] In light of these circumstances, the preeminent Jamaican historian Barry Higman has argued that "First Empire optimism" persisted only into the 1780s.[159]

Interestingly, the Creole house came to popularity in these very same decades. By the late eighteenth century, Jamaicans began to embrace their lack of refinement as a distinctively "local" feature. The era of rebuilding Renaissance villas was over; there are no major monumental houses in any distinctively British elite form begun in the 1770s or after. Divorced from British America and socially and culturally assaulted from the British mainland, white Jamaicans began in the late eighteenth century to warmly embrace their circumstances; in doing so, they formulated a material and social life that stood in stark contrast to the refinement that defined the broader British world. As chapter 5 argued, a British oligarchy enjoyed social and political authority over Jamaica through the middle decades of the eighteenth century; by the end of the century they had thrown in the towel, making their primary residence in Britain. Those left behind fashioned for themselves a set of distinctive cultural practices, including material cultural practices, that set them apart from British elites, and in so doing they became "Creoles."[160]

8   Architectures of Freedom

Ms. Rosie's house is only two blocks from Water Square, Falmouth's central public space (fig. 8.1). Standing to the front of a deep but narrow lot, the house serves as her residence, and the small nogged kitchen building to the rear is her hair-braiding studio. Now surrounded on two sides by a small piazza, close analysis of the building suggests that it was originally a small two-room frame building with a slightly larger chamber in front of a smaller chamber (fig. 8.2). The front room was lit by a single sash window on the street-front elevation and was accessed by a door that opened to the side yard. The building materials and detailing indicate that the house was built in the early nineteenth century; the documentary record reveals it was probably built by Elizabeth Somerville, a free woman of color, soon after she purchased this lot in 1836. Sometime in the decades following, Somerville or a later owner transformed the front room into a shop by changing the front window into the double door now in that opening and by erecting the piazza that allowed sheltered access into the shop from the street.[1]

As a building erected by a free woman of color, Elizabeth Somerville's house is an important survival. But remarkably, Falmouth has a number of examples sharing a similar history. Suggesting some specialization of function, the two rooms in Somerville's and other examples are usually differentiated in size, with the larger toward the street. Often the street-front elevation has a more elaborated window illuminating the front chamber. The primary entrance into the building is almost always a side door into the same front chamber. The rooms are separated by an interior partition with a door communicating between chambers shifted to one side of the partition. The rear space usually has a door through the rear elevation into the yard. The surviving early nineteenth-century examples all boast very high quality box framing with substantial beaded members secured by pegged mortise and tenon joinery (fig. 8.3).[2] Such quality is striking in buildings so small. They all comprise two rooms, with one of the two short ends of the building addressing the street. Notably, the chambers almost always measure to the exact foot on external dimensions; ten by twelve, ten by ten, and eleven by twelve are typical sizes. Such consistency among dimensions likely points to the processes shaping each building's design and construction. The clean external dimensions of these buildings suggest that carpenters and patrons agreed on pricing based on room

FIG. 8.1 Elizabeth Somerville House, 8 Trelawny Street, Falmouth, Jamaica, ca. 1840.

dimensions, which were almost always measured to the foot.

If slavery was the hegemonic institution in Jamaica, these buildings were and are the physical evidence of an alternative black landscape, a landscape of free blacks marked most particularly by small buildings that represented neither white and elite nor black and enslaved. Many of those slaves who became artisans had the capacity to earn an income and eventually could purchase their own freedom or freedom for members of their families.[3] Advertisements in the Kingston newspapers regularly advertised jobs available to "Free Persons," implying free people of color.[4] Additionally, many slave women bore mulatto children by white men. Although born slaves, these children had greater chances of eventually being freed, sometimes through manumission at the time of the owner's death. As a result, Jamaica saw increasing numbers of free people of color over the course of the eighteenth century.[5] Depending on their circumstances, their legal status was sometimes unstable, as described in the late eighteenth century: "The inhabitants of this colony consist

of four classes: white, free people of color having special privileges granted by private acts, free people of color not possessing such privileges, and slaves."[6] As many historians have suggested, the free black community was kept separate from the white population, especially in cities, wherever possible.[7] Similarly, free blacks worked hard to differentiate themselves physically, socially, and politically from the slave population.[8]

Narratives on slavery in the Caribbean necessarily emphasize plantations and the enslaved, but historians have noted that free blacks were often a substantial minority of Jamaica's urban populace by the later eighteenth century.[9] As early as 1754, one census of Spanish Town on Jamaica's south coast reported a total free population of twelve hundred, a full one-third of which were "Negroes and Mulattoes."[10] In 1788, Kingston had a free black population of 3,280, nearly one-third of the entire population of Jamaica.[11] While no specific demographic data have yet surfaced that outline the proportion of free blacks in Falmouth, it seems safe to assume that free blacks were a substantial minority. Analysis of the free black population

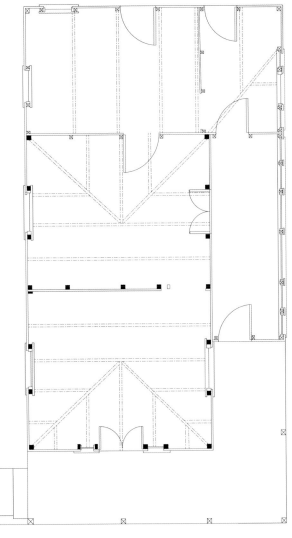

FIG. 8.2 Plan of 8 Trelawny Street, Falmouth, Jamaica.

in Kingston suggests that over the course of the century increasing numbers of free blacks had wealth enough to pay the parish tax and to own land.[12] Examination of Falmouth's early land deeds indicates that by the turn of the nineteenth century a number of free blacks already owned lots in town.[13] These included carpenters Samuel Reeves and John Sylvester, brickmason Thomas Love, tavern keeper Thomas Neale, and the spinster Rebecca Lake.[14] Free blacks in Falmouth and elsewhere were artisans, small planters, tavern keepers, shopkeepers, and bookkeepers.[15] Much of the work on black architecture in the early Americas has focused on finding African-derived forms, materials, and technologies.[16] By considering buildings constructed or owned by free blacks in their immediate context, this chapter does something quite different, and argues that these buildings resolved practical constraints while also marking status in a complex racial landscape.[17]

AFRICANS' ARCHITECTURE

One of the questions that has long dominated discussions of the architecture of enslaved Africans asks the extent to which mud-walled slave quarters continued African building practices.[18] This question is even more important given the fact that even as late as the 1770s approximately 75 percent of the enslaved laborers in Jamaica were African born.[19] Put simply, the vast majority of enslaved Africans in Jamaica knew African architecture. And it is certainly true that examples such as contemporary mud-walled Ewe

FIG. 8.3 Detail of wall plate, 54 Duke Street, Falmouth, Jamaica.

FIG. 8.4 Ewe House, vicinity of Cape Coast, Ghana.

houses now in Ghana have much in common with the African houses described in Jamaica's early written record and those that surface in the archaeological record (fig. 8.4).

Yet, a number of facts undermine any rigorous attempt to make these connections. The first is that Africans came from a wide swath of Africa, a space encompassing a bewildering diversity of cultures. Since many Africans traveled a huge distance from their point of capture to their point of sale to white traders, even those Africans sold from a single port were not necessarily from similar or related cultures. Secondly, the paucity of surviving eighteenth-century everyday architecture in West Africa means that the evidence available for use consists of written descriptions and twentieth-century buildings, often substituted for their eighteenth-century counterparts. Such substitutions wrongly presume a stability of cultural practice that anthropology has resoundingly demonstrated to be untenable. And, lastly, there is little evidence in Jamaica that Africans were doing anything more than simply building shelter in the most practical and efficient methods available. One period observer notes that there was only "trifling variation" between the house of a new poor white settler and an enslaved African.[20] In his careful examination of the quarters at Montpelier, Barry Higman finds some clear evidence of African architectural practices.[21] There does appear to be a slight preference among African-born slaves for wattled houses—a broadly popular African technology—while Creole slaves appear to prefer board or shingle houses.[22] Furthermore, the installation of the raised platform in House 37 at Montpelier and the construction of family house groups both have African architectural precedents.[23] The search for African connections ends there; the evidence suggests that enslaved Africans enlisted various known and new strategies to negotiate their circumstances. Their houses were not attempts—conscious or otherwise—to recreate an "African" architectural identity.

But if the connections between Jamaica and West Africa are to remain unclear, the differentiation between houses among the enslaved is demonstrable. Over the course of the eighteenth century, some of the relatively privileged among the enslaved—if the reader will allow the solecism—learned marketable skills and used them to their own advantage through jobbing, or hiring out.[24] Justin Roberts has estimated that on a typical sugar plantation, 6 to 8 percent of the enslaved labor—usually tradesmen and drivers—ranked among "the slave elite."[25] Enslaved artisans and tradesmen often had the wherewithal to improve the quality of their housing; especially by the early nineteenth century, visitors to plantations began to note the change. One observer expressed a fairly commonly held assumption that "the wealth of the Negro was chiefly amongst the tradesmen; in going through a Negro village I could always tell a tradesman's house from its external appearance."[26] Bryan Edwards argued that "tradesmen and domestics are in general vastly better lodged and provided. Many of these have larger houses with boarded floors, and are accommodated (at their own expense it is true) with very decent furniture."[27] In describing his own plantation, Matthew Lewis noted that the houses of the cooper, carpenter, and blacksmith could be "reckoned picturesque," but that many of the other buildings were "ugly enough."[28]

Barry Higman has argued that the emerging variation in quality of housing only loosely correlates with the privileged status of the building's occupants.[29] The shift might also have reflected the rising preferences of the plantation owner or overseer for certain slaves over others. The first reference to a wooden slave quarter in Thomas Thistlewood's journals, for example, is a 1768 reference to a new house for Abba, Thistlewood's laundress and one of his preferred sexual partners in those years.[30] As Trevor Burnard has shown, Jamaican planters and overseers demonstrated clear preferences among their slaves, especially the women.[31] Preferential treatment might have been desirable enough to convince some enslaved women, usually house slaves, to consent to sexual relations with their masters; a benefit of this sexual servitude might have been improved housing.

It is clear that later eighteenth- and early nineteenth-century planters offered plantation resources for improved quartering for the enslaved. Most plantations had enslaved carpenters; their scope of work occasionally included repairs or new construction in the village. Billy and George, two Jamaican-born enslaved carpenters on John Tharp's plantations, likely spent much of their time building board houses for their peers.[32] But if the extent of correlation of improved housing to tradesmen or to favorite slaves is in question, the emerging differentiation among the quality of housing is not. According to Higman, "Boarded walls became increasingly common after 1800 and after 1838 they gradually replaced wattle and plaster."[33] This observation is broadly substantiated by archaeologists working on plantation sites in Jamaica.[34] By the early nineteenth century, some few enslaved laborers were living in houses that differed markedly from the earthfast post wattle and mud houses that dominated the eighteenth-century landscape.

As Barry Higman's extensive analysis of the 1825 "Report of the state and condition of Old Montpelier

FIG. 8.5 Artist unknown, sketch of a slave quarter, from the Storer Sketchbook, 1820s. Private collection.

FIG. 8.6 Artist unknown, sketch of a slave village, from the Storer Sketchbook, 1820s. Private collection.

Negro houses and provision grounds" makes clear, enslaved laborers occupied a much wider range of houses in the early nineteenth century than they had through most of the eighteenth century. Plantation villages increasingly boasted houses of frame sheathed in boards or shingles and houses of the intermixture of frame construction and brick or masonry infill called "Spanish wall." Furthermore, thatch roofing slowly gave way to shingled roofs.[35] These changes are evident in the collection of early nineteenth-century drawings of such quarters in the Storer family sketchbook. One sketch shows a house in the foreground with board walls clearly nailed to vertical posts that terminate on a sill (fig. 8.5). The presence of a sill meant that the interior had a board floor rather than the earthen floor of earlier examples and that the whole house frame was elevated on earthfast piers, which could be easily replaced when they began to rot. It is also clear that these houses were outfitted with louvered window

openings and a board door conveniently positioned adjacent to an end post, rather than opening through the middle of a wall. Another sketch from the same collection shows a number of houses with very similar features (fig. 8.6). But this view also shows that a number of houses were of mixed building materials, one chamber wattled and another boarded, indicative of the aggregate nature of self-improved housing.

Yet, even in the early nineteenth century these changes were still very much the minority; of the Montpelier houses described in 1825, 64 percent were still wattled and almost half were still covered in thatch.[36] A postemancipation account from 1873 suggests that wattled, earthfast buildings were still the predominant mode of building by that date.[37] The appearance of board-walled and shingled houses in the early nineteenth century reflects an adoption of a European building technology in both the use of boards and shingles and in the preference of nails over lashing. If the Montpelier lists are at all indicative, very few quarters in the early nineteenth century were built in Spanish wall.[38]

The body of evidence on the architecture of eighteenth-century quarters in Jamaica finds some important correlations with those from other Caribbean and mainland colonies. What seems quite clear is that wattle-and-daub, thatch-roofed, one- and two-room quarters were ubiquitous not only in eighteenth-century Jamaica but also elsewhere in the Caribbean and on the British American mainland.[39] Slave quarter sites excavated in South Carolina, for example, revealed a number of eighteenth-century wattle-and-daub earthfast houses; their features correspond quite closely with those described here. The Carolina examples were also of one or two chambers with earthen floors and presumably thatch roofs. Evidence of interior and exterior fires corresponds with practices described in Jamaica. One distinction is the appearance in late eighteenth-century South Carolina of external wattle-and-daub chimneys, features absent from the archaeological, documentary, or pictorial record in Jamaica.[40] Evidence from eighteenth-century Virginia suggests that enslaved Africans there were housed almost exclusively in quarters built of log with rooms larger in scale than those found in South Carolina. Diversity among these quartering practices points to a variety of conditions among these locales. The first is climate. The climate in Jamaica and to a lesser degree in South Carolina meant that enslaved people could spend a greater portion of their time at home out-of-doors, while winters in Virginia required that quarters be able to accommodate all the occupants inside the house for weeks or months at a stretch. As a result, chambers in Virginia were likely larger to accommodate this need. The differences in building materials and the emergence of chimneys in South Carolina record differing rates of adaptation of European building practices; this might well reflect the degrees of engagement between Europeans and Africans in daily life. While Virginia never had an enslaved majority, South Carolina had such a majority by the early eighteenth century. Jamaica, by contrast, had not just a majority but an eight-to-one black-to-white ratio through most of the eighteenth century. Furthermore, Africans in Jamaica—especially field slaves—had far less exposure to the daily lives of whites than did those in South Carolina and Virginia. These differences in density and exposure helped enslaved Africans in Jamaica resist the adoption of British lifeways.

If the typical eighteenth-century quarter was of two chambers, as the documentary record seems to suggest, those of the early nineteenth century reveal far greater planning complexity. Alexander Barclay, writing in the 1820s, noted that quarters commonly measured seventeen by twenty-eight feet, organized into three to four rooms.[41] Writing a few years later, William Taylor described typical quarters as two or three rooms. The two-room quarters consisted of a hall and a partitioned sleeping chamber while the three-room version boasted a larger hall in the center flanked on each side by smaller sleeping chambers.[42] The most common footprint size for nineteenth-century quarters at Montpelier was eighteen by twenty-seven feet.[43] The stone quarter called House 37 at New Montpelier, as excavated and recorded by Barry Higman, measured nineteen by twenty-two, organized into three rooms in addition to a longitudinal platform raised eighteen inches above the floor that probably functioned as a sleeping alcove.[44] The floors were extensively plastered, which appeared in places to turn up walls as well. Accounts from the early nineteenth century also suggest that quarters were by then commonly supplemented with separate kitchens or a kitchen shed, often extending off the rear of the house.[45] By the end of the eighteenth century, Africans had been erecting piazzas across one or more elevations of their houses. Describing the houses of the Maroons at Charlestown, Maria Nugent noted that each had "a piazza in front."[46]

While the evidence for the accommodations of urban slaves before the late eighteenth century is thin, the few references do suggest that urban slaves were often housed in mud-walled and thatch-roofed houses, much like their rural counterparts, only in towns and cities those buildings sat in urban back lots.[47] In his examination of early Spanish Town, James Robertson has determined that urban slaves occupied fenced-in yards, often segregated in their own district of the city, even in the early eighteenth century.[48] In his assessment of urban slavery in Bridgetown, Barbados, Pedro Welch also finds that the majority of urban slaves lived in clustered compounds around the edges of the city.[49] While no documentary evidence for such yards has yet surfaced in Falmouth's archival record, an extraordinary compound of four individual houses at 11 Queen Street—all early twentieth century—might be a material echo of the urban yard tradition from the previous century (fig. 8.7). While the buildings are certainly of a later period, the clustering of

four individual houses on a single lot corresponds closely to urban slave house yards described by James Robertson for early Spanish Town.

But by the very late eighteenth and early nineteenth centuries, urban slaves—especially house slaves—often lived in barracks-like buildings that stood along the side or rear property line of their owner's house lot.[50] A remarkable surviving example is the barracks range along the south property line of 18 Pitt Street in Falmouth. The main house on the lot is a three-room framed house, the front hall later divided by a partition, likely built in the early nineteenth century (fig. 8.8; see fig. 6.12). The aspiring nature of the building is reinforced by the early masonry foundation wall, which supports the front elevation only. The rest of the building is supported by earth-fast posts. But more importantly, immediately to the side of this building is a service range that similarly fronts the street. Built of timber-framing and nogged infill, the range comprises four early chambers. The two larger chambers to the front of the lot were likely kitchen and washhouse; the two smaller to the rear were likely bedchambers for house slaves. A few other examples of such ranges, usually of brick, survive in ruinous condition elsewhere in town. A larger but now less complete set of urban quarters was built by James Hardyman around the perimeter of his large Duke Street lot, between his purchase of the lot in

1797 and the drafting of his insurance policy on the same property in 1799. In that policy he denotes a series of timber and shingle "offices" along two of the exterior walls of the property, likely individual rooms used to accommodate some of his house slaves. Sadly, almost all of the evidence for this range has now been lost.

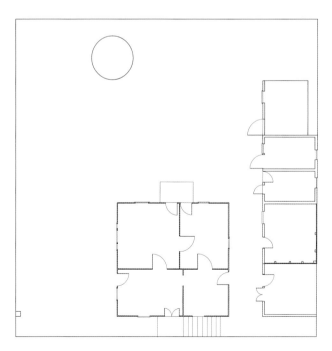

FIG. 8.8 Plan of 18 Pitt Street showing kitchen and slave quarter, Falmouth, Jamaica.

FREE BLACK HOUSING

In contradistinction to the mud-walled houses or urban barracks occupied by the enslaved community, urban free blacks chose to build in a manner that set them apart. Elizabeth Somerville's house is similar in form to many other examples surviving from the very early nineteenth century. In all cases, they are small frame houses situated on a lot with a yard. One contemporary observer noted that "Adjoining to the house is usually a small spot of ground, laid out into a sort of garden and shaded by various fruit trees."[51] This correspondence of house to food-bearing shade tree enlisted the yard as a living space. While board houses are carefully crafted buildings, they are often no more than 150 square feet. But to assume that this was the whole house is to misunderstand life in the tropics. The two chambers of these buildings functioned as the storage and sleeping quarters of a house that encompassed both interior and exterior spaces. The size of these buildings forced the major part of everyday life outdoors. And in fact some of these spaces are still occupied in these very same ways. Standing in the side

yard of 7 Lower Harbour is a large mango tree that creates a shaded social space toward the front of the lot (fig. 8.9). In the rear, by contrast, is a swept dirt yard with access to a station for food preparation and an external shower and privy. The cleared swept space around this board house is indicative of these early houses, where so much activity took place outside in the unobstructed spaces of the yard.

The early board houses are all sheltered with a shingled, hipped roof. Wood shingles appear on the vast majority of roofs in early townscapes of Jamaica, clearly the preferred roofing material over the palm thatch used for most slave quarters, which probably shed water just as effectively but required a great deal more maintenance. The hipped roof form presented a lower roof profile to the raging hurricane-force winds that struck the island with notable frequency. Some of these buildings also had glazed, sash windows with side jalousies. While the sash windows were certainly fashionable and clearly differentiated these houses from slave quarters, the most constant ventilation came through the jalousies, which

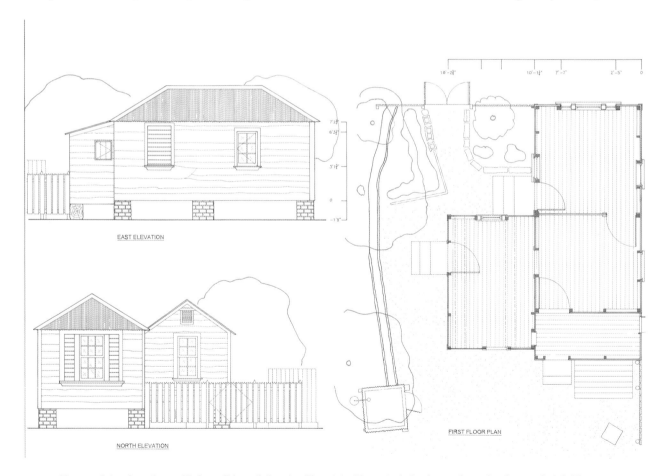

EAST ELEVATION

NORTH ELEVATION

FIRST FLOOR PLAN

FIG. 8.9 House and site plan, 7 Lower Harbour, Falmouth, Jamaica. The original house includes the two front chambers to the left. The narrow rear chamber is a twentieth-century kitchen and the larger chamber to the right is a second bedroom, also twentieth century.

FIG. 8.10 Partition ventilator, board house, northwest corner of Duke and Pitt Streets, Falmouth, Jamaica.

kept out the sun and allowed some air circulation even when the window sashes were closed.

Attempts to mediate the climate extended to the interior as well. The lack of any internal sheathing for walls and the exposed roof framing meant that the building envelope was only one board-width thick, reduced to a single, fairly thin skin. Builders were also concerned about circulation of air within the house. That portion of the interior partition above the wall plate transitions from the solid board below to a series of horizontal slats that allow air to move between chambers within the exposed roof framing system (fig. 8.10). From elevated foundations to interior ventilators, these buildings incorporate a wide range of architectural strategies adapted to Jamaica's climate.

With access to a greater range of resources, Jamaica's free blacks embraced English box-framing technology that was not only longer lasting than the earthfast architecture of their enslaved counterparts but also directly associated with the dominant—but more importantly free—white cultural tradition. The shingle or clapboarding of these buildings presumed a regular system of sills, posts, braces, plates, and joists, all secured with mortise and tenon joinery; to the early nineteenth-century eye, the association of this framing technology with whites would have been particularly apparent in the Caribbean, where carpenters often left the framing exposed to the interior, even in the grandest spaces. The interiors of almost any Jamaican planter's house, laying bare these framing members, differentiated the alternative technologies of the slave quarter from the English box framing of the big house. The marked differences between the framed board houses of free blacks in Falmouth and the earthfast, wattle and thatch architecture of their enslaved counterparts would have served as a clear signal of social disparity among early black Jamaicans.[52]

One remarkably important feature of these houses is that they are almost universally outfitted with two exterior doors, one opening from the side yard into the front chamber and another opening through the back wall of the rear chamber. Through the late eighteenth and early nineteenth centuries, the incorporation of that rear door was in direct defiance of Jamaican law. Although they were legally free, free blacks lived in a world defined by racial disenfranchisement, and, as a result, resisting the institution of slavery was a reality of everyday life. While their architecture certainly functioned to distinguish them from slaves, free blacks actively resisted the institution of slavery by harboring runaways.[53] In the Kingston newspapers, for example, one ad seeking a runaway complained that Cudjoe, who was well known in Kingston, "was last year harboured about eight months by a mulatto woman in St. Mary's named Lydia Small."[54] When the free black community worked together to harbor a runaway,

such neighborhoods could become a labyrinth of small, highly permeable spaces known intimately by those colluding but bewildering to authorities. This cat and mouse game played out in a real landscape of densely occupied neighborhoods filled with small, two-chamber houses and their associated gardens and yards. In an effort to frustrate these attempts to gain freedom, the Colonial Assembly enacted legislation that limited the houses of all blacks to a single exterior door.[55] With only a single point of egress, allowing more effective surveillance over multiple buildings during a search for a runaway, the escapee could not slip out the rear door and into an adjacent house that had already been searched. That the legislation was passed on multiple occasions—and that the vast majority of surviving examples still have rear door openings and historic doors intact—is sufficient evidence that Jamaica's free blacks ignored this legislation and built into their houses a conscious strategy for harboring runaways (fig. 8.11).

As Trevor Burnard has noted, enslaved Africans were "trapped in a dehumanizing life of exhausting labor, debilitating disease, and demeaning social relationships; they were constantly tired, frequently frightened, and subject to continual flux in their living and work arrangements."[56] He further argues that these conditions were not a natural result of the machinery of the sugar plantation; rather, they were conditions cultivated by masters. The lives of the enslaved presented innumerable opportunities to oppose or press against their condition within

FIG. 8.11 Rear yard of 7a Lower Harbour Street, Falmouth, Jamaica.

the contours of their everyday lives, a practice generally referred to as "resistance."[57] An extraordinary example is the song reported by a new English arrival in Port Royal. Immediately upon anchor, a canoe of three slave women came to the side of the ship selling oranges. As they departed, the women sang:

> New-come buckra,
> He get sick,
> He tak fever,
> He be die
> He be die
> New-come buckra . . .[58]

While this song did little to upset the machinery of slavery, it certainly opposed the institution by instilling fear in the hearts and minds of new arrivals, many of them potential overseers or masters. Furthermore, Douglas Hall has outlined the many acts of opposition possible on the plantation: "planting potato slips in the wrong way . . . maiming animals . . . damaging or losing tools and equipment, allowing livestock in the canefields," among others.[59] But in reaction to explicit oppression, Africans also actively resisted slavery by obscuring surveillance, running away, practicing Obeah, and inciting rebellion. In many cases, the buildings and landscapes of the plantation played a critical role.

Many slaves resisted slavery by stealing themselves (and their labor) from the plantation by running away. One historian has estimated that as many as ten thousand slaves in Jamaica at any point in time were or had been runaways.[60] This is a remarkable number given that the island's total white population peaked at thirty thousand. And in these efforts to resist, the landscape played a key role. Africans traversed a plantation landscape that differed in important ways from that known by whites.[61] Archaeological evidence certainly suggests that slave villages were the genesis of paths that never appear on period plats of those same plantations; the plantation routes used by whites were only one set of routes that marked the landscape.[62] Many plantations incorporated or abutted large tracts of wetlands that remained generally uncharted and avoided by planters and overseers. Called morasses, these wetlands became safe havens for runaways. Thistlewood complained in 1776, for example, that Lincoln, his fisherman, had returned from a day's work without "enough for a cat." Suspecting him of having sold his fish for personal profit, Thistlewood ordered Pompey, another slave, to restrain Lincoln in the cookroom. "But while I was getting the bilboes he escaped

from Pompey & ran into the morass." Pompey, sent in after Lincoln, "could not come up with him."[63] As a fisherman, Lincoln knew very well the particularities of the morass and he also knew that Thistlewood did not.

Like Lincoln, Jamaican slaves most frequently ran away for short periods of time, intending to avoid an immediate task or the violence of a whipping.[64] This meant that runaways likely had favored hiding places to which they fled for brief seasons. The fact of such places was not unknown to planters. In a 1797 account published in the *Columbian Magazine,* the author notes that "in this seclusion from society, and in want of many of the common conveniencies of life, [runaways] are obliged to practice various shifts at which they are expert." One described in the article was the practice of cooking in the earth "for want of a pot." "Having made a hollow in the clayey soil and smoothed the surface of the cavity with their hands, they line the same with plantain leaves, and deposit their food and water. They cover all with plantain leaves, sticks, and a layer of earth, on which they make a fire which answers the purpose intended." Such sites were not uncommonly discovered by white travelers through "remote and uncultivated mountains."[65] In his research on Barbados, Frederick Smith has also described at length the evidence that slaves hid in remote caves to drink rum as a temporary escape from the grind of sugar labor.[66]

But sometimes, slaves were able to run away for good. Edward Long reports that given the regular illicit commerce between planters in St. Ann Parish on the north coast and the Spanish in Cuba, every year hundreds of slaves in that parish attempted to flee by boat to Cuba. Since Spaniards were able to cross the distance "in one night's time in very small vessels, and not seldom in open boats," Long asserted that slaves, "perceiving the facility of this passage . . . [take] every opportunity to desert in canoes, and withdraw to Cuba, in hopes of obtaining their freedom."[67] The remote settlements of the Maroons, however, were the far more common destination.

While there is no data to begin to estimate the number of slaves who fled to Maroon settlements in hope of freedom, the simple fact that treaties between the Maroons and the English included the responsibility to return runaways suggests that Maroon towns were intended destinations for large numbers of Jamaican runaways throughout the eighteenth century.[68] Maroons located their settlements in Jamaica's most difficult terrain, the Blue Mountains to the east and the Cockpit Country to the west. The latter is extraordinarily rough terrain marked by a series of steep-sided hollows formed from collapsed limestone caves, some with sides over three hundred feet high. Such features made traversing this area nearly impossible, save for those with an intimate knowledge of the land. Even today, these regions of Jamaica are very difficult to access, some still only by foot. By the late eighteenth century, some of the footpaths to the major Maroon settlements were discernible from heavy use; contemporaries indicated that since these towns usually had only a single point of access, footpaths usually led to a settlement.[69] Minor settlements were usually lower in elevation and more easily accessible. More important political centers were nearly inaccessible and as a result, runaways surely found themselves at the mercy of peripheral settlements as they sought out sanctuary. And upon arrival, runaways could very easily discover that their labor was in vain; Maroons often—though not always—returned runaways for profit.

◆ ◆ ◆

Although they are the most common and easily identifiable types, small, two-room board houses were not the only building type erected by or for Jamaica's free blacks. While studies on the architecture of free blacks in Jamaica are few, recent fieldwork and archival research in Falmouth has shown that free blacks built and owned many of the buildings of that town and that those buildings exhibit remarkable variation. Documents list many whites in the blocks of Duke Street between Market and Princess Streets, most of which sold between 1775 and 1785, including four carpenters, three gentlemen, two spinsters, a merchant, a planter, a tavern keeper, a butcher, and a mason, but also numerous free people of color, including a free mulatto woman and three free mulatto men, none of whom were listed by trade.

Sometime in the 1780s, Thomas Neale and his wife, Eleanor, both free people of color, built and opened a tavern on Duke Street, a building that survives to the present in ruinous condition (fig. 8.12). In its building materials, the tavern was quite typical of architecture in Falmouth, with a strong masonry foundation and a timber-framed upper story. But in its plan, it was quite distinctive. Occupying an important corner lot on Duke Street, the major road connecting towns along the north coast, the building responds to its site in a distinctive manner. It takes the form of an *L*, creating a protected (north-facing), stone-paved forecourt fronting Duke Street. Large double doors and substantial windows opened through the rear

wall of the forecourt into the tavern rooms of the interior, creating what must have been a lively and fluid space with a regular flow between outdoor patio and interior tavern room. Although the poor condition of the building has prevented careful investigation of the interior and the upper floors, the regular sequence of evenly disposed windows along the eastern elevation suggests that the upper floor was dominated by rentable chambers. Neale's tavern rooms were richly appointed with twenty mahogany tables and numerous fine mahogany and Windsor chairs, as well as a backgammon table and other gaming pieces. The upper-story chambers included ten bedsteads, six featherbeds, six mattresses, and six mosquito nets. But Neale and his wife held investments that reached well beyond their tavern and its furnishings. By the time of his death in 1796, Neale owned a plantation of over two hundred acres, twenty-three mules, six horses, and thirty-two head of sheep, in addition to his ninety-six slaves.[70]

In October 1793, Sarah McGhie, a free woman of color, bought the lot at the northwest corner of Duke and Princess Streets for ninety pounds.[71] McGhie was likely the mistress of James McGhie, a wealthy white planter who owned three plantations and over three hundred slaves.[72] That James McGhie served as executor of Thomas Neale's will demonstrates the familiarity between whites and the free black community in Falmouth. Sarah McGhie was a well-kept woman, if indeed being a mistress was her means to prosperity. Her house appears today to be a single-story masonry building set slightly back from the street, built sometime after 1800 (fig. 8.13). But physical examination of the building and an early street view suggest that the house originally took the form of a mixed-material merchant house. The surviving masonry ground floor was originally fronted by the tall columns of a sidewalk piazza that supported the residential quarters of the original upper wooden story. The current form of the building is likely the result of rebuilding after some catastrophe, as the only early materials to survive are three of the four ground-floor masonry walls.

Some decades later, in 1838, Thomas Davidson erected a large mansion house on a lot overlooking Falmouth Harbor (see fig. 6.11). He inherited this lot and its "Bay Creole house" from his mother, who bequeathed it to him in her 1837 will.[73] Like a number of free women of color in town, Mary Gairdner was an extensive landowner in Falmouth. In October 1800, she purchased part of lot 55 on Upper Parade Street in the Reid Town section from John

FIG. 8.12 Neale Tavern, Duke Street, Falmouth, Jamaica, late 1780s.

Baillie for £150.[74] Her will provided for each of her four children to remain in the houses where they were living at the time of her death in 1837.[75] Davidson's spectacular new house was matched by equally grand houses of free blacks elsewhere in the Caribbean. In his examination of urban slavery in Bridgetown, Barbados, Pedro Welch has uncovered numerous references to free blacks of

FIG. 8.13 McGhie House, Duke Street, Falmouth, Jamaica, early nineteenth century.

surprising wealth in that city.[76] Visitors to the house of free black merchant Joseph Thorne, for example, observed that it demonstrated his interest in the arts and learning, as it had "a large library of religious, historical, and literary works." Opposite his library, Thorne displayed a cabinet filled with minerals and artifacts from Amerindian sites on the island.[77] From Elizabeth Somerville's small, two-room board house, to Thomas Neale's large tavern, to Mary Gairdner's "Bay Creole house," and Thomas Davidson's grand two-story house, Falmouth's free blacks built for themselves a wide range of houses, some distinguishing free blacks from their enslaved counterparts, others revealing the extraordinary wealth of a small portion of Jamaica's free black population.

Even so, the predominant form was the small two-room timber-framed house. In their careful analysis of early nineteenth-century missionary records, Natalie Zacek and Laurence Brown tracked the persistence of this house type past emancipation. Freedmen's villages appearing across Jamaica in the late 1830s were described as populated with "comfortable cottages" and "neat and substantial" houses. The Jamaican *Baptist Herald* asserted that each freedman's family required a small house not of two rooms but three, one for the parents and one each for the male and female children, possibly accounting for the prevalence of three-room examples from the middle and later nineteenth century. Unsurprisingly, the alignment of neat framed houses and respectability marked the aspirations of free blacks before and after emancipation.[78]

Along with Lydia Small, Sarah McGhie, and Elizabeth Somerville, many other free black owners of small houses were women. This pattern appears across the Caribbean; Pedro Welch has determined that women made up more than half of free black property owners in Bridgetown, Barbados.[79] One of the ways that these women generated enough real and social capital to build their own house was by serving as a mistress to a wealthy white man.[80] As suggested by an early nineteenth-century author, "It is quite common for an attorney to keep a favorite black or mulatta girl on every estate, which the managers are obliged to pamper and indulge like goddesses."[81] What was true of attorneys on plantations was also true in towns and in Kingston; white men commonly "kept" one or more black mistresses. Kingston's "kept mistresses" were, in the words of one critical observer:

> generally more expensive in their habiliments than wives; indeed their sole motive for cohabitating with white men, is the gratification of their extravagant desires. They value themselves on the number and ample dimensions of their coats . . . the dress of such a Delilah is a Holland shift, cambric handerchiefs, a chintz bed-gown, Morocco slippers, a beaver or silk hat richly laced, with a broad cloth laced cloak.[82]

While the assertion of "sole motive" is certainly less than generous, this commentator reinforces not only the existence of mistresses in Kingston but also their very public status and recognition.

Trevor Burnard's analysis of Phibbah, the long-term mistress of Thomas Thistlewood, offers a richly detailed look into the life of one of these women.[83] Phibbah, born in Jamaica, first met Thistlewood when he became the overseer on the plantation where she served but where she was owned not by the white planter but by his mulatto mistress. Thistlewood took her as his mistress in 1754, two years after they first met and after he had already flogged her once and suspected her of plotting to kill him. Once they took up together, Phibbah remained Thistlewood's mistress for thirty-three years, until his death in 1787.

Phibbah was allowed to own not only livestock but also land and other slaves; she also undertook to punish or forgive the transgressions of other slaves in Thistlewood's absence.[84] It is clear that this condition generated for Phibbah a distinct economic advantage in her accumulation of wealth through gifting from Thistlewood, vending merchandise, and working as a baker and seamstress. At one point Thistlewood even borrowed money from Phibbah, demonstrating her personal control of her wealth.[85] Phibbah was a remarkably strong woman, for she remained throughout those decades well-respected in the local slave community. In Burnard's words, Phibbah "transcended" slavery, achieving for herself a lifestyle that more closely resembled freedom than slavery. And most importantly for our purposes here, Thistlewood named her in his will, in which he gifted her not only her manumission but also "the sum of One Hundred Pounds . . . in the purchase of a Lot of piece of land for the said Phibba wherever she shall chose and that they [the executors] do build thereon a dwelling-house for the said Phibbah suitable to her station."[86] One wonders whether that house might have approximated Elizabeth Somerville's. As a mistress, Phibbah spent her life moving toward an eventual reality of living as a free woman of color in her own house.

Evidence abounds for the presence of "kept" mistresses in Falmouth. An excellent example is the 1797 will of George Goodin Barrett, son of Edward Barrett. The will authorizes his trustees to free Eliza Peters, his mulatto woman, and to give her £50 from his estate. Furthermore, Barrett's estate was to expend £100 to erect a dwelling house for Eliza together with ten acres of provision land within five miles of the sea. Eliza was also to have the use and services of an enslaved girl named Rachel. And, maybe most importantly, Barrett's will named each of Eliza's children—Thomas, William, Ann, Samuel, and Richard. That they were all his own children is made evident by the fact that he directed his executors to deliver to each a handsome sum of £2000, fortyfold the amount given to their mother.[87] All four sons were to be sent to England at age seven for their education. Although born of an enslaved mulatto woman, Thomas, William, Ann, Samuel, and Richard were not going to grow up in Jamaica as slaves. If they returned to Jamaica, they would join the increasingly wealthy contingent of Jamaica's free black population.

In some ways, the publicly accepted nature of keeping a black or mulatta mistress parallels the practice of *placage* in French Louisiana, wherein a (usually light-skinned) free black woman could be "contracted" to a white man for a few years. He was expected to deliver her a stipend and construct for her a small house. He was also expected to financially support their children. In exchange he enjoyed her company until (or sometimes well beyond) the time of his marriage to a white woman.[88] While the historical record offers no institutional parallel in Jamaica to Louisiana's *placage*, the tradition of women's ownership of small houses in Falmouth and elsewhere suggests that some or many of these were the result of having served as a mistress to a white man.

The houses of free blacks were largely indistinguishable from the rest of the built environment, and in this way they further blurred the lines between the enslaved and black and free and white. By the late eighteenth century, these individuals were often described by visitors to Jamaica as "Creoles," the same word used to describe Jamaican-born whites. Their manners, their dress, and their architecture were by the early nineteenth century indistinguishable from one another; British visitors spent more time differentiating themselves not from the enslaved Africans but from the Creoles, both white and mixed race.

PAN-CARIBBEAN FREE BLACK ARCHITECTURE

Small board houses were not limited to Jamaica. An early nineteenth-century view of a Sunday market in St. John's, Antigua, shows a small board house in the background, standing along the edge of the square (see fig. 6.16). The 1829 will of Elizabeth Goodwin, a free black woman in Bridgetown, Barbados, bequeathed to her aunt "a board and shingled house in Bay Street," and "£20 to purchase a spot of land to put the house on."[89] The indication that the timber house would be moved corresponds to its small scale. Similar buildings appear in the early nineteenth century across the Caribbean, but the densest collection survives on the small island of Nevis in the Leeward Islands of the eastern Caribbean.[90] Like their rural counterparts in Jamaica, the oldest small houses on Nevis include two chambers sheltered under a hipped roof with long-side access into one chamber, an interior partition with a communicating door, and a short-end door from the inner chamber to the side yard (fig. 8.14). Rather than board sheathing, the Nevis examples are often shingled on the walls as well as the roof. While their form and plan are quite similar to the Jamaican examples, Nevisian houses boast richly ornamented interior partitions. Where Jamaican ventilators are simple horizontal boards,

FIG. 8.14 Board house, Cotton Ground, Nevis.

Nevisian carpenters found in the ventilator the opportunity for remarkable artistic improvisation (fig. 8.15). Such elaboration resulted in details that can only be described as spectacular. If, in fact, these other small wooden houses that mark the landscapes of Nevis, Antigua, Jamaica, Barbados, and elsewhere across the Caribbean also date from the early nineteenth century, then the board houses of Falmouth's free blacks are not alone.

FIG. 8.15 Interior partition, board house, near Fort Charles, Nevis.

FIG. 8.16 Shotgun house, 1636 Fourth Street, Columbus, Georgia. Library of Congress.

The New Orleans shotgun house was equally burdened with the responsibility of communicating free black identity (fig. 8.16).[91] As a building type long associated with the free black population in New Orleans, the shotgun house has some distinctive characteristics, most particularly its one-story timber-frame construction and its linear organization of rooms. The reassessment of the shotgun house by Jay Edwards, which suggested that these houses were associated with that city's population of free black mistresses, established connections between the small houses of French Louisiana and British Jamaica less through form and more through the politics of gender and slavery.[92] As the southern American city with the largest free black population throughout the first half of the nineteenth century and the city most closely associated with the Caribbean, it is no surprise to find this tradition manifest in early New Orleans just as it was in Kingston and Falmouth. If we follow the lead of historians and consider the coastal regions of the early American South to be the landside perimeter of the greater Caribbean, then the New Orleans shotgun house is a regional variant that expands the landscape of free blacks to the American mainland. These buildings are regionally differentiated examples of a shared phenomenon: free blacks struggling to marshal available resources to build houses that mediate the climate and signal their status as free blacks in a region where everything was overshadowed by the specter of slavery.

◆ ◆ ◆

What do we learn from examining the board houses of free blacks in Falmouth? They help us lay to rest the persistent assertion that the value of early African and African American material expressions resides in their capacity to manifest African cultural survivals.[93] The significance laid on surviving Africanisms is still overplayed in the scholarship on early African American cultural production. Far too often interpretations of early American architecture embrace an immutable cultural determinism that assumes buildings will naturally emulate deeply imbedded cultural structures. Some scholars have linked the formal features of both Caribbean board houses and the New Orleans shotgun house to the traditional architectures of West Africa, citing the similarity of room dimensions and continuities in living patterns. Other scholars find direct parallels between the translation of West African languages through a reductive pidgin language to a mature Creole and the literal structural transformation of architectural traditions. In this view, the Caribbean board house is the literal materialization of Creole language.[94] But if their value lies in their connections to Africa, Falmouth's board houses are an utter failure; they reflect little of the architectural technologies or lifeways of western Africa. The proportions of their interiors speak less to structuralist models of African spatial patterning or linguistic models of cultural identity and formation and more to the practical concerns of construction.

Instead, the built environment of early free black Jamaica is better understood as a pragmatic, creative, and resourceful resolution of fundamental social, economic, and climatic considerations. What do we think defined these buildings? Certainly not some shared African survivalism. They are extraordinary examples of appropriation by a disenfranchised margin of the resources of the majority. They are examples of creative architectures generated by the intense pressures of colonialism in the context of at least an Atlantic if not global economy. They demonstrate sensitive accommodation to the climate. And they are material acts of resistance to a fairly consistent set of circumstances; in that way they have much in common.[95] These buildings represent strategies by free blacks to fashion a way of life in critical material circumstances, shaped by challenging climatic conditions and profound racial injustices. They remind us of the resilience of the human spirit to resist oppression through sheer strength of will and to reach out and assist others in circumstances worse than our own.

9 Building in Britain

Canary Wharf is now a posh district of hotels, business centers, and condominiums in the East End of London easily accessible from downtown via a new above-ground light rail. Elegantly detailed towers overlook spacious open plazas with outdoor restaurant seating and quays harboring small yachts. Here Gucci bags, truffle burgers, and Cuban cigars comfortably commingle. But along the northwest edge of the complex stands a range of five-story brick warehouses that suggest this place has a very different past (fig. 9.1). Begun in 1799 and largely completed by 1806, the district that is now Canary Wharf was once the West India Docks, at the time of its construction the world's largest and most sophisticated complex of wet docks. The project had a profound impact on shipping and trade between London and the British West Indies and was so successful that merchants trading to East India followed suit in 1806. The scheme was driven to fruition largely through the efforts of Robert Milligan, a Jamaican planter with West Indian shipping interests who had been resident in London since 1780. In the early 1790s, Milligan enlisted George Hibbert, nephew and heir to Thomas Hibbert, Kingston's most prosperous later eighteenth-century slave trader (and builder of the Kingston harbor

merchant house and slave trading headquarters that closed chapter 1). Born in Jamaica, George Hibbert had first partnered with his uncle and then inherited the slave trading business at his uncle's death in 1780. By the early 1790s Hibbert was living in London, joining the swelling ranks of absentee Jamaicans, those with significant interests in Jamaica but resident in the motherland. Together Milligan and Hibbert spearheaded a scheme for the new docks, and by June of 1799, their plan received royal assent. Over the next six years, the West India Dock Company, with Hibbert as chairman, Milligan as deputy chairman, and thirteen other West Indians as the board of elected stockholders, undertook the largest public works program yet imagined in Britain. The West India Docks complex was Jamaican architecture, a Jamaican building program that transformed the capital city.[1]

◆ ◆ ◆

Earlier chapters explored the architectural interdependence of West Africa and Jamaica, and analyzed castles, merchant houses, and plantations as embodiments of the architectural and social impact of Britain on Jamaica. This final chapter examines the impact of Jamaica on the

FIG. 9.1 Warehouses of the West India Docks, London, England, 1799–1806.

architecture and landscapes of Great Britain, and argues that Jamaican life and architecture extended beyond the shores of that island to the motherland.[2] These chapters collectively resist any linear interpretive model that leads from Jamaica to Britain or vice versa. After the transfer of the Ceded Islands—Grenada, St. Vincent, Dominica, and Tobago—to Britain through the Treaty of Paris and the growing interest in the late eighteenth century in India and Australia, Jamaica would become only one of many colonial actors. As many scholars have now come to recognize, these places were in constant dialogue; people and ideas were constantly moving back and forth across and around the empire. As Jamaica's continuing role in the project of empire moved into the early nineteenth century, the subject field simply shifts to Britain. Barry Higman's article "The Sugar Revolution" significantly reframes our understanding of the phenomenon of Jamaican absenteeism: rather than a static condition of colonials having removed to Britain, Higman demonstrates that many Jamaican absentees moved freely between Jamaica and Britain; they were, to use David Hancock's phrase, "citizens of the world."[3] Following this trajectory, this final chapter demonstrates the transatlantic scope of Jamaican architecture.

Jamaica shaped the architecture and landscapes of Britain in myriad ways. When the British Empire had expanded into Africa and Jamaica, those with interests in these ventures began to signal their global connections by collecting and exhibiting curiosities. The earliest examples of this impulse took the form of black bodies, as enslaved African servants, attributes in portraits, and blackamoor figures. Another form was the collection of exotic tropical plants, necessarily grown in greenhouses. And after the early 1720s, numerous houses began to exhibit the conspicuous display of Jamaican mahogany, the gold standard of tropical hardwoods through the eighteenth century. Through this display of natural exotica, late seventeenth- and early eighteenth-century Britons proclaimed their participation in empire.

COLONIAL OFFICIALS AND THE IMPERIAL *WUNDERKAMMER*

By the late seventeenth century, Jamaica played a role in reshaping Britain's elite domestic interiors, most especially through the collection of African and Caribbean exotica. One collector was William Blathwayt. Of undistinguished heritage, Blathwayt made his career as a civil servant deeply involved in the administration of Britain's plantations.[4] After his education and a brief stint as an English emissary to The Hague, Blathwayt began his long career as an administrator over the colonies. By the early 1670s, he was serving as a clerk of the privy council and by 1680 he was England's first auditor-general over revenues from the American colonies. But in 1685 he received his most important post as secretary of the Committee on Trade and Foreign Plantations, which effectively positioned him as the leading English official involved in colonial administration. The following year he married Mary Wynter, heiress to the Dyrham estate, and by 1692, after his wife's death, he began the construction of the west front of the house at Dyrham Park, the first stage in an extensive reconstruction that would last more than a decade (fig. 9.2).

In his reconstruction at Dyrham Park, Blathwayt signaled his participation in the global project of empire through collection, a late echo of the *Wunderkammer,* or cabinet of curiosities. Generally comprising *naturalia,* or specimens from exotic places, and *artificialia,* including artifacts of historical interest or technical virtuosity, the Wunderkammer had a long history in northern Europe before the late seventeenth century.[5] In her introductory essay on this collecting impulse, Joy Kenseth makes clear that the collection of natural marvels—primarily animals, plants, and people—was closely connected to the exploration of the Americas, Africa, and the Orient, the sites of empire.[6] But taking this observation a step further, the act of collection makes a personal and individual claim to participation in empire; the ownership of objects from across the empire betrayed a presumed personal authority over the places and peoples represented by the artifacts collected.[7] And while Dyrham Park did not exactly have a room reserved as a cabinet for his curiosities—although it does include one small closet with a seventeenth-century depiction of a Jamaican cocoa tree—Blathwayt built into

his new house the spoils of empire, including black bodies, brown woods, and green plants. Certainly in the late seventeenth century and for many through the eighteenth century as well, all three categories would have been understood to be *naturalia.*

An inventory of Dyrham Park from 1700 recorded in the upstairs balcony room two "blackamore figures," statues of African slaves wearing red tunics, their bondage made explicitly clear by the shackles around their ankles and the metal bands around their necks (fig. 9.3).[8] The location of these figures in this room is significant. As the first chamber in the suite of rooms that served as Blathwayt's private chambers, this was just as much private office for important colonial business as it was the central room of the upper floor from which one might survey the garden. These two objects, silenced and subservient black bodies, have knelt in this room for more than three hundred years. These objects were for Blathwayt not just objects of general curiosity but evidence of the benefits of his post; one of Blathwayt's primary and more lucrative activities was the promotion of the African slave trade. As Jamaican Edward Long argued a century later, even "the sovereign of Great Britain holds an interest in Negroes . . . for his revenue is very greatly benefited and supported by the produce of their personal labor."[9] Purchased and installed by Blathwayt and unmoved since, these blackamoor figures raise important questions about the place of the black body in the British imagination through the eighteenth century, first more generally as the

FIG. 9.2 Dyrham Park, Gloucestershire, England, begun 1692.

anonymous servant and then, more specific to Caribbean planters, reduced to the African head as heraldic device.

Blathwayt's blackamoor figures correlate closely with the later seventeenth-century portrait practice of including black servants as anonymous attributes of the sitter.[10] Africans, generally identified as slaves by silver collars, commonly appear in British portraiture by the middle of the seventeenth century.[11] As Susan Amussen has argued, the appearance of these figures was not random. African slaves appeared as servants earliest in the portraits of British royalty and military leaders, demonstrating the direct connections between the representation of anonymous Africans and the expanding empire in the British visual imagination.[12] As David Bindman points out, the

increasing presence of blacks in later seventeenth-century portraits is likely a result of the 1663 charter of the Company of Royal Adventurers to Africa and the rise of Charles II and the return of courtly culture and its association with black pages.[13] In these seventeenth-century portraits, many wear silver collars, explicitly reminiscent of the shackles of the slave trade. In later decades, the fashion for including a black "servant" in a portrait—generally those of elite or aristocratic women—became widespread, suggesting broader participation in the project of empire and the sense that ownership of an African posed little moral anxiety in the minds of Englishmen and women into the eighteenth century. African bodies—black bodies—were objects of wonder to seventeenth-century

FIG. 9.4 Candlestick, Bow Porcelain Manufactory, ca. 1770. Porcelain with enamels and gilded. Victoria and Albert Museum, London.

Britons, and were portrayed as objects first collected by the court of Charles II and by those deeply involved with the Atlantic trade. The manifestation of this collecting impulse was first the representation of black pages in portraits but soon thereafter the production and purchase of blackamoor figures like Blathwayt's. Through the seventeenth century, black figures often appeared on the stems of elaborate cups, such as those made from nautilus shells or coconuts, as collectible emblems of exotic Africa.[14]

The most popular manifestation of this form by the middle of the eighteenth century was the production of figurines depicting Africans as decorative objects for table and mantel; two porcelain manufactories, Bow and Chelsea, were both producing such figures by the

1760s. In a more emblematic manner, dark bodies represented Africa—and sometimes America as well—in sets of the "four continents." Commonly "America" wore an imagined Native American headdress while "Africa" wore an elephant's head as a cap. Otherwise the figures were nearly interchangeable. But these manufactories also produced figures that were more explicitly enslaved Africans (fig. 9.4). In 1765 Bow produced a pair of figures—one male and one female—who were cast with upraised arms supporting a pierced porcelain basket over their head, intended to hold sweetmeats during a dessert course of a meal.[15] Meissen versions of the same object types were commonly produced for the French market with blackamoor figures alongside a sugar bowl, simultaneously referencing the enslavement of the black body and the source of great wealth.[16] By the middle of the eighteenth century the black body and white sugar were inextricably linked in the British (and European) imagination. In this way, these black bodies were simultaneously exotic, collectible, and—as with Blathwayt's figures—working. In all manifestations—live bodies, portrait attributes, and sculptural figure—the black body in late seventeenth- and eighteenth-century Britain represented simultaneously exotic wonder and imperial aspiration. They also served to reinforce by contrast the whiteness, and by extension the authority, of the British elite. Standing at the very center of the entire project of Atlantic empire was the fact of slavery and object of the black body.

Over the course of the eighteenth century the presence of black bodies in Britain rapidly increased and by extension so too their frequency in British portraiture.[17] But by the later eighteenth century—in the generations after Blathwayt—the blackamoor and the African slave both became subjects of deep anxiety. The British imagining of the blackamoor was profoundly shaped by the reprinting of "The Blackamoor in the Wood," a ballad that appeared first in print in the sixteenth century but was reproduced extensively after the 1770s. In the telling of the narrator,

FIG. 9.5 Josiah Wedgwood and Sons, medallion, ca. 1787. White jasper with black relief. Victoria and Albert Museum, London.

the blackamoor is a villainous figure who enacts revenge for the corrections of his master, vengeance that includes the rape of his mistress and the bloody murder of her two sons, followed by his own suicide.[18] These increasingly popular anxieties map onto the increasing presence of actual black bodies in Britain. As Madge Dresser has made very clear, the increased trade with Africa and the West Indies meant that late eighteenth-century Bristol had a substantial black population, although not so large as that in contemporary London, which had a population of five thousand blacks by the 1770s.[19]

It seems not coincidental that the appearance of porcelain collectible versions of black bodies began to appear in the middle decades of the century, just as racist sentiments increased in the public sphere, the fashion for black servants declined, and the numbers of black persons in British cities began to rapidly increase. In the 1760s, newspapers in Bristol, Liverpool, and other port cities regularly printed advertisements for the sale of slaves or requesting the recovery of a runaway, closely linking the public spaces of Britain with those of the British Caribbean, at least until the Somerset Act of 1772, which hindered legal slavery in England and raised the specter of moral shame associated with the trade.[20] By the end of the century, the moral critique of slavery launched by abolitionists diminished the popularity of black bodies in British elite portraiture; where they continued, the presence of the black body became allied with the ostentatious display of wealth and lax morality associated with absentee or returning West Indian planters.[21] The close visual similarity of the kneeling blackamoor and the final version of the famous Wedgwood image of the kneeling slave surrounded by the text "Am I Not a Man and Brother?" seems not accidental (fig. 9.5). Josiah Wedgwood and others working to end the African slave trade would surely have known kneeling forms similar to those in Dyrham Park.

In his substantial reconstruction of the house at Dyrham Park, William Blathwayt installed two very grand staircases, each rising within one of the two major flanks of the house. The first, a component part of the earlier west range of the house from the early 1690s, was originally devised of exposed Virginia walnut, although later painting has obscured the wood's natural richness (fig. 9.6). In his slightly later campaign in the east range of the house (1698–1704), Blathwayt again selected an exotic foreign wood, this time American cedar. While grand staircases such as these had been incorporated

FIG. 9.6 Walnut staircase, Dyrham Park.

FIG. 9.7 Mahogany floors and doors of Marble Hill House, outside London, ca. 1720.

into British country houses for decades, those in Dyrham Park are among the earliest to intentionally utilize exotic colonial woods. Blathwayt's conspicuous consumption of these woods signaled his participation in the production of empire, as did the display of blackamoor figures in his upper chambers.

The cachet of American walnut and cedar, however, would not last long. As Jennifer Anderson has documented, mahogany would by the 1720s become the exotic wood of choice, and through the eighteenth century the leading supplier of mahogany was Jamaica. This rapid transformation was a result of both supply and demand. As Anderson has so deftly demonstrated, the early eighteenth-century abundance of Jamaican mahogany was in part the result of the rapid clearing of land in those same decades for the planting of sugar. When the Board of

Trade lifted all duties on the importation of timber from British holdings in the Americas, including the Caribbean, in 1721, this customs change opened the floodgates for the introduction of Caribbean mahogany into the English market and its subsequent lavish use. By the late 1720s any mahogany in Britain would have been rightly understood to derive from the Caribbean trade.[22] But at the same time, the introduction of the rich new wood played a critical role in the refashioning of British and American elites as consumers in a phenomenon called by most historians the "consumer revolution." Through the first half of the eighteenth century, elites used the conspicuous consumption of luxury goods as a mechanism of establishing social standing. What in the 1710s was a largely unknown material became by the 1730s the wood of choice among the elite. Spurred by supply and demand, mahogany exports

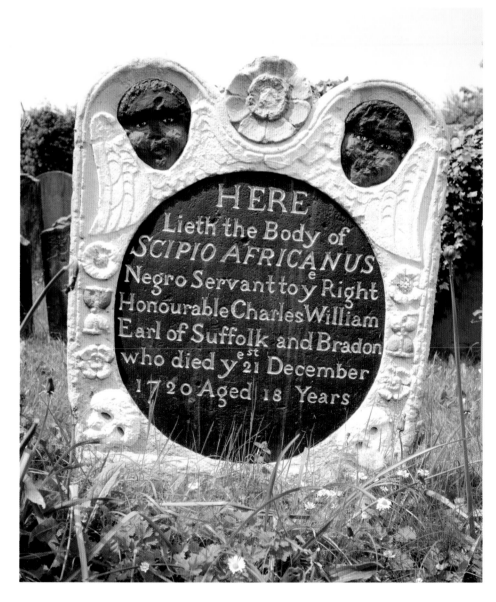

FIG. 9.8 Gravemarker for Scipio Africanus, Henbury Churchyard, Gloustershire, England, 1720.

from Jamaica climbed steadily from the 1720s through the 1760s. As Anderson makes clear, the great age and size of mahogany trees felled through these decades—the result of the clearing of forests for sugar fields—produced an extraordinarily rich and sophisticated finish. By the 1760s Jamaica was supplying 92.5 percent of all West Indian mahogany to England.[23]

The embrace of mahogany as a building material is nowhere better demonstrated than in Marble Hill House, under construction through the late 1720s. One of the most striking characteristics of the house is the very extensive use of this wood, especially the unpainted mahogany of the entire staircase and the mahogany floors of the great room (fig. 9.7). Lawrence Brown's recent research on Marble Hill House makes quite clear that the patron, Harriett Howard, depended on investments in both the South Sea Company and other slaving ventures to fund the construction of her new house.[24] Significantly, her ownership of stock in the South Sea Company rose dramatically in 1722, after the fall of stock prices and just as the company was escalating its investment in the African slave trade.[25] While Howard was not herself Jamaican, the construction of her house depended heavily on a financing scheme that profited from the Atlantic trade. And her novel and conspicuous use of mahogany—likely from Jamaica—not only for doors but also for the floors and staircase, sent a very clear signal of her profit from the expanding British Empire. And her connection to enslaved Africans was likely made personal through her familiarity with the slave Scipio Africanus, an African manservant owned by her nephew, Charles William Howard (fig. 9.8).[26] Harriett Howard's material world was profoundly shaped by the African and Caribbean trade.

If Blathwayt's blackamoor figures and exotic hardwoods failed to signal his colonial responsibilities, his greenhouse, begun in 1701, surely succeeded (fig. 9.9). Described as "one of the most beautiful and commodious Piles for its Purpose," according to one contemporary, the building was in winter "replete with all Manner of fine Greens, as Oranges, Lemons, Mirtles, etc. set in the most beautiful order." By the end of the seventeenth century, English plant collections included specimens from Africa, Persia, India, and the Caribbean, most delivered via merchant traders and sea captains.[27] In order to sustain orange trees as well as exotic flowers and vegetables, Blathwayt's greenhouse was fitted out with the most advanced heating system.[28] His appetite for exotic fruits had likely been piqued by his regular receipt of oranges, casks of preserved ginger, and even pickled peppers from West Indians hoping to curry his favor.[29] Greenhouses were fairly common among royalty and the nobility by the end of the seventeenth century, but such a feature on a country house of the gentry was quite unusual; even more so, Blathwayt's was far finer than most, signaling his particular interest in tropical exotica.

But Blathwayt's greenhouse was also a place of social and political performance. In the summer, when many of the heartiest plants were moved into the gardens, the greenhouse retained "two or three rows of Oranges &, the Length of the House, which make the most beautiful and fragrant Walks within Doors; and the whole house is whitewash'd, and hung round with the most entertaining Maps, Sculptures, & furnished with fine Chairs of Cane for the Summer."[30] The maps noted by this visitor are part of the enormous and extensive collection of maps of English America, Africa, and the Caribbean assembled by Blathwayt in the 1680s.[31] The combination of greenhouse, orange trees, and maps of the expanding empire conspired to create a space of extraordinary imperial power, here expressed not through fortifications or royal authority but through cartography and consumption.

An earlier chapter of this volume explored the attempts by Jamaicans to transform their tropical environs into picturesque landscapes; the gardens of Charles Price were among the most spectacular attempts. But in a remarkable move that Jill Casid has called the colonial intermixing of landscapes that fueled the production of empire, tropical exotica also transformed British landscapes, in and out of greenhouses.[32] While the significance of the imperial gardens at Kew are well understood, the cultivation of tropical varieties reached well beyond.[33] The seventy-six mahogany doors of Harewood House, built in Yorkshire through the 1760s by the Lascelles—whose money derived from Leeward Islands investments—have long been understood to be a signal of their West Indian wealth.[34] This message was reinforced by the exotics of the Harewood gardens and hothouse, which included pineapple plants, palms, aloes, and banana trees.[35] William Blathwayt's proclivity for collecting exotica—from black bodies to colonial hardwoods to exotic plants and foodstuffs—is just an early example of a practice of collection from the colonies that profoundly reshaped the spaces of Britain. While this discussion only begins to

FIG. 9.9 Greenhouse at Dyrham Park, Gloucestershire, England, begun 1701.

scratch the surface, the architecture and material worlds of colonial dignitaries like Blathwayt are likely to prove rich fodder for examination of the impact of the colonies on the spaces, forms, and lives of the motherland.

PORT CITIES AND ATLANTIC MERCHANTS

Sugar was Britain's largest single import from 1750 to 1820.[36] As Ralph Davis has argued, sugar consumption in England expanded rapidly over the first half of the eighteenth century. It was consumed only by the most elite in late seventeenth-century England, but by 1750 "even the poorest English farm laborer's wife took sugar in her tea."[37] England imported three thousand hogsheads of sugar in 1660; by 1753 that number rose to 110,000.[38] And the growth only escalated over the second half of the century.[39] This massive consumption was largely fed by Jamaica, the largest producer. In the peak year of production, 1805, Jamaica produced 100,000 *tons* of sugar; the following year Jamaica exported 6,760,000 gallons of rum, a by-product of sugar and a strong secondary export.[40] This trade had a profound impact on Great Britain, especially in the port cities, closely connecting them to the West Indies and especially to Jamaica. In 1753, Kingston's merchants proposed the removal of the seat of government from Spanish Town—the social and political center for Jamaica's planters—to Kingston, the larger port city and seat of the island's merchants. Hoping to increase profits,

Kingston's merchants sought out and received vigorous political support from merchants in London, Liverpool, and Bristol. As members of the mutually dependent transatlantic community of trade, British merchants claimed a stake in trade-related colonial affairs.[41]

Some of the earliest buildings in Great Britain to manifest the interdependence between the Caribbean and the motherland were the seventeenth-century sugar houses of Bristol. Especially through the seventeenth century, many Caribbean sugar planters found it easier to produce only muscavado, or unrefined brown sugar, which was stable enough to transport to Great Britain for finishing. Upon arrival in Bristol, these unrefined sugars would be returned to a line of coppers and refined into white sugar, which demanded a much higher sale value. The port city's first sugar refinery—indeed the first sugar refinery in England—was opened in 1616 near St. Peter's churchyard, but this early enterprise was devoted to refining sugar imported from the Portuguese Azores and Brazil.[42] In 1654, however, John Knight established a sugar refinery in a rented great house in Bristol to process raw sugar imported from Barbados and the Leeward Islands. As an absentee owner of a plantation in Nevis, Knight was invested in both ends of the trade.[43] Competitors emerged in the following decade or two, and by the years following the Restoration, Bristol claimed a number of sugar refineries.[44] John Hine's new sugar house, built in 1662 on the edge of the city in an already industrial area, established the model for purpose-built sugar houses through the rest of the century. Hine's sugar refinery eventually filled the site of a brewery and seven adjacent house sites. In addition to the newly built bakery (the seventeenth-century term for a refinery), the site included a warehouse with a counting house, a cooperage, stables, large houses for the two major proprietors, and eventually a house for the works' manager.[45] The refinery was not fundamentally different from a West Indian boiling house, with a series of coppers and ladles used to boil and extract impurities.[46] These sugar refineries were industrial sites that first emerged and flourished in Bristol.[47]

The numbers and size of sugar refineries grew through the eighteenth century in Bristol, where by the middle of the century they were six and seven stories in height.[48] None of the earlier sugar houses survive, but the brick shell of Lewin Meade's eighteenth-century sugar house has been repurposed as a luxury hotel (fig. 9.10). By the time of its construction it was one of at least twenty sugar houses that lined waterfront locations around Bristol.[49] The profitability of sugar refining was so clear that the premier historian of the industry has argued that by 1720 there were no waterfront sites available for new sugar houses, although the demand continued.[50] And by the 1730s, sugar refiners built into their estates pleasure gardens and extensive libraries as evidence of their transition from artisans to gentlemen.[51]

The sharp rise in shipping into and from the west coast of Britain also had a direct impact on Bristol's docking capacity. Bristol and London dominated the Africa and West Indies trade through the opening decades of the eighteenth century. Economic historian David Richardson has indicated that Bristol played a leading role in the expansion of the African slave trade before 1730, and eclipsed London and Liverpool into the 1740s.[52] His work, expanded by that of Madge Dresser, provides a compelling narrative of Bristol's expanding financial interest in and benefit from the slave trade through the first half of the eighteenth century, embroiling not just slave traders but also those involved in supplying the ships departing for Africa with necessities and trade goods and employing many in the refining of sugar upon its arrival in Bristol.[53] The increasing scope of shipping through Bristol over the course of the eighteenth century is well indicated by the rise in port traffic: 240 ships cleared the port of Bristol in 1687; that number was almost doubled a century later. Trade with Jamaica was the most profitable dimension of that shipping by far.[54]

The expanding interest in this trade reshaped the Bristol waterfront. As early as 1692, the construction of a major new quay in Bristol was underwritten by William Swymmer, one of Bristol's earliest slave merchants.[55] In 1765, William Champion built what he hoped would be a privately operated wet dock, but the venture collapsed and the dock was purchased by the Merchant Venturers and was thereafter known as the Merchants' Dock.[56] The demand for berthing was always greater than the accommodation, keeping a constant pressure on expansion and improvement. As suggested by one visitor in 1767, "the docks are flanked with commodious quays, surrounded by handsome brick houses, inhabited for the most part by seafaring people, and communicating with the down by drawbridges and floodgates."[57] Not until the opening years of the nineteenth century was any major change approved, this including the construction of a floating harbor and a new cut, or canal, that allowed ships two tracks up and down the waterfront. The project was completed in 1809, but by then Bristol had long lost its preeminence.

Owners of seventeenth-century sugar works often lived adjacent to their source of income; those making their wealth off the slave trade in Bristol began to build houses near one another. Edmund Saunders was one of the original builders on Guinea Street, newly laid out in early eighteenth-century Bristol. Saunders was one of the leading Bristol slave traders of his age, and while his house does not survive, an inventory includes rich furniture, jewelry, and exotica including gold-tipped

FIG. 9.10 Lewin Meade Sugar House, Bristol, England.

FIG. 9.11 Nathaniel Day House, Queen Square, Bristol, England, begun 1709.

antelope horns and "a blackamore's head in gold." He also had items intended for the Africa trade, including "Negro caps" and bales of textiles specifically intended for trade in West Africa.[58] Others followed and Guinea Street was soon densely populated by those engaged in the African slave trade.

The development of Bristol's first urban square meant that Queen Square quickly became Bristol's most fashionable address, that city's first "socially exclusive urban enclave," to quote one historian.[59] Emulating one of London's new urban squares, Queen Square was laid out in 1699 in formerly marginal land, the marshes at the edge of the town. Largely completed by the late 1720s, Queen Square was a major transformation of Bristol's cityscape. As Madge Dresser has argued, the development of Queen Square was closely connected to the rising wealth of that city's merchants, especially those who undertook (or provisioned) slaving voyages. Woodes Rogers was an infamous Bristol privateer who invested in numerous slaving voyages and served late in life as Governor of the Bahamas. He was also one of the very first to secure a plot on Queen Square. Also on Queen Square lived Isaac

Elton, who owned a plantation in Jamaica, and Henry Bright, who had previously lived in Jamaica as a factor before his return to Bristol. Thomas Freke, also a resident, was a major slave trader to Jamaica. One of the few surviving early houses was built by Nathaniel Day, a part owner of one of Bristol's sugar houses (fig. 9.11). Serving as alderman and eventually mayor, Day actively resisted the imposition of taxes on the slave trade. Soon after the completion of the square, at least ten of the twenty-four major residents were in some way involved in the slave trade or with interests in the Caribbean. Queen Square was just the earliest of such developments; by the later eighteenth century, builders with West Indian interests developed Bristol's Royal York Crescent and Berkeley and Portland Squares.[60]

After Queen Square became the most fashionable address in the opening decades of the eighteenth century, midcentury merchants with West Indian interests began building villas in the newly expanding suburbs. The best examples are the collection of elegant houses in the newly developed suburb of Clifton; Paul Fisher, a linen draper, built the grand Clifton Hill House sometime before 1747.

FIG. 9.12 Gothic tower garden folly, Henbury estate, outside Bristol, 1766.

Fisher was the son of a merchant involved in the Africa trade, a member of the Merchants Trading to Africa, and he held financial interests in West Indian plantations. Other houses in that district that were built with money derived from Africa or the West Indies include Cornwallis House, Fremantle House, Beaufort House, and St. Vincent's Rocks. But among the most interesting is the work of Thomas Farr. In 1762, Farr, sugar merchant and later mayor of Bristol, purchased the Henbury estate, just outside the city. One of Farr's interests was clearly in the property's high hillock overlooking Bristol and its harbor,

for the only major alteration he made to the property was the construction in 1766 of a tall Gothic tower on the crest of the hillock, providing spectacular, uninterrupted views over the city and its shipping (fig. 9.12).

Jamaica shaped Great Britain's cities through public buildings as well as domestic architecture. In the middle years of the century, merchants in Bristol hired architect John Wood to erect the Exchange Building (fig. 9.13). A public building to facilitate the regular transactions of merchants, the exchange also symbolized the increasing authority of Bristol's merchants, especially Africa and

West India merchants.[61] The merchants of Bristol had been considering the possibility of replacing their old exchange since at least 1717, but conversations appear to have escalated through the late 1730s.[62] In early 1741, representatives approached John Wood for designs to build the largest public building in the city in centuries. The plan of the building included an open "Egyptian Hall" courtyard surrounded by flanks on four sides housing a wide variety of functions, including counting rooms, a coffee house, and taverns. And while the plans and elevations are features that have captured the attention of architectural historians, it is the ornamental program that concerns us here. In the courtyard, sculptor Thomas Paty filled the tympanum of three pediments with figural representations of Asia, Africa, and America, each embellished with animals that symbolize these various realms, from penguins, to crocodiles, to camels (figs. 9.14, 9.15). In Wood's words, "The spaces between the Capitals of the Columns and the Pilasters of this Front, are filled with Festoons which represent Great Britain and the Four Quarters of the World, with the chief products and manufactures of every country."[63] Bristol's merchants understood their exchange to be a nexus of global trade. The huge scale of the building and the global vision of the decorative scheme left nothing to the imagination. And it was Jamaican sugar that fueled that developing global market and its residual impact on sugar houses, wharves, townhouses, and the Exchange of Bristol.

But the greater urban transformation took place in Liverpool, which after midcentury overtook Bristol as the major center for trade with Africa and the West Indies.[64] The African and Caribbean trade comprised at least a third or perhaps one half of Liverpool's revenue by that time and until the abolition of the slave trade in 1807.[65] If Liverpool sent out only fifteen ships per year as slavers in the 1730s, by the early 1770s that number crested one hundred per year and by the final decades of the century three quarters of all ships involved in the English slave trade departed from Liverpool.[66] One of the reasons for this dramatic escalation was the capacity of Liverpool merchants to outfit those ships with necessary supplies, shaping a regional economy—from fishing to textiles—that depended on the slave trade.[67]

An early history of the city reports on the construction of a new dock in 1710 in the form of an artificial harbor, intended to attract new shipping interests to Liverpool.[68] By the 1720s, Liverpool was also benefiting broadly from the slave trade, especially those producing coarse cloth from Manchester to be used for provisioning African slaves.[69] In 1738, Liverpool embarked on the construction of a second major dock, called the Salthouse Dock, for the exportation of salt from the south end of the city. But the rapid increase of shipping meant that the dock, completed in 1753, was quickly loaded with ships of various interests, including those trading to Africa and the West Indies.[70] The city's intentional work to attract shipping trade is probably best realized in a 1765 map and advertisement for the city of Liverpool (fig. 9.16). The published map celebrated the city's docks, which are described as "not inferior to any in Great Britain." The map boasts of Liverpool's dominance in the trade with Ireland and Scotland, but interestingly does not mention either the Africa trade or the West India trade that was certainly

FIG. 9.13 John Wood, Bristol Exchange, Bristol, England, 1741–43.

FIG. 9.14 Thomas Paty, Detail of figural representation of Africa, Bristol Exchange, Bristol, England.

by that point a major component of the city's shipping economy. In fact, the only reference to the Africa trade is the name of the quay adjacent to a newly intended dock: Goree, referring directly to a trading fort off the coast of modern Senegal. This dock, the largest yet, completed by 1771, was even outfitted with lighthouses.[71] One of the clearest surviving expressions of this growing economic reality was the 1793 construction of the Goree Warehouses. The continual expansion and enlargement of Liverpool's docks was in part a result of that city's increasing investment in the African and West Indian trades.

By the middle of the century, Liverpool's merchants had begun to outpace their rivals in Bristol and in doing so they built an exchange, also designed by Wood with ornament by Paty. The Liverpool Exchange, originally intended to serve as town hall, exchange, and assembly rooms, was begun in 1749 and was largely completed by 1754. Although later changes have transformed the building, the east elevation survives intact, and a drawing and description of the pediment scheme of the southern elevation shed light on the original design. A close analysis of Paty's ornamental schemes on these facades reveals Liverpool's global vision.

FIG. 9.15 Thomas Paty, Detail of figural representation of America, Bristol Exchange, Bristol, England.

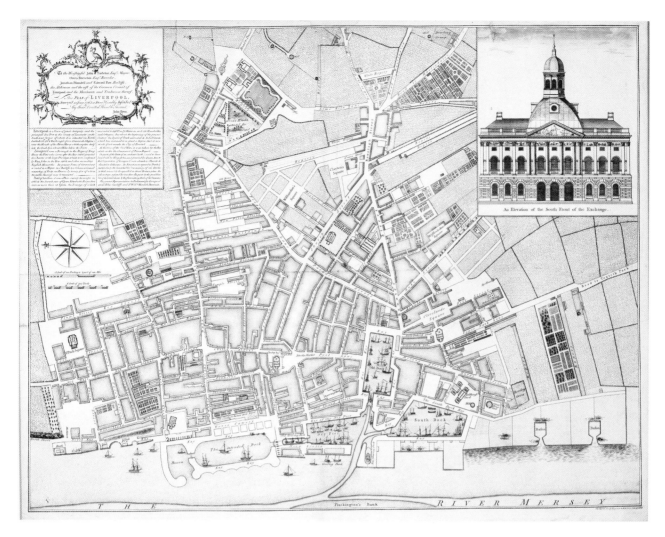

FIG. 9.16 John Eyer's map of Liverpool, 1765.

The south front included a pediment over the portico and carved relief panels along the entablature. An 1810 description of the exchange indicates that the sculpture of the pediment—no longer extant but visible in Wood's elevation—was framed around a central figure, the Genius of Liverpool. To Liverpool's right stood the Genius of Commerce, the Genius of Liberty, and a sculptural rendition of a liver; to her left rose Neptune with his trident and an aqueous urn (fig. 9.17).[72] The program here likely depends in part on the 1650s program in the pediment of the Amsterdam Town Hall, in which the four continents, including Africa framed by a lion and elephant, pay homage to the city of Amsterdam represented as a standing female figure crowned by a mast and crow's nest. Much like the Liverpool example, Neptune lies at Amsterdam's feet.[73]

But if the pediment generically asserts Liverpool's mercantile dominance, the east entablature makes clearer reference to the source of her wealth. Comprising nine

panels, the east entablature is organized into three sets of three. Each of the sets is organized similarly with a female allegorical figure in the central panel and supporting attributes to either side. The far left set represents Africa (fig. 9.18). An African woman's head surmounted with feathers sits amid ivory tusks, gourds, and an umbrella. The rightmost panel presents a huge elephant head with raised tusks and trunk. The panel to the left has a beast of burden surrounded by crates, hogshead barrels, and sacks all interconnected by interweaving ropes, emulative of the stuff of wharves. The far right set represents America, with a female head amidst bows, slingshots, and a quiver full of arrows (fig. 9.19). The panel to the right includes a boar surrounded by blossoms, but it is the panel to the left that is of greater import. This panel includes a camel's head and a crocodile with a sea monster behind (fig. 9.20). The camel, commonly represented on maps of Barbados, and the crocodile, which surmounted the great seal of

An Elevation of the South Front of the Exchange.

FIG. 9.17 Liverpool Town Hall, detail of John Eyer's map of Liverpool, 1765.

FIG. 9.18 Thomas Paty, entablature of Liverpool Town Hall, Liverpool, England, ca. 1754. Left side panels as "Africa."

FIG. 9.19 Thomas Paty, entablature of Liverpool Town Hall, Liverpool, England, ca. 1754. Right side panels as "America," or, more specifically, the Caribbean.

Jamaica, indicate that "America" here is specifically the Caribbean. Connecting Africa and America, the middle three panels represent the Atlantic Ocean, with a central female head surrounded by seashells. That she connects Africa and America is made clear by the gourds nearer to Africa and the sunflower nearer to America. The sculptural program is in fact the Atlantic trade, but not just any Atlantic trade. As this program was intended to be read from left to right, the route began in Africa and ended in America, or more precisely, the Caribbean.

By the early 1750s, when this program was installed, Liverpool had just overtaken Bristol as the leading port in the African slave trade. A decade later, Liverpool merchants argued that "the West Indian and African trade is by far the largest branch of the great and extensive commerce of this kingdom."[74] The interpretation of the sculptural program as referring to the slave trade would have been reinforced by the occasional sale of African slaves very near the building, as suggested in this 1765 advertisement:

> To be sold by auction at George's Coffee-house, betwixt the hours of six and eight o'clock, a very fine negro girl about eight years of age, very healthy, and hath been

FIG. 9.20 Detail of crocodile in America panel, Liverpool Town Hall.

some time from the coast. Any person willing to purchase the same may apply to Capt. Robert Syers, at Mr. Bartley Hodgett's Mercer and Draper, *near the Exchange, where she may be seen until the time of sale.*[75]

Even so, the sculptural program makes no obvious reference to slaves, offering instead nondescript crates and barrels, suggesting that even by the 1750s British merchants harbored some anxiety about the moral legitimacy of the slave trade.[76]

As was the case in Bristol, the expansion of the African and Caribbean trade also played a key role in reshaping the houses of Liverpool's elite, the best surviving examples of which all date from the close of the century. Sometime between 1785 and 1790, John Blackburn built for himself a grand house then just beyond the dense urban core of the city of Liverpool. The construction of the house might have been an affirmation of his increasing political and social capital, as Blackburn was elected mayor in 1788. His wealth was largely derived from inheritance; his father, also John, had been one of Liverpool's most prominent mid-eighteenth-century slave traders, working in the years that Liverpool drew increased trade away from Bristol. In 1799, one of Liverpool's wealthiest slave traders, Thomas Parr, built for himself an extraordinarily grand five-part house, a three-story urban villa (fig. 9.21). As noted in chapter 1, Parr was the builder of the largest slave ship on record. Clearly responsive to the Palladian-Whiggish aesthetics of a much earlier generation, the house seems more closely aligned with mid-eighteenth-century houses of Annapolis, Maryland, than with urban townhouses of contemporary Britain. Immediately behind

his house, Parr erected a massive five-story warehouse, making explicit the fact that his wealth derived from trade.

Although Glasgow is often thought of as having primary linkages to the tobacco colonies of the American South, it also benefited from trade with the Caribbean.[77] By the middle of the eighteenth century, Glasgow's interests in the Caribbean had outpaced those in the tobacco colonies, although much of this interest was in plantation ownership and provisioning and less in the African slave trade.[78] The later rise of Glasgow and Liverpool meant that the wealthiest Africa and West Indies merchants in those cities tended to build free-standing townhouses and suburban villas, the more fashionable option of the middle and later decades. Anthony Cooke's recent research has identified at least fourteen Glasgow townhouses or villas on estates owned by Scots with major financial investments in the Caribbean through the late eighteenth and into the nineteenth century.[79] Early examples of suburban villas in Glasgow include Pollock House, built in 1752, and Greenbank house of a decade later. The builder of Greenbank, Robert Allaston, began building his fortune in the Atlantic trade, but by the time he built his great house in the Glasgow suburbs he was also a Caribbean plantation owner.

It is worth noting here that as wealthy Atlantic merchants became even wealthier, John Wood's connections to those engaged in the Atlantic trade naturally extended to Bath, Britain's emerging eighteenth-century resort city. Although Wood's connections to the rebuilding of Bath begin in the 1720s, his work envisaging King's Circus, begun in 1754, is what concerns us here (fig. 9.22). Widely

FIG. 9.21 Thomas Parr House and warehouse, Liverpool, England, 1799.

FIG. 9.22 John Wood Sr. and John Wood Jr., King's Circus, Bath, England, 1754–68.

recognized as a triumph of urban residential architecture, the perfectly round circus inverted the imperial ancient Roman Colosseum to create an inner, unified elevation of three stacked orders—Doric, Ionic, and Corinthian—masking individually designed townhouses behind. The format of the leasing structure undergirding the construction meant that while the curved facades were all perfectly unified, the townhouses were each built for a particular lessee.[80] This individualism is expressed on the elevations only in the extremely interesting carved metopes of the Doric order fronting the various houses. While Timothy Mowl and Brian Earnshaw have identified George Wither's 1635 emblem book as the visual source for many of the metopes, they also rightly note that the extraordinary variation of the designs—526 individually carved metopes—is likely tied to the identities of the original lessees; William Pitt, one of the first lessees of a house in King's Circus, built a townhouse ornamented with trophies of arms and symbols of triumph.[81] Another townhouse decorated with an easel and painter's palette was likely the house and studio of Thomas Gainsborough.

This raises very interesting questions about the occupation of the house ornamented by a metope sequence that includes a palm tree, a crocodile, and what is likely a royal African umbrella, a closed version of the type seen in the earlier vignette of the *Southwell Frigate* (fig. 9.23, compare to fig. 1.15). Versions of the first two devices appear in Wither's *Emblemes* but the latter certainly does not. Other curious gestures include an overshot waterwheel, a windmill, sugarcane, and metopes on three different townhouses that all appear to represent a cluster of round African huts with thatched conical roofs (fig. 9.24). The appearance of the overshot wheel appears just years after John Smeaton's 1759 publication of his findings of its greater efficiency. While the overshot waterwheel was certainly found in the British landscape, as chapter 4 suggested, its greatest distribution was in Jamaica. Taken together, these references strongly suggest that King's Circus in Bath—that city's most exclusive urban development until the construction of the Bath Crescent later in the century—was occupied by those benefiting from the Atlantic trade and from Caribbean plantations.

FIG. 9.23 Detail of metopes, King's Circus, Bath, England.

The African and Caribbean trade reshaped Britain's port cities through the late seventeenth and eighteenth centuries; those involved in the trade quickly found their place among the local elite, first in urban contexts like Guinea Street and Queen Square in Bristol but eventually in many of the suburban villas that encircled Bristol, Liverpool, and Glasgow. The prominence of the African and Caribbean trade triggered the construction of public architecture in the form of exchanges in Bristol and Liverpool, prominent buildings that declared the importance of the Atlantic trade in scale, materials, and ornament, but the greatest impact was surely in London in the decades around 1800, a subject addressed later in this chapter.

FIG. 9.24 African huts metopes, King's Circus, Bath, England.

COUNTRY HOUSES AND ABSENTEE JAMAICANS

In 1778, Lord Shelbourne declared that "there were scarcely ten miles together throughout the country where the house and estate of a rich West Indian was not to be seen."[82] While Shelbourne might have been given to exaggeration, his general observation that late eighteenth-century Britain was increasingly marked by West Indian absentees was certainly true. Simon Smith's *Slavery, Family, and Gentry Capitalism in the British Atlantic* is a worthy examination of the rise of the Lascelle family from mercantile rank, through ownership of plantations in Barbados, to landed gentry and the construction of Harewood House, a spectacular Yorkshire country house built in the 1760s to the designs of architects John Carr and Robert Adam.[83] Yet as suggested by Shelbourne's comment, Harewood was not a singular instance but a prominent example of a widespread reality, one that deserves much closer inspection. Another case study is Richard Oswald's 1760s country house at Auchincrive, in the former county of Ayrshire, Scotland. In his close examination of Oswald's career, David Hancock lays bare Oswald's efforts to purchase land and build a country house "to gain respect and station."[84] But among the earliest and most spectacular of the country houses built by absentee Jamaicans was surely William Beckford's Fonthill.

Also known as Alderman Beckford, William was born in Jamaica in 1709 to an already wealthy Jamaican planter. His grandfather, a clothworker named Peter, had settled in Jamaica in the 1660s, eventually becoming a planter and slave owner and thereafter rising to the post of lieutenant governor. William's father, also named Peter, had inherited great wealth and would become Speaker of Jamaica's House of Assembly. William was his second son. In 1723 William traveled to England for his education; he returned to Jamaica in 1735 to settle his father's estate. In 1737 Beckford, at the time of his elder brother's death, became Jamaica's largest landholder, the sole owner of eleven plantations, including the well-researched Drax Hall plantation, and part owner of five more and the owner of over seventeen hundred slaves.[85] In 1744, Beckford returned to England, and drawing upon his vast wealth from Jamaican plantations, he purchased Fonthill estate in Wiltshire. His new property was already graced with an Elizabethan house surrounded by a large, more recent picturesque garden. He soon began his architectural work, first building a chapel in the "style of Inigo Jones," together with an open temple and rotunda in the gardens.[86] By 1755 he had

begun the project of replacing the recently burned great house, following upon a marriage that moved him into the ranks of the aristocracy. After the completion of his house, Beckford was twice elected lord mayor of London. His status among England's elite was secure.

Beckford's Fonthill House was impressive enough to be published in six plates of the 1767 edition of *Vitruvius Britannicus*, which described it as a "magnificent edifice."[87] Including its two large pavilion wings, the building stretched 390 feet, dominated by a large nine-bay central block with a giant Ionic portico. The interior was equally lavish. "Its apartments," it was recalled in later years, "were numerous and splendidly furnished. They displayed the riches and luxury of the east and on particular occasions were superbly brilliant and dazzling."[88] The coffers of the stateroom ceilings were inset with vignettes by Italian painter Andrea Casali, and the walls were covered in crimson velvets and blue damask and lined with gilded furniture. The chimneypieces in the dining parlor and library were rescued from the burned house and reinstalled in the new. Comic in nature, they satirized physicians and lawyers and would have complemented the original paintings for the two Hogarth series *A Rake's Progress* and *A Harlot's Progress* that hung in those rooms.[89] The grand entrance hall was a thirty-six-foot cube with stone-colored walls, a white and black checkerboard floor, a grand Crag organ, and two antique porphyry busts. Niches flanking the doors into the grand salon held John Wilton copies of the Apollo Belvedere and the Venus de' Medici. The great dining room was hung with biblical tapestries by Gobelins. But among this splendor, there was one feature that received regular comment. Beckford's half-sister described the lavish interior: "I must here remark that all the doors of the Grand Apartment (of which there are at least forty) are all of the finest mahogany. The floors are of fine oak and the panes of the window sashes of large plate glass with very neat brass frames covered with mahogany."[90] Complete with the requisite mahogany finishes, Beckford's house was a clear statement of his intentional engagement with the arts, and he used it effectively. Beckford was famous for extravagant banquets; the grandson of a clothworker, William Beckford rose into the ranks of the English aristocracy, and his house was clear demonstration of his wealth and political stature. His fortune, wholly derived from sugar, allowed him the means to construct an extraordinary house; its mahogany details were quite possibly fashioned from trees cleared to allow the planting and production of sugar.

Fonthill was only the most spectacular of the houses of the first wave of mid-eighteenth-century Jamaicans to remove—either permanently or temporarily—to Britain. But as suggested in chapter 7, the greater wave took place in the decades flanking the turn of the century. A remarkably useful tool for understanding this later wave of absenteeism is the University College of London's *Legacies of British Slave-ownership,* an extraordinarily comprehensive assessment of the beneficiaries of the £20 million paid by the British government as compensation to former slave owners with the Slavery Abolition Act of 1833. The various individuals—most but not all of them men—and their houses named in the following discussion emerged as the result of a search through this database for all individuals resident in Britain who received compensation for one hundred or more Jamaican slaves. Of the hundreds of individuals whose names appeared on this list, only a few dozen were identified as having built or purchased major country houses. Even so, that research identified one pattern of construction worthy of note: a penchant among absentee Jamaicans toward towered or castellated architecture.

One of the most striking patterns is the construction or purchase of country houses with four corner towers, not unlike elite houses erected in early eighteenth-century Jamaica. The most prominent among these is Hagley Hall, in Worcestershire, built by George Lyttleton (ca. 1751; see fig. 2.25). The Lyttleton connection to Jamaica was longstanding. George's grandfather, Sir Charles Lyttleton, was Jamaica's third governor, from 1662 to 1664; his coat of arms was surmounted by the head of a black man in profile. As Trevor Burnard has shown, English governors of Jamaica quickly became landowners, often acquiring plantations and then passing them on to later generations.[91] The family's close link to Jamaica persisted well into the eighteenth century, as George's brother William Henry Lyttleton was appointed governor of Jamaica in 1760. Hagley Hall's corner towers were already out of fashion in the 1750s, but the distinctive floor plan is very similar to that in William Beckford's house at Fonthill, rising in exactly the same years.[92] Both houses are organized in five flanks with a central flank of salon and hall, with chambers divided by stairhalls to either side. And both houses have a gallery dominating one full end of the building. Given the fact that both men moved in England's elite Jamaican community and that the houses are almost exact contemporaries, the similarity between these house plans is surely not coincidental.

The association between Jamaican absentees and houses with corner towers persisted through to the end of the century. Sometime in the early 1790s, James Wildman left Jamaica for England and soon purchased Chilham Castle, a spectacular Jacobean house in Kent (fig. 9.25).[93] Begun in 1616, Chilham is laid out on a polygonal plan, but one dominated by prominent corner towers. Wildman had served as overseer for William Beckford's Jamaican plantations through much of the late eighteenth century. Having made a fortune in that post, Wildman retired to England late in life to enjoy the benefits of his wealth. While Chilham is certainly far grander than anything

FIG. 9.25 Chilham Castle, Kent, England, begun in 1616.

FIG. 9.26 Bodiam Castle, Sussex, England, begun 1385.

Wildman would have known in Jamaica, the allusions to a castellated house with prominent towers would have been quite familiar. A second, similar example is the 1540s house called Michelgrove in Sussex purchased by Richard Walker. Walker was a Liverpool merchant who invested in the Atlantic trade to Jamaica and by the 1780s owned a substantial portion of Potosi plantation in St. James Parish.[94] Walker's son, Richard Watt Walker, added the Gothic ornamentation to the building's exterior in 1814. As a final example, John Fuller, heir to numerous Jamaican plantations in the early nineteenth century, undertook the extraordinary act of purchasing and partly restoring Bodiam Castle in 1828.[95] Built in east Sussex in the late fourteenth century, Bodiam Castle is among that era's most visually spectacular castles, positioned as it is in the center of an artificial lake (fig. 9.26). In this setting, its towered corners are all the more pronounced. Interestingly, Fuller's purchase of the castle appears to have been romantic. "Slighted" or partially demolished in the English Civil War, Bodiam was already a tourist destination by the early eighteenth century. Fuller began the process of stabilizing the ruin, apparently, without ever intending to occupy it as a residence.[96] Fuller was a staunch defender of slavery and had no apprehensions about the source of his wealth, a fact reinforced by his construction, not far from Bodiam, of a folly in the form of a sugarloaf (fig. 9.27).

In the same years that these Jamaican absentees were purchasing castles or houses with corner towers in the southeast of England, a few of their Scottish compatriots were building new houses in the same form in Scotland. In the 1790s, Charles Gordon began the construction of Cairness House, in Aberdeenshire, in form quite similar to Hagley Hall. Like Lyttleton's, Gordon's connections to Jamaica started with an older generation; his uncles had both lived in Jamaica and undertaken business there since the 1720s. Likely building on their previous investments and social network, Charles was living in Jamaica when in 1778 he purchased Georgia plantation in Trelawny Parish.[97] By the 1790s, he had returned to Scotland, where he began the construction of Cairness House. With four prominent corner towers, the masonry pile was well out of fashion when it was built in the 1790s. The same could be said of Kilgraston House, also built in Scotland at the end of the century. John Grant had served as the chief justice of Jamaica from 1783 to 1790. After the completion of his term, he returned to Scotland and purchased Kilgraston estate. Upon his death in 1793, his brother Francis undertook to build a house on the estate; its finished form included four prominent corner towers.[98] And while the building form is more explicitly "castellated," George Pennant's 1820 construction of the massive Penrhyn Castle in northern Wales is also worthy of note. Pennant inherited a number of Jamaican plantations from his father's cousin in 1808 and in the years following was an active member of the West India Committee, working to undermine efforts toward emancipation.[99]

FIG. 9.27 John Fuller, Sugarloaf folly, Sussex, England, 1820s.

From the purchase of older towered houses to the construction of new examples, even when that form was well out of fashion, returning Jamaican absentees of the late eighteenth and early nineteenth centuries demonstrated an architectural kinship with elites in Jamaica.

But surely the most famous of all the absentee Jamaican constructions was the fanciful Gothic rebuilding of Fonthill House into Fonthill Abbey by William Thomas Beckford, son of the lord mayor, builder of Fonthill House. At the death of his father in 1771, Beckford, then ten years old, inherited an enormous fortune, likely the largest among British commoners. In 1796, Beckford began to work with James Wyatt to imagine what would become one of the most extraordinary houses of its day, Fonthill Abbey (fig. 9.28). Beckford at first lived in his father's house, making numerous changes to that building. The abbey was initially conceived as a ruin, a picturesque feature of the garden landscape.[100] The dramatic expansion of the building from ruin to massive cathedral-scaled house

was driven largely by Beckford. The speed of construction and the frequent changes to the design resulted in multiple collapses of the soaring central tower. The interiors were nothing short of vast; the scale of the great entrance hall is made most evident in contemporary prints. As is made clear by most scholars who work on the subject, understanding Beckford's motivations is a very complex business, but the extensive presentation of armorial bearings in the hall—earned through his mother's aristocratic heritage—suggests that acceptance among her peerage played a role. Simon Gikandi and others have suggested that William Thomas Beckford, builder of Fonthill Abbey, labored under a deep desire to erase the morally implicated source of his wealth in a way that his father, William Beckford, builder of Fonthill House, did not. Slavery, Gikandi argues, was "the hidden cause—the political unconscious, as it were—of Beckford's aesthetic being."[101] Beckford did not entirely deny his Caribbean connections; one corner of his house contained a contorted blackamoor figure whose feet were raised over its head to support a cushion.[102] But even in his spectacular eccentricities, Beckford was not entirely unique. In 1817, Col. Thomas Wildman purchased Newstead Abbey in Nottinghamshire, which had been an abbey from the fifteenth century until the dissolution of the monasteries; it also served as home to Lord Byron. Wildman's father was a lawyer for the Beckfords, and his uncle was the Beckford overseer who had earlier purchased Chilham Castle. After his purchase of the medieval pile in 1817, Wildman spent years restoring and expanding the complex. The penchant for Gothic or castellated architecture among absentee Jamaicans is a curious and surely multivalent practice; for some it might have been an extension of the fortified landscapes that so marked Jamaica, but surely for most it was a material strategy to position themselves as integrated into the social landscape of British antiquity, a common strategy among the nouveau riche.

A second thread that appears to run through the country house architecture of absentees is the introduction of the piazza and the cultivation of corresponding picturesque landscapes. In 1724 Francis Dashwood inherited West Wycombe Park, together with the circa 1698 manor house that had been built on the property by his father.[103] In that same year he departed on an eleven-year tour of Europe and the Mediterranean. In 1732 he was a founding member of the Society of the Dilettanti, and remained a major figure in their support of the midcentury

VIEW OF THE WEST, & NORTH FRONTS.

FIG. 9.28 Fontill Abbey, reprinted from John Rutter, *Delineations of Fonthill* (London, 1823), Plate 11.

archaeological expeditions to Athens and later Ionia. Beginning in about 1750, Dashwood extensively remodeled the house at West Wycombe. The entrance hall has four columns in the form of a Roman atrium, complete with a marble floor, and the ceiling includes scenes taken directly from Robert Wood's *Ruins of Palmyra,* published in 1753, which Dashwood would have known firsthand through his Jamaican friend James Dawkins.[104] But if the house incorporates Dashwood's fascination with the exoticism of ancient sites in the eastern Mediterranean, it also gestured toward Jamaica. The grand entrance hall with its marble floors, atrium plan, and ancient Roman ceiling also boasted a grand staircase fashioned from Jamaican mahogany. Dashwood—like Blathwayt before him—owned a pair of blackamoor figures, which survive today in the main dining room. But in a new move, the south front was graced with a full, open double-elevation portico, unique to eighteenth-century British architecture (fig. 9.29). A compelling case has been made that the double portico was possibly the work of French architect Maurice-Louis Jolivet; since the drawings for the portico are in the otherwise undistinguished hand of John Donowell, Dashwood's clerk of the works at West Wycombe from 1755 to 1764, it seems much more likely

that the idea for the double portico lies with Dashwood.[105] In the same years (1753–1755) that Dashwood was poring over the pages of *The Ruins of Palmyra* and beginning to reimagine West Wycombe, he welcomed into his circle the Jamaican James Dawkins, who funded and launched the expedition that resulted in that publication. And while double porticos are entirely unfamiliar to the English landscape—architectural historians have struggled to find contemporary or ancient sources—they were quite common in Jamaica.

John Gladstone began his career as a Liverpool merchant trading first in India and then in Virginia, but by 1803 he had begun to make substantial investments in the West Indies. By the time of British compensation to slave owners at the passage of the Slavery Abolition Act in 1833, Gladstone owned three hundred Africans who labored on Holland estate in St. Elizabeth Parish in Jamaica. His deep investment in Jamaica is evidenced by the fact that, beginning in 1809, he served as chairman of the Liverpool branch of the West Indies Association.[106] Gladstone's strong West Indies connections might have determined the shape of Seaforth House, begun in 1813 in Lancashire. Although long demolished, the house was described in the early twentieth century as "well remembered by

FIG. 9.29 South front of West Wycombe, Buckinghamshire, England, late 1750s.

many—a long, somewhat low building, having a veranda along the front, facing Elm-road."[107] Similarly, John Jarrett, grandson and heir to the owner of Golden Grove and Kent plantations in Jamaica, began construction in 1838 of Camerton Court, a country house in Somerset defined primarily by its long garden-front piazza.[108] While some absentees, especially those who had lived in Jamaica, preferred castellated architecture, others appended to their houses the more exotic form of the gallery, making a romantic gesture to the Jamaican piazza.

As Victoria Perry has recently demonstrated, West Indians also played a key role in the formation of the eighteenth-century British landscape tradition. The connections between the Caribbean and England were not just in the collection of exotic plants. As Perry argues, "The growing prosperity of provincial 'Atlantic' ports such as Bristol, Liverpool, Lancaster, Whitehaven, and Glasgow had a profound effect on what might best be called Britain's cultural geography: a shift toward the Atlantic west that was manifest in a new aesthetic attitude toward wild, uncultivated landscapes."[109] She notes that the shift to the wilder west of Britain also had economic dimensions; those made wealthy by Caribbean plantations could use their far less profitable land in Britain in nonproductive ways, freeing them to dedicate large tracks of land for

the new late-century leisure activity of nature walking. She demonstrates how returning West Indian planters and wealthy Atlantic merchants from Bristol and Liverpool purchased large estates in Wales. Similarly, she argues that the increasing popularity of Bath as a resort town was triggered by new construction financing that depended almost entirely on banks founded on West Indian capital and the mortgaging of West Indian plantations. But this was equally true in Scotland; returning Scottish Jamaican planters, for example, began to buy up large tracts of land in the western Highlands of Scotland in the late eighteenth century, further displacing the Gaelic-speaking Scots of the Highlands in the decades following the Jacobite Rebellion. And finally, Perry makes the point that Edmund Burke, the author and theorist who gave voice to the sublime, in the same years that he was writing his treatise on landscapes—*An Enquiry into the Origin of Our Ideas of the Sublime and the Beautiful*—was also drafting his treatise on the colonies entitled *An Account of the European Settlements in the Americas.* Landscape tourism and the taste for the sublime, Perry argues, were made possible by Britain's investments in the West Indies.

The infrequency of piazzas on houses of absentee Jamaicans is perhaps not surprising; the piazza as a distinctively "West Indian" form in Britain pales in comparison to the construction of fortified or castellated architecture. But the latter decades of the eighteenth century were a difficult season for absentee Jamaican planters. The increasing arrivals of wealthy absentees over the closing decades of the century began to generate an unflattering stereotype of the "Creole." One of the first expressions of this was Richard Cumberland's comic play *The West Indian*, first performed in London in 1771, in which a wealthy but awkward West Indian planter fails to navigate London society. This play and others would be followed by a rash of publications in the 1790s illustrating "Creole" life in the Caribbean as unrefined or exotic.[110] Abraham James published three satirical prints in 1803: "The Torrid Zone, or Blessings of Jamaica," "A Grand Jamaica Ball!" and "Segar Smoking Society in Jamaica!" (fig. 9.30). James was a military officer stationed in Jamaica in 1801, just two years before the prints appeared from the press of radical London publisher William Holland.[111] By the end of the eighteenth century, Jamaican absentees faced a clear and particularly unflattering social stereotype. The challenges

were also political. As early as the 1760s, a debate had emerged over the legality of slavery in Britain. In that decade, Granville Sharp began his persistent legal defense of the rights of black people in Britain.[112] In 1787, William Wilberforce began his public campaign to end the African slave trade. In 1791 on the French island of Saint-Domingue (Santo Domingo, or Haiti), slaves broke out in what would eventually become a successful revolution against slavery and white rule in French colonies in the West Indies. And, of course, 1807 would bring the abolition of the African slave trade to British colonies (in the same year in the United States, Congress also brought an end to the transport of African slaves); 1833 saw the abolition of slavery under British law, and over the next five to seven years emancipation came to the British colonies. By the late eighteenth and early nineteenth centuries, successful integration into elite British social and political circles meant distancing oneself from the clear markers of Caribbean identity. Certainly one of those markers was the piazza and its culture of leisure, informality and, to some, impropriety.

FIG. 9.30 "Segar Smoking Society in Jamaica!" Etching and aquatint with hand coloring, 11¹³⁄₁₆ × 18⅝ in. (30 × 47.2 cm). The Lewis Walpole Library, Yale University.

LONDON AND THE WEST INDIA COMMITTEE

In the context of increasing social and political criticism, West Indian absentees and merchants involved in the Atlantic trade—especially those with interests in the trade in enslaved Africans—began in the late eighteenth century to cohere as a social and political block. West Indian absentees banded together in solidarity with West India merchants for the first time in response to the pending American War of Independence.[113] This action would formally cement what had already become the most powerful lobby in London, the West Indian interest.[114] While there is clear evidence that West Indian planters and merchants each had their own societies in the decade or so before the war, they formally united in 1775. On New Year's Day of that year, a group of West Indian planters all resident in London wrote a collective letter to the Society of West India Merchants, requesting that they not respond to the pending crisis as separate bodies. Rather, the planters requested that the merchants "join with us, in calling a General Meeting of the whole Body of Planters, and West India Merchants, to deliberate on the Steps necessary to be taken by us jointly on the present important crisis."[115] More than half of the West Indians involved in the meeting were Jamaicans.[116] The West India Committee, a political action group comprising planters and merchants, was born. And the social and political center of their work was Portman Square.

In 1773, the Countess of Home hired Robert Adam to build a townhouse on the north side of Portman Square in the newly developed London district of Marylebone (fig. 9.31).[117] The house would later be described by the eminent historian of British architecture Sir John Summerson as one of Adam's finest London townhouses.[118] One of the most important chambers in the house was a grand drawing room, described by Lady Home as "my Capital Room."[119] Adam designed a spectacular ceiling for this room and looking glasses in elegant neoclassical style for the chimneypiece and for the spaces between the various doors. He positioned the drawing room to be in direct communication with a music room, for which he designed an elaborate organ case. These remain among the most spectacular late eighteenth-century rooms in London in one of the capital city's grandest houses of the age. Its importance was recognized into the twentieth century when in 1932 it became the home of the newly minted Courtauld Institute of Art; today it houses an exclusive private club.

Lady Home was Jamaican. Born circa 1704 and the only surviving child of William Gibbons, Elizabeth

FIG. 9.31 Robert Adam, Home House, Portman Square, London, late 1770s.

Gibbons was the heiress to a substantial Jamaican plantation in Vere Parish, on the island's south coast.[120] In 1720 she married James Lawes, elder son of Sir Nicholas Lawes, then governor of Jamaica. In 1732, when Elizabeth was twenty-eight years old, the couple moved to England; the next year she was widowed, receiving a life interest in her late husband's large Jamaican estates. In 1742 she married the Earl of Home, but her husband abandoned her the following year. She remained single through the next thirty years of her life, and in 1773 at the age of sixty-nine embarked upon the construction of her spectacular townhouse on Portman Square. Lady Home replaced her first architect, James Wyatt, with the newly fashionable Robert Adam. The construction of this house demands some explanation, as Elizabeth was in those years already living in a fairly grand townhouse on the south side of the same square. Lesley Lewis has convincingly argued that Lady Home built the new house as a reception hall and grand city palace for the Duke and Duchess of Cumberland. The duke, George III's brother, had enraged his brother and caused a permanent rift by marrying a young widow named Anne Horton. Lewis points to the fact that Lady Home's "Capital Room" was adorned with full-length portraits of the duke and duchess, very likely those painted by Thomas Gainsborough and now in the royal collection.[121] Officially shunned by George III's court, the duke and duchess found social refuge in Lady Home's grand new townhouse.

Five bays wide—much more imposing than the usual three-bay townhouse—Home House would become the center for lavish entertainments on Portman Square and would give the square a very distinctive persona. Portman Square was the heart of the highly fashionable Marylebone district of London.[122] Largely fields and open space through the first half of the eighteenth century, the land north of what is now Oxford Street saw rapid development after midcentury. Streets were laid out in the 1750s and soon thereafter houses began to rise.[123] In addition to Home House by Robert Adam and Lady Home's slightly earlier house on the south side of Portman Square, there was also a range of houses by James Wyatt, among the earliest uses of Coade stone in London.[124] Montagu House, built by James Stuart for Elizabeth Montagu, was on the northwest corner. But for our purposes it is not the work of the architects but the profile of the residents that is of greater interest. The 1760s and 1770s were the same decades that witnessed the rising tide of absenteeism from

Jamaica. Diarist John Gwynn noted in 1766 that a "rage of building" has expanded London "in an astonishing manner." A key reason for the growth was, in his mind, "the arrival of others, who, having acquired fortunes in the plantations, come to spend them here."[125]

Portman Square provided recent wealthy arrivals from Jamaica the opportunity to purchase newly built and highly fashionable housing, and it simultaneously provided a social safety net of the company of other West Indians, with Lady Home and her connections to the (disenfranchised) Duke and Duchess of Cumberland at the fore.[126] By 1784, Portman Square was home to William Thomas Beckford (the younger), his mother, Mrs. William Beckford, Lady Home, Lord Maynard, Erle Drax, Sir Peter Parker, and Admiral Lord Rodney, all of whom owned West Indian plantations.[127] George Hibbert, champion of the West India Docks, purchased a house in Portland Place, a few blocks to the west, in 1782. The clear association of Portman Square with Jamaican and other West Indian absentees is best demonstrated in the words of William Beckford, the largest Jamaican landowner in London, also lord mayor of London and Member of Parliament. In spite of his position of respect in the city, Beckford felt compelled to band together with his very wealthy and less well-respected Jamaican compatriots to create a powerful lobby to protect West Indian interests. By 1782, he moved from his house elsewhere in the city to Portman Square, an event memorialized in a letter in which he described the party thrown by Lady Home in honor of his "accession to Portman Square." He indicated that Lady Home assumed that since he was "a West Indian potentate I ought to receive distinguished homage."[128] Until her death in 1784, Lady Home stood at the center of West Indian society in London, presiding from her grand house on Portman Square. And this association with absentees persisted; by the late 1790s, newly arrived Jamaican John Tharp—one of Jamaica's wealthiest planters—paid £3000 to refashion his London townhouse on Portman Square.[129] In the same years Edward Moulton-Barrett, of the planter merchant family from Falmouth, Jamaica, would purchase a house in Marylebone as well.[130] This establishment of a clearly subversive West Indian contingent in London sheds light on the oft-repeated if apocryphal outburst of George III to William Pitt upon seeing the lavish equipage and outriders of an absentee Jamaican: "Sugar, sugar, hey? All that sugar! How are the duties, hey Pitt, how are the duties?"[131]

FIG. 9.32 William Daniell, "An Elevated View of the New Docks & Warehouses now constructing on the Isle of Dogs near Limehouse for the reception & accommodation of shipping in the West India Trade . . . ," 1802. Colored aquatint and etching, 1½ × 30½ in. (40 × 77.6 cm). National Maritime Museum, Greenwich, London.

Portman Square became the political and social center of Jamaican absentees in London, but the most substantial work of the West India Committee was manifested in the construction of the West India Docks, then the largest dock-building program in the world.[132] Having weathered the economic crisis of the American Revolution—and countering the uncertainty of slavery's future—the West India Committee launched in the opening years of the nineteenth century a new, more secure facility for arriving sugar ships. An extraordinary 1802 view of the West India Docks as intended upon completion presented the scheme from a bird's-eye view, exaggerated in scale (fig. 9.32). In this west-facing view, the import dock, a twenty-eight-acre basin (now West India Quay), is seen to the right, while the adjacent export dock, which spanned fifteen acres, occupies the middle. A canal to the south of the two quays allowed passage cutting across the Isle of Dogs. And to prevent the rampant theft that so characterized the older docks in the City of London, a thirty-foot-high perimeter wall was to surround the whole complex. The facility's main gate, which has been reconstructed in the new development scheme, was called the Hibbert Gate—as much for the chairman of the West India Committee as

for the ship model of the *Hibbert* that crested the design (fig. 9.33). The first buildings to be built were the eight sugar warehouses complete with rum vaults along the north edge, part of the surviving span. Five stories in height, each of the warehouses required more than two million bricks; the walls of the docks and locks required another forty million. Supplying bricks to keep pace with construction became an enormous challenge. But in late August of 1802, tens of thousands of onlookers watched as the first two ships sailed into the quay with great pomp and circumstance. At the provisional opening in 1802, *The Times* celebrated the "stupendous scale" of the project, noting that it appeared "like a great lake . . . an object of beauty and astonishment."[133] By 1815, stevedores were unloading 165,000 tons of sugar at the West India Docks per annum.[134] Sugar could be unloaded to docks and warehouses with far greater speed and efficiency than before—down from a full month to thirty hours—and each ship could undertake more voyages per year than had been previously possible. As the surviving memorial tablet proclaims, the scheme was "An Undertaking which, under the favor of God, shall contribute Stability, Increase and Ornament to British Commerce."[135]

In the capital city the loose affiliation of those benefiting from the trade had coalesced into the political lobby known as the West India Committee, whose work focused on defending and expanding the system that had made them all so very wealthy. In addition to lobbying for tax policy and trade regulations that preserved the status quo, their construction of the West India Docks—to better accommodate and protect ships loaded with sugar, the source of their wealth—was a monumental feat with a profound impact on the city's urban infrastructure. At the very center of the building programs of Portman Square and most especially the West India Docks, we find Jamaicans. Throughout the eighteenth century the changing architecture and infrastructure of Britain's port cities can and should be considered Jamaican architecture. These wharves, townhouses, villas, and mercantile exchanges stood at the periphery of a massive global system that by the later eighteenth century centered almost entirely on Jamaica.

◆ ◆ ◆

Jamaicans in Britain left their own indelible and now largely forgotten mark, but whatever the architectural

FIG. 9.33 Hibbert Gate, West India Docks, London.

form, what is clear is that Jamaican plantation owners removed the focus of their opulence from the source of their wealth back to the motherland. The wealthiest Jamaicans understood their island to be the front edge of empire through the first half of the eighteenth century. They consumed Africans by the thousands to clear lowlands of mahogany stands and install sugar fields in their stead; such consumption fueled the construction of the massive fortifications along the west coast of Africa now collectively called the slave castles. They invested substantial capital in the construction of sugar works and experimented through the century to discover new techniques to increase efficiency and profit. All the while the wealthiest launched extraordinary programs in the arts—in architecture, archaeology, and landscape architecture—to demonstrate their mastery of the refinement essential to an empire's elite. And throughout the century, Jamaicans participated in the empire of goods, purchasing fine goods and consumables from Britain and across her empire. But Tacky's Rebellion and other insurrections of the 1760s changed Jamaica forever. That decade saw the rapid increase of actually defensible houses along the north and west coast, and the same decade saw the end of grand house construction on the island and the egress of many of the elite. So much so that even by the 1770s, commentators complained that one could not travel more than ten miles in Britain without finding an absentee West Indian planter. This departure of the wealthiest landowners also helped to facilitate the generation of a more clearly realized Creole culture in Jamaica. The departure of the Beckfords, Hibberts, and many others to Britain left Jamaican-born overseers, attorneys, aspiring planters, and others in positions of social authority, allowing the fluorescence of island culture and architecture. An important component of this new culture was the ever-growing free black population. And as Creole culture was forming in the final decades of the century, it did so in the context of the island's worst decades of hurricane damage in its history as a British colony. By 1800, Jamaica was quite different. It was "Creole" in ways that were just emerging in the 1750s; race had become an incredibly complicated phenomenon; racial categories were more easily legible in earlier decades. Elite Jamaicans who had the wherewithal to do so continued to migrate to Britain, where they built or purchased new estates, stages for a new life. And in this way, West Africa, Jamaica, and Britain were inextricably linked, the tribulations of two directly shaping the fortunes of the third.

Notes

INTRODUCTION

1. The study of the British Caribbean as a region rests on the work of a handful of historians and anthropologists, most of whom published critical analyses in the 1970s: Brathwaite, *Development of Creole Society in Jamaica;* Bridenbaugh and Bridenbaugh, *No Peace Beyond the Line;* Dunn, *Sugar and Slaves;* Sheridan, *Sugar and Slavery;* and Higman, *Slave Population and Economy in Jamaica.* This early work focused largely on one of three themes: (1) the political and military turmoil of the seventeenth and early eighteenth century; (2) the economic implications of the Sugar Revolution; or (3) the study of slavery under a sugar regime. The most culturally sophisticated of these works is Brathwaite's *Development of Creole Society in Jamaica.* After a lull in scholarship on the history of the British Caribbean, the past decade or so has witnessed a significant resurgence, with major histories by Hillary Beckles, David Buisseret, Trevor Burnard, Barry Higman, Andrew O'Shaughnessey, Verene Shepherd, and Natalie Zacek, all appearing since 2000. These new works are fine-grained studies that attend more to social history than to institutional or political history, and they favor the histories of the enslaved over the enslavers.

2. This understanding of space depends on that formulated by Henri Lefebvre in which space is at once physical, socially produced, and imagined. Lefebvre, *The Production of Space.*

3. Burnard, *Mastery, Tyranny, and Desire,* 66, 155, 270.

4. Moreton, *Customs and Manners,* 60.

5. Sheridan, *Sugar and Slavery,* 152; see also Higman, *Slave Populations of the British Caribbean.*

6. See Craton and Walvin, *A Jamaican Plantation;* Craton and Greenland, *Searching for the Invisible Man;* Armstrong, *The Old Village and the Great House;* Higman, *Plantation Jamaica, 1750–1850;* Delle, Hauser, and Armstrong, eds., *Out of Many, One People;* and Satchell, *Hope Transformed.* For a broader overview of the concept of the plantation, see Curtin, *Rise and Fall of the Plantation Complex.*

7. Burnard, "Prodigious Riches," 505–23. See also McCusker and Menard, *The Economy of British America, 1607–1789,* table 3.3, p. 61.

8. On wealth disparity, see Mann, "Becoming Creole," 44.

9. For Atlantic histories, see Bailyn, *Atlantic History;* Zahedieh, *The Capital and the Colonies;* Liss, *Atlantic Empires;* Hornsby, *British Atlantic, American Frontier;* Elliott, *Empires and the Atlantic World;* Jasanoff, "Loyalists in the British Empire"; Hancock, *Citizens of the World;* Smith, *Slavery, Family, and Gentry Capitalism;* and Jarvis, *In the Eye of All Trade.*

10. One exception is Herman, *Town House.*

11. Gilroy, *The Black Atlantic.* One architectural historian to attend to the architectural implications of the Black Atlantic before Gilroy's thesis was John Michael Vlach, who launched his career with a dissertation and then numerous articles exploring African identity and agency in the architecture of early Haiti through to the shotgun houses of Louisiana.

12. See Marshall, "First British Empire," and Bayly, "Second British Empire," in *Oxford History of the British Empire,* vol. V, *Historiography,* 43–72.

13. For example, Jamaica is largely absent from Cain and Hopkins, *British Imperialism, 1688–2000.*

14. The most important work on this front is Armitage, *Ideological Origins of the British Empire.* See July 2011 *William and Mary Quarterly* for recent discussions of empire from the early American perspective.

15. See Bayly and Fawaz, *Modernity and Culture from the Mediterranean to the Indian Ocean.*

16. For an excellent architectural history using this model, see Celik's *Empire, Architecture and the City.*

17. See Fordham, "State, Nation and Empire." Books ranging in subject from memorial art—Coutu, *Propaganda and Persuasion*—to popular visual culture—Quilley and Kriz, *An Economy of Colour*—have demonstrated that art played a critical role in shaping the imagined community of the British Empire.

18. Buckridge, *Language of Dress;* Berringer et al., *Art and Emancipation in Jamaica.* See also Kay Dian Kriz, *Slavery, Sugar, and the Culture of Refinement.*

19. Two important volumes are worth noting. Scriver, *Colonial Modernities,* demonstrates the power of architecture in the writing on colonial (and theoretically postcolonial) sites in the later British Empire. And most recently Rajagopalan and Desai, eds., *Colonial Frames, Nationalist Histories,* have provided a strong critical foundation for a broad understanding of the role of architecture in empire. The most rigorous assessment of early Jamaican architecture is James Robertson's "Jamaican Architectures before Georgian."

20. An important volume that connects the architecture of the Spanish Caribbean to that of Spain is Chias and Abad, *The Fortified Heritage.*

21. This field-based method is best exemplified by the winners of the Abbot Lowell

Cummings Award given by the Vernacular Architecture Forum. This use of the everyday derives from Pierre Bourdieu's theoretical formulation of habitus; see Bourdieu, *Outline of a Theory of Practice*, 78.

22. In this way, my understanding of space depends on that formulated by Henri Lefebvre, one in which space is at once a physical thing, a thing discursively imagined and constructed, and a thing socially produced. See Lefebvre, *The Production of Space*, 1974.

23. Bailyn, *Atlantic History*, 62–81.

24. Long, *History of Jamaica*, II, 87.

25. St. George, "Introduction," in *Possible Pasts*, 4–5.

26. Burnard, *Mastery, Tyranny, and Desire*, 75–77.

27. On these processes, see Brathwaite, *Development of Creole Society in Jamaica*. More recent work on these forms of cultural change enlists hybridity and transculturation as theoretical models. See Papastergiadis, "Tracing Hybridity in Theory," in *Debating Cultural Hybridity*. On transculturation, see Pratt, *Imperial Eyes*.

28. See Brown's extraordinary digital history of this event, "Slave Revolt in Jamaica, 1760–61," at http://revolt.axismaps.com/.

29. The most recent discussion of the impact of the American Revolution on the Caribbean is O'Shaughnessy, *An Empire Divided*, esp. ch. 10.

30. Higman, *Plantation Jamaica*, 18–19.

31. Higman, *Plantation Jamaica*, 111.

CHAPTER 1. COFFLE, CASTLE, DECK, DOCK

1. The best sources on the slave forts of West Africa include St. Clair, *Door of No Return*, 2006; Lawrence, *Trade Forts of West Africa*; Van Danzig, *Forts and Castles of Ghana*, 1980; see also Kea, *Settlements, Trade, and Polities in the Seventeenth-Century Gold Coast*.

2. The term "slave hole" was used in the middle of the eighteenth century to refer specifically to a chamber within the strong walls of a bastion used to contain slaves. These were often ventilated by holes in the paved surface of the bastion. By the 1790s, these spaces were universally referred to as prisons. See Lawrence, *Fortified Trade Posts*, 181, 223 (for slave holes), 69, 70, 148, 168 (for slave prison).

3. Scholarship on the internal African slave trade includes Northrup, *Trade without Rulers*; Der, *The Slave Trade in Northern Ghana*; Howell, *The Slave Trade and Reconciliation*; Bailey "Anlo Oral Histories"; A. B. Stahl "Atlantic Slave Trade in Banda"; Boachie-Ansah, "Archaeological Research at

Kasana, 35–57; Miller, "The Slave Trade in Congo and Angola."

4. The only other scholar to address the connections between space and slave making is Simon Gikandi, who asserts that "spatial disorientation . . . led to an acute crisis of identity and a sense of moral devaluation." See Gikandi, *Slavery and the Culture of Taste*, 208–11.

5. There are also many historical issues that do not concern me here. The economic implications of changes in markets or the preferences of planters for Africans from different regions, for example, are both important components of the historiography but as they do not directly implicate the experience of the enslaved in space they play no role in this telling. On these, for example, see Galenson, *Traders, Planters, and Slaves*, and Littlefield, *Rice and Slaves*, ch. 2.

6. See Davies, *Royal African Company*, 1957.

7. Davies, *Royal African Company*.

8. Barbot, quoted in Perbi, *History of Indigenous Slavery in Ghana*, 29. Barbot, *Description of the Coasts of North and South Guinea*.

9. Northrup, *Trade without Rulers*, 68–80.

10. Bowman and Owen quotes cited in Hansen, *Coast of Slaves*, 48.

11. Edwards, *A History, Civil and Commercial*, II, 107.

12. Cugoano tells his story in *Thoughts and Sentiments*, 7–9.

13. Transcribed from Asa-Asa's telling and printed in Prince, *The History of Mary Prince*, 51.

14. Northrup, *Trade without Rulers*, 66, 78.

15. Edwards, *A History, Civil and Commercial*, II, 107.

16. For recent work on the internal slave trade and the impact of European involvement, see ch. 3, "African Paths to the Middle Passage," in Rediker, *The Slave Ship*; also Perbi, *A History of Indigenous Slavery in Ghana*. See also work on Antera Duke, Hugh Thomas, and others. The essay by Christopher Fyfe in the *African Diaspora* is a good cautionary essay on assessments of numbers and economic impact as well as the use of guns.

17. See Mouser, *A Slaving Voyage to Africa and Jamaica*.

18. Curtin, *Economic Change in Precolonial Africa*, 272–73.

19. Clarkson, *Letters on the Slave Trade*, 34–37.

20. One such yoke, probably from the early nineteenth century, survives in the collections of the International Slavery Museum in Liverpool. The base of the yoke has an indentation a few inches from the end that

would have been used to secure a cord between the yoke and the neck or waist of the captive. The crutched end of the yoke does not have any evidence of such mechanisms for fastening, suggesting that it simply rested on the shoulders of the person before.

21. Monrad, *Description of the Guinea Coast*, 219.

22. Cited in Thomas, *The Slave Trade*, 381.

23. Estimates of mortality before even boarding the slave ship range from highs of 25 percent to lows of 5 percent. See Miller, *Way of Death, Merchant Capitalism and the Angolan Slave Trade, 1730–1830*, and Manning, *The African Diaspora*.

24. Thomas, *The Slave Trade*, 381.

25. Monrad, *Description of the Guinea Coast*, 218.

26. On the internal trade in these areas, see Miller, "The Slave Trade in Congo and Angola."

27. Perbi, *History of Indigenous Slavery in Ghana*, 40, see also map III.

28. Perbi, *History of Indigenous Slavery in Ghana*, 37–38. Over the past two decades a number of African historians have partnered with UNESCO to better understand these markets and the slave routes that connected them under the aegis of The National Slave Route project. Okoro, "An archaeological and ethnohistorical investigation of the slave market and baobab site of Saakpuli, N. Ghana"; Longi, "Oral history of the slave trade at Kasana and Gwollu"; Nkumbaan, "Archaeological Study at Kasana"; and "Archaeological Reconnaissance at Sankana"; see also Nkumbaan, "Historical Archaeology of Slave Route Case Study of Kasana and Sankana," 2003.

29. Edwards, *History, Civil and Commerical* II, 69, 107.

30. Asa-Asa, quoted in Prince, *The History of Mary Prince*, 52.

31. On Salaga, see Perbi, *History of Indigenous Slavery in Ghana*, 44–47.

32. On the importance of the Asante to the internal slave trade, see Perbi, *History of Indigenous Slavery in Ghana*, 20–23. See also the source cited, Rediker, *The Slave Ship*, 87, n. 16.

33. Okoro, "Indigenous Water Management, Slavery and Slave Trade in Salaga," 2003.

34. See the 1705 account reprinted in Anquandah, "Researching the Historic Slave Trade in Ghana," 23–56. Quote on 28–29.

35. On slave camps, see Perbi and Bredwa-Mensah, "Slave Camps in Pre-Colonial Ghana,"138–47.

36. Norman, "Hueda (Whydah) Country and Town." See also Kelly, "Change and Continuity in Coastal Benin," 81–100.

37. Behrendt, Latham, and Northrup, *The Diary of Antera Duke*, 110–13.
38. Northrup, *Trade without Rulers*, 64.
39. Northrup, *Trade without Rulers*, 101.
40. Sparks, *Two Princes of Calabar*, 49. For a broad study of the African canoe, see Smith, "The Canoe in West African History," 4.
41. Lambert, ed., "Account of Isaac Parker," in *House of Commons Sessional Papers*, vol. 73, 126.
42. Equiano (Gustavus Vassa), *Interesting Narrative*, 32.
43. Lambert, ed., "Account of David Henderson," in *House of Commons Sessional Papers*, vol. 69, 139.
44. Rask, *A Brief and Truthful Description*, 156–57.
45. For a comprehensive study of a castle town, see DeCorse, *Archaeology of Elmina*.
46. St. Clair, *Door of No Return*, ch. 5.
47. This complexity is made clear in ch. 5, "Soldiers and Workers," in St. Clair, *Door of No Return*.
48. Monrad, *Description of the Guinea Coast*, 258.
49. Monrad, *Description of the Guinea Coast*, 216.
50. Monrad, *Description of the Guinea Coast*, 220.
51. Monrad, *Description of the Guinea Coast*, 221.
52. The majority of Africans traded by English and American slavers never saw a fort. Modern histories of the transatlantic African slave trade break the west coast of Africa into six regions running from northwest to southeast: Senegambia, Sierra Leone (also called the Windward Coast), the Gold Coast, the Bight of Benin, the Bight of Biafra, and west-central Africa. Although the English built substantial slaving forts all along the Gold Coast, only one in five Africans sold into slavery—approximately 22 percent—passed through the forts of the Gold Coast, most now in modern Ghana. The greatest concentration came from the Bight of Biafra, approximately 860,000 or 29 percent, and most of those during the second half of the eighteenth century. There are a number of excellent works on the history, economics, and social structures of Old Calabar: Behrendt, Latham, and Northrup, *The Diary of Antera Duke*; Northrup, *Trade without Rulers*; and Sparks, *Two Princes of Calabar*. On the importance of Calabar to Jamaica, see Burnard and Morgan, "Dynamics of the Slave Market and Slave Purchasing Patterns in Jamaica, 1655–1788," 205–28, esp. 208.
53. Davies, *Royal African Company*, 241–43.
54. Martin, *British West African Settlements*, 7. For a full account of the financial management of the British West African forts see also Davies, *Royal African Company*.
55. See Inikori and Engerman, *Atlantic Slave Trade*, 173–74, and Postma, *The Dutch in the Atlantic Slave Trade 1600–1815*, 103–4.
56. Monrad, *Description of the Guinea Coast*, 212. The records of the Company of Merchants offer a very similar list. See Martin, *British West African Settlements*, 45. See also ch. 2, "The 'Fredensborg' is Fitted Out for the Slave Trade," in Svalesen, *The Slave Ship Fredensborg*, 31–44.
57. As scholars of early West African history and the slave trade have come to argue, the internal African slave trade was much exacerbated by European involvement, especially through the introduction of guns. On this see Inikori, "Changing Commodity Composition of Imports into West Africa, 1650–1850," 57–80, and Inikori, "The Import of Firearms into West Africa." See also Owen, *Journal of a Slave-Dealer*, 45.
58. Martin, *British West African Settlements*, 50.
59. Rask, *A Brief and Truthful Description*.
60. Lawrence, *Trade Forts*, 298.
61. Lawrence, *Trade Forts*.
62. Davies, *Royal African Company*, 226.
63. Cape Coast is described in 1710 as having "repositories for one thousand slaves." Davies, *Royal African Company*, 241.
64. St. Clair, *Door of No Return*, 77
65. Barbot, 1732, quoted in Lawrence, *Trade Forts*.
66. St. Clair, *Door of No Return*, 223.
67. Davies, *Royal African Company*, 241.
68. For a full account, see Richardson, *Bristol, Africa, and the Eighteenth-Century Slave Trade to America*.
69. Letterbook of the Company of Merchants Trading to Africa, 1751–1769, May 28, 1756. From the collections of The Royal Geographical Society, London.
70. Letterbook of the Company of Merchants Trading to Africa, 1751–1769, 24, no date.
71. Letterbook of the Company of Merchants Trading to Africa, 1751–1769, 141, June 24, 1761.
72. Letterbook of the Company of Merchants Trading to Africa, 1751–1769, 135, September 5, 1760.
73. Hansen, *Coast of Slaves*, 50.
74. St. Clair, *Door of No Return*, 220.
75. Simmonds, "A Note on the Excavations in Cape Coast Castle," 267–69.
76. St. Clair, *Door of No Return*, 212–13.
77. For the capacity for two thousand captives, St. Clair, *Door of No Return*, 80. For the *Voyages* database, Eltis and Halbert, *Voyages: The Transatlantic Slave Trade Database*, http://www.slavevoyages.org/tast/index.faces.
78. Monrad, *Description of the Guinea Coast*, 221.
79. Cugoano, *Thoughts and Sentiments*, 9
80. Monrad, *Description of the Guinea Coast*, 222. See also Hansen, *Coast of Slaves*, 82, 171.
81. St. Clair, *Door of No Return*, 81. Monrad suggests only once a day; Monrad, *Description of the Guinea Coast*, 222.
82. St. Clair, *Door of No Return*, 72–73.
83. St. Clair, *Door of No Return*, 75.
84. St. Clair, *Door of No Return*, 63.
85. Monrad, *Description of the Guinea Coast*, 266.
86. St. Clair, *Door of No Return*, 129.
87. Monrad, *Description of the Guinea Coast*, 228.
88. Monrad, *Description of the Guinea Coast*, 222. A very similar description from the 1690s suggests that this was common practice throughout the period of the slave trade. See Hansen, *Coast of Slaves*, 29–30.
89. Quoted in Beckles "African Resistance," 81–91.
90. John Barbot, 1746, as cited in Hansen, *Coast of Slaves*, 31; Svalesen, *The Slave Ship Fredensborg*, 99.
91. St. Clair, *Door of No Return*, 78; Lawrence, *Trade Forts*, 190
92. Letterbook of the Company of Merchants Trading to Africa, 1751–1769, 96–97, November 6, 1767.
93. Equiano, *Interesting Narrative*, 33.
94. The most important source for accurate information on the middle passage and ship-board experience of the slave is Rediker, *The Slave Ship*. An interesting comparison to the transportation of slaves is the transportation of convicts. See Morgan, "The Organization of the Convict Trade to Maryland," vol 42, no. 2, 201–27.
95. Rediker, *The Slave Ship*, 70.
96. St. Clair, *Door of No Return*, 14.
97. Monrad, *Description of the Guinea Coast*, 223; St. Clair, *Door of No Return*, 25.
98. Law, *Ouidah*, 135.
99. Monrad, *Description of the Guinea Coast*, 223; Rediker, *The Slave Ship*, 38.
100. Monrad. *Description of the Guinea Coast*, 223.
101. Cited in Thomas, *The Slave Trade*, 404–5.
102. Law, *Ouidah*, 143. For a fascinating discussion of the cultural perceptions of nakedness and the use of nudity in power relations, see Buckridge, *The Language of Dress*, 26–46.
103. Rediker, *The Slave Ship*, 143, 233–34.
104. Equiano, *Interesting Narrative*, 33.
105. St. Clair, *Door of No Return*, 223; see also Mouser, *A Slaving Voyage*, 104.
106. Handler, "On the Transportation of Material Goods by Enslaved Africans during the Middle Passage: Preliminary Findings from Documentary Sources." *African Diaspora Archaeology Newsletter* (December 2006).
107. St. Clair, *Door of No Return*, 11; Rediker, *The Slave Ship*, 234; Davies, *Royal African Company*, 186.

108. See Sheridan, "Resistance and Rebellion," 181–205. Quote on 190.

109. Davies, *Royal African Company*, 293.

110. For statistical information on the slave trade, see Curtin, *The Atlantic Slave Trade, a Census*. For a detailed discussion of the conditions on slave ships, see Rediker, *The Slave Ship*, and Garland and Klein, "The Allotment of Space for Slaves," 238–48.

111. As will be plainly evident in my notes through this section, the critical source on the slave ship is Rediker's recent and excellent book, *The Slave Ship*; see also Davies, *Royal African Company*, 192.

112. Rediker, *The Slave Ship*, 62.

113. Rediker, *The Slave Ship*, 63. See also Stewart-Brown, *Liverpool Ships in the Eighteenth Century*.

114. Galenson, *Traders, Planters, and Slaves*, 31.

115. See Richardson, *Bristol, Africa and the Eighteenth-Century Slave Trade to America*. See also Richardson, "Liverpool and the English Slave Trade."

116. Rediker, *The Slave Ship*, 53.

117. Jane Webster has edited a collection of essays that stands as the definitive work on underwater archaeology of slavers. See Webster, "Slave Ships and Maritime Archaeology," 6–19. See also Moore and Malcom, "Seventeenth-Century Vehicle of the Middle Passage," 20–38; Svalesen, *The Slave Ship Fredensborg*, 177–86.

118. Rediker, *The Slave Ship* 53, 66.

119. Lambert, ed., "Account of David Henderson," in *House of Commons Sessional Papers*, vol. 69, 115.

120. Riland, *Memoirs of a West-Indian Planter*.

121. Rediker, *The Slave Ship*, 54. For more on the economic importance of slaver construction in Liverpool, see Williams, "The Shipping of the British Slave Trade in its Final Years, 1798–1807," 1–25. See also Behrendt, "Markets, Transaction Cycles, and Profits: Merchant Decision Making in the British Slave Trade," 171–204.

122. Galenson, *Traders, Planters, and Slaves*, 29.

123. Rediker, *The Slave Ship*, 51. For the full account, see Elizabeth Donnan, *Documents Illustrative of the History of the Slave Trade to America*. See also Svalesen, *The Slave Ship Fredensborg*, 92.

124. Malcom, "The Iron Bilboes of the *Henrietta Marie*," 81–100.

125. Rediker, *The Slave Ship*, 72.

126. Falconbridge, *Account of the Slave Trade on the Coast of Africa*.

127. Equiano, *Interesting Narrative*, 37.

128. Mouser, *A Slaving Voyage*, 79.

129. *House of Commons*, 115; Monrad, *Description of the Guinea Coast*, 223. Riland, *Memoirs of a West-Indian Planter*.

130. Riland, *Memoirs of a West-Indian Planter*.

131. For a detailed discussion, see Garland and Klein, "The Allotment of Space for Slaves," 238–48.

132. Rediker, *The Slave Ship*, 61–62.

133. Davies, *Royal African Company*, 194.

134. Equiano, *Interesting Narrative*, 37.

135. Rediker, *The Slave Ship*, 235.

136. Marcus Wood first addressed this image as a polemic in *Blind Memory*. More extensive discussions appear in McInnis, *Slaves Waiting for Sale*, and Rediker, *The Slave Ship*.

137. Rediker, *The Slave Ship*, 235.

138. Rediker, *The Slave Ship*, 71, esp. n. 56; Svalesen, *The Slave Ship Fredensborg*, 106.

139. Rediker, *The Slave Ship*, 148.

140. John Riland, *Memoirs of a West-Indian Planter*.

141. Mouser, *A Slaving Voyage*, 105.

142. Rediker, *The Slave Ship*, 30

143. Klein, *The Atlantic Slave Trade*, 155. By contrast, David Galenson reports that only 3.8 percent of those boarding ships bound from the German states to Pennsylvania would die in the same decades. Galenson, *Traders, Planters, and Slaves*, 38–39.

144. Rediker, *The Slave Ship*, 37–40. Quote from p. 38.

145. Rediker, *The Slave Ship*, 238; Riland, *Memoirs of a West-Indian Planter*.

146. Rediker, *The Slave Ship*, 234

147. See Falconbridge, *Account of the Slave Trade on the Coast of Africa*, 6.

148. Carpenters took six days in October to build the barricade on the Sandown in 1794. See Mouser, *A Slaving Voyage*, 77–78.

149. Newton, *Journal of a Slave Trader, 1750–54*, 22.

150. Monrad, *Description of the Guinea Coast*, 225.

151. Svalesen, *The Slave Ship Fredensborg*, 86.

152. Rediker, *The Slave Ship*, 233.

153. Rediker, *The Slave Ship*, 51.

154. Equiano, *Interesting Narrative*, 39.

155. On shipboard food for slaves, see Svalesen, *The Slave Ship Fredensborg*, 112.

156. Thomas, *The Slave Trade*, 417.

157. Thomas, *The Slave Trade*, 422–28; see also Rediker, *The Slave Ship*, 16

158. Wax, "Negro Resistance to the Early American Slave Trade," 1–15; Piersen, "White Cannibals, Black Martyrs," 147–59; Rathbone, "Some Thoughts on Resistance to Enslavement in Africa," 3–22.

159. Surprisingly, David Galenson's assessment of the Royal African Company's records suggests that there was no correlation between the length of the voyage and average mortality rates. See Galenson, *Traders, Planters, and Slaves*, 41.

160. Burnard and Morgan, "Dynamics of the Slave Market," 205–28, esp. 205–7. For work on the slave trade in the late seventeenth century, see Thornton, "The Organization of the Slave Trade in the English West Indies, 1660–1685," 399–409.

161. Burnard and Morgan, "Dynamics of the Slave Market," 209.

162. Burnard and Morgan, "Dynamics of the Slave Market," 209. For a broader discussion of the economic impact of the slave trade on the Atlantic economy, see Inikori and Engerman, *The Atlantic Slave Trade*.

163. Writing about Barbados in the 1650s, Richard Ligon noted that indentured servants were sold right from the decks of ships. See Ligon, *History of the Island of Barbados*. John Taylor implies the same in his description of Jamaica in the 1680s. Quoted in Buisseret, *Jamaica in 1687*, 68.

164. *Jamaica Mercury and Kingston Weekly Advertiser*, May 1, 1779, 32.

165. *Royal Gazette*, June 10, 1780, Kingston, 363.

166. *Savanna-la-Mar Gazette*, August 15, 1788, 2.

167. Burnard, "Who Bought Slaves in Early America?," 68–92, esp. 73.

168. Besson, *Martha Brae's Two Histories*, 72

169. Conolley, "Deployment of Forced Labor."

170. Emma Christopher has written on the process of transforming a slave into a commodity for sale in *Slave-Trade Sailors*, ch. 5.

171. Burnard and Morgan, "Dynamics of the Slave Market," 218

172. Ligon, *History of the Island of Barbados*, 68.

173. Cugoano, *Thoughts and Sentiments*, 95.

174. Donnan, "The Slave Trade into South Carolina," 824; Morgan, "Slave Sales in Colonial Charleston," 914.

175. Equiano, *Interesting Narrative*, 41.

176. Cugoano, *Thoughts and Sentiments*, 95.

177. Rediker, *The Slave Ship*, 152.

178. Equiano, *Interesting Narrative*, 41.

179. Galenson, *Traders, Planters, and Slaves*, 71–91. See also Burnard and Morgan, "Dynamics of the Slave Market," 222.

180. *Jamaica Mercury and Kingston Weekly Advertiser*, May 15, 1779, 82.

181. Galenson, *Traders, Planters, and Slaves*, 71–91.

182. Burnard and Morgan, "Dynamics of the Slave Market," 216

183. Mouser, *A Slaving Voyage*, 113. Sales of Africans from ships in Charleston appear to have transpired more quickly, rarely lasting more than three weeks. See Morgan, "Slave Sales in Colonial Charleston," 916.

184. Burnard and Morgan, "Dynamics of the Slave Market," 206-7; Burnard, "Who Bought Slaves in Early America?," 68, 87.

185. Davies, *Royal African Company*, 59.

186. Galenson, *Traders, Planters, and Slaves*, 85, n. 25.

187. Burnard, "Who Bought Slaves in Early America?," 68, 71. See also Burnard and Morgan, "Dynamics of the Slave Market," 217.

188. For a summary of sicknesses that afflicted newly arrived slaves, see Craton and Greenland, *Searching for the Invisible Man*, 200. See also Burnard and Morgan, "Dynamics of the Slave Market," 214–21. For seasoning see Sheridan, *Doctors and Slaves*, 131–34.

189. Beckford, *A Descriptive Account of the Island of Jamaica*, 342–43, quoted in Burnard and Morgan, "Dynamics of the Slave Market," 221.

190. Edwards, *A History, Civil and Commercial*, II, 115–16.

191. Burnard, "Who Bought Slaves in Early America?," 88; Burnard and Morgan, "Dynamics of the Slave Market."

192. Burnard and Morgan, "Dynamics of the Slave Market," 220–22.

193. For an extensive discussion of slave pens in antebellum New Orleans, see Johnson, *Soul by Soul*.

194. *Jamaica Mercury and Kingston Weekly Advertiser*, May 1, 1779, 104.

195. *Jamaica Mercury and Kingston Weekly Advertiser*, May 1, 1779, 117.

196. *South Carolina Gazette*, 1739.

197. Donnan "The Slave Trade into South Carolina," 805

198. *South Carolina Gazette*, 1739.

199. *South Carolina Gazette*, October 18, 1761.

200. On Hibbert, see Oliver, *Caribbeana*, 193–99. On the morality debate, see Robertson, "Eighteenth-Century Jamaica's Ambivalent Cosmopolitanism," 629.

201. Burnard and Morgan, "Dynamics of the Slave Market," 212–13.

202. *Royal Gazette*, Kingston, March 30, 1780, 215.

203. Thomas Hibbert had no legitimate sons; the house passed to George Hibbert who continued the trade through the 1790s, the decade in which Jamaica consumed a full one-half of all British slave imports from Africa.

204. Craton and Greenland, *Searching for the Invisible Man*, 199.

CHAPTER 2. CASTLES OF FEAR

1. The best summary of the house site is found in Panning, "Exploring Stewart Castle Estate," 172–79 and 199–205. See also Galle, "Stewart Castle Main House Background"; Bates, "Surveillance and Production on Stewart Castle Estate."

2. Galle, "Stewart Castle Main House Background."

3. See Galle, "Stewart Castle Main House Chronology," 2007, http://www.daacs.org/sites/stewart-castle-main-house/#chronology.

4. Hodges, "Private Fortifications in 17th-Century Virginia."

5. St. George, *Conversing by Signs*, 22–31.

6. Bailyn, *Atlantic History*, 62–81.

7. Kelso, *Captain Jones's Wormsloe*, 1979.

8. Dunbar, *Historic Architecture of Scotland*, 36, 66.

9. Dunbar, *Historic Architecture of Scotland*, 44.

10. Cruft, Dunbar, and Fawcett, *Borders*, 45–47.

11. Z-plan houses with towers at two corners were first identified as a type by MacGibbon and Ross, *Castellated and Domestic Architecture of Scotland*. The Z-plan house also took on a nondefensive form among elites in the seventeenth century in the northeast of Scotland. See Glendenning, MacInnes, and MacKechnie, *A History of Scottish Architecture*, 46–49.

12. Dunbar, *Historic Architecture of Scotland*, 42; Howard, *Scottish Architecture*, 51–53.

13. Tuan, *Landscapes of Fear*.

14. Long, *History of Jamaica*, II, 100

15. Long, *History of Jamaica*, I, 419.

16. Long, *History of Jamaica*, II, 192.

17. Hall, *In Miserable Slavery*, 13, 252.

18. Stewart, *An Account of Jamaica and Its Inhabitants*, 185.

19. For a discussion of the 1757 purchase of Hamden by the Stirling family, see Karras, *Sojourners in the Sun*, 74–79.

20. Scotus, *Reminiscences of a Scottish Gentleman*, 188.

21. See Robertson, "Late Seventeenth-Century Spanish Town, Jamaica," *Early American Studies*, 346–90.

22. Long, *The History of Jamaica*, II, 19–20.

23. See Robertson, "Reinventing the English Conquest of Jamaica in the Late Seventeenth Century," *English Historical Review* 118 (2002): 813–39. See also Buisseret, "The Taylor Manuscript and Seventeenth-Century Jamaica," in *West Indies Accounts* (Kingston), 48–63.

24. See the use of the term "conquest" in the *The Weekly Jamaica Courant*, 1722.

25. Burnard and Morgan state decisively that "Jamaica had the largest demand for slaves of any British colony in the Americas." Burnard and Morgan, "Dynamics of the Slave Market," 205. See also Dunn, *Sugar and Slaves*, 164–65. On increasing rates of absenteeism see Douglas Hall, "Absentee-Proprietorship in the British West Indies to about 1850," *The Jamaican Historical Review*, vol. 4 (1964): 15–35.

26. Dunn, *Sugar and Slaves*, 226; Wood, *Black Majority*, 131.

27. Rhys, *Transformation of Virginia*, 12.

28. Dunn, *Sugar and Slaves*, 164–65.

29. Burnard and Morgan, "Dynamics of the Slave Market," 205–6; Petley, "Plantations and Homes," 445.

30. Oldmixon, *The British Empire in America*, 120. The typical eighteenth-century slave quarter, earthfast, thatched, and plastered inside, is described in detail in Stewart, *An Account of Jamaica and Its Inhabitants*, 231.

31. Knight, *Portions of a History of Jamaica*.

32. Craton, *Testing the Chains*, 125–39; Robert Napier, "Tacky's War," *Jamaican Historical Society Bulletin* 2 (1960); Campbell, *Maroons of Jamaica*, 156.

33. Long, *History of Jamaica*, II, 447.

34. Cited in Burnard, *Mastery, Tyranny, and Desire*, 171.

35. Higman, *Plantation Jamaica*, 197.

36. Hall, *In Miserable Slavery*, 243.

37. Craton, *Testing the Chains*, 335–39.

38. Dunn, *Sugar and Slaves*, 256.

39. Long, *History of Jamaica*, II, 446.

40. *Jamaican Journal of Alexander Innes*, 17.

41. Craton, *Testing the Chains*, 125–39; see also Burnard, *Mastery, Tyranny, and Desire*, 10.

42. On Jamaica's Maroons, see Campbell, *The Maroons of Jamaica*.

43. Campbell, *The Maroons of Jamaica*, 54.

44. Lilly to Gen. Hunter at Jamaica, September 20, 1728, *Journal and Letterbook of Christian Lilly*.

45. Knight, *Portions of a History of Jamaica*, 16.

46. *Jamaican Journal of Alexander Innes*, 38.

47. Knight, *Portions of a History of Jamaica*, 77.

48. Knight, *Portions of a History of Jamaica*, 71.

49. Hall, *In Miserable Slavery*, 124, 126, 239, 240, 253, 267, 269, 289.

50. Long, *History of Jamaica*, II, 100.

51. Long, *History of Jamaica*, II, 171–72.

52. Pares, *War and Trade in the West Indies*, viii.

53. Burnard, *Mastery, Tyranny, and Desire*, 33.

54. Moody et al., *A New History of Ireland*, III, 31.

55. Moody et al., *A New History of Ireland*, III, 39–48.

56. Quoted in Moody et al., *A New History of Ireland*, III, 102.

57. Moody et al., *A New History of Ireland*, III, 102.

58. An excellent introduction to the theory and practice of colonization in Munster is ch. 3 of Canny, *Making Ireland British*.

59. On the population of Munster with settlers from the southwest of England, see Dunlop, "The Plantation of Munster 1584/9," *English Historical Review* 9, (1880), 250. See also Dunlop, "An Unpublished Survey of the Plantation of Munster in 1622," *Journal of the Royal Society of Antiquaries of Ireland* 54 (1924), 143.

60. Johnson, *Ireland: Land of Troubles*, 31–32.

61. Moody et al., *A New History of Ireland*, III, 115–41.

62. Moody et al., *A New History of Ireland*, III, 146.

63. See Fitzpatrick, *Seventeenth-Century Ireland;* on the architecture of this period, see Leask, *Irish Castles and Castellated Houses*, 137.

64. See Moody et al., *A New History of Ireland.*

65. Quoted in Johnson, *Ireland: Land of Troubles*, 28.

66. Quoted in Johnson, *Ireland: Land of Troubles*, 31.

67. Bailyn, *Atlantic History*, 67.

68. St. George, "Bawns and Beliefs," 89–125; St. George, *Conversing by Signs*, 26–35.

69. Delle, *An Archaeology of Social Space.*

70. Bailyn, *Atlantic History*, 71.

71. I am not the first to argue for a connection between the built environment of early Jamaica and Ireland. See Delle, "Extending Europe's Grasp," 106–16.

72. Knight, *Portions of a History of Jamaica*, 77.

73. Long, *History of Jamaica*, II, 159.

74. For a brief introduction to the militia that populated the barracks, see Brathwaite, *Development of Creole Society*, 27–31.

75. On military installations, Long, *History of Jamaica*, II, 51, 80, 118, 171, 175, 204, 205, 309. On public buildings and houses, Long, *History of Jamaica*, I, 422 and plate 2.

76. Long, *History of Jamaica*, II, 84–85.

77. Klinglehofer, "Colonial Castles: The Architecture of Social Control."

78. Girouard, *Robert Smythson and the Elizabethan Country House*, 34–36 and 206–30; see also "A Martial Face," in Thompson, *Decline of the Castle*, ch. 5; and Platt, *The Castle in Medieval England and Wales*, chs. 7 and 8.

79. Mark Girouard described it as participating in the "mysterious Spenserian world, neither Gothic nor classic." See Girouard, *Robert Smythson*, 225.

80. McKean, *The Scottish Chateau*, 41.

81. Recognizing the increasing significance of landholding as a sign of status, those whose wealth derived primarily from trade or business were especially motivated to purchase large tracts of land in the two centuries following the dissolution of the monasteries by Henry VIII. See Cooper, "Social Distribution of Land and Men in England," 419–40; Clay, "Marriage, Inheritance and the Rise of Large Estates in England," 503–18.

82. Arnold, *The Georgian Country House*, 18; see Arnold's chapter "Living off the Land: Innovations in Farm Practices and Farm Design," in *The Georgian Country House.*

See also Mingay, "The Size of Farms in the Eighteenth Century," 469–88; Clemenson, *English Country Houses and Landed Estates;* Thompson, "Patrician Society, Plebian Culture," 382–405.

83. Malcolm Airs notes the increasing power of the country house, newly erected on recently acquired tracts of land, to fashion and communicate the identity of the patron and his family. Airs, *The Tudor and Jacobean Country House*, ch. 1.

84. Avery, *Tattershall Castle, Lincolnshire*, 5. See also Johnson, *Behind the Castle Gate*, 60.

85. Girouard, *Robert Smythson*, 4–5.

86. Girouard, *Robert Smythson*, 83; Durant, *The Smythson Circle*, 71.

87. Durant, *The Smythson Circle*, 71.

88. Pevsner, *Buildings of Wales*, 377.

89. For other examples, including unexecuted plans for houses, see Maguire and Colvin, "A Collection of Seventeenth-Century Building Plans," 140–69; Harris, "Kneller Hall, Middlesex." See also Summerson, "Class B: Single Block Plans with Corner Towers," 27–28.

90. Johnson, *Behind the Castle Gate*, 133.

91. Johnson, *Behind the Castle Gate*, 173–74,

92. McKean, *The Scottish Chateau*, 27, and ch. 3; see also Howard, *Scottish Architecture*, 48–65; Glendinning, *History of Scottish Architecture*, 71–102.

93. Thompson, *Decline of the Castle*, 158.

94. Summerson, *The Unromantic Castle*, 93.

95. Summerson, *The Unromantic Castle*, 14.

96. Thompson, *Decline of the Castle*, 158.

97. For Scotland, see McKean, *The Scottish Chateau*, 130.

98. Thompson, *Decline of the Castle*, 2.

99. See Thompson, *Decline of the Castle*, 22.

100. Bunratty, built in the fifteenth century in County Clare by the O'Briens of Thomond, appears to be another rare pre-1580 example. Leask, *Irish Castles*, 116, 121. Gomme suggests the possibility that the towers are not fifteenth century but were added in 1581 by the fourth Earl of Thomond. See Gomme, *Design and Plan in the Country House*, 38.

101. See Jope, "Cornish Houses, 1400–1700," and Waterman, "Some Irish Seventeenth-Century Houses and Their Architectural Ancestry," in Jope et al., eds., *Studies in Building History*, 192–222, 251–74.

102. For more on Rathfarnham, see McParland, "Rathfarnham Castle," 734.

103. Other Protestant-built examples include Manorhamilton, also built in the north, in 1634. See Craig, *The Architecture of Ireland*, 117.

104. See Craig, "Portumna Castle, County Galway," in *The Country Seat*, 36–41.

105. MacMahon, *Portumna Castle and Its Lords*, 18–19.

106. Craig, *Architecture of Ireland*, 118.

107. Craig, *Architecture of Ireland*, 127.

108. On "The Graces" and confiscation of old English land, see Clarke, *The Old English in Ireland.*

109. For more on the Archdeacon family in Jamaica, see Higman, *Plantation Jamaica*, 147.

110. For this chronology, see Panning, "Exploring Stewart Castle Estate."

111. Panning, "Edinburgh Castle," Jamaica National Heritage Trust Report, 2005.

112. Aarons, "Auchindown Excavation 1983–84."

113. National Archives of Jamaica, 1B/11/3 vol. 28, folios 58-63, 7 November 1748. Special thanks to Robert Barker for bringing this source to my attention.

114. For distribution, consider the presence of the same building types in Oman, some built by the Portuguese, but many built by the Omanis. (Special thanks to Dell Upton for making this observation.) The connection between Scotland and Jamaica has been previously addressed, although with a very different focus, by Drinkall in "The Jamaican Plantation House: Scottish Influence," 56–68.

115. Karras, *Sojourners in the Sun.* For a comparable assessment of the rise of Scottish merchants in the Chesapeake tobacco trade, see Price, *Tobacco in Atlantic Trade.*

116. Karras, *Sojourners in the Sun.* For a profile of typical sojourners, see 4, 49–50. By contrast less affluent Scots, he notes, would settle plantations on the American mainland, which offered broader opportunities and required less start-up capital for success. On Scottish immigration to and trade with the colonies, see Devine, *Scotland's Empire and the Shaping of the Americas.*

117. Karras, *Sojourners in the Sun*, 122–29.

118. Karras, *Sojourners in the Sun*, 120, 139.

119. Glendenning, MacInnes, and MacKechnie, *A History of Scottish Architecture*, chs. 3 and 4; Dunbar, *Historic Architecture of Scotland*, 81–87.

120. Jope, "Scottish Influences in the North of Ireland, 31–47. See also Jope, "Moyry, Charlemont, Castleraw, and Richhill," 111.

121. Johnson, "Settlement and Architecture in County Fermanagh, 1610–41," *Ulster Journal of Archaeology* 43, 79–89.

122. Salter, *Castles and Stronghouses of Ireland*, 159.

123. In County Fermanagh, other examples include Portora, Crom, Enniskillen, and Balfour; elsewhere Brackfield in County Derry, Roughan in County Tyrone, and Ballinafad in County Sligo. For work on these buildings see Weadick, "How Popular

Were Fortified Houses in Irish Building History?" in *Plantation Ireland*, 61–85. For Scottish precedents in Ireland, see McKean, *The Scottish Chateau*, and Salter, *Castles and Stronghouses of Ireland*.

124. Jope, "Scottish Influences in the North of Ireland, 31–47. See also Leask, *Irish Castles*, 138.

125. Tuan, *Landscapes of Fear*, 5.

126. See Vincent Brown's digital history of this event, "Slave Revolt in Jamaica, 1760–61: A Cartographic Narrative," at http://revolt.axismaps.com/.

CHAPTER 3. HEAT AND HURRICANES

1. An excellent introduction to John Tharp appears in Pearsall, "The Late Flagrant Instance of Depravity in My Family," 145.

2. Hart, "Good Hope, Jamaica, 1744–1994" (unpublished manuscript), 57–58, partially reprinted in Besson, *Martha Brae's Two Histories*, 72.

3. Such quality dissolves, however, in portions of the foundations not originally intended to be seen. When the house was built, the majority of the western elevation of the foundation was under water or blocked by a dock along that side of the house. Now visible, the masonry there is fairly rough-cut coursed stone of much lower quality than the more visible northern and eastern elevations.

4. For an assessment of Tharpe's architectural production see Bryant and di Valmarana, "Legacy of a Sugar Baron." For architects' work in Britain, see chapter 9.

5. Thomas Thistlewood, who plays a key role in later chapters, is a very important observer of climatological data for the eighteenth-century Caribbean. See Chenoweth, *The 18th-Century Climate of Jamaica Derived from the Journals of Thomas Thistlewood, 1750–1786*.

6. Gragg, "First Impressions of Barbados," 189.

7. Taylor quoted in Buisseret, *Jamaica in 1687*, 239.

8. Kupperman, "Fear of Hot Climates" 213–40.

9. Kupperman, "Fear of Hot Climates," 221–23.

10. Quoted in Mulcahy, *Hurricanes and Society*, 119.

11. Quoted in Buisseret, *Jamaica in 1687*, 114.

12. Quoted in Mulcahy, *Hurricanes and Society*, 120.

13. *The Weekly Jamaica Courant*, September 12, 1722.

14. Knight, *Portions of a History of Jamaica*; Robertson, "A Short Account of the Hurricane, that pass'd thro' the English Leeward Caribbee Islands, on Saturday the 30th of June 1733, 12." Using a vast body of documentary evidence, Matthew Mulcahy

has recently argued that late seventeenth-century British colonials in the Caribbean began to note the ways architecture responded more or less successfully to the region's regular hurricanes. Mulcahy, *Hurricanes and Society in the British Greater Caribbean, 1624–1783*, ch. 5, "Building for Disaster."

15. All uncited references to eighteenth-century storms derive from Chenoweth, "A Reassessment of Atlantic Basin Tropical Cyclone Activity, 1700–1855," *Climatic Change* (2006).

16. Edwards, "The Complex Origins of the American Domestic Piazza-Veranda-Gallery," 3–58; Oszuscik, "Passage of the Gallery and Other Caribbean Elements," 1–14; Buisseret, *Historic Architecture of the Caribbean*; Crain, *Historic Architecture in the Caribbean Islands*. As a counterpoint, John Crowley has demonstrated that the more important questions frame the piazza's social and cultural functions. See Crowley, *The Invention of Comfort*.

17. Thornton, "The Probate Inventories of Port Royal, Jamaica," 117–18. The words *hammock* and *hurricane* came into English in the mid-sixteenth century via Spanish from the Taino language.

18. Ligon, *History of the Island of Barbados*, 65.

19. Quoted in Buisseret, *Jamaica in 1687*, 239.

20. Quoted in Gragg, "First Impressions of Barbados," 208.

21. Robert Thurger (1712) and Robert Nedham (1739), National Archives of Jamaica, Wills and Inventories, Series 1B.

22. Hall, *In Miserable Slavery*, 62, 67.

23. Ligon, *History of the Island of Barbados*, 59–60.

24. Ligon, *History of the Island of Barbados*, 60, 141.

25. Ligon, *History of the Island of Barbados*, 63, 141.

26. Ligon, *History of the Island of Barbados*, 142.

27. Cooper, *Houses of the Gentry*, 142.

28. Robertson, "Jamaican Architectures before Georgian," 75.

29. Quoted in Hobson, "Domestic Architecture," 140.

30. Quoted in Hobson, "Domestic Architecture," 52; the Sevion and Abbot citations come from the 1706 St. Kitts claims, which were registered by English colonials on St. Kitts (St. Christopher) to the Crown for reimbursement from losses in the previous year from a French raid on the island. St. Kitts claims, Public Record Office, Kew, London.

31. Ligon, *History of the Island of Barbados*, 59.

32. Quoted in Hobson, "Domestic Architecture," 53.

33. Rochefort and Davies, *History of the Caribbee-Islands*, 23.

34. Quoted in Robertson, "Jamaican Architectures before Georgian," 92.

35. Samuel Dickens to Board of Trade, November 16, 1757, quoted in Douglas Mann, "Becoming Creole," 26.

36. See OED, 1624 J. Smith *Virginia* iii. vii. 73. See also Lounsbury, *An Illustrated Glossary*, 326.

37. See also fig. 9 in Dunn's *Sugar and Slaves*, from Du Tertre, *Histoire générale des Antilles*, II, 419.

38. St. Kitts claims, Public Record Office, Kew, London.

39. A full transcription of the glebe house in Barbados appears in Bridenbaugh and Bridenbaugh, *No Peace Beyond the Line*, appendix 4.

40. Originally named Consett plantation, the property was purchased by Christopher Codrington I, a wealthy royalist who departed for Barbados in 1649 after the fall of the royalist army in that year. J. A. Kenworthy-Browne, *Dodington*, 19.

41. On rear stair towers, see Hall, *The Rural Houses of North Avon and South Gloucestershire, 1400–1720*, 27.

42. Quoted in Hobson, "Domestic Architecture," 53.

43. Cited in Crowley, *Invention of Comfort*, 236.

44. See "Port Royal's Excavated Buildings," in Donny Hamilton, "The Port Royal Project," http://nautarch.tamu.edu/portroyal/archives/buildings.htm.

45. Robertson, "Jamaican Architectures before Georgian," 81, 92.

46. For more examples, see the St. Kitts claims, Public Record Office, Kew, London.

47. Hall, *In Miserable Slavery*, 11.

48. Hobson, "Domestic Architecture," 218–19.

49. Pawson and Buisseret, *Port Royal*, 106.

50. Robertson, "Jamaican Architectures before Georgian," 76.

51. Rochefort and Davies, *History of the Caribbee-Islands*, 177.

52. "Answers to the Inquiries sent to Colonel Stapleton, Governor of the Leeward Islands," November 22, 1676, *Calendar of State Papers: Colonial Series*, 499. Quoted in Mulcahy, *Hurricanes and Society*.

53. Quoted in Hobson, "Domestic Architecture," 156.

54. Leech, "Impermanent Architecture," 153–68.

55. Rochefort and Davies, *History of the Caribbee-Islands*, 145–46. See also Peyssonnell, "Observations upon the Currents of the Sea, at the Antilles of America," 624–30; Jeaffreson, *A Young Squire of the Seventeenth Century*, 275–76;

Oldmixon, *The British Empire in America*, 2: 235.

56. The most recent and comprehensive work on the architecture of Tainos is Ramcharan, "Caribbean Prehistoric Domestic Architecture." For the Drake manuscript see Pierce, *Histoire Naturelle des Indes*.

57. Fernández de Oviedo y Valdés, *La Historia general y natural de las Indias . . .* (Seville, 1535).

58. The smaller circular house form is called a caney in most of the historical and archaeological literature. Irving Rouse, *The Tainos*, 9.

59. Special thanks to Kirk Martini for this observation.

60. Ramcharan, "Caribbean Prehistoric Domestic Architecture," 89. Recent archaeological excavations of a Taino site in Cuba have uncovered an oval communal building more than sixty feet in diameter with a roof supported by vertical posts of twenty feet in length, offering for the first time physical evidence of du Tertre's description. See www.archaeology.org/9809/newsbriefs/ taino.html.

61. For archaeological evidence of comparative examples from eighteenth-century South Carolina, see Ferguson, *Uncommon Ground*, 63–82.

62. Armstrong, "Reflections on Seville," 84.

63. Armstrong, *The Old Village and the Great House*, 101–4.

64. Edwards, *A History, Civil and Commercial*, II, 164.

65. Lewis, *Journal of a West-India Proprietor*. See also the description by R. C. Dallas quoted in Higman, *Montpelier*, 150.

66. Edwards, *A History, Civil and Commercial*, II, 164; evidence from South Carolina suggests that early eighteenth-century African builders laid their posts in line in a single trench while later eighteenth-century builders dug individual holes for each post. No such differentiation has surfaced in the Jamaican evidence. See Ferguson, *Uncommon Ground*, 65–66.

67. Much of this paragraph depends on *Columbian Magazine or Monthly Miscellany*, April 1797.

68. Edwards, *A History, Civil and Commercial*, II, 164.

69. *Columbian Magazine or Monthly Miscellany*, April 1797.

70. Higman, *Montpelier*, 153.

71. Higman, *Montpelier*, 158.

72. *Columbian Magazine or Monthly Miscellany*, April 1797. See also Edwards, *A History, Civil and Commercial*, II, 164.

73. *Columbian Magazine or Monthly Miscellany*, April 1797.

74. *Columbian Magazine or Monthly Miscellany*, April 1797.

75. Edwards, *A History, Civil and Commercial*, II, 164.

76. *Columbian Magazine or Monthly Miscellany*, April 1797.

77. Higman, *Montpelier*, 156–57.

78. Jeaffreson, *A Young Squire of the Seventeenth Century*, 275–76.

79. Quoted in Mulcahy, *Hurricanes and Society*, 121.

80. Quoted in Mulcahy, *Hurricanes and Society*, 122.

81. "Henry Whistler's Journal, March 1655," quoted in Firth, ed., *Narrative of General Venables*, 168–69.

82. *The Weekly Jamaica Courant*, September 12, 1722.

83. Knight, *Portions of a History of Jamaica*, 86.

84. I am indebted to the work of Edward Barnes on this point. He first made the observations about houses worth less than £200 in his unpublished paper, "Continuity: The Traditional Architecture of Saba." See also Rochefort and Davies, *History of the Caribbee-Islands*; St. Kitts claims, Public Record Office, Kew, London.

85. Hobson, "Domestic Architecture," 193. Daphne Hobson's dissertation is the most comprehensive analysis of the St. Kitts claims to date. While many of my conclusions agree with hers, my conclusions depend on an independent transcription and analysis of the data. Scholars of seventeenth-century Virginia have noted that the two-room house predominated in that colony as well. See Graham, "Adaptation and Innovation," 510.

86. For examples see the St. Kitts claims, Public Record Office, Kew, London.

87. Rochefort and Davies, *History of the Caribbee-Islands*, 11.

88. Welch, "A Journal of my Voyage with ye Sundry passages thereof as I travel'd into divers parts of the West Indies, 1671," 80–81, microfilm copy of manuscript, American Philosophical Society, Philadelphia. Quoted in Mulcahy, *Hurricanes and Society*, 125.

89. Hall, *Earthquakes in Jamaica from 1688 to 1919*; Sykes and Ewing, "The Seismicity of the Caribbean Region," 5065–74.

90. "Answers to the Inquiries sent to Colonel Stapleton, Governor of the Leeward Islands," November 22, 1676, *Calendar of State Papers: Colonial Series*, 500. Quoted in Mulcahy, *Hurricanes and Society*, 126.

91. Special thanks to Kirk Martini for his help in understanding the structural performance of buildings in seismic circumstances.

92. *An Account of the Late Dreadful Earthquake in the Island of Nevis, 1690*. Quoted in Leech, "Impermanent Architecture," 6.

93. Quoted in Hobson, "Domestic Architecture," 289.

94. Quoted in Buisseret, *Jamaica in 1687*, 118–19.

95. Pawson and Buisseret, *Port Royal*, 123.

96. Sloane, *The Philosophical Transactions of the Royal Society of London*, vol. 3, 625.

97. Knight, *Portions of a History of Jamaica*, 82.

98. Pawson and Buisseret, *Port Royal*.

99. Leslie, *A New History of Jamaica*, 30.

100. Jacobs, *A Short History of Kingston*, 9; see also Young, "The Founding of Kingston."

101. Roberts, "Who Planned Kingston?," 144–53.

102. Piazzas appear in Kingston probate inventories from the early 1710s. Robert Lodge inventory, National Archives of Jamaica, Wills and Inventories, Series 1B.

103. *The Importance of Jamaica to Great Britain Considered*, 5.

104. Knight, *Portions of a History of Jamaica*.

105. On the Laws of the Indies, see Crouch, Garr, and Mundigo, *Spanish City Planning in North America*.

106. Laws of the Indies, 1573, quoted in Donahue-Wallace, *Art and Architecture of Viceregal Latin America*, 74.

107. Bailey, *Art of Colonial Latin America*, 138, 142, 200–201.

108. Llanes, *The Houses of Old Cuba*, 33, 62, 65, 71, 77, 87. For an eighteenth-century example of an urban colonnade in Puerto Rico, see Castro, *Arquitectura en San Juan de Puerto Rico*, 145.

109. By the early 1760s, even the houses in the remote city of St. Augustine, Florida, were described as "built of Masonry: their entrances are shaded by Piazzas supported by Tuskan Pillars or Pillasters against the South Sun." See Manucy, *The Houses of St. Augustine*, 28–29.

110. Jamaican Journal of Alexander Innes, 16.

111. Zahedieh, "The Merchants of Port Royal," 570–93. See also Stephen, *Merchants and Jews*, 142–43; Christelow, "Contraband Trade between Jamaica and the Spanish Main," 309–43.

112. See Curtin, *Atlantic Slave Trade*, 26; see also McNeill, *Atlantic Empires of France and Spain*, 44, 169; Pares, *Merchants and Planters*, 33.

113. James and Roberts, "Winchester and Late Medieval Urban Development"; see also Beacham, *Devon Building*, 113–15; Lawson and Smith, "The Rows of Chester," 1–42. Andrew Brown et al., *The Rows of Chester*, 55–62, provides an up-to-date review of current thinking on the origins of The Rows.

114. James and Roberts, "Winchester and Late Medieval Urban Development," 10.

115. Robertson, "Jamaican Architectures before Georgian," 90.

116. Pawson and Buissere, *Port Royal*, 88.

117. Dan Cruicksshank and Peter Wyld, *London: The Art of Georgian Building*, 212.

118. Manucy, *Sixteenth-Century St. Augustine*, 93, 112, 115, 119; see also Llanes, *Houses of Old Cuba*, 108–9.

119. *Royal Gazette*, Kingston, April 29, 1780, 271.

120. Long, *History of Jamaica*, II, 103.

121. Anon., "London Apprentices Declar.," in *The Harleian Miscellany* 8, 571/2 (1746).

122. Burnet, *Some Letters*, 167.

123. Thomas Belchkin, 1719; George Walden, 1727. National Archives of Jamaica, Wills and Inventories, Series 1B.

124. Long, *History of Jamaica*, II, 21.

125. Manucy, *Sixteenth-Century St. Augustine*, 91, 115, 119.

126. Manucy, *Sixteenth-Century St. Augustine*, 63; Llanes, *Houses of Old Cuba*, 42–45, 71. See also Castro, *Arquitectura en San Juan de Puerto Rico*, 61.

127. Sloane, *A Voyage to the Islands* I: xxi; Deagan, *Puerto Real*, 434–36.

128. See Sloane, *A Voyage to the Islands* I: xxi; Wright, ed., "The English Conquest of Jamaica," 3; David Buisseret, "Fresh Light on Spanish Jamaica," 72–75.

129. See Lancaster, *American Bungalow*, 51. For more on the Spanish Caribbean see Palm, *Los monumentos arquitectónicos de la Espanola*; Joplin, *Puerto Rican Houses*; Manucy, *Sixteenth-Century St. Augustine*; Kubler, *Mexican Architecture of the Sixteenth Century*; Deagan, *Puerto Real*.

130. Leslie, *A New History of Jamaica*, 30.

131. Quoted in Crowley, *Invention of Comfort*, 238.

132. Edwards, "The Complex Origins," 40–41; Oszucik, "Passage of the Gallery," 1.

133. Edwards, "The Complex Origins," 11–15, 41.

134. John Crowley has suggested that the piazza is common in the Caribbean only by the mid-eighteenth century. Crowley, "The Invention of Comfort," 287.

135. See A. Picon, *French Architects and Engineers in the Age of Enlightenment*.

136. An extensive account of Belidor's book appears in Underwood, "The Pombaline Style."

137. Loriot, *A Practical Essay, on Cement and Artificial Stone*.

138. Sloane, quoted in Hobson, "Domestic Architecture," 44.

139. Long, *History of Jamaica*, II, 19–20.

140. Mullin, "The Reconstruction of Lisbon," 157–79.

141. Underwood, "The Pombaline Style" 100–101, 180.

142. Shiping, "The Earthquake Resistant Properties of Chinese Traditional Architecture," 355–89.

143. Tobriner, "A gaiola pombalina," 164.

144. For an extensive analysis of the system and its modern preservation, see Paula and Coias, "Rehabilitation of Lisbon's Old 'Seismic Resistant' Timber Framed Buildings."

145. Coias e Silva, "Using Advanced Composites to Retrofit Lisbon's Old 'Seismic Resistant' Timber Framed Buildings."

146. Tobriner, "La Casa Baracata," 131–38.

147. M. D'Albaret, *Différents projets relatifs au climat*, 5.

148. Oldendorp, *A Caribbean Mission*, 151.

149. Long, *History of Jamaica*, II, 627.

150. Lilly to Capt. Simon Clarke, April 14, 1731. *Journal and Letter Book of Christian Lilly*, p. 59 recto.

151. Hall, *In Miserable Slavery*, 163.

152. Craton and Walvin, *A Jamaican Plantation*, 55–56.

153. Beckford, *A Descriptive Account of the Island of Jamaica*, 135. There are occasional references to purpose-built hurricane houses in eighteenth-century Jamaica but physical evidence for them has yet to surface. See Hall, *In Miserable Slavery*, 20, 285.

154. Stewart, *An Account of Jamaica*, 14.

155. Quoted in Buisseret, *Jamaica in 1687*, 113.

156. Quoted in Mulcahy, *Hurricanes and Society*, 121.

157. *The Weekly Jamaica Courant*, Port Royal, September 5, 1722

158. Oszuscik, "Eighteenth-Century Concerns for 'Healthy Buildings' on the North Gulf Coast," 3.

159. Long, *History of Jamaica*, III, 617–18.

160. *Savanna-la-Mar Gazette*, July 15, 1788, 4.

161. This has already been noted in Bridenbaugh and Bridenbaugh, *No Peace Beyond the Line*, 94, 370.

162. Journals of the Assembly of Jamaica, 1663/4–1826 14 vols., I: 3, cited in James Robertson, "Jamaican Architectures before Georgian," 76, note.

163. Thanks to Kirk Martini for his understanding of the performance of roof framing.

164. Hall, *In Miserable Slavery*, 310.

165. Burnard, *Mastery, Tyranny, and Desire*, 65.

166. Hall, *In Miserable Slavery*, 277.

167. Sources for the frequency of seventeenth-century storms are derived primarily from Poey, "Chronological Table, Comprising 400 Cyclonic Hurricanes," 291–328. Poey has been supplemented with many other sources, including Mulcahy, *Hurricanes and Society*; Fraser, *Charleston! Charleston!*

168. Burnard, *Mastery, Tyranny, and Desire*, 65.

CHAPTER 4. PLANTATIONS AND POWER

1. The best published history of Good Hope is Tenison, *Good Hope Jamaica: A Short History*. An important manuscript source on the history of the plantation is Hart, "Good Hope, Jamaica, 1744–1994." Some of Hart's information and arguments are published in Besson, *Martha Brae's Two Histories*. For more intensive studies of individual Jamaican plantations, see Craton and Walvin, *A Jamaican Plantation*; Armstrong, *The Old Village and the Great House*; Higman, *Plantation Jamaica*; and Satchell, *Hope Transformed*. For a broader overview of the concept of the plantation, see Curtin, *Rise and Fall of the Plantation Complex*. For the most recent examination of the institution of slavery, see Roberts, *Slavery and the Enlightenment*.

2. Roberts, *Slavery and the Enlightenment*, 231.

3. Conolley, "Deployment of Forced Labor," 130.

4. The original land patent for Good Hope plantation was for one hundred acres from George II to Thomas Williams, August 2, 1742. Cambridgeshire Archives.

5. On Tharp's wealth, see Higman, *Plantation Jamaica*, 57, 141. See also Burnard, *Mastery, Tyranny, and Desire*, 64; Conolley, "Deployment of Forced Labor."

6. This bridge replaced the direct gutter shown on the 1794 plat. Likely supported by posts in the river, the gutter was probably compromised in the surging waters of the Martha Brae, especially in the rainy season.

7. Anon., *Art of Making Sugar*, 6.

8. While this chapter examines only sugar production, Jamaica also had coffee plantations, pimento walks, cattle pens, and other forms of productive farming. For an excellent investigation of the spaces of a late eighteenth-century Jamaican coffee plantation, see Delle, *An Archaeology of Social Space*. The number of slaves at Good Hope is taken from the 1829 Inventory of Good Hope in the National Archives of Jamaica, vol. 148, folio 154–57.

9. Wright, ed., *Lady Nugent's Journal*, 63; Stedman, *Narrative of a Five Years' Expedition against the Revolted Negroes of Surinam*, 315.

10. Quoted in Roberts, *Slavery and the Enlightenment*, 39.

11. Long, *History of Jamaica*, I, 435, 439.

12. Long, *History of Jamaica*, I.

13. Higman, *Plantation Jamaica*, 225.

14. Higman, *Plantation Jamaica*, 190.

15. An early example is Martin on Antigua. See Sheridan, "Samuel Martin," 126–39.

16. Higman, *Plantation Jamaica*, 194; Higman,

"Spatial Economy of Jamaican Sugar Plantations," 17–39, citation p. 18.

17. Galloway, "Tradition and Innovation in the American Sugar Industry," 334–51, esp. 341.

18. Watts, *The West Indies,* 392. See also Devine, *The Transformation of Rural Scotland.*

19. On sugar planters and agricultural reform, see Sheridan, "Samuel Martin." See also Warde, "The Idea of Improvement," 128–29.

20. Dunn has noted a few examples of sharing in seventeenth-century Barbados, see Dunn, *Sugar and Slaves,* 194.

21. Higman, *Jamaica Surveyed,* 16–17.

22. Sheridan, *Sugar and Slavery,* 212, 219–20.

23. Anon., *Art of Making Sugar,* 8.

24. Anon., *Art of Making Sugar,* 7.

25. Anon., *Art of Making Sugar,* 7.

26. Ligon, *History of the Island of Barbados,* 79.

27. Roberts, *Slavery and the Enlightenment,* Appendix B, Table A2 and A3.

28. The most recent examination of the sugar plantation as a machine appears in Roberts, *Slavery and the Enlightenment,* 32–35.

29. Higman, *Jamaica Surveyed,* 85; see also Higman, "Spatial Economy of Jamaican Sugar Plantations," 21–24.

30. Higman, *Jamaica Surveyed,* 80. More statistical analysis appears in Higman, "Spatial Economy of Jamaican Sugar Plantations," 27.

31. Higman, *Jamaica Surveyed,* 82–89.

32. Roberts, *Slavery and the Enlightenment,* 30, 69–72.

33. Galloway, "Tradition and Innovation ," 339.

34. While the exact place of origin of this form of sugar mill technology remains uncertain, it appeared first in the opening years of the seventeenth century and quickly became the standard mill used in American sugar production, appearing in Brazil by the 1610s and in Barbados by the 1640s. Buisseret, *Jamaica in 1687,* 254. The recognition of the vertical rollers as an important innovation in sugar production is realized in the numerous images of that new mill form published in the seventeenth and early eighteenth centuries. Examples include Charles de Rochefort, *Histoire naturelle et morale des Îles Antilles de l'Amérique* (Rotterdam, 1665).

35. Watts, *The West Indies,* 408.

36. Palmer and Neaverson, *Industry in the Landscape,* 20.

37. Anon., *Art of Making Sugar,* 10.

38. Edwards, *A History, Civil and Commercial,* II, 292; Anon., *Art of Making Sugar,* 10.

39. Watts, *The West Indies,* 409.

40. Satchell, "Innovations in Sugar-cane Mill Technology," 98.

41. Satchell, "Innovations in Sugar-cane Mill Technology," 105–8.

42. Satchell, "Early Use of Steam Power in the Jamaican Sugar Industry," 518–26.

43. Higman, *Jamaica Surveyed,* 81.

44. Higman, *Plantation Jamaica,* 180.

45. Satchell, "Early Use of Steam Power in the Jamaican Sugar Industry," 519. There were thirty-six plantations also using windmills but wind required a very particular terrain and was highly variable; as a result it was never a major power source. Watts, *The West Indies,* 407.

46. Reynolds, *Stronger Than a Hundred Men,* 289.

47. Edwards, *A History, Civil and Commercial,* II, 292.

48. Stewart, *A View of the Past and Present State of the Island of Jamaica,* 122.

49. Roughley, *Jamaica Planter's Guide,* 187.

50. Higman, *Plantation Jamaica,* 184.

51. Cundall, *Historic Jamaica,* 217–18. Special thanks to Robert Barker for bringing this to my attention.

52. Watts, *The West Indies,* 410–11. Digital images of the 1804 map of Jamaica can be found on the online catalogue of the National Library of Scotland: http://maps.nls.uk/jamaica/index.html.

53. Smeaton, "An Experimental Enquiry Concerning the Natural Powers of Water and Wind," 100–174, esp. 124.

54. Beckford, *A Descriptive Account of the Island of Jamaica,* 167.

55. Watts, *The West Indies,* 393–95. See also Anderson, *Mahogany.*

56. Edwards, *A History, Civil and Commercial,* 294.

57. Roughley, *Jamaica Planter's Guide,* 191–92.

58. Probate inventory of Sarah Houghton, 1767, National Archives of Jamaica.

59. Lindsay (1788), quoted in Higman, *Proslavery Priest,* 212.

60. Roberts, *Slavery and the Enlightenment,* 50, 163–67.

61. Conolley, "Deployment of Forced Labor," 125.

62. Conolley, "Deployment of Forced Labor," 131.

63. Edwards, *A History, Civil and Commercial,* II, 294.

64. Roughley, *Jamaican Planter's Guide,* 186–87.

65. Brathwaite, *Development of Creole Society,* 243.

66. Buisseret, *Jamaica in 1687,* 269.

67. On sleeping out of doors, see Buisseret, *Jamaica in 1687,* 269; Brathwaite, *Development of Creole Society,* 235. On bedsteads, see Edwards, *A History, Civil and Commercial,* II, 164. See also *Columbian Magazine or Monthly Miscellany,* April 1797.

68. *Columbian Magazine or Monthly Miscellany,* April 1797.

69. See Armstrong, "Reflections on Seville," 83.

70. Edwards, *A History, Civil and Commercial,* II, 164.

71. *Columbian Magazine or Monthly Miscellany,* April 1797.

72. Edwards, *A History, Civil and Commercial,* II, 164; *Columbian Magazine or Monthly Miscellany,* April 1797.

73. *Columbian Magazine or Monthly Miscellany,* April 1797.

74. Hall, *In Miserable Slavery,* 155; see also Higman, *Montpelier,* 218; Edwards, *A History, Civil and Commercial,* II, 164.

75. *Columbian Magazine or Monthly Miscellany,* April 1797.

76. Hall, *In Miserable Slavery,* 69–71.

77. Higman, *Montpelier,* 219.

78. Edwards, *A History, Civil and Commercial,* II, 279.

79. Higman, *Montpelier,* 197.

80. Higman, *Montpelier,* 221.

81. Brathwaite, *Development of Creole Society,* 213–14.

82. Brathwaite, *Development of Creole Society,* 216.

83. Armstrong, "Reflections on Seville," 95–97.

84. Armstrong, "Reflections on Seville," 95–97; see also Hall, *In Miserable Slavery,* 185.

85. Hall, *In Miserable Slavery,* 145.

86. Quoted in Brathwaite, *Development of Creole Society,* 217.

87. Burnard, *Mastery, Tyranny, and Desire,* 138.

88. Bilby and Handler, "Obeah: Healing and Protection," 154–83.

89. Williams, *A Tour through the Island of Jamaica,* 19.

90. Brathwaite, *Development of Creole Society,* 162.

91. Lambert, ed., "Account of David Henderson," in *House of Commons Sessional Papers,* vol. 69, 219.

92. Brathwaite, *Development of Creole Society,* 162.

93. Lambert, ed., "Account of David Henderson," in *House of Commons Sessional Papers,* vol. 69, 218.

94. Quoted in Higman, *Montpelier,* 147.

95. See the quote in Higman, *Montpelier,* 148. Chappell, "Accommodating Slavery in Bermuda"; Farnsworth, "Negroe Houses Built of Stone Besides Other Watl'd and Plaistered."

96. Chapman, "Slave Villages in the Danish West Indies."

97. Chapman, "Slave Villages in the Danish West Indies," esp. 115–19; see Mingay, *The Agricultural Revolution;* Wood, *A Series of Plans for Cottages or Habitations of the Labourer.*

98. Hayden Bassett, personal communication, August 28, 2014, based on summer 2014 excavation season.

99. Chapman, "Slave Villages in the Danish West Indies," 112.

100. Higman, *Montpelier*, 178.

101. Higman, *Montpelier*, 150–51, 167–68.

102. Higman, *Montpelier*, 141–43; Armstrong, *The Old Village and the Great House*, 88.

103. One of the best recent sources on agricultural improvement. Hoyle, ed., *Custom, Improvement, and the Landscape*.

104. Drayton, *Nature's Government*, xv.

105. Drayton, *Nature's Government*, 54.

106. See Hagelberg, "Sugar in the Caribbean," in Mintz, *Caribbean Contours*, 85–126. For the power of the boiling house as social metaphor in Creole Jamaica, see Higman, *Plantation Jamaica*, 143.

107. Roberts, *Slavery and the Enlightenment*, 72.

108. Quoted in Roberts, *Slavery and the Enlightenment*, 233.

109. Dunn, *Sugar and Slaves*, 194. For an extensive discussion of the role of the boiler, see Roberts, *Slavery and the Enlightenment*, 230–33.

110. Price is the first slave listed on the inventory, has the highest value of any slave in the full list of 393, and precedes a long list of fifty-two male slaves and fifty-three female slaves who are all listed alphabetically. From the 1829 Inventory of Good Hope in the National Archives of Jamaica, vol. 148, folio 154–57.

111. Buisseret, *Jamaica in 1687*, 254–55.

112. On the Jamaica train, see Anon., *Art of Making Sugar*, 13–14; see also Watts, *The West Indies*, 399; Galloway, "Innovation and Tradition."

113. Hobson, "Domestic Architecture," 261; Edwards, *A History, Civil and Commercial*, II, 292.

114. Names extracted from the 1829 Inventory of Good Hope in the National Archives of Jamaica, vol. 148, folio 154–57.

115. For more see Smith, *Caribbean Rum*.

116. Buisseret, *Jamaica in 1687*, 256.

117. Buisseret, *Jamaica in 1687*, 256.

118. Anon., *Art of Making Sugar*, 23.

119. Ligon, *History of the Island of Barbados*, 166.

120. Anon., *Art of Making Sugar*, 23.

121. Edwards, *A History, Civil and Commercial*, II, 292.

122. Quoted in Higman, *Plantation Jamaica*, 217.

123. Dunn, *Sugar and Slaves*, 197. By the late eighteenth century, a few Jamaican foundries were likely provisioning plantations with some equipment. See Satchell, "Innovations in Sugar-cane Mill Technology," 103.

124. Long, *History of Jamaica*, I, 457.

125. Beckford, *A Descriptive Account of the Island of Jamaica*, 64.

126. Edwards, *A History, Civil and Commercial*, II, 288.

127. Ligon, *History of the Island of Barbados*. Quoted in Buisseret, *Jamaica in 1687*, 79.

128. Ligon, quoted in Buisseret, *Jamaica in 1687*, 79.

129. Anon., *Art of Making Sugar*, 12.

130. *Jamaican Journal of Alexander Innes*, 20.

131. For a detailed discussion of time discipline on the sugar plantation, see Roberts, *Slavery and the Enlightenment*, 26–79.

132. Quoted in Amussen, *Caribbean Exchanges*, 98.

133. Roberts, *Slavery and the Enlightenment*, 200.

134. Martin, *Essay upon Plantership*, 9, 30.

135. Palmer and Neaverson, *Industry in the Landscape*, 134.

136. For the older view, see Hobsbawm, *Age of Revolution*. For a summary of the gradualist view, see Berg and Hudson, "Rehabilitating the Industrial Revolution," 24–50.

137. Mintz, *Sweetness and Power*, 47–52. See also Dunn, *Sugar and Slaves*, 189, 198; Higman, *Plantation Jamaica*, 8–10, 15; Fogel, *Without Consent*, 23–26; Watts, *The West Indies*, 385; Pritchard, *In Search of Empire*, 171.

138. Higman, *Plantation Jamaica*, 198–201.

139. For discussion of Robertson's paintings of both Jamaica and Coalbrookdale, see Quilley, "Pastoral Plantations," 121.

140. See Higman, "The Sugar Revolution," 213–36, esp. 223.

141. Delle, "The Habitus of Jamaican Plantation Landscapes," 122–43.

142. Beckford, *A Descriptive Account of the Island of Jamaica*; Roughley, *Jamaica Planter's Guide*, 184.

143. Bates, "Surveillance and Production on Stewart Castle Estate."

144. Long, *History of Jamaica*, II, 169; See also Casid, *Sowing Empire*, 197–213.

145. Quoted in Higman, *Jamaica Surveyed*, 243.

146. Edwards, *A History, Civil and Commercial*, II, 164; Long, *History of Jamaica*, II, 510.

147. Edwards, *A History, Civil and Commercial*, II, 164.

148. Higman, *Montpelier*, 217–57; see also Hauser, *An Archaeology of Black Markets*; Delle, "The Governor and the Enslaved," 488–512.

149. Hauser, "Of Earth and Clay," 163–82.

150. Higman, *Montpelier*, 217–57.

151. Galle, "Assessing the Impacts of Time," 211–42.

152. Galle, "Assessing the Impacts of Time"; Buckridge, *The Language of Dress*.

153. Howson, "Colonial Goods and the Plantation Village"; Reeves, "By Their Own Labor."

154. Hall, *In Miserable Slavery*, 152.

155. Higman, *Montpelier*, 176.

156. Edwards, *A History, Civil and Commercial*, II, 164.

157. *Columbian Magazine or Monthly Miscellany*, April 1797.

158. Higman, *Montpelier*, 174.

159. Long, *History of Jamaica*, II, 510.

160. Long, *History of Jamacia*, II, 510.

161. *Columbian Magazine or Monthly Miscellany*, April 1797.

162. *Columbian Magazine or Monthly Miscellany*, April 1797.

163. See Armstrong, "The Afro-Jamaican House Yard," 51–63.

164. Knight, *Portions of a History of Jamaica*, 80.

165. Edwards, *A History, Civil and Commerical*, II, 163.

166. In his monograph on Montpelier plantation, Barry Higman undertakes an extended discussion of the remarkable lists of slave households produced in 1825 for three interrelated plantations: New Montpelier, Old Montpelier, and Shettlewood. These lists include the names of the slaves with their family relationships to other residents and a fairly detailed description of the house they occupied. This is a unique document and a remarkably valuable record of slave housing conditions in the early nineteenth century. On family yards, see Higman, *Montpelier*, 135. For archaeological evidence, see Delle, "The Habitus of Jamaican Plantation Landscapes," 139.

167. *Columbian Magazine or Monthly Miscellany*, April 1797.

168. Robertson, *Gone Is the Ancient Glory*, 86.

169. Mintz, *Caribbean Transformations*, 231.

170. *Columbian Magazine or Monthly Miscellany*, April 1797.

171. Higman, *Montpelier*, 177.

172. *Columbian Magazine or Monthly Miscellany*, April 1797.

173. Armstrong, *The Old Village and the Great House*, 88.

174. Higman, *Montpelier*, 177. See also Handler, "Plantation Slave Settlements in Barbados."

175. Hakewill, *A Picturesque Tour of the Island of Jamaica*, 73. See also Burnard, *Mastery, Tyranny, and Desire*, 153–54.

176. Brathwaite, *Development of Creole Society*, 133; Armstrong, *The Old Village and the Great House*, 98–99; Hall, *In Miserable Slavery*, 238.

177. Lewis, *Journal of a West-India Proprietor*, January 10, 1816, 56. See also Edwards, *A History, Civil and Commercial*, II, 163.

178. Burnard, *Mastery, Tyranny, and Desire*, 154.

179. Williams, *A Tour through the Island of Jamaica*, 17.

180. Higman, *Montpelier*, 145.

181. Long, *History of Jamaica*, II, 269.

182. Quoted in Burnard, *Mastery, Tyranny, and Desire*, 138.

183. Edwards, *A History, Civil and Commercial*, I, 13

184. Quoted in Buisseret, *Jamaica in 1687*, 269.

185. Hall, *In Miserable Slavery*, 73, 192.

186. Quoted in Burnard, *Mastery, Tyranny, and Desire*, 104.

187. Burnard, *Mastery, Tyranny, and Desire*, 96–97, 183–84.

188. Hall, *In Miserable Slavery*, 204; for stock rooms, see Delle, "The Habitus of Jamaican Plantation Landscapes," 137.

189. Quoted in Hall, *In Miserable Slavery*, 133, 142, 161, 165.

190. Hall, *In Miserable Slavery*, 97.

191. Hall, *In Miserable Slavery*, 235.

192. Delle, "The Habitus of Jamaican Plantation Landscapes," 128.

193. Higman, *Plantation Jamaica*, 198

194. Wright, ed., *Lady Nugent's Journal*, 165.

195. Burnard, *Mastery, Tyranny, and Desire*, 3, 7.

196. From the 1829 Inventory of Good Hope in the National Archives of Jamaica, vol. 148, folio 154–57.

197. See "Sex and Social Control," in Burnard, *Mastery, Tyranny, and Desire*, 160–62, 219.

198. Burnard, *Mastery, Tyranny, and Desire*, 156, 157, 160, 210, 219.

199. Burnard, *Mastery, Tyranny, and Desire*, 159.

200. Hall, *In Miserable Slavery*, 20, 122, 155.

201. Burnard, *Mastery, Tyranny, and Desire*, 167.

202. Brathwaite, *Development of Creole Society*, 292.

203. Roberts, *Slavery and the Enlightenment*, 44–56.

204. Anon., *Art of Making Sugar*, 6.

205. Probate inventory of Thomas Belchkin for an overseer's room on the plantation, 1719, National Archives of Jamaica.

206. Probate inventory of Mathias Pilpsale for an overseer's house, 1750, National Archives of Jamaica.

207. See Ligon, *History of the Island of Barbados*, 79; Higman, *Plantation Jamaica*, 18.

208. Hall, *In Miserable Slavery*, 64, 264.

209. Beckford, *A Descriptive Account of the Island of Jamaica*.

210. Hall, *In Miserable Slavery*, 140.

211. Roberts, *Slavery and the Enlightenment*, 30, 72.

212. Quoted in Roberts, *Slavery and the Enlightenment*, 27.

213. Probate inventory of John Lord, 1788, National Archives of Jamaica.

214. 1750, John Vere, telescope in counting house; 1761, John Robert, plantation, spyglass in the hall; 1767, Sarah Houghton, overseer's house has a two-hour glass; 1769, William Matthews, plantation, spyglass; 1769, Beecher Fleming, plantation, spyglass and two-hour glass in hall; 1768, Robert Dellap, spyglass on piazza. See also Anon., *A Short Journey in the West Indies*, II, 26; Williams, *A Tour through the Island of Jamaica*, 154.

215. Williams, *A Tour through the Island of Jamaica*, 239.

216. On time discipline and plantations, see Smith, *Mastered by the Clock*.

217. Simon Taylor inventory as reprinted in Higman, *Jamaica Surveyed*, 242.

218. Hall, *In Miserable Slavery*; on ticketing, 101, 151, 197; regarding trespass, 174. For the legislation on ticketing, see Jamaica Council Minutes Ms. 60, vol. 26, p. 132, National Library of Jamaica.

219. Hall, *In Miserable Slavery*, 124, 150, 191.

220. Burnard, *Mastery, Tyranny, and Desire*, 217.

221. *Cornwall Chronicle*, Trelawny, Gibraltar, November 5, 1781; *Cornwall Chronicle*, March 28, 1810; *Cornwall Chronicle*, March 21, 1811.

222. Higman, *Jamaica Surveyed*, 244

223. Quoted in Higman, *Montpelier*, 130.

224. Armstrong, "Reflections on Seville," 87.

225. On village planning and the agency of the enslaved, see Higman, *Montpelier*, 127, 129; see also Delle, "Habitus of Jamaican Plantation Landscapes," 141.

226. Vlach, "Snug Li'l House with Flue and Oven," 118–32.

227. Quoted in Higman, *Montpelier*, 147.

228. Quoted in Higman, *Montpelier*, 128.

229. Foucault, *Discipline and Punish*, 184–87.

230. Hall, *In Miserable Slavery*, 54–55.

CHAPTER 5. THE ARTS OF EMPIRE

1. Three William Beckfords are central to the story of colonial Jamaica. William Beckford (1709–70) was the principal heir of the family fortune. Born in Jamaica, he traveled to England for his education in 1723 and later returned there, eventually becoming lord mayor of London. For his biography, see "Beckford, William," in *Appletons' Cyclopaedia of American Biography*. (On this William Beckford and William Pitt, see Peters, *Pitt and Popularity*.) His cousin, William Beckford of Somerley (1744–99), was an illegitimate son of the family and author of *A Descriptive Account of the Island of Jamaica*; see Sheridan, "Planter and Historian," 36–58. William Thomas Beckford (1760–1844) was the son of the lord mayor and a famous aesthete. There are numerous biographies on this Beckford; on his aesthetics, see Hewat-Jaboor, "Fonthill House," and McLeod, "A Celebrated Collector."

2. See Burnard, "Elephants Colliding," 17. See also Greene, "The Jamaica Privilege Controversy," 16–53. For a brief profile of the assembly, see Brathwaite, *Development of Creole Society*, 40.

3. Greene, "The Jamaica Privilege Controversy," 48.

4. Burnard, "Elephants Colliding," 5.

5. For an excellent discussion of the politics of "British" identity in the early modern era, see the introduction in Lawrence, *Archaeologies of the British*.

6. Armitage, *Ideological Origins*, ch. 8; 181.

7. On Jamaicans self-identifying as Britons, see Canny and Padget, eds., *Colonial Identity in the Atlantic World*.

8. Ingamells, *Dictionary*, 284, 787.

9. See Ingamells, *Dictionary*: Dawkins, Jr. [1744–51], 283; Swymmer [1753], 921; Cuzzens [1762], 265; Pennant [1765], 755; James [1761–72], 550; Beckford [1773–74], 71; Blagrove [1773–74], 97; Taylor [1773], 931; Goulburn [1777], 413; Ellis [c. 1780s], 336; Lyttleton [1785–86], 619; Hibbert [1787], 496; and Pinnock [1791–94] 769.

10. Cundall, *Historic Jamaica*, 33; Hancock, *Citizens of the World*.

11. Armitage, *Ideological Origins*, 172.

12. Browne, *The Civil and Natural History of Jamaica*, 23.

13. Land grants reveal that the Dawkins family were among the earliest of Jamaica's English settlers and that they continuously expanded their landholdings with each generation. See Sheridan, *Sugar and Slavery*, 224–27. Another excellent source on Dawkins is the *Oxford Dictionary of National Biography*.

14. On Dawkins's politics, see Lewis, *Connoisseurs and Secret Agents*, 24, 131, 134, and 141.

15. Pace, "Gavin Hamilton's *Wood and Dawkins Discovering Palmyra*."

16. Higman, *Jamaica Surveyed*, 93.

17. Wood, *Ruins of Palmyra*, preface.

18. Wood, *Ruins of Palmyra*, preface.

19. Kelly, *Society of Dilettanti*, 146–49.

20. See the diaries and sketchbooks belonging to Wood, Dawkins, Borra, and Bouverie, Joint Library of the Hellenic and Roman Societies, Senate House, London.

21. Wood, *Ruins of Palmyra*, preface.

22. See Kelly, *Society of Dilettanti*, 120–43.

23. Kelly, *Society of Dilettanti*, 137.

24. Harris and Savage, *British Architectural Books and Writers*, 50–51; Summerson, *Architecture in Britain*, 381; see also Kelly, *Society of Dilettanti*, 136–37.

25. Kelly, *Society of Dilettanti*, 109.

26. Kelly, *Society of Dilettanti*, 149.

27. Harris and Hind, "A Greek Revival Detective Story," 141–50.

28. The definitive study is Kelly, *Society of Dilettanti*.

29. His English estate was at Laverstoke, Hampshire.

30. See Dawkins and Beckford in *The History of Parliament*, ed. L. Namier.

31. Cundall, *Historic Jamaica*, 383, 395, 396.

32. Will and Testament of James Dawkins, National Archives of Jamaica, Wills and Inventories, Series 1B 11/835, transcribed by Robert B. Barker, October 15, 2004. Special thanks to Robert for bringing this to my attention and for sharing his transcription with me. The same information was later published in Harris and Hind, "A Greek Revival Detective Story," 141–50.

33. Will and Testament of James Dawkins, National Archives of Jamaica, Wills and Inventories, Series 1B 11/835. Dawkins and Price likely knew each other in England; Dawkins had just returned from his excursions through the Mediterranean when Price was studying at Trinity College, Oxford.

34. For more on the governors of Jamaica see Metcalf, *Royal Government and Political Conflict*.

35. Long, *History of Jamaica*, II, 62.

36. Cundall, *Historic Jamaica*, 396.

37. Kelly, *Society of the Dilettanti*, 152.

38. Special thanks to Robert Barker for this observation.

39. For biographical data on Price, see Stuart Handley, "Price, Sir Charles, first baronet (1708–1772)," http://www.oxforddnb.com/view/article/22743 (accessed May 7, 2013). Another source on Price is Craton and Walvin, *A Jamaican Plantation*, ch. 4, esp. 79.

40. Cundall, *Historic Jamaica*, 260–65.

41. Cundall, *Historic Jamaica*, 174.

42. Such elevation to and integration with the nobility was not new to Jamaica; earlier English settlers on the island had been so elevated. Furthermore, seemingly innumerable Jamaican daughters married into the English aristocracy over the course of the eighteenth century. And, of course, most royal governors were nobility. See Burke, *General and Heraldic Dictionary of the Peerage and Baronetage of the British Empire* (1832), 5, 41, 45, 62, 78, 83, 120, 126, 127, 143, 167, 204, 211, 222, 257, 260, 281, 296, 322, 327, 339, and 366.

43. Long, *History of Jamaica*, II, 76–77.

44. Long, *History of Jamaica*, II, 82.

45. Long, *History of Jamaica*, II, 84–85.

46. Long, *History of Jamaica*, II, 137.

47. Art historical analysis suggests that Du Simitière's works are on-site sketches of real views, not manufactured scenes. Crawford, "Transient Painters, Traveling Canvases."

48. Coutu, *Persuasion and Propaganda*, 52.

49. Bermingham, *Landscape and Ideology*, 13. See also Di Palma, *Wasteland: A History*, and Andrews, *The Search for the Picturesque*.

50. Casid, *Sowing Empire*. On Thistlewood's garden see Burnard, *Mastery, Tyranny, and Desire*, 106–12. See also Hall, "Botanical and Horticultural Enterprise in Eighteenth-Century Jamaica," 101–25. On Weston, see Robertson, "Eighteenth-Century Jamaica's Ambivalent Cosmopolitanism," 614.

51. Long, *History of Jamaica*, II, 95.

52. Sir Charles Price, National Archives of Jamaica, Inventory Series. No. 77: 1791–92, p. 54.

53. John Gale, National Archives of Jamaica, Inventory Series 1B 11-3.

54. Long, *History of Jamaica*, II, 76–77.

55. Originally printed in *Columbian Magazine or Monthly Miscellany*, 1796; reprinted in Cundall, *Historic Jamaica*, 262.

56. Hall, "Planters, Farmers, and Gardeners in Eighteenth-Century Jamaica," 97–114.

57. See introduction to Long, *History of Jamaica*, not paginated. See also Brathwaite, *Development of Creole Society*, 73.

58. Higman, *Jamaica Surveyed*, 84.

59. Higman, *Jamaica Surveyed*, 92.

60. Cundall, *Historic Jamaica*, 174.

61. Quoted in Greene, "The Jamaica Privilege Controversy," 16–53, citation on 20.

62. For assessments of Long's *History*, see Metcalf's introduction to the 1970 reprint of Long, *History of Jamaica*. See also Fryer, *Staying Power*, 70. I'm not the first to address Long's capacities for landscape description. See Casid, *Sowing Power*, 13–21.

63. Jamaican Caves. The Underground World of Jamaican Caves—Part II (Guidance Part VI) 2003. August 25, 2006. http://www.jamaicancaves.org/article_2.htm.

64. Long, *History of Jamaica*, II, 95–100.

65. Long, *History of Jamaica*, II, 159–67.

66. Cundall, *Historic Jamaica*, 248.

67. Long, *History of Jamaica*, II, 184.

68. Long, *History of Jamaica*, II, 185.

69. See Andrews, *Search for the Picturesque*.

70. Long, *History of Jamaica*, II, 208–9.

71. See Casid, *Sowing Empire*; Kriz, *Slavery, Sugar and the Culture of Refinement*, esp. ch. 5; Andrews, *Search for the Picturesque*. See also Crowley, "The American Republic Joins the British Global Landscape," 89–127. On the use of landscape to tame the Scottish Highlands, see Withers, "The Historical Creation of the Highlands," 143–56.

72. Long, *History of Jamaica*, II, 76–78.

73. Hall, *In Miserable Slavery*, 239.

74. Beckford, *A Descriptive Account of the Island of Jamaica*, 50–51, 65. For more on Beckford and landscape description, see Quilley, "Pastoral Plantations," 108–11.

75. *Jamaica Mercury and Kingston Weekly Advertiser*, May 1, 1779, 94.

76. Wright, ed., *Lady Nugent's Journal*, 66; see also Higman, *Montpelier*, 132; for a larger discussion in English culture see Barrell, *The Dark Side of the English Landscape*.

77. Jamaican Journal of Alexander Innes, 18.

78. Long, *History of Jamaica*, II, 22.

79. As quoted in Burnard, "Elephants Colliding," 8. For more on Kingston's wealth, see Burnard, "Elephants Colliding."

80. Through the late seventeenth century, this position was claimed by the famed Port Royal, positioned at the end of a long spit of land that sheltered a huge natural harbor. But the 1692 earthquake, which collapsed the city under leagues of water, shifted that urban history to the large open plain on the landside of the harbor. Laid out in 1703 according to a large grid plan with a massive central square, Kingston grew rapidly over the first half of the new century.

81. For a profile of Kingston merchants, see Brathwaite, *Development of Creole Society*, 111–17.

82. Robert Barker, "Mid Eighteenth-Century Jamaican House Design."

83. For more on MacFarlane and his house see Bryden, "The Jamaican Observatories." See also chapter 3 of Clarke, *Reflections on the Astronomy of Glasgow*.

84. Long, *History of Jamaica*.

85. *Genealogical collections concerning families in Scotland, made by W. Macfarlane, 1750–1751.* Edited from the original manuscripts in the Advocate's library, Edinburgh, by James Toshach Clark, v. 33–34. See also an abstract of MacFarlane's will at http://lib-operations.sonoma.edu/fin/aaa-0065.html.

86. The house is called "the Great House" in a 1780 diary entry of James Pinnock. British Library, Add. Ms. 33316, Diary of James Pinnock (July 24, 1780), cited in Mann, "Becoming Creole," 43. For a biography of Pinnock, see DuQuesney, "Phillip Pinnock," 95–97.

87. On the Jamaican Association, see Metcalf, *Royal Government and Political Conflict in Jamaica*, 120–21. See also Knowles, *The Jamaican Association Develop'd*.

88. Comparison of the sketch with Archibald Campbell's 1782 "Survey of the South Coast of Jamaica," now in the British Library, suggests that Du Simitière was looking west–southwest from the St. Andrews Church tower toward the house labeled "Pinnock's" to the southwest of Half-Way Tree on the map. Such a view would capture the slope

of Long Mountain seen to the west of Half-Way Tree on the map and the aggregations of mountains behind.

89. Pusey and Stauffenburg, "The Cipher Book of Pierre Eugène du Simitière," 33–41.

90. Long, *History of Jamaica*, II, 124. Special thanks to Robert Barker for bringing this passage to my attention.

91. Andrea Palladio, *Four Books of Architecture*, 51.

92. *Royal Gazette*, Kingston, March 20, 1786.

93. Knight, *Portions of a History of Jamaica*, 100.

94. Long, *History of Jamaica*, II, 22; Robertson, "Eighteenth-Century Jamaica's Ambivalent Cosmopolitanism," 610.

95. Hickey, *Memoirs of William Hickey*.

96. Cundall, *Historic Jamaica*, xvii, xviii.

97. Long, *History of Jamaica*, II, 64.

98. Jill Casid has noted how in this particular passage Long seeks "to naturalize slavery as part of a Georgic plantation of Eden." Casid argues rightly that Long's casting of Jamaica as picturesque was motivated by the impulse for political control over the exotic and the foreign. See Casid, *Sowing Empire*, 13, 47.

99. Long, *History of Jamaica*, II, 64–65.

100. Cundall, *Historic Jamaica*, 291. For a biography, see the archival entry for John Blagrove, Jr. on the Royal Bank of Scotland Group online archives: http://heritagearchives.rbs.com/wiki/John_Blagrove_junior_(17531824),_West_Indian_plantation_owner. Accessed September 17, 2012. See also Shakespear, *John Shakespear of Shadwell and His Descendants*, 82–96; Venn (compiler), "*Alumni Cantabrigiensis*" II, vol. I, 285.

101. Ingamells, *Dictionary of British and Irish Travelers in Italy*, 97.

102. Hakewill, *A Picturesque Tour of the Island of Jamaica*, 73.

103. *Morning Post and Daily Advertiser* (London), Wednesday, December 4, 1776.

104. M. D'Albaret, *Différents projets relatifs au climat*, 5.

105. Long, *History of Jamaica*, II, 84.

106. M. D'Albaret, *Différents projets relatifs au climat*, 9.

107. Wright, ed., *Lady Nugent's Journal*, 12; Palladio, *Four Books of Architecture*, 45.

108. Long reports that the King's House was designed during the tenure of Henry Moore and constructed "under the inspection of" English engineer Thomas Craskell. The elevation and plans were agreed upon by November 1759 and completed by 1762 at an expense of £30,000. The Ionic portico, outfitted with solid stone columns, was not realized until 1770. Long, *History of Jamaica*, II, 6.

109. *Journals of the Assembly of Jamaica*, 353.

110. Cundall, *Historic Jamaica*, 292.

111. See Probates and Wills, Island Record Office, vol. 137, p. 41, Bernard Henry to John MacLeod, November 22, 1749. We know that John MacLeod of Colbeck, an "eminent planter," died on May 12, 1775 at "his seat." See *General Evening Post* (London, England), July 22, 1775–July 25, 1775, issue 6488; *London Evening Post* (London, England), July 22, 1775–July 25, 1775, issue 8322. MacLeod's will outlines his specific intentions for the "mansion-house" on his estate. See Wills, Island Record Office, folio 111, no. 42, John MacLeod, Proved May 18, 1775, p. 112. The exact site of the building is identified as a square house and labeled "Colbecks" on Archibald Campbell's 1782 "Survey of the South Coast of Jamaica," now in the British Library. In 1789, after MacLeod's death, the building, described as "Colbeck Castle," was offered for sale to the government for use as a barracks for the accommodation of British troops. In that ad, the castle was described as costing its proprietor £70,000 sterling. See *Morning Star* (London, England), Tuesday, June 2, 1789; Issue 94. A mid-eighteenth-century construction date was also offered by Concannon in "Diggin up the Past." See Lumsden, 133. Archaeological assessments of the house and outbuildings appear in Concannon, "The Masterbuilder" (June 1965), and Panning, "Colbeck Castle Outbuildings and Environs," 33–38.

112. Genealogical records on the MacLeod family suggest that one John MacLeod was "of Colbeck, planter in Jamaica," in 1762, when he applied for arms as the chief of a branch of the MacLeod clan. See http://www.clanmacleod.org/genealogy/macleod-genealogy-research/the-macleods-of-lewis.html.

113. Anon., *The Laws of Jamaica, 1760–1772*, 107.

114. Hart and Hicks, *Sebastiano Serlio on Architecture*, 240–43.

115. Long, *History of Jamaica*, II, 33.

116. Wooten, *Elements of Architecture* (editor's introduction, lxi). See Isaac Ware, cited in Bushman, *Invention of Comfort*, 119, notes 24, 25, 28.

117. Special thanks to Jackie Ranston for finding and sharing this inventory with me. See probate inventory of John MacLeod of St. Dorothy, National Archives of Jamaica, 1B/11/3, vol. 56, ff. 72–81. 1 August, 1775.

118. The presence of stew stoves helps to date the building since such stoves first appear in France in the 1730s.

119. This assessment of the kitchen at Colbeck depends heavily on a field report produced by Ed Chappel on-site with the Falmouth Field School in 2006.

120. Special thanks to Hayden Bassett for sharing his observations about the workings of the water systems at Colbeck.

121. Dunn, *Sugar and Slaves*, 307.

122. On Weston, see Robertson, "Eighteenth-Century Jamaica's Ambivalent Cosmopolitanism," 613–14; Long, *History of Jamaica*, II, 273.

123. Smith, *Clean*, 219, 241–42; For public baths in early America see Eberlin, "When Society First Took a Bath." See also Smollett, *An Essay on the External Use of Water*.

124. Long, *History of Jamaica*, II, 135.

125. Long, *History of Jamaica*, II, 32.

126. Quoted in Burnard, "Elephants Colliding," 17.

127. See Sheridan, *Sugar and Slavery*, 458–63.

CHAPTER 6. MERCHANT STORES AND THE EMPIRE OF GOODS

1. This lithograph is derived from a daguerreotype taken by Duperly in 1843. For information on Adolphe Duperly, see Boxer, *Duperly*. See also Barringer et al., *Art and Emancipation in Jamaica*, 420. See also Macmillan, *The West Indies*.

2. Wesler, "Excavations at the Barrett House, Falmouth." Archaeology also revealed heavy deposits of fine early nineteenth-century tablewares, but light deposits of utilitarian wares used in the preparation of meals. This suggests the possibility that the site was full-time commercial space—possibly selling these very same fine tablewares—and only a part-time residence. This migration toward full-time commercial functions in domestic buildings is addressed in the Philadelphia context by Dell Upton. See Upton, "Commercial Architecture in Philadelphia Lithographs."

3. This history of the house depends heavily on archival research completed by Emilie Johnson and published in Nelson et al. *Falmouth, Jamaica: Architecture as History*, 60–63.

4. The most recent work on the house-shop as a building form is Davis, *Living over the Store*. For additional work on this building form, see Klepper, "The Merchant's House in the Caribbean." For the importance of port towns and the Atlantic economy, see O'Flanagan, "Port Cities"; Knight and Liss, eds., *Atlantic Port Cities*; Burnard, "The Grand Mart of the Island," 225–241; and Jacob Price, "Economic Function and the Growth of American Port Towns," 123–86.

5. Ainslie, *Reminiscences of a Scottish Gentleman*, 28.

6. Stewart, *An Account of Jamaica,* 193 (italics in original); Mann also argues that elite women were actively purchasing fine goods for their houses by the 1770s. See Mann, "Becoming Creole," 160–64.

7. For a useful examination of the social implications of urban space see Çelik, Favro, and Ingersoll, eds., *Streets: Critical Perspectives on Urban Space.* For information on enslaved populations elsewhere in the urban Caribbean see Welch, *Slave Society in the City.*

8. For examples from the seventeenth century, see Pawson and Buisseret, *Port Royal,* 107. For work on even older examples, see Schofield, *Medieval London Houses,* 71–74.

9. The significance of Caribbean port cities in the early modern Atlantic world has become increasingly recognized among historians. As early as 1991, for example, a volume on Atlantic port cities included five essays that address the Caribbean, four essays on Central and South America, and only one on a port city in North America. See Knight and Liss, eds., *Atlantic Port Cities.*

10. Edwards, *A History, Civil and Commercial,* II, 263–64.

11. Higman, "Jamaican Port Towns" 125. For evidence of the correlation of slave population growth and free port status, see Hall, "Slavery in Three West Indian Towns," 437–53, esp. 439.

12. For a discussion of the political competition between merchants in Kingston and planters in Spanish Town, see Metcalf, *Royal Government and Political Conflict in Jamaica,* 122–40. For a discussion of that contest's impact on urban history, see Robertson, *Gone Is the Ancient Glory.*

13. Higman, "Jamaican Port Towns," 119.

14. Higman, "Jamaican Port Towns," 133.

15. Evidence for such overlap appears as early as the late seventeenth century. See Dunn, *Sugar and Slaves,* 182–83. Emma Hart has offered a similar assessment of the economic interdependence of plantations and city trades and services in her discussion of later eighteenth-century Charleston. See Hart, *Building Charleston,* ch. 2.

16. This formulation of social and economic landscapes depends on models offered by both Dell Upton and Bernard Herman. For landscapes of race, see Upton, "White and Black Landscapes," 357–69, and for embedded social and economic landscapes, see Herman, "The Embedded Landscapes of the Charleston Single House," 41–57. "House and store" is a phrase used in the period to describe this building type. For example, see the rental advertisements in the *Cornwall Chronicle,* Montego Bay, December 27, 1854, for "the house and store on the corner of Duke and King Streets, Falmouth."

17. Breen, *The Marketplace of Revolution,* 75–76.

18. Breen, "An Empire of Goods," 472.

19. Herman, *Town House.*

20. Breen, "An Empire of Goods," 467–99.

21. Davis, *Living over the Store,* 12–13.

22. Davis, *Living over the Store,* 70.

23. Davis, *Living over the Store,* 182.

24. For a parallel account of the Caribbean hall see Chapman, "Irreconcilable Differences," 162, 166–71.

25. Bayley, *Four Years Residence in the West Indies,* as cited in Mann, "Becoming Creole," 174.

26. Hall, "Slavery in Three West Indian Towns," 439–41.

27. Higman, *Slave Populations of the British Caribbean,* 227–32.

28. Hall, *In Miserable Slavery,* 168.

29. Long, *History of Jamaica,* II, 21.

30. *Royal Gazette,* Kingston, 1 May 1779, 282.

31. Higman, *Slave Populations of the British Caribbean,* 255.

32. Mann, "Becoming Creole," 84.

33. See probate inventory for Jonathan Gale, St. Andrews, 1728, National Archives of Jamaica.

34. Williams, *A Tour through the Island of Jamaica,* 45.

35. On these, see McInnis, *The Politics of Taste,* 160–94.

36. See Joseph, "From Colonial to Charlestonian," in *Another's Country,* 215–34.

37. Higman, *Slave Populations of the British Caribbean,* 256.

38. Cited in Mann, "Becoming Creole," 57–58. On slaves "living out" in Bridgetown, Barbados, see Welch, *Slave Society in the City,* 158–59.

39. Higman, *Slave Population and Economy in Jamaica,* 60–61.

40. See Thomas Robert Vermont will, January 14, 1865, Wills, Island Record Office, vol. 130, folio 28.

41. Davis, *Living over the Store,* 182.

42. These warehouses were probably not unlike the historic warehouses that have survived along the careenage in Bridgetown, Barbados.

43. Special thanks to Emilie Johnson for bringing this document to my attention.

44. John Stogdon ship manifest, April 15, 1794. National Archives of Jamaica.

45. Stewart, *An Account of Jamaica,* 14.

46. 1854 newspaper account, cited in Robinson, *Rise and Fall of Falmouth,* 71.

47. See Geggus, "Major Port Towns of Saint-Domingue," 99.

48. Thomas Atwood, *History of the Island of Dominica,* 179–80.

49. The best scholarly source on urban pushcarts is Daniel Bluestone's article on the pushcarts in New York, although Bluestone argues they did not become a major vending strategy there until the final quarter of the nineteenth century. See Bluestone, "The Pushcart Evil," 68–92.

50. Atwood, *History of the Island of Dominica,* 176.

51. See Geggus, "Major Port Towns of Saint-Domingue," 99.

52. November 7, 1798, a petition of the merchants, traders, and other inhabitants of Trelawny presented to the House of Assembly. Quoted in Robinson, *Rise and Fall of Falmouth,* 14.

53. "Report of Laws Regarding Wharves," *South Carolina Gazette,* May 16, 1743.

54. Data extracted from Calhoun, Zierden, and Paysinger, "The Geographic Spread of Charleston's Mercantile Community," 183–220.

55. *South Carolina Gazette,* 1740, number 357.

56. For examples in Philadelphia, see Watson, *Annals of Philadelphia,* vol. 1, 221; Upton, "Commercial Architecture."

57. Smith and Watson, "Western Bridgetown and the Butchers' Shambles," 185–98.

58. For more on everyday life on eighteenth-century wharves see Gildjie, *Liberty on the Waterfront.*

59. *The Mariner's Church* (New York, 1818), 7, as quoted in Gildjie, *Liberty on the Waterfront,* 203. For discussions of the unsavory reputation of the wharves, see esp. ch. 7, "The Proper Objects of Christian Compassion."

60. Data taken from Hall, "Nefarious Wretches, Insidious Villains, and Evil-Minded Persons," 151–68.

61. Higman, "Jamaican Port Towns," 140.

62. Markets were a locus of slave communication. See Hauser, "Linstead Market before Linstead?," 90. See also McDonald, "Urban Crime and Social Control."

63. September 13, 1826, no. 30, Cornwall correspondent in *The Gossip.*

64. Atwood, *History of the Island of Dominica,* 176.

65. See numerous witness testimonies in Pearson, *Designs against Charleston.* Soon after the Vesey trials, the state legislature passed the Negro Seaman Acts, requiring the incarceration of all black sailors while in port. On the architectural implications of the Vesey insurrection see 'The Public Landscape of Racial Control," in McInnis, *The Politics of Taste.*

66. This phenomenon of merchants retreating from wharves happened in port cities across the early modern world. For an

extensive discussion of the emergence of dedicated commercial spaces in early nineteenth-century Philadelphia, see Upton, "Commercial Architecture." For a discussion of the same in New York, see Scobey, *Empire City.*

67. For a historian's perspective on the importance of West Indian trade with the U.S. in this period, see Carrington, "United States and the British West Indies Trade" 149–68.

68. *Cornwall Chronicle,* December 20, 1815. National Library of Jamaica.

69. That this abundance is a marked change over the last century is evidenced in the difference in ship cargo reported in the late seventeenth century. Such listings include mostly alcohol and essentials, with only a few luxury items. See the cargo list of the 1671 voyage of the *Friendship,* republished in Dunn, *Sugar and Slaves,* 209.

70. See probate inventory for Jonas Hart, May 13, 1805. National Archives of Jamaica.

71. Higman, "Jamaican Port Towns," 135.

72. Inventory reprinted as appendix A in Hudgins, "The Probate Record of William Wilson, Charleston Merchant." On the integrated house and shop of eighteenth-century merchants and artisans see Upton, "Commercial Architecture."

73. Stobart et al., *Spaces of Consumption,* 117.

74. Show glasses were cabinets with glass tops fitted out for display, often positioned in the shop window. For early eighteenth-century shop counters and shelves, see Sindry Account Books and also Crawford daybook, South Carolina Historical Society.

75. Stobart et al., *Spaces of Consumption,* 16, 126–27, and ch. 5. On fittings in English shops, see Walsh, "Shop Design" 157–76; Stobart, "Shopping Streets as Social Space," 19. For a discussion of bulk windows in early Philadelphia, see Upton, "Commercial Architecture."

76. Such shop refinement and differentiation was common in London through the eighteenth century. See Walsh, "Shop Design," 160.

77. See Stobart et al., *Spaces of Consumption,* 128, for English examples. For a detailed discussion of refined retail spaces in early nineteenth-century Philadelphia, see Upton, "Commercial Architecture." On the rise of specialization, see Porter and Livesay, *Merchants and Manufacturers.*

78. For a discussion of the differentiation between wholesale and retail shop interiors, see Upton, "Commercial Architecture."

79. For Philadelphia, see Upton, "Commercial Architecture." For New York, see Rosebrock, *Counting-House Days in South Street,* 27.

80. See Walsh, *Shop Design,* 167.

81. On the significance of artisans in early Charleston, see Hart, *Building Charleston,* ch. 2.

82. Stobart et al., *Spaces of Consumption,* 136-38.

83. *The Falmouth Gossip,* June 14, 1826. National Library of Jamaica.

84. Buisseret, *Jamaica in 1687,* 231

85. Knight, *Portions of a History of Jamaica.*

86. Long, *History of Jamaica,* II, 21.

87. See Yin, "The Singapore Shophouse," 115–34, and Tjoa-Bonatz, "Shophouses in Colonial Penang," 122–36. See also ch. 1 of Davis, *Living over the Store.*

88. The Spanish *Laws of the Indies*—sixteenth-century guidelines intended to govern city planning in the Spanish New World—dictated that new cities should have arcaded streets.

89. See Kostof, *The City Assembled,* 216–18.

90. For other work on comparative urban form, see Burnard and Hart, "Kingston, Jamaica, and Charleston, South Carolina," 1–21.

91. *South Carolina Gazette,* 1740, number 357.

92. *South Carolina Gazette,* November 15, 1760.

93. See Upton, "Commercial Architecture."

94. Bowden, "Three Centuries of Bridgetown."

95. Stobart et al., *Spaces of Consumption,* chs. 3 and 4.

96. Geismar, "Patterns of Development in the Late Eighteenth- and Nineteenth-Century American Seaport," 175–84.

97. Williams, *A Tour through the Island of Jamaica,* 221.

98. Calhoun, Zierden, and Paysinger, "The Geographic Spread of Charleston's Mercantile Community," 183–219. For a detailed discussion of the merchants positioned along the early nineteenth-century waterfront of Philadelphia, see Ritter, *Philadelphia and Her Merchants.* For a discussion of this phenomenon in Philadelphia, see Upton, "Commercial Architecture."

99. Stobart, "Shopping Streets as Social Space."

100. Stobart, "Shopping Streets as Social Space," 16. On the quest for urban order, see Upton, *Another City,* 133–44. For a discussion of the broader remaking of the refined English town, see Borsay, *English Urban Renaissance.*

101. Perotin-Dumon, "Cabotage, Contraband, and Corsairs," 75.

102. Stobart, "Shopping Streets as Social Space,"18.

103. For more on consumption by women in this period, see Walsh, "Shops, Shopping, and the Art of Decision Making," and Martin, "Ribbons of Desire."

104. For work on the representation of race in Brunias, see Bagneris, *Coloring the Caribbean.*

105. On this point, I differ from William Chapman, who argues that genteel women were constrained to the spaces of the parlor through the day and were allowed access to the social spaces of the street only in the evening. See Chapman, "Irreconcilable Differences," 129–72.

106. For the emergence of a consumer society, see McKendrick, Brewer, and Plumb, eds., *Birth of a Consumer Society;* Miller, ed., *Acknowledging Consumption,* 164–62; Brewer and Porter, *Consumption and the World of Goods;* on the increasing number of shops, see Mitchell, "Development of Urban Retailing," 259–83.

107. Chapman, "Irreconcilable Differences," 167.

108. Stobart, "Shopping Streets as Social Space" 14–15.

109. On Jamaica's free black population, see chapter 8. On the Jonkonnu festival, see Bettelheim, "The Afro-Jamaican Jonkonnu Festival"; Bilby, "More Than Meets the Eye," 121–36; Bettelheim "Jonkonnu and Other Christmas Masquerades"; Ryman, "Jonkonnu," 13–23, 50–61; Craton, "Decoding Pitchy-Patchy, 14–44; and Gikandi, *Slavery and the Culture of Taste,* 270–81.

110. Bettelheim, "Jonkonnu and Other Christmas Masquerades," 45.

111. Quoted in Patterson, *The Sociology of Slavery,* 238.

112. John Dauling, 1780, "A Negroe mask," National Archives of Jamaica, Inventory Series 1B 11–3.

113. Davis, *Parades and Power;* for festivals and resistance in the Caribbean, see Burton, *Afro-Creole.*

114. Quite obviously, the Jonkonnu festival bears the character of Homi Bhabha's double discourse. See Bhabha, "Of Mimicry and Man," 88–91.

115. On the whole collection, see Barringer et al., *Art and Emancipation.*

116. Williams, *A Tour through the Island of Jamaica,* 21–27.

117. Williams, *A Tour through the Island of Jamaica,* 21–27

118. James Kelly, *Voyage to Jamaica,* 20–21.

119. Quoted in Craton, "Decoding Pitchy-Patchy," 28.

120. Bilby, "More Than Meets the Eye," 121.

121. Anon., "Characteristic Traits of the Creolian and African negroes in Jamaica, &c &c," *Columbian Magazine* April–October, 1797. Quoted in Abrahams and Swed, *After Africa,* 233.

122. See Thompson, "Charters for the Spirit"; Martinez-Ruiz, "Sketches of Memory"; and Bilby, "More Than Meets the Eye."

123. Robert Blair St. George has addressed the

body–building analogy and the house as surrogate in his work on seventeenth-century New England. See St. George, *Conversing by Signs*, ch. 2, "Embodied Spaces," and ch. 3, "Attacking Houses."

124. See Bilby, "More Than Meets the Eye."

125. This secondary meaning has also been briefly noted by Martinez-Ruiz, "Sketches of Memory," 114.

CHAPTER 7. THE JAMAICAN CREOLE HOUSE

1. Jay Edwards and Philippe Oszuscik are the two primary scholars working to understand Creole architecture; they both focus on French Creole. See Edwards, "Creole Architecture"; Edwards, "Origins of Creole Architecture," 155–89; Oszuscik, "French Creoles on the Gulf Coast," 136–56; Oszuscik, "Comparisons between Rural and Urban French Creole Housing," 1–36.

2. Higman, *Plantation Jamaica*, 192.

3. Long, *History of Jamaica*, II, 21.

4. Wright, *Lady Nugent's Journal*, 25–26, 55–57.

5. Lewis, *Journal of a West-India Proprietor*.

6. For recent scholarship on the complexities of creolization as an interpretive model, see Stewart, *Creolization*. See also Allen, "Creole: The Problem of Definition," 47–66. Work on material creolization is limited; see Mann, "Becoming Creole"; Greving, "Accounting for Lady Nugent's Creole House," 16–27; and Finneran, "'This Island Is Inhabited with All Sorts,'" 319–51.

7. Brathwaite, *Development of Creole Society*, xiv.

8. Storrow, quoted in Mann, "Becoming Creole," 118.

9. Long, *History of Jamaica*, II, 261–74.

10. Long, *History of Jamaica*, II, 261–62.

11. Long, *History of Jamaica*, II, 273, 279.

12. Long, *History of Jamaica*, II, 541.

13. Stewart, *An Account of Jamaica*, 177.

14. Greving, "Accounting for Lady Nugent's Creole House."

15. Wright, *Lady Nugent's Journal*, 76.

16. Petley, "Plantations and Homes," 446–48.

17. Fryer, *Staying Power*, 70.

18. On free blacks in Jamaica, see Brathwaite, *Development of Creole Society*, 167–75.

19. Moreton, *West India Customs*, 105.

20. Anon., *The Importance of Jamaica to Great Britain Considered*, 8.

21. Burnard, "Passengers Only."

22. The material history of Seville depends on a site analysis and field report by Ed Chappell, summarized in the Falmouth Field Guide, 2011. Chappell's assessment is verified by Armstrong. See Armstrong, "Reflections on Seville," 90–91.

23. Wright, *Lady Nugent's Journal*, 81.

24. Lewis, *Journal of a West-India Proprietor*, 56.

25. Other examples include Hamden, Minard, Arcadia, and Montpelier.

26. Stewart, *An Account of Jamaica*, 14.

27. Gosse, *A Naturalists's Sojourn in Jamaica*, 156–57.

28. Williams, *A Tour through the Island of Jamaica*, 237.

29. Other examples appearing in prints or paintings include Hamden, Arcadia, Hyde Hall, and Vale Royal.

30. For examples of this plan in the English context, see Guirard, *Life in the English Country House*, 119–40.

31. Upton, "Vernacular Domestic Architecture in Eighteenth-Century Virginia," 102–4; Wenger, "Central Passage Plan in Virginia," 137–49. For a similar discussion of these same changes on a much grander scale, see Guirard, *Life in the English Country House*, 119–62.

32. Diary of Philip Vickers Fithian (1773–74), quoted in Wenger, "Central Passage Plan in Virginia," 139.

33. *Royal Gazette*, Kingston, April 1, 1780, 211.

34. *Royal Gazette*, Kingston, April 8, 1780, 219.

35. *Jamaica Mercury and Kingston Weekly Advertiser*, May 1, 1779, 430; December 21, 1779.

36. *Jamaica Mercury and Kingston Weekly Advertiser*, May 1, 1779, 430; December 21, 1779.

37. *Royal Gazette*, Kingston, February 18, 1781, 283.

38. Moreton, *West India Customs*, 114.

39. Gosse, *A Naturalists's Sojourn in Jamaica*, 156–57.

40. Stewart, *An Account of Jamaica*, 186.

41. Jamaican Journal of Alexander Innes, 36.

42. Stewart, *An Account of Jamaica*, 186.

43. Edwards, *A History, Civil and Commercial*, II, 8.

44. Edwards, *A History, Civil and Commercial*, I, 255.

45. Cited in Burnard, *Mastery, Tyranny, and Desire*, 82.

46. Hall, *In Miserable Slavery*, 223, 302, 309.

47. Stewart, *An Account of Jamaica*, 191; see also Edwards, *A History, Civil and Commercial*, II, 279.

48. Moreton, *West India Customs*, 128.

49. Stewart, *An Account of Jamaica*, 207.

50. Hall, *In Miserable Slavery*, 252.

51. See probate inventory of James Tebber, planter, St. Andrews, 1719. National Archives of Jamaica.

52. For eighteenth-century inventories with examples of this plan, see James Herbert (1726), James Willsdon (1728), William Johnston (1740), Joseph Millward (1740), Joseph Heiser (1740), Thomas Francis (1741),

Thomas Kidd (1742), John McNeil (1750), John Wallen (1751), William Parker (1753), Sarah Houghton (1767), Sarah Seymour (1788), Series 1B 11-3, National Archives of Jamaica.

53. *The Weekly Jamaica Courant*, July 18, 1718.

54. Hall, *In Miserable Slavery*, 16.

55. Long, *History of Jamaica*, II, 21.

56. Long, *History of Jamaica*, II, 21.

57. Edwards, "The Origins of Creole Architecture," 156–89.

58. Hobson, "Domestic Architecture," 59–60.

59. Quoted in Hobson, "Domestic Architecture," 59–60.

60. See Sloane, *A Voyage to the Islands*, I: I xxi; Irene A. Wright, ed., "The English Conquest of Jamaica," in *Camden Miscellany* XIII, 3rd ser., 34 (1924): 3; Buisseret, "Fresh Light on Spanish Jamaica," 72–75.

61. Hall, *In Miserable Slavery*, 13.

62. Hall, *In Miserable Slavery*, 55, 64, 100.

63. Other examples of houses with single elevation open piazzas include: Seville, Hyde Hall, Swansey, and the Pinnacle.

64. Woods, *Glass Houses*, 39. Guirard, *Life in the English Country House*, 100–101.

65. Moreton, *West India Customs*, quoted in Buisseret, *Historic Architecture*, 22.

66. Long, *History of Jamaica*, II, 538–40.

67. Wright, *Lady Nugent's Journal*, 113, 114, 116, 125, 128, 168.

68. Wright, *Lady Nugent's Journal*, 169.

69. Quoted in Poesch, *The Art of the Old South*, 53

70. Whitefield, *An Account of the Money*, 3; Whitefield, *George Whitefield's Journals*.

71. Whitefield, *George Whitefield's Journals*, entry for June 6, 1740, 431.

72. Cashin, *Beloved Bethesda*, ch. 2.

73. Wright, *Lady Nugent's Journal*, 164.

74. *Jamaica Mercury and Kingston Weekly Advertiser*, May 1, 1779.

75. *Jamaica Mercury and Kingston Weekly Advertiser*, May 1, 1779, 360.

76. Williams, *A Tour through the Island of Jamaica*, 314.

77. Long, *History of Jamaica*, II, 313. Interestingly, Spanish builders in the Caribbean built frame houses in the sixteenth and seventeenth centuries and transitioned to stone in the eighteenth century. See Llanes, *Houses of Old Cuba*; Manucy, *Sixteenth-Century St. Augustine*.

78. Long, *History of Jamaica*, II, 313.

79. On causes of death see "Death in the Tropics," in Dunn, *Sugar and Slaves*, 300–34.

80. Burnard, "European Migration to Jamaica," 775–77.

81. Dunn, *Sugar and Slaves*, 329.

82. Leslie, *A New History of Jamaica*, 21.

83. A recent article published by Philippe Oszuscik suggests that the practices of healthfulness in architecture learned by the British in Jamaica were transferred to British West Florida after 1763. Oszuscik, "Eighteenth-Century Concerns for 'Healthy Buildings,'" 5–27.

84. Long, *History of Jamaica,* II, 509.

85. Long, *History of Jamaica,* II, 510.

86. Lilly to Ashworth, July 29, 1729, *Journal and Letterbook of Christian Lilly.*

87. Williams, *A Tour through the Island of Jamaica,* 2.

88. Phillippo, *Jamaica,* 68–69.

89. Dr. Thomas Trapham (1679), quoted in Dunn, *Sugar and Slaves,* 289.

90. Crowley, *Invention of Comfort,* 288–89.

91. Probate inventory for Robert Thurger, 1712, National Archives of Jamaica, Inventory Series 1B 11–3.

92. Probate inventory for William Sampson, 1741, National Archives of Jamaica, Inventory Series, 1B 11–3.

93. Probate inventory for William Lodge, 1714, National Archives of Jamaica, Inventory Series 1B 11–3.

94. Probate inventory for Hannah Sanders, 1742; probate inventory for George Roberts, 1750, National Archives of Jamaica, Inventory Series 1B 11–3.

95. Probate inventory for Mathias Philpsale, 1750, National Archives of Jamaica, Inventory Series 1B 11–3.

96. Probate inventory for Sarah Seymour, 1788, National Archives of Jamaica, Inventory Series 1B 11–3.

97. Williams, *A Tour through the Island of Jamaica,* 8.

98. Williams, *A Tour through the Island of Jamaica,* 314.

99. Long, *History of Jamaica,* II, 21

100. Wright, *Lady Nugent's Journal,* 110–11, 162–63.

101. Wright, *Lady Nugent's Journal,* 53, 90, 95, 154, 156, 158-59, 162, 167.

102. Higman, *Jamaica Surveyed,* 242.

103. Wright, *Lady Nugent's Journal,* 122.

104. Storrow to sister, 1792, quoted in Mann, "Becoming Creole," 81.

105. Wright, *Lady Nugent's Journal,* 84.

106. Wright, *Lady Nugent's Journal,* 54.

107. Wright, *Lady Nugent's Journal,* 208.

108. Long, *History of Jamaica,* II, 47.

109. Wright, *Lady Nugent's Journal,* 225.

110. Long, *History of Jamaica,* II, 21.

111. Anon., *A Short Journey in the West Indies,* 34.

112. Wright, *Lady Nugent's Journal,* 117.

113. John MacLeod, *Narrative of a voyage in his majesty's late ship* Alceste, *to the Yellow Sea* (1817), cited in Wright, *Lady Nugent's Journal,* 155.

114. Williams, *A Tour through the Island of Jamaica,* 44

115. Probate inventory for Richard Moore, 1739, National Archives of Jamaica.

116. Probate inventory for George Roberts, 1750, National Archives of Jamaica.

117. Probate inventory for Mathias Philpsale, 1750, National Archives of Jamaica.

118. *Jamaica Mercury and Kingston Weekly Advertiser,* May 1, 1779.

119. *Jamaica Mercury and Kingston Weekly Advertiser,* May 1, 1779.

120. National Archives of Jamaica, 1B/11/3, vol. 28, folios 58–63, November 7, 1748.

121. Gontar, "The Campeche Chair," 183–212. For recent work on Thomas Jefferson's Campeche chairs, see Priddy, Erby, and Huffman, "The one Mrs. Trist would chuse."

122. Long, *History of Jamaica,* II, 84.

123. Stewart, *An Account of Jamaica,* 14.

124. Lewis, *Journal of a West-India Proprietor,* 84–85.

125. Moreton, *West India Customs,* 129.

126. Moreton, *West India Customs,* 129.

127. Burnard, *Mastery, Tyranny, and Desire,* 156–60.

128. Brathwaite, *Development of Creole Society,* 110.

129. Burnard, *Mastery, Tyranny, and Desire,* 160–61. See also Hall, *In Miserable Slavery,* 118.

130. Higman, *Plantation Jamaica,* 79, 80, 144.

131. Robertson, *Gone Is the Ancient Glory;* for the Spanish Caribbean, see Manucy, *Sixteenth-Century St. Augustine,* 87; Llanes, *The Houses of Old Cuba,* 41.

132. *Jamaica Mercury and Kingston Weekly Advertiser,* May 1, 1779, 430; December 21, 1779.

133. Stewart, *An Account of Jamaica,* 14.

134. Other examples include Minard, Georgia, Belle Isle, and Fontabelle.

135. Moreton, *West India Customs,* 24.

136. Moreton, *West India Customs,* 109.

137. Williams, *A Tour through the Island of Jamaica,* 45.

138. See another account in Williams, *A Tour through the Island of Jamaica,* 8.

139. Long *History of Jamaica,* II, 114.

140. Long, *History of Jamaica,* II, 22.

141. Williams, *A Tour through the Island of Jamaica,* 2.

142. Lewis, *Journal of a West-India Proprietor,* January 28, 1816, 149.

143. Pocius, *A Place to Belong.* See also Pocius, "Parlors, Pump Houses and Pickups."

144. Examples from the Storer Sketchbook include Blackheath and Ashton.

145. Inventories of William Sampson (1741), Matthias Philpsale (1750), William Duncan (1751), William James (1811), nos. 22, 30, 111, Series 1B 11-3, National Archives of Jamaica.

146. Burnard, *Mastery, Tyranny, and Desire,* 80.

147. Beckford and Thistlewood quoted in Burnard, *Mastery, Tyranny, and Desire,* 79, 80.

148. Burnard, *Mastery Tyranny, and Desire,* 250.

149. Quoted in Burnard, *Mastery, Tyranny, and Desire,* 74–79.

150. Burnard and Morgan, "Dynamics of the Slave Market," 205. See also Dunn, *Sugar and Slaves,* 164–65.

151. Dunn, *Sugar and Slaves,* 256.

152. Hayden Bassett, personal communication, August 28, 2014, based on summer 2014 excavation season.

153. Long, *History of Jamaica,* II, 279.

154. Special thanks to Fraser Neiman and Jillian Galle for numerous conversations that led us to these hypotheses.

155. For the impact of the American Revolution on the Caribbean, see O'Shaughnessy, *An Empire Divided.*

156. The introduction of mangos and breadfruit from India to Jamaica was a partial response to the need for inexpensive foodstuffs for enslaved Africans. O'Shaughnessey, *An Empire Divided.*

157. Higman, *Plantation Jamaica,* 18–19.

158. Ragatz, *Fall of the Planter Class.*

159. Higman, *Plantation Jamaica,* 111.

160. Stewart, *Creolization,* 8.

CHAPTER 8. ARCHITECTURES OF FREEDOM

1. This history of Somerville's house depends on documentary research undertaken by a 2010 University of Virginia research team and on-site analysis by the Falmouth Field School. Somerville purchased this lot unimproved in 1836; careful examination of the material fabric of the building indicates that it was built soon thereafter. See Samuel Barrett Moulton Barrett to Elizabeth Somerville. Deeds, Island Record Office, vol. 806, folio 172.

2. The documentary evidence points to a shift toward box framing in the early nineteenth century among slave quarters as well. See Armstrong, *The Old Village and the Great House,* 96. On box framing, see Upton, "Traditional Timber Framing," 35–93. See also Graham, "Preindustrial Framing in the Chesapeake," 179–96; Graham, "Timber Framing," in Carson and Lounsbury, *The Chesapeake House,* 206–38.

3. Brathwaite, *Development of Creole Society,* 167–75. Long suggests that free blacks were either favored domestics or skilled slaves who purchased their own freedom. See Long, *History of Jamaica,* II, 322.

4. Mann, "Becoming Creole," 41.

5. For seventeenth-century free blacks in

Spanish Town, see Robertson, *Gone Is the Ancient Glory*, 50. On free blacks in the Caribbean, see Cohen and Green, eds, *Neither Slave nor Free*. See also Welch and Goodridge, *"Red" and Black over White*.

6. Quoted in Brathwaite, *Development of Creole Society*, 105.

7. Brathwaite, *Development of Creole Society*, 186, 187, 191, 196; Burnard, *Mastery, Tyranny, and Desire*, 81.

8. Heuman, *Between Black and White*, 9.

9. Higman, *Slave Population and Economy in Jamaica*, 101, 146. See also Brathwaite, *Development of Creole Society*, 169. For comparative data on free blacks in urban centers see Welch, *Slave Society in the City*, 177–80.

10. Robertson, *Gone Is the Ancient Glory*, 91.

11. Mann, "Becoming Creole," 40. See also Pons, *History of the Caribbean*, 205, 317.

12. Bailey, "Social Control in the Pre-Emancipation Society of Kingston," 95–105.

13. For a similar examination in a different West Indian town, see Geggus, "Major Port Towns of Saint-Domingue," 87–116.

14. Conolley and Parrent, "Land Deeds That Tell the Story," 383–409.

15. For published work on free blacks in Falmouth, see Conolley and Parrent, "Land Deeds That Tell the Story."

16. The canonical work, of course, is Vlach, "The Shotgun House: An African American Legacy" (1976). More recent work includes Jones, "The African-American Tradition in Vernacular Architecture"; Sobel, *The World They Made Together*; Ferguson, *Uncommon Ground*; Vlach, *By the Work of Their Hands*; and Anthony, "The Big House and the Slave Quarters."

17. Thus far the Falmouth Field School has identified and recorded seven small board houses that are convincingly of an early nineteenth-century date. On the Jamaican board house as an early nineteenth-century building type, see Hennings, "Miss Rosie's House." The small houses recorded in Falmouth are part of a larger architectural phenomenon across the Caribbean. For broad discussions of the Caribbean board house, see Doran, "West Indian Hip-Roofed Cottage," 97–104; Edwards, "The Evolution of Vernacular Architecture," 291–92; and Berthelot and Gaume, *Caribbean Popular Dwelling*. Broader popular histories of architecture that touch on these buildings include Crain, *Historic Architecture in the Caribbean Islands*; Buisseret, *Historic Architecture of the Caribbean*, 1–4; Gravette, *Architectural Heritage of the Caribbean*, 38–43.

18. See Vlach, "Shotgun House" (1976);

Ferguson, *Uncommon Ground*; Armstrong, *The Old Village and the Great House*, 93; Pabon, "Por la encendida calle antilana," 14–32.

19. Burnard and Morgan, "Dynamics of the Slave Market," 207.

20. *Columbian Magazine or Monthly Miscellany*, April 1797.

21. Higman, *Montpelier*, 183.

22. Higman, *Montpelier*, 184.

23. Higman, *Montpelier*, 184–85.

24. Brathwaite, *Development of Creole Society*, 155.

25. Roberts further points out that this trend of increasing rates of skilled labor ran contrary to the prevailing trends among laborers in industrial England. Roberts, *Slavery and the Enlightenment*, 209.

26. Quoted in Higman, *Montpelier*, 180.

27. Edwards, *A History, Civil and Commercial*, II, 165.

28. Lewis, *Journal of a West-India Proprietor*, January 10, 1816, 56.

29. Higman, *Montpelier*, 180.

30. Hall, *In Miserable Slavery*, 149.

31. Burnard, *Mastery, Tyranny, and Desire*, 190, 231–33.

32. Conolley, "Deployment of Forced Labor," 130.

33. Higman, *Montpelier*, 160

34. Jillian Galle believes that her archaeological evidence suggests that Stewart Castle had more wattle and daub in the eighteenth century and timber-framing with brick or masonry infill, or Spanish wall, in the nineteenth century. Personal communication, 2011.

35. Higman, *Montpelier*, 151.

36. Higman, *Montpelier*, 152.

37. Armstrong, *The Old Village and the Great House*, 95.

38. Higman, *Montpelier*, 162–63.

39. Ferguson, *Uncommon Ground*, 62–83; Chapman, "Slave Villages in the Danish West Indies"; Handler and Lange, *Plantation Slavery in Barbados*; Goveia, *Slave Society in the British Leeward Islands*.

40. Ferguson, *Uncommon Ground*, 62–83; see also Wheaton, "Colonial African American Plantation Villages," 30–44.

41. Higman, *Montpelier*, 150.

42. Higman, *Montpelier*, 171.

43. Higman, *Montpelier*, 148.

44. For more on platforms, see Higman, *Montpelier*, 173–74.

45. Phillippo, *Jamaica*, 221.

46. Wright, *Lady Nugent's Journal*, March 18, 1802, 75.

47. For a South Carolina example, see Joseph, "From Colonial to Charlestonian," 215–34.

48. Robertson, *Gone Is the Ancient Glory*, 86.

49. Welch, *Slave Society in the City*, 179.

50. Higman, *Slave Populations of the British Caribbean*, 255. See also Welch, *Slave Society in the City*, 49.

51. Stewart, *A View of the Past and Present State*. Quoted in Pulsipher, "The Landscapes and Ideational Roles of Caribbean Slave Gardens," 213.

52. For a discussion of the competition between the least prosperous of the free blacks and urban enslaved laborers, see Hall, "Slavery in Three West Indian Towns," 445.

53. Slaves also harbored runaways for long periods of time. See Burnard, *Mastery, Tyranny, and Desire*, 165.

54. *Jamaica Mercury and Kingston Weekly Advertiser*, May 14, 1779, 32, "Kingston May 14, 1779."

55. Robertson, *Gone Is the Ancient Glory*, 87.

56. Burnard, *Mastery, Tyranny, and Desire*, 210.

57. For discussions of "passive resistance," see Patterson, *Sociology of Slavery*, and Schuler, "Day to Day Resistance," 57–75. For an interesting example of passive resistance, see Buckridge, *The Language of Dress*, 67–110. The definitive work on resistance, however, is Craton, "Forms of Resistance to Slavery," 222–70, and Craton, *Testing the Chains*. In using the term "resistance," I do so familiar with Michel de Certeau's distinction between resistance and opposition; see de Certeau, "On the Opposition," 3–43, and de Certeau, *Practice of Everyday Life*. A recent revision of the concepts of resistance, slavery, and freedom appears in Dunkley, *Agency of the Enslaved*.

58. As quoted in Brathwaite, *Development of Creole Society*, 223. *Buckra* was a common term for white overseer or master.

59. Hall, *In Miserable Slavery*, 92.

60. Brathwaite, *Development of Creole Society*, 201.

61. Upton, "White and Black Landscapes," 59–72.

62. Higman, *Montpelier*, 144.

63. Hall, *In Miserable Slavery*, 183.

64. Delle, "Habitus of Jamaican Plantation Landscapes," 138.

65. *Columbian Magazine or Monthly Miscellany*, April 1797.

66. Smith, *Caribbean Rum*.

67. Long, *History of Jamaica*, II, 85.

68. See Campbell, *The Maroons of Jamaica*, and Thompson, *Flight to Freedom*, 308–9.

69. Dallas, *History of the Maroons*, 40–41.

70. Thomas Neale inventory. Inventories, National Archives of Jamaica, vol. 83, folio 262.

71. Edward Barrett to Sarah McGhie, October 10, 1793. Deeds, Island Record Office, vol. 416, folio 68.

72. James McGhie inventory, April 18, 1807. Inventories, National Archives of Jamaica, vol. 108, folio 131.

73. Mary Gairdner will, March 3, 1837. Wills, Island Record Office, vol. 117, folio 143.

74. John Baillie to Mary Gardner [sic], October 1, 1800. Deeds, Island Record Office, vol. 505, folio 154.

75. Mary Gairdner will, March 3, 1837. Wills, Island Record Office, vol. 117, folio 143.

76. Welch, *Slave Society in the City*, 18, 48.

77. Welch, *Slave Society in the City*, 178.

78. Zacek and Brown, "Unsettled Houses."

79. For small houses in early nineteenth-century New Orleans and free women of color, see Edwards, "Shotgun," 62–96. See also Welch, *Slave Society in the City*, 169.

80. Welch, *Slave Society in the City*, 187–89.

81. Moreton, quoted in Brathwaite, *Development of Creole Society*, 305.

82. *Columbian Magazine or Monthly Miscellany*, quoted in Mann, "Becoming Creole," 202.

83. Burnard, *Mastery, Tyranny, and Desire*, 57, 211, 228–37.

84. Hall, *In Miserable Slavery*, 198.

85. Hall, *In Miserable Slavery*, 219.

86. Burnard, *Mastery, Tyranny, and Desire*, 237.

87. George Goodin Barrett will, March 6, 1797. Wills, Island Record Office, 63–157.

88. Martin, "*Placage* and the Louisiana *Gens de Couleur Libre*," 57–70. Jay Edwards has found a compelling correspondence between small, well-built houses in early nineteenth-century New Orleans and free women of color. He hypothesizes that these houses were built for free women of color by white men bound to these women through the institution of *placage*, not quite marriage or concubinage. The evidence is thus far inconclusive for a similar relational dynamic in Falmouth. See Edwards, "Shotgun," 62–96.

89. Welch, *Slave Society in the City*, 182.

90. For work on these buildings across the Caribbean, see Berthelot and Gaume, *Caribbean Popular Dwelling*. See also Pulsipher and Wells-Bowie, "Domestic Spaces of Daufuskie and Monserrat," 2–29. For an argument that the building type is European in origin, see Doran, "West Indian Hip-Roofed Cottage," 97–104.

91. Vlach, "Shotgun House: An African Architectural Legacy" (1986), 58–78.

92. Edwards, "Shotgun."

93. The persistence of an Afrocentric view of Afro-Caribbean culture has been critiqued in the very sensitive and thoughtful introduction by Carolyn Allen in Shepherd and Richards, *Questioning Creole*. For a critique of finding Africanisms in the work of African American artisans, see Prown, "The Furniture of Thomas Day," 215–49.

94. For examples, see Berthelot and Gaume, *Caribbean Popular Dwelling*, and Vlach, "Shotgun House (1976)." See also Gravette, *Architectural Heritage of the Caribbean*, 38–43.

95. For a broad overview of black resistance to British slavery, see Craton, *Testing the Chains*.

CHAPTER 9. BUILDING IN BRITAIN

1. The history of the West India Docks is best told in the survey by English Heritage: Hobhouse, ed., "The West India Docks: Historical Development," *Survey of London: Poplar, Blackwell, and Isle of Dogs*, vols. 43 and 44, 248–68.

2. Harewood House is often touted as the great British country house built on a fortune made in the Caribbean. See Smith, *Slavery, Family, and Gentry Capitalism*.

3. Higman, "The Sugar Revolution," 213–36. Hancock, *Citizens of the World*.

4. Jacobsen, *William Blathwayt*.

5. See Kenseth, *Age of the Marvelous*; Impey and MacGregor, eds., *The Origins of Museums*.

6. Kenseth, *Age of the Marvelous*, 29–36. On the "naturalness" of Africans see Jordan, *White over Black: American Attitudes towards the Negro*, 3–44.

7. The presumption of authority and control embedded in collection proceeded from the earlier Wunderkammer drive toward universal knowledge. See Kenseth, *Age of the Marvelous*, 83–84.

8. Garnett, *Dyrham Park*, 9.

9. Long, *History of Jamaica*, II, 87.

10. An excellent and sophisticated discussion of this subject appears in Molineux, *Faces of Perfect Ebony*.

11. See Bindman, "The Black Presence in British Art," 253–70, and Massing, *The Image of the Black in Western Art*, 225–60. On African slaves as exotics, see Walvin, *Making the Black Atlantic*, 105–7.

12. Amussen, *Caribbean Exchanges*, 191–217.

13. Bindman, "The Black Presence in British Art," 255–56.

14. Massing, *The Image of the Black in Western Art*, 384–94.

15. Peter Bradshaw, *Bow Porcelain Figures, 1748–1774* (London: Barrie and Jenkins, 1992), fig. 216.

16. Childs, "Sugar Boxes and Blackamoors," 159–78.

17. Bindman and Weston, "Court and City: Fantasies of Domination," 133–48, 159–70.

18. Molineux, *Faces of Perfect Ebony*, 67–72.

19. Dresser, *Slavery Obscured*, 72–81; Walvin, *Making the Black Atlantic*, 113.

20. Walvin, *Making the Black Atlantic*, 107–12.

21. Bindman and Weston, "Court and City: Fantasies of Domination," 147–48, 160–64.

22. Anderson, *Mahogany*; Bowett, "The Commercial Introduction of Mahogany," 42–56; Bowett, "The English Mahogany Trade."

23. Anderson, *Mahogany*, 65.

24. Brown, "Atlantic Slavery and Classical Culture at Marble Hill and Northington Grange," 91–101.

25. Anes, "Accounting and Slavery," 441–52; Brown, "Atlantic Slavery and Classical Culture at Marble Hill," 10.

26. Brown, "Atlantic Slavery and Classical Culture at Marble Hill," 17.

27. Casid, *Sowing Empire*, 45–94; Woods and Warren, *Glass Houses*, 34.

28. Jeffery, "The Flower of All the Private Gentlemen's Palaces in England," 14–15. On Dyrham Park and early modern greenhouses, Woods and Warren, *Glass Houses*, 43–46.

29. Dunn, *Sugar and Slaves*, 278.

30. Stephen Switzer, quoted in Woods and Warren, *Glass Houses*, 46.

31. This collection became the *Blathwayt Atlas* and forms the core of the huge Blathwayt collection now in the John Carter Brown Library at Brown University. See Black, ed., *The Blathwayt Atlas*.

32. Casid, *Sowing Empire*.

33. Brockway, *Science and Colonial Expansion*.

34. Mauchline, *Harewood House*, 101–5.

35. Casid, *Sowing Empire*, 53–57.

36. Ward, "British West Indies in the Age of Abolition," 421–22.

37. Davis, *Rise of the Atlantic Economies*, 251.

38. Mintz, *Sweetness and Power*, 39.

39. Palmer, "Port Economics in an Historical Context."

40. Higman, "Jamaican Port Towns," 120.

41. Despite transatlantic involvement, the dispute was eventually settled in favor of Spanish Town. On the wealth of Kingston, see Burnard, "'The Grand Mart of the Island," 225–41. See also Burnard, "Elephants Colliding," 9–10. A lengthy account appears first in Metcalf, *Royal Government and Political Conflict in Jamaica*. On the relationship of this dispute and the rebuilding of Spanish Town, see Robertson, *Gone Is the Ancient Glory*, 89–93.

42. Hall, "John Knight" 110–64.

43. Hall, "John Knight," 119.

44. Dresser, *Slavery Obscured*, 20.

45. Hall, "Temple St. Sugar House," 118–40.

46. Hall, "Temple St. Sugar House," 128–30.

47. Hall, "Whitson Court Sugar House," 49–52.

48. Refineries were not limited to Bristol. Glasgow's first manifestation of the Caribbean trade was also the construction of a series of sugar refineries, the first in 1667, the second in 1669, and another in 1700. Smout, "Early Scottish Sugar Houses," 240–53. See also Nisbet, "The Sugar Adventurers of Glasgow," 26–33.

49. The same is also true of Glasgow. Hall, "Whitson Court Sugar House," 56.

50. Hall, "Whitson Court Sugar House," 1–97.

51. Hall, "Whitson Court Sugar House," 61.

52. Richardson, *Bristol, Africa, and the Eighteenth-Century Slave Trade to America*, I, xv. For a discussion of the port of London in the late seventeenth century, see Zahedieh, *The Capital and the Colonies*, 166–73.

53. Dresser, *Slavery Obscured*, esp. ch. 1.

54. Minchinton. *The Port of Bristol*, 2–3.

55. Dresser, *Slavery Obscured*, 100.

56. Minchinton. *The Port of Bristol*, 11.

57. Quoted in Picton, *Memorials of Liverpool*, 225.

58. Dresser, *Slavery Obscured*, 101–2.

59. Dresser, *Slavery Obscured*, 105. See also Borsay, *English Urban Renaissance*, 73–75.

60. Dresser, *Slavery Obscured*, 100–111.

61. The most comprehensive discussion of the Bristol Exchange is Roger Leech, "An Historical and Architectural Analysis of the Exchange Building, Corn Street, Bristol" (unpublished report for the City of Bristol, 1999).

62. On the history of the Bristol Exchange, see Mowl and Earnshaw, *John Wood*, 149–64. For the architect's view of the design and construction, see Wood, *A Description of the Exchange of Bristol*.

63. Wood, *A Description of the Exchange of Bristol*, 22.

64. Minchinton. *The Port of Bristol*, 18–22.

65. Richardson, *Bristol, Africa, and the Eighteenth-Century Slave Trade to America*.

66. Richardson, "Liverpool and the English Slave Trade," 73.

67. Wadsworth and Mann, *The Cotton Trade of Industrial Lancashire*, 212, 227–28.

68. Corry, *History of Liverpool*, 101–3.

69. Corry, *History of Liverpool*, 109.

70. Corry, *History of Liverpool*, 114.

71. Corry, *History of Liverpool*, 123.

72. Corry, *History of Liverpool*, 286–87.

73. Freemantle, *The Baroque Town Hall*, 28–32.

74. Quoted in Burnard, "Elephants Colliding," 18.

75. Italics mine. Cited in Picton, *Memorials of Liverpool,* 225. For other examples, see Baines, *History of the Commerce and Town.*

76. For a similar anxiety in English portraiture, see Massing, *The Image of the Black in Western Art*, vol. III, pt. 3, "The Eighteenth Century," 135.

77. See Hamilton, *Scotland, The Caribbean, and the Atlantic World.*

78. Smith, *Slavery, Family, and Gentry Capitalism*, 179.

79. Cooke, "An Elite Revisited," 148.

80. Green, *The Eighteenth-Century Architecture of Bath.*

81. Mowl and Earnshow, *John Wood*, 198–204.

82. Quoted in Walvin, *Making the Black Atlantic*, 106.

83. Smith, *Slavery, Family, and Gentry Capitalism.*

84. One of the first historians to gesture to the clear socioeconomic implications of the interconnectedness of motherland and colony was David Hancock. His monumental *Citizens of the World* unveiled the social and financial lives of a circle of British-born, mid-eighteenth-century merchants, revealing their involvement in numerous overseas financial ventures, including ownership of Jamaican plantations. Hancock, *Citizens of the World*, 279. And most recently, in preparation for the bicentenary of the 1807 abolition of the slave trade, English Heritage hosted a groundbreaking conference, "Slavery and the British Country House," in which a range of scholars pointed to the extensive network of interconnections between the British elite and the Caribbean. This project has resulted in the recent publication of Madge Dresser and Andrew Hann's important edited collection. See Dresser and Hann, eds., *Slavery and the British Country House.*

85. By the time of his death in 1770 Beckford owned thirteen plantations and three thousand slaves. For the wealth of the Beckford family, see an article on his cousin of the same name in Sheridan, "Planter and Historian," 36–58. See also Sheridan's entry on Alderman William Beckford in the *Oxford Dictionary of National Biography*. On Drax Hall, see Armstrong, *The Old Village and the Great House.*

86. Ostergard, ed., *William Beckford*, 140.

87. The most complete discussion of the house appears in Hewat-Jaboor, "Fonthill House," 51–71.

88. Britton, *Graphical and Literary Illustrations of Fonthill Abbey*, 25.

89. Hewat-Jaboor, "Fonthill House," 53.

90. Quoted in Hewat-Jaboor, "Fonthill House," 55.

91. Burnard, "Passengers Only," 186.

92. Hewat-Jaboor, "Fonthill House," 56.

93. For Wildman's biography, see James Beckford Wildman in the Database of British Slave-ownership: http://www.ucl.ac.uk/lbs/person/view/16372. See also Hasted, *History and Topographical Survey of Kent*, vol. VII, 1798, p. 276; vol. VIII, p. 544; see also Killingray, "Kent and the Abolition of the Slave Trade," 107–25.

94. See Richard Walker in James Watt Walker biography in the Database of British Slave-ownership: http://www.ucl.ac.uk/lbs/person/view/43237.

95. See John Fuller biography in the Database of British Slave-ownership: http://www.ucl.ac.uk/lbs/person/view/-1047169191.

96. Thackray, *Bodiam Castle*, 25.

97. For Gordon's biography, see entry for Charles Gordon seventh of Buthlaw and first of Cairness (1747–1797), on http://www.clanmacfarlanegenealogy.info.

98. For the biographies of John and Francis Grant, see Francis Grant in the Database of British Slave-ownership: http://www.ucl.ac.uk/lbs/person/view/1317639698. See also Burke's *Commoners*, vol. 2, p. 613, "Grant of Kilgraston."

99. See George Pennant biography in the Database of British Slave-ownership: http://www.ucl.ac.uk/lbs/person/view/22227.

100. For Beckford's changes to his father's house, see Hewat-Jaboor, "Fonthill House," 59–71.

101. Gikandi, *Slavery and the Culture of Taste*, 131–32.

102. Lees-Milne, *William Beckford*, 113.

103. On the history of the house see Purchas, "Maurice-Louis Jolivet's Drawings at West Wycombe Park," 68–79.

104. Knox, *West Wycombe Park*. On James Dawkins, see Kelly, *Society of the Dilettanti*, 195–203.

105. See Purchas, "Maurice-Louis Jolivet's Drawings at West Wycombe Park," 68–79. For Donowell, see Colvin, *A Biographical Dictionary of British Architects*, 269–70.

106. See John Gladstone biography in the Database of British Slave-ownership: http://www.ucl.ac.uk/lbs/person/view/8961.

107. *Liverpool Post*, April 9, 1913.

108. See John Jarrett biography in the Database of British Slave-ownership: http://www.ucl.ac.uk/lbs/person/view/23686.

109. Perry, "Slavery and the Sublime," 102–12.

110. These include Beckford, *A Descriptive Account of the Island of Jamaica: with Remarks Upon the Cultivation of the Sugar-cane . . . and Chiefly Considered In a Picturesque Point of View; Also, Observations and Reflections Upon What Would Probably Be the Consequences*

of an Abolition of the Slave-trade, and of the
Emancipation of the Slaves, published in 1790;
Edwards, A History, Civil and Commercial,
of the British Colonies in the West Indies
(1793); and Moreton, West India Customs and
Manners (1793).

111. Barringer et al., Art and Emancipation in
Jamaica, 335.

112. Walvin, Making the Black Atlantic, 111.

113. Burnard has offered an extensive assessment of the interconnectedness of Kingston
and London merchants. See Burnard,
"Passengers Only," 189–91.

114. O'Shaughnessey, An Empire Divided, 15.

115. January 1, 1775, letter cited in Hall, A Brief
History of the West India Committee, 5.

116. See Penson, "The London West India
Interest in the Eighteenth Century," 373–92;
and Higman, "The West India Interest in
Parliament, 1807–1833," 1–19.

117. Whinney, Home House: No. 20 Portman
Square.

118. Summerson, Georgian London. See also
Lewis, "Elizabeth, Countess of Home,"
443–51, 453. For a deeper examination of the
interior, see Harris, The Genius of Robert
Adam: His Interiors.

119. Cited in Lewis, "Elizabeth, Countess of
Home," 447.

120. A thorough biography of Lady Home
appears in the opening pages of Lewis,
"Elizabeth, Countess of Home."

121. Lewis, "Elizabeth, Countess of Home."
Surviving in Sir John Soane's museum is a
Robert Adam drawing entitled "Frame for
the Duke of Cumberland's Picture for the
Countess of Home," complete with a canopy
and surely intended for the only open
spaces left by Robert Adam in the grand
drawing room. And, most convincingly,
Anne, the Duchess of Cumberland, was the
daughter of Lady Home's sister-in-law via
her first husband. See Tait, "Home House."

122. See Thorold, The London Rich, 134–45.

123. Thorold, The London Rich, 137.

124. Robinson, James Wyatt, Architect to
George III.

125. Cited in Hayes, "The Black Atlantic and
Georgian London," 150.

126. See Hayes, "The Black Atlantic and
Georgian London," 137–60, esp. 150–57.

127. Thorold, The London Rich, 143–44.

128. Quoted in Hayes, "The Black Atlantic and
Georgian London," 155–56.

129. Pearsall, "The Late Flagrant Instance of
Depravity in My Family," 572.

130. Thorold, The London Rich, 145.

131. Pares, Merchants and Planters, 38.

132. Hobhouse, "The West India Docks," 248–68.

133. The Times of London, August 28, 1802, 2–3.

See also The Morning Chronicle, London,
August 28, 1802.

134. Ward, "British West Indies in the Age of
Abolition," 421–22.

135. Substance of the Memorial, 1822, p. 12, cited
in Barringer et al., Art and Emancipation in
Jamaica, 273.

Bibliography

UNPUBLISHED PRIMARY SOURCE MATERIALS
The Bodleian Library, Oxford
Letterbook of the Company of Merchants Trading to Africa

British Library
CAMPBELL, ARCHIBALD. "Survey of the South Coast of Jamaica," 1782.
KNIGHT, JAMES. *Portions of a History of Jamaica to 1742*, BL, Add. Ms. 12417.
Columbian Magazine or Monthly Miscellany
General Evening Post
Journal and Letter Book of Christian Lilly, BL, Add. Ms. 12427.
London Evening Post
Morning Post and Daily Advertiser
Morning Star
The Weekly Jamaica Courant, September 12, 1722.

Cambridgeshire Archives
George II to Thomas Williams, August 2, 1742.

Institute of Jamaica
HART, RICHARD. "Good Hope, Jamaica, 1744–1994."

Island Record Office, Kingston, Jamaica
Deeds, Probates and Wills

Jamaica National Heritage Trust
National Archives of Jamaica, Spanish Town
John Stogdon ship manifest, April 15, 1794.
Wills and Inventories, Series 1B

National Library of Jamaica
Cornwall Chronicle
The Falmouth Gossip
Jamaica Council Minutes Ms. 60

Public Record Office, Kew, London
1706 St. Kitts. CO 243/2/34.

South Carolina Historical Society
Alexander Crawford daybook

Elizabeth Sindry Account Books
South Carolina Gazette

University of the West Indies (UWI), West Indies Collections
Jamaican Journal of Alexander Innes of Loanhead near Rathven, Banffshire, 1823–1834. National Library of Scotland Ms. 17956 (UWI Library, West Indies Collections, Microfilm 3518).
Jamaica Mercury and Kingston Weekly Advertiser, Microfilm 962.
Royal Gazette, Kingston, Microfilm 983.
Savanna-la-Mar Gazette

PUBLISHED MATERIALS
D'ALBARET, M. *Différents projets relatifs au climat et à la manière la plus convenable de bâtir dans les pays chauds, et plus particulièrement dans les Indes occidentales* (Paris, 1776).
ANONYMOUS. *The Art of Making Sugar*. London: R. Willock, 1752.
ANONYMOUS. *The Importance of Jamaica to Great Britain Considered.* London, 1740.
ANONYMOUS. *Journals of the Assembly of Jamaica*, vol. 5 (1757–1766), Jamaica, 1798.
ANONYMOUS. *The Laws of Jamaica, 1760–1792.* St. Jago de la Vega, Jamaica: Printed by A. Aikman, 1792.
ANONYMOUS. "London Apprentices Declar." In *The Harleian Miscellany* 8, 571/2 (1746).
ANONYMOUS. *A Short Journey in the West Indies in which are interspersed, curious anecdotes and characters. In two volumes*, vol. 2. London: Printed for the author, and sold by J. Murray and J. Forbes, 1790.
ATWOOD, THOMAS. *The history of the island of Dominica, containing a description of its situation, extent, climate, mountains, rivers, natural productions etc. etc., together with an account of the civil government, trade, laws, customs and manners of different inhabitants of that island, its conquest by the French and restoration to the British Dominions.* London, 1791.
BAINES, THOMAS. *History of the commerce and town of Liverpool, and of the rise of the manufacturing industry in the adjoining counties.* London: Longman, Brown, Green, and Longmans, 1852.
BARBOT, JOHN. *A Description of the Coasts of North and South Guinea*, 5 vols. London, 1732.
BAYLEY, FREDERICK WILLIAM NAYLOR. *Four Years Residence in the West Indies.* London: W. Kidd, 1830.

BECKFORD, WILLIAM. *A Descriptive Account of the Island of Jamaica: with Remarks Upon the Cultivation of the Sugar-cane, Throughout the Different Seasons of the Year, and Chiefly Considered In a Picturesque Point of View; Also, Observations and Reflections Upon What Would Probably Be the Consequences of an Abolition of the Slave-trade, and of the Emancipation of the Slaves.* London: Printed for T. and J. Egerton, 1790.

BRITTON, JOHN. *Graphical and Literary Illustrations of Fonthill Abbey, Wiltshire: with heraldical and genealogical notices of the Beckford family.* London: Printed for the author, 1823.

BROWNE, PATRICK. *The Civil and Natural History of Jamaica.* London: Sold by B. White and Son, 1756.

BURKE, JOHN. *A genealogical and heraldic history of the commoners of Great Britain and Ireland enjoying territorial possessions or high official rank; but uninvested with heritable honours.* London: Colburn, 1836.

BURKE, JOHN. *A General and Heraldic Dictionary of the Peerage and Baronetage of the British Empire.* London: H. Colburn and R. Bentley, 1832.

BURNET, GILBERT. *Some letters, containing an account of what seemed most remarkable in travelling through Switzerland, Italy, some parts of Germany, &c. in the years 1685 and 1686.* London: Printed and to be sold by J. Robinson, 1689.

CLARKSON, THOMAS. *Letters on the Slave-Trade: And the State of the Natives in Those Parts of Africa, Which Are Contiguous to Fort St. Louis and Goree, Written at Paris in December 1789, and January 1790. By T. Clarkson.* London: Printed and sold by James Phillips, George Yard, Lombard Street, 1791.

CORRY, JOHN. *The History of Liverpool: From the Earliest Authenticated Period Down to the Present Times.* Liverpool: W. Robinson, 1810.

CUGOANO, OTTOBAH. *Thoughts and Sentiments on the Evil and Wicked Traffic of the Slavery and Commerce of the Human Species: Humbly Submited to the Inhabitants of Great-Britain by Ottobah Cugoano, a Native of Africa. London, July 1787.* London: Sold by T. Becket, bookseller, Pall-Mall; also by Mr. Hall, at No. 25, Princes-Street, Soho; Mr. Phillips, George-Yard, Lombard-Street; and by the author, at Mr. Cosway's, No. 88, Pall-Mall, 1787.

EDWARDS, BRYAN. *A History, Civil and Commercial, of the British Colonies in the West Indies.* 2nd ed. Dublin, 1793.

EDWARDS, BRYAN, ED. *Journals of the Assembly of Jamaica*, vol. 5 (1757–1766). Alexander Aikman, Jamaica, 1798.

EQUIANO, OLAUDAH. *Interesting Narrative of the Life of Olaudah Equiano: Or Gustavus Vassa the African. Written by Himself.* Norwich, 1794.

FALCONBRIDGE, ALEXANDER. *Account of the Slave Trade on the Coast of Africa.* London: J. Phillips, 1788.

GOSSE, PHILIP. *A Naturalist's Sojourn in Jamaica.* London: Longman, Brown, Green and Longmans, 1851.

HAKEWILL, JAMES. *A Picturesque Tour of the Island of Jamaica.* London: Hurst and Robinson, 1834.

HASTED, EDWARD. *History and Topographical Survey of Kent.* Canterbury: Printed by Simmons and Kirkby, 1778.

HICKEY, WILLIAM. *Memoirs of William Hickey*, edited by Alfred Spencer. London: Hurst & Blackett, 1913.

KELLY, JAMES. *Voyage to Jamaica, and seventeen years' residence in that island: chiefly written with a view to exhibit Negro life and habits; with extracts from Sturge and Harvey's "West Indies in 1837."* Belfast: Printed by J. Wilson, 1838.

KNOWLES, CHARLES. *The Jamaican Association Develop'd.* London, 1757.

LAMBERT, SHEILA, ED. "Account of David Henderson." In *House of Commons Sessional Papers of the Eighteenth Century, 1714–1805*, vol. 69. Wilmington, DE: Scholarly Resources, 1975.

LAMBERT, SHEILA, ED. "Account of Isaac Parker." In *House of Commons Sessional Papers of the Eighteenth Century, 1714–1805*, vol. 73. Wilmington, DE: Scholarly Resources, 1975.

LESLIE, CHARLES. *A New History of Jamaica from the Earliest Accounts to the Taking of Porto Bello: Thirteen Letters from a Gentleman to His Friend.* London, 1740.

Letterbook of the Company of Merchants Trading to Africa, 1751–1769, gb 0402 ssc/22, 2 vols. Vol. 1: Letters from the Company to the Governor and Council of Cape Coast Castle, 1751–68, London, May 28, 1756.

LEWIS, MATTHEW GREGORY. *Journal of a West-India Proprietor, kept during a residence in the island of Jamaica.* London: J. Murray, 1834.

LIGON, RICHARD. *History of the Island of Barbados.* London, 1657.

LONG, EDWARD. *The History of Jamaica, or, General survey of the antient and modern state of that island: with reflections on its situations, settlements, inhabitants, climate, products, commerce, laws, and government.* London: T. Lownudes, 1774. (Reprint, London: F. Cass, 1970.)

LORIOT, ANTOINE-JOSEPH. *A Practical Essay, on Cement and Artificial Stone.* Translated from Loriot, *Mémoire sur une découverte dans l'art de bâtir.* St. Jago de la Vega: printed by order of the honourable House of Assembly, by Robert Sherlock, 1775.

MARTIN, SAMUEL. *Essay upon Plantership humbly inscribed to his excellency George Thomas, Esq., Chief Governor of all the Leeward Islands, as a monument to antient friendship.* 2nd ed. London, 1750.

MORETON, J. B. *West India Customs and Manners.* London, 1793.

OLDENDORP, C. G. A. *A Caribbean Mission: History of the Evanglical Brothers on the Caribbean Islands of St. Thomas, St. Croix, and St. John,* edited by Johann Jakob Bossard, 1770. Translated by Arnold R. Highfield and Vladimir Barac. Reprint, Ann Arbor, MI: Karoma, 1987.

OLDMIXON, JOHN. *The British Empire in America*, vol. 11. London, 1708.

DE OVIEDO Y VALDÉS, FERNÁNDEZ. *La Historia general y natural de las Indias.* Seville, 1535.

PALLADIO, ANDREA. *Four Books of Architecture.* London: Printed for Benj. Cole, 1733–35.

PALSGRAVE, JOHN. *Lesclarcissement de la langue francoyse compose par maistre Iohan Palsgraue Angloyse natyf de Londres, et gradue de Paris.* London, 1530.

PEYSSONNELL, DR. "Observations upon the Currents of the Sea, at the Antilles of America." *Philosophical Transactions of the Royal Society* 49 (1756): 624–30.

PHILLIPPO, JAMES M. *Jamaica, Its Past and Present State.* London: John Snow, 1843.

POEY, ANDRES. "Chronological Table, Comprising 400 Cyclonic Hurricanes Which Have Occurred in the West Indies and in the North Atlantic from 1493 to 1855." *Journal of the Royal Geographical Society of London* 25 (1855): 291–328.

RASK, JOHANNES. *A Brief and Truthful Description of a Journey to and from Guinea* (1708–1713). Accra: Sub-Saharan, 2009.

RILAND, JOHN. *Memoirs of a West-Indian Planter.* London: Hamilton, Adams, 1827.

DE ROCHEFORT, CHARLES. *Histoire naturelle et morale des Îles Antilles de l'Amérique.* Rotterdam, Chez A. Leers, 1665.

DE ROCHEFORT, CHARLES, AND JOHN DAVIES. *The history of the Caribbee-Islands, viz, Barbados, St Christophers, St Vincents, Martinico, Dominico, Barbouthos, Monserrat, Mevis [sic], Antego, & c in all XXVIII: in two books: the first containing the natural, the second, the moral history of those islands: illustrated with several pieces of sculpture representing the most considerable rarities therein described: with a Caribbian vocabulary.* Translated and edited by John Davies. London: Printed by J. M. for Thomas Dring and John Starkey, 1666.

ROBERTSON, ROBERT. "A Short Account of the Hurricane, that pass'd thro' the English Leeward Caribbee Islands, on Saturday the 30th of June 1733." London, 1733.

ROUGHLEY, THOMAS. *A Jamaica Planter's Guide: Or A System for Planting and Managing a Sugar Estate.* London, 1823.

SLOANE, SIR HANS. *The Philosophical Transactions of the Royal Society of London*, vol. 3. London: W. Boyer and J. Nichols, 1776–1886.

SLOANE, SIR HANS. *A Voyage to the Islands Madeira, Barbados . . . and Jamaica.* 2 vols. London, 1707 and 1725.

SMEATON, JOHN. "An Experimental Enquiry Concerning the Natural Powers of Water and Wind to Turn Mills, and Other Machines, Depending on a Circular Motion." *Philosophical Transactions* 51 (January 1759): 100–74.

SMITH, JOHN. *The generall historie of Virginia, New-England, and the Summer Isles: with the names of the adventurers, planters, and governours from their first beginning, anno: 1584 to this present 1624: with the proceedings of those severall colonies and the accidents that befell them in all their journyes and discoveries: also the maps and descriptions of all those countryes, their commodities, people, government, customes, and religion yet knowne: divided into sixe bookes.* Vols. 3 and 4. London: Printed by I. D. and I. H. for Michael Sparkes, 1624.

SMOLLETT, TOBIAS. *An Essay on the External Use of Water.* London, 1752.

STEDMAN, JOHN. *Narrative of a Five Years' Expedition against the Revolted Negroes of Suriname.* 1796.

STEWART, JOHN. *An Account of Jamaica and Its Inhabitants.* London: Longman, Hurst, Rees, and Orm, 1808. Reprint, Freeport, NY: Books for Libraries, 1971.

STEWART, JOHN. *A View of the Past and Present State of the Island of Jamaica; with remarks on the moral and physical condition of the slaves, and on the abolition of slavery in the colonies.* Edinburgh: Oliver & Boyd, 1823.

DU TERTRE, JEAN-BAPTISTE. *Histoire générale des Antilles habitées par les François.* Paris: Thomas Lolly, 1667.

WILLIAMS, CYNRIC R. *A Tour through the Island of Jamaica: From the Western to the Eastern End in the Year 1823.* London: Hunt and Clarke, 1826.

WHITEFIELD, GEORGE. *An Account of the Money Received and Disbursed for the Orphan House in Georgia.* London: Printed by W. Strahan for T. Cooper, and sold by R. Hett, 1741.

WOOD, JOHN. *A Description of the Exchange of Bristol.* Bath, 1745.

WOOD, JOHN. *A Series of Plans for Cottages or Habitations of the Labourer: either in husbandry, or the mechanic arts, adapted as well to towns, as to the country. Engraved on thirty plates. To which is added, an Introduction, containing many useful Observations on this Class of Building; tending to the Comfort of the Poor and Advantage of the Builder: with Calculations of Expences. By the late Mr. J. Wood, of Bath, Architect.* London: Printed for I. and J. Taylor, 1792.

WOOD, ROBERT. *The Ruins of Palmyra, otherwise Tedmor, in the desart.* London: Robert Wood, 1753.

SECONDARY SOURCES

AARONS, G. A. Unpublished report on Auchindown Castle, "Auchindown Excavation 1983–84," for the Center for Archaeological and Conservation Research, Port Royal, JA.

ABRAHAMS, ROGER D., AND JOHN F. SWED. *After Africa: Extracts from British Travel Accounts and Journals of the Seventeenth, Eighteenth, and Nineteenth Centuries Concerning Slaves, Their Manners, and Customs in the British West Indies.* New Haven: Yale University Press, 1983.

AINSLIE, PHILLIP BARRINGTON. *Reminiscences of a Scottish Gentleman*, reprinted in Georgian Society of Jamaica, *Falmouth, 1791–1970*. Jamaica: Lithographic Printers Limited, 1970.

AIRS, MALCOLM. *The Tudor and Jacobean Country House: A Building History.* Stroud: Sutton Pub, 1995.

ALLEN, CAROLYN. "Creole: The Problem of Definition." In *Questioning Creole: Creolization Discourses in Caribbean Culture.* Kingston: Ian Randle, 2002.

AMUSSEN, SUSAN DWYER. *Caribbean Exchanges: Slavery and the Transformation of English Society, 1640–1700.* Chapel Hill: University of North Carolina Press, 2007.

ANDERSON, JENNIFER L. *Mahogany: The Costs of Luxury in Early America.* Cambridge, MA: Harvard University Press, 2012.

ANDREWS, MALCOLM. *The Search for the Picturesque: Landscape Aesthetics and Tourism in Britain, 1760–1800.* Aldershot: Scholar, 1989.

ANES, RAFAEL DONOSO. "Accounting and Slavery: The Accounts of the English South Sea Company, 1713–22." *European Accounting Review* 11, no. 2 (2002): 441–52.

ANQUANDAH, JAMES. "Researching the Historic Slave Trade in Ghana—An Overview." In *The Transatlantic Slave Trade: Landmarks, Legacies, Expectations*, edited by James Kwesi Anquandah, 23–56. Accra: Sub-Saharan, 2007.

ANQUANDAH, JAMES KWESI, ED. *The Transatlantic Slave Trade: Landmarks, Legacies, Expectations.* Accra: Sub-Saharan, 2007.

ANTHONY, CARL. "The Big House and the Slave Quarters: African Contributions to the New World," reprinted in *Cabin, Quarter, Plantation: Architecture and Landscapes of North American Slavery*, edited by Clifton Ellis and Rebecca Ginsburg. Charlottesville: University of Virginia Press, 2010.

ARMITAGE, DAVID. *The Ideological Origins of the British Empire.* Cambridge: Cambridge University Press, 2000.

ARMSTRONG, DOUGLAS V. "The Afro-Jamaican House Yard: An Archaeological and Ethno-Historical Perspective." *Florida Journal of Anthropology* 7 (1991): 51–63.

ARMSTRONG, DOUGLAS V. *The Old Village and the Great House: An Archaeological and Historical Examination of Drax Hall Plantation, St. Ann's Bay, Jamaica.* Urbana: University of Illinois Press, 1990.

ARMSTRONG, DOUGLAS V. "Reflections on Seville: Rediscovering the African Jamaican Settlements at Seville Plantation, St. Ann's Bay." In *Out of Many, One People: The Historical Archaeology of Colonial Jamaica*, edited by James A. Delle, Mark Hauser, and Douglas V. Armstrong. Tuscaloosa: University of Alabama Press, 2011.

ARNOLD, DANA. *The Georgian Country House: Architecture, Landscape and Society.* Sutton, 1980, reprinted 1998.

AVERY, TRACEY. *Tattershall Castle, Lincolnshire.* London: Country Life for the National Trust, 1997.

BAGNERIS, MIA. "Coloring the Caribbean: Agostino Brunias and the Painting of Race in the British West Indies, 1765–1800." Ph.D. diss., Harvard University, 2009.

BAILEY, ANNE C. "Anglo Oral Histories of the Slave Trade." In *Synopses of the Papers of the 2003 National Conference on the Historic Slave Trade.* Accra, 2003.

BAILEY, GAUVIN ALEXANDER. *Art of Colonial Latin America.* London: Phaidon, 2005.

BAILEY, WILMA. "Social Control in the Pre-Emancipation Society of Kingston." *Boletín de Estudios Latinoamericanos y del Caribe* 24 (June 1978): 97–110.

BAILYN, BERNARD. *Atlantic History: Concept and Contours.* Cambridge, MA: Harvard University Press, 2005.

BARKER, ROBERT. "Mid Eighteenth-Century Jamaican House Design." Unpublished paper.

BARRELL, JOHN. *The Dark Side of the English Landscape: The Rural Poor in English Painting, 1730–1840.* Cambridge: Cambridge University Press, 1980.

BARRINGER, T. J., GILLIAN FORRESTER, AND BARBARO MARTINEZ-RUIZ, EDS. *Art and Emancipation in Jamaica.* New Haven: Yale University Press, 2007.

BATES, LYNDSEY. "Surveillance and Production on Stewart Castle Estate: A GIS-Based Analysis of Models of Plantation Spatial Organization." Master's thesis, University of Virginia, 2007.

BAYLY, C. A., AND LEILA TARAZI FAWAZ. *Modernity and Culture from the Mediterranean to the Indian Ocean, 1890–1920.* New York: Columbia University Press, 2002.

BEACHAM, P. *Devon Building.* Devon County Council, 1990.

BECKLES, HILLARY. "African Resistance to the Transatlantic Slave Trade." In *The Transatlantic Slave Trade: Landmarks, Legacies, Expectations,* edited by James Kwesi Anquandah, 81–91. Accra: Sub-Saharan, 2007.

BEHRENDT, STEPHEN. "Markets, Transaction Cycles, and Profits: Merchant Decision Making in the British Slave Trade." *William and Mary Quarterly* 58, no. 1 (January 2001): 171–204.

BEHRENDT, STEPHEN, A. J. H. LATHAM, AND DAVID NORTHRUP. *The Diary of Antera Duke, an Eighteenth-Century African Slave Trader.* New York: Oxford University Press, 2010.

BERG, MAXINE, AND PAT HUDSON. "Rehabilitating the Industrial Revolution." *Economic History Review* 45, no. 1 (February 1992): 24–50.

BERMINGHAM, ANN. *Landscape and Ideology: The English Rustic Tradition, 1740–1860.* Berkeley: University of California Press, 1986.

BERTHELOT, JACK, AND MARTINE GAUME. *Kaz Antiye: jan moun ka rete (Caribbean popular dwelling / L'Habitat populaire aux Antilles).* Translated by Karen Bowie, Robert Jean-Pierre, and Juliette Sainton. Paris: Éditions Perspectives Créoles, 1982.

BESSON, JEAN. *Martha Brae's Two Histories: European Expansion and Caribbean Culture-Building in Jamaica.* Chapel Hill: University of North Carolina Press, 2002.

BETTELHEIM, JUDITH. "The Afro-Jamaican Jonkonnu Festival: Playing the Forces and Operating the Cloth," Ph.D. diss., Yale University, 1979.

BETTELHEIM, JUDITH. "Jonkonnu and Other Christmas Masquerades." In *Caribbean Festival Arts: Each and Every Bit of Difference,* edited by John W. Nunley and Judith Bettleheim. Seattle: University of Washington Press, 1988.

BHABHA, HOMI. "Of Mimicry and Man." In *The Location of Culture.* London: Routledge, 1994.

BILBY, KENNETH. "More Than Meets the Eye: African-Jamaican Festivities in the Time of Beliario." In *Art and Emancipation in Jamaica,* edited by T. J. Barringer, Gillian Forrester, and Barbaro Martinez-Ruiz, 121–36. New Haven: Yale University Press, 2007.

BILBY, KENNETH, AND JEROME HANDLER. "Obeah: Healing and Protection in West Indian Slave Life." *Journal of Caribbean History* 38, no. 2 (2004): 154–83.

BINDMAN, DAVID. "The Black Presence in British Art: Sixteenth and Seventeenth Centuries." In Massing, Jean Michel. *The Image of the Black in Western Art.* Vol. III of *The "Age of Discovery" to the Age of Abolition, Part 1: Artists of the Renaissance and Baroque,* edited by David Bindman and Henry Louis Gates, Jr. Cambridge, MA: Harvard University Press, 2011.

BINDMAN, DAVID, AND HELEN WESTON. "Court and City: Fantasies of Domination." In Massing, Jean Michel. *The Image of the Black in Western Art.* Vol. III of *The "Age of Discovery" to the Age of Abolition, Part 3: The Eighteenth Century,* edited by David Bindman and Henry Louis Gates, Jr. Cambridge, MA: Harvard University Press, 2011.

BLACK, JEANNETTE D., ed. *The Blathwayt Atlas: A collection of 48 manuscript and printed maps of the 17th century relating to the British overseas empire in that era, brought together about 1683 for the use of the Lords of Trade and Plantations.* Providence: Brown University Press, 1970–75.

BLUESTONE, DANIEL. "The Pushcart Evil: Peddlers, Merchants, and New York City's Streets, 1890–1940." *Journal of Urban History* 18, no. 1 (1991): 68–92.

BOACHIE-ANSAH, J. "Archaeological Research at Kasana: A Search for Evidence on the Historic Slave Trade in the Upper West Region of Ghana." *Journal of Environment and Culture* 2, no. 1 (2005): 35–57.

BORSAY, PETER. *The English Urban Renaissance and Society in the Provincial Town, 1660–1770.* Oxford: Clarendon, 1991.

BOURDIEU, PIERRE. *Outline of a Theory of Practice.* Translated by Richard Nice. Cambridge: Cambridge University Press, 1977.

BOWDEN, MARTYN. "The Three Centuries of Bridgetown: An Historical Geography." *Journal of the Barbados Museum and Historical Society* 49 (2003).

BOWETT, ADAM. "The Commercial Introduction of Mahogany and the Naval Stores Act of 1721." *Furniture History* 30 (1994): 43–56.

BOWETT, ADAM. "The English Mahogany Trade, 1700–1793." Ph.D. diss., Brunel University, 1997.

BOXER, DAVID. *Duperly: An Exhibition of the Works of Adolphe Duperly and His Sons and Grandsons Mounted in Commemoration of the Bicentenary of His Birth.* Kingston: National Gallery of Jamaica, 2001.

BRATHWAITE, KAMAU. *The Development of Creole Society in Jamaica, 1770–1820.* Oxford: Clarendon, 1971.

BREEN, T. H. "An Empire of Goods: The Anglicization of Colonial America, 1690–1776." *Journal of British Studies* 25, no. 4 (October 1986): 467–99.

BREEN, T. H. *The Marketplace of Revolution: How Consumer Politics Shaped American Independence.* New York: Oxford University Press, 2004.

DE BREFFNY, BRIAN. *Castles of Ireland.* London: Thames and Hudson, 1977.

BREWER, JOHN, AND ROY PORTER. *Consumption and the World of Goods.* London: Routledge, 1993.

BRIDENBAUGH, CARL, AND ROBERTA BRIDENBAUGH. *No Peace beyond the Line: The English in the Caribbean, 1624–1690.* New York: Oxford University Press, 1972.

BROCKWAY, LUCILE. *Science and Colonial Expansion: The Role of the British Royal Botanic Gardens.* New York: Academic, 1979.

BROWN, ANDREW, ET AL. *The Rows of Chester: The Chester Rows Research Project.* English Heritage Archaeological Research Report, 16, London, 1999.

BROWN, LAWRENCE. "Atlantic Slavery and Classical Culture at Marble Hill and Northington Grange." In *Slavery and the British Country House,* edited by Madge Dresser and Andrew Hann. Swindon: English Heritage, 2013.

BROWN, VINCENT. "Slave Revolt in Jamaica, 1760–61: A Cartographic Narrative." http://revolt.axismaps.com/.

BRYANT, PEREGRINE, AND ALEXANDRA DI VALMARANA. "Legacy of a Sugar Baron." *The Georgian* 2 (2014): 28–31.

BRYDEN, D. J. "The Jamaican Observatories of Colin Campbell, F.R.S. and Alexander Macfarlane, F.R.S." Notes and Records of the Royal Society of London 24/2 (April 1970), 261–72.

BUCKRIDGE, STEEVE. *The Language of Dress: Resistance and Accommodation in Jamaica, 1760–1890.* Kingston: University of the West Indies Press, 2004.

BUISSERET, DAVID. "Fresh Light on Spanish Jamaica." *Jamaica Journal* 16 (1983): 72–75.

BUISSERET, DAVID. *Historic Architecture of the Caribbean.* London: Heineman, 1980.

BUISSERET, DAVID. *Jamaica in 1687: The Taylor Manuscript at the National Library of Jamaica.* Kingston: University of the West Indies Press, 2008.

BUISSERET, DAVID. "The Taylor Manuscript and Seventeenth-Century Jamaica." In *West Indies Accounts: Essays on the History of the British Caribbean and the Atlantic Economy in Honour of Richard Sheridan,* edited by Roderick A. McDonald. Kingston, University of the West Indies Press, 1996.

BURNARD, TREVOR. "Elephants Colliding: Conflict and Cooperation between Kingston Merchants and Jamaican Planters on the Eve of the Seven Years War." Paper delivered at "A War for Empire: The Seven Years War in Context." National Maritime Museum, July 13–14, 2006.

BURNARD, TREVOR. "European Migration to Jamaica, 1655–1780." *William and Mary Quarterly* 53, no. 4 (October 1996): 769–96.

BURNARD, TREVOR. "'The Grand Mart of the Island': The Economic Function of Kingston, Jamaica, in the Mid-Eighteenth Century." In *Jamaica in Slavery and Freedom: History, Heritage, and Culture,* edited by Kathleen E. A. Monteith and Glen Richards. Kingston: University of the West Indies Press, 2002.

BURNARD, TREVOR. *Mastery, Tyranny, and Desire: Thomas Thistlewood and His Slaves in the Anglo-Jamaican World.* Chapel Hill: University of North Carolina Press, 2004.

BURNARD, TREVOR. "Passengers Only: The Extent and Significance of Absenteeism in Eighteenth-Century Jamaica." *Atlantic Studies* 1, no. 2 (2004): 178–95.

BURNARD, TREVOR. "Prodigious Riches: The Wealth of Jamaica before the American Revolution." *Economic History Review* 54, no. 3 (2001): 505–23.

BURNARD, TREVOR. "Who Bought Slaves in Early America? Purchasers of Slaves from the Royal African Company in Jamaica, 1674–1708." *Slavery & Abolition: A Journal of Slave and Post-Slave Studies* 17, no. 2 (August 1996): 68–92.

BURNARD, TREVOR, AND EMMA HART. "Kingston, Jamaica, and Charleston, South Carolina: A New Look at Comparative Urbanization in Plantation Colonial British America." *Journal of Urban History.* Published online, June 22, 2012, 1–21.

BURNARD, TREVOR, AND KENNETH MORGAN. "The Dynamics of the Slave Market and Slave Purchasing Patterns in Jamaica, 1655–1788." *William and Mary Quarterly* 58, no. 1 (January 2001): 205–28.

BURTON, RICHARD. *Afro-Creole: Power, Opposition, and Play in the Caribbean.* Ithaca, NY: Cornell University Press, 1997.

BUSHMAN, RICHARD. *The Refinements of America: Persons, Houses, Cities.* New York: Vintage, 1992, 119, see notes 24, 25, 28.

CALHOUN, JEANNE, MARTHA ZIERDEN, AND ELIZABETH PAYSINGER. "The Geographic Spread of Charleston's Mercantile Community, 1732–1767." *South Carolina Historical Magazine* (1985), 183–220.

CAMPBELL, MAVIS. *The Maroons of Jamaica, 1655–1796: A History of Resistance, Collaboration, and Betrayal.* Trenton, NJ: Africa World Press, 1990.

CANNY, NICHOLAS. *Making Ireland British, 1580–1650.* Oxford: Oxford University Press, 2001.

CANNY, NICHOLAS, AND ANTHONY PADGET, EDS. *Colonial Identity in the Atlantic World, 1500–1800.* Princeton: Princeton University Press, 1987.

CARRINGTON, SELWYN H. H. "The United States and the British West Indies Trade." In *West Indies Accounts: Essays on the History of the British Caribbean and the Atlantic Economy,* edited by Roderick McDonald, 149–68. Kingston: University of the West Indies Press, 1996.

CASHIN, EDWARD J. *Beloved Bethesda: A History of George Whitefield's Home for Boys, 1740–2000.* Macon, GA: Mercer University Press, 2001.

CASID, JILL H. *Sowing Empire: Landscape and Colonization.* Minneapolis: University of Minnesota Press, 2005.

CASTRO, MARÍA. *Arquitectura en San Juan de Puerto Rico.* Rio Piedras: Editorial Universitaria, Universidad de Puerto Rico, 1980.

ÇELIK, ZEYNEP. *Empire, Architecture and the City: French Ottoman Encounters, 1830–1914.* Seattle: University of Washington Press, 2008.

ÇELIK, ZEYNEP, DIANE FAVRO, AND RICHARD INGERSOLL, EDS. *Streets: Critical Perspectives on Urban Space.* Berkeley: University of California Press, 1994.

DE CERTEAU, MICHEL. "On the Opposition of Practices of Everyday Life." *Social Text* no. 3 (Autumn 1980): 3–43.

DE CERTEAU, MICHEL. *The Practice of Everyday Life.* Cambridge, MA: Harvard University Press, 1994.

CHAPMAN, WILLIAM. "Irreconcilable Differences: Urban Residences in the Danish West Indies, 1700–1900." *Winterthur Portfolio* 30 (Summer–Autumn 1995): 129–72.

CHAPMAN, WILLIAM. "Slave Villages in the Danish West Indies: Changes of the Late Eighteenth and Early Nineteenth Century." In *Perspectives in Vernacular Architecture IV,* edited by Thomas Carter and Bernard Herman. Columbia: University of Missouri Press for the Vernacular Architecture Forum, 1991.

CHAPPELL, EDWARD. "Accommodating Slavery in Bermuda." In *Cabin, Quarter, Plantation: Architecture and Landscapes of North American Slavery,* edited by Clifton Ellis and Rebecca Ginsburg. New Haven: Yale University Press, 2010.

CHENOWETH, MICHAEL. "A Reassessment of Atlantic Basin Tropical Cyclone Activity, 1700–1855." *Climatic Change* 76, no. 1–2 (2006): 169–240.

CHENOWETH, MICHAEL. *The 18th-Century Climate of Jamaica Derived from the Journals of Thomas Thistlewood, 1750–1786.* Philadelphia: American Philosophical Society, 2003.

CHIAS, PILAR, AND TOMAS ABAD. *The Fortified Heritage: Cadiz and the Caribbean, A Transatlantic Relationship.* Alcalá de Henares, Madrid: Universidad de Alcalá, 2011.

CHILDS, ADRIENNE L. "Sugar Boxes and Blackamoors: Ornamental Blackness in Early Meissen Porcelain." In *The Cultural Aesthetics of Eighteenth-Century Porcelain,* edited by Alden Cavanaugh and Michael Yonan. Farnham, Surrey: Ashgate, 2010.

CHRISTELOW, ALLAN. "Contraband Trade between Jamaica and the Spanish Main, and the Free Port Act of 1766." *Hispanic American Historical Review* 22 (1942): 309–43.

CLARKE, ALDAN. *The Old English in Ireland, 1625–42.* Ithaca, NY: Cornell University Press, 1966.

CLARKE, DAVID. *Reflections on the Astronomy of Glasgow: A Story of Some Five Hundred Years.* Edinburgh: Edinburgh University Press, 2013.

CLAY, CHRISTOPHER. "Marriage, Inheritance and the Rise of Large Estates in England, 1660–1815." *Economic History Review* 21, no. 3 (1968): 503–18.

CLEMENSON, HEATHER. *English Country Houses and Landed Estates.* London: Croom Helm, 1982.

COHEN, DAVID, AND JACK GREENE, EDS., *Neither Slave nor Free: The Freedman of African Descent in the Slave Societies of the New World.* Baltimore: Johns Hopkins University Press, 1972.

COIAS E SILVA, VITOR. "Using Advanced Composites to Retrofit Lisbon's Old 'Seismic Resistant' Timber Framed Buildings." In *European Timber Buildings as an Expression of Technological and Technical Cultures,* edited by Bertolini Cestari, Faria Amorim, and Anu Soikkeli, 109–24. Paris: Elsevier, 2002.

COLVIN, HOWARD. *A Biographical Dictionary of British Architects, 1600–1840.* 3rd ed. New Haven: Yale University Press, 1998.

CONCANNON, TOM. "Diggin up the Past." *Daily Gleaner,* June 8, 1965.

CONCANNON, TOM. "The Masterbuilder." *Jamaica Historical Society Bulletin* (June 1965).

CONOLLEY, IVOR. "Deployment of Forced Labor: An Analysis of the Role of Slaves on Ten Tharp Properties in 1805 Trelawny, Jamaica." *Jamaica Historical Society Bulletin* 12, nos. 7 and 8 (April and October 2012): 115–35.

CONOLLEY, IVOR, AND JAMES PARRENT. "Land Deeds That Tell the Story of the Birth of Falmouth." *Jamaican Historical Society Bulletin* 11 (2005): 383–409.

COOKE, ANTHONY. "An Elite Revisited: Glasgow West India Merchants, 1783–1877." *Journal of Scottish Historical Studies* 32, no. 2 (2012): 127–65.

COOPER, J. P. "Social Distribution of Land and Men in England, 1436–1700." *Economic History Review* 20 (1967): 419–40.

COOPER, NICHOLAS. *Houses of the Gentry, 1480–1680.* New Haven: Yale University Press, 1999.

COUTU, JOAN. *Persuasion and Propaganda: Monuments and the Eighteenth-Century British Empire.* Montreal: McGill–Queen's University Press, 2006.

CRAIG, MAURICE. *The Architecture of Ireland: From the Earliest Times to 1800.* Dublin: B. T. Batsford, 1989.

CRAIG, MAURICE. "Portumna Castle, County Galway." In *The Country Seat: Studies in the History of the British Country House Presented to Sir John Summerson on His Sixty-fifth Birthday Together with a Select Bibliography of His Published Writings,* edited by John Summerson, Howard Colvin, and John Harris. London: Allen Lane, 1970.

CRAIN, EDWARD E. *Historic Architecture in the Caribbean Islands.* Gainesville: University Press of Florida, 1994.

CRATON, MICHAEL. "Decoding Pitchy-Patchy: The Roots, Branches, and Essence of Junkanoo." *Slavery and Abolition* 16, no. 1 (1995): 14–44.

CRATON, MICHAEL. "Forms of Resistance to Slavery." In *General History of the Caribbean: The Slave Societies of the Caribbean,* vol. 3, edited by Franklin Knight. London: UNESCO, 1997.

CRATON, MICHAEL. *Testing the Chains: Resistance to Slavery in the British West Indies.* Ithaca, NY: Cornell University Press, 1982.

CRATON, MICHAEL, AND GARRY GREENLAND. *Searching for the Invisible Man: Slaves and Plantation Life In Jamaica.* Cambridge, MA: Harvard University Press, 1978.

CRATON, MICHAEL, AND JAMES WALVIN. *A Jamaican Plantation: The History of Worthy Park, 1670–1970.* Toronto: University of Toronto Press, 1970.

CRAWFORD, KATELYN. "Transient Painters, Traveling Canvases: Portraiture and Mobility in the British Atlantic, 1750–1780." Ph.D. diss. in process, University of Virginia.

CROUCH, DORA P., DANIEL J. GARR, AND AXEL I. MUNDIGO. *Spanish City Planning in North America.* Cambridge, MA: Massachusetts Institute of Technology Press, 1982.

CROWLEY, JOHN E. "The American Republic Joins the British Global Landscape." In *Shaping the Body Politic: Art and Political Formation in Early America,* edited by Maurie Dee McInnis and Louis P. Nelson. Charlottesville: University of Virginia Press, 2011.

CROWLEY, JOHN E. *The Invention of Comfort: Sensibilities and Design in Early Modern Britain and Early America.* Baltimore: Johns Hopkins University Press, 2001.

CRUFT, KITTY, JOHN DUNBAR, AND RICHARD FAWCETT. *Borders: The Buildings of Scotland.* New Haven: Yale University Press, 2006.

CRUICKSHANK, DAN, AND PETER WYLD. *London: The Art of Georgian Building.* London: Architectural Press, 1975.

CUNDALL, FRANK. *Historic Jamaica.* London: Published for the Institute of Jamaica by the West India Committee, 1915.

CURTIN, PHILIP D. *The Atlantic Slave Trade, a Census.* Madison: University of Wisconsin Press, 1969.

CURTIN, PHILIP D. *Economic Change in Precolonial Africa: Senegambia in the Era of the Slave Trade.* Madison: University of Wisconsin Press, 1975.

CURTIN, PHILIP D. *The Rise and Fall of the Plantation Complex: Essays in Atlantic History.* Cambridge: Cambridge University Press, 1990.

DALLAS, ROBERT. *The History of the Maroons from their Origins to the Establishment of Their Chief Tribe at Sierra Leone.* London: Longman and Rees, 1803, I.

Database of British Slave-ownership: http://www.ucl.ac.uk.

DAVIES, K. G. The Royal East Africa Company: *The Emergence of International Business, 1200–1800,* vol. 5. London: Royal African, 1957.

DAVIS, HOWARD. *Living over the Store: Architecture and Local Urban Life.* Abingdon, England: Routledge, 2012.

DAVIS, RALPH. *The Rise of the Atlantic Economies.* Ithaca, NY: Cornell University Press, 1973.

DAVIS, SUSAN. *Parades and Power: Street Theatre in Nineteenth-Century Philadelphia.* Philadelphia: Temple University Press, 1986.

DEAGAN, KATHLEEN. *Puerto Real: The Archaeology of a Sixteenth-Century Spanish Town.* Gainesville: University Press of Florida, 1995.

DECORSE, CHRISTOPHER R. *An Archaeology of Elmina: Africans and Europeans on the Gold Coast, 1400–1900.* Washington, DC: Smithsonian Institution Press, 2001.

DELLE, JAMES. *An Archaeology of Social Space: Analyzing Coffee Plantations in Jamaica's Blue Mountains.* New York: Plenum, 1998.

DELLE, JAMES. "Extending Europe's Grasp: An Archaeological Comparison of Colonial Spatial Process in Ireland and Jamaica." In *Old and New Worlds,* edited by R. L. Michael and G. Egan. Oxford: Oxbow, 1999.

DELLE, JAMES. "The Governor and the Enslaved: An Archaeology of Colonial Modernity at Marshall's Penn, Jamaica." *International Journal of Historical Archaeology* 12, no. 4 (2009): 488–512.

DELLE, JAMES. "The Habitus of Jamaican Plantation Landscapes." In *Out of Many, One People: The Historical Archaeology of Colonial Jamaica,* edited by James Delle, Mark Hauser, and Douglas V. Armstrong. Tuscaloosa: University of Alabama Press, 2011.

DELLE, JAMES, MARK HAUSER, AND DOUGLAS V. ARMSTRONG, EDS. *Out of Many, One People: The Historical Archaeology of Colonial Jamaica.* Tuscaloosa: University of Alabama Press, 2011.

DER, BENEDICT G. *The Slave Trade in Northern Ghana.* Accra: Woeli, 1998.

DEVINE, THOMAS MARTIN. *Scotland's Empire and the Shaping of the Americas, 1600–1815.* Washington, DC: Smithsonian, 2004.

DEVINE, THOMAS MARTIN. *The Transformation of Rural Scotland: Social Change and the Agrarian Economy, 1660–1815.* Edinburgh: Edinburgh University Press, 1994.

DONAHUE-WALLACE, KELLY. *Art and Architecture of Viceregal Latin America, 1521–1821.* Albuquerque, NM: University of New Mexico Press, 2008.

DONNAN, ELIZABETH. *Documents Illustrative of the History of the Slave Trade to America.* New York, Octagon Books, 1965.

DONNAN, ELIZABETH. "The Slave Trade into South Carolina before the Revolution." *The American Historical Review* 33, no. 4 (July 1, 1928): 804–28.

DORAN, JR., EDWIN. "The West Indian Hip-Roofed Cottage." *The California Geographer* 3 (1962): 97–104.

DRAYTON, RICHARD. *Nature's Government: Science, Imperial Britain, and the "Improvement" of the World.* New Haven: Yale University Press, 2000.

DRESSER, MADGE. *Slavery Obscured: The Social History of the Slave Trade in an English Provincial Port.* London: Continuum, 2001.

DRESSER, MADGE, AND ANDREW HANN, EDS. *Slavery and the British Country House.* Swindon: English Heritage, 2013.

DRINKALL, SOPHIE. "The Jamaican Plantation House: Scottish Influence." *Architectural Heritage: The Journal of the Architectural Heritage Society of Scotland* 2, no. 2 (November 1991): 56–68.

DUNBAR, JOHN. *The Historic Architecture of Scotland.* London: Batsford, 1966.

DUNKLEY, D. A. *Agency of the Enslaved: Jamaica and the Culture of Freedom in the Atlantic World.* Lanham: Lexington, 2013.

DUNLOP, R. "The Plantation of Munster 1584/9." *English Historical Review* 9 (1880): 250–69.

DUNLOP, R. "An Unpublished Survey of the Plantation of Munster in 1622." *Journal of the Royal Society of Antiquaries of Ireland* 54 (1924): 128–46.

DUNN, RICHARD S. *Sugar and Slaves: The Rise of the Planter Class in the English West Indies, 1624–1713.* Chapel Hill: Published for the Institute of Early American History and Culture at Williamsburg, Va. by the University of North Carolina Press, 1972.

DUQUESNEY, F. J. "Phillip Pinnock." *Jamaican Historical Society Bulletin* (March 1966), 95–97.

DURANT, DAVID. *The Smythson Circle: The Story of Six Great English Houses.* London: Peter Owen, 2011.

EBERLIN, HAROLD DONALDSON. "When Society First Took a Bath." In *Sickness and Health in America: Readings in the History of Medicine and Public Health,* edited by J. Walter Leavitt and Ronald L. Numbers. Madison: University of Wisconsin Press, 1978.

EDWARDS, JAY. "The Complex Origins of the American Domestic Piazza-Veranda-Gallery." *Material Culture* 21 (1989): 3–58.

EDWARDS, JAY. "Creole Architecture: A Comparative Analysis of Upper and Lower Louisiana and Saint Domingue." *International Journal of Historical Archaeology* 10, no. 3 (Sept. 2006): 241–71.

EDWARDS, JAY. "The Evolution of Vernacular Architecture in the Western Caribbean." In *Cultural Traditions and Caribbean Identity: The Question of Patrimony,* edited by Jeffrey K. Wilkerson. Gainesville: University Press of Florida, 1980.

EDWARDS, JAY. "The Origins of Creole Architecture." *Winterthur Portfolio* 29 (Summer–Autumn 1994): 156–89.

EDWARDS, JAY. "Shotgun: The Most Contested House in America." *Buildings and Landscapes* 16 (Spring 2009): 62–96.

ELLIOTT, JOHN. *Empires and the Atlantic World Empires of the Atlantic World: Britain and Spain in America, 1492–1830.* New Haven: Yale University Press, 2006.

ELTIS, DAVID, AND MARTIN HALBERT. *Voyages: The Transatlantic Slave Trade Database.* http://www.slavevoyages.org/tast/index.faces.

FARNSWORTH, PAUL. "Negroe Houses Built of Stone Besides Other Watl'd and Plaistered." In *Island Lives: Historical Archaeologies of the Caribbean,* edited by Paul Farnsworth. Tuscaloosa: University of Alabama Press, 2001.

FERGUSON, LELAND. *Uncommon Ground: Archaeology and Early African America, 1650–1800.* Washington, DC: Smithsonian Institution Press, 1992.

FINNERAN, NIALL. "'This Island Is Inhabited with All Sorts': The Archaeology of Creolization in Speightstown, Barbados, and Beyond, AD 1650–1900." *Antiquaries Journal* 93 (2013): 319–51.

FIRTH, C. H., ed. *Narrative of General Venables.* London, 1900.

FITZPATRICK, BRENDAN. *Seventeenth-Century Ireland: The War of Religions.* Dublin: Gill and MacMillan, 1988.

FOGEL, ROBERT. *Without Consent or Contract: The Rise and Fall of American Slavery.* New York: Norton, 1989.

FORDHAM, DOUGLAS. "State, Nation and Empire in the History of British Art." *Perspective: La revue de l'INHA,* no. 1 (2013): 723-42.

FOUCAULT, MICHEL. *Discipline and Punish: The Birth of the Prison.* Translated by Alan Sheridan. London: Allen Lane, 1977.

FRASER, JR., WALTER J. *Charleston! Charleston!: The History of a Southern City.* Columbia: South Carolina University Press, 1989.

FREEMANTLE, KATHERINE. *The Baroque Town Hall of Amsterdam.* Utrecht: Haentjens Dekker & Gumbert, 1959.

FRYER, PAUL. *Staying Power: The History of Black People in Britain.* London: Pluto, 1984.

FYFE, CHRISTOPHER. "The Dynamics of African Dispersal: The Transatlantic Slave Trade." In *The African Diaspora: Interpretive Essays,* edited by Martin L. Kilson and Robert I. Rotberg. Cambridge, MA: Harvard University Press, 1976.

GALENSON, DAVID. *Traders, Planters, and Slaves: Market Behavior in Early English America.* Cambridge: Cambridge University Press, 1986.

GALLE, JILLIAN. "Assessing the Impacts of Time, Agricultural Cycles, and Demography on the Consumer Activities of Enslaved Men and Women in Eighteenth-Century Jamaica and Virginia." In *Out of Many, One People: The Historical Archaeology of Colonial Jamaica,* edited by James Delle, Mark Hauser, and Douglas V. Armstrong, 211–42. Tuscaloosa: University of Alabama Press, 2011.

GALLE, JILLIAN. "Stewart Castle." In *Vernacular Architecture Forum Field Guide.* Unpublished field guide, 2011.

GALLE, JILLIAN. "Stewart Castle Main House Background." 2007. *The Digital Archaeological Archive of Comparative Slavery,* http://www.daacs.org/resources/sites/background/30/. Accessed April 7, 2013.

GALLOWAY, J. H. "Tradition and Innovation in the American Sugar Industry, 1500–1800: An Explanation." *Annals of the Association of American Geographers* 75, no. 3 (September 1985): 334–51.

GARLAND, CHARLES, AND HERBERT S. KLEIN. "The Allotment of Space for Slaves aboard Eighteenth-Century British Slave Ships." *William and Mary Quarterly* 42, 3rd ser., no. 2. Williamsburg, VA: Omohundro Institute of Early American History and Culture, April 1985, 238–48.

GARNETT, OLIVER. *Dyrham Park.* London: National Trust, 2000.

GEGGUS, DAVID. "The Major Port Towns of Saint-Domingue in the Later Eighteenth Century." In *Atlantic Port Cities: Economy, Culture, and Society in the Atlantic World, 1650–1850,* edited by Franklin W. Knight and Peggy K. Liss. Knoxville: University of Tennessee Press, 1991.

GEISMAR, JOAN H. "Patterns of Development in the Late Eighteenth- and Nineteenth-Century American Seaport: A Suggested Model for Recognizing Increasing Commercialism and Urbanization." *American Archeology* 5 (1985): 175–84.

GIKANDI, SIMON. *Slavery and the Culture of Taste.* Princeton: Princeton University Press, 2011.

GILDJIE, PAUL. *Liberty on the Waterfront: American Maritime Culture in the Age of Revolution.* Philadelphia: University of Pennsylvania Press, 2004.

GILROY, PAUL. *The Black Atlantic: Modernity and Double Consciousness.* Cambridge, MA: Harvard University Press, 1993.

GIROUARD, MARK. *Robert Smythson and the Elizabethan Country House.* New Haven: Yale University Press, 1983.

GLENDINNING, MILES. *A History of Scottish Architecture: From the Renaissance to the Present Day.* Edinburgh: Edinburgh University Press, 1996.

GLENDENNING, MILES, RANALD MACINNES, AND AONGHUS MACKECHNIE. *A History of Scottish Architecture: From the Reformation to the Present Day.* Edinburgh: Edinburgh University Press, 1996.

GOMME, A. H., AND ALISON MAGUIRE. *Design and Plan in the Country*

House: From Castle Donjons to Palladian Boxes. New Haven: Yale University Press, 2008.

GONTAR, CYBELE. "The Campeche Chair in the Metropolitan Museum of Art." *Metropolitan Museum Journal* 38 (2003).

GOVEIA, ELSO V. *Slave Society in the British Leeward Islands at the End of the Eighteenth Century.* New Haven: Yale University Press, 1969.

GRAGG, LARRY. "First Impressions of Barbados: England's Most Attractive Seventeenth-Century Imperial Locale." *Locus: Regional and Local History of the Americas* 8, no. 2 (Spring 1996): 189.

GRAHAM, WILLIE. "Adaptation and Innovation: Archaeological and Architectural Perspectives on the Seventeenth-Century Chesapeake." *William and Mary Quarterly* 64, no. 3 (July 2007): 451–522.

GRAHAM, WILLIE. "Preindustrial Framing in the Chesapeake." In *Constructing Image, Identity and Place: Perspectives in Vernacular Architecture IX,* edited by Alison Hoagland and Kenneth Breisch. Knoxville: University of Tennessee Press, 2003.

GRAHAM, WILLIE. "Timber Framing." In *The Chesapeake House,* edited by Cary Carson and Carl Lounsbury. Chapel Hill: University of North Carolina Press, 2013.

GRAVETTE, ANDREW. *Architectural Heritage of the Caribbean.* Kingston: Ian Randle, 2000.

GREEN, MOWBRAY. *The Eighteenth-Century Architecture of Bath.* Bath: Gregory, 1904.

GREENE, JACK. "The Jamaica Privilege Controversy, 1764–66: An Episode in the Process of Constitutional Definition in the Early Modern British Empire." *Journal of Imperial and Commonwealth History* 22, no. 1 (1994): 16–53.

GREVING, JUSTIN. "Accounting for Lady Nugent's Creole House." *Arris* 23 (2012): 16–27.

GUIRARD, MARK. *Life in the English Country House.* New Haven: Yale University Press, 1978.

HAGELBERG, G. B. "Sugar in the Caribbean: Turning Sunshine into Money." In *Caribbean Contours,* edited by Sally Price and Sidney Wilfred Mintz. Baltimore: Johns Hopkins University Press, 1985.

HALL, DOUGLAS. "Absentee-Proprietorship in the British West Indies to About 1850." *The Jamaican Historical Review* 4 (1964): 15–35.

HALL, DOUGLAS. "Botanical and Horticultural Enterprise in Eighteenth-Century Jamaica." In *West Indies Accounts: Essays on the History of the British Caribbean and the Atlantic Economy in Honour of Richard Sheridan,* edited by Roderick A. McDonald. Barbados: University of the West Indies Press, 1966, 101–25.

HALL, DOUGLAS. *A Brief History of the West India Committee.* St. Lawrence, Barbados: Caribbean Universities Press, 1971.

HALL, DOUGLAS. *In Miserable Slavery: Thomas Thistlewood in Jamaica, 1750–86.* London: Macmillan, 1989.

HALL, DOUGLAS. "Planters, Farmers, and Gardeners in Eighteenth-Century Jamaica." In *Slavery, Freedom, and Gender: The Dynamics of Caribbean Society,* edited by Brian L. Moore et al. Kingston: University of the West Indies Press, 2001.

HALL, DOUGLAS. "Slavery in Three West Indian Towns." In *Caribbean Slavery in the Atlantic World,* edited by Verene Shepherd and Hillary Beckles. Kingston: Ian Randle, 2000.

HALL, I. V. "John Knight, Junior, Sugar Refiner at the Great House on St. Augustine's Back (1654–67): Bristol's Second Sugar House." *Transactions of the Bristol and Gloucester Archaeological Society* 68 (1949): 110–64.

HALL, I. V. "Temple St. Sugar House under the First Partnership of Richard Land and John Hine (1662–78)." *Transactions of the Bristol and Gloucester Archaeological Society* 76 (1957): 118–40.

HALL, I. V. "Whitson Court Sugar House, Bristol." *Transactions of the Bristol and Gloucester Archaeological Society* 65 (1944): 49–52.

HALL, JOHN A. "Nefarious Wretches, Insidious Villains, and Evil-Minded Persons: Urban Crime Reported in Charleston's City Gazette in 1788." *South Carolina Historical Magazine* 88 (July 1987): 151–68.

HALL, LINDA J. *The Rural Houses of North Avon and South Gloucestershire, 1400–1720.* Bristol: City of Bristol Museum and Art Gallery, 1983.

HALL, MAXWELL. *Earthquakes in Jamaica from 1688 to 1919.* Kingston: Government Printing Office, 1922.

HAMILTON, DONNY. "Port Royal's Excavated Buildings." In "The Port Royal Project," http://nautarch.tamu.edu/portroyal/archives/buildings.htm.

HAMILTON, DOUGLAS. *Scotland, The Caribbean, and the Atlantic World, 1750–1820.* Manchester: Manchester University Press, 2005.

HANCOCK, DAVID. *Citizens of the World: London Merchants and the Integration of the British Atlantic Community, 1735–1785.* Cambridge: Cambridge University Press, 1995.

HANDLER, JEROME. "On the Transportation of Material Goods by Enslaved Africans during the Middle Passage: Preliminary Findings from Documentary Sources." *African Diaspora Archaeology Newsletter* (December 2006).

HANDLER, JEROME. "Plantation Slave Settlements in Barbados, 1650s to 1834." In *In the Shadow of the Plantation: Caribbean History and Legacy,* edited by Alvin Thompson. Kingston: Ian Randle Publishers, 2002.

HANDLER, JEROME, AND FREDERICK LANGE. *Plantation Slavery in Barbados: An Archaeological and Historical Investigation.* Cambridge, MA: Harvard University Press, 1978.

HANSEN, THORKILD. *Coast of Slaves.* Translated by Kari Dako. Accra: Sub-Saharan, 2002.

HARD, FREDERICK, ED. "Introduction." In Henry Wotten, *Elements of Architecture.* Charlottesville: Published for the Folger Shakespeare Library by the University Press of Virginia, 1968.

HARRIS, A. E., AND N. SAVAGE. *British Architectural Books and Writers, 1556–1785.* Cambridge: Cambridge University Press, 1990.

HARRIS, EILEEN. *The Genius of Robert Adam: His Interiors.* New Haven: Yale University Press, 2001.

HARRIS, JOHN. "Kneller Hall, Middlesex." In *The Country Seat: Studies in the History of the British Country House.* London: Allen Lane, 1970.

HARRIS, JOHN, AND CHARLES HIND. "A Greek Revival Detective Story." *The Georgian Group Journal* XX (2012): 141–50.

HART, EMMA. *Building Charleston: Town and Society in the Eighteenth-Century British Atlantic World.* Charlottesville: University of Virginia Press, 2010.

HART, VAUGHAN, AND PETER HICKS. *Sebastiano Serlio on Architecture.* New Haven: Yale University Press, 1996.

HAUSER, MARK. *An Archaeology of Black Markets, Local Ceramics and Economics in Eighteenth-Century Jamaica.* Gainesville: University Press of Florida, 2008.

HAUSER, MARK. "Linstead Market before Linstead? Eighteenth-Century Yabbas and the Internal Market System of Jamaica." *Caribbean Quarterly* 55, no. 2 (June 2009): 89–111.

HAUSER, MARK. "Of Earth and Clay: Locating Colonial Economies and Local Ceramics." In *Out of Many, One People: The Historical Archaeology of Colonial Jamaica,* edited by James Delle, Mark Hauser, and Douglas V. Armstrong, 163–82. Tuscaloosa: University of Alabama Press, 2011.

HAYES, RICHARD. "The Black Atlantic and Georgian London." In *Colonial Frames, Nationalist Histories: Imperial Legacies, Architecture, and Modernity,* edited by Mrinalini Rajagopalan and Madhuri Desai. Burlington, VT: Ashgate, 2012.

HENNINGS, KRISTIN. "Miss Rosie's House and the Jamaican Vernacular." Master's thesis, University of Virginia, 2008.

HERMAN, BERNARD. "The Embedded Landscapes of the Charleston Single House." In *Exploring Everyday Landscapes: Perspectives in Vernacular Architecture VII*, edited by Annmarie Adams and Sally McMurry. Knoxville: University of Tennessee Press (1997): 41–57.

HERMAN, BERNARD. *Town House: Architecture and Material Life in the Early American City, 1780–1830.* Chapel Hill: University of North Carolina Press, 2005.

HEUMAN, GAD. *Between Black and White: Race Politics and Free Coloreds in Jamaica, 1792–1865.* Westport, CT: Greenwood, 1981.

HEWAT-JABOOR, PHILIP. "Fonthill House: 'One of the Most Princely Edifices in the Kingdom.'" In *William Beckford, 1760–1844: An Eye for the Magnificent*, edited by Derek E. Ostergard, 50–71. New Haven: Yale University Press, 2002.

HIGMAN, BARRY W. *Jamaica Surveyed: Plantation Maps and Plans of the Eighteenth and Nineteenth Centuries.* San Francisco: Institute of Jamaica Publications, 1988.

HIGMAN, BARRY W. "Jamaican Port Towns in the Early Nineteenth Century." In *Atlantic Port Cities: Economy, Culture, and Society in the Atlantic World, 1650–1850*, edited by Franklin W. Knight and Peggy K. Liss. Knoxville: University of Tennessee Press, 1991.

HIGMAN, BARRY W. *Montpelier, Jamaica: A Plantation Community in Slavery and Freedom, 1739–1912.* Kingston: University of the West Indies Press, 1998.

HIGMAN, BARRY W. *Plantation Jamaica, 1750–1850: Capital and Control in a Colonial Economy.* Kingston: University of the West Indies Press, 2005.

HIGMAN, BARRY W. *Proslavery Priest: The Atlantic World of John Lindsay, 1728–1788.* Kingston: University of the West Indies Press, 2011.

HIGMAN, BARRY W. *Slave Population and Economy in Jamaica, 1807–1834.* Cambridge: Cambridge University Press, 1976.

HIGMAN, BARRY. *Slave Populations of the British Caribbean, 1807–1834.* Baltimore: Johns Hopkins University Press, 1984.

HIGMAN, BARRY W. "Spatial Economy of Jamaican Sugar Plantations: Cartographic Evidence from the Eighteenth and Nineteenth Centuries." *Journal of Historical Geography* 13 (1987): 21–24.

HIGMAN, BARRY W. "The Sugar Revolution." *Economic History Review* 5, no. 2 (2000): 213–36.

HIGMAN, BARRY W. "The West India Interest in Parliament, 1807–1833." *Historical Studies* 12 (1967): 1–19.

HOBHOUSE, HERMIONE, ED. "The West India Docks: Historical Development." *Survey of London: Poplar, Blackwell, and Isle of Dogs*, vols. 43 and 44. London: English Heritage, 1994. http://www.british-history.ac.uk/report.aspx?compid=46494. Accessed October 22, 2007.

HOBSBAWM, ERIC. *Age of Revolution: 1789–1848.* London: Abacus, 1962.

HOBSON, DAPHNE. "The Domestic Architecture of the Earliest British Colonies in the American Tropics: A Study of the Houses of the Caribbean Leeward Islands." Ph.D. diss., Georgia Institute of Technology, 2007.

HODGES, CHARLES. "Private Fortifications in 17th-Century Virginia: A Study of Six Representative Works." In *The Archaeology of Seventeenth-Century Virginia*, edited by Theodore Reinhart and Dennis Pogue. Archaeology Society of Virginia Special Publication no. 30, Richmond, 1993.

HORNING, AUDREY. "Archaeology, Conflict and Contemporary Identity in the North of Ireland: Implications for Theory and Practice in Comparative Archaeologies of Colonialism." *Archaeological Dialogues* 13, no. (December 2006): 183–200.

HORNSBY, STEPHEN J. *British Atlantic, American Frontier: Spaces of Power in Early Modern British Atlantic.* Hanover, NH: University Press of New England, 2005.

HOWARD, DEBORAH. *Scottish Architecture: Reformation to Restoration, 1560–1660.* Edinburgh: Edinburgh University Press, 1995.

HOWELL, ALLISON M. *The Slave Trade and Reconciliation: A Northern Ghanaian Perspective.* Bible Church of Africa, 1998.

HOWSON, JEAN. "Colonial Goods and the Plantation Village: Consumption and the Internal Economy in Montserrat from Slavery to Freedom." Ph.D. diss., New York University, 1995.

HOYLE, RICHARD, ED. *Custom, Improvement, and the Landscape in Early Modern Britain.* Farnham, Surrey: Ashgate, 2011.

HUDGINS, LISA R. "The Probate Record of William Wilson, Charleston Merchant." Unpublished report. Charleston: Museum of Early Southern Decorative Arts, 2008.

IMPEY, OLIVER, AND ARTHUR MACGREGOR, EDS. *The Origins of Museums: The Cabinet of Curiosities in Sixteenth- and Seventeenth-Century Europe.* Oxford: Clarendon, 1985.

INGAMELLS, JOHN. *Dictionary of British and Irish Travelers in Italy, 1701–1800.* New Haven: Yale University Press, 1997.

INIKORI, JOSEPH E. "Changing Commodity Composition of Imports into West Africa, 1650–1850: A Window into the Impact of the Transatlantic Slave Trade on African Societies." In *Transatlantic Slave Trade: Landmarks, Legacies, Expectations: Proceedings on the International Conference on Historic Slave Routes*, Accra, Ghana, August 30–September 2, 2004, edited by James Kwesi Anquandah, 57–80. Accra: Sub-Saharan, 2007.

INIKORI, JOSEPH E. "The Import of Firearms into West Africa" in *Forced Migration: The Impact of the Export Slave Trade on African Societies.* London: Hutchinson, 1982.

INIKORI, JOSEPH E., AND STANLEY L. ENGERMAN, EDS. *The Atlantic Slave Trade: The Effects on Economics, Societies, and Peoples in Africa, the Americas, and Europe.* Durham, NC: Duke University Press, 1992.

JACOBS, H. P. *A Short History of Kingston.* Kingston: Ministry of Education Publications Branch, 1976.

JACOBSEN, GERTRUDE. *William Blathwayt: A Late 17th-Century English Administrator.* New Haven: Yale University Press, 1932.

JAMES, TOM BEAUMONT, AND EDWARD ROBERTS. "Winchester and Late Medieval Urban Development: Palace to Pentice." *Medieval Archaeology* 44 (2000): 181–200.

JARVIS, MICHAEL. *In the Eye of All Trade: Bermuda, Bermudians, and the Maritime Atlantic World, 1680–1783.* Chapel Hill: University of North Carolina Press, 2010.

JASANOFF, MAYA. "The Other Side of Revolution: Loyalists in the British Empire." *William and Mary Quarterly* 65, no. 2 (April 2008): 205–32.

JEAFFRESON, JOHN CORDY. *A Young Squire of the Seventeenth Century: From the Papers, 1676–1686, of Christopher Jeaffreson.* London: Hurst and Blackett, 1878.

JEFFERY, SALLY. "'The flower of all the Private Gentlemen's Palaces in England': Sir Stephen Fox's 'extraordinarily fine' garden at Chiswick." *Garden History* 32: 1 (2004).

JOHNSON, J. D. "Settlement and Architecture in County Fermanagh, 1610–41." *Ulster Journal of Archaeology* 43 (1980): 79–89.

JOHNSON, MATTHEW. *Behind the Castle Gate: From Medieval to Renaissance.* London: Routledge, 2002.

JOHNSON, PAUL. *Ireland: Land of Troubles.* London: Methuen, 1980.

JOHNSON, WALTER. *Soul by Soul: Life inside the Antebellum Slave Market.* Cambridge, MA: Harvard University Press, 1999.

JONES, STEVEN. "The African-American Tradition in Vernacular Architecture." In *The Archaeology of Slavery and Plantation Life*, edited by Theresa Singleton. Orlando: Academic Press, 1985.

JOPE, E. M. "Cornish Houses, 1400–1700." In *Studies in Building History: Essays in Recognition of the Work of B. H. St. J. O'Neil,* edited by E. M. Jope et al. London: Odhams, 1961.

JOPE, E. M. "Moyry, Charlemont, Castleraw, and Richhill: Fortification to Architecture in the North of Ireland." *Ulster Journal of Archaeology* 3 (1960): 97–123.

JOPE, E. M. "Scottish Influences in the North of Ireland: Castles with Scottish Features, 1580–1640." *Ulster Journal of Archaeology* 14 (1951): 31–47.

JOPLIN CAROL F. *Puerto Rican Houses in Sociohistorical Perspective.* Knoxville: University of Tennessee, 1988.

JORDAN, WINTHROP D. *White over Black: American Attitudes towards the Negro, 1550–1812.* Chapel Hill: Published for the Institute of Early American History and Culture at Williamsburg, Va. by the University of North Carolina Press, 1968.

JOSEPH, J. W. "From Colonial to Charlestonian: The Crafting of Identity in a Colonial Southern City." In *Another's Country: Archaeological and Historical Perspectives on Cultural Interactions in the Southern Colonies,* edited by J. W. Joseph and Martha A. Zierden. Tuscaloosa: University of Alabama, 2002.

KARRAS, ALAN L. *Sojourners in the Sun: Scottish Migrants in Jamaica and the Chesapeake, 1740–1800.* Ithaca, NY: Cornell University Press, 1992.

KEA, RAY A. *Settlements, Trade, and Polities in the Seventeenth-Century Gold Coast.* Baltimore: Johns Hopkins University Press, 1982.

KELLY, JASON M. *The Society of Dilettanti: Archaeology and Identity in the British Enlightenment.* New Haven: Yale University Press, 2009.

KELLY, KENNETH. "Change and Continuity in Coastal Benin." In *West Africa during the Atlantic Slave Trade: Archaeological Perspectives,* edited by Christopher DeCorse. Leicester University Press, 2001.

KELSO, WILLIAM M. *Captain Jones's Wormsloe: A Historical, Archaeological and Architectural Study of an Eighteenth-Century Plantation Site near Savannah, Georgia.* Athens: University of Georgia Press, 1979.

KENSETH, JOY, ED. *The Age of the Marvelous.* Hanover, NH: Hood Museum of Art, 1991.

KENWORTHY-BROWNE, J. A. *Dodington: The Home of the Codrington Family.* Derby: English Life Publications, n.d.

KILLINGRAY, DAVID. "Kent and the Abolition of the Slave Trade: A County Study, 1760s–1807." *Archæologia Cantiana,* CXXVII (2007): 107–25.

KLEPPER, KATHERINE. "The Merchant's House in the Caribbean." Master's thesis, University of Virginia, 2008.

KLEIN, HERBERT. *The Atlantic Slave Trade.* Cambridge: Cambridge University Press, 1999.

KLINGLEHOFER, ERIC. "Colonial Castles: The Architecture of Social Control." In *Material Culture in Anglo-America: Regional Identity and Urbanity in the Chesapeake, Tidewater, and Caribbean,* edited by David Shields. Columbia: University of South Carolina Press, 2009.

KNOX, TIM. *West Wycombe Park.* Bromley, Kent: The National Trust, 2001.

KOSTOF, SPIRO. *The City Assembled: Elements of Urban Form through History.* Boston: Little, Brown, 1992.

KRIZ, KAY DIAN. *Slavery, Sugar and the Culture of Refinement: Picturing the British West Indies, 1700–1840.* New Haven: Yale University Press, 2008.

KUBLER, GEORGE. *Mexican Architecture of the Sixteenth Century.* New Haven, CT: Yale University Press, 1948.

KUPPERMAN, KAREN. "Fear of Hot Climates in the Anglo-American Colonial Experience." *William and Mary Quarterly,* 3rd ser., vol. 41, no. 2 (April 1984): 213–40.

LANCASTER, CLAY. *American Bungalow, 1880–1930.* New York: Abbeville, 1985.

LAW, ROBIN. *Ouidah: The Social History of a West African Slaving "Port," 1727–1892.* Athens, OH: Ohio University Press, 2004.

LAWRENCE, A. W. *Fortified Trade-Posts: The English in West Africa, 1645–1822.* London: Cape, 1969.

LAWRENCE, SUSAN. *Archaeologies of the British: Explorations of Identity in Great Britain and Its Colonies, 1600–1945.* London: Routledge, 2003.

LAWSON, P. H., AND T. SMITH. "The Rows of Chester: Two Interpretations." *Chester Archaeological Society* XLV (1958): 1–42.

LEASK, HAROLD GRAHAM. *Irish Castles and Castellated Houses.* Dundalk: Dundalgan Press, 1951.

LEECH, ROGER. "An Historical and Architectural Analysis of the Exchange Building, Corn Street, Bristol." Unpublished report for the City of Bristol, 1999.

LEECH, ROGER. "Impermanent Architecture in the English Colonies of the Eastern Caribbean: New Contexts for Innovation in the Early Modern Atlantic World." In *Building Environments: Perspectives in Vernacular Architecture X,* edited by Kenneth Breisch and Alison Hoagland, 153–68. Knoxville: University of Tennessee Press, 2005.

LEES-MILNE, JAMES. *William Beckford.* Montclair, NJ: Alanheld, 1979.

"Legacies of British Slave Ownership." http://www.ucl.ac.uk.

LEWIS, LESLEY. *Connoisseurs and Secret Agents in Eighteenth-Century Rome.* London: Chatto & Windus, 1961.

LEWIS, LESLEY. "Elizabeth, Countess of Home, and Her House in Portman Square." *Burlington Magazine* 109, no. 773 (August 1967).

LISS, PEGGY K. *Atlantic Empires: The Network of Trade and Revolution.* Baltimore: Johns Hopkins University Press, 1983.

LITTLEFIELD, DAVID. *Rice and Slaves: Ethnicity & the Slave Trade in Colonial South Carolina.* Baton Rouge: Louisiana State Press, 1981.

LLANES, LLILIAN. *The Houses of Old Cuba.* London: Thames and Hudson, 2001.

LOUNSBURY, CARL R. *An Illustrated Glossary of Early Southern Architecture and Landscape.* New York: Oxford University Press, 1994.

LUMSDEN, JOY. "Notes on Three Historic Buildings and/or Sites." *Jamaica Historical Society Bulletin* 10, no. 12 (October 1995): 130–33.

MACGIBBON, DAVIS, AND THOMAS ROSS. *Castellated and Domestic Architecture of Scotland from the Twelfth to the Eighteenth Century,* 5 vols., 1887–92.

MACMAHON, MICHAEL. *Portumna Castle and Its Lords.* Co. Clare: Kincora, 2000.

MACMILLAN, ALLISTER. *The West Indies Illustrated: Historical and Descriptive, Commercial and Industrial Facts, Figures, and Resources.* London: W. H. and L. Collingridge, 1909.

MAGUIRE, ALISON, AND HOWARD COLVIN. "A Collection of Seventeenth-Century Building Plans," *Architectural History* 35 (1992): 140–82.

MALCOLM, COREY. "The Iron Bilboes of the *Henrietta Marie*." *The Navigator: Newsletter of the Mel Fisher Maritime Heritage Society* 13, no. 10 (October 1998): 81–100.

MANN, DOUGLAS. "Becoming Creole: Material Life and Society in Eighteenth-Century Kingston, Jamaica." Ph.D. diss., University of Georgia, 2005.

MANNING, PATRICK. *The African Diaspora: A History through Culture.* New York: Columbia University Press, 2008.

MANUCY, ALBERT. *The Houses of St. Augustine, 1565–1821.* Gainesville: University Press of Florida, 1992.

MANUCY, ALBERT. *Sixteenth-Century St. Augustine: The People and Their Homes.* Gainesville: University Press of Florida, 1997.

MARSHALL, P. J. *The Oxford History of British Empire.* Oxford: Oxford University Press, 1998.

MARTIN, ANN SMART. "Ribbons of Desire: Gendered Stories in the

World of Goods." In *Gender, Taste, and Material Culture in Britain and North America, 1700–1830,* edited by John Styles and Amanda Vickery. New Haven: Yale University Press, 2006.

MARTIN, EVELINE. *The British West African Settlements, 1750–1821: A Study in Local Administration.* New York: Longmans, 1927.

MARTIN, JOAN M. *"Placage* and the Louisiana *Gens de Couleur Libre."* In *Creole: The History and Legacy of Louisiana's Free People of Color,* edited by Sybil Kein. Baton Rouge: Louisiana State University Press, 2000.

MARTINEZ-RUIZ, BARBARO. "Sketches of Memory: Visual Encounters with Africa in Jamaican Culture." In *Art and Emancipation in Jamaica,* edited by T. J. Barringer, Gillian Forrester, and Barbaro Martinez-Ruiz. New Haven: Yale University Press, 2007.

MASSING, JEAN MICHEL. *The Image of the Black in Western Art.* Vol. III, pt. 2 of *The "Age of Discovery" to the Age of Abolition,* edited by David Bindman and Henry Louis Gates, Jr. Cambridge, MA: Harvard University Press, 2011.

MAUCHLINE, MARY. *Harewood House: One of the Treasure Houses of Britain.* Ashbourne: Moorland, 1992.

MCCUSKER, JOHN J., AND RUSSELL R. MENARD. *The Economy of British America, 1607–1789.* Chapel Hill, 1985.

MCDONALD, RODERICK. "Urban Crime and Social Control in St. Vincent during the Apprenticeship." In *West Indies Accounts: Essays on the History of the British Caribbean and the Atlantic Economy in Honour of Richard Sheridan,* edited by Roderick A. McDonald. Kingston: University of the West Indies Press, 1996.

MCINNIS, MAURIE. *The Politics of Taste in Antebellum Charleston.* Chapel Hill: University of North Carolina Press, 2005.

MCINNIS, MAURIE DEE. *Slaves Waiting for Sale: Abolitionist Art and the American Slave Trade.* Chicago: University of Chicago Press, 2011.

MCKEAN, CHARLES. *The Scottish Chateau: The Country House of Renaissance Scotland.* Stroud, England: Sutton, 2001.

MCKENDRICK, NEIL, JOHN BREWER, AND J. H. PLUMB, EDS. *The Birth of a Consumer Society: The Commercialisation of Eighteenth-Century England.* London: Hutchinson, 1982.

MCLEOD, BET. "A Celebrated Collector." In *William Beckford, 1760–1844: An Eye for the Magnificent,* edited by Derek E. Ostergard. New Haven: Yale University Press, 2002.

MCNEILL, ROBERT. *Atlantic Empires of France and Spain.* Chapel Hill: University of North Carolina Press, 1985.

MCPARLAND, EDWARD. "Rathfarnham Castle." *Country Life* 172 (September 1982): 734–37.

METCALF, GEORGE. *Royal Government and Political Conflict in Jamaica, 1729–1783.* London: Longmans, 1965.

MILLER, DANIEL, ED. *Acknowledging Consumption: A Review of New Studies.* London: Routledge, 1995.

MILLER, JOSEPH. "The Slave Trade in Congo and Angola." In *The African Diaspora: Interpretive Essays,* edited by Martin Kilson and Robert Rotberg, 75–113. Cambridge, MA: Harvard University Press, 1976.

MILLER, JOSEPH. *Way of Death, Merchant Capitalism and the Angolan Slave Trade, 1730–1830.* Madison: University of Wisconsin Press, 1988.

MINCHINTON, WALTER. *The Port of Bristol in the Eighteenth Century.* Bristol: Bristol Historical Association, 1962.

MINGAY, G. E. *The Agricultural Revolution: Changes in Agriculture, 1750–1880.* London: A. and C. Black, 1977.

MINGAY, G. E. "The Size of Farms in the Eighteenth Century." *Economic History Review* 14, no. 3 (1962): 469–88.

MINTZ, SIDNEY. *Caribbean Transformations.* Chicago: Aldine, 1974.

MINTZ, SIDNEY. *Sweetness and Power: The Place of Sugar in Modern History.* New York: Penguin, 1985.

MITCHELL, S. IAN. "The Development of Urban Retailing, 1700–1815." In *The Transformation of English Provincial Towns, 1600–1800,* edited by Peter Clark, 259–83. London: Hutchinson, 1984.

MOLINEUX, CATHERINE. *Faces of Perfect Ebony: Encountering Atlantic Slavery in Imperial Britain.* Cambridge, MA: Harvard University Press, 2012.

MONRAD, HANS CHRISTIAN. *Description of the Guinea Coast and Its Inhabitants.* Accra: Sub-Saharan, 2009.

MOODY, T. W., F. X. Martin, and F. J. Byrne, eds. *A New History of Ireland: Early Modern Ireland, 1534–1691,* vol. 3. Oxford: Oxford University Press, 1976.

MOORE, DAVID, AND COREY MALCOM. "Seventeenth-Century Vehicle of the Middle Passage: Archaeological and Historical Investigations on the *Henrietta Marie* Shipwreck Site." *International Journal of Historical Archaeology* 12, no. 1 (March 2008): 20–38.

MORGAN, KENNETH. "The Organization of the Convict Trade to Maryland: Stevenson, Randolph, and Cheston, 1768–1775." *William and Mary Quarterly,* 3rd ser., vol. 42, no. 2 (April 1985): 201–27.

MORGAN, KENNETH. "Slave Sales in Colonial Charleston." *The English Historical Review* 113, no. 453 (September 1, 1998): 905–27.

MOUSER, BRUCE L. *A Slaving Voyage to Africa and Jamaica: The Log of the Sandown, 1793–1794.* Bloomington: Indiana University Press, 2002.

MOWL, TIM, AND BRIAN EARNSHAW. *John Wood: Architect of Obsession.* Bath: Millstream, 1988.

MULCAHY, MATTHEW. *Hurricanes and Society in the British Greater Caribbean, 1624–1783.* Baltimore: Johns Hopkins, 2006.

MULLIN, J. R. "The Reconstruction of Lisbon following the Earthquake of 1755: A Study in Despotic Planning." *Planning Perspectives* 7 (1992): 157–79.

NAMIER, L. B., ED. *The History of Parliament: The House of Commons, 1754–1790.* New York, Published for the History of Parliament Trust by Oxford University Press, 1964.

NELSON, LOUIS, EDWARD CHAPPELL, BRIAN COFRANCESCO, AND EMILIE JOHNSON. *Falmouth, Jamaica: Architecture as History.* Kingston: University of West Indies Press, 2014.

NEWTON, JOHN. *Journal of a Slave Trader 1750–54,* edited by Bernard Martin and Mark Spurrell. London: Epworth Press, 1962.

NISBET, S. "The Sugar Adventurers of Glasgow, 1640–1740." *History Scotland* 9:3 (2009): 26–33.

NKUMBAAN, S. N. "Historical Archaeology of Slave Route Case Study of Kasana and Sankana." M. Phil. thesis, University of Ghana, Legon, 2003.

NORMAN, NEIL. "Hueda (Whydah) Country and Town: Archaeological Perspectives on the Rise and Collapse of an African Atlantic Kingdom." *The International Journal of African Historical Studies* 42, no. 3, Current Trends in the Archaeology of African History (2009): 387–410.

NORTHRUP, DAVID. *Trade without Rulers: Pre-Colonial Economic Development in Southeastern Nigeria.* Oxford: Clarendon, 1978.

O'FLANAGAN, PATRICK. "Port Cities: Engines of Growth in an Emerging Atlantic System." In *Port Cities: Dynamic Landscapes and Global Networks,* edited by Carola Hein. New York: Routledge, 2011.

OKORO, J. A. "An Archaeological and Ethno-Historical Investigation of the Slave Market and Baobab Site of Saakpuli, N. Ghana"; F. Y. T. Longi, "Oral History of the Slave Trade at Kasana and Gwollu"; S. N. Nkumbaan, "Archaeological Study at Kasana" and "Archaeological Reconnaissance at Sankana." UNESCO National Slave Route Project, 2002.

OKORO, J. A. "Indigenous Water Management, Slavery and Slave Trade in Salaga." Unpublished paper, Department of Archaeology, Legon, 2003.

OLIVER, VERE LANGFORD. *Caribbeana: Being Miscellaneous Papers Relating to the History, Genealogy, Topography, and Antiquities of the British West Indes.* London: Mitchell, Hughes and Clarke, 1910–1919.

O'SHAUGHNESSY, ANDREW. *An Empire Divided: The American Revolution and the British Caribbean.* Philadelphia: University of Pennsylvania Press, 2000.

OSTERGARD, DEREK E., ED. *William Beckford, 1760–1844: An Eye for the Magnificent.* New Haven: Yale University Press, 2002.

OSZUSCIK, PHILIPPE. "Comparisons between Rural and Urban French Creole Housing." *Material Culture* 26, no. 3 (1994): 1–36.

OSZUSCIK, PHILIPPE. "Eighteenth-Century Concerns for 'Healthy Buildings' on the North Gulf Coast." *Arris* 22 (2011).

OSZUSCIK, PHILIPPE. "French Creoles on the Gulf Coast." In *To Build in a New Land: Ethnic Landscapes in North America,* edited by Allen Noble. Baltimore: Johns Hopkins University Press, 1992.

OSZUSCIK, PHILIPPE. "Passage of the Gallery and Other Caribbean Elements from the French and Spanish to the British in the United States." *Material Culture* 15 (1992): 1–14.

OWEN, NICHOLAS, AND EVELINE CHRISTIANA MARTIN. *Journal of a Slave-Dealer: "A View of Some Remarkable Axcedents In the Life of Nics: Owen On the Coast of Africa and America from the Year 1746 to the Year 1757."* London: G. Routledge, 1930.

PABON, ARLEEN. "*Por la encendida calle antilana:* Africanisms and Puerto Rican Architecture." *CRM: The Journal of Heritage Stewardship* (Fall 2003): 14–32.

PACE, CLAIRE. "Gavin Hamilton's *Wood and Dawkins Discovering Palmyra:* The Dilettante as Hero," *Art History,* 4 (1981): 271–90.

PALM, EDWIN WALTER. *Los monumentos arquitectónicos de la Espanola con una introducción a America.* 2 vols. Ciudad Trujillo [Santo Domingo]: Publicaciones de la Universidad de Santo Domingo, 1955.

DI PALMA, VITTORIA. *Wasteland: A History.* New Haven: Yale University Press, 2014.

PALMER, MARILYN, AND PETER NEAVERSON. *Industry in the Landscape, 1700–1900.* New York: Routledge, 1994.

PALMER, SARAH. "Port Economics in an Historical Context: The Nineteenth-Century Port of London." *International Journal of Maritime History* 15 (June 2003).

PANNING, STEVEN. "Colbeck Castle Outbuildings and Environs," *Jamaica Historical Society Bulletin* 11, no. 2 (1998), 33–38.

PANNING, STEVEN. "Edinburgh Castle." Jamaica National Heritage Trust Report, 2005.

PANNING, STEVEN. "Exploring Stewart Castle Estate," *Jamaican Historical Journal* (1995).

PAPASTERGIADIS, NIKOS. "Tracing Hybridity in Theory." In *Debating Cultural Hybridity: Multi-Cultural Identities and the Politics of Anti-Racism,* edited by Pnina Werbner; Tariq Modood. London: Zed, 1997.

PARES, RICHARD. *Merchants and Planters.* Cambridge: Published for the Economic History Review, Cambridge University Press, 1960.

PARES, RICHARD. *War and Trade in the West Indies, 1739–1763.* Frank Cass, 1963.

PATTERSON, ORLANDO. *The Sociology of Slavery: An Analysis of the Origins, Development and Structure of Negro Slave Society in Jamaica.* London: MacGibbon and Kee, 1967.

PAULA, RAQUEL, AND VITOR COIAS. "Rehabilitation of Lisbon's Old 'Seismic Resistant' Timber Framed Buildings Using Innovative Techniques." Paper delivered at the International Workshop on Earthquake Engineering on Timber Structures, Coimbra, Portugal (2006).

PAWSON, MICHAEL, AND DAVID BUISSERET. *Port Royal, Jamaica.* Kingston: University of the West Indies Press, 2002.

PEARSALL, SARAH M. S. "'The Late Flagrant Instance of Depravity in My Family': The Story of an Anglo-Jamaican Cuckold." *William and Mary Quarterly* 60, no. 3 (July 2003): 549–82.

PEARSON, EDWARD. *Designs against Charleston: The Trial Record of the Denmark Vesey Slave Conspiracy of 1822.* Chapel Hill: University of North Carolina Press, 1999.

PENSON, LILLIAN M. "The London West India Interest in the Eighteenth Century." *English Historical Review* 36 (1921): 373–92.

PERBI, AKOSUA ADOMA. *A History of Indigenous Slavery in Ghana: From the 15th to the 19th Century.* Accra: Sub-Saharan, 2004.

PERBI, AKOSUA, AND YAW BREDWA-MENSAH. "Slave Camps in Pre-Colonial Ghana: The Case of Jenini in the Brong Ahafo Region." In *The Transatlantic Slave Trade: Landmarks, Legacies, Expectations,* edited by James Kwesi Anquandah. Accra: Sub-Saharan, 2007.

PEROTIN-DUMON, ANNE. "Cabotage, Contraband, and Corsairs: The Port Cities of Guadeloupe and Their Inhabitants, 1650–1800." In *Atlantic Port Cities: Economy, Culture, and Society in the Atlantic World, 1650–1850,* edited by Franklin W. Knight and Peggy K. Liss. Knoxville: University of Tennessee Press, 1991.

PERRY, VICTORIA. "Slavery and the Sublime: The Atlantic Trade, Landscape Aesthetics, and Tourism." In *Slavery and the British Country House,* edited by Madge Dresser and Andrew Hann. Swindon: English Heritage, 2013.

PETERS, MARIE. *Pitt and Popularity: The Patriot Minister and London Opinion during the Seven Years' War.* Oxford: Clarendon, 1980.

PETLEY, CHRISTER. "Plantations and Homes: The Material Culture of the Early Nineteenth-Century Jamaican Elite." *Slavery & Abolition* 35, no. 3 (2014): 437–57.

PEVSNER, NIKOLAUS. *The Buildings of Wales: Clwyd, Denbighshire, and Flintshire.* Harmondsworth, England: Penguin, 1986.

PICON, ANTOINE. *French Architects and Engineers in the Age of Enlightenment.* Translated by Martin Thom. Cambridge: Cambridge University Press, 1992.

PICTON, J. A. *Memorials of Liverpool.* London: Longmans, Green, 1873.

PIERCE, CHARLES. *Histoire Naturelle des Indes: The Drake Manuscript in the Pierpont Morgan Library.* New York: Norton, 1996.

PIERSEN, W. D. "White Cannibals, Black Martyrs: Fear, Depression, and Religious Faith as Causes of Suicide among New Slaves." *Journal of Negro History* 62, no. 2 (April 1977).

"Place for Macleods." *The Associated Clan MacLeod Societies.* http://www.clanmacleod.org/genealogy/macleod-genealogy-research/the-macleods-of-lewis.html. Accessed September 11, 2012.

PLATT, COLIN. *The Castle in Medieval England and Wales.* New York: Scribner, 1982.

POCIUS, GERALD L. "Parlors, Pump Houses, and Pickups: The Art of Privacy in a Newfoundland Community." Paper delivered at the annual meeting of the American Folklore Society, Baltimore, 1986.

POCIUS, GERALD L. *A Place to Belong: Community Order and Everyday Space in Calvert, Newfoundland.* Montreal: McGill-Queen's University Press, 2001.

POESCH, JESSIE. *The Art of the Old South: Painting, Sculpture, Architecture, and the Products of Craftsmen, 1560–1860.* New York: Harrison House, 1989.

PONS, FRANK MOYA. *History of the Caribbean: Plantations, Trade and War in the Atlantic World.* Princeton: Markus Weiner, 2007.

PORTER, GLENN, AND HAROLD C. LIVESAY. *Merchants and Manufacturers: Studies in the Changing Structure of Nineteenth-Century Marketing.* Baltimore: Johns Hopkins University Press, 1971.

POSTMA, JOHANNES. *The Dutch in the Atlantic Slave Trade, 1600–1815.* Cambridge: Cambridge University Press, 1990.

PRATT, MARY LOUISE. *Imperial Eyes: Travel Writing and Transculturation.* New York: Routledge, 1992.

PRICE, JACOB. "Economic Function and the Growth of American Port Towns in the Eighteenth Century." *Perspectives in American History* 8 (1974): 123–86.

PRICE, JACOB. *Tobacco in Atlantic Trade: The Chesapeake, London, and Glasgow, 1675–1775.* Brookfield, VT: Variorum, 1995.

PRIDDY, SUMPTER III, ADAM T. ERBY, AND JENNA HUFFMAN. "'The one Mrs. Trist would chuse': Thomas Jefferson, the Trist Family, and the Monticello Campeachy Chair." *American Furniture* (2012), 24–56.

PRINCE, MARY. *The History of Mary Prince: A West Indian Slave.* Rev. ed. Edited by Moira Ferguson. Ann Arbor: University of Michigan Press, 1997.

PRITCHARD, JAMES. *In Search of Empire: The French in the Americas, 1670–1730.* Cambridge: Cambridge University Press, 2004.

PROWN, JONATHAN. "The Furniture of Thomas Day: A Reevaluation." *Winterthur Portfolio* 33, no. 4 (Winter 1998): 215–49.

PULSIPHER, LYDIA. "The Landscapes and Ideational Roles of Caribbean Slave Gardens." In *Archaeology of Garden and Field,* edited by Naomi Miller and Katheryn Gleason. Philadelphia: University of Pennsylvania Press, 1994.

PULSIPHER, LYDIA, AND LAVERNE WELLS-BOWIE. "The Domestic Spaces of Daufuskie and Monserrat: The Cross-Cultural Comparison." In *Traditional Dwellings and Settlements Working Paper Series,* VII (1989).

PURCHAS, ANNE. "Maurice-Louis Jolivet's Drawings at West Wycombe Park." *Architectural History* 37 (1994): 68–79.

PUSEY, MARY FAITH, AND ANN STAUFFENBURG. "The Cipher Book of Pierre Eugène du Simitière." *Serif* 11 (Winter 1975): 33–41.

QUILLEY, GEOFF. "Pastoral Plantations: The Slave Trade and the Representation of British Colonial Landscape in the Late Eighteenth Century." In *An Economy of Colour: Visual Culture and the Atlantic World, 1660–1830,* edited by Geoff Quilley and Kay Dian Kris, 106–28. Manchester: Manchester University Press, 2003.

QUILLEY, GEOFF, AND KAY DIAN KRIZ. *An Economy of Colour: Visual Culture and the Atlantic World, 1660–1830.* Manchester: Manchester University Press, 2003.

RAGATZ, LOWELL JOSEPH. *The Fall of the Planter Class in the British Caribbean, 1763–1833.* New York: Century, 1928.

RAJAGOPALAN, MRINALINI, AND MADHURI DESAI, EDS. *Colonial Frames, Nationalist Histories: Imperial Legacies, Architecture, and Modernity.* Burlington, VT: Ashgate, 2012.

RAMCHARAN, SHAKU. "Caribbean Prehistoric Domestic Architecture: A Study of Spatio-Temporal Dynamics and Acculturation." Master's thesis, Florida State University, 2004.

RASK, JOHANNES. *A Brief and Truthful Description of a Journey to and from Guinea.* Accra: Sub-Saharan, 2009.

RATHBONE, RICHARD. "Some Thoughts on Resistance to Enslavement in Africa." *Slavery and Abolition* 6, no. 3 (December 1985): 11–22.

REDIKER, MARCUS. *The Slave Ship: A Human History.* London: John Murray, 2007.

REEVES, MATTHEW BRUCE. "By Their Own Labor: Enslaved Africans' Survival Strategies on Two Jamaican Plantations." Ph.D. diss., Syracuse University, 1997.

REYNOLDS, TERRY. *Stronger Than a Hundred Men: A History of the Vertical Water Wheel.* Baltimore: Johns Hopkins University Press, 1983.

RHYS, ISAAC. *The Transformation of Virginia, 1740–90.* Chapel Hill: University of North Carolina Press, 1982.

RICHARDSON, DAVID. "Liverpool and the English Slave Trade." In *Transatlantic Slavery: Against Human Dignity,* edited by Anthony Tibbles. Liverpool: Liverpool University Press, 1994.

RICHARDSON, DAVID, ED. *Bristol, Africa, and the Eighteenth-Century Slave Trade to America.* Bristol: Bristol Record Society, 1986–1996.

RITTER, ABRAHAM. *Philadelphia and Her Merchants, as Constituted Fifty to Seventy Years Ago.* Philadelphia: Published by the author, 1860.

ROBERTS, ADOLPHE. "Who Planned Kingston?" *Jamaican Historical Review* I (1946): 144–53.

ROBERTS, JUSTIN. *Slavery and the Enlightenment in the British Atlantic, 1750–1807.* Cambridge: Cambridge University Press, 2013.

ROBERTSON, JAMES. "Eighteenth-Century Jamaica's Ambivalent Cosmopolitanism." *History* 99, no. 337 (October 2014): 607–31.

ROBERTSON, JAMES. *Gone Is the Ancient Glory: Spanish Town, Jamaica, 1534–2000.* Kingston: Ian Randle, 2005.

ROBERTSON, JAMES. "Jamaican Architectures before Georgian," *Winterthur Portfolio* 36, no. 2–3 (Summer/Autumn 2001): 73–95.

ROBERTSON, JAMES. "Late Seventeenth-Century Spanish Town, Jamaica: Building an English City on Spanish Foundations." *Early American Studies* 6, no. 2 (Fall 2008): 346–90.

ROBERTSON, JAMES. "Reinventing the English Conquest of Jamaica in the Late Seventeenth Century." *English Historical Review* 118 (2002).

ROBINSON, CAREY. *The Rise and Fall of Falmouth: Urban Life in 19th-Century Jamaica.* Kingston: LMH, 2007.

ROBINSON, JOHN MARTIN. *James Wyatt, Architect to George III.* New Haven, Yale University Press, 2012.

ROSEBROCK, ELLEN FLETCHER. *Counting-House Days in South Street: New York's Early Brick Seaport Buildings.* New York: South Street Seaport Museum, 1975.

ROUSE, IRVING. *The Tainos: The Rise and Decline of the People Who Greeted Columbus.* New Haven: Yale University Press, 1993.

RYMAN, CHERYL. "Jonkonnu: A Neo-African Form." *Jamaica Journal* 17, nos. 1 and 2 (1984): 13–23, 50–61.

SALTER, MIKE. *Castles and Stronghouses of Ireland.* Malvern, England: Folly, 1993.

SATCHELL, VERONT. "The Early Use of Steam Power in the Jamaican Sugar Industry, 1768–1810." In *Caribbean Slavery in the Atlantic World,* edited by Verene Shepherd and Hillary Beckles. Kingston: Ian Randle, 2000.

SATCHELL, VERONT. *Hope Transformed: A Historical Sketch of the Hope Landscape, St. Andrew, Jamaica, 1660–1960.* Kingston: University of the West Indies Press, 2012.

SATCHELL, VERONT. "Innovations in Sugar-cane Mill Technology in Jamaica." In *Working Slavery, Pricing Freedom: Perspectives from the Caribbean, Africa, and the African Diaspora,* edited by Verene Shepherd. Kingston: Ian Randle, 2001.

SCHOFIELD, JOHN. *Medieval London Houses.* New Haven: Published for the Paul Mellon Center for Studies in British Art by Yale University Press, 1994.

SCHULER, MONICA. "Day to Day Resistance to Slavery in the Caribbean during the Eighteenth Century." *African Studies Association of the West Indies* 6 (1973): 57–75.

SCOBEY, DAVID M. *Empire City: The Making and Meaning of the New York City Landscape.* Philadelphia: Temple University Press, 2002.

SCOTUS, PHILO. *Reminiscences of a Scottish Gentleman.* London: Arthur Hall, Virtue, 1861.

SCRIVER, PETER. *Colonial Modernities: Building, Dwelling and Architecture in British India and Ceylon.* London: Routledge, 2007.

SEYMOUR, SUSANNE, AND SHERYLLYNNE HAGGERTY. "The Slavery Connections of Bolsover Castle." English Heritage, July 21, 2010. https://www.historicengland.org.uk/images-books/publications/slavery-connections-bolsover-castle/.

SHAKESPEAR, JOHN. *John Shakespear of Shadwell and His Descendants, 1619–1931.* Newcastle upon Tyne: Northumberland Press, 1931.

SHEPHERD, VERENE, AND GLEN RICHARDS. *Questioning Creole: Creolozation Discourses in Caribbean Culture.* Kingston: Ian Randle, 2002.

SHERIDAN, RICHARD. *Doctors and Slaves: A Medical and Demographic History of Slavery in the British West Indies, 1680–1834.* Cambridge: Cambridge University Press, 1985.

SHERIDAN, RICHARD. "Planter and Historian: The Career of William Beckford of Jamaica and England, 1744–1799." *The Jamaican Historical Review* 4 (1964): 36–58.

SHERIDAN, RICHARD. "Resistance and Rebellion of African Captives in the Transatlantic Slave Trade." In *Working Slavery, Pricing Freedom: Perspectives from the Caribbean, Africa, and the African Diaspora,* edited by Verene Shepherd. Kingston: Ian Randle, 2002.

SHERIDAN, RICHARD. "Samuel Martin: Innovating Sugar Planter of Antigua, 1750–1776," *Agricultural History* 34, no. 3 (July 1960): 126–39.

SHERIDAN, RICHARD. *Sugar and Slavery: An Economic History of the British West Indies, 1623–1775.* Baltimore: Johns Hopkins University Press, 1973.

SHIPING, H. "The Earthquake Resistant Properties of Chinese Traditional Architecture." *Earthquake Spectra* 7 (1991): 355–89.

SIMMONDS, D. "A Note on the Excavations in Cape Coast Castle." *Transactions of the Historical Society of Ghana* (Historical Society of Ghana) 14, no. 2 (1973): 267–69.

SMITH, FREDERICK. *Caribbean Rum: A Social and Economic History.* Gainesville: University Press of Florida, 2008.

SMITH, FREDERICK H., AND KARL WATSON. "Western Bridgetown and the Butchers' Shambles in the Seventeenth–Nineteenth Centuries." *Journal of the Barbados Museum Historical Society* 53 (2007): 185–98.

SMITH, MARK. *Mastered by the Clock: Time Slavery and Freedom in the American South.* Chapel Hill: University of North Carolina Press, 1997.

SMITH, ROBERT. "The Canoe in West African History." *Journal of African History* 11, No. 4 (1970): 515–33.

SMITH, SIMON. *Slavery, Family, and Gentry Capitalism in the British Atlantic: The World of the Lascelles, 1648–1834.* Cambridge: Cambridge Studies in Economic History, Cambridge University Press, 2006.

SMITH, VIRGINIA. *Clean: A History of Personal Hygiene and Purity.* Oxford: Oxford University Press, 2007.

SMOUT, T. C. "The Early Scottish Sugar Houses, 1660–1720." *Economic History Review* 14, no. 2 (1961): 240–53.

SOBEL, MECHAL. *The World They Made Together: Black and White Values in Eighteenth-Century Virginia.* Princeton: Princeton University Press, 1987.

SOMERSET FRY, PLANTAGENET. *Castles of Britain and Ireland: The Ultimate Resource Book.* New York: Abbeville Press, 1997.

SPARKS, RANDY. *The Two Princes of Calabar: An Eighteenth-Century Atlantic Odyssey.* Cambridge, MA: Harvard University Press, 2004.

ST. CLAIR, WILLIAM. *The Door of No Return: The History of Cape Coast Castle and the Atlantic Slave Trade.* New York: BlueBridge, 2007.

ST. GEORGE, ROBERT BLAIR. "Bawns and Beliefs: Architecture, Commerce and Conversion in Early New England," *Winterthur Portfolio* 25/4 (1990): 89–125.

ST. GEORGE, ROBERT BLAIR. *Conversing by Signs: The Poetics of Implication in Colonial New England Culture.* Chapel Hill: University of North Carolina Press, 1998.

ST. GEORGE, ROBERT BLAIR. Introduction. In *Possible Pasts: Becoming Colonial in Early America.* Ithaca, NY: Cornell University Press, 2000.

STAHL, A. B. "Historical Process and the Impact of the Atlantic Slave Trade in Banda, Ghana c. 1800–1920." In *West Africa during the Atlantic Slave Trade: Archaeological Perspectives,* edited by C. R. De Corse. London: Leicester University Press, 2001.

STEPHEN, ALEXANDER FORTUNE. *Merchants and Jews: The Struggle for British West India Commerce, 1650–1750.* Gainesville: University Press of Florida, 1984.

STEWART, CHARLES. *Creolization: History, Ethnography, Theory.* Walnut Creek, CA: Left Coast, 2007.

STEWART-BROWN, RONALD DAVID. *Liverpool Ships in the Eighteenth Century: Including the king's ships built there, with notes on the principal shipwrights.* University Press of Liverpool; London: Hodder & Stoughton, 1932.

STOBART, JON. "Shopping Streets as Social Space: Leisure, Consumerism and Improvement in an Eighteenth-Century County Town." *Urban History* 25, no. 1 (May 1998): 3–21.

STOBART, JON, ANDREW HANN, AND VICTORIA MORGAN, EDS. *Spaces of Consumption: Leisure and Shopping in the English Town, c. 1680–1830.* London: Routledge, 2007.

SUMMERSON, JOHN. *Architecture in Britain, 1530–1830.* Harmondsworth, England: Penguin, 1970.

SUMMERSON, JOHN. "Class B: Single Block Plans with Corner Towers" In "The Book of Architecture of John Thorpe in John Soane's Museum," *Journal of the Walpole Society* 40 (1966).

SUMMERSON, JOHN. *Georgian London.* New York: Scribner's, 1946.

SUMMERSON, JOHN. *The Unromantic Castle and Other Essays.* London: Thames and Hudson, 1990.

SVALESEN, LEIF. *The Slave Ship Fredensborg.* Translated by Pat Shaw and Selena Winsnes. Kingston: Ian Randle, 2000.

SYKES, LYNN R., AND MAURICE EWING. "The Seismicity of the Caribbean Region." *Journal of Geophysical Research* 70, no. 20 (1965): 5065–74.

TAIT, A. A. "Home House," *Apollo* 126, no. 306 (August 1987).

TENISON, PATRICK J. *Good Hope Jamaica: A Short History.* Edinburgh and London, Waddie, 1971.

THACKRAY, CHARLES. *Bodiam Castle.* London: National Trust, 2004.

THOMAS, HUGH. *The Slave Trade: The Story of the Atlantic Slave Trade, 1440–1870.* New York: Simon & Schuster, 1997.

THOMPSON, ALVIN. *Flight to Freedom: African Runaways and Maroons in the Americas.* Kingston: University of the West Indies Press, 2006.

THOMPSON, E. P. "Patrician Society, Plebian Culture." *Journal of Social History* 7 (Summer 1974): 382–405.

THOMPSON, FARRIS. "Charters for the Spirit: Afro-Jamaican Music and Art." In *Art and Emancipation in Jamaica,* edited by T. J. Barringer, Gillian Forrester, and Barbaro Martinez-Ruiz. New Haven: Yale University Press, 2007.

THOMPSON, MICHAEL. *Decline of the Castle.* Cambridge: Cambridge University Press, 1987.

THORNTON, A. P. "The Organization of the Slave Trade in the English West Indies, 1660–1685." *William and Mary Quarterly* 12, no. 3 (July 1955).

THORNTON, DIANA. "The Probate Inventories of Port Royal, Jamaica." Master's thesis, Texas A&M University, 1992.

THOROLD, PETER. *The London Rich: The Creation of a Great City, from 1666 to the Present.* New York: St. Martin's, 2000.

TJOA-BONATZ, MAI-LIN. "Shophouses in Colonial Penang." *Journal of the Royal Asiatic Society* 71, no. 2 (1998): 122–36.

TOBRINER, STEPHEN. "La Casa Baracata: Earthquake Resistant Construction in Eighteenth-Century Calabria." *Journal of the Society of Architectural Historians* XLII 2 (May 1983): 131–38.

TOBRINER, STEPHEN. "A gaiola pombalina: o sistema de construção antissísmico mais avançado do século XVIII," *Monumentos* 21 (September 2004).

TUAN, YI-FU. *Landscapes of Fear.* New York: Pantheon Books, 1979.

UNDERWOOD, DAVID. "The Pombaline Style and International Neoclassicism in Lisbon and Rio de Janeiro." Ph.D. diss., University of Pennsylvania, 1988.

UPTON, DELL. *Another City: Urban Life and Urban Spaces in the New American Republic.* New Haven: Yale University Press, 2008.

UPTON, DELL. "Commercial Architecture in Philadelphia Lithographs." In *Philadelphia on Stone: Commercial Lithography in Philadelphia, 1828–1878,* edited by Erika Piola. University Park: Pennsylvania State University Press, 2012.

UPTON, DELL. "Traditional Timber Framing." In *Material Culture of the Wooden Age,* edited by Brooke Hindle. Tarrytown, NY: Sleepy Hollow, 1981.

UPTON, DELL. "Vernacular Domestic Architecture in Eighteenth-Century Virginia." *Winterthur Portfolio* 17 (1982): 102–4.

UPTON, DELL. "White and Black Landscapes in Eighteenth-Century Virginia" *Places* 2, no. 2 (1985): 59–72.

UPTON, DELL, AND JOHN MICHAEL VLATCH. *Common Places: Readings in American Vernacular Architecture.* Athens: University of Georgia Press, 1986.

VAN DANZIG, ALBERT. *Forts and Castles of Ghana.* Accra: Sedco, 1980.

VENN, J. A., COMPILER. "Alumni Cantabrigiensis" II, vol. I. Cambridge: Cambridge University Press, 1940.

VLACH, JOHN MICHAEL. *By the Work of Their Hands: Studies in Afro-American Folklife.* Charlottesville: University of Virginia Press, 1992.

VLACH, JOHN MICHAEL. "The Shotgun House: An African American Legacy." *Pioneer America: Journal of Historic American Material Culture* 8 (January 1976): 47–70.

VLACH, JOHN MICHAEL. "The Shotgun House: An African Architectural Legacy," *Common Places: Readings in American Vernacular Architecture.* Athens: University of Georgia, 1986.

VLACH, JOHN MICHAEL. "'Snug Li'l House with Flue and Oven': Nineteenth-Century Reforms in Plantation Slave Housing." In *Gender, Class and Shelter: Perspectives in Vernacular Architecture* V, edited by Elizabeth Cromley and Carter Hudgins. Knoxville: University of Tennessee Press, 1995.

WADSWORTH, ALFRED, AND JULIA MANN. *The Cotton Trade of Industrial Lancashire, 1600–1780.* Manchester: Manchester University Press, 1931.

WALSH, CLAIRE. "Shop Design and the Display of Goods in Eighteenth-Century London." *Journal of Design History* 8 (1995): 157–76.

WALSH, CLAIRE. "Shops, Shopping, and the Art of Decision Making in Eighteenth-Century England." In *Gender, Taste, and Material Culture in Britain and North America, 1700–1830,* edited by John Styles and Amanda Vickery. New Haven: Yale University Press, 2006.

WALVIN, JAMES. *Making the Black Atlantic: Britain and the African Diaspora.* London: Cassell, 2000.

WARD, J. R. "British West Indies in the Age of Abolition, 1745–1815." In *Oxford History of British Empire,* edited by Nicholas Canny et al. Oxford: Oxford University Press, 1998.

WARDE, PAUL. "The Idea of Improvement, c. 1520–1700." In *Custom, Improvement, and the Landscape in Early Modern Britain,* edited by Richard Hoyle. Farnham, Surrey: Ashgate, 2011.

WATERMAN, D. R. "Some Irish Seventeenth-Century Houses and Their Architectural Ancestry." In *Studies in Building History: Essays in Recognition of the Work of B. H. St. J. O'Neil,* edited by E. M. Jope et al. London: Odhams, 1961.

WATSON, JOHN. *Annals of Philadelphia and Pennsylvania in the Olden Time,* 3 vols. Philadelphia: E. Stuart, 1900.

WATTS, DAVID. *The West Indies: Patterns of Development, Culture, and Environmental Change since 1492.* Cambridge: Cambridge University Press, 1987.

WAX, D. D. "Negro Resistance to the Early American Slave Trade." *Journal of Negro History* 51, no. 1 (January 1966): 1–15.

WEADICK, SHARON. "How Popular Were Fortified Houses in Irish Building History?" In *Plantation Ireland: Settlement and Material Culture, c. 1550–c. 1700,* edited by James Lyttleton and Colin Rynne. Dublin: Four Courts, 2009.

WEBSTER, JANE. "Slave Ships and Maritime Archaeology: An Overview." *International Journal of Historical Archaeology* 12 (2008): 6–19.

WELCH, PEDRO. *Slave Society in the City: Bridgetown, Barbados, 1680–1834.* Kingston: Ian Randle, 2003.

WELCH, PEDRO, AND RICHARD A. GOODRIDGE. *"Red" and Black over White: Free Coloured Women in Pre-Emancipation Barbados.* Bridgetown: Carib, 2000.

WENGER, MARK. "The Central Passage Plan in Virginia: Evolution of an Eighteenth-Century Living Space." In *Perspectives in Vernacular Architecture II,* edited by Camille Wells. Columbia: University of Missouri Press, 1986.

WESLER, KIT W. "Excavations at the Barrett House, Falmouth, Jamaica, 2006, Preliminary Report." Unpublished report for the Jamaica National Heritage Trust, November 2006.

WHEATON, THOMAS. "Colonial African American Plantation Villages." In *Another's Country: Archaeological and Historical Perspectives on Cultural Interactions in the Southern Colonies,* edited by J. W. Joseph and Martha Zierden. Tuscaloosa: University of Alabama Press, 2002.

WHINNEY, M. *Home House: No. 20 Portman Square.* Feltham: Country Life, 1969.

WHITEFIELD, GEORGE. *George Whitefield's Journals (1737–1741),* edited by William V. Davis. Gainsville, FL: Scholars' Facsimilies and Reprints, 1969.

WILLIAMS, DAVID. "The Shipping of the British Slave Trade in Its Final Years, 1798–1807." *International Journal of Maritime History* 12 (2000): 1–25.

WITHERS, CHARLES. "The Historical Creation of the Highlands." In *The Manufacture of Scottish History,* edited by I. Donnachie and C. Whateley, 143–56. Edinburgh: Polygon, 1992.

WOOD, PETER. *Black Majority: Negroes in Colonial South Carolina from 1670 through the Stono Rebellion.* New York: Norton, 1996.

WOODS, MAY. *Glass Houses: A History of Greenhouses, Orangeries and Conservatories.* New York: Rizzoli, 1988.

WOODS, MAY, AND ARETE WARREN. *Glass Houses: A History of Greenhouses, Orangeries, and Conservatories.* London: Aurum, 1996.

WRIGHT, IRENE A., ED. "The English Conquest of Jamaica." In *Camden Miscellany* XIII, 3rd ser., 34 (1924).

WRIGHT, PHILIP, ED. *Lady Nugent's Journal of Her Residence in Jamaica from 1801 to 1805.* Kingston: Institute of Jamaica, 1966.

YIN, LEE HO. "The Singapore Shophouse: An Anglo-Chinese Urban Vernacular." In *Asia's Old Dwellings: Tradition, Resilience, and Change,* edited by Ronald G. Knapp, 115–34. New York: Oxford University Press, 2003.

YOUNG, J. G. "The Founding of Kingston." In *The Capitals of Jamaica,* edited by W. Adolphe Roberts. Kingston: Pioneer, 1955.

ZACEK, NATALIE, AND LAURENCE BROWN. "Unsettled Houses: The Material Culture of the Missionary Project in Jamaica in the Era of Emancipation." *Slavery & Abolition* 35, no. 3 (2014): 493–507.

ZAHEDIEH, NUALA. *The Capital and the Colonies: London and the Atlantic Economy.* Cambridge: Cambridge University Press, 2010.

ZAHEDIEH, NUALA. "The Merchants of Port Royal, Jamaica, and the Spanish Contraband Trade, 1655–1692." *William and Mary Quarterly,* 3rd ser., vol. 43, no. 4 (October 1986): 570–93.

Index

Numbers in *italics* indicate images.

Abbot, John, 71
absenteeism, 8, 191–92, 217, 257, 258, 265, 267
absentees: architectural preferences of, 258–60; stereotypes of, 263
"Actor Boy" (Belisario), *184*
Adam, Robert, 8, 135, 257, 264, 265
adobe, reinforced, 90
African architecture, 220–21
African house, 31; under construction (1820s), *76*
Africanus, Scipio, 244; gravemarker for, *243*
"A Front View of Hamden House" (n.d.), *43*
"A Grand Jamaica Ball! or the Creolean Hop à la Muftee," *202*
agricultural improvement, 103, 115
A Harlot's Progress (Hogarth), 257
Ainslie, Phillip Barrington, 42
air, quality of, architectural response to, 205–6
airflow, increasing, 70
A Linen Market in Dominica (Brunias, 1770), *182*
A Liverpool Slave Ship (Jackson, 1780s), *27*
Allaston, Robert, 254
American Revolution, 8, 216–17
Amsterdam Town Hall, 251, *252*, 253
Amussen, Susan, 238
Anderson, Benedict, 4
Anderson, Jennifer, 243–44
"An Elevated View of the New Docks . . ." (Daniell; 1802), *266*
Anglo-Georgian building tradition, 194
Anglo-Scottish Union of 1707, 132
animal mill (Labat; 1714), *103*
Ankerwycke House, 147
Antigua, 73, 78, 178
Antiquities of Athens, 134, 135
anxiety, 6, 8, 64; British, 240; moral, 127
"A Plan of Good Hope Estate" (Schroeder; 1794), *101*, *111*
Appleby, John, 18
aqueducts, 107, *108*

A Rake's Progress (Hogarth), 257
arcades, 81, 178
arcade stair (1820), *195*
Arcadia plantation (ca. 1820), *114*, 115, 196, 193
archaeology: as interest of Jamaica's elites, 134–36; classical, 135
Archdekin, John, 59
Archdekin family, 59
Archedekne, Andrew, 146
architectural engineering, 88
architecture: antiseismic, 88–96; as evidence of everyday life, 4–5; experimentation in, 3, 6; hurricane resilience of, 6, 8, 88, 89, 192, 194; Jamaica's elites' interest in, 142–50; responding to Caribbean climate, 67–96
Armitage, David, 132
Armstrong, Douglas, 74, 112, 125, 129
Arnold, Dana, 50
Arnold's Repository, 175
Art and Emancipation in Jamaica (ed. Barringer et al.), 4
artificialia, 237
Art of Making Sugar, 127
Asante, 15
Asiento, 81
Atkinson, Mary, 168
Atkinson, Wilhemina, 168
Atwood, Thomas, 171
Auchincrive, 257
Auchindown Castle, 60
"A View of the Houses at Bath" (Du Simitière; early 1760s), 141
"A View in the Island of Jamaica, of Roaring River Estate . . ." (Robertson; 1778), *128*

back lots, 7
Bacon, Francis, 47
Bacon's Castle, 71
Baillie, John, 113, 129–30, 230–31
Bailyn, Bernard, 3, 6, 37, 47
Balcaskie, 53

balconies, 82–83, 179
balcony houses, 83
Bantanon, Godwin, 71
Baptist rebellion of 1831, 45
Barbot, John, 12
Barclay, Alexander, 224
barmkin, 39
barracoons, 19
Barrett, Edward, 158
Barrett, George Goodin, 232
Barrett House, 158–65, 168, 175, 183
Barrett's wharf, 169, 170
barricado, 29–30
Barringer, Tim, 4
Barrycourt, 55
Bartram, William, 204
Bassett, Hayden, 115
Bates, Lyndsey, 124
bathing houses, 156
Battle of Kinsale, 56, 57
bawns, 47, 63
Beastall, W. E., 171
Beaufort House, 248
Beckford, Mary Ballard, 140
Beckford, Mrs. William, 264
Beckford, Peter (the elder), 257
Beckford, Peter (the younger), 257
Beckford, Richard, 157
Beckford, William (cousin to Lord Mayor), 122, 142, 203; on building quarters in straight lines, 129; on domesticating slaves, 32; on hospitality, 215; house of, 257; in hurricane, 91; on overseer's house, 128; on sugar works, 120;
Beckford, William (Lord Mayor), 131, 134, 135n Portman Square, 265; status of, 257; working on Fonthill Abbey, 260
Beckford, William (of Somerley), 279n1
Beckford, William Thomas, 260, 265, 279n1
Beeston, William, 140
Belchin, Thomas, 84
Belidor, Bernard Forest de, 88, 90, 91

Belisario, Isaac Mendes, 183, 184
Belle Isle House, Jamaica (unknown; ca. 1820), *197*
Belle Isle plantation, 196
Bentham, Jeremy, 130
Berkeley Square, 247
Biet, Antoine, 68
Bindman, David, 238
Bindon, Howard, 49
blackamoor: British imagining of, 240; figures of, 237–39, 240, 260, 261
"Blackamoor in the Wood, The," 240
Black Atlantic, 3
black bodies, British collection of, 236–40
Blackburn, John, 254
Blackburn, John (the elder), 254
Blagrove, John, 147–51, 157
Blagrove, William, 198
Blair, James, 105
Blaney, Edward, 56–57
Blathwayt, William, 236–38, 240–45
Blathwayt Atlas, 287n31
Blenheim Palace (Vanbrugh; 1705–24), 53
Blount, Charles, 46, 56–57
Bluehole, 41
board houses, 8, *171*, 221, 226–28, 230, 233
Bodiam Castle (begun 1385), 259
boiling house, 97, *98*, 118–21, 246: plan for (Good Hope; 18th cent.), *118;* plan of (Labat; 1714), *104*
booths (small shops), 170–71, *172*
Borra, Giovanni, 134–35
botany, 138–39
Bourdieu, Pierre, 269n
Bourton House, 51–52
Bouverie, John, 134
Bow Porcelain Manufactory, 239
box framing, 227–28, 285n2
branding, 129
Brathwaite, Kamau, 112, 268n1
Brazilian Landscape with a Worker's House (Post; ca. 1665), *87*
Breen, T. H., 7, 161–62
Bright, Henry, 247
Bristol: docking capacity of, 246; merchants of, 248–49; slave trade and, 246–47; suburbs of, 247–48; sugar refining in, 245–46; waterfront capacity of, 246
Britain: cultural geography of, 262; white West Indians in, 192. *See also* England
British Caribbean, studies of, 268n1
British Empire: contested frontiers of, 64; early modern British art and, 4; improved workers' housing in, 115; Jamaica's architectural role in, 3; Jamaica's importance to, 4, 6–7; slavery as element of, 1
British identity, 132
Britons in Jamaica, identity of, 132–33
Bromley, 40, *41*
Brookes, 28
Brookes, James, Jr., 28

Brown, Capability, 137
Brown, Laurence, 231
Brown, Lawrence, 244
Bruce, William, 53
Brunias, Augustino, 172, 181, 182
Bryan Castle, 211
Buckridge, Steeve, 4
Bunratty, 273n100
Burke, Edmund, 157, 262
Burke, Richard, 57
Burke, William, 157
Burlington, Lord (Richard Boyle), 149
Burnard, Trevor, 132, 258; on absenteeism, 192; on egalitarian tyranny, 8; on hospitality, 215; on Jamaica's mortality rate, 205; on Jamaica as society at war, 46; on Phibbah, 232; on preferred slaves, 222; on rape, 126, 210; on slave sale process, 31, 32; on slaves' conditions, cultivated by masters, 228; on wealth of white Jamaicans, 13; on worth of slave trade, 30
Burnet, Gilbert, 83
Butterwalk, the, 81

cage (jail), 90
Cairness House, 259
Camerton Court, 262
Campbell, Archibald, 110
Campeche chairs, 7, 209–10
Canary Wharf, 235
candlestick (ca. 1770), *239*
caning, for walls, 71
canoes, 15–16, 24
Cape Coast Castle, 16–23
capital flow, importance of, to early modern Atlantic studies, 3
capture, of slaves, 10, 12–16
Cardiff Hall (1789), 147, 151, 198
Caribbean, climate of, 67–78, 206; architectural response to, 227; effect of, on slaves' housing, 224. *See also* heat; hurricanes
Carr, John, 257
Carter's Grove, 194, *195*
Carvalho, Sebastião José de, 89–90
casa baraccata, 90
Casali, Andrea, 257
Casid, Jill, 139, 244
castellated architecture, 6, 49, 53–54, 60, 258–60, 262–63
castles, 16–22: mock, 49; northern Ireland, 47; towers in, 36
Catesby, Robert, 52
cattle mills, 103, 106–8
Ceded Islands, 236
cement, 88
central passages, 62, 122, 164, 196–97, 215
chambers, 201–3, 210; for free blacks, 226; on piazzas, 215
Champion, William, 246
Chapman, William, 115, 163–64
Charles I, 59

Charles II, 80, 238
Charleston (SC), 167–68, 172–74, 176, 179–80
Chastleton, 52
Chelsea Porcelain Manufactory, 239
Chilham Castle (begun 1616), 258–59, 260
Chippenham Park, 67; entrance lodges and gates (Sandys, 1790s), *67;* workers' housing (late 18th cent.), *116*
Chippenham Village, 115
Chiswick House, 145
churches, 70, 71
Churchill, John, 53
Clark, William, 122
Clarkson, Thomas, 14, 15, 27
Clifton Hill House, 247
Clifts Plantation, 37
clock time, used to measure slaves' shifts, 128
Codrington, Christopher, I, 274n40
Codrington, Christopher, II, 78
Codrington College, principal's house, 72
coffles, 14, *15*, 16
Colbeck, John, 152
Colbeck Castle (ca. 1750–75), 7, 48–49, *50*, 131, *132*, *133*, 142, 149, 151, 152–57, 281n111
cold water bathing, 155–56
collecting, 236–45
Colonial Frames, Nationalist Histories (Rajagopalan and Desai, eds.), 268n19
Colonial Modernities (Scriver), 268n19
colonnaded commercial streets, 181–82
colonnades, 177–78
colony, motherland and, 288n84
Colyear, Juliana, 135
commercial spaces, as social spaces, 160, 161
Company of Merchants Trading to Africa, 17–19, 21, 22
Company of Royal Adventurers to Africa, 238
consumer revolution, 243–44
consumption, patterns of, 161
containment, 10
Cooke, Anthony, 254
cookery, 112
cookhouses, used for solitary confinement, 126
coppers, 118–19, 121
corner features, houses with, 48–49
corner pavilions, 149–51
corner towers, 6, 47–54, 258–60; on Palladian houses, 54; square, 54–55, 63
Cornwallis House, 248
"Cottages with One Room" (Wood), *117*
counters, 176
country houses, 7, 50–53, 257, 273n83
courtyard, Cape Coast Castle, *19*, 22
Covent Garden (Jones), 83, 178
"Covent Garden" (Nichols; ca. 1720), *85*
Covey plantation, 97
Craskell, Thomas, 281n108
Craton, Michael, 45
Crawford, Alexander, 176
crenellations, 54, 56, 57

Creoles, 217; British stereotypes of, 263; characterizations of, 190–92; dancing, 201; food, 201; free blacks described as, 233; housing, 7, 8 (*See also* Jamaican Creole houses); racial blurring and, 216; social ambivalence associated with, 210

creolizing, 7, 207–10

Cromwell, Ralph, 50

Croome Court, garden rotunda (Brown; 1754–57), *137*

Crowley, John, 206

Cugoano, Ottobah, 10, 12, 13, 16, 22

Cumberland, Duke of, 265

Cumberland, Richard, 263

curing houses, 118, 120

D'Alberet, M., 42, 44, 90–91, 147–49, 151, 157

dancing, 201

Daniell, William, 266

Dashwood, Francis, 260–61

Davidson, Thomas, 230

Davidson (Thomas) House, 166, *167*

Davis, Howard, 162, 169

Davis, John, 71, 72

Davis, Ralph, 245

Davis, Susan, 183

Dawkins, Elizabeth Pennant, 134

Dawkins, Henry, 134, 135

Dawkins, James, 134–36, 261

Dawkins, William, 135, 157

Dawkins family, 140, 279n13

Day, Nathaniel, 247

Day (Nathaniel) House (begun 1709), *247*

Deagan, Kathleen, 86

Decoy, The, 137, 139, 142, 156

defensive architecture, 8, 36–42, 47–49, 60–62. *See also* fortified houses; loopholes; palisades houses; tower houses

deforestation, 108

Dellap, Robert, 203

Delle, James, 47

Derby's Dose, 126

Desborough, Samuel, 37

Descriptive Account of the Island of Jamaica, A (Beckford), 91, 120, 142

Desmond Rebellions, 46

Development of Creole Society in Jamaica (Brathwaite), 268n1

Dictionary of British and Irish Travelers in Italy, 1701–1800, 133

Différents projets relatifs au climat . . . (D'Albaret), 44, *91*, 148

dining rooms, 200, 203

Discipline and Punish (Foucault), 130

diseases, 205

Dixcove Castle (Ghana), 5, 10, *11, 12*, 16, 17

Doblen Act (1788), 28

donjon, 50–51

Donowell, John, 261

door surround, rusticated (ca. 1740s), *194*

double arcades, 152

double house, 70

double porticos, 261

Drake, Francis, 73

drawbridges, 42

Drax, Erle, 265

Drax Hall plantation, 74, 75, 125, 146, 256

Drax family, 146

Drayton, Richard, 116

Dresser, Madge, 240, 246, 247

Drumlanrig Castle, 53

dry docks, *26*

Duke, Antera, 15

Duke Street (Falmouth), 230

Duncan, William, 215

dungeons, 17, 19–22

Dunkinfield, Robert, 83

Duperly, Adolphe, 158–59, 171, 172

Du Simitière, Pierre Eugène, 82, 127, 137, 139, 141, 145, 190, 280–81n88

Dyrham Park (begun 1692), 237, 240–43, *245*

early modern Atlantic, studies of, 3

Earnshaw, Brian, 255

earthfast construction, 74–75, 77–78

earthfast framing systems, 88

earthquakes, 78–79, 88–96

Edge of Empire (Jasanoff), 4

Edinburgh Castle (late 18th cent.), 60, *62*, 214, 216

Edwards, Bryan, 14, 120, 160; on boiling houses, 119; on Falmouth's growth, 160; on fear, 125; on hospitality, 215; on Jamaica's crops, 201; on slave hospitals, 109; on slaves' housing, 75, 221; on trash houses, 109; on water mills, 106–7

Edwards, Jay, 284n1

egalitarian tyranny, 8

Egypt, 4

Egyptian Hall, 149, 201, 249

18 Pitt Street (Falmouth; ca. 1820), *167*, 225

"Elevation of the South front of the row of buildings on the market wharf" (1793), *174*

Elizabeth I, 46, 56

Elliott, William, 173

Eltis, David, 20

Elton, Isaac, 247

Emblemes (Wither), 255

empire of goods, 7, 161–62

empires: through collection, 237; interconnected worlds of, 4; making of, through visual culture, 4; prevailing view of (17th cent.), 132

England: agricultural improvement in, 115; corner towers in, 49, 50–54; covered walkways in, 81; industrialization emerging in, 121; landscape of, reorganized (16th–18th cent.), 50; occupation of Ireland, 55–56; sugar refineries in, 245

English South Sea Company, 81

entertainment, West Indian style, 200–201

entrance halls, 196–203

Equiano, Olaudah, 16, 23, 24, 26–27, 28, 30, 31, 32

Essay on Prints (Gilpin), 141

European slaver's house, *16*

Ewe houses, 220–21

Exchange Building, 248–49

executions, public, following slave riots, 45

exercise, 204

exotica, British collecting of, 236–38, 244

exploitation, capitalist, 140

"Exterior of a boiling house" (Clark), *122*

Eyer, John, 251

Facey, Laura, 1–2

Faerie Queen (Spenser), 47, 49

Falconbridge, Alexander, 27

Falmouth: free blacks in, 218–20; growth of, 160; house-stores in, 162–69; imports to, 169–70, 175; piazzas and galleries in, 84; plan of (1844), *161*; stores of, 160, 161, 175–77; streets of, 177–83; wharves of, 169–75

Falmouth Field School, 285n1, 286n17

Farr, Thomas, 248

fear, landscape of, 214

Fearon, Thomas, 140, 147, 157

Ferraresi, Vincenzo, 90

figural representation of America (Paty), *250*

figurines, depicting Africans, 239–40

First Empire optimism, 8

Fisher, Paul, 247–48

five-foot way, 178

floods, architectural response to, 92–93

floors, in Creole houses, 200, 201

Floyd, Thomas, 173

Floyer, John, 156

Fonthill Abbey, 260, *261*

Fonthill House, 257, 258

food: Creole, 201; West India style, 201

Fordham, Douglas, 4

Forrester, Gillian, 4

Forsythe, John, 151

Fort Balcarres, 170

fortified houses, 6; in English building strategies, 47; in mainland colonies, 37

forts, 16–20

Foucault, Michel, 130

foundations, masonry, 91–92

Four Books of Architecture (Palladio), 145, 149

framing, exposed, 198

Fredensborg, 25

free blacks: agency of, 8; architectural practices of, 4; described as Creoles, 233; distancing from the slave population, 219; frame houses of, 8; harboring runaway slaves, 228; housing for, 218–20, 226–28, 230–34; shotgun houses and, 234; villages of, 231–32; wealth among, 230–31; women homeownership among, 218, 230–33

free women of color, houses built for, 287n88

Freke, Thomas, 247

Fremantle House, 248

French Caribbean, house planning tradition in, 202

Illustration Credits

The photographers and the sources of visual material other than the owners indicated in the captions are as follows. Every effort has been made to supply complete and correct credits; if there are errors or omissions, please contact Yale University Press so that corrections can be made in any subsequent edition.

Unless otherwise noted, photos are by the author.

Fig. 0.1. Photo by Donnette Zacca

Figs. 0.2, 1.19. Image reproduced by permission of The Huntington Library, San Marino, California

Fig. 1.2. Image Courtesy Public Record Office, London (MPG 1/237)

Figs. 1.4, 1.18, 3.12, 9.32. Image courtesy National Maritime Museum, Greenwich, London

Figs. 1.5, 2.16, 3.21, 4.13, 4.24. Image courtesy Harvard Libraries

Fig. 1.7. Image courtesy Public Record Office, London (MPG 1/233)

Fig. 1.9. Digital model by Jason Truesdale

Fig. 1.12. Drawn by Jason Truesdale based on 1944 drawings produced by the University of Ghana and field work undertaken by the author in July of 2012

Fig. 1.15. Bristol Museum and Art Gallery. Bequest of Harold Bolles Bowles, 1909

Fig. 1.17. National Museums, Liverpool

Figs. 1.21–1.23, 2.2, 2.3, 2.6, 5.2, 5.16. Drawn by Jason Truesdale (2.6 based on drawings by Robert Carney)

Fig. 2.4. Image courtesy Colonial Williamsburg Foundation

Figs. 2.7, 3.10, 3.14, 4.6, 4.17, 4.30, 5.6, 5.7, 5. 10, 7.5, 7.14, 7.21–7.23, 8.5, 8.6. Private collection

Fig. 2.13. Image Courtesy Glasgow City Archives and Special Collections (T-SK22/14)

Figs. 2.14, 3.23, 5.12, 5.13. Image courtesy University of Maryland Library

Fig. 2.17. Reprinted from Frank Cundall, *Historic Jamaica* (1915)

Figs. 2.18, 3.11, 3.15–3.17, 5.8, 8.16. Image courtesy Library of Congress (8.16. courtesy Historic American Buildings Survey)

Fig. 2.26. Reprinted from Michael Thompson, *Decline of the Castle* (Cambridge: Cambridge University of Press, 1987), 22

Figs. 2.34, 4.20, 7.3, 7.4. Measured by author, drawn by Jason Truesdale

Fig 3.2. Drawn by KeVaughn Harding

Fig. 3.4. Image courtesy Pierpont Morgan Library

Figs. 3.6, 4.32. Courtesy of the John Carter Brown Library at Brown University

Figs. 3.9, 3.19. Image courtesy of the National Gallery of Jamaica

Fig. 3.20. Image courtesy Los Angeles County Museum of Art

Figs. 3.30, 7.6. Image courtesy Sotheby's

Figs. 4.3–4.5, 4.29. Drawn by Falmouth Field School, 2009 (4.4 by Jessica Vanacek; 4.5 by Leeann Dickerson)

Figs. 4.9–4.11, 4.27, 5.3, 5.11, 5.17, 5.18. Image courtesy University of Virginia Special Collections

Fig. 4.14. Photo by KeVaughn Harding

Fig. 4.15. Image courtesy Cambridgeshire Archives

Fig. 4.28. Image courtesy Yale Center for British Art

Fig. 4.31. Image courtesy Library Company of Philadelphia

Fig. 5.4. Image courtesy National Gallery of Scotland

Figs. 5.19, 6.6, 6.7. Drawn by Falmouth Field School

Figs. 6.1, 6.9, 6.10. Photo by Jeff Klee

Figs. 6.2, 6.4, 6.17. National Library of Jamaica

Fig 6.3. Drawn by John Kupstas

Fig. 6.15. Image courtesy National Archives, Kew, UK

Figs. 6.16, 7.18, 7.20, 9.30. Courtesy Lewis Walpole Library, Yale University

Fig. 6.19. Register of Mesne Conveyance, Charleston, South Carolina

Fig. 6.26. Yale Center for British Art, Paul Mellon Collection

Figs. 6.27, 6.28. Courtesy Yale Center for British Art

Figs. 7.8, 7.10, 8.2, 8.8. Drawn by Zhifei Cheng (fig. 7.10 drawn from Historic American Buildings Survey)

Fig. 8.9. Plan by Falmouth Field School, 2007

Fig. 9.3. Image courtesy The National Trust

Figs. 9.4, 9.5. Image courtesy Victoria and Albert Museum

Figs. 9.14, 9.15. Photo by Roger Leech

Figs. 9.16, 9.17. Photo R. Philpott © Trustees of National Museums, Liverpool

Figs. 9.18–9.20. Photo by Robert Philpott

Fig. 9.28. Reprinted from John Rutter, *Delineations of Fonthill* (London, 1823), plate 11